THE
VOYAGER'S
HANDBOOK

International Marine
Camden, Maine

THE VOYAGER'S HANDBOOK

THE ESSENTIAL GUIDE TO BLUEWATER CRUISING

by Beth A. Leonard

Drawings by Lyanne Schuster

To my father,
who gave me the courage to dream,
and to Evans,
who gave me the strength to live my dreams.

International Marine/
Ragged Mountain Press
A Division of The McGraw-Hill Companies

10 9 8 7 6 5 4 3

Library of Congress Cataloging-in-Publication Data
Leonard, Beth.
     The voyager's handbook : the essential guide to bluewater
cruising / Beth Leonard
        p.   cm.
     Includes index.
     ISBN 0-07-038143-7 (alk. paper)
     1. Sailing. 2. Ocean travel.   I. Title.
GV811.L426   1997
910'.2'02--dc21   97-23130
                                   CIP

If you have questions or comments regarding the content
of this book, or suggestions for topics to discuss in future editions,
please contact:
International Marine, P.O. Box 220, Camden, ME 04843
We will forward any such comments to the author.

Questions regarding the ordering of this book should be addressed to:
The McGraw-Hill Companies, Customer Service Department
P.O. Box 547, Blacklick, OH 43004
Retail customers: 1-800-262-4729
Bookstores: 1-800-722-4726

This book is printed on acid-free paper.

Printed by Quebecor Printing, Fairfield, Pennsylvania
Design by Mary Brown, Brown Design & Co., Portland, Maine
Production by Deborah Krampf, Pentagöet Design, Brooksville, Maine
Edited by Jonathan Eaton, Kathryn Mallien, Cynthia Flanagan Goss

Drawings by Lyanne Schuster unless otherwise noted.
Photography by Beth Leonard unless otherwise noted.

Portions of this book previously appeared in *Cruising World*
and *SAIL* magazines.

CONTENTS

PART I: THE ESSENTIAL INGREDIENTS

Successful long-term voyaging depends first and foremost on a realistic and enthusiastic crew. The dream often belongs to one crewmember at the start, but among successful crews every crewmember has embraced the dream and made it his or her own. Differences in crewmembers' attitudes often reflect fundamentally different expectations about the cruising lifestyle.

Too many would-be voyagers launch a never-ending quest for the "perfect" boat that keeps them from living their dream. Everyone wants a larger, more modern, more seaworthy boat, but many small, simple boats have completed epic voyages. The ideal boat must fit within your budget while allowing you to meet your voyaging goals.

One of the first questions would-be voyagers ask us is, "How much did it cost?" Here I analyze each of our expense categories in detail and discuss the lifestyle decisions that make the difference between living expenses of $10,000 and $20,000 per year.

PART II: EQUIPPING THE YACHT FOR BLUEWATER VOYAGING

When sailing stops being a weekend diversion and becomes your primary means of traveling long distances, the sail inventory becomes the most important gear aboard. To highlight the requirements for a trade wind sail inventory, I examine the wind speeds and wind angles we actually experienced as recorded in Silk's three-year log.

PART V: FOREIGN SAVVY

When we started voyaging, one of the biggest surprises was the amount of time we spent dealing with bureaucracy—a minimum of a half a day clearing in and out in every one of the 35 countries we visited. Voyagers must know the paper requirements for entering and leaving countries as well as other bureaucratic pitfalls—from getting spares into foreign countries to avoiding import taxes on the boat.

When you arrive in port, you'll want to get ashore and explore. However, experience taught us that we were better off getting the boat back in shape before rushing ashore and signing up for a tour of the island. The tasks for the first week or so in port are myriad, from cleaning up and airing out the boat to adjusting to a new culture to getting mail and money.

One of the most rewarding aspects of traveling by boat is the unavoidable interactions with many different cultures. To make these magical encounters most rewarding and enjoyable, you need to understand and respect some general protocols and be prepared for the different customs you will encounter along the tradewind route.

Sailors have shared many traditions for generations. The most basic is to always assist a vessel in distress. Modern voyagers have added other traditions as the number of boats has increased, including traditions concerning treading softly in the environment and respecting local cultures.

APPENDICES

ACKNOWLEDGMENTS

Many midwives helped this book along its journey and into your hands. I want to thank the readers who offered me valuable advice, constructive criticism, and unbounded enthusiasm: Walker and Ginny Vought, Joe and Kathy Möeller, Scott and Kitty Kuhner, Dale and John Dalgliesh, and Ray and Linda Baker. Thanks to Steve Corenman for his offshore racing perspective and to Dr. Pat LaFrate and Dr. Susan Kline for their assistance on medical issues. I also want to thank Clive Shute and Laila Stjerndrüp not only for their comments and ideas, but also for their friendship and sharing across two oceans.

Some of the chapters in this book were originally shorter articles in *SAIL* magazine, *Cruising World,* and *Sailing.* Thanks to Tom Linskey at *SAIL,* Lynda Morris Childress at *Cruising World,* and Micca Hutchins at *Sailing* for their interest and encouragement as I made my first forays into the marine market.

Thank you to the many voyagers we met along the way who shared their wisdom and their joy. In the spirit of their giving, I pass this book on to you, the reader. May you too discover that the beauty of the dream does not even begin to compare to the magic of the reality.

FOREWORD | BY GEORGE DAY

Ocean cruising and world voyaging have a way of changing a person, or a couple, in ways that never occur ashore. Once you have sailed across an ocean, watching the moon move through a whole cycle and meeting the great sea mammals on their own turf, you never see our home planet and our little place in it quite the same way again.

And when you get to the far islands and continents at the end of a long passage, when you drop the anchor off a white coral beach and stroll through coconut groves where you have to guard your toes from the claws of coconut crabs, you begin to forget the things that were once so important at home. You happily exist without phones, fax, and e-mail, without a daily mainline of news, without roadrage and Prozac and attention deficit disorder. You become a self-sufficient citizen of the sea. You realize the importance and beauty in small things. You become, in a way, less civilized and more human as you develop voyaging skills and a cruising state of mind.

But the leap from casual coastal sailing to world cruising is a long one that demands the acquisition of a certain body of knowledge and a new attitude. The life aboard a small ship is not for everyone, yet it is one that can be adopted successfully by the most woods-bound landlubber if his or her attitude is right. Making the leap does not require an expensive boat, the latest electronics, or a million dollars. It does require an adventurous spirit, a flexible mind, and a persistent willingness to learn.

In the pages of this book, Beth Leonard will open many doors for you. Being a comparatively recent convert to the world-cruising life who jumped in with both feet by setting off immediately on a circumnavigation, she brings a fresh zeal to the subject, tossing out tired old notions and reinforcing practices that really work. An international management consultant, she has a gift for seeing into the heart of a problem, while organizing solutions in simple, logical ways. There are many chapters in this book that you will want to keep as ready reference, even after many years of bluewater sailing.

When I think of the transition a sailor makes from coastal to offshore cruising, I always think of the Maine yarn about an MIT mathematics professor who adopted cruising as a summer pastime. One afternoon he found himself hard aground on a submerged ledge off his harbor entrance and had to hail a nearby lobsterman for help. After being hauled off the ledge, the professor exclaimed, "How illogical of them to put the buoys over there, when the ledges are over here!"

The lobsterman looked the man in the eye and said, "You know, professor, you sure do know a lot, but you don't realize nuthin'."

In the pages of *The Voyager's Handbook* you'll find a lot of knowledge that will help you prepare for offshore cruising. You'll also find many realizations that are keys to really enjoying and being successful in the voyaging life.

Fair winds,

George Day
Publisher, *Blue Water Sailing*

PROLOGUE

We finished our circumnavigation and sailed into our home port on the Sunday of Memorial Day weekend in 1995. As we approached the Newport Bridge in Rhode Island, most people would have seen one of hundreds of boats enjoying the late spring sunshine of a holiday weekend. But a few people would have taken a second look.

They would have noticed the battered hard dinghy lashed securely to Silk's coach roof and the rust-spotted wind vane on her transom. They would have noted the sea-silvered teak, the plastic jugs lashed to the mizzen mast, and the gooseneck barnacles growing just above the waterline. They might have looked closely enough at the sailors onboard to see deeply burnished tans and sun-bleached hair. They would have wondered where we had been, what places we had visited, and what tales we had to tell.

If you are one of those people who would have noticed us that Sunday and thought even fleetingly of your own dream, this book is written for you.

It was a brilliant June day three years earlier, in 1992, when my partner Evans Starzinger and I boarded our Shannon 37 ketch Silk, untied our docklines, and headed off to sea. We sailed out under the Newport Bridge like dozens of other pleasure boats. Like those boats, we could have turned back to our snug berth as sunset colored the water and an evening chill arrived. But we had spent the last two years preparing for this day. Rather than head for home, we kept sailing and began a three-year odyssey that would take us to three continents.

For the five years before our departure, we spent almost every waking minute living the life of successful 1980s baby boomers. We worked 70-hour weeks, traveled to different cities and countries weekly, and saw each other for only a few hours each weekend. When we were asked to stand for partnership election in our firm, we both took a hard look at ourselves and considered what we wanted to do with the rest of our lives. Despite the applause and accolades, neither of us had ever accomplished anything we considered worthwhile. We knew we were on the wrong track. With that realization, we took the first step toward our journey and a new life.

No one can be completely prepared for a change of such magnitude, and we were less prepared than most. Just two months before putting to sea, we had left our jobs in Sweden as international management consultants. We came back to the United States, to a boat we had purchased but never seen. Silk had been refit during the winter for offshore sailing, and we started sailing her less than two weeks before our departure. We had taken some liveaboard courses, but our offshore sailing experience was minimal. On that June day, we sailed under the Newport Bridge for our shakedown cruise to Bermuda. Our journey had begun, but we had not left our old lives behind.

Three days later, we were in the worst gale of our entire voyage. We ran under bare poles dragging warps while the rigging shredded the wind and waves crashed on the coach roof. The motion below felt like a roller coaster jumping its tracks. For the preceding 36 hours, we had both been so seasick we couldn't keep water down. Lying in my bunk, I realized my jaw ached from clenching my teeth against the tension. All I wanted was to get off the boat. It was then that I suddenly understood what this was all about. I wasn't hiking in the woods or sailing on a lake where rescue was never far away. I had chosen this, and no one could come and take me back to shore. I had to live with my choice.

I didn't recognize the person thinking that way. I had never thought of myself as brave, but I hadn't considered myself a coward either. I thought I took responsibility for my actions. But there in *Silk*'s belly—as I fought nausea, apathy, and fear—I took a hard look at myself. I understood the true meaning of responsibility. I saw who I had been and what I wanted to become.

When I returned three years later, a different person sailed back under the Newport Bridge. The person who left had viewed time as something to be constantly filled or lost forever; the person who returned understood that time is the only space within which the soul can expand. The person who left was too busy earning money to do simple tasks such as cleaning the house or baking bread; the person who returned had learned that no amount of money can compare with the value of self-sufficiency. The person who left had never spent more than 48 hours alone with her partner over the course of their four-year relationship; the person who returned trusted her partner with her life and had been trusted with his.

If you are one of those people who would have noticed us returning that day, then you too have dreamed of the infinite possibilities voyaging holds. When other boats scurry back to their berths just ahead of the setting sun, you want to keep sailing. You want your tracks to be the only ones on a perfect sand beach of a deserted tropical island. You want to see the green flash, taste coconut milk from the husk, watch the fish dance at dusk, and share a feast with new friends from other cultures.

This book can help you get there. It is written for coastal and limited offshore cruisers who want to make the transition to long-term voyaging. I have tried to capture everything I wish I had known when we set sail that June day.

Perhaps you have cruised for a few months along one of the coasts, for a season in the Caribbean, or for a year in the Atlantic. You probably returned relaxed and contented—full of plans for *someday*. Even though you tasted cruising and found it appealing, you wonder whether you are ready to step away from your current life and become a voyager.

To make that decision, you need to understand the differences between several weeks of cruising and several years of voyaging. You have many questions about how much money it will cost, what boat is best, what equipment you should carry, and what skills you will need. Most of all, you wonder what the life of a voyager is really like.

To answer your questions, this book is divided into five major sections.

■ *The Essential Ingredients.* Before you can do more than dream, you need three things—a willing crew, an offshore-capable boat, and enough money. Shortcomings in your boat and finances can be made up for with enthusiasm, but not vice versa.

■ *Equipping the Yacht for Bluewater Voyaging.* Once you find the right boat, you need to decide what you require on board, from sails to clothes. The trade-offs of optional equipment, such as generators and watermakers, are discussed. The last chapter in this section covers all of the little things you need to find a place for on board, as well as the items that are not worth the stowage space.

■ *Liveaboard Skills.* Many of the skills you need have nothing to do with sailing and everything to do with voyaging: maintenance, provisioning, keeping your boat watertight, managing fresh water, maintaining your health, and staying entertained and safe. You need to master each of these skills and set your boat up to make them easier.

■ *Shorthanded Passagemaking Skills.* To the long-distance voyager, passagemaking is a major part of life aboard. You need to learn how to manage the routines of passagemaking and make them as comfortable and straightforward as possible. I discuss passagemaking skills for the shorthanded voyager, including preparing the boat, managing seasickness, effective watchkeeping, and accurate weather forecasting.

■ *Foreign Savvy.* Traveling by boat offers a unique opportunity to experience other cultures and customs. To make the most of your stay in different countries, you will want to acclimate quickly. You need to learn how to deal with different cultures, manage your boat while traveling ashore, and leave a "clean wake" for those who follow.

Throughout the book, advice and conclusions are supported by data from our three-year circumnavigation and from outside sources. For example, the chapter on finances analyzes our expenditures and compares them to other published figures. The chapter on provisioning provides a detailed list of what is available in foreign ports so you can decide what you need to stow before you go. The relevant facts will help you reach your own conclusions. Many chapters contain boxed features that cover pretrip skill-building and onboard improvements. Numerous tables provide quick references for everything from maintenance schedules to departure checklists.

To help you decide if voyaging makes sense for you, the prologue offers perspective on the voyaging life, and sections titled "A day in the life" give you glimpses into our experiences as cruisers.

The decision to embark on a major voyage in a small sailing boat should not be taken lightly. The dangers are real and should never be underestimated. You must take responsibility for yourself and your vessel at all times.

Almost every element of preparing for and undertaking a voyage involves decisions about the risks and hazards you will face at sea. Should you purchase an EPIRB or spend the money on better storm sails? Will you take on extra crew to ensure a constant watch if someone is incapacitated? Will you insist on a 50-foot boat with a collision bulkhead before you are willing to head out to sea? No book can make these decisions for you. Each of us has his or her own risk tolerance. This book will help you define yours. It covers solutions that worked for us and other voyagers.

Then, like every sailor before you, you will have to accept responsibility for your decisions and live with the consequences. The reward will be a self-sufficiency and independence that will change your life.

INTRODUCTION | IS THIS THE LIFE FOR YOU?

A never-ending series of extreme highs and intense lows ■ *A simpler, cleaner, more self-sufficient way of life*
■ *A voyage of self-discovery* ■ *A process of growth and change in relationships*

"To me, this feels very much like the beginning. A new life, so unlike the old. Exciting and a little frightening—the start of a literal voyage into a new and enchanting future. Looking back, I cannot pinpoint the real beginning. Two years ago, sailing around the world sounded like a crazy and impossible venture but a great reason to start saving as much money as possible. I find it impossible to say when the dreaming turned to scheming, when the phantom boat that Evans was nursing to some future rendezvous with reality took on an urgency, a solidity—a life of its own.

"But even now as we embark on our adventure, I still cannot quite picture the life that goes with this dream—only snapshots of moments not tied together with the thread of routine. I wonder what it is that will define me as we begin our new life, what activities will become a regular part of my day, what thoughts will reflect my new way of being. Right now, I simply do not know the nature of the thread that will bind day to day to create a lifestyle.

"So after weeks of good-byes, a month of physicals, vaccinations, bank accounts, and trivia, we are finally poised for an adventure—our adventure. A fairy tale of our own making, of epic proportions if we so will it. The witches and demons are as yet stage left, awaiting their cues. Who knows what form or shape they will take, how or when they will come? I am certain that many of them will be of our own manufacture, but no less fearsome for that. As in all good fairy tales, much of our success will lie with us—with our cleverness and resourcefulness, our tenacity and our faith."—journal entry, May 2, 1992, the night before we moved aboard *Silk*.

To step aboard your boat and head off to sea takes a leap of faith. You must have faith in your vessel, in your partners, and most of all in yourself. To some extent, the act requires blind faith—for no one can fully understand such a different life before they live it.

Most people draw an image of the voyaging life from glossy magazine photos, boatshow advertisements, and a few boat charters in paradise. While golden moments exist and are wonderful beyond description, voyaging consists of more than these spontaneous highs. Having been sold on the dream, many couples find the reality less enchanting. Some quit. Others learn to love the reality and end up living the dream.

Is voyaging for you? You cannot know what the life will be like before you go, but you can begin to develop a realistic view of what voyaging is and is not. Picture yourself drinking a rum cooler anchored off a sand beach fringed by swaying palm trees. Then picture yourself sweating over a hot diesel engine, trying to figure out why your batteries aren't charging. Both pictures are accurate. Cruising is a vocation, not a vacation. If you make the mistake of selling yourself and your crew on the vacation, conflict will follow when reality intrudes.

If you want only to travel, you would be well advised to look for a simpler, less risky, and less time-consuming way to visit exotic places. Voyaging is not even primarily about sailing. Sailing is only one element of the life, and you can not understand the nature of voyaging from a two-week charter in the Caribbean. Voyaging is not temporary, and that makes all the difference.

Voyaging is a way of life. It changes everything: from your interactions with other people, to how you think about time, to the value you place on convenience and comfort. Most people take a year or more to begin to understand these differences—to slow down and live life. You may sun on deck and snorkel in exotic waters, but other activities will take priority. A typical day mixes the following activities, depending on whether you are on passage or in port.

■ **Keeping the boat going.** For every person aboard, this is a key focus that includes everything from engine repair to reprovisioning. In addition to daily "household" chores, we spent an average of 20 crew hours per week fixing and maintaining the boat, plus 80 crew hours at haulout time. The boat has to come first—your life depends on it every minute you are at sea. Even in port, the boat is your escape hatch if you need to leave land and head back to sea. When we reached port, we spent the first few days making the boat seaworthy again: refueling, reprovisioning, completing minor maintenance, and initiating major repairs.

■ **Managing basic household chores without modern conveniences.** When you go voyaging, you give up much of what Americans consider modern conveniences. Conveniences become something different: bakery bread rather than homemade, catching rain in a rainstorm rather than filling your tank using the dinghy and jerry cans. Voyagers step back several decades. How far back you step depends on your finances and your boat's level of complexity, but many voyaging boats function at a convenience level equivalent to the 1950s. Without a dishwasher or a clothes washer and dryer, household chores take longer. Every day is full, in part because nothing is easy.

■ **Unwinding red tape.** Logistics and bureaucracy took more time and effort than we ever imagined before we left. When entering different countries, we spent a minimum of a half-day clearing in and a half-day clearing out, plus a day or more arranging visas when they were required. We also had to manage the logistics of functioning in a foreign place so far from home. In most ports, we needed to receive mail, send faxes, and pay bills.

■ **Passagemaking.** Over our three-year voyage, we spent one-quarter of our time at sea. Few long-term voyagers spend less than eight weeks at sea annually.

Most make a minimum of two major passages a year in order to be out of the tropics during hurricane (or typhoon) season. Passagemaking is a life unto itself where everything is more difficult and the wear and tear on the boat is more extreme. When you are on a passage, your first priority is to keep the boat moving well. Then you can consider the needs of the crew and enjoy the solitude of being at sea.

■ **Enjoying the cruising community.** Voyaging offers the opportunity to meet a wide variety of interesting people. Offshore boats form a tightly knit, small community. Because of the hurricane seasons, cruising boats tend to travel in waves; you will see the same boats in key crossroads, such as New Zealand or Australia, the Mediterranean, or South Africa. The relationships among cruisers are based on shared adventure, which makes them intense and lasting. The ties begin in one anchorage and end thousands of miles later with tearful good-byes.

■ **Seeing the places along the way.** When you travel as a tourist, you are insulated from the frustrations and fascinations of everyday life. When you travel by boat, you must interact with the people you encounter as you buy food in the market, get diesel at the same dock that serves the fishing fleet, check in with the local police and customs. These interactions can lead to rewarding relationships and insights into rich cultures. But the very best experiences take additional effort: Once you arrive in paradise, you still have to make the magic happen.

■ **Entertaining yourself.** When not otherwise occupied, you must rediscover the art of entertaining yourself. In developed countries, we have lost this talent under the onslaught of television, VCRs, video games, computer networks, and movies. At sea, we reacquaint ourselves with old friends—books, handicrafts, radio, and nature. It is a wonderful chance to free your imagination and stimulate your creativity, but we knew more than one crew who quit because they found the life boring. Faced with unstructured time, they could not find ways to entertain themselves.

Voyaging has its share of work and worry. But it is a way of life, and its rewards make the glossy photos in the magazines pale in comparison. Our initial image of tropical beaches and swaying palm trees is not what we came to love, nor why we are preparing to go again. What is the voyaging life really like? What are its rewards and challenges?

A NEVER-ENDING SERIES OF EXTREME HIGHS AND INTENSE LOWS

The essence of voyaging lies in trading the comforts of shore life for a wide range of vivid experiences. Voyaging is a life of extreme highs and intense lows—from drinking French red wine in the cockpit as the sun is setting behind the twin peaks of Bora Bora, to being hove-to in a gale off Durban while seawater drips into your bunk. Distilling these extremes into words like "fun" or "pleasant" misses the essence of the life.

Emotional extremes are the antithesis of what we strive for ashore. The average American or European equates success with security, stability, comfort, and convenience. Extremes are kept to manageable and predictable levels. But when you cut out the lows, you also truncate the highs. When we headed offshore, we put aside the adult quest for financial and physical security and rediscovered the intoxicating euphoria of youth. Most voyagers become addicted to the extremes, to the emotional intensity and vividness of the life. When they return to land, most find shore life sterile in comparison. But this transition does not occur overnight, and some never adjust to the unpredictable nature of the voyaging life.

We left stressful jobs hoping to find peace and tranquillity. While we did find inner peace, we also found that voyaging is at times more stressful than life ashore. But the stress is real, not manufactured. Questions about navigation and boat handling demand immediate action—unlike deadlines and performance evaluations. This stress of voyaging is unambiguous: You do what you have to do. If you get it wrong, you know.

Stress exists even in port. At anchor, the boat cannot take care of itself. Without you on board, your boat is vulnerable to everything from a poorly set anchor to a wayward barge. When you go ashore, you must determine the country's rules for checking in, learn a new culture and its customs, and find the market and the post office. For those who value familiarity, the lack of routine creates its own stress. But for those who enjoy

adventure, every day is a revelation and every small task is a discovery.

Finally, most voyagers give up the safety nets we take for granted ashore. The majority of crews we knew did not carry health or boat insurance. Many younger cruisers lived by a thread financially. Many older voyagers worried about the quality of health care in foreign countries. But too much security robs us of taking responsibility for ourselves. Letting go of that security frees us to develop a sense of self-control that is life changing.

If you expect to find a tropical paradise and a care-free existence, you will find both. But if that is all you expect, the more stressful times will come as a bitter disappointment. If you can accept that voyaging poses unique challenges and rewards, and if you can appreciate the highs and work through the lows, then you too will end up living the dream and loving the reality.

A SIMPLER, CLEANER, MORE SELF-SUFFICIENT WAY OF LIFE

There are no smoke and mirrors at sea. Things are very simple and immediate. Sailors are impressed by good seamanship and sailing accomplishments—not by job titles, possessions, or wealth. When you arrive in Durban, South Africa, and see a foreign flag flying from a salt-scrubbed yacht, you won't care what the crew did in their previous lives. But you can be fairly certain that the crew aboard will be accomplished, self-sufficient sailors—people you will enjoy getting to know.

The voyager's focus on what is important touches every aspect of day-to-day activities. After we had been out for several months, I even changed the way I thought about time. I let my watch run fast on land, hoping to squeeze an extra five minutes out of each day. On the boat, I fixed our position with the sextant and prided myself on having the exact time, to the second. Time had become a means to an end—not an end in itself.

Voyagers must learn to do everything for themselves. These skills go far beyond mechanical know-how. All crewmembers need to be well versed in first aid and disease prevention. Even with a GPS aboard, every crewmember should know how to navigate with a sextant. Someone has to master culinary skills such as baking bread, making pies, and preserving food. Someone has to learn the art of rain catching, and everyone needs to learn how to conserve water. The challenge lies not in the difficulty of any given task, but in the range of tasks a crew must perform.

Mastering new skills is one of the most thrilling aspects of voyaging. As you start to manage everything in your own small world, you will create satisfaction and build confidence. You will eventually achieve a degree of self-sufficiency that very few people ever attain.

This transition changes who we are and how we interact with our world. In an age when environmentalism has become a fashionable cliché, voyagers are a living demonstration of how to tread lightly on the planet. During our three years of voyaging, we generated virtually all our electricity, primarily by pollution-free solar panels. Our water consumption, even when we had access to shore water, rarely exceeded five gallons per day, per person. We consumed less than 500 gallons of fuel while traveling some 35,000 miles over three years (about what an American family uses for a single car in a year).

Whether you go for three years or thirty, voyaging frees you by offering an alternative. Your newly acquired skills let you make choices about how you want to live your life. Your increased sense of responsibility allows you to deal with your choices realistically. Your newfound simplicity frees you from the misconception that material goods make you feel productive or fulfilled. Your view of yourself and your place in the world radically alters, and you tread more lightly, think more deeply, and breathe more easily.

A VOYAGE OF SELF-DISCOVERY

Voyaging is not just about physical travel. As you voyage, you move deeper and deeper into your own heart and soul. But you may not like what you see: Nothing can prepare you for coming face to face with your true self.

At some point, everyone on board a small boat at sea must come to terms with their deepest fears. We all possess a cherished image of ourselves, of how we will behave when tested. That image can be tarnished by reality—laid out for you in stark relief in a moment of fear. Then the process begins as you work to change those aspects of yourself that you do not like.

We also come face to face with our true selves in the desert of unstructured time that surrounds us at sea. Only a lucky few are fulfilled by work alone, or by their home. For most of us, what we choose to do with our free time gives us depth as individuals. When there are no other demands, the demands of your own heart and soul can be heard. Some people are disappointed to discover they would rather read a mystery novel than devour great literature, do a crossword puzzle rather than write a book.

A few people find themselves uncomfortable with who they really are. But most learn to love the solitude of the sea and appreciate the infinite vistas of their hearts. The literal voyage, with its pulling up of roots, is accompanied by a figurative voyage and the pulling apart of the self. Both teach you what defines you and fulfills you. If you are ready to face yourself as you are, then you will find this spiritual growth to be vastly satisfying and energizing.

A PROCESS OF GROWTH AND CHANGE IN RELATIONSHIPS

When they dream about a future life with no outside demands, some couples envision a continuous honeymoon. For those who make the transition, the reality far exceeds the fantasy. But the first year or so presents many challenges. Most couples on land typically see very little of each other—a few hours each evening after work, a smattering of longer periods over the weekend. Almost everyone finds it a shock to spend 24 hours a day with someone, even the person they have pledged to spend the rest of their lives with. Despite all that time together, many couples find that the boat can drive them apart. The boat and her crew form a family. In that family the skipper is the boat's husband, and the first mate is the boat's wife. Your relationship with one another can get lost in the middle.

Voyaging will not fix a deteriorating relationship. Thinking otherwise is not only foolish, but potentially dangerous. You will be dependent on your partner for your life. Total dependency implies tremendous trust, which can be very fragile. If you understand that you may discover aspects of your own personality you do not like when you go to sea, you should also understand that you may discover things about your partner—even a partner of decades—that you do not like. The sea finds all weaknesses eventually—in boats, in people, and in relationships.

Crew interactions require a delicate balance. Most long-term voyaging couples agree that in an emergency, where second-guessing and argument can lead to disaster, there can only be one captain. Yet every crewmember must be capable of sailing the boat to the nearest port if the skipper is incapacitated. Balancing this equality of skill against the need for hierarchy challenges every crew, especially couples. And there are no safety valves aboard a small boat—no supportive friend or family member to listen while you vent. Crewmembers must address the situation directly.

Voyaging will not replicate a honeymoon. But for those who meet the challenge, voyaging will strengthen and deepen their relationship in ways they may never fully understand. In the end, you must trust one another with your lives. In a February 1996 *Outside* article by Trip Gabriel, filmmaker Mike Hoover, who lost his wife Beverly in a heli-skiing accident, captured the essence of it: "Beverly and I did everything together. On our trips to Antarctica, we wouldn't be more than a rope-length apart for three months. Something happens when you're together like that. You become infused, like in metallurgy when you meld a chunk of iron with a chunk of brass. The molecules combine and they become one."

If you have done some extensive coastal cruising or offshore passagemaking, you have a sense of what the voyaging life is like. You may have dealt with some of the issues outlined above and tasted the rewards. Don't make the mistake of believing that voyaging will be easier. When cruising changes from being your time-out to being your life, the rewards and challenges become more intense—not less so.

Voyaging is not for everyone. If you take your shoreside values with you when you head off to sea, you will find yourself burdened by unrealistic expectations and impossible goals. But if you are able to let go of your old values and open yourself to unexpected challenges and rewards, then voyaging offers you a new and different way of living.

PART  THE ESSENTIAL INGREDIENTS

CHAPTER 1 | COMMITTED CREW

Basic elements for a successful voyaging crew ▪ Willing and realistic crewmembers ▪ Confident and competent skipper ▪ Toward successful voyaging partnerships ▪ **Laying the groundwork** ▪ Adjusting expectations ▪ Agreeing on a lifestyle ▪ Defining clear roles ▪ Some additional preparations ▪ Setting goals ▪ **Breaking the ties that bind** ▪ Timing issues ▪ Timing options ▪ Letting go ▪ Additional resources

In most cases, the human element determines whether a long-term voyage is a success or a failure. Yet this is often the last aspect considered by would-be voyagers and marine writers. Of the dozens of crews we knew who quit, none of their dreams foundered on anything as solid as a tropical reef. They lost their dream to such intangibles as poor communication and unrealistic expectations. They failed to make the transition from a workable relationship on land to a successful voyaging partnership.

To make that transition, each crewmember must be willing to invest in the dream. The crew must embark on a journey together before the actual voyage, evaluating themselves and their relationship with each other, planning their dream together, and supporting one another every step of the way. By the time they begin their voyage, each crewmember should be committed to a future afloat—whether for one year or ten.

BASIC ELEMENTS FOR A SUCCESSFUL VOYAGING CREW

What types of crews are out there on long-distance voyages?

During our circumnavigation, we met 30 crews who completed circumnavigations. Two-thirds were couples or families, and the remaining third consisted of men only (half were singlehanders, and half were groups of men). Only two boats took on crewmembers as they traveled. This proportion of couples and families to other crew mixes was consistent from ocean to ocean and at every major port where cruisers congregated.

We can learn several things from these statistics.

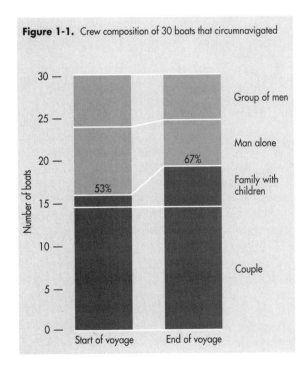

Figure 1-1. Crew composition of 30 boats that circumnavigated

Number of boats (y-axis: 0, 5, 10, 15, 20, 25, 30)

Start of voyage — End of voyage

Group of men
Man alone
67%
Family with children
53%
Couple

First, the majority of crews on long-distance voyages consist of couples and families. Most people do not choose to invite nonfamily members to live with them ashore for weeks or months. Aboard, with less space and greater stress, close-knit families succeed where other types of relationships often fail. Relying on outsiders can also jeopardize the freedom and independence that most voyagers prize. For each situation where a nonfamily crewmember worked out, we heard three horror stories.

3

Second, women are under-represented on cruising boats. Of the several hundred boats we met, only three were sailed by a single woman. No boats were crewed by a group of women. In contrast, we met nearly two dozen boats singlehanded or crewed by men who had left reluctant spouses behind. In some cases, their dream had cost these men their marriages—marriages that had lasted for decades ashore. We met only one couple in which the woman acted as skipper. Though most long-distance voyaging couples had achieved a general level of equality aboard, the man was still the captain.

There is no reason why women should be less common or less competent than men aboard offshore boats. Voyaging does not require great physical strength or a masculine approach. Most couples, however, don't start out on equal footing. Among the crews we met, in all but one case the man was the one who initiated the dream and the woman was the one who reluctantly committed to voyaging. Based on my discussions with voyaging women and my own experience, I detected four issues that contribute to this reluctance.

■ *Skill levels.* Today, more girls are learning to sail at a young age. But like most women over 30, I was introduced to serious sailing by my partner. Teaching a spouse to sail can be worse than teaching a spouse to drive. As a result, some women never master basic skills and are afraid to venture offshore.

■ *Onboard interactions.* When things get hairy, many men yell and many women overreact. Whether we were coming into a dock or dousing a sail in a gale, Evans' voice would go up three decibels if something went wrong, and I would react as if personally attacked. While most men brush off such incidents once everything is under control, many women want an apology or an explanation. Over time, Evans learned to yell less, and I learned to shrug off his lapses.

■ *Lifestyle decisions.* Some men revel in the machismo of sleeping in damp sleeping bags and eating beans from a can. Most women want a home, not a base camp. This difference in attitude extends to all aspects of voyaging, from the comfort level aboard to safety procedures. Evans and I had to balance my need for a home and his willingness to camp out, as well as my cautious approach to sailing and his tendency to take more risks.

■ *Wanderlust.* While men often define themselves through their work, many women define themselves through their homes, community activities, and family roles. Most men who dream of voyaging possess a natural wanderlust, reinforced by discontent with their jobs. Women faced with uprooting themselves can feel as if they are losing their identity. Most women need to become comfortable with their new role aboard before the magic of travel works its spell.

You may not fit these patterns, but being aware of potential conflicts in your approach to voyaging makes resolving them possible. The only way to resolve them is to work through them together. To become partners in adventure, you must take this first step.

Willing and realistic crewmembers

As Evans and I readied for our voyage, I often felt overwhelmed by the choice I had made. How could I weigh the tradeoffs between two different futures? I knew what to expect ashore, but voyaging remained an abstraction. I couldn't picture what this new life would offer, despite the books I had read and people I had talked to. I was not an adventurer, but I enjoyed traveling and nature. Would that be enough? I wanted to understand what defines a good crewmember.

I learned that little is required beyond an enthusiastic attitude and a curious nature. Ask yourself one question: Do you possess a sense of adventure? If you hike into the mountains with a smile on your face even in the rain, enjoy traveling and seeking out local people, learn about sailing by stepping forward and pitching in, and thrive on change and new experiences, then you will make an excellent crewmember. If you cannot picture yourself enjoying any of these situations, reconsider voyaging as a way of life.

I approached my voyaging life one step at a time. I reacted to a situation when I had to, and only later did I wonder where my fear had gone. We met dozens of women who had been transformed by voyaging. You cannot know what the voyaging life will offer until you live it. But almost everyone we knew who voyaged for a period of two years or more, including the most reluctant first mates, wanted to go again.

Does this life sound appealing to you? If so, take a hard look at your companions and yourself and consider your answers to the following questions.

■ *Do you trust your skipper with your life?* To answer yes, you must trust not only your captain's sailing skills, but also his or her courage: the ability to act rather than react. If you have any doubts about your skipper's competence, you will always be a little afraid and, in reality, you may be in physical danger. If trust is an issue, learn as much as you can to determine if your fear is justified. Get your skipper to take an offshore sailing course or act as crew on a delivery. Above all, share your concerns. Don't head offshore until you can answer this question positively.

■ *Can you deal constructively with fear?* Offshore sailing, like any adventure, has an element of risk. If you are truly given to hysterics, then you should not head offshore. For most people, having a plan to deal with emergencies helps avert panic. By the time you head offshore, you should understand every piece of survival gear and every emergency procedure. After that, if you still feel your stomach tighten when the wind goes above 20 knots, the cruising life may not be for you.

■ *Can you learn from your partners?* The cruising life demands constant experimentation and growth. You may know how to sail the boat, but can you take a sextant sight, row a laden dinghy, change the oil, operate the self-steering gear? Each of you will learn new skills, and you will need to share those with your partners. If you have difficulty learning from one another, you won't operate as a team. If one of you is injured, the others won't be able to manage the boat. So take a Sunday and have the most experienced person try to teach the others about the electrical system. If by day's end the least experienced partner knows where to start to fix a problem, go for it. If you are not speaking to each other, reconsider.

Successful crewmembers share an attitude. That attitude includes a cheery disposition, enthusiastic outlook, and a curious nature. But it also includes a sense of responsibility for themselves. Passive crewmembers are worse than no crewmembers. Voyaging takes strength and demands realism. In return, it gives you self-confidence, skills, and satisfaction.

Confident and competent skipper

A captain must be able to accept ultimate responsibility for the boat and crew. The "loneliness of command" extends to all captains, including those whose only crew is themselves. You must judge when you, your boat, and your crew are ready to leave. You must decide if you have adequate skills to manage an emergency. Most people who have only crewed underestimate the burden they will shoulder as skipper. One day the sea will judge you. Until then, you can never be certain how you will react.

Skippers with crew aboard need to be good leaders. They need to share their responsibility without relinquishing it. Many behaviors that work on a day sail are destructive to crew relations on a voyage. The following questions address leadership aboard. Consider whether you need to change before leading your crew to sea.

■ *Do you handle stressful situations aboard calmly?* A skipper must earn the right to be entrusted with the crew's lives. Crewmembers never trust skippers who appear susceptible to panic. Good skippers plan ahead, quietly inform their crews, and then react calmly and confidently. If you are unsure of your reactions in an emergency, try to get some firsthand experience. Crew on a passage or take a bluewater sailing course. If you find that you are not susceptible to panic, start acting like it. You'll be amazed how willingly people follow a competent skipper who is calm and confident.

■ *Are you able to make your crewmembers partners in the adventure?* If you want your crew to be comfortable voyaging, you should want them to know as much as you do. Encourage less skilled crewmembers to take a sailing course. As they build skills, give them additional responsibilities and trust them when they're alone on deck. Nothing made me more certain of my capabilities than the first night Evans slept soundly through my watch during a squall.

■ *Do you share the highs and lows?* Successful partners share the highs and lows, and for them voyaging becomes an adventure that brings them together—not a wedge that drives them apart. Next time you're struggling with a recalcitrant bolt, let your crew know why your vocabulary is causing the paint to blister! They might offer suggestions or a helping hand. At least they can share your frustration and help you see the humor in it later.

And finally, some advice from Evans: "When you are feeling unable to share the things that are bothering you or your mate is unhappy with something aboard, hugs work better than words."

The final measure of your ability as a skipper is the crew's confidence in you. Until they believe you are capable, you will be skipper in name only and uncertain whether your crew will respond calmly to your orders in an emergency.

Toward successful voyaging partnerships

A willing crew and an able skipper do not guarantee harmony onboard. The relationships between individuals can create a strong crew or destroy the dream. How do you build successful voyaging partnerships?

Debbie Cantrell researched this issue for her Ph.D. dissertation in psychology. Liveaboard cruisers were a perfect illustration of major lifestyle change. To contact cruising couples, she wrote a letter to the editor of *Cruising World* magazine. Her letter requested that first mates contact her, and it was carefully worded to be gender neutral. Of the 110 people who responded, only 2 were men. Of the 50 crews she interviewed in depth, all were couples. In all but two cases, the man initiated the sailing dream, and the woman embraced it only after a period of reluctance.

The successful voyaging partners had solid, long-standing relationships on land with open and honest communication, supportive interactions, and trust in one another's skills and decision-making abilities. But these were only necessary, not sufficient, attributes. Their voyaging partnerships also encompassed the following elements.

■ *Joint ownership of the plan.* Most successful couples could pinpoint the moment the reluctant first mate became committed. From then on, both partners knew they would benefit from voyaging—both in their relationship and as individuals. The transition became one of joint cooperation and mutual investment. Generally, the woman's increasing knowledge led her to take ownership of the plan. Her self-confidence led to enjoyment and ultimately to success.

■ *Shipboard roles.* Ashore, most of the women saw their marriages as equal partnerships characterized by clearly defined roles and mutual respect. Aboard, many women felt the partnership was no longer equal. Successful couples supported each other's efforts to acquire additional skills. They appreciated the difficulties of each person's role, respected each other's contributions, and moved quickly to an equal partnership while still recognizing the need for a skipper.

■ *Sense of identity.* If the dream is the man's, the boat embodies that dream. Much of what defines him can be found aboard. Women need to establish their own identity on board and make the boat home. Successful couples take along the items that matter most to each person. That might mean stoneware dishes and crystal wine glasses, or computers and cameras.

■ *Independence and control.* Living together in a small space can be confining, and being together all the time can lead to a loss of independence. Every crewmember needs to maintain a sense of control in his or her personal life. Each person needs private stowage spaces, some personal money, and an area where he or she won't be disturbed. That area does not have to be a separate cabin, only a place that is recognized as a "do not disturb" space.

Among the crews who failed to make the transition to voyaging partners, Cantrell found several contributing factors. In cases where women never became joint owners of the plan, they had nothing to lose if the dream failed. Where risk tolerances differed markedly, safety became a source of conflict. When a man did not recognize a woman's effort to increase her skills, the woman gave up and played a passive role. When expectations were unrealistic, couples found it difficult to share their fears and misgivings.

Finally, Cantrell found that couples who spent little time together on land had difficulty making the transition. Once alone with one another, some couples decided they didn't enjoy each other's company. If you would enjoy a weekend alone with your partner locked in your apartment without power and water, then you will love voyaging together. If careers and kids mean that you don't really know each other, spend as much time alone together as you can before you go. Embark on your adventure with your partner and friend—not a complete stranger.

LAYING THE GROUNDWORK

Once you and your crewmates take an honest look at yourselves and your relationships and find things are workable, if not perfect, you can take the next step toward voyaging. You need to lay the groundwork for cruising, which includes realistic expectations, shared goals, clear roles, and agreed-upon timelines. Discuss your approaches to voyaging and determine where they are compatible and where you need to compromise. Nothing is cast in stone. For example, saving money for your dream does not irretrievably commit you to that dream. Continue moving forward together, one step at a time.

Adjusting expectations

The prologue of this book presents one view of what the voyaging life is like. But don't stop there. Find people who have been voyaging. Attend liveaboard and cruising forums at boat shows. If you have access to CompuServe and America Online, participate in their online sailing discussions. Join the Seven Seas Cruising Association (SSCA) and read their monthly bulletins (see "Additional resources" in this chapter, page 16).

Learn about the joys and challenges of voyaging and build a realistic picture of what the life entails. With your partners, talk about the aspects of voyaging that attract or concern you. Discuss the pros and cons for each of you as individuals and for your relationship. If you create realistic expectations before you leave, you will avoid investing in an unachievable dream and minimize the conflict between crewmembers while you adjust to your new life.

Agreeing on a lifestyle

A major source of friction on many boats centers on how each crewmember wants to live on board. Determine the level of comfort, convenience, social interaction, and safety you will aspire to before you leave. Choose together what items you will bring along and what things you can do without. Your decisions affect every aspect of your voyaging life—from the size of your boat, to the level of your budget, to the type of gear you carry.

Before we left, I told Evans I was willing to "camp" on passage. But at anchor, I wanted *Silk* to be close to a floating five-star hotel. To me that meant plenty of water, a large double berth, a well-designed galley, a good icebox, adequate electricity, and a comfortable salon. None of these requirements entailed expensive equipment or major modifications.

Decisions about your lifestyle onboard are personal, and no one can make them for you. I would recommend, however, that you keep everything as simple as possible—at least to start. You'll never know you can live without something unless you try.

Creature comforts

What does it mean to you to be comfortable? A burrow or a luxurious featherbed? A utilitarian space or a designer interior? Most people feel strongly about their level of creature comfort, yet most crewmembers do not think about this issue until their own assumptions collide with someone else's. I wanted to sleep in a bunk made up with dry, clean-smelling sheets on passage and in port; Evans was comfortable as long as deck leaks weren't dripping on his head.

Someone with a high tolerance for discomfort rarely minds if things are luxurious and comfortable, but the person with a low tolerance for discomfort may feel resentful if comforts are missing. You need to agree on standards. It is unreasonable to insist you drink from crystal goblets on passage, but it is equally unreasonable to refuse to take them along if a crewmember feels strongly about having them.

Convenience levels

Like creature comforts, everyone defines convenience differently. On a boat, conveniences fall into two categories: incremental improvements and major investments. Making a place to stow suntan lotion near the companionway is a small change that protects your health by increasing the chances you'll use sun protection. Installing a watermaker, on the other hand, requires much more time and money. But the addition can dramatically change the quality of life on board.

Will you carry a GPS? Do you want radar? Will you install headsail roller furling? What about mainsail handling? Do you need a windlass? Self-steering? How about refrigeration? A microwave? A watermaker? Perhaps a washer or dryer? If so, will you need a generator? Do you want a single-sideband radio in addition to a VHF? How about an emergency beacon? An outboard motor for the dinghy? What about the smaller yet still expensive items: binoculars, night vision scopes, celestial calculators, and computers? All of these items make life easier aboard a sailing boat, but they are not equal. Experienced sailors will have already divided this list into necessities and luxuries, but the line each one draws will not fall in the same place. Therein lies the potential for conflict.

With limited resources, we are forced to make choices. Even with unlimited wealth, these conveniences come at a price. Each piece of equipment on board increases a boat's complexity and the likelihood that something will break. All equipment requires maintenance, and you may end up spending time on a convenience intended to save time.

You and your crewmates need to agree on the line between necessity and luxury after you research gear and equipment, refine your budget, and evaluate your boat.

Social life vs. solitude

What do you want to get out of cruising? During cockpit cocktails one evening in the Caribbean, we got into a discussion with friends on what we valued most about voyaging. For two couples, the answer centered on their interactions with other voyagers and the fellowship of the cruising community. They talked of the magical bond they felt with voyagers in every ocean and of deep, lasting friendships. For the other two couples, independence and self-reliance were at the top of their list. They talked of the freedom of voyaging, their increasing self-confidence, and their joy in the solitude of the sea. These answers illustrate two sides of voyaging: the individual and communal aspects of cruising.

If the idea of community attracts you, you can participate in amateur radio nets, join cruising rallies and travel in a mobile community, and even buddy cruise. But such activities compromise what others view as the essence of voyaging: independence, isolation, adventure, self-reliance, and interactions with people of foreign cultures. If one partner wants to be the Lone Ranger and the other partner wants to be the life of the party, compromise will be required. Be honest about your feelings from the start and find a balance everyone can live with.

Safety and acceptable risk levels

Individual views on safety and acceptable risk levels vary a great deal. These decisions entail the highest level of emotional content, for a wrong decision can carry a major consequence.

Choosing to voyage at all means you accept a certain amount of risk: It is impossible to avoid risk altogether. What you and your crew need to do is agree on an acceptable level of safety and risk. A more safety-conscious skipper can make for a happier crew. Most of us don't mind being overprotected, but few of us can cope with a constant sense of danger.

Nearly every decision about your boat and gear affects safety. For example, your maintenance program, such as how often you replace halyards, makes your boat more or less safe.

Decide when you will wear safety harnesses, if the on-watch person can leave the cockpit, whether you will reef with only one person on deck, what safety gear you will carry, and what emergency procedures you will follow. Most successful voyaging crews work within a well-defined set of safety boundaries.

Most crews also follow a basic rule on risk. When there is no immediate danger, any crewmember can veto the risky alternative. For example, when faced with the choice of entering a reef pass at night or heaving-to and waiting for daylight, all crewmembers have to agree to make the night entry. If one crewmember feels uncomfortable, the crew waits until daylight. I believe this approach has saved more offshore cruising vessels than any single piece of safety gear.

Defining clear roles

When you first head offshore, keeping your boat in seaworthy condition can seem like an overwhelming task. Defining clear roles and areas of responsibility is a practical approach to managing life aboard. For example, if each crewmember does some of the provisioning, how will you know exactly what is on board and whether essentials have been purchased?

Dividing responsibilities also allows each crewmember to focus on a few essential skills. The roles aboard demand specialization. To function at sea, every boat needs a captain, cook, engineer, ship's surgeon, navigator, sailmaker, meteorologist, and watch captains. In port, you need a cruise director, cultural ambassador, naturalist, and interpreter. To succeed, you need to divide and conquer, at least at first.

Before you embark on your voyage, each crewmember should try different onboard tasks. You will discover which tasks you do well, enjoy, and care about. Though couples tend to divide skills along traditional lines, you don't have to. Every crewmember should focus on the skills they can use to make a contribution.

Assess each of your skills and how they translate to voyaging. Does one of you enjoy sewing? That person should manage sail and canvas repairs. Does one of you enjoy planning trips and sightseeing? That crewmember should manage the logistics of traveling at each landfall. Hopefully, one of you will have some mechanical aptitude and one will have the patience necessary to deal with bureaucracy. Parts III, IV, and V cover the skills you need to make your voyage a success. Some skills can be developed as you go, but some you will need from the very start.

Some additional preparations

Beyond mastering new skills, you should start to develop a voyaging mindset. Above all else, start saving. Budget every dollar and account for every penny. Your success as a voyager depends on your self-discipline.

The first test comes in freeing yourself from consumerism. Don't move into a bigger house, buy a new car, upgrade your computer, or replace your washing machine. Stop eating out, going to movies, and buying non-boat-related books. Rediscover your local library, factory outlet stores, and consignment shops. Instead of watching television, read books about sailing and practice your splicing skills. Learn to do without wherever possible, or learn to do with less where you cannot do without. With the money you save, pay off your debts. If you can put 50 to 60 percent of your take-home pay into a bank account, you will be able to afford your dream. The rest of the preparations come easily after you have learned the

self-discipline necessary to live frugally in our society.

If you have studied another language, brush up by taking an adult education class or find a native speaker and start practicing. If not, start learning one. If your travels will take you to the Pacific and Indian Oceans, focus on French. For South America, study Spanish or Portuguese. For Europe, either French or Spanish helps. Yes, you can get along with English almost everywhere in the world, but talking to local people in their native tongue provides unique social interactions and cultural insights. If you are serious about voyaging, learning a language will pay off in a thousand different ways.

If you haven't been offshore, you and your crewmembers should get some experience. Take a course or join a delivery crew with a reputable skipper. Use the trip to understand how you and your partners interact at sea—not to acquire new skills. Find out how you react to boredom and stress at sea. Watch how the skipper handles the crew and evaluate the general level of morale and comfort aboard. Afterwards, debrief with your partners on what worked and what didn't. Consider the issues raised in this chapter on skipper and crew relations.

If you lack skills relative to your partners, take a basic coastal or dinghy sailing course. If you can learn with your partners present, you may want to take a course together. A more experienced crewmember can always use a review of the basics. Taking the course together will also help you develop a shared vocabulary and agreed-upon procedures.

Offshore sailing may be the most solitary of sports. Voyagers rarely sail on other boats or with other offshore sailors aboard. We can get locked into our own way of doing things without seeking better alternatives. To see how another skipper manages a boat benefits any sailor, no matter how experienced. Afterwards, you and your partners can decide together whether or not to change your procedures aboard.

Spend time together aboard the boat. Whether installing new gear, doing maintenance, sailing in heavy weather, or just socializing, you will learn about how you interact on board. Work on resolving conflicts that arise. Learn to discuss problems calmly and recognize situations that lead to tension. The better you function as a team before you leave, the better you will manage the adjustment to the voyaging life.

Setting goals

When will you go and for how long? Too many people talk about this first, and the dream vanishes against the hard reality of careers and caretaking. Tackle some of the other issues before you devote much time to this one. Your dream will take on some substance and be better able to stand comparison to your current life.

Don't feel pressured to commit at the very beginning. One step at a time will get you there. Decide together what you each need to accomplish to move on to the next step. If you need to spend time offshore, make that your goal and act on it before you begin to buy offshore gear for the boat. At each stage, you should be working toward shared objectives and personal ones, and toward small goals and major milestones. Keep your goals realistic with respect to your current life, but start putting a priority on voyaging. If you cannot find the time to invest, you lack the commitment to be successful.

The first commitment most people make is financial. Create a financial plan and determine how much money you should be saving. The saving will take years, so there is plenty of time for other things—at least at first. Set goals for the boat skills you want to perfect and the boat refitting you must complete.

For most couples, a turning point will arrive when the reluctant partner embraces the dream and starts to participate actively. Only then should you take your first steps away from land life. At that point, you can decide when to put your house on the market, when to have a massive garage sale, when to move aboard, and when to quit your job.

A point will come when you will know it is time. The boat won't be quite ready and you won't have quite as much money as you want, but you'll realize you need to set a departure date or risk losing another year to the cycle of the hurricane (or typhoon) season and winter storms. No matter how thorough your preparations, you will be overwhelmed by the list of provisions to stow, gear to install, and small chores to complete. But you will get there, because the time has come and you are ready.

When you leave the dock for the last time, you should have agreed-upon, realistic goals for your first year of voyaging. You might want to complete a fast-paced Atlantic circle or a slow cruise to the Caribbean. A common goal helps get you through some of the early lows.

The chance to recommit after the first year lets you assess what is working and what isn't. Once you slip into the voyaging mentality, you may no longer need to set goals. After our first year, goals became more like reference points—important as beacons, less important as milestones.

BREAKING THE TIES THAT BIND

Together you and your crewmates have walked step by step down a path that leads to a new life. You have chosen a branch at every fork in the road, and after several months or years you find yourselves committed to the voyaging dream. Now you need to make the transition from shore to sea. As you consider when to go and for how long, you must weigh the very real constraints of jobs, family, and money. But no such thing as a perfect time to leave exists. You must pick the best window of opportunity. Once you have decided *when,* you will be faced with *how.* As a last step, you need to break the ties that bind you to home and community and head off to sea.

Timing issues

You can always find a reason not to go. The children are either too young or too old. When the children can take care of themselves, elderly parents cannot. If your career demands attention early on, then you won't be able to leave later without risking your status and position. If you keep saving for one more contingency, you will never be satisfied with your cruising kitty.

If you wait too long, time or health may preclude your ever leaving. We heard many heartbreaking stories of couples who spent their careers planning to retire aboard, only to lose their dream to declining health or sudden death. Leaving your voyage for last means that you get no second chances. If you leave too early and must return because your kids are too young or your parents are too old, you will pay a financial penalty. But you will still have time to realize your dream.

Age is the only true constraint. Physical strength and agility are required to raise an anchor or douse a mainsail, especially if equipment fails. Circumnavigators we met ranged in age from 20 to 60. Improvements in boat-handling gear continue to extend voyaging time for seniors. But somewhere between age 60 and 70, the combination of physical demands aboard and grandchildren at home translates to the end of voyaging for most people.

Age aside, most of us must juggle three major constraints to determine when we can go:

■ *Caretaking.* If you have children, you have to decide whether or not to take them along. And if so, at what age (see the sidebar "Cruising with kids—what age is best?" in this chapter). You may have little choice if you seriously want to go voyaging. Most people who choose to have children spend the majority of their adult years caretaking. They finish caretaking their children only to find that their parents require care. If this could be your situation, then you should take your children and go while you have the opportunity.

■ *Careers.* Can you afford to leave your job for an extended period of time? The answer depends upon your field, ambitions, success, and skills. If you are in a technology-driven field, you probably cannot afford to be gone for more than a few months. You may have to wait until retirement to live your dream. If your field changes more slowly and depends on skills rather than cutting-edge concepts, you risk little in leaving for up to five years. Beyond that, no matter what the field, your resumé will be stale and you will have to start over.

Case study of a reluctant first mate

In 1990, when Evans first suggested we sail around the world, we were both at the apex of our careers as international management consultants. Evans had been a charter skipper during his business school summers, but my sailing experience was limited to day sails on Lake Ontario. My first reaction to his suggestion was, "Are you crazy?"

Yet we were both tired of 70-hour work weeks and constant travel. We had begun to question the cost of our success in terms of our relationship and our values. We were both ready for a change. I knew I lacked the skills to head off to sea. Evans did not ask me to commit to voyaging at the outset. He asked only two things: that we agree to save money toward his dream, and that I stay open to learning more about what it would be like.

Throughout the winter and spring of 1990–1991, I read all the cruising classics—books by world voyagers Eric and Susan Hiscock and Lin and Larry Pardey, *Maiden Voyage, American Promise,* Chapman on seamanship, and Adlard Coles on heavy weather. Evans taught me celestial navigation from our apartment window. Ropes sprawled around the living room in various stages of bowlines and rolling hitches. Sailing magazines found their way into my briefcase. We discussed boat designs and gear. But none of that convinced me that voyaging was in my future. By the spring of 1991 I had three key concerns:

I wanted to know if I was prone to seasickness, I wanted to sail in heavy weather, and I wanted to decide if I trusted Evans as a skipper.

That was what Evans had been waiting for—for me to gain enough knowledge so I had specific questions. Within a few weeks, Evans had arranged two liveaboard sailing courses. But we did not head for the Caribbean. Evans was just as eager as I to see if I could handle the worst before we sampled the best. During the summer of 1991, we spent three weeks along the southern coast of England, living in foul-weather gear and braving 20-foot tides, 5-knot currents, and several half gales. While surfing on decent-sized waves running in front of Force 8 winds, I took the helm and suddenly thought, "I can do this!" In that instant, I went from reluctant observer to active participant. Within six months we had purchased a 1988 Shannon 37, *Silk.* Four months after that we embarked on our new life, one full year ahead of schedule.

Since then, I've asked Evans if he thought much about how to convince me. He told me he had developed a sales plan at the very beginning. "If this is the man's dream, he has to market the idea to his partner. I took the approach of building up your comfort level with the schools and the books. Then I tried to sell you on seeing the world since I knew that you loved to travel." The things you learn after the fact!

■ *Cash flow.* If you are serious about voyaging, you will make the adjustments in careers and caretaking. But for most people, cold hard cash determines when they can leave. Yet money is the most flexible constraint. While every voyager would love limitless resources, you can voyage successfully on limited funds. You need to be debt free and have a cruising kitty that reflects your voyaging preferences. If you don't have enough money and you want to voyage badly enough, you can take a smaller boat with fewer conveniences, or you can work and earn money along the way.

Timing options

How do you juggle these three elements to come up with the time period when you can live your dream? You must balance voyaging against the demands of career and family. Only you can place a financial value on voyaging. Yet most people resolve these constraints in one of three ways—by leaving before they start a career, taking a sabbatical, or waiting for retirement. Their choice dictates almost everything about their voyaging life— from the boat they sail, to how much money they spend, to whether or not they sail with children.

Precareer

About 15 percent of the circumnavigators we met were young people voyaging before or after college. These people had no children and little money. They went in small boats, often 30 feet or less, with almost no gear. Most of them worked part of the time while they were voyaging. They accepted a lower level of comfort and convenience than most of us, but they anchored in the same harbors, saw the same sights, shared the same beach barbecues, and gained the same insights into themselves and their world.

We met some people who fell into this category after they had been voyaging for a decade or more. Generally, they were aboard the same boat, working three or four months of the year, living modestly, and enjoying life. One precareer couple we met had two children along the way, and the children were growing up happy and healthy aboard a 25-foot boat.

The major advantage of this option is simplicity; cash flow requirements are minimal, and there is no need to juggle caretaking and careers. This approach requires

only minor resources, but it demands great adaptability and flexibility. Precareer voyagers tend to be young or young at heart—people who have not learned to love their creature comforts. For those who return to the "real world" within four or five years, their sojourn is often viewed favorably by potential employers and college admissions officers alike.

Sabbatical or job change

Almost half the circumnavigators we met had taken a sabbatical from their career. Most of these people had no guarantee of re-employment, but they assumed they could resume their careers when they returned. Some people had been laid off during corporate restructuring, and their severance pay played a large role in the financial equation. Perversely, this option is most difficult for the self-employed and small-business owners. Many businesses run down in the absence of the entrepreneur. Selling the business seemed to be the best alternative. We met several people who had built up sizable companies and traded them in for a boat and the voyaging lifestyle.

Those on sabbatical tended to be between 30 and 40 years old. A few left with children on board, and many had children during their voyage. Their resources varied widely, and their boats reflected this range. But their boats were almost always larger and better equipped than those of the precareer crowd. They left with more money than that group as well, and most of them did not work along the way. None of them became permanent voyagers. Having invested a decade or more in a career, they didn't want to leave the work force completely. They wanted their children to receive a high school education ashore to safeguard their college opportunities and future careers.

Upon returning, most people who took a sabbatical experienced few problems resuming their careers. We were offered several interesting opportunities in consulting and the corporate world within weeks of returning. Friends of ours in marketing and stock brokerage jumped right back on the career track. Those with a trade found employment just as easily. We knew of no one who left and came back to find themselves unemployable. Most people had work within a few months of ending their sojourn.

A sabbatical provides a much higher level of comfort

Cruising with kids—what age is best?

Of the 30 crews we knew who circumnavigated, 6 voyaged with children. We also met dozens of boats with kids aboard doing more limited cruising. Discussions with these crews revealed differences in cruising with kids of different ages.

Most people agreed that babies fit well into shipboard life. They sleep a great deal, stay where you put them, and keep hours that are consistent with changes of the watch. For many women, the worst aspect of having a baby while living aboard was morning sickness compounded by seasickness in the first trimester. But infants turn into toddlers quickly, and toddlers are not as well suited to life aboard. For that reason, several couples had babies during the last year of their voyage and returned to the relative safety of shore before the child reached the "terrible twos."

Toddlers are too young to understand why they can't play with the gimbaled stove and too old to stay where you put them. Their mobility is astonishing, their curiosity unquenchable. To keep toddlers safe, you must child-proof an area of your boat. If you have any choice, avoid having children of this age aboard.

Those with pre-school-age children aboard generally enjoyed the experience. At this age, children are more flexible and adapt better than when they get older. They can be taught to swim and understand the word "no!" You do not need to worry about schooling, but you will spend time inventing ways to keep them entertained. Pre-school–age children are more work and worry and less help than older children. They are too young to get the full benefit of voyaging and may not remember much of their trip. Still, most people preferred going with children this age to not going at all.

Once children reach school age, you become responsible for their education. With the increasing popularity of home schooling, an array of high quality programs have become available. Most parents we've met used the Calvert system (see "Additional Resources" in this chapter) and were very pleased

with the results. Everyone commented on how well they could focus their teaching and how much less time was required than in public school. Self-teaching takes discipline, especially in paradise. On most boats, the first two to four hours of every day were devoted to school; then kids were free to do whatever they pleased. Children home educated for several years generally score well on standardized tests. If you can work out the logistics of schooling, most voyaging parents agree that between 6 and 12 is ideal for taking your children and heading offshore.

We met only a few boats with teens aboard. Some teens loved it, and some hated it. On boats with unhappy adolescents, no one had a good time. Children over 12 are old enough to have their own opinions about voyaging. Ask them and listen to what they say. Consider them crewmembers and take their issues and concerns as seriously as any other crewmember's.

Taking a break from high school needs to be considered even more carefully than taking a break from a career. A few teenagers joined their parents for a year after graduating from high school. But if your older children don't buy in, wait until you can go on your own. Otherwise, you risk permanently damaging relationships.

Most people found the experience of voyaging with children very positive. None of the families we met regarded voyaging as a disadvantage to the children, though many felt it was harder for the parents. The children thrived on the natural life and the relationship with their parents. Voyaging made them more mature and self-confident than their shore-based peers. Most children returned to school and did well academically. Some children's social development suffered, due to a lack of interaction with peers. For that reason, boats with children aboard tended to travel together. Having kids aboard opened doors ashore. Children can be a bridge, connecting naturally to local people in port and initiating many magical experiences effortlessly.

and financial security than precareer voyaging—but at a price. You are unlikely to reach the very top of your profession after taking three to five years off in the middle of your career. Only you can decide if voyaging is worth that tradeoff.

Early retirement

About one-third of the circumnavigators we knew had taken early retirement and headed off to sea somewhere between ages 45 and 55. Many of these people had worked in fields where retirement on partial pay is possible after 20 years of service, such as the military, firefighting, or policing. Others had accepted severance pay and early retirement as part of corporate downsizing. None of the circumnavigators we met had waited until a normal retirement age of 62 or 65, though we met many people that age and older doing limited cruising in areas such as the United States East Coast.

As with precareer voyaging, a major advantage of this option is simplicity. Career issues no longer exist for retirees. And most of these early retirees found themselves in that comfortable in-between time with newly independent children and not-yet-dependent parents. Financially, they were at least on a par with those taking a career sabbatical, with the added benefit of continuing income. Retirement income, though less than what they might have been used to, stretched a long way aboard a cruising boat and ensured that they did not need to work as they voyaged. Early retirees' boats had many comforts and conveniences, and these voyagers had invested much thought and money to reduce physical demands on board.

Health risks represent the largest downside to this option. These are the people whose voyaging dreams may come to an end after a sudden stroke, a heart attack, or the insidious progress of a condition such as rheumatoid arthritis. You must evaluate your own health and physical condition honestly to make this choice. If you are healthy and physically fit, you don't risk much by waiting for early retirement.

Part-time voyaging

For those with flexible careers and adequate finances, part-time voyaging may be a viable option. While we knew only one couple who circumnavigated this way, some people do extensive Mediterranean and Pacific voyages by working six to nine months and sailing the rest of the year. Teaching fits in nicely with this approach. Consultants who accept client work for a few months of every year can pursue this option. Doctors and nurses can arrange part-time work through agencies that supply practices with qualified personnel on a temporary basis. One person we knew ran a landscaping service on Long Island in the summer and sailed the tropics throughout the winter.

Virtual offices and telecommuting make this option feasible for other occupations. Freelance computer programmers, accountants, and writers, for example, are able to work by phone, fax, and e-mail for several months at a time. Easy and inexpensive worldwide satellite communication should become a reality in the near future, and many options that are impractical today will then become feasible.

Not everyone will prefer the option of taking their career with them or leaving for only a few months at a time. If ringing phones and e-mail had followed us to sea, we would have compromised what to us was the essence of voyaging. This option represents neither shore life nor ship life, but a blend of both. The disadvantage of part-time voyaging comes in the cost and complexity of the life. Flying back and forth twice a year, storing the boat for several months, and maintaining a residence ashore increase the cost of voyaging. But this option can offer a way to go voyaging without sacrificing careers or caretaking. For now, few can realistically consider this option. But if it sounds attractive and you have a suitable career, be flexible and perhaps you can make it work.

Permanent change of life

No one we met had originally thrown it all in and left permanently, though some never got around to going back. Becoming permanent voyagers was achieved year by year, not wholesale. Don't leave thinking that you won't return, and don't set it up so you can't.

You need an escape hatch—financially and emotionally. Many would-be voyagers want to free themselves from the tyranny of time clocks through early retirement and a low-income, low-cost lifestyle. But you may discover that voyaging is not for you. Even if you love it, any number of things—from health to relationships—could make voyaging unattractive in the future. If your income just covers voyaging expenditures, you will face a serious financial shortfall if you are forced to move back ashore.

You also need an emotional escape hatch. As we moved aboard, a friend who had been a lieutenant commander in the Coast Guard told me, "Never feel you can't come back. The sea can be a terrifying place. We won't think any less of you if you return earlier than you expect." Those words stayed with me throughout our circumnavigation. The more time went on, the more I appreciated them. You need goals to get you through some of the low points, but you also need the reassurance that those you left behind will still take joy in your accomplishments and support you if you quit. If the escape hatch exists, you are less likely to use it. Don't close the door forever by planning on a permanent change.

Whether you are a precareer, sabbatical, or early retirement voyager, your cruise may lead to a permanent change. But don't start there. Assume you will return to a shore-based existence and make sure you have the resources to do so. Then take it year by year, as most successful voyagers do.

Letting go

You've worked together to become a cruising team. You've purchased your boat, fitted her out, and sailed her in everything from flat calms to gales. You've taken courses in engine repair and first aid, dusted off your French, and gotten a Ham radio license. You're close to your goal for your cruising kitty, and you can leave this season or next. How do you make the final break?

Move aboard

If you've reached this stage, you are ready to cut the ties that bind you to shore. The first step is to move aboard. Rent your house or put it on the market. Sell your furniture or put it into storage. Have a massive garage sale for those treasures that have sat for decades in your attic or basement.

This can be a traumatic time, especially if one partner is still ambivalent about the sailing dream. You can ease the transition by making it reversible. If certain possessions mean a great deal to you, don't give them up completely. Invite your friends and family to temporarily adopt your pottery, paintings, and books. If you are not

ready to sell your house, rent it. But make an honest effort to simplify your life and move from a shore mindset to a sea mindset. You need to unload the baggage from decades of too much space, too much money, and too many things.

Once aboard, simplifying your life continues to be the theme. See if you can make do with one car instead of two. Declare it taboo to hire outside help for anything except electronic repairs. Eat aboard, sleep aboard, live aboard—just as you will in foreign ports all over the world. Don't take refuge in a friend's house if it is rainy and cold. Anchor out on a weekend when it is blowing 20 knots and listen to the wind whistling in the rigging. Sail the boat as often as possible, despite the time it takes to convert a liveaboard boat at rest to a shipshape boat in motion. Start to live the life.

Quit your job

Exactly when you will quit your job to prepare for voyaging depends primarily on how much money you are earning. You have to weigh the income lost from quitting early against the expenses saved from working on the boat yourself. You may decide to stagger your schedule with crewmates. For example, one partner may quit a year early to work full-time on the boat.

We quit two months to the day before we headed off to sea. That two months proved to be just barely enough time. Even if you pay professionals to fit your boat out, you will need to be there to supervise at least twice a week.

Count on all crewmembers working full time on trip preparations the month before you depart. You may be fixing the refrigeration, installing the liferaft, or putting your medical kit together. You will also need to organize your passports and visas, have physical and dental check-ups, get vaccinations, arrange your finances and mail forwarding, and update your will. All of this takes time.

Make one final round of family and friends

Right before you leave, take a week or two to see family and close friends. Though you may have to travel to do it, this is money well spent. Seeing those closest to you for a concentrated period of time keeps the pain of departure from cutting too deep.

Talk through any lingering concerns friends and family have about your new life. Reassure them that you have considered every aspect of safety. Tell them how and when you will communicate. If you are going to have a Ham or SSB radio aboard, see if you can arrange to pass messages to your family regularly. Plan on a rendezvous somewhere in paradise that fits their schedules and finances. If that looks unlikely, plan your first visit home.

Do not offer them a schedule. Schedules only cause anxiety for all of you. Stick to your one-step-at-a-time philosophy. Tell them when you plan to leave and where your first landfall will be. The day you leave, call and confirm that you are on your way. Offer a generous range of dates for your landfall. Reassure them that you will call or fax when you arrive—and make certain to do so.

After years of planning, saving, and scheming, it is time to leave. The moment of tearful good-byes you have been dreading is upon you, and you must make the final break and say your farewells. But by the time you make this final round of visits, your sadness at leaving should be overshadowed by excitement over your new venture. Those close to you will feel this energy, and they will become enthused. They have watched while you started to spend all your free time aboard your boat. They helped at the garage sale and carried boxes when you moved aboard. They have already accepted your departure.

You have long since given up the conveniences you thought you could never do without: the dishwasher and clothes dryer, the television and VCR, the plumber and TV repairer. Friends and family plan to join you in the tropics in a few short months. As you gradually moved toward your new life, you were slowly uprooting yourself. Now, the hard fact of leaving makes almost no difference at all. In that moment of realization, you are free to start your new life.

Additional resources

The Seven Seas Cruising Association (SSCA) is a non-profit organization that encourages voyaging. One of their functions is to act as a clearinghouse for information relevant to cruisers. In their monthly bulletin, members share letters that cover everything from diesel prices to local health hazards. An average issue covers areas as diverse as the Caribbean and Greenland. One year of bulletins costs about $35.

Blue Water Insurance offers reasonably priced boat and health insurance to SSCA members, designed to meet the peculiar needs of offshore voyagers.

To become an associate member, write SSCA for an application—Seven Seas Cruising Association, Inc., 1525 S. Andrews Avenue, Suite 217, Fort Lauderdale, Florida, 33316; phone 954-463-2431, fax 954-463-7183, e-mail: sscaassn@aol.com

Similar organizations in the U.K. are The Cruising Association, CA House, 1 Northey Street, Limehouse Basin, London E14 8BT; phone 44(0)171-537-2828, and The Little Ship Club, Bell Wharf Lane (off Thames Street), London EC4R 3TB; phone 44(0)171-236-7729.

To inquire about home schooling programs offered through the Calvert system, contact the Calvert School, 105 Tuscany Road, Baltimore, MD, 21210; phone 410-243-6030.

CHAPTER 2 | BLUEWATER-CAPABLE YACHT

Key parameters for a bluewater voyager ■ *Seaworthiness* ■ *The question of size* ■ *The question of cost* ■ **Survey of a bluewater boat** ■ *General* ■ *On deck* ■ *Below* ■ *Additional resources*

Marine books and magazines devote tremendous amounts of time and effort describing the perfect offshore yacht. But for those of us with finite resources and a desire to do more than dream, this endless discussion offers little in the way of useful advice. In fact, there is no such thing as the perfect boat for bluewater voyaging. Every boat balances hundreds of tradeoffs, and no amount of design improvements, complicated gear, or modern materials will ever change that.

The perfect offshore yacht must be two boats—a luxury hotel in port and a sailing machine on passage. The elements that contribute to one often detract from the other. So don't waste time seeking the perfect boat. Find *your* ideal boat—the one that meets your criteria for comfort and safety and fits your budget.

KEY PARAMETERS FOR A BLUEWATER VOYAGER

The range of boats voyaging right now almost defies description. Every conceivable combination of hull material, rig, and size can be found (see the sidebar "Some data on offshore-capable yachts" in this chapter).

We crossed the southern Indian Ocean with a group of voyagers all completing circumnavigations by way of South Africa. These boats included a 60-foot fiberglass catamaran; a 45-foot, French, open-sterned racing boat; a 37-foot, rebuilt, 30-year-old steel ketch; and a 24-foot fiberglass production boat. None of the crews were completely satisfied with their boat. But each knew their boat's strengths and weaknesses, and none regretted the compromises they had made. The fact that they were still voyaging was proof enough.

How do you go about selecting an offshore yacht?

Your dream boat lies at the intersection of three parameters: seaworthiness, size, and cost. All successful offshore sailboats share a minimum level of seaworthiness, even if they have nothing else in common. Size and cost depend on you—your goals, your budget, your crew.

These three parameters are basically independent. There are cheap, small, seaworthy boats and large, expensive, unseaworthy ones. Every boat will need some reinforcement, minor modifications, and additional equipment. You will have to learn the strengths and weaknesses of whatever boat you buy to understand and respect its limits.

Seaworthiness

A boat you take offshore must perform well at sea. Seaworthiness consists of three basic elements: sailing performance, stability, and durability.

Sailing performance includes windward and light-air capabilities and balance. Most coastal sailors readily understand these attributes. Stability and durability are more difficult to evaluate before heading off to sea. Stability, or the ability to stay upright even when the sea would have it otherwise, can be considered synonymous with safety offshore. Durability allows a boat to stand up to the punishment of the sea—mile after mile, day after day. A good bluewater yacht relies on strength, simplicity, and redundancy to reduce the likelihood of breakage and make failures easier to fix.

Offshore sailing performance

Sailing performance means nothing until it is tested in offshore conditions. Offshore conditions are distinguished from coastal by wind speeds and wave conditions.

Some data on offshore-capable yachts

To determine what today's successful offshore boats have in common, I analyzed two sets of boats in terms of length, hull material, rig, and boat manufacturer.

The first sample consists of the 30 circumnavigating boats we met, which I call the circumnavigators. To study a larger sampling and look for contradictions to the first sample, I used the Seven Seas Cruising Association bulletins for a 12-month period. For the SSCA sample, I selected 127 boats that had sailed at least 5,000 nautical miles.

The circumnavigating boats ranged from the Cal 25 *Direction,* a 25-foot California-built production boat intended for daysailing, to the Tayana *Bluewater,* a 50-foot modern Taiwanese yacht designed for offshore voyaging. *Direction*—which carried a family of four, including two children aged five and two—had been structurally reinforced by her skipper. At the time we knew the boat, *Direction* was on her ninth year of voyaging. *Bluewater,* crewed by a couple, had just completed an 18-month circumnavigation and won her division as part of Europa '92 cruising rally when we met her. The SSCA boats proved equally diverse. They ranged from a Norsea 27 to a Sundeer 78. No single manufacturer or designer dominated either sample.

Among the circumnavigators, 11 of the 30 boats were one-off custom designs. The remaining 19 production boats included 2 Valiants and a single boat each from 17 other designers, including Pearson, Westerly, Roberts, Van de Stadt, and Stevens.

The 127 SSCA boats included a staggering 94 different models and designs. Six Westsails topped the list as the largest number of boats from one manufacturer. Also included were 5 Tayanas, 3 each from Stevens, Norseman, and Valiant, and 2 each from 18 other manufacturers. The brands traditionally marketed to offshore sailors were represented, including Mason, Bristol Channel Cutter, Hallberg-Rassy, Swan, Shannon (not us!), and Pacific Seacraft. The SSCA sample also included many boats marketed to coastal sailors, including Catalina, Beneteau, and Tartan. Less traditional boats included a single Freedom and

7 catamarans. Both samples prove that many types of boats make successful bluewater voyagers.

In terms of length, Figure 2-1 shows that in both samples about 40 percent of the boats were between 40 and 45 feet long. Of the circumnavigators, 6 were under 35 feet and 7 were over 45 feet in length. Of the SSCA sample, 15 were under 35 feet and 37 were over 45 feet. Almost three-quarters of the boats in both samples fell between 35 and 50 feet. At the extreme, boats under 30 feet had completed circumnavigations (we knew two 25 feet or under).

In terms of material, fiberglass dominated both samples. An estimated 70 percent of the circumnavigators and 77 percent of the SSCA boats were made of fiberglass. Other materials were all represented, however, with steel being the second most common.

With respect to rig, almost 80 percent of the circumnavigators were cutters, with the remainder being ketches or yawls (except for a single junk-rigged boat). Among the SSCA boats, two-thirds of

Figure 2-1. Size distribution of voyaging boats

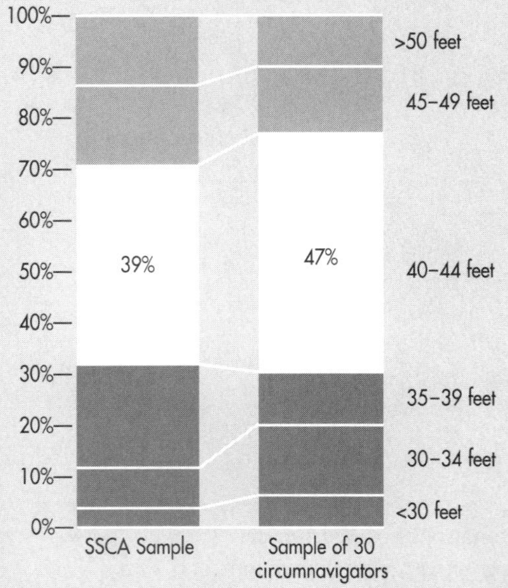

the rigs were cutters. A junk-rigged fiberglass boat, a ferrocement cutter, and a steel ketch completed circumnavigations.

Keel configurations varied almost as much. While traditional full keels dominated among the circumnavigators, 8 boats had medium-length, moderate-displacement keel designs and 3 had centerboards. Three boats had modern underbodies, with a fin keel and a partial skeg or no skeg at all. One French boat had a flat bottom with a centerboard and a detach-able rudder for drying out on beaches or riding the ice in Antarctica.

What can we conclude from all of this data? Based on these samplings, if there were an "average" voyaging boat, it would be a 40-foot fiberglass production cutter with a traditional keel from any of a dozen different manufacturers. But the sampling proves that a wide range of boats successfully voyage. Their success does not depend on boat length, rig type, hull material, keel design, manufacturer, or designer.

Most coastal sailors have experienced strong winds, though probably for hours but not days. Few coastal sailors have encountered offshore waves, and most have difficulty appreciating the impact waves have on sailing performance. A large ocean swell in less than 10 knots of breeze will stop forward progress on many boats. When you are beating to windward, large waves can increase leeway by 10 degrees or more, even on an excellent offshore boat. Waves will also cause a poorly balanced boat to come off course more quickly and to take longer to recover. Most damage to boats in heavy weather results from dangerous breaking waves, not high winds. At the extreme, waves also cause knockdowns—when boats are rolled through 90 degrees or more. To perform well at sea, an offshore boat must perform well on all points of sail in large waves. She must possess the following attributes:

■ *Downwind/light-air performance.* Offshore, a boat must be able to make good daily runs in light air with the wind on the aft quarter or dead over the stern. About one-quarter of our time at sea, we sailed with an apparent wind of less than 10 knots aft of 115 degrees. In these conditions, a normal ocean swell rolls the wind out of the sails. While it helps to have lighter displacement and a keel design with less wetted surface, a heavy displacement full keel can be offset by lots of sail area. An offshore boat needs sufficient mast height to carry enough sail to keep moving in these conditions.

■ *Windward performance.* Trade wind sailing tends to be about running downwind under double headsails. But once you leave the trades, you will have to go to weather. To sail efficiently to weather in big waves, nothing beats a deep fin keel. However, deep keels pose problems in poorly charted harbors. At a minimum, an offshore boat needs to have enough of a keel that it can manage close to a 100-degree tacking angle (including leeway), even in large waves.

■ *Balance.* In theory, the amount of helm required to hold a well-balanced boat on course does not change as the boat heels. Reliable self-steering depends on a well-balanced boat. A poorly balanced boat will round up or fall off as the wind gusts and the angle of heel changes. The amount of force required to hold such a boat on course increases with the wind speed. The crew will be constantly adjusting the steering or the sails to stay on course. The boat will have to be reefed early for the self-steering to operate without breaking. An offshore yacht must be balanced on all points of sail. Her self-steering must function reliably with the appropriate amount of sail for the wind conditions.

How does your boat perform against these criteria? You may know your boat's light-air and windward capabilities in coastal conditions. To really test your boat's light-air abilities, take her out in a big swell on a calm day and see if you can make 4 to 5 knots of boat speed in 5 knots of apparent wind. To evaluate her to windward, determine her tacking angle against a 20-knot breeze and 7- to 10-foot waves with two minutes between tacks. To test her balance, see how your autopilot or wind vane steers when the wind is on the beam and gusty, and when it is light and over the stern. If your boat passes these tests, then her sailing performance measures up to offshore standards.

An offshore boat must be balanced. She must sail to weather reasonably well and keep moving decently in light airs. If any of these attributes are missing, she will be a danger to herself and her crew. If all these attributes are in place, she may prove to be an outstanding passagemaker. For that, she must do more than sail well. She must also be stable in extreme conditions and be able to stand up to the rigors of the sea—the constant motion, wear and tear, and strains on every part of her structure and gear.

Stability

Stability, or the ability to resist a knockdown, determines an offshore boat's ultimate measure of safety. Much has been written about stability, but few unequivocal conclusions have been reached. In theory, a boat's stability is determined by her hull shape, center of gravity, buoyancy, and a host of other factors. In practice, many dynamic factors affect stability, including the force and form of the waves and the momentum created by the mast and keel in a roll.

As poorly understood as it is, stability represents one of the only measures of how well a boat will stand up to extreme conditions. Coastal sailors encounter stability issues when they don't put enough weight on the rail during a heavy-weather race or when they broach carrying a chute. Inshore, such events are exciting; offshore, they are terrifying. An offshore boat needs to stay upright. If she is rolled by an exceptionally large wave, she needs to come back upright.

Designers use different measures to describe a boat's stability. The righting moment or stability curve shows how much force is necessary to heel the boat one more degree through a 180-degree roll (Figure 2-2). The amount of force to get her to heel the first degree is her initial stability, what most sailors call "stiffness." The point where the greatest force is required to roll the boat one more degree is the boat's angle of maximum stability (about 50 degrees of heel in Figure 2-2). As the boat continues rolling, it reaches a point where it is more likely to continue over than it is to come upright. This occurs where the curve crosses the x-axis and is called the angle of vanishing stability or the limit of positive stability (about 125 degrees in the diagram). Once the boat is completely upside down, her tendency to stay that way is measured by her inverted stability. Ideally, in-verted stability is low—the weight of the keel acts as a pendulum that tends to right the boat if it is rolled by a wave. The stability ratio, or the ratio of the area under the positive part of the curve to that above the negative part, offers another measure of the boat's stability.

The factors that contribute to stability are complex and not always consistent. A low center of gravity, high coach roof and topsides, and heavy displacement all contribute to specific measures of stability. But a deep hull will increase the angle of maximum stability, while a shallow hull will increase the amount of force the boat can withstand at that angle. A narrow beam decreases inverted stability, but a wide beam increases maximum stability. Even a low center of gravity, which appears to always increase stability, can contribute to a capsize. The inertia of the weight low in the keel can create a flywheel effect that carries the boat past the point of positive stability. Designers end up with few clear rules to follow.

The governing bodies of offshore racing agree that a 40-foot boat should be able to withstand a 120-degree knockdown without capsizing. That means a point of vanishing stability of at least 120 degrees. Smaller boats require a higher limit because their lower displacement makes them more vulnerable to being knocked down beyond the horizontal. The proper limit of vanishing stability for traditional designs under 40 feet can be approximated by 160 degrees minus the waterline length of the boat.

How do you go about evaluating the stability of your hull? While you can contact the boat designer or manufacturer and ask them for a stability curve like the one shown in Figure 2-2, differences in calculation methods make these difficult to compare. Currently the only source of consistent data is US Sailing (see "Additional resources" in this chapter).

US Sailing's data come from physical measurements and roll tests that are carried out exactly the same way on each boat. The resulting IMS certificate (based on the International Measurement System, a handicap rating rule used for racing boats) includes a calculated limit of positive stability, righting moments at various heel angles, and a calculated ratio of stability. They also offer fairly complete information on how well the boat should sail at various wind speeds and angles—enough to construct a polar diagram for a given boat. While measurements are always open to interpreta-

Figure 2-2. Stability curve for a 47-foot offshore boat

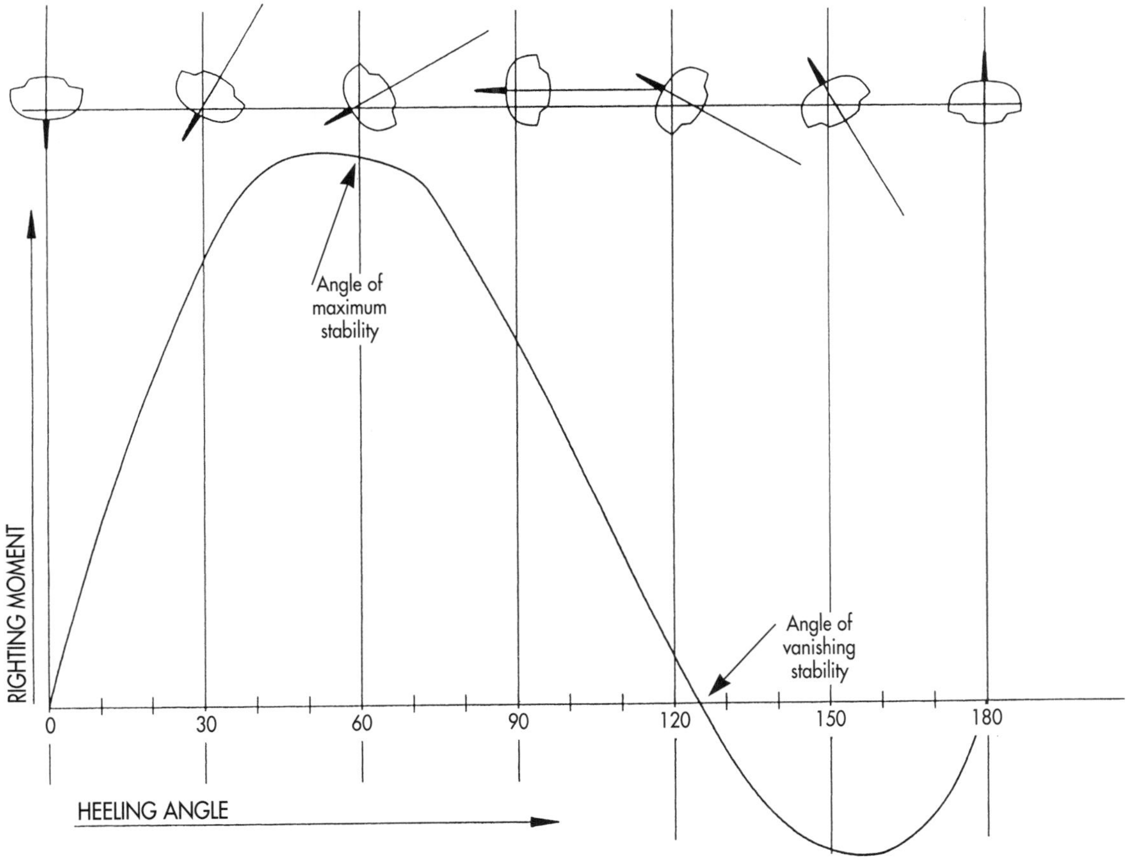

Angle of maximum stability

Angle of vanishing stability

RIGHTING MOMENT

0   30   60   90   120   150   180

HEELING ANGLE

tion, US Sailing offers comparable data for evaluating many boats.

If you are interested in examining the stability characteristics of a wide variety of boats, US Sailing publishes a document titled, "Performance Characteristics of the North American IMS Fleet." This summarizes stability and measurement data for every boat that has been IMS certified. Many of the boats out voyaging are represented in this list: Aldens, Bristols, Cals, Crealocks, Hinkleys, Irwins, Little Harbors, Morgans, Petersons, Swans, Tartans, and Valiants, among others. The data allow quick comparisons between boat brands and show how stability varies among sisterships.

The US Sailing data let you compare boats on a set

of consistent but static measurements. No widely available measurement technique can model the dynamic process of a boat being rolled by a wave. On an average trade wind circumnavigation timed to avoid both tropical cyclones and winter gales, the chances are minimal that you will ever get knocked down beyond the horizontal. But you want to evaluate your boat's ability to deal with such events. The number of sisterships that have successfully completed offshore voyages provides one positive indication of a given boat's stability.

Long-term durability

Seaworthiness also means a boat sails well and weathers gales even after many ocean miles. Gear aboard seldom breaks. If it does, it is fixed easily or a backup is readily available. This is the essence of durability, which includes the following attributes:

■ **Strength.** The strength of the hull determines how well a boat will stand up to voyaging. An offshore cruising boat must have a well-built hull that can take a minor grounding without serious damage. She must be able to sit on her keel and be hauled on a marine railway without stressing her structure. Her hull must have some rigidity, so the constant flexing at sea does not result in stress cracks and deck leaks. Strength includes a well-stayed rig with chainplates that are securely bolted to key structural members; high quality deck fit-

tings—cleats, stanchions, and handholds—that won't break when your life depends on them; and special reinforcement in key structural areas, such as in the bow and under the maststep.

Most of us lack the expertise to recognize and reinforce a weak hull. A brand name offshore boat offers some assurance of hull quality. If a sistership has completed long voyages, that is a clue that your boat can meet the same offshore challenges.

That does not mean you will not discover a few problem areas that need to be fixed or reinforced. Taking a production boat voyaging, no matter how well built, can be compared to taking a stock Jeep in the Paris-to-

Multihulls as offshore voyagers

We knew of two catamarans that completed circumnavigations, both of them 60 feet or over. Over the three years we were out voyaging, catamarans were becoming increasingly common, and their advantages were becoming more evident. While we were in New Zealand, the 80-foot catamaran *ENZA* was being readied for her second try at the Trophée Jules Verne. This French race challenged boats to sail around the world in less than 80 days. *ENZA* succeeded, proving that catamarans are the fastest open-ocean sailing machines yet devised.

While stability comes from the keel on monohulls, large catamarans depend on their beam and overall size to stay upright. To realize their potential for speed, catamarans use lightweight construction. That means that a multihull for bluewater voyaging needs to be big (over 40 feet) and well built. These requirements translate to large amounts of money: $500,000 and up for a new 40-foot catamaran.

The decision between a multihull and a monohull comes down to specific tradeoffs. Most people are put off by the fact that on a catamaran, what goes down doesn't necessarily come back up. Think of it like this: A multihull is like a Cracker Jack box—it will float just as well on either side. The multihull (like the low, flat Cracker Jack box) has enormous *initial* stability. Even so, once it reaches the point of vanishing stability, it will turn over—and you need to be prepared to live

upside down until you are rescued. Yet a large, wellbuilt multihull is about as likely to capsize as a large, well-built monohull is likely to *sink*—which catamarans are far less likely to do than monohulls.

The true advantage of a multihull is its generous layout and commodious space, combined with its general lack of heel and roll in all but the most extreme seaway. You can also clean the bottom of a multihull by beaching the craft.

The few cruising multihulls we knew were not significantly faster than similar-sized monohulls in true offshore conditions. Their performance is more dependent on a light load, and they tend not to do well to windward or in large seas. Also, while heel and roll are greatly reduced in most circumstances, the motion in heavy weather is much more up and down: "Like a golf ball teed off in a bathroom," as one offshore multihull sailor put it.

Improvements in materials mean that multihulls are just now coming into their own. They are likely to increase in numbers among offshore voyagers over the next decade. The choice between the multi- and monohulls reflects two approaches to voyaging. If you prefer gunkholing and coastal cruising to long offshore passages and deep anchorages, the catamaran may be ideal. But any offshore yacht must meet the criteria listed in this section. Put a catamaran to the same test as any monohull and see how it scores.

Dakar race. Production boats are built for the requirements of the average buyer and, with very few exceptions, for the demands of coastal cruising. No boat will be trouble free, and every boat will have its weaknesses. You will discover them when you head offshore and reinforce and upgrade as you go along.

To determine if a specific hull can take offshore punishment, seek out objective information. Contact the manufacturer or the designer and ask about sisterships that have made long-distance voyages. Contact the owners of these boats. Ask them about the strengths and weaknesses of the hull. Find out if they had any mast compression, delamination, or osmosis problems. Take advantage of *Cruising World* magazine's "Another Opinion" section to learn how well boats perform offshore and purchase the *Practical Sailor* or *Blue Water Sailing* review of the boat (see "Additional resources" in this chapter). Ask local marine surveyors and boatyards what problems have appeared in sisterships. By the time you have exhausted all these sources, you should have a sense of the strength of a particular hull. If you are still in doubt, pay a surveyor to go through a structural analysis of the hull.

■ *Simplicity.* An offshore cruising boat should be simple in her design and construction. Simple means uncluttered side decks that allow you to move freely from bow to stern, an efficient foredeck layout that lets you deploy an anchor in seconds, and an easy system for reefing that can be handled by one person.

Below, simplicity means accessibility to every deck fitting, every part of the bilge, and every piece of equipment. With a little thought and effort, simplicity is easy to achieve on any boat. Next time you remove trim pieces inside a locker to get at wiring or deck fittings, don't bother to put them back. Add access panels in cabinetry to reach plumbing and seacocks. Cut additional openings in the cabin sole to increase access to the bilge. After a year or so, you will be amazed at how much simpler your boat will be.

■ *Redundancy.* If a critical piece of gear fails, you need options. You can create redundancy if it doesn't already exist on board. For example, redundancy can mean multiple shrouds that run to different chainplates, a staysail stay in addition to a headstay, and more than one water tank below.

Redundancy also translates to strong sailing performance. If your engine dies, your sailing performance is your backup system. If your boat needs the engine to punch her way through a heavy sea or to enter a crowded anchorage, then she may prove to be a hazard if her engine fails. As long as your boat sails reasonably well, the proper amount of backup can be created.

A bluewater-capable yacht starts with a well-made, durable hull that sails well. Many yachts fall into this category. Your budget and your preference for size will help you narrow down your choices.

The question of size

Almost everybody wants a bigger boat. But *everything* aboard a cruising boat is a tradeoff, and size is no exception.

Beyond more space below, larger boats benefit from increased stability for better seakeeping ability, a longer waterline for more speed, and greater displacement for more comfort at sea. Smaller boats cost less to buy, outfit, and maintain. They can be sailed into a crowded anchorage or even into a marina slip, and sails and anchors can be managed by hand.

Given that there is no right answer, what size will best meet your needs? Most of us want the biggest boat we can afford and still sail shorthanded. With the equipment available today, a shorthanded crew can manage boats 60 feet and more in length. However, if the windlass fails, two people will not be able to get the anchor up by hand; if roller furling breaks, two people would be hard-pressed to get a large genoa down in a moderate breeze.

The findings presented in the sidebar "Some data on offshore-capable yachts" show that many long-distance voyagers found 40 to 45 feet the right length. Forty-seven percent of the circumnavigators and 39 percent of the SSCA boats fell into this size range. On a boat over 40 feet, you can stow the basics and some luxuries, such as spare light-air sails and extra fuel and water; carry a generator and a watermaker without making major compromises in other areas; and offer guests some measure of privacy without using the main salon as a sleeping area.

But the average may not be your ideal. Going from a 35- to a 45-foot boat will more than double your costs.

If you really want to go, a smaller boat may make it feasible. The many voyagers managing well on smaller boats prove that size does not correlate to success.

The question of cost

Don't fall into the trap of spending too much on your boat and ending up with too little money to go voyaging. Instead of buying your dream boat and then seeing how much money is left, work backwards. Figure out what you can afford to spend on your boat in light of what you'll need to support yourself as a voyager.

What is a realistic number for buying and fitting out a boat for voyaging? We met people on boats that cost less than $50,000 and more than $500,000. Half of the circumnavigators we knew spent between $100,000 and $200,000 to buy and outfit their boat. Most of these boats ranged from 35 to 45 feet. Larger boats tended to be older, and their owners did more of the work themselves. The majority of these people had bought a used boat for $75,000 to $150,000, and then spent $25,000 to $50,000 on gear.

Plan on investing one-quarter to one-third of the purchase price in a new or used boat less than 5 years old to ready it for offshore sailing. The initial cost may be less for an older boat, but the cost of additional gear and modifications will be higher. One of our friends bought a 20-year-old used fiberglass boat for $60,000 and then invested $50,000 to upgrade it for his circumnavigation. Typically, our friends in boats 10 years old and older spent an additional 50 percent of the purchase price refitting the boat for offshore.

One-quarter of the boats that circumnavigated cost less than $100,000, and one-quarter cost over $200,000. The less expensive boats were either older or smaller, or both. A 30-year-old, 30-foot fiberglass Van de Stadt design (see the sidebar on *Isa Lei* on page 36) and a 20-year-old, 37-foot steel ketch rebuilt from a bare hull both fell into this category. By comparison, a 20-year-old Nicholson 32 would cost £17,000 to £20,000, and you would need to add £2,000 for re-rigging and £3,000 to £5,000 for added batteries and the means to charge them. Over 35 feet, this figure increases considerably. The largest and newest boats in the under-$100,000 range had been built by their owners, including one 40-foot steel boat. For every such boat that ends up voyaging, a dozen sit ashore abandoned. Those owners who went to sea in their own homebuilt boats had owned several boats before, knew enough to supervise a nonmarine welder in welding the hull, and finished out the interior themselves.

Plan to spend over $200,000 to buy and outfit a new boat. A new Pacific Seacraft 40 lists for $285,000, not including sails, GPS, windlass, and refrigeration. A new Island Packet 40 lists for $218,950 not including instruments, GPS, VHF, and bottom paint. Most of the boats we met that fell between $200,000 and $300,000 in price were new or less than three years old. Among the boats in the over-$200,000 category were custom designs built for offshore voyaging. A few had price tags starting at $400,000.

If these numbers shock you, don't despair. Most cruisers cannot afford to buy new. Most boats appear in faraway anchorages when their design is already a bit dated and their gelcoat has a few cracks. But they are proven offshore vessels with sisterships that have traveled the world over.

No one can tell you what boat to take to sea. Whatever boat you eventually choose will balance your requirements and tradeoffs. Like the cruisers we met sailing across the Indian Ocean, you will never find the perfect boat. But you will find a boat that combines seaworthiness, spaciousness, and affordability to satisfy your definition of a bluewater voyager, your *ideal* boat.

SURVEY OF A BLUEWATER BOAT

Once you have decided what you are looking for in terms of size, cost, and seaworthiness, you will have a subset of boats to consider for offshore voyaging. You will probably find that dozens of boats fall into the parameters you have set. The way to decide between the different boats is to scrutinize their details. Perform the following survey on any boat you are considering. If your current boat is at least 30 feet long and meets the general requirements outlined above, see how it fares against the criteria below.

The survey pinpoints critical differences between a successful offshore voyager and a coastal cruiser. These are the details that distinguish a safe, workable, comfortable offshore voyager. Consider these attributes, as well as the things that matter to you in your coastal boat—from an extra-long double berth to a four-burner stove.

The overall size and basic hull shape are the only details that cannot be modified. Given a seaworthy hull capable of accommodating you and your proposed crew, almost everything else can be upgraded, changed, or fixed. But if the boat lacks most of the items in the survey, the cost to make it offshore capable may prove prohibitive. Most of the items on the list are unrelated to size. We met several boats 30 feet and under that met these criteria better than many boats over 40 feet.

As you consider the boats you can afford, bear in mind that even the most luxurious boat cannot offer the level of comfort and convenience of a moderate-sized apartment. If you start by expecting shoreside comforts, every boat will fall short. It is far better to start with a bare minimum of necessities and add the comforts that prove worthwhile as you go along.

General

Beyond a solid hull, an easily handled rig, and a keel that will give you adequate windward and light-air performance, a few additional considerations make or break an offshore voyager:

■ *Adequate ventilation.* Many production boats lack sufficient ventilation for the heat and humidity of the tropics. Poor ventilation contributes to the growth of mold and mildew and produces damp berths at sea. Offshore boats need large opening hatches (ideally, one for each major living space aboard). High quality, operable ports should be located throughout the boat, but at a minimum in the head and galley.

Ports and hatches cannot replace ventilation for use in boisterous conditions at sea. On most boats, Dorade vents are the only source of ventilation in heavy weather. Four large Dorades should be considered the minimum on a 35-foot boat. All ventilation, including Dorades, must be watertight in extreme conditions.

■ *Adequate light below.* Many traditional, all-wood interiors are so dark they become claustrophobic. If you can't see into lockers or work on the engine without turning on a light on a rainy day, consider using white surfaces to increase the light below. A white roof liner of molded plastic, or white paint on the cabin trunk, can

change the entire feel of a boat (Figure 2-3). Beyond that, make certain every area has good lights for reading and working. Fluorescent lights stay cooler, last longer, and use less electricity than conventional bulbs.

■ *Handholds and footholds.* Safety aboard an offshore boat depends on handholds and footholds. Whether you are on deck or below, heeled at 20 degrees or flat, you should be able to stand anywhere and reach a good handhold (Figure 2-3). Handholds do not include lifelines and stanchions, which should never be knowingly trusted with your entire weight. In the galley and around the mast where "one hand for the boat, one hand for yourself" can be impossible, good footholds become critical. Walk around the boat and consider some common problem areas: around the companionway, stepping onto the side deck over the coaming, in the galley, between the coach roof and the staysail stay, and at the mast. Handholds and footholds are inexpensive and easy to install. View them as cheap insurance against serious injury or crew overboard.

■ *Adequate stowage.* An offshore boat must be able to carry an average of 2,000 pounds per crewmember. The boat's design determines the amount of stowage onboard. For example, center cockpit designs tend to sacrifice stowage for accommodations.

Silk had fewer areas devoted to stowage than many boats her size. Her tankage was located in the settee and quarter berths, because it would not fit in her shallow bilge. Whatever stowage might have been available under the floorboards was taken up by her centerboard. We created additional stowage areas to carry enough supplies to cross an ocean. When comparing several boats, take a good look at the amount, location, and accessibility of stowage.

■ *Storm-proof stowage.* Stowed items can cause serious injury in a knockdown if they are not adequately secured. An offshore boat needs strong, lockable floorboards to hold heavy items in the bilge, even if the boat is upside down. Batteries must be strapped to structural mounts. Latches on drawers and lockers need to lock positively and hold even when contents are thrown against them. The stove must be held in place, even during a capsize. Heavy icebox lids must be securable.

Figure 2-3. *Silk's* white headliner and cabin trunk provide a bright interior; many solid handholds make for a safe platform in a seaway.

Picture the boat upside down and consider ways to correct potential problem areas.

On deck

The boat's decks are your working platform at sea. They must offer a safe, comfortable environment even when chaos reigns just beyond. Each area needs to be well designed to meet its function: The bow platform must facilitate anchoring, the side decks must allow free movement fore and aft, and the cockpit must keep crewmembers secure and comfortable. Beyond that, details ranging from nonskid to watertight ports and hatches protect you and your boat at sea.

Bow platform and anchoring arrangement

True offshore voyagers can be distinguished from their coastal counterparts by their bow platforms and anchoring setups. Many round-the-buoys racers and daysail boats have no anchor ready to drop. They lack bow rollers, solid bow cleats, and good fairleads. Even small offshore voyagers can drop or retrieve an anchor at a moment's notice.

A good bow platform has adequate room to flake a sail or an anchor rode. It includes two good bow rollers far enough forward of the stem of the boat to keep an anchor from hitting the hull when being dropped or retrieved. It includes at least two solid cleats, each large enough to hold two docklines cleated in a proper figure eight. A line passing over the bow rollers leads fair to the bow cleats. Each cleat also has a solid fairlead to minimize chafe on docklines. Boats over 35 feet will be equipped with a windlass, which feeds the rode through a hawser to the chain locker. From the bow platform described above, you can efficiently set or retrieve two anchors.

If the foredeck isn't set up well for anchoring, you will have to add a small anchoring platform with proper bow rollers and solid cleats. This modification greatly improves anchoring ability, but it tends to add weight at the bow.

Clean side decks

How easily can you move from stern to bow? Do you have to duck around stays or climb on the coach roof? Are there handholds at every point along the way? Can you run a jackline from bow to stern? In a safety harness, could you stay clipped to the jackline while you traveled the length of the boat?

A good offshore side deck measures at least 18 inches wide and is unobstructed from bow to stern. With a high coach roof and steep cabin sides, even this may be inadequate when heeled. If you can walk down the lee side deck when the boat is heeled over at 20 to 30 degrees, then the side decks will offer plenty of security at sea.

Handholds must be mounted all the way along the coach roof. A high toerail or bulwark offers footholds when the boat is heeled. This should be at least four inches high, have drain holes so it doesn't trap water, and be strong enough to easily support several hundred

Figure 2-4. *Silk's* bow platform allows for the easy stowage and deployment of two properly sized anchors and includes two large cleats with excellent fairleads.

Figure 2-5. From this bow platform on a 40-foot coastal boat, you could deploy only one anchor using the undersized bow roller.

Figure 2-6. *Silk's* side decks are exceptionally wide and clean with good handholds from the cockpit all the way to the end of the coach roof.

Figure 2-7. This side deck could prove problematic at sea with its stay attachments in the middle of the deck and the ratlines coming down at an angle above the coach roof.

Figure 2-8. Many production boats fall short with respect to good fairleads that lead both fore and aft from the spring cleats.

Figure 2-9. *Silk's* spring cleat is large enough to hold several over-sized docklines and has a solid fairlead that works for both fore and aft springlines.

pounds of weight. Side decks need to drain well. That means an open toerail on at least one large scupper at their widest point. At midships, look for oversized spring cleats with proper fairleads for fore and aft springlines.

Narrow or cluttered side decks, particularly when the clutter comes from rigging, are difficult to change (Figure 2-7). Poor deck drainage can eventually lead to deck leaks. Improving deck drainage can be a major project, but it is possible on most boats. Increasing the number of handholds or upgrading undersized cleats are quick and easy fixes.

Comfortable cockpit with good drainage

The cockpit undergoes constant use, at sea and in port. You will use the cockpit for many hours of watchkeeping and spend time there enjoying exotic views and entertaining friends. In port, you want a comfortable cockpit that holds a decent-sized crowd. At sea, you want a small cockpit that drains quickly. *Silk's* cockpit offered a reasonable compromise (Figure 2-10), though we felt it was slightly big offshore. On a boat between 35 and 40 feet, a properly sized cockpit can seat up to seven people comfortably without resorting to coamings or the coach roof. Cockpits larger than that could prove dangerous offshore.

A good offshore cockpit has a bridge deck or high sill to prevent a boarding wave from going below. The first or second hatchboard should come level with the top of the coamings, and you should be able to enter the boat without removing those boards. Large scuppers

Figure 2-10. We generally found *Silk's* cockpit to be a good compromise, although it was a bit too large in the worst offshore conditions. Her engine control panel was particularly vulnerable to water in the cockpit and had to be replaced in South Africa.

few minutes. If you have electronics below the level of the bridge deck, cover them with acrylic or, better yet, move them to a more protected spot.

On most boats, the single biggest openings through the deck are for the cockpit lockers. Locker hatches should be fairly watertight, reasonably sized, well secured, and fully protected by the coamings. Ideally, the lockers should not communicate directly with spaces below and should be drained overboard. Otherwise, a lost locker hatch could lead to sinking in heavy weather.

On a daytime watch in the tropics, your primary concern will be shade. Many voyagers' second offshore boat includes a well-ventilated hard dodger or pilothouse. Short of a permanent structure, the cockpit must include some provision for rigging canvas for shade. This should be securely stowed in storm conditions.

Many coastal cruisers want sail controls near the helm to facilitate shorthanded sailing. But long-distance sailors don't drive. They use self-steering almost all the time, including to control the boat while all hands carry out sail changes. On watch, you will spend most of your time under the dodger. Having the controls there makes far more sense. If you can put an autopilot control head under the dodger, that will benefit watchkeeping far more than having the traveler or primary winches aft by the helm.

If you feel the cockpit is too small, little can be done. However, too small is preferable to too large. If your cockpit is too large, or if you do not have a bridge deck, create a new locker by decking in a portion of the cockpit. If the cockpit is too wide, particularly when you are heeling, put footholds or a granny bar in the middle of the cockpit floor for crewmembers to brace against. Be sure the cockpit drains quickly at all angles of heel, or that it can be modified to do so. Otherwise, consider another boat for offshore voyaging.

The devilish details

The devil is in the details. The major things on a boat may be right, but the rest can still be wrong. The following details make a workable boat a pleasure to sail offshore:

■ *Excellent nonskid.* Good nonskid keeps you and your crew aboard the boat. To test your nonskid, spill a little diesel on it, then try to rinse it off with a bucket of

should drain the cockpit in two to three minutes when filled to the tops of the coamings. Water up to the level of the bridge deck may occur frequently in heavy weather. Water to the tops of the coamings occurs occasionally with a freak wave.

Imagine your cockpit is filled with water to the bridge deck or to the top of the coamings. What potential problems exist? Would any electronics be underwater? Ports? On *Silk,* our engine starting panel (Figure 2-10) and our autopilot control head were located by the helm at knee level. Both had to be replaced after several rough passages when boarding waves half-filled the cockpit every

Figure 2-11. Stanchion bases mounted on top of toerails keep bolts from sitting in water, minimizing leaks.

saltwater. Many surfaces that are supposed to be nonskid immediately become a skating rink. If your nonskid does not pass this test, replace it with one of many excellent nonskid products. Consider it your first investment in crew overboard gear.

■ *Deck fittings that discourage leaks.* Deck leaks are the bane of many voyagers. Fittings mounted slightly above deck level leak less because they do not sit in water. Stanchion bases can be mounted to the top or side of the toerail to minimize leaks.

■ *Watertight ports, hatches, and Dorades.* Every opening through the hull creates a potential hazard to the boat's buoyancy. Most boats that sink do so not because their hull has been compromised, but because they have been broached or rolled so far that they take

in water through hatches or companionways. All openings need to be watertight when sealed and capable of withstanding the force of a breaking wave. The companionway hatch should have a seahood to break water sweeping aft (Figure 2-12). All hatches and ports should have flexible gaskets to create a watertight seal.

■ *Strong attachments with backing plates.* All deck hardware on fiberglass boats should be through-bolted to large backing plates. The backing plates spread the load across a greater area of fiberglass, minimizing the chance that the fitting will be pulled from the deck. They also stabilize the bolts and decrease the probability of leaks.

■ *Protected diesel tank and water tank breathers.* *Silk's* diesel tank breather was located in the cockpit, below the level of the cockpit seats (Figure 2-14). On one occasion, a breaking wave filled the cockpit and saltwater siphoned through the breather into the diesel tank. It took us half a day in rolly seas to pump out the diesel tank sump and bleed the engine. *Silk's* water tank breathers were well protected in the cockpit coamings.

■ *Place to stow gasoline.* Dangerous gasoline engines have largely been replaced on boats by safer marine diesels. However, most voyagers still carry gasoline for their dinghy outboards. Gasoline is just as dangerous aboard as propane, but it is rarely shown as much respect. Many people stow gasoline in their cockpit lockers without considering the potential danger of a spark from electrical wiring or batteries. Stowing jerry cans on deck in the hot sun is not particularly safe ei-

Figure 2-12. A solid sea hood on a coastal boat

Figure 2-13. The wooden plinths on which both hatches are mounted will help direct water over or around the hatches instead of into them.

ther. Gasoline requires a separate compartment that does not contain any electrical wiring and drains overboard just as propane does.

Below

When you are looking at boats, notice how few differences there are between interior layouts. Details such as ventilation and lighting vary significantly, but the interior plans for boats between 35 and 45 feet vary only slightly. Fore to aft, most boats have a forepeak double berth, head, midship salon, aft galley across from nav station, and quarter berth or aft cabin. Are all layouts created equal? The answer is no, and many production boats lack vital elements that make an offshore voyager safe and livable. After a few long passages, you will appreciate how much your safety and well-being offshore depend on the specific points in this section.

Engine and diesel tank access

Easy engine work becomes difficult when you cannot reach a filter or put a wrench on a recalcitrant bolt. An aggravation in harbor, poor engine access becomes a nightmare at sea. Good engine access means you can reach the following elements through engine access panels: oil dipstick; fuel and oil filters; air filter; water, fuel, and oil pumps; injectors; gear box. You can improve your engine access by replacing solid panels with removable ones.

A good engine installation will keep oil and diesel out of the bilge (where it could foul bilge pump fittings). The engine should be mounted over a solid fiberglass or metal engine pan. The engine should be bolted to mounts, which are in turn bolted and glassed to structural frames. In the event of a capsize, there must be no chance of your engine breaking loose.

Contaminated fuel causes most engine problems. The diesel tank needs to have a sump—an indentation in the bottom of the tank where the dirt and water that settle out of the diesel can pool. The outflow from the diesel tank should be located above this level. This sump must be drainable, even at sea. Otherwise, a fuel problem could result in an engineless passage or you could ruin your engine with seawater or dirt. If you do not have a sump in your diesel tank, or if it is not drainable in a rolling sea, consider adding a small day tank

Figure 2-14. *Silk's* diesel tank breather was located on the cockpit locker and proved to be a problem on one occasion when a breaking wave filled the cockpit with water.

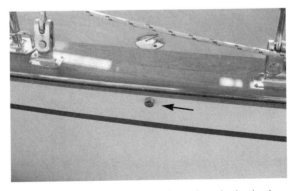

Figure 2-15. On another offshore production boat, the diesel tank breather is located just below the toerail; problems with siphoning have been reported when the rail is under water on an upwind sail.

Figure 2-16. The engine access on a Swan 47 is exceptional; panels can also be removed to reach the side and rear of the engine.

between the diesel tank and the engine equipped with a stopcock to drain off contaminated fuel.

Bilge drainage and access

A well-constructed bilge channels water to a deep sump and keeps it there until it is pumped overboard. On many flatter-bottom modern designs with small sumps, water tends to overflow the sump. Take a good look at the bilge and ask yourself three questions.

Can you access the entire bilge from bow to stern? Pull up floorboards and open the chain locker and the area under the forepeak bunk and uncover as much of the bilge as possible. You should be able to access every area of the bilge along the centerline of the boat—if not with your hand, then with a short length of wire rod. Limber holes should be drilled in all structural members that might otherwise trap water. You need to be able to inspect those limber holes and clear them of trapped silt and sand. If the head has its own shower pan and separate drain overboard, can you still access the bilge un-

derneath? If not, you need to find a way to clear the limber holes under the head pan liner.

Will the bilge drain from bow to stern without trapping water anywhere along the way? Take several buckets or a hose and pour water down the chain hawser. Start from the chain locker and work back to the sump. Trace the path the water takes and see where it pools and sits. Mold and mildew will grow in any area that traps water and will eventually result in rot and unpleasant odors. Find ways to channel the water to the sump. Drill more limber holes, stow items strategically in the bilge, and add fiberglass to low areas.

What happens to bilge drainage when the boat is heeled over? Turn your bilge pump off, fill your sump, and take the boat out sailing in some wind. While beating on either tack, go below and figure out where the water has gone: It won't be in the sump! On most boats, water will pool midships under settee berths or aft under the galley stove or nav station. Don't worry if a small amount of water is involved and it returns to the sump quickly when you come back upright. But if more than a few gallons finds its way out of the sump and doesn't return when the boat comes upright, you will need to locate and drain the area that is retaining the water.

Seagoing galley

Galley design has taken tremendous leaps forward in the last decade. Boat designers have freed themselves from the British concept of a gas ring for tea and a single shallow sink for washing the tea cup. Most newer galleys border on the luxurious: a real four-burner stove and an oven large enough for a Christmas turkey, a good safety bar with padeyes for a cook's belt, double stainless steel sinks, and adequate counter space. But some of these galleys fall short in how workable they are offshore. Consider the following areas as you inspect the galley:

■ ***Deep double sinks as close to the centerline as possible.*** For offshore work, the sinks need to be at least 10 to 12 inches deep so you can keep enough water in them to wash dishes when heeled over. They should be located close to the centerline. This makes it less likely they will backfill when the boat is heeled. The sinks will provide one of your few secure places to put dishes, bowls, and ingredients when cooking at sea. Don't settle for just one!

■ **Footholds and bracing.** Picture yourself getting something out of the hot oven that is swinging in a rolly sea. Few safety belts can be used when you are crouched in front of the stove. A good galley needs to have either solid footholds or something the cook's back can brace against. Try it sometime when you are heeled 20 degrees with the stove on the windward side. For some real excitement, spill olive oil on the cabin sole first. On any boat that passes this test, you'll always have hot meals and fresh bread—unless you're too seasick to make and eat them.

■ **Accessible lockers.** From the safety-belted position in front of the stove, the cook should be able to reach to the back of every galley locker and to the far corners of the icebox. Lockers located behind the gimbaled stove should not jeopardize important parts of the cook's anatomy, especially when the burners are lit. Lockers need high fiddles to prevent everything from sliding out when they are opened. Sliding doors limit how far open the locker must be to retrieve frequently used items. Positive latches on sliding doors hold them shut during gales.

A U-shaped or aisle-way galley with sinks on the centerline offers bracing in almost all conditions (Figures 2-17 and 2-18). You can refit a less-than-perfect galley, or you can stick with quick and simple offshore meals.

Seaworthy berths

Boat manufacturers tout how many people their boats can sleep, but they sometimes overlook the need for good sea berths. Sea berths are vital equipment: They determine how well you sleep at sea, which in turn determines your level of alertness and ultimately your safety. Curved settee seats and large double berths may be enjoyable in port, but they make terrible sea berths.

Each regular crewmember needs a good sea berth. When hove-to, all crewmembers are likely to be below and in sea berths—at least part of the time. Sharing bunks destroys any sense of personal space. They are fine for a race boat but are not recommended on a voyage that may last several years. Extra sea berths give you the option of taking on extra crew, something you may do for a particularly difficult passage.

Figure 2-17. *Silk's* U-shaped galley includes sinks close to the centerline, good access to all lockers, and lots of places to brace yourself on all angles of heel.

Figure 2-18. An aisle-way galley on a Swan 47 also offers a secure work space for the offshore cook.

A good sea berth allows a sleeper to stretch out, which means the berth must be several inches longer than the sleeper's height. Sea berths are relatively narrow: between 20 and 22 inches. If they are any wider, the sleeper will be rolled mercilessly in a heavy sea. On some berths you can alter the width by sliding them in and out. Others can be set at different angles depending on the amount of heel. A berth must lock securely in place and be equipped with a heavy lee cloth or board to hold the sleeper in place. Berths that lack either of these features will only be good on one tack or in calm conditions.

Pilot berths—berths located outboard against the hull and above settee berths—provide a sense of private space out of the main traffic flow. They allow the main salon to be used for its primary purpose, rather than becoming a tent camp during a passage. They make excellent sea berths for boats over 40 feet where the stowage space won't be missed.

For smaller boats, quarter berths can make good sea berths and take up less prime stowage area than pilot berths. Many quarter berths are too wide and poorly ventilated. Their location next to the engine makes them hot when the engine is running. By adding a Dorade vent or a port and dividing quarter berths with a lee cloth, you can turn a useless quarter berth into an excellent sea berth.

The devilish details

Even if the general layout works well, the fine details ultimately determine a boat's comfort and safety offshore. The following areas can be upgraded or improved in an existing boat. A few small changes will greatly simplify life at sea.

■ *Accessibility of fittings.* Deck fittings should be easily accessible from below so that they can be rebedded. You should be able to reach all seacocks within a minute. If fittings are not accessible, you may have to add access panels through bulkheads, ceiling liners, or locker trim pieces. Boats with no interior trim or moldings will be simpler to work on, but they won't be as aesthetically appealing. You will need to find a balance between appearance and convenience.

■ *Place for wet clothes near companionway.* Saltwater in clothing and bedding absorbs additional water, making everything damp and promoting mold and mildew. To control moisture below, we shed clothes and rinsed thoroughly before entering the main living space of the boat. Ideally, you want a place to drop your clothes or towel yourself off at the bottom of the companionway. This could be a head, a "damp" seat and wet locker, or a square of nonskid and a rod suspended over the sink.

■ *Inspection ports for fuel and water tanks.* The interiors of water and fuel tanks need to be accessible. All tanks should have removable hatches for inspection and cleaning. Dirty tanks are an occupational hazard of offshore voyaging. You cannot be certain of the quality of water and fuel. Different types of minerals result in scaling. The only way to get tanks clean is to open them up and hand clean or steam clean them once every few years. If your boat does not have inspection hatches, install some before you go.

■ **Stowage spaces.** An offshore boat needs more of its interior volume devoted to stowage than a coastal cruiser. That stowage should be divided up into small compartments. You will appreciate the wisdom of this when you are searching for a stainless steel bolt in a cavernous space when the boat is rolling.

■ **Locker ventilation.** Your lockers require good ventilation to limit mold and mildew. If they are not ventilated, you can improve air circulation either by cutting out large areas and replacing them with cane or by installing louvered openings.

Figure 2-19. All of *Silk's* locker doors were louvered, as seen in this photo of her forepeak.

Additional resources

The following sources offer more information on specific topics in this chapter:

■ **"Recommendations for Offshore Sailing," US Sailing.** This brochure offers specific recommendations on construction and equipment used to make an offshore boat seaworthy. Nonmembers can purchase it from US Sailing for $7.50, plus postage and handling. US Sailing will also provide IMS certificates of sisterships for $14 to nonmembers. To order, or to obtain membership information, contact US Sailing (PO Box 1260, Portsmouth, Rhode Island, 02871; phone 1-800-877-2451).

■ **Practical Sailor.** Based on a *Consumer Reports*-type format, this publication tests equipment and boats and reports on their performance. They are not dependent on advertising income, so their reporting is more objective than many sailing magazines'. Their boat reviews are available by fax for 80 different boat brands. You do not have to subscribe to purchase boat reviews. The fax number for boat reviews is 203-661-4802. If you wish to subscribe, write *Practical Sailor* (Box 420235, Palm Coast, Florida, 32142-0235; phone 1-800-829-9087).

■ *Cruising World's* **"Another Opinion."** National sailing magazine *Cruising World* has created a clearinghouse for owners' opinions on different boat brands. For a $5 fee, you can get the names and addresses of owners willing to share information on their boat with prospective buyers. To participate, you will need to look at an edition of *Cruising World* to find the four-digit code identifying the boat you are considering. The magazine is available in most major bookstores. You can also call *Cruising World* at 401-847-1588. If you have a fax, the number for "Another Opinion" is 1-900-988-2775. Or send a check or money order for $5 to "Another Opinion" (*Cruising World,* PO Box 3400, Newport, Rhode Island, 02840-0992).

■ *The Complete Offshore Yacht*, **by** *Yachting Monthly* **magazine (IPC Magazines Ltd).** Written in 1990 when the disaster of the Fastnet Race was still fresh in offshore sailors' minds, this concise paperback is a summary of the lessons learned from the Fastnet and covers a variety of topics including definitions of seaworthiness, the importance of stability, and achieving watertight integrity.

■ *Blue Water Sailing.* This is a new publication targeted toward the offshore voyager. The publishers regularly test and review new and used boats. To subscribe, write *Blue Water Sailing*, 5 Marina Plaza, Newport, Rhode Island, 02840; phone 888-800-SAIL.

■ *Practical Boatowner* and *Yachting Monthly* in the U.K. publish regular monthly features on designs and will provide back issues. Contact IPC Magazines Ltd, King's Reach Tower, Stamford Street, London SE1 9LS.

Potential buyers of established classes can also contact owners' associations. The major yachting magazines provide details of these.

Isa Lei: A small boat *can* do it better

If you are convinced you need a 50-footer to do the job, consider just one example of a small, successful offshore yacht. Clive Shute and Laila Stjerndrüp have been cruising aboard *Isa Lei* for seven years. She is a 30-foot, Van de Stadt Pioneer design built in 1965 out of fiberglass and launched in 1968. Her waterline length is 24 feet, and her draft is 4 feet 6 inches.

She has clean side decks and a good anchoring arrangement. Her cockpit is sized well for her length (nearly a dozen people have fit for a party at anchor). She has excellent engine access, even when compared to boats twice her length, and her bilge is accessible and well designed. Both her engine access and bilge drainage benefit from her small size: Things are simpler and require less space. Her galley lacks an oven, but it offers excellent bracing for the cook working at the gimbaled kerosene stove. She has two good sea berths with lee cloths for her two crewmembers.

This boat scores well on all the devilish details, mainly by being devilishly simple. Deck fittings are accessible because there is no trim aboard. A few handholds provide good coverage for her entire interior and deck. All fittings are smaller and less expensive than on a 40-footer, but they are still oversized for the job they need to do.

Isa Lei meets all the criteria for a bluewater voyager with the added advantage of affordability. She represents an ideal cruiser for those who have less than $50,000 to spend on a boat. But she also requires a crew willing to inhabit a small space and live at a basic comfort level. If you and your partners want to go cruising badly enough, a boat like *Isa Lei* offers you the chance to realize your dreams.

Figure 2-20. *Isa Lei* rests at anchor on Cocos Keeling.

Length on deck: 30 feet		
Length at waterline: 24 feet		
Draft: 4 feet 6 inches		
Displacement: 4.5 tons		
Sail area:		
Main:	19.5	square meters
Genoa:	23.5	square meters
Total:	43	square meters
Spinnaker:	47	square meters
Storm jib:	6.5	square meters

Figure 2-21. Clive and Laila relax in *Isa Lei's* simple but seaworthy interior.

CHAPTER 3

FINANCING THE DREAM: THE BOTTOM LINE

How much does voyaging really cost? ■ *Ongoing living expenses* ■ *Annual boat expenses* ■ *Capital costs* ■ *Discretionary spending* ■ *How much boat can you afford?* ■ ***Alternative approaches to financing the dream*** ■ *Precareer: earn as you go* ■ *Sabbatical: earn enough to finance several years* ■ *Early retirement: stretching the retirement income*

One of the first questions prospective voyagers ask us is, "How much did it cost?" While it is true you tend to spend as little or as much as you have, some guidelines will help you determine how much you will need.

The two of us spent an average of $12,000 per year on non-boat-related expenses. Half of that was spent on food, and the other half was spent in other categories. Most of our friends spent about the same, plus or minus 10 percent.

The amount voyagers spent on their boats varied widely. These expenditures reflected a vessel's size and complexity, as well as the cruisers' attitude toward insurance. For a medium-sized, moderately complex boat, we spent about $5,000 per year on maintenance and insurance.

To help you develop a realistic estimate of what voyaging will cost you, I organized the financial records from our three-year circumnavigation by expense category. I discuss each category, and make comparisons to other boats' budgets. I also examine how different voyagers financed their ventures and suggestions on the feasibility of earn-as-you-go alternatives. Throughout this chapter, prices are from the period 1992 to 1995. The SSCA bulletins (see "Additional resources" in Chapter 1) offer the best source for up-to-date prices, though the information is not systematic.

HOW MUCH DOES VOYAGING REALLY COST?

Before Evans and I headed off to sea, we wanted to set aside enough money for five years of voyaging. But the information available regarding voyaging budgets was

sketchy. The few sources that discussed finances at all quoted a standard figure of $1,000 per month for a medium-sized, moderately complex boat with a couple aboard. No one discussed how that money was allocated. To start, we annualized this number and added in a 25-percent safety margin to arrive at a figure of $15,000 per year. We set aside an additional $25,000 reserve for emergencies and for job hunting when we returned. For five years of cruising, that brought us to a cruising kitty of $100,000.

We learned that $1,000 per month covered our living expenses but did not stretch to include boat maintenance, insurance, and additional capital invested in the boat. We averaged just under $17,000 per year (almost $1,500 per month) including maintenance and boat insurance but not including capital costs. We knew many people on smaller boats who chose not to carry insurance, did all their own maintenance, and did not buy expensive gear. They spent well under $10,000 per year, almost all on living expenses.

Table 3-1 summarizes our costs from the time we moved on board until we sold *Silk* and moved ashore three years later.

Table 3-1. Summary of expenses by type (U.S. dollars)

	Year 1	Year 2	Year 3	Total	Average
Living expenses	13,372	10,228	11,622	35,222	11,740
Boat expenses	5,750	4,601	4,964	15,315	5,105
Total expenses	19,122	14,829	16,586	50,537	16,845
Capital costs	24,000	17,000	4,000	45,000	15,000

The basic definition of each category follows. These categories are discussed in further detail later in the chapter.

- **Living expenses:** food, communication, entertainment, dockage and fees, diesel, and other day-to-day living expenses

- **Boat expenses:** ongoing maintenance and boat insurance

- **Capital costs:** investments to upgrade or fundamentally change the boat

The only items not included in these numbers are photography, gifts, souvenirs, health insurance, and two Christmas trips home. We budgeted these as discretionary expenses, a category you may want to include in your overall budget.

Ongoing living expenses

Figure 3-1 shows that we spent two-thirds of our budget (about $12,000 per year) on living expenses. Our friends averaged a similar amount, plus or minus 10 percent. For everyone we knew, food was the single largest budget item, totaling about one-third of noncapital expenses. How money was allocated for nonfood categories constituted the biggest difference between boats.

Our budget numbers for the first year (see Table 3-2) reflect the higher costs of cruising in the Atlantic and our transition from spending freely to being frugal. If we had continued voyaging, we would have planned on $12,000 per year for living expenses.

Food

Food costs comprised one-third of our total expenses and just under one-half of our living expenses. Food was the single largest category and the most stable category in our budget. Food costs varied from place to place. For example, our food costs for the first year reflected the higher living costs of the Atlantic and Caribbean islands.

To minimize food costs, provision where it's cheapest. Mainland ports in developed countries are less expensive than island ports. In the islands, major ports where you clear customs are the least expensive and have the most variety. If you need to restock after having been away from developed countries for many months, places like Las Palmas in the Canaries, Suva in Fiji, Pago Pago in Western Samoa, and Port Louis in Mauritius offer reasonable prices. The French islands are outrageously expensive except for staples that are subsidized, such as pasta, rice, flour, and dried milk. Additional guidelines for minimizing food expenses follow.

- **Find inexpensive sources.** Try to find out where good quality, inexpensive provisions can be purchased. Subscribe to the Seven Seas Cruising Association's (SSCA) bulletin and ask other voyagers you meet along the way. Find out what goods islanders will trade for in your next landfall. Trade goods, however, can change

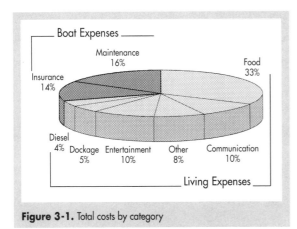

Figure 3-1. Total costs by category

Table 3-2. Detail of living expenses by category (U.S. dollars)					
	Year 1	Year 2	Year 3	Total	Avg.
Food	6,331	4,628	5,406	16,365	5,455
Communication	1,885	1,792	1,438	5,115	1,705
Entertainment	1,432	1,034	2,350	4,816	1,605
Other	1,539	1,559	1,178	4,276	1,425
Dockage/fees	1,513	501	730	2,744	915
Engine fuel & fluids	672	714	520	1,906	635
Total living expenses	13,372	10,228	11,622	35,222	11,740

year to year and place to place. When we left Panama, we stocked up on sugar only to find that the Polynesian islanders wanted Beta videotapes in French! If you can take along the right items, you will be able to trade for fish or fresh fruit to liven up your diet and preserve your canned stores.

■ *Buy in quantity.* When you find something you need at a good price, buy, buy, buy. I never regretted being overstocked, but I was often annoyed with myself for not taking advantage of a good deal. Buy in quantity, but don't buy in bulk. If there are only two aboard, lots of small amounts mean less spoilage. Make sure you try one can of something before you buy a dozen. We left New Zealand with a drawer full of canned chili and baked beans that turned out to be so sweet we couldn't eat them!

■ *Eat inexpensive meals ashore.* In most places, eating aboard is cheaper. But exceptions do exist. In Fiji we could buy huge plates of rice smothered in curry for under $2, and on Christmas Island we got heaping plates of lo mein for about $1.50. In general, islands with large Indian, Indonesian, or Chinese communities offer inexpensive restaurant meals.

■ *Buy duty-free alcohol.* Of all food items, alcohol costs varied the most widely from boat to boat and from place to place. We rarely had more than a bottle of wine or sherry aboard and seldom drank. Other boats carried a variety of beers, wines, and liquors. With the exception of rum in the Caribbean, alcohol is very expensive on most islands: two to three times U.S. prices for questionable quality. You can keep costs down by buying in quantity before you leave the States and restocking in New Zealand, Australia, South Africa, and Europe. However, liquor is often bonded—sealed by Customs so it can't be used while you are in port. One alternative is to buy duty-free alcohol as you check out of many island nations.

Communication

Staying in touch with loved ones accounted for approximately 10 percent of our total expenditures (Figure 3-1). This amount was high compared to what most of our friends spent. We communicated often. When in port,

we traded weekly faxes with our families. When it was reasonable (less than $2 per minute), we indulged in a 15-minute phone call every few weeks. We mailed tapes, letters, and packages weekly. Communication is discretionary. But if you are leaving a close-knit family behind, you'd be wise to overbudget for it. The following ideas will help you control your communication costs.

■ *Use faxes when available.* We found fax services nearly everywhere, and they were often cheap. Over the six-month period when we traveled from Panama to Tonga, we relied exclusively on faxes and were charged from $1 to $3 per page. Make sure to ask what it costs to receive faxes. Some upscale marinas in the Caribbean charge up to $5 per page for incoming faxes.

■ *Watch phone expenses carefully.* We used an AT&T calling card and the AT&T USA Direct service in many places, particularly where language was an issue. We found that it was sometimes very expensive on a per-minute basis (up to $4 per minute from halfway around the world), and we didn't know how much we were spending until we were billed months later. Where language was not an issue, we preferred to call from the local post office and specify a time limit. We knew exactly how much we had spent, and we talked for only as long as we intended.

■ *Take advantage of cheap postal rates.* Postage varied from country to country more than any other communication expense. A first-class letter to the United States from South Africa was $.30. The same letter from parts of the Caribbean cost up to $2. Where postage was inexpensive, we sent home boxes of souvenirs and items we no longer wanted aboard.

Entertainment

We considered off-the-boat activities as entertainment. This category covered cook's night out, a Fijian feast, an island tour, and a safari in South Africa. We spent about 10 percent of our total budget on entertainment (Figure 3-1). Some of our friends spent almost nothing, while others spent over $5,000 per year.

More than any other category, entertainment defined the difference between big spenders and budget-minded voyagers. Couples on tight budgets toured the island on the local bus; cruisers with money to spend rented cars or went in a van with a guide. In port, those with money ate ashore weekly; those without ate off the boat only when it was less expensive than eating aboard. Both types of voyagers had the joy of seeing the country and experiencing the culture. In the end, how much you get out of cruising has more to do with your attitude than your bank account.

We invested in touring when we could not use our boat to explore. In New Zealand, we bought a car for about $1,000 and sold it six months later for $900. In South Africa, we went on two tours that doubled our

The cruising community

As Evans and I approached the Azores, I experienced all the emotions of landfall for the first time. We had spent weeks on the open ocean, limited physically to a piece of fiberglass and wood 37 feet long and 11 feet wide, where a trip to the bow and back could seem like a voyage to the moon. Yet our visual environment spanned horizon to horizon, acres of nothing except the blue and white tumble of the ocean speaking to itself. We were going from that full emptiness, that eternal waste, to seeing lights? An island? Suddenly we had a focus between the ever-so-close and the oh-so-far-away of a sensible scale, or at any rate a scale that made sense to the human psyche. The isolation of a sea voyage fell away, to be replaced by trepidation. Would we get ashore safely? What complexities awaited us there? How would we manage in a culture where we didn't speak the language? It suddenly seemed better to be alone, isolated but safe, rather than risk nearing a dangerous shore.

But then the smell! Faial reached out to us with the scent of the earth itself; black, fertile earth full of secrets and promises—full of life. Senses heightened by over two weeks in the austere sea environment tasted forgotten meals on the offshore breeze, smelled the bucolic odor of cedar from the dark hills, felt the warmth of the night air breathed off the land. As the sky lightened, we started to make out the features of land. Doubts and hesitations were cast aside. We entered the breakwall and within a few hours found ourselves tied up in the marina, surrounded by dozens of other boats that had arrived by sea.

Within half a day we were completely enmeshed in the life of the harbor. We had traded stories with and gotten advice from dozens of other cruisers. A Swiss couple showed us the tiny store where we could buy Pico wine for a dollar a gallon if we supplied our own jug. A British skipper with a Swedish first mate taught us the wonders of Softscrub in removing stains from the hull. A French couple let us borrow their handcart when we reprovisioned. We spent evenings in other people's cockpits discussing everything from the islands we planned to visit next to how to handle customs officials. The wealth of information and the generosity of other sailors came as a revelation. The voyaging community itself offsets and complements the isolation of sailing.

For those who haven't experienced it, it can be difficult to understand both how small and how closely knit this community is. At any given time, a couple hundred boats are in the process of circumnavigating. In most major ports, fifty or sixty boats congregate during the appropriate season. The seasons themselves dictate that most boats arrive at certain places at about the same time and stay for several months. We got to know a group of about two dozen boats extremely well despite the mobility of our community. Since we have returned, we have met many people who did extensive offshore sailing in the decade before us, and we almost always find people we know in common. Even more often, we have shared experiences—cruising in the Azores, Daniel's Bay in the Marquesas, the Galapagos, Cocos Keeling, and dozens of others.

Within this community, helping each other is a way of life. Throughout this book I suggest that you ask other cruisers in the harbor about everything from water to how to send packages home. While that may seem odd right now, you'll understand the first time you make landfall in a place like the Azores, concerned about how you will get along in a new culture, and you see a boat with an American or British or French flag. When the next boat appears, you will row out with a loaf of bread from ashore to tell the new arrivals where to find the post office.

entertainment costs in the final year. But these trips were once-in-a-lifetime opportunities to see the fantastic wildlife of this beautiful country, and we considered the money well spent.

Other

This category includes miscellaneous items such as prescription drugs and medicines, clothing, laundry, cleaning supplies, paper products, haircuts, batteries, and other nonboat hardware items. This category came to less than 10 percent of our total budget (see Figure 3-1).

Clothing costs substantially less aboard compared to shoreside life. Living aboard is hard on clothes. But you can get away without wearing much at all for long periods of time. In the tropics, you'll need a couple pairs of new shorts, an occasional tee-shirt, and several hats a year.

Dockage and fees

This category includes marina costs, harbor fees, visa fees, and charges for water and propane. At about five percent of our total, this category was not that significant. But it was more variable than most categories (see Table 3-2, page 38). The high costs in our first year reflected marina fees in the United States, Europe, and the Caribbean, where being rafted six boats out along a marina wall could run up to $40 per night. Once you leave the Atlantic, marinas are few and far between. When available, they are much cheaper. For example, our marina costs in South Africa were on the order of $7 per night (Figure 3-3). In this category, our first year included the $250 we spent to transit the Panama Canal. Since we went through in 1993 the fees have doubled, but they're still a bargain compared to going around the horn.

Be aware that this expense category is likely to increase, both in absolute terms and as a percentage of the total cruising budget. Panama Canal fees are slated to increase to $800 at the end of 1997 and to $1,500 at the end of 1998. As the number of offshore boats grows, harbor authorities and governments are finding ways to ensure that voyagers pay their fair share. For example, English Harbour in Antigua has a park and anchor-

Figure 3-2. A $35-per-night marina on Madeira Island in the North Atlantic

age fee that comes to about $35 per week. While this is minimal compared to marina fees in the United States, it represents almost 15 percent of your budget at $12,000 per year. The Galapagos are even more extreme, and voyagers are now charged $100 per day to visit the islands.

Engine fuel and fluids

Besides diesel, this category includes engine and transmission oils. We were frugal in engine use: We put fewer than 1,000 hours on our Yanmar in the 35,000 nautical miles we traveled in just over three years. This category was less than 5 percent of our total budget. Friends who relied on their engines to generate electricity and cool refrigerators ran closer to 10 or 20 percent.

On average, we paid $2 per gallon for diesel. Use this figure to estimate your diesel costs. If you plan to run your engine two hours per day for charging and refrigeration, you will spend a minimum of $850 per year (i.e., two hours per day @ 0.6 gallons per hour @ $2.00 per gallon @ 365 days per year).

Annual boat expenses

Boat insurance and ongoing maintenance were about one-third of our noncapital expenditures (see Figure 3-1). These expenses vary widely from boat to boat. The level of upkeep, boat size and complexity, boat insurance, and a couple's skills all influence total expenditures. We spent about $5,000 per year to maintain a medium-sized, moderately complex boat that we insured. The sum of $1,000 per year (or the equivalent in your labor) is about the minimum to keep a cruising boat up to the demands of offshore passagemaking.

Boat insurance

Insuring your boat is a major decision that must reflect your personal financial situation. At almost 15 percent of our total budget, insurance represented a sizable commitment of our resources. We chose to be insured because *Silk* was our only asset. We could not, however, get insurance from June through October 1994 after the program associated with SSCA folded. This ex-

Figure 3-3. A $7-per-night marina at Durban, South Africa

plains our low insurance expense in the third year (Table 3-3).

If you decide to insure, expect to pay from one to two percent of hull value. This estimate will not cover liability in U.S. waters and assumes you will be out of the tropics during the hurricane season. Make sure to check your policy for a "named storm exclusion," which excludes coverage for damage from any named storm (i.e., a hurricane). Hurricanes Luis, Marilyn, and Bertha reminded insurance companies about hurricane risks. Expect increasing restrictions or higher premiums associated with staying in hurricane-prone areas during the season.

When we finished our trip, we knew of only two major players in the long-distance, couple-on-board, cruising insurance market: Lloyds of London, and Pantaenius, a German company with a British subsidiary. Since then, Blue Water Insurance has begun providing SSCA members with boat insurance tailored to liveaboard voyagers. If you are ex-military, you may be able to get insured at favorable rates through USAA, the insurance company for military personnel (phone 800-531-8222).

Many boats we knew chose to carry no insurance at all. They argued that money was better spent on safety equipment than on premiums, and not having the safety net made them more prudent sailors. We did not sail the boat any better when we were uninsured, but our stress level went up and our enjoyment went down. We were both relieved when we got reinsured in South Africa for the trip home.

The value of a boat has bearing on an owner's attitude toward insurance. Friends who were uninsured by choice had generally spent less than $50,000 on their boats and had done most of the work aboard themselves. Those of us who chose to be insured had generally spent $150,000 and up on the boat. We could not replace our boat without returning to work for a long period of time. For those who had invested between $50,000 and $150,000 in their boats, the decision to insure varied from boat to boat and reflected personal considerations.

If you cannot afford the insurance premiums for worldwide coverage but would prefer to be insured, there is a partial alternative. If you leave the tropics during hurricane season, you will be coastal cruising somewhere for a period of several months. In the Atlantic, that means Venezuela, Maine, or the Mediterranean; in

Table 3-3. Detail of boat expenses by category (U.S. dollars)

	Year 1	Year 2	Year 3	Total	Avg.
Boat insurance	3,500	2,190	1,572	7,262	2,421[1]
Maintenance	2,250	2,411	3,392	8,053	2,684
Total boat expenses	5,750	4,601	4,964	15,315	5,105

[1]Comparable sterling prices would be approximately £1,500 per year for a £50,000 boat.

the Pacific, that means New Zealand or Australia; in the Indian Ocean, that means Thailand or South Africa. In these places you can get coastal insurance through a local insurance broker or one of the brokers mentioned above. This way, you are protected under a coastal policy for up to six months of the year at reasonable rates compared to the premiums for offshore voyaging.

We most appreciated being insured when we were navigating reef-strewn waters and approaching harbors bustling with freighters and fishing boats. While the partial approach may not help with tropical reefs, the largest harbors tend to be in more developed countries. This alternative approach will cover some risks, and it may be a compromise worth investigating.

Maintenance

This category includes moneys spent fixing or replacing gear and equipment on the boat, plus the costs associated with the annual haulout. We considered any modifications or additions that added significantly to the value of the boat to be capital expenditures. For example, we called replacing our sails in New Zealand a capital expenditure because we installed full battens on the mainsail and mizzen and added lazyjacks to the main. These upgrades enhanced the value of the boat.

Maintenance is another category that reflects your approach to cruising. Our goal was to maintain the resale value of our boat, and we wanted some comforts aboard. In addition, we were fairly safety conscious. While we rarely used our refrigeration and did not have an SSB for most of the trip, we did replace halyards and jacklines every year and had the rig inspected annually. At over 15 percent of our total budget (see Figure 3-1), our costs reflected our philosophy.

A comparison to other published numbers

In the May 1992 issue of *Cruising World* magazine, the article titled "Tallying the Bottom Line" explored cruising costs. Two boats' expenses for one year of cruising were detailed. I adjusted their expense categories to make them comparable to ours in Table 3-4. The analysis reveals similarities in the proportion of most expenses to overall costs.

Clover was a reasonably equipped Mason 45 with George and Rosa Day and their two preteenage sons aboard. Their cruising costs covered their first year sailing from Jamestown, Rhode Island, to Auckland, New Zealand, beginning in October 1990. *Sparrow* was a well-equipped Crealock 37 with Tor Pinney and his wife aboard. Their costs covered one year in the Atlantic and Mediterranean, beginning in Fort Lauderdale in May 1990.

This comparison confirms many observations made earlier. Boat expenses and food expenses are each about one-third of the total, and nonfood living expenses make up the final third on all three boats. The greatest variation between the boats is in nonfood living expenses. *Clover* and *Sparrow* spent 14 and 22 percent of their overall budgets respectively on entertainment, compared to *Silk's* 10 percent. The consistency of boat insurance and maintenance numbers reflects the similarity of the three boats in terms of size, complexity, general level of maintenance, and overall value.

NOTE: *Sparrow's* numbers do not include $3,900 for shoreside living expenses for the six weeks prior to departure (including $1,100 for dental work); or $2,300 for outfitting the boat with new gear, books, and equipment, which we would have classed as capital expenses.

Table 3-4. Comparison of expenses for three cruising boats (figures in U.S. dollars)

	Clover	Sparrow	Silk (avg.)
Food	7,488	5,000	5,455
Communication	381	1,200	1,705
Entertainment	2,899	3,750	1,605
Other	1,931	900	1,425
Dockage/fees	852	150	915
Engine fuels & fluids	1,598	1,000	635
Total living expenses	15,149	12,000	11,740
Boat insurance	2,124	2,400	2,421
Maintenance	2,923	3,000	2,684
Total boat expenses	5,047	5,400	5,105
Total expenses	20,196	17,400	16,845
Additional expenses not comparable to *Silk's*:			
Calvert School for two	1,195		
Airfare from Europe		1,200	

Figure 3-4. Comparison of expenses for three voyagers (figures in U.S. dollars)

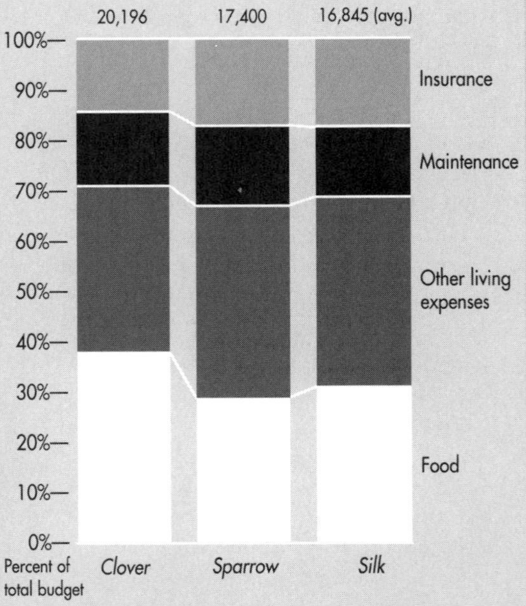

If you want to minimize your maintenance costs, simplicity is the key. Aboard a boat like *Isa Lei* (profiled in Chapter 2), you can do all your own work and still have time to enjoy voyaging. Owners Clive Shute and Laila Stjerndrüp spent about one-quarter the amount we spent on maintenance.

Most voyagers spend a minimum of $1,000 per year on maintenance. Half that amount paid for an annual haulout. We did a haulout in South Africa in 1995 and spent $135 to be hauled, $100 to have the hull polished, and $250 to have the bottom painted with paint we supplied. Someone willing to do their own work could have gotten away with less than $200, plus several hundred dollars for paint.

The increase in maintenance costs in our third year reflects equipment replacements. The wear and tear of sailing thousands of miles a year and living aboard necessitates continual investments in cushions, sails, and other gear. These costs can be ignored on a boat making an Atlantic circle or spending a year in the Caribbean, but they need to be included in the long-term budget of the bluewater voyager.

Capital costs

Capital costs consisted of expenditures to upgrade or fundamentally change the boat. There are a variety of ways to approach the cost of buying a boat and fitting it out. Financially, our time was better spent earning money than working on a boat before we left. Once we were sailing, *Silk* was our only asset, and we invested heavily to keep her in good shape. We expected to partially recoup these costs when we sold *Silk*. Other cruisers buy older boats, refit them themselves, and do not expect to resell them for much money. Their capital costs per year are a fraction of ours. If they include the value of their own time, however, their figures may be comparable to ours. Either way, capital costs should fall off quickly after the first year or two of teething problems.

The capital costs shown in Table 3-5 include all investments made in the boat beyond the purchase price. Many couples spend years fitting out a coastal boat for offshore cruising, but we left on our trip within four months of purchasing *Silk*. While we would not advise others to do the same, the result is that the numbers in Table 3-5 include all expenditures to convert *Silk* from

Table 3-5. Capital costs by year (U.S. dollars)

	Year 1	Year 2	Year 3	Total	Avg.
Capital costs	24,000	17,000	4,000	45,000	15,000

a coastal cruiser to an offshore voyager.

In the first year, about two-thirds of the $24,000 reflects large capital investments in equipment such as a windlass, a hard dinghy, an upgraded electrical system, a wind vane, an autopilot, an EPIRB, and a GPS. About one-sixth represents costs associated with fixing early teething problems after our first passage. The final sixth represents a range of smaller items, including our medical kit, fitting out the galley, bedding, charts, and cruising guides. Charts and cruising guides are expensive but worth investing in. You can trade for charts as you go along, particularly in the Caribbean and the Mediterranean where boats beginning and ending long voyages cross paths. Photocopied charts can save you hundreds of dollars, but the lack of color makes it difficult to pick out shoal water. Many of our friends who purchased photocopied charts colored in the reef and shoal areas with Magic Markers.

Had we known more about offshore sailing, we could have done the work ourselves and done it better. Almost half of the initial $24,000 was poorly spent, either on inappropriate items or shoddy work. One boatyard, for example, advised us to install a helm-mounted autopilot and not use a wind vane. The autopilot turned out to be undersized for the boat: We broke it and a spare crossing the North Atlantic. We then paid a small fortune in Madeira to have a wind vane and an appropriately sized autopilot shipped to us. These worked flawlessly. But had they been put on the boat originally, we would have saved at least 30 percent of the purchase price by avoiding freight and duties, plus the cost of the defunct autopilot and its spare (about $3,000).

After our second year and 17,000 nautical miles, we took advantage of the high quality, low-cost boat work available in New Zealand to do a major refit. We invested in a brand new set of full-battened sails and a new cruising chute; the only sails we did not replace were the staysail and the Yankee. The sails cost half what they would have in the United States. We installed a feathering prop and a below-decks autopilot. After sailing halfway around the world, *Silk* was well suited to our idea of offshore voyaging.

In the third year, we added an SSB radio. If we had continued voyaging on *Silk,* our capital costs would have stayed at or below our third-year level. By this time, however, maintenance costs had already started to rise as we began to replace existing equipment (see Table 3-3).

Discretionary spending

One voyager's discretionary spending is another voyager's idea of necessary spending. Many would consider boat insurance to be discretionary. But boat insurance can be quantified in terms of something concrete—the value of your boat. The expenses discussed in this section are both discretionary and very difficult to quantify meaningfully. The cost of flying home at Christmastime, for example, can radically alter a budget, but the *actual* cost will depend on where you are flying from. The following categories represent sizable expenses you may choose to incur, so you will want an idea of the amounts involved. In our case, these expenses were funded out of the crew's personal money—not the cruising kitty.

Travel home

I went home for Christmas two of the three years that we were voyaging. My family's sanity and mine demanded an annual reunion. Despite good intentions, few family members or friends traveled to spend time with us aboard. If you want to see family and friends while you are voyaging, chances are you will have to go to them. The journey home recharged me emotionally, renewed my sense of wonder at our life aboard, and allowed me to restock our library and our larder.

I flew home from the Caribbean for our first Christmas, and the roundtrip airfare ran $300. You can often find inexpensive fares from the Caribbean if you book them early enough. I flew home from New Zealand the second year, and even the discounted fare was close to $2,000. If you intend to travel home once a year from the Pacific or Indian Oceans, be prepared to spend a great deal of money.

There are alternatives to normal airfares, and a few of our friends took advantage of them. Courier services

pay for your flight if you carry documents or packages with you. This arrangement works well if you can be flexible. Major newspapers in most cities include advertisements for couriers. As a courier, the luggage you can carry is sometimes limited—no peanut butter and Ziploc bags for next year! Flying standby can also be an option. Contact the local air carriers and inquire. Charter flights are another possibility. A travel agency in the country you wish to fly from will be able to find the best deals.

Souvenirs and gifts

You will be able to buy local arts and crafts along the way for a fraction of what they cost at home. Handmade baskets and wood carvings, colorful garments, and painted cloth—every culture practices traditional arts, and samples are always for sale. Scott and Kitty Kuhner, who have completed two circumnavigations (see the sidebar in Chapter 7, "A tale of two cruises") regretted not buying much local art on their first voyage. On their second voyage, they budgeted for souvenirs and artwork and spent freely. Their home is decorated with colorful molas from the San Blas islands, intricate carvings from the Solomons, and kava bowls from Fiji. They spent several thousand dollars on handicrafts and art.

I spent several hundred dollars on souvenirs during our trip. Like Scott and Kitty after their first trip, I wished I had bought more and will budget for these purchases when we go again. I bought or traded for baskets in Tonga and South Africa, molas in Panama, and tapa cloth in the Marquesas. A can of corned beef can be traded for most handicrafts in the Pacific. Stowing the souvenirs proved more difficult than acquiring them. When we reached a country with low-cost mail service, we shipped our purchases home.

Health insurance

The decision to buy health insurance is as difficult an issue as buying boat insurance—and the answer is every bit as individual. Health-care costs around the world are much cheaper than in the United States. For example, a doctor's visit in Tahiti ran $10, and an appointment with an ear specialist in New Zealand, including several tests, totaled $40. Given that medical costs around the world usually run one-third of U.S. rates, very few voyagers we

How much boat can you afford?

The money you save before you leave will have to cover both the purchase price of the boat and your cruising kitty. Most people spend more than they need to on their boat and end up cutting their voyage short when funds run out. It is better to allocate money to the cruising kitty first and then decide how much boat you can afford.

For a rough estimate, start with what you have already saved and add what you can realistically expect to save before you head off to sea. To allocate that total between the cruising kitty and the boat, start by calculating how much you need for the cruising kitty. Based on the information in this chapter, set aside between $1,000 and $2,000 per month for living expenses for the period you plan to voyage without working. Add an additional $1,000 to $5,000 per year for maintenance and boat insurance. If you want one, set aside an emergency fund. The total makes up your cruising kitty.

You can afford to spend what's left on purchasing the boat and on capital costs. If you plan to buy a boat less than 5 years old, set aside 30 percent for fitting out. For a boat over 10 years old, set aside 50 percent. You are left with what you can afford to pay for a boat. The section in Chapter 2 titled "The question of cost" gives you an idea of what that money will buy.

For example, assume you will take early retirement in five years. You and your crewmembers have saved $30,000 and are saving $2,000 per month. Using a conservative assumption that interest and inflation cancel each other out, you will have saved $150,000 by the time you retire. You plan to sell a house and other assets worth $80,000. Your cruising budget will be $2,000 a month. Your social security and pension will cover that monthly budget, but this income won't start until three years after you retire. You will need just over $70,000 to cover that three-year gap. In addition, you want a $20,000 emergency fund. That leaves you with about $140,000 for the boat. After setting aside 40 percent for fitting out, you can afford to spend about $100,000 to buy the boat. According to the sidebar in Chapter 2, most people in your situation choose a 35- to 45-foot boat between 5 and 10 years old with a purchase price between $75,000 and $100,000 and modification and equipment costs of $25,000 to $50,000.

For a different example, assume you are a precareer couple. You have no savings, but you also have no debt. You both work, and together you save close to $1,000 per month. You are fairly handy and willing to try almost any type of work along the way. You would like to leave as soon as possible, and you plan to cruise for three years. Your cruising budget will be about $750 per month ($4,500 for six months of cruising). After six months, you plan to earn money as you go. If you worked for two years and got a loan of $30,000 from parents or friends to be repaid upon sale of the boat, you could afford to invest $50,000 in total. You could buy a 25-year-old, 30- to 35-foot hull for $35,000 and use the rest to refit it.

knew carried health insurance.

On the other hand, Scott and Kitty Kuhner had a terrifying experience at the end of their first four-year circumnavigation when Scott developed a malignant melanoma. They were in their late 20s and healthy, so they had not chosen to carry insurance. The financial and emotional trauma of that situation, plus the difficulty of getting health insurance afterwards, convinced them that they needed insurance for their second trip. Despite a doubling in premiums over the course of their second four-year circumnavigation with their two children, they never regretted their decision. They used the insurance in New Zealand, where Kitty ended up with a serious compound fracture of her leg. She would have been covered under the socialized medical system, but the insurance allowed her to go to a specialist. "While we are probably unusual given our experiences, we feel that, at the very least, people should have some sort of catastrophic insurance," Kitty says.

I got major medical insurance for the last year of our voyage. I selected a plan with a $5,000 deductible. At age 33 and in good health, I was able to get catastrophic insurance that cost $800 a year and covered the cost of flying me home plus up to $2,000,000 in medical expenses. Before you make a decision, research your health insurance options. Make sure to find out whether a given plan will cover you outside of the United States. Few plans actually do. Blue Water Insurance provides three health insurance plans to SSCA members—all tailored to the specific needs of cruisers sailing in foreign countries. For those on Medicare, travelers' policies exist that cover just the costs of getting you home. If you do purchase insurance, have everything spelled out in writing—especially the provisions covering health costs incurred abroad.

Photography

If you plan to take a few shots for your photo album or make a dozen videotapes, you can ignore the cost of photography. But if you are planning to write for marine magazines or make presentations when you return, you should use slide film (not print film or videotapes) and be prepared for the expense. You will also need a good camera with telephoto capabilities: You won't be able to capture beach scenes from the deck of your boat without a high quality, 300-mm lens.

You cannot buy slide film in most countries. When it is available, it can cost $10 to $15 per roll. We found slide film in New Zealand, Australia, and South Africa. But only South African camera stores stocked the professional quality slide films that magazines prefer. Professional quality slide film always ended up in my overstuffed luggage at Christmastime.

Avoiding budget busters

Evans and I came to the voyaging life directly from high-paying jobs and expense accounts. After two months, we had spent six months' worth of money. If we were going to make it to the Pacific, we needed to make a major change in our spending habits. We started tracking every dollar we spent and evaluating every spending decision we made.

To live within our means, we simplified our lives and paid attention to our budget. We learned to enjoy life at anchor and avoid marinas. We sought out the village hardware store instead of the marina chandlery. We avoided taxis and tours and used the local bus system. We wrote letters to keep our frequent phone calls and faxes brief.

Our spending was cyclical: On passage we spent nothing for weeks; on shore we lost track of how much we were spending. Once we noted the pattern, we created strategies to control our expenditures. We determined what we could afford to spend per day, based on our annual budget. At sea, we accumulated this daily budget to create reserves. When provisioning, we purchased necessities first and then decided how much more we could spend based on our remaining reserves. We used that "mad money" to buy the special treats that gave us some variety while at sea.

We never carried more than $10 or $15 for the first few days after reaching port. In a developed country, we could easily spend in a single day what we had spent in the last two months of island cruising. Before we walked around with cash in hand, we needed to rebuild our defenses against the overwhelming temptations of grocery stores and chandleries.

When we discovered something we thought we needed, we wrote it down on a wish list. An item had to appear on that list three times before we talked about buying it. This simple rule prevented us from making impulse purchases and ending up with items we rarely used and had to stow aboard.

Each crewmember should have some money, aside from the cruising kitty, to spend as they please. Most of my money went toward photography and souvenirs, which Evans appreciates more now that we are back ashore. Most of Evans' money went toward small luxuries for the boat, such as expensive binoculars and a celestial calculator.

You should factor in some money to handle emergencies. We knew voyagers who did not, and they had to quit due to an engine that died or a first mate who needed surgery. Our emergency fund could have handled either of those contingencies, but probably not both.

If you consider every possible calamity and try to factor it into your budget, you will never go cruising. Don't let the fact that you haven't got all the money you want stop you. Decide what you can get along without, or figure out how to earn money along the way, and go cruising. You'll learn that you need less than you think.

Developing slides is also problematic. In the Pacific, we could develop slides only in Papeete (Tahiti) and Suva (Fiji). The quality of processing was poor and the cost was outrageous—$20 and up for a 36-exposure roll. Cruisers who sent their film to U.S. labs and had the slides forwarded home paid less for better quality.

The sea environment can also destroy expensive camera gear. Heat, humidity, and salt air corrode the electronics, and the constant motion plays havoc with fine mechanics. You will need to store the camera to protect it from motion and moisture. The camera should also be fully serviced once a year to keep it in good working condition. Servicing can run $300 to $500, but the investment could save you the cost of buying a new camera. When I had my telephoto lens serviced in New Zealand after a year at sea, mold was growing inside the lens body—even after storing it in a watertight case with desiccant.

During our voyage, I spent a total of $6,000 on photography—for film and development of about 4,000 slides and for camera servicing.

ALTERNATIVE APPROACHES TO FINANCING THE DREAM

How do you finance your cruising kitty? What can you do to generate income after you set sail? The answers to these questions are related to the timing options outlined in Chapter 1. If you take time out before starting college or a career, you will need to earn money as you go. If you plan to voyage part-time, you will earn money from your chosen career when you return home each year. The following sections cover the financial side of the equation for each timing option in Chapter 1.

If you want to cruise badly enough, you will find a way—even if it means scaling back your expectations. But whichever option you choose, don't close the door on returning. Make sure you have an escape hatch financially if voyaging does not work for you.

Precareer: earn as you go

Precareer voyagers are not likely to have any income or savings to offset their voyaging costs, except for an occasional check from family. Those who cruise when they are young and financially insecure tend to leave with savings for six months to a year of cruising and a boat full of provisions. They start looking for work as their food and money supply dwindles. Most younger voyagers we knew worked four to six months for every year of cruising. Others anchored off a resort, got jobs, and worked for two to three years before heading off again for a long adventure.

Working in foreign countries has changed a great deal over the last few decades, and the situation is likely to change more in the decades to come. Fifteen years ago, you could get temporary visas that allowed you to work in almost any country. These days, countries guard their jobs for their own citizens. Tourist visas expressly prohibit working. Work permits are granted only if you have specific skills, which those traveling before starting careers are unlikely to possess. Many voyagers work "under the table." Without the tax bite, they can save quickly. If caught, however, they are politely but firmly asked to leave the country.

What types of jobs are available when you are working your way around the world? Voyagers pursue a variety of temporary occupations to fill the cruising kitty. These job opportunities are available to anyone—not just the precareer cruiser. If you have the self-discipline and adaptability to voyage, you will be able to find work as you go. Whether it will be enjoyable is another question. But you will find you can put up with a great deal if your cruising kitty is growing rapidly.

Working for resorts and charter companies

When cruising, most voyagers prefer quiet anchorages away from the bustling tourist centers. But when the time comes to earn money, head for the tourist resorts. You can find work in the resort itself: running the waterfront, teaching sailing or sailboarding, waiting tables, tending bar, or selling in a boutique. With luck you may work your way into a position managing a shop, a restaurant, or the resort's recreational program. As the number of top-quality resorts increases in island groups around the world, there is more demand for people to fill these types of positions.

Charter companies are usually located near these resort areas as well. There are opportunities at charter outfits to repair fiberglass, paint boats, maintain engines, fix refrigeration, and install electronics. If you are good with people, you can take a position as a skipper or cook aboard a charter boat. With the right clientele, the tips can make this lucrative for a couple working together. One couple we knew managed the Moorings' charter base in Tonga for a season. But be warned: The French have passed a law requiring that the skipper of any French-flagged charter boat operating in French waters must be French. For most of us, that law rules out acting as a charter skipper in half of the Caribbean, much of the South Pacific, and some of the Indian Ocean. In other countries, including the United States, charter captains must be licensed. Violators face stiff fines.

Most of these positions are in the tropical regions of the Caribbean or the Pacific islands. Unless you limit your stay to a few months, you will find yourself in these areas during hurricane season. Friends of ours working on St. Martin in the Caribbean sat through hurricanes Luis and Marilyn in 1995 so they wouldn't lose their lucrative jobs ashore. If you find yourself in this position, consider putting your boat on the hard in a hurricane pit. Otherwise, factor in the hurricane risk when accepting a job.

Deliveries

Few precareer voyagers consider chartering their own boats, because their boats are too small. But delivery work is always available. Most deliveries pay by the mile or by the day. Delivery skippers generally receive $1 to $2 per mile, plus airfare back to their point of origination. Additional crew usually get airfare only, so taking your partners with you reduces the financial attraction. Earning $100 to $200 a day for sailing may sound wonderful, but deliveries can be a difficult and sometimes dangerous way to earn money. Delivery skippers are hired for the upwind slogs—not the downwind sleigh rides. You may be hired to deliver a boat during hurricane season or find yourself in a winter gale. The quality of the boat and gear can run the gamut, from spectacular to spectacularly bad. Take a good look at the condition of the boat and safety gear before you agree to do a delivery.

If you take on a delivery, your own boat needs to be looked after while you are gone. This is not a problem if your crewmates are not joining you. But if they are, or if you sail alone, you will have to ensure your boat's safety for several weeks.

If you are an accomplished sailor who can adapt quickly to a strange boat and sail safely in the worst weather, deliveries offer a way to earn a decent daily wage and expand your skills. Make sure taking on a delivery does not compromise your safety or the safety of your own boat.

Offer services to other cruisers

When it comes to earning money by offering services to other cruisers, remember that most voyagers are just like you: They have built up their skills so they can limit the amount of money spent on repairs. To find a marketable service, consider what you would be willing to pay for in Tonga or Mauritius. The list won't be very long.

To be successful, you need to have skills beyond those of the average cruiser. You also need to make it clear that there is a fee for your expertise. One of the unwritten rules of the cruising community is that we all help each other as insurance against the day when we will need help.

What does that leave? The most successful venture appears to be sail and canvas work. Most cruisers will not pay someone else to fix popped stitches or a ripped seam. But they will pay to have a sail recut, to have the sun protection replaced on their genoa, or to have a new dodger made. To be successful, you must carry a sewing machine, spare sail material, and spare canvas. The condition of your own sails and canvas must also reflect your level of skill.

Skilled technicians may be able to make money as a diesel mechanic, refrigeration expert, or electronics guru. This works best in medium-sized yachting centers where spares are available and competition is limited.

Sometimes the simplest skills prove valuable in a faraway place. In Tonga, one woman made pocket money doing professional haircuts. Most of us trimmed our partners' hair with rusty scissors, so a salon-quality haircut on a sand beach under a palm tree was a luxury. Another woman with an old-fashioned, hand-crank washing machine aboard did laundry for reasonable prices. Another cruiser with a store of rye flour offered fresh-baked rye bread to order several mornings a week.

Teaching

Teaching, particularly teaching English, is another possibility. In the United States, you need to take a TEFL (Teaching English as a Foreign Language) or an ESL

(English as a Second Language) course to become certified. In other countries, your ability to speak the language qualifies you for informal tutoring and sometimes for more formal situations. If you have some proficiency in an area where there is a local need, you may find other teaching opportunities. (One of our friends was offered a position teaching shop at the high school in Vava'u, Tonga.)

Serendipity plays a large role in finding teaching opportunities, unless you have specialized training. For informal tutoring, such as teaching English to other cruisers, post a sign on the bulletin board at the local yachtie hangout to advertise your services.

Writing and photography

Almost every couple we met had considered submitting articles to sailing magazines. About 1 in 10 cruisers we knew tried it, but only 1 in 10 who tried had anything published. Good photographs sell articles, but photography itself constitutes a major expense. Magazines pay between $400 and $600 for articles (between £250 and £350 in the U.K.). You can supplement your cruising kitty by selling several articles a year, but you can't finance your entire trip.

If you are considering writing a book, take a hard look at the economics. It took the Hiscocks 25 years and five books before they were earning enough in royalties to support a modest lifestyle afloat. A marine book is considered a bestseller when it hits 5,000 to 10,000 copies over three or more years. At a 10-percent royalty rate on the net price, you will have an annual income around $5,000 for three years versus the year or so invested in writing.

The marine market is small, and sailors have the time to write. There is too much competition for writing to be lucrative. But don't let that stop you if you enjoy writing and hope to use the marine market to launch a broader career. Chapter 14 discusses professional writing in more detail.

Other artists

If you have an artistic talent, consider creating on board. If your art is portable, then you can probably earn something while you voyage.

One friend of ours is an oil painter who specializes in marine paintings. He has the talent to capture the feel of a boat on the open ocean—something that most boatowners find irresistible. He set up his cruising boat with painting in mind and financed his voyage with commissions from cruisers and megayacht owners. Another cruising artist in Antigua specialized in small watercolors. He painted local scenes and sold them to the tourist shops and boutiques. Some voyagers made jewelry with shells; others produced note cards using pressed and dried wildflowers. You can also do your craft in remote anchorages and sell your work when you get back to civilization.

Trading

When you purchase local crafts, the idea of buying a hundred instead of a dozen and selling them along the way may cross your mind. Every voyager has been tempted. Some profited handsomely, and others rued the day they ever had the thought.

To be successful, you must understand the value of what you are buying and know where you plan to sell these goods. If you do not know the works' quality and value, you may end up with a boatload that you cannot unload. But if you have spent a few months learning about the individual styles and quality levels of baskets made in South Africa, for example, and you have seen which baskets sell in the tourist shops, then you may want to buy some from local artisans and take them to your next port.

You are still not home free. Many countries, the United States being one, have laws about importing plants or plant material, including wood carvings, tapa cloth, baskets, etc. Technically, you must apply for a license to bring the goods in, in which case you will be faced with import taxes and duties.

Most voyagers quietly sell their treasures to friends and fellow cruisers. When the scheme works, you can supplement your cruising kitty for several months. For example, friends of ours stuffed their forepeak with brightly colored hammocks they bought in Brazil for $5 each and sold them in the Caribbean for $50 to $100 each.

Sabbatical: earn enough to finance several years

If you are planning to take a sabbatical for several years, save as much as you can before you leave. But don't get trapped ashore saving for one more year or one more contingency. In the end, you have to take the money you have, the boat you have, and the gear you have and go. You will never have as much money as you would like; however, you need to reach the point where lack of financial resources will not interfere with your enjoyment of voyaging.

Sabbatical takers have to decide whether to sell their home. The decision to sell is an individual one, and it depends on the current value of your house versus the purchase price, the tax implications of a sale, your attachment to the house and community, your feelings about having someone else live in your home, and your ability to manage a rental situation from halfway around the world. Voyagers who keep their homes may earn supplemental income from rental payments. But don't depend on the rental income to fund your voyaging each month: A six-month vacancy could end your trip. Most cruisers were satisfied if the rent covered the mortgage, taxes, insurance, and upkeep. They treated additional moneys as a windfall—not an integral part of their cruising budget. Cruisers who kept their homes also recommended hiring someone to manage the rental property.

We met a few people who were financing their cruise by taking on paying crew for six months to a year. While this sounds like a wonderful idea if you have a spare cabin or two, the few cases we saw firsthand did not work out. The realities of life aboard make the likelihood that you will find compatible crewmembers slim to nil. Moreso, paying crew expect to be treated as guests. They want to enjoy a vacation, which leaves you with even more work. And even the densest of paying crewmembers will realize that there are dozens of people doing what they are doing simply for a contribution toward expenses, for free, or—worse yet—for a paid fee. At that point, you can kiss your crewmember good-bye.

Most people taking the sabbatical option do not have to work along the way, but some choose to do so. Any of the money-earning options outlined in the precareer section are open to the sabbatical group. In addition, many sabbatical takers have marketable skills. Professionals have the easiest time finding positions and getting temporary work permits. For example, a teacher of disabled children arranged a job in New Zealand for the hurricane season before leaving the United States. That way, she and her husband could enjoy the Pacific without financial worries.

Doctors can always set up shop, especially if they carry a well-stocked medical kit. Some doctors chose not to announce their vocation to limit the amount of free medical advice solicited during cocktails in the cockpit! Others established office hours once or twice a week and remained off duty at other times.

Many countries seek professionals with skills in computer technology and financial markets. Before you leave, investigate some of the countries where you intend to spend time. Find out what areas of expertise are sought after and how difficult it is to obtain a temporary work permit.

Early retirement: stretching the retirement income

Most retired voyagers receive monthly income from some sort of pension. Many had rental income from real estate that was owned free and clear. Given their income, few retirees worked along the way.

As a group, these people had the largest, best-equipped boats. With these vessels, retirees may consider chartering their own boats as a way to earn additional income. While you can make some money taking a dozen people a day to a reef from a local hotel, chartering your own boat cannot be taken casually. Aside from the regulations mentioned earlier, most successful chartering businesses take years to build up and are dependent on good connections with the travel agents and charter brokers who find clients. Unless you plan to spend considerable time in one place and are committed to building a business, don't count on chartering your boat as a way to earn money as you go.

PART

EQUIPPING THE YACHT FOR BLUEWATER VOYAGING

CHAPTER 4

SAILS AND SAIL HANDLING

Our average wind speeds and conditions ■ *Summary of a circumnavigation* ■ *A closer look: trade winds vs. temperate latitudes* ■ **Implications for the voyaging sail inventory** ■ *Trade wind passagemaking: maximizing downwind performance* ■ *Temperate latitude passagemaking: managing variability* ■ **Putting it all together: sail inventory and sail-handling equipment for voyaging** ■ *Pretrip preparations: beyond the sail inventory*

Sails are the engine of a sailing boat. Good sails can improve an average day's run by 25 percent. A sail inventory tailored to the demands of trade wind passagemaking also makes life aboard safer, easier, and more enjoyable. In heavy air, proper sails and good sail-handling equipment will protect your rig. In light air, the right sails will keep you moving without turning on the engine.

Before we left, we based our sail inventory on the open-ocean wind conditions we expected to experience. We overestimated the amount of time we would spend at high wind speeds and didn't consider how large ocean swells would affect us in light air. After 18,000 nautical miles, we reconfigured our sail inventory in New Zealand. These changes contributed to a 25-percent increase in our average day's run. We stretched our daily average from 109 to 130 nautical miles-made-good toward our destination.

To illustrate the lessons we learned, I have analyzed the wind conditions we experienced during our three-year voyage. These findings define the optimal sail inventory for tropical and nontropical passages.

OUR AVERAGE WIND SPEEDS AND CONDITIONS

Shortly before we left on our trip, Evans gave me Lin and Larry Pardey's *Self-Sufficient Sailor*. The authors discuss analyzing their log over ten and a half years of voyaging. Their data points to the relative infrequency of heavy weather. They experienced gale force conditions (Force 8 or higher; see Table 4-1) less than one percent of the time. I had sailed in Force 7 gusting to Force 8

off the coast of southern England, and I could visualize what that meant. While I didn't underestimate how much worse higher wind speeds would be, I was relieved to see data proving heavy weather to be a small part of offshore voyaging.

My analysis confirms the Pardeys' findings. But I have also looked at the differences in wind conditions on passages made in the trade wind belt and those made in latitudes north and south of 25 degrees. The wind speeds and angles differ significantly, depending on latitude, and dictate different sail combinations for maximum efficiency.

Summary of a circumnavigation

What are open-ocean wind conditions really like? The charts in this chapter summarize our log entries made every four hours during the 266 days we spent on passage. These are average, sustained wind speeds that lasted for at least two watch periods. This overview of our log reveals three key insights with respect to open-ocean voyaging with the prevailing winds.

■ *Predominance of downwind conditions.* During our three-year trade wind circumnavigation, we spent close to two-thirds of our time going downwind (Figure 4-1). This finding surprised us—largely because we tended to remember when the trades weren't behaving themselves. In fact, the trade winds are remarkably consistent in direction, if not in strength.

■ *Relative infrequency of heavy weather.* We encountered apparent winds of Force 6 or higher just over 10 percent of the time (Figure 4-2). Like the Pardeys,

Figure 4-1. Percentage of time at various apparent wind angles

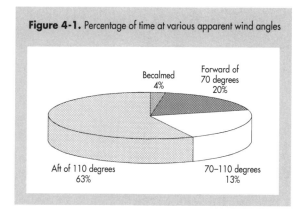

Becalmed
4%

Forward of
70 degrees
20%

Aft of 110 degrees
63%

70–110 degrees
13%

we found that winds of Force 8 and higher accounted for less than 1 percent of our time at sea. While offshore sailors must always be prepared for storm conditions, they will not encounter them very often. Our two storms with sustained winds over 45 knots made up less than a fraction of a percent of our time at sea, even though they loom large in our memories.

■ *Relative frequency of light air.* On the basis of true wind, it appears as if we spent an equal amount of time at less than 10 knots and over 22 knots (Figure 4-2). However, so much of our time was spent going downwind that we experienced apparent winds of less

Table 4-1. The Beaufort wind scale

Beaufort number	Mean velocity (knots)	Descriptive term	Deep sea criterion
0	Less than 1	Calm	Sea like a mirror
1	1–3	Light	Ripples with appearance of scales, but without foam crests
2	4–6	Light breeze	Small wavelets, still short but more pronounced; crests have glassy appearance
3	7–10	Gentle breeze	Large wavelets; crests begin to break; foam of glassy appearance; perhaps scattered white horses
4	11–16	Moderate breeze	Small waves, becoming longer; fairly frequent horses
5	17–21	Fresh breeze	Moderate waves with more pronounced long form; many white horses; chance of some spray
6	22–27	Strong breeze	Large waves begin to form; white foam crests more extensive everywhere; probably some spray
7	28–33	Near gale	Sea heaps up and white foam from breaking waves begins to blow in streaks along direction of the wind
8	34–40	Gale	Moderately high waves of greater length; edges of crests begin to break into spindrift; foam is blown in well-marked streaks along direction of the wind
9	41–47	Strong gale	High waves; dense streaks of foam along direction of the wind; crests of waves begin to topple, tumble, roll over; spray may affect visibility
10	48–55	Storm	Very high waves with long overhanging crests; resulting foam in great patches blown in dense white streaks along direction of the wind; surface of sea takes on general white appearance; tumbling of sea becomes heavy and shock-like; visibility affected
11	56–63	Violent storm	Exceptionally high waves; small- and medium-sized ships can be lost to view behind waves for a time; sea is completely covered with long, white patches of foam lying along direction of the wind; everywhere the edges of wave crests are blown into froth; visibility affected
12	63+	Hurricane	Air filled with foam and spray; sea completely white with driving spray; visibility seriously affected

than 10 knots almost one-third of the time. We encountered extremely light conditions more than twice as often as we experienced moderate and heavy winds over Force 6.

A closer look: trade winds versus temperate latitudes

This overall summary masks the very different conditions we experienced in different latitudes. We made 14 passages within the tropical latitudes between 25 degrees north and south of the equator. We made a dozen passages either completely in temperate latitudes (around South Africa) or between the tropics and temperate latitudes (New Zealand to New Caledonia). Breaking the data down shows both how consistent trade wind conditions are and how much variability cruisers face once they go above 25 degrees in either hemisphere.

We planned our route and timed our weather windows to avoid headwinds. We still ended up with the wind forward of the beam more than one-third of the time in higher latitudes. In contrast, we sailed downwind almost three-quarters of the time in the tropics (Figure 4-3). True wind speeds did not differ that much. However, downwind sailing in the trades made for less varied apparent wind speeds than in the higher latitudes. We experienced apparent wind speeds of Force 5 or less 90 percent of the time in the tropics (Figure 4-4).

Apparent wind speeds are more evenly distributed above 25 degrees, with 19 percent over Force 6 as opposed to only 9 percent in the tropics (Figure 4-4). Of that 19 percent, 9 percent was Force 7 or higher as opposed to only 1 percent in the tropics. Our log suggests that the higher the latitude, the greater the frequency of gale-force winds. While we did not venture much north or south of 40 degrees, we met others who had. Jo Hunter, a woman who had sailed singlehanded in the Southern Ocean aboard her Contessa 32, told us she had experienced winds of Force 7 or higher 30 percent of the time.

This greater variability in wind speeds and wind angles outside the tropics demands more sail handling aboard. We almost never experienced the same conditions over two consecutive 24-hour periods once we left the tropics. In contrast, on several trade wind passages we did not touch the sails for days at a time. When we

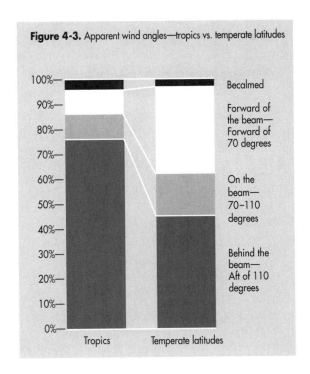

Figure 4-2. Percentage of time at various wind speeds

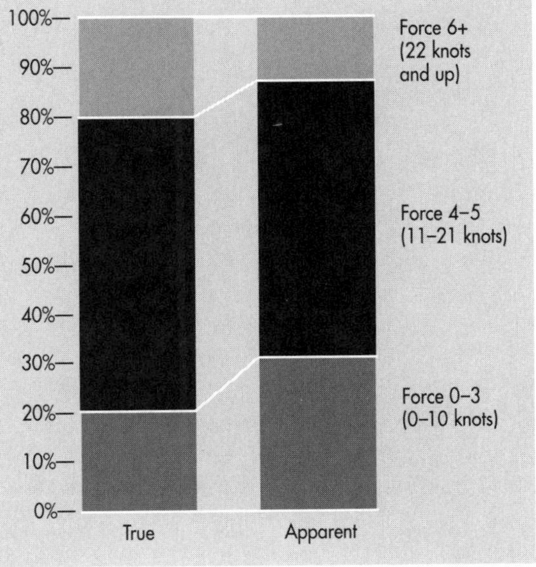

Force 6+ (22 knots and up)

Force 4–5 (11–21 knots)

Force 0–3 (0–10 knots)

True   Apparent

Figure 4-3. Apparent wind angles—tropics vs. temperate latitudes

Becalmed

Forward of the beam— Forward of 70 degrees

On the beam— 70–110 degrees

Behind the beam— Aft of 110 degrees

Tropics   Temperate latitudes

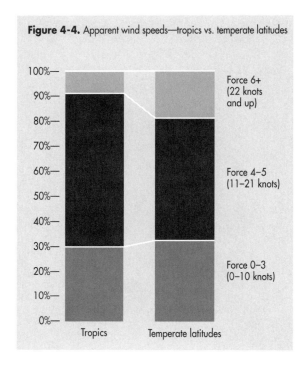

Figure 4-4. Apparent wind speeds—tropics vs. temperate latitudes

expected. Twenty percent of the time, we were moving downwind in Force 3 or less apparent. Successful sailing in the tropics depends on effective downwind sail combinations for apparent winds from 3 to 30 knots (Figure 4-5).

When running downwind in the trades day after day, three requirements dictate optimal sail combinations:

■ ***Minimize chafe.*** The constant motion of a boat rolling in ocean swells when running in front of the wind causes chafe on running rigging, sails, and even hardware. Running downwind on the passage from the Canaries to the Caribbean in 3 to 4 knots of apparent wind, we chafed through a one-quarter-inch hardened stainless steel shackle between our spinnaker block and the masthead crane. To control chafe, you must apply sail tape at all chafe points, reinforce and sew shut batten pockets, and protect sails from UV with sail covers whenever possible. Above all, use sail combinations to minimize chafe.

■ ***Maintain helm balance.*** Nothing drains a crew faster than hand steering the hours of their watch, day after day. The boat must be well balanced without significant weather or lee helm for self-steering to operate well, even in gusty or rolly conditions. Sail combinations should improve balance.

■ ***Minimize the risk of jibes.*** An uncontrolled jibe can endanger crewmembers and damage the rig. A preventer should be used on every boom anytime the wind goes behind the beam. But mechanical prevention can fail in an extreme situation. Sail combinations that can prevent jibes, or cause little harm if a jibe occurs, create an additional margin of safety.

Most coastal cruisers sail downwind "wing and wing," using a main and poled-out genoa. But this method of sailing does not work well with the above guidelines. The main must be eased to the point where it is against the spreaders, which causes chafe. On many boats, a slight change in wind speed or direction will affect the main at or near the center of effort more than the poled-out genoa. The boat will then tend to round up, making self-steering difficult. Finally, an uncontrolled jibe of the main is never a minor event.

For these reasons, all-headsail sail combinations continue to be many voyagers' first choice for offshore

left St. Helena in the South Atlantic for Antigua in the Caribbean, we put up our asymmetrical spinnaker an hour out of the harbor and left it up for 12 blissful days.

IMPLICATIONS FOR THE VOYAGING SAIL INVENTORY

Figures 4-3 and 4-4 suggest that an offshore yacht intended to sail only in the trade winds would be significantly different from one built and fitted out for higher latitudes. The sail inventories would also be completely different. But a trade wind circumnavigation involves passagemaking in both. The combination of average wind conditions dictates the sail combinations and sail-handling requirements for the offshore voyager.

Trade wind passagemaking: maximizing downwind performance

Even though all voyagers remember times when the trade winds refused to cooperate, the trades do live up to their downwind reputation. With respect to wind speed, however, the trades are less consistent than we

trade wind conditions. Chafe is minimized because the headsails are not in contact with any part of the boat. Double headsails tend to be extremely well balanced. Whenever the boat moves too far off the proper wind angle, the change in relative pressure on the two headsails acts to bring her back on course. Under all-headsail combinations, our wind vane steered dead downwind flawlessly down to 2 knots of boat speed. The rig tends to self-correct, making a jibe unlikely. If one does occur, it will do little more than damage a pole.

The sail combinations we used aboard *Silk* when running downwind in different wind and wave conditions follow.

Light-air sail combinations

Open-ocean light air is often characterized by localized squalls with wind gusts and shifts that require constant vigilance and frequent sail changes. These conditions will try the patience of the most sanguine crew and

wear or break gear. Over one-quarter of our time in the trade winds, we experienced apparent winds of Force 3 or less aft of the beam (Figure 4-5). Most of the time, these conditions were accompanied by an ocean swell. To keep moving without resorting to the engine, we needed a large but stable sail area that would hold the air as the boat rolled.

Light-air passages—not heavy weather—prove the true sailing ability of a boat and her crew. We sailed 1,980 nautical miles from Cocos Keeling to Rodrigues with Force 7+ conditions most of the time. The group of boats we left with, ranging from 24 to 45 feet, arrived within a few days of each other, their passage times dictated by their waterline length. When we sailed from Cape Town to St. Helena through the South Atlantic high, passage times for the group of boats that left with us varied significantly. Most of this 1,690-nautical mile passage was sailed in average winds of Force 3 or less, with apparent winds of 3 to 5 knots for the last

Figure 4-5. Apparent wind speeds and wind angles between 25 degrees north and south

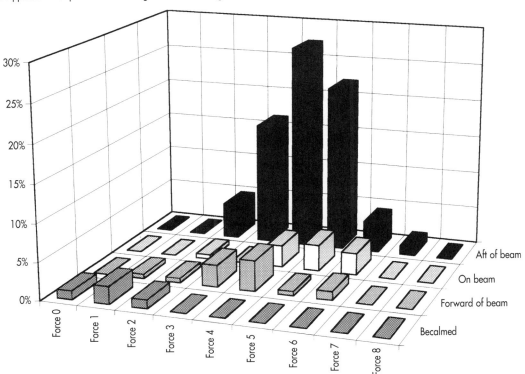

few days. Table 4-2 compares the performance of various boats on this passage.

In these light-air conditions, a spinnaker (symmetrical or asymmetrical) allowed boats to achieve a higher percentage of their hull speed and even allowed boats with less waterline to sail faster than much larger boats. Spinnakers hold the air to keep a boat moving forward when other sail combinations would be slatting uselessly, even in a heavy ocean swell. Equipped with a sock, the chute can be doused quickly as a squall line approaches. An asymmetrical spinnaker does not require a pole. Its airfoil-shaped cross section works more effectively than a conventional spinnaker over a wider range of wind angles. An asymmetrical chute is, however, less efficient than a conventional spinnaker dead downwind.

Like many coastal sailors, we were intimidated by managing a chute at sea. We started our trip with a slightly oversized, mid-weight (0.75 oz.) asymmetrical spinnaker, which came with the boat. After several passages, we discovered that this sail lacked enough stability to hold the air in an ocean swell. Its size kept us from using it at night and caused us to douse it whenever a squall approached. We replaced this sail with one that was cut fuller, three-quarters of the size, and twice the material weight (1.5 oz.) than the recommended coastal spinnaker for our boat. What we lost in the air being rolled out of the heavier material was offset by the better shape of the smaller sail in light winds. The smaller size allowed us to douse the sail without fuss, even after the wind had picked up. And we felt safe leaving the chute up overnight—even in the puffy, doldrums-like conditions of open-ocean light air.

We could carry our new asymmetrical spinnaker in wind angles as high as 60 degrees apparent down to 150 degrees apparent. At that point, we would set the tack on a pole and fly it like a symmetrical spinnaker.

To control an asymmetrical chute, rig a downhaul for the tack instead of tacking the sail to the bow with a fixed pendant. This allows you to control sail shape by lengthening or shortening the luff. On *Silk,* we used a shackle on the end of a 10-foot, small-diameter line. We attached the tack of the chute to our second headstay with the shackle, then we ran the line through a block at the bottom of the stay and back to a bow cleat (Figure 4-6). This arrangement would work with any hank-on stay attached to the stemhead. If you only have a roller furler at the stemhead, one alternative is to use the spinnaker pole. Attach a guy to the tack as on a conventional spinnaker; then set the pole up a foot or so to windward of the headstay and use its height to control the luff. Many sail lofts sell a sleeve with D-rings that rides up and down the roller-furling sail. The tack and the downhaul line are attached to the D-rings (Figure 4-7). The friction in this system makes it work less well, but the system does offer some degree of sail control.

Even a smaller, heavier, better-shaped sail can benefit from a few special tricks in light air and a big swell. Under 6 knots apparent, we stowed the mainsail. Its slatting accentuated the roll from the swell and disturbed the air in the chute. We used an extra-light Spectra sheet attached with a bowline to the clew to keep the sail from drooping. In rolly conditions, we ran the Spectra sheet through a plastic hose that was tied to the end of the fully eased main boom (see Figure 4-8, page 63). This arrangement poled out the clew without causing chafe to the sheet or the flaked mainsail. The setup worked well whether the tack was attached to the second headstay or flying from the pole.

Table 4-2. Performance of various boats between Cape Town and St. Helena (January 1–20, 1995)

Boat type	Length (waterline)	Days on passage	Hours motoring	Average speed	% of hull speed	Light-air sails aboard
43-foot steel cutter	40	15	80	4.7	55%	Spinnaker, blown out second day of light air
37-foot steel ketch	30	16	40	4.4	60%	None
30-foot fiberglass cutter	24	13.5	0	5.2	78%	Spinnaker with pole
37-foot fiberglass ketch	30	12	20	5.9	80%	Asymmetrical spinnaker

Medium-air sail combinations

Nearly half of our time in the tropics was spent with the apparent wind behind the beam at Force 4 to 5 (see Figure 4-5). In these conditions, double headsails are a safe, effective sail combination. They require very little in the way of specialized gear and offer thousands of worry-free, chafe-free, jibe-free downwind miles.

Many people assume that double headsails result in a rolly downwind ride. Eric Hiscock described *Wanderer III's* "fast and furious rolling" under twin headsails. He attributed this motion to the boat's narrow beam and low initial stability—uncommon design factors in today's offshore voyagers. Aboard *Silk*, we were most comfortable downwind under double headsails. Compared to flying the genoa alone, they reduced our roll by up to a third. The wind acting in each sail dampened down the roll while correcting the boat's course.

A boat needs two things to fly double headsails: a second stay arrangement and a pole. Before roller furlers, two sails could be hanked on and flown from a single stay. *Silk* had a second headstay next to her roller furler that we used to fly a hanked-on headsail. She also had rod rigging, which minimized the chafe from side-by-side headstays. Other boats were equipped with forward and aft headstays, two genoas furled around a single stay, or a smaller headsail on its own Kevlar or wire luff. A cutter can fly a second sail on the staysail stay, but the boat will not balance as well given the difference in size and position between the two sails.

The windward sail needs to be flown from a pole. The pole must be strong enough to handle an accidental jibe and fittings on both ends need to be releasable. We had a telescoping pole, which we never used extended. We would have preferred a proper pole the length of the boat's *J* measurement with a sufficient diameter to sup-

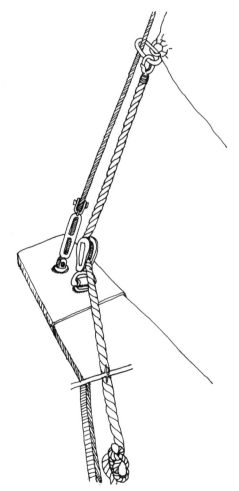

Figure 4-6. A tack downhaul increases light-air performance by allowing you to shape the luff of the sail.

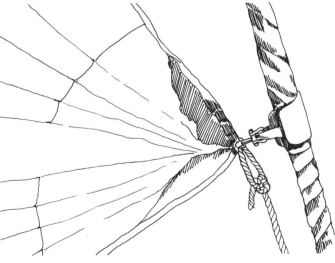

Figure 4-7. Sleeves like this offer a last resort for a tack downhaul.

port the loads of a spinnaker. We did not carry a second pole, and 90 percent of the time the leeward sail needed no support. In extremely rolly conditions, we used the main boom to pole out the clew of the leeward sail (as described for the asymmetrical spinnaker). We ran the genoa sheet through a length of plastic hose tied to the end of the fully eased boom (Figure 4-8).

We left with a 150-percent, 9-ounce roller-furling headsail. We found this genoa too big and too heavy below 15 knots apparent. In New Zealand, we replaced this headsail with a smaller, 130-percent, 5.5-ounce furling sail. This sail held the air better in a heavy fol-

lowing sea. We recut our old roller-furling genoa into a 110-percent hank-on sail.

After that, we flew the 130-percent furling headsail to leeward and poled out the 110-percent sail to windward in winds from 10 to 15 knots apparent (Figure 4-9). When the wind went over Force 5 apparent or the wind angle increased above 135 degrees, we switched down to our 88-percent, 9-ounce Yankee for the windward sail. The smaller sail to windward allowed us to fly double headsails up to 120 degrees apparent in moderate seas. As the wind increased toward Force 6 apparent, we reefed the roller-furling genoa until we were

Taking the drama out of setting and dousing a chute

Many sailors are intimidated by the prospect of flying a chute on a shorthanded offshore passage. To handle a chute with fewer than three people, you need a snuffer or a sock. But even with a sock, getting the sail off in a sudden squall can be traumatic. After a few scary incidents, we learned several tricks to manage our biggest sail.

Setting the sail

For a symmetrical spinnaker, set the pole up first. The pole jaw needs to be a comfortable reach from the bow, which means 5 to 6 feet above the deck and 2 to 3 feet to windward of the headstay. The guy should be in the pole fitting, but not attached to the sail. The pole should be held firmly in place by its afterguy, foreguy, and topping lift. For an asymmetrical spinnaker, set up the tack downhaul without attaching the sail to it.

Next, set the self-steering to steer an apparent wind angle of about 130 degrees. Tie the end of the sock control lines to a cleat. With the tack and clew free, attach the halyard and hoist the sail in its sock. Once the head is at the proper hoist, free the tack and clew from the bottom of the sock and spin the sail around within the sock until the control lines are free of the sail and are inboard of the tack and clew. Attach the sheet to the leeward clew. Pull the tack around the headstay and attach it to the tack down-

haul. On a symmetrical spinnaker, attach the guy to the windward clew.

While one crewmember raises the sock using the control lines, the other pulls in the sheet. Once the sail fills, trim the sheet and the guy or tack downhaul to get the proper sail shape. Then relax!

Dousing the sail

The sock cannot be pulled down when the sail is still full. Brute force does not help. Before you try to douse the sail, it needs to be streaming. Many people get the air out of the sail by releasing the sheet, but if the wind is aft of 150 degrees the sail will stream out in front of the boat and get wrapped around the headstay. The sock will get caught on stays and roller-furled sails before you can get it over the chute. To take the drama out of the takedown, you need to release the tack or guy, not the sheet. That requires a shackle or pole arrangement that can release the tack or guy under load.

To douse a chute with a sock easily in strong winds, return the boat to the 130-degree wind angle and set the self-steering. For a symmetrical spinnaker, return the pole to the setup position and trip the jaws to release the guy. For an asymmetrical spinnaker, release the tack. The chute will collapse and flop around until the sock is pulled down. Pulling in the sheet will keep the chute aft until it is under control.

running with a 100-percent sail to leeward and the 88-percent sail to windward. We marked the foot of the furling headsail with reflective tape at 100 percent and 88 percent to facilitate reefing at night.

When it came to a day's run, double headsails produced the best results. Between the Galapagos and the Marquesas, we managed 178 nautical miles in a 24-hour period. We sailed 183 nautical miles the first day out from Cape Town enroute to St. Helena with a half-knot current. In both cases, we maintained hull speed for 24 hours without feeling overcanvassed or out of control. Several times we averaged up to 95 percent of hull speed for five days in a row.

Heavy-air sail combinations

In the tropics, we sailed downwind in apparent winds of Force 6+ 5 percent of the time. In these conditions, you need a way to fly a small headsail without depending on a roller furler.

Roller furling has become accepted as standard offshore equipment. Today, the lack of a colored sail wrapped around the headstay causes comment. This is a testament to the simplicity and reliability of today's roller furlers when used in appropriate conditions. We would not sail offshore without a good roller furler for our primary headsail—but even today's furlers are not bulletproof.

When we were in the Azores after our first Atlantic crossing, about one-third of the boats that arrived had experienced gear failure. Half of those failures were self-steering; the other half were roller furlers. Friends of ours sailing transatlantic had their furler jam in a gale, which caused a shroud to part. Roller furlers are dependable, but they cannot be depended on implicitly. In heavy weather or in the event of a failure, an offshore boat needs an alternate way to fly a small headsail. We used our second headstay with hank-on sails. A staysail stay is another option.

To protect our equipment, we never used the roller furler in more than about Force 6 apparent wind. Instead, we ran downwind with our hanked-on Yankee to leeward and our 50-percent staysail boomed out to windward. When the wind went over Force 8 apparent, we dropped the Yankee and continued on our staysail alone, now to leeward.

Figure 4-8. The poor sailor's second spinnaker pole: a plastic hose attached to the end of the fully eased main boom.

Figure 4-9. *Silk's* primary downwind sail combination after New Zealand: our new 130-percent, 5.5-ounce genoa on the roller furler and our old 9-ounce genoa recut to 110 percent, hanked to our second-headstay, and flown from a pole.

Temperate latitude passagemaking: managing variability

Above 25 degrees latitude, no wind angle–wind speed combination dominated (Figure 4-10). We encountered more extreme conditions and greater variability once we left the tropics. In this region, a boat must be equipped to manage a wider range of conditions, and sail handling must be easy and efficient—even when you are shorthanded. Windward sail combinations need to power the boat well. You must perfect your sail inventory and sail-handling techniques for heavy weather before you leave.

Efficient sail handling

Sail changes could be an hourly event when we were north and south of 25 degrees latitude, and they often occurred in deteriorating conditions and poor visibility.

Simple, bulletproof sail-handling gear enable a short-handed crew to douse a sail quickly. Such equipment is not a luxury: It is an absolute requirement for safety. Even with a ketch rig, we found the mainsail difficult to handle in heavy weather. In New Zealand we switched to a full-battened mainsail and mizzen with lazyjacks on the main. The full battens offered four main advantages over a sail with partial battens or no battens.

■ *Increased sail life.* Full battens extend sail life by reducing flogging when reefing or dousing. Our first set of partial-batten sails lasted for about 20,000 miles. By that point, the sails had lost their shape even though the material showed few signs of weakness. We sailed the next 20,000 miles using full-battened sails and sold the boat with those sails. Their shape remained excellent, and the material showed little wear. We could have sailed at least another year before replacing them.

Figure 4-10. Apparent wind speeds and angles north and south of 25 degrees latitude

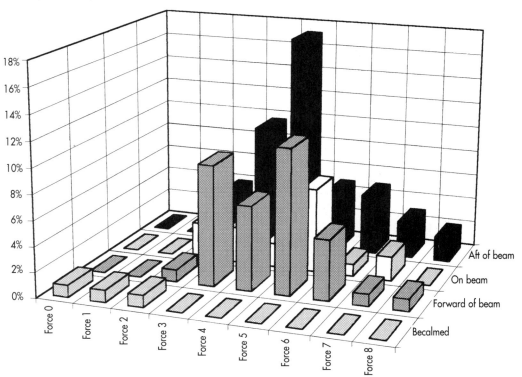

■ **Better sail shape.** The full battens improved sail shape at almost all wind angles and made the sails less sensitive to perfect trim. When the wind was veering or gusting every few minutes, the boat would keep powering along without constant attention to the sail controls.

■ **More efficient reefing.** We placed each of our reef points just below one of the full-length battens. The battens allowed us to reef both sails quickly and efficiently and improved the reduced sail's shape. They also extended material life by reducing the amount of stretch in the belly of the sail once it was reefed.

■ **Easier dousing.** Ease of sail handling can be defined by how well you can douse a sail at night in heavy winds and a rolling sea. Doing a poor furling job in these conditions invites disaster later. With full battens, we could get the entire sail down with more ease in any condition and furl it well with minimum effort. In calmer conditions, we could drop the sail into the lazyjacks, tug on it a few times, throw a few sail ties around it, and we were done.

The disadvantage of full battens and lazyjacks is chafe. But we found we could minimize chafe with careful thought and a few precautions. To prevent the battens from chafing the sail, we had the sailmaker reinforce each batten pocket with extra stitching and cover all edges with sail tape. After being properly tensioned, the batten ends were sewn in to ensure that they did not pop out. After every passage, we inspected the sail for any broken stitches or signs of chafe and repaired any damage immediately. Our lazyjacks were attached to the boom only when we dropped the sail; the rest of the time they were led forward to a stay and fastened to a small cleat so they would not foul the sail as we raised it (Figure 4-11). This location also kept them from chafing the sail and prevented them from being chafed by any part of the mast.

The other disadvantage of a full-battened mainsail is the expense. The cost can be greatly reduced by avoiding the separate track and cars favored by many sailmakers. When we refit *Silk* in New Zealand, we installed a system of Battslides from North Sails (Figure 4-12) that combined a sail slug that worked on our existing track with a fitting attached to the batten ends. This option worked well on *Silk* and ran less than one-third

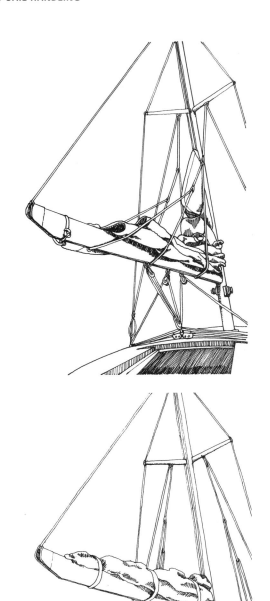

Figure 4-11. Our lazyjacks cost less than $50 and worked well for 20,000 offshore miles. Because we stored them along the shroud, they never chafed on the sail or mast and never became fouled.

the price of the separate track-and-car system. For ketches up to 40 feet and cutters up to the mid-30s, this option offers a practical, inexpensive way to attach the batten end to the mast. For boats above those lengths, there will be too much friction in the system to make it workable. Larger boats will need to install the separate track and cars. Before selecting any system, be sure the fittings are well made. Obtain references from sailors who have used them offshore.

While headsail roller furling has come of age for offshore work, mainsail furling has not. We met only a handful of boats voyaging with mainsail furlers, and only one crew was satisfied with the system's perfor-

Figure 4-12. The Battslide arrangement that we used for our full-battened sails was about one-third the cost of the separate track and car alternative.

mance. These systems are still too complex and unreliable, but that will change. Other than lazyjacks, flaking systems are not in general use aboard offshore boats. While perfectly acceptable for coastal cruising, many have too much friction for two people to raise and lower the sail quickly and easily in heavy weather. When it comes to mainsail handling, simpler is still better.

Few boats were set up to be reefed from the cockpit. Again, many of the systems have too much friction for a shorthanded crew to manage them easily. We had slab reefing with two reef points on both the main and the mizzen on *Silk,* and this system is practically foolproof. Our first reef reduced the sail area by about 20 percent, our second by an additional 15 percent. With the ketch rig, we used our mizzen as our primary storm sail. A cutter needs either a third reef or a trysail, preferably both. The trysail should have its own mast track. If your main blows out or the track rips from the mast, the trysail and track provide essential backup. Using the trysail also reduces the stretch and wear that occur when reefing the main.

Racers know that regularly cleaning and lubricating the mast track eases sail handling. Cruisers may not care how quickly a sail goes up, but extra lubrication will save you time and effort when you bring a sail down. It may even allow you to get a sail off in extreme conditions when you cannot turn head to wind.

After a week at sea, the mast track will be coated with salt. To clean the mast track while on passage without going up the mast, tie a damp, soapy piece of cloth securely to a spare sail slide. Attach the halyard to one side of the slide and a downhaul to the other and use the two controls to pull the slide up and down in the track until the cloth does not pick up any more dirt and salt. In port, wash the track thoroughly with soap and water while aloft and then lubricate it. Silicone tends to attract dirt and collect on the sail slides, turning your lovely white sail black along the luff. Liquid soap works well as a lubricant and cleans as it greases. Of course, it must be applied more frequently. The new dry lubricant products last longer but are hard to find outside the United States.

You must have an easy way to get someone up the mast if something goes wrong. Halfway between St. Helena and Antigua, we went to reef the main one evening in deteriorating conditions, and it wouldn't come down.

Luckily, we had fitted a large, self-tailing winch on the main mast. I used that winch to haul Evans up the mast in big seas on the pitching boat. He discovered that the stainless steel slide attached to the headboard had become welded to the aluminum mast after several days of beating to weather in 25 to 30 knots of apparent wind.

Beyond the need to be able to get up the mast at sea, this incident illustrates the danger from mixed metals in the presence of salt. Mixed metals can often be found on standing rigging and deck hardware. The pins that held our aluminum furler together were stainless steel. The pins in our traveler cars were stainless and became welded to the aluminum track. If problem areas cannot be eliminated, lubricate and inspect them frequently.

Windward performance

If gentlemen never sail to weather, they must never leave the tropics. Despite our efforts to plan our passages to avoid headwinds, we still spent over one-third of our time with the wind ahead of the beam (Figure 4-4). Windward ability depends on the basic hull shape and sail plan of the boat. But assuming your boat goes to windward at all, you can improve her performance with the right sails.

We were able to point 10 degrees higher and carry more sail comfortably after our New Zealand sail refit. Sailing 10 degrees closer to the wind over several days can save a day on an already uncomfortable passage.

With our refit, we increased the roach of the main and mizzen, which improved their efficiency. The additional sail area on the mizzen eliminated the slight lee helm we had previously experienced in light headwinds. The smaller, lighter, better-cut headsail allowed *Silk* to point higher. The better sail shape made us heel less, so more of the sails' effort translated into forward movement through the water. Working below was easier because *Silk* was flatter.

With her new sails, *Silk* could sail 35 degrees off the wind in flat water, but we could generally only make 45 degrees in windy, open-ocean conditions. If the winds fell and the waves didn't, we sometimes were unable to do better than 60 degrees off the wind.

Heavy weather techniques

In the tropics, heavy air was on our stern. Outside the tropics, gales came from every direction. In nontropical regions, 9 percent of our time was spent in apparent winds of Force 7+. For heavy weather, offshore boats and crews must have efficient reefing systems, storm sails, and practice with heavy weather techniques.

We saw no reason to kill ourselves in heavy weather. If the wind was behind the beam, we would reach or run on our Yankee or staysail up to Force 9, unless the waves became unmanageable. If the wind was around 60 degrees apparent, we would forereach on a small headsail and our mizzen until the wind dropped. If the wind was over Force 6 and dead on our nose with big seas, we hove-to and waited 6 to 12 hours for a wind shift.

Over the course of our entire circumnavigation, we were in winds Force 9 or over only a half-dozen times; most of those lasted less than 12 hours. The small percentages shown in Figure 4-10 don't reduce the risk of even an hour spent in storm conditions. Every boat heading offshore has to be prepared for heavy weather.

Being prepared means having a staysail stay and a storm jib to fly from it. Each tactic mentioned above requires a small headsail on almost all boats. On a cutter, dropping to the staysail moves the center of effort toward the mast, complementing the reefed main. The location of the staysail inboard from the bow platform is safer in heavy weather. The smaller sail and lower attachment point of the stay put less force on the mast. If a headstay ever parts, the staysail stay offers essential backup. If you don't have a staysail stay, fit one before you depart.

On *Silk*, we dropped the main completely when the wind went over 25 knots. We could continue on the mizzen and our 88-percent Yankee, as long as the waves were manageable. We reefed the mizzen at 30 knots. Like many ketches, *Silk* hove-to on her mizzen alone without a backed headsail. We would drop the Yankee and heave-to on the reefed mizzen in up to 45 knots of wind. We could remain hove-to in winds over 50 knots with a second reef in the mizzen, unless the waves became threatening.

Our mizzen was our primary storm sail in gale-force winds. Most offshore cutters fly a trysail in 30 knots apparent and up, and some will heave-to nicely on the trysail alone in extreme conditions.

When you switch down to the staysail, you need to secure the roller furler so it does not unroll. Furl the sail with several wraps of the sheets around it, cleat off the

Ode to the ketch

When we purchased *Silk,* we saw her ketch rig as a liability. We even considered converting her to a cutter. But within 5,000 ocean miles, we came to appreciate the virtues of a ketch rig.

Downwind, a ketch can carry more sail area than a cutter. The mizzen can be flown without blanketing a headsail. A mizzen staysail adds 20 percent more sail area (Figure 4-13). Ketches have won many round-the-world races, including the Whitbread and the original Golden Globe, which proves their speed off the wind. They also offer the ultimate cruising benefit: less stress in a building breeze. Many small sails offer dozens of sail combinations to keep the boat moving without being overcanvassed. These sails are easy to handle, even for a shorthanded crew. When the wind goes over 25 knots, the boat is left with two small working sails that can be handled by one crewmember.

A ketch rig can be likened to four-wheel drive in a car. In normal conditions, it complicates life unnecessarily and can never compete with dedicated racing machines. But when you head into the untamed wilds, a ketch will carry you over the rough spots and make life aboard easier.

To understand the benefits of the ketch rig, we had to learn how to sail it. We initially made the mistake of trying to sail *Silk* like a cutter. We would keep the mizzen up too long, then drop it and reef the main in stages. The result was poor performance and weather helm. By the end of our first year, we had learned four lessons that vastly improved *Silk's* sailing performance.

■ *General reefing sequence.* The storm sails on a cutter balance the boat from the middle—the storm jib and trysail are located either side of the mast. On a ketch, small sails balance the boat from the ends. When the wind first starts to build, dropping the mizzen makes for a quick and easy first reef. But as the wind goes over Force 6, the sail to get rid of is the main. Under a small headsail and mizzen, the boat is well balanced and the remaining sails are easy to handle in almost any wind.

■ *Windward work.* Ketches do not sail to windward as well as sloops and cutters do. Mizzen efficiency is often spoiled by dirty air from the main, leaving less effective sail area than on a comparable cutter. To sail as close to the wind as possible, we learned to drop the mizzen completely—no matter what the wind speed. When we first discovered this, it felt like releasing a hand brake: Without the drag from the mizzen, the boat picked up 2 knots of speed. When slightly off the wind, the mizzen helps sailing performance. In that situation, we found the best reefing sequence to be: first reef in the main; first reef in the mizzen; second reef in the main; drop the main altogether.

■ *Heaving-to.* When conditions reach the point where you need to heave-to, you will be sailing under the mizzen and a small headsail. To heave-to on most ketches, all you need to do is drop the headsail. *Silk* lay at about 45 degrees off the wind with the mizzen sheeted just off the centerline and the helm centered. Once hove-to this way, the crew can stay in the safety of the cockpit.

■ *Power sailing.* Ketches have always done well on offshore, off-the-wind races because they can carry some extra sail on their second mast. For fast passages off the wind, a ketch equipped with a mizzen staysail will outperform a comparable cutter (Figure 4-13). In winds too strong for a spinnaker and too far forward to carry double headsails, a cutter's main can blanket the genoa. The mizzen and a large headsail do not interfere with one another, and they create a balanced, efficient rig.

Various rigs offer different advantages. For a westabout trade wind circumnavigation, the benefits of a ketch rig outweigh the costs. For a ketch rig to perform well, the mizzen needs to be between one-third and one-half the sail area of the main. Many ketches have undersized mizzens, which offer all the disadvantages of the rig with none of the advantages. But if you have found a boat that you like with a proper ketch rig, don't rule it out. If you buy a ketch, experiment with the ideas above to see what works. By the time you have learned to sail the boat well, you too will be convinced of a ketch's merits.

Figure 4-13. A ketch powers along under mizzen staysail in the Gulf of Carpentaria north of Australia.

reefing line, and lock the drum in place with a shackle. If your drum does not have this provision, find a way to lock it in place so it cannot swivel if the roller-furling line chafes through.

Before you sail offshore, practice heavy weather techniques aboard your own boat. That may sound obvious, but it is advice that we ignored. On our first offshore passage we were forced to run downwind trailing warps when we could not get *Silk* to heave-to with a headsail. That time we had plenty of sea room. We made sure there wasn't a next time.

PUTTING IT ALL TOGETHER: SAIL INVENTORY AND SAIL-HANDLING EQUIPMENT FOR VOYAGING

During the course of a normal trade wind circumnavigation, you will encounter both tropical and temperate latitude conditions. Table 4-3 summarizes a minimal sail inventory for voyaging. This list balances the trade-offs between the limited stowage space aboard a medium-sized cruising boat and the need for a range of sails to handle the mix of conditions offshore.

For sail handling, at minimum, you will need a pole and preventers. This means a strong spinnaker pole sized for the boat's J measurement and the largest sail aboard with the appropriate fittings. Every boom should have a preventer. A vang with a minimum purchase of

Table 4-3. A minimal sail inventory for offshore voyaging

Types of sails	Minimal requirements	Comments
Working sails	Main (plus mizzen for ketch rig) with two to three reef points	Triple-stitched, moderate weight, reinforced at all chafe points with sail tape
	100–150% mid-weight genoa	Hank-on or roller furling with sun protection
Heavy weather	88% heavyweight Yankee	Second headsail for downwind or heavy weather; flown on separate stay or wire luff
	9–10 oz. 50% staysail	Flown from staysail stay or baby stay; storm/emergency sail
	9–10 oz. storm trysail (or second reef in mizzen for ketch)	Flown on separate mast track; storm/emergency sail
Light air	Asymmetrical or symmetrical spinnaker	Three-quarters the size and twice the weight of the recommended

3:1 that can be attached from a bale on the boom to a stanchion base makes a convenient, temporary preventer or a regular preventer for small booms. A preventer that runs from the boom forward to a bow fitting should be used offshore. The boom can be rigged with a permanent line led forward to the mast so you don't have to bring the sail back in to set up the preventer (Figure 4-14).

All equipment to control sail shape—including outhauls, travelers, leech lines, vangs, reefing winches, and sheet winches—should be well placed, adequately sized, and in good working order. Traveler cars that are held by a pin (instead of controlled by a block and tackle) are useless, as are underpurchased vangs and undersized, non-self-tailing primary winches. To get the most out of the boat, equip it with gear that can do the job.

Handling heavy weather will always be a key concern for every offshore yacht. However, our experience suggests that most people will spend far more time trying to make a respectable day's run in under 10 knots apparent and rolly seas. By focusing on the actual conditions you will encounter in the areas where you plan to

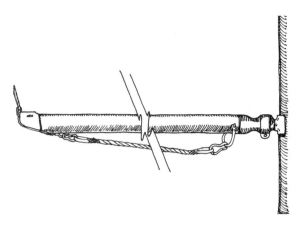

Figure 4-14. To make sure the preventer gets used whenever it is needed, rig a line along the boom with an eye splice. You can attach the preventer even when the boom is fully eased.

sail, you can optimize your sail inventory to maximize safety and speed while minimizing frustration. Perhaps you will avoid a major sail refit in New Zealand when you have half the world in your wake!

Pretrip preparations: beyond the sail inventory

When considering your boat's sail and sail-handling arrangements, the following list will help you cover all the bases.

■ *Rigging.* Many offshore cruisers avoid rod rigging because it does not strand like wire or offer other warning before it fails. Compared to wire, rod rigging does reduce chafe on sails and running rigging and creates less windage aloft. *Silk* was equipped with rod rigging, and it gave us no major problems, though we found few riggers who knew how to tune it or had the equipment to work on it. After our trip, we don't have a strong preference for rod or wire. Regardless of type, if the rigging is more than 10 years old, you should replace it before leaving. Otherwise, inspect it and all fittings thoroughly using a magnifying glass. Pay particular attention to terminal ends, spreader tips, and the masthead crane welds. If you have any concerns, pay for a professional rig survey.

■ *Halyard accessibility.* You should be able to reach the head of each sail to attach a halyard without having to perform gymnastic feats. If you find you have to climb like a monkey up the main mast or balance precariously on the companionway hatch to reach the mizzen, picture that maneuver when the boat is rolling through 30 degrees. A foldable maststep or a well-placed deck locker can easily prevent a hair-raising experience aboard.

■ *Tack pendants.* Check every sail at full hoist to see if it chafes at or near the tack. Many Yankees and cruising chutes need to be set up with a wire pendant so that they clear the bow pulpit. Some roller-furling genoas will need the same treatment. Trysails should be outfitted with a pendant that will keep them from chafing on the furled main. Roller-furling sails are particularly vulnerable to chafe on their tack grommet. Lashing the grommet to the roller-furling foil reduces the movement that causes this chafe.

■ *Spare halyards.* Every mast must have a spare halyard for situations when a halyard is lost up the mast or a sail jams. If you want to avoid weight and windage aloft, use a Spectra messenger line. But rig it so that it cannot chafe; otherwise your spare halyard won't last through your first passage.

■ *Shackles.* You need to be able to operate shackles without actually looking at them. The type that requires you to line up a pin and screw it into threads is almost impossible to operate in bad conditions. Except where they could be accidentally tripped, snap shackles should be fitted with a lanyard that makes them releasable with one hand. All shackles should be oversized. Many offshore racing boats use bowlines instead of shackles on sheets and halyards to save money, weight, and aggravation.

■ *Winches.* The boat should have a minimum of two oversized self-tailing winches, preferably the primary sheet winches. If you cannot afford more, consider how you will take someone up the mast in the event of an emergency. On *Silk,* we added an oversized, self-tailing main halyard winch on the mast. Other people used electric windlasses or led the halyard through blocks back to a primary winch. Whatever your solution, you need to be able to set it up in less than five minutes.

■ *Spinnaker halyards.* For spinnaker halyards, your boat should have either a single sheave at the top of the masthead crane on the boat's centerline or two bails on either side of the masthead crane for port and starboard halyards. Do not plan on flying a spinnaker from the sheave for a staysail or Yankee halyard. Besides not giving you a full hoist, these halyards will quickly chafe through due to the lateral pull of a spinnaker. Our Yankee halyard chafed through at the masthead in less than two hours of light-air spinnaker flying.

■ *Sail covers.* Good sail covers protect your canvas from the devastating effects of UV radiation. But most materials stop screening the sun's rays long before they start looking worn out. If your covers are more than two years old, replace them before you leave. And make sure to use them whenever a sail is furled. They do no good stowed down below.

You will also want to bring along some light-air sheets, lengths of plastic hose for chafe protection, and a downhaul for the asymmetrical spinnaker.

Finally, practice, practice, practice. Take your boat out when there is no wind and when the wind is slapping the halyards against the masts in the marina. Try heaving-to and learn how your boat behaves in storm conditions. Figure out how to balance your boat downwind. Give the double headsails a try. Practice setting and dousing the chute. Get to know your boat's idiosyncrasies. Sailing your boat in everything from Force 3 to Force 9 will prove one of the best investments of time and energy you can make before you leave.

CHAPTER 5

GROUND TACKLE AND ANCHORING ARRANGEMENTS

The basics for successful anchoring ■ *Ground tackle for the bluewater voyager* ■ *Anchoring technique* ■
Real-world anchoring solutions ■ *Basic gear* ■ *Actual situations* ■ *Pretrip preparations: beyond anchors and rodes*

Recommendations on the "best" anchor and the "best" anchoring system spawn passionate debate in sailing magazines and online sailing forums. Everyone agrees on certain basic principles: Heavier rodes and more scope are always desirable; chain is more chafe resistant than nylon, even though its weight reduces sailing performance. Beyond these conclusions, the arguments degenerate into discussions on complex catenary curves, obscure trigonometric functions, and unrealistic anchor tests.

In the real world, anchors and anchoring are rarely discussed by experienced voyagers during cockpit cocktails. Anchoring is more straightforward than the convoluted theories. Successful anchoring starts with the right gear and ends with good technique.

THE BASICS FOR SUCCESSFUL ANCHORING

One of the most common sea stories among coastal cruisers starts, "It was blowing like stink," and ends, "Then we reset the anchor and sat watches for the rest of the night." But offshore voyagers don't talk about dragging at anchor because, in all but the most extreme conditions, they don't drag. We sat out a gale in St. George's harbor in Bermuda with 30 other boats. Winds went over 45 knots, then shifted so we were exposed to the anchorage's two-mile fetch. Throughout the night, the crews sat anchor watches and adjusted their scope—just as we did. But not one single boat dragged.

There is no magic involved. Getting a good night's sleep at anchor depends on selecting the right gear to do the job and setting the anchor in the right spot with the proper scope. Every cruiser we met who had been out there for more than a few months had mastered it.

Ground tackle for the bluewater voyager

The anchoring arrangements on an offshore boat need to be flexible, because no one anchor can do it all. They need to be strong, because at some point shock loads will exceed the design strength of standard ground tackle. Once you leave the Atlantic, you will be anchored most of the time. At some point, your life could depend on your ground tackle. As with sails, this is an area where it does not pay to stint.

Use the right anchor for the conditions

Despite the profusion of anchors on the market, no one anchor sets and holds perfectly in all conditions. Almost all anchors work well in a good sand bottom, but very few work at all in soft mud, clay, or heavy grass. As shown in Table 5-1, fluke-type anchors offer the best holding power for their weight in sand and soft mud, but they are close to useless in grass, rock, or clay. Plow anchors need to be heavier to achieve the same holding power as their fluke equivalents, but they hold well in a wide range of bottoms. Bruce anchors also work well across a wide range of bottoms, but they can be fouled by large pieces of rock or coral that get jammed in the claw.

You may encounter one or two bottom types in your local cruising grounds, so you can afford to carry one type of anchor suitable for the anchorages in your area. But a voyaging boat must be prepared to anchor in any type of bottom, even in strong tidal or river currents. To cope with this range of conditions, offshore boats must carry several different types of anchors. In practice, most of our friends had from three to five anchors aboard including a Bruce, a CQR, and a fluke-type model. Some boats also carried a fisherman-type anchor that was stowed in the bilge and used only in storm conditions.

Size all ground tackle for shock loads

While the exact numbers are debatable, the loads on an anchor under normal conditions are surprisingly modest. Anchored in 10 knots of wind on a sand bottom, we would snorkel over our ground tackle to find that we were held by a 10- to 15-foot length of chain. No pull at all was exerted on the anchor's shank, even when the boat swung through a complete circle. The anchor would be dug in, but its flukes and shank would still be visible.

When the wind increases, the loads increase with the square of the change in wind velocity (e.g., the force in 20 knots of wind will be four times the force in 10 knots). In these conditions, about half our chain would be pulled steadily off the bottom and the rest would be pulling against the anchor, parallel to the bottom. The anchor would be dug in well with only the tip of the shank visible.

This constant force on the anchor in higher winds is a steady-state load but not the maximum load the anchor has to hold. If you are anchored where there is some fetch and your boat is pitching in a small chop, or if your boat is sailing at anchor and then fetching up hard on the chain, your ground tackle is receiving shock loads of thousands of pounds. Every piece of your ground tackle must be able to withstand such loads—not just the anchor and rode, but also the shackles, bow rollers, cleats, snubber, and even the bowsprit.

For anchors, that means at least one size larger than normal for your boat's size. For instance, a 35-pound CQR is generally recommended for a 40-foot boat. If you

Table 5-1. Attributes of different anchor types for a 40-foot coastal boat

Anchor type	Fluke-type	Plow	Large claw type	Fisherman-type
Brand names	Danforth, Fortress	CQR, Delta	Bruce	Paul Luke
Holding-to-weight ratios	Excellent	Moderate	Moderate	Poor
Recommended size	25 lb.	35 lb.	40 lb.	70 lb.
Performs well in:	Sand, soft mud	Weeds, grass, hard-packed sand	Sand, coral, rock	Rock, coral, kelp, weed
Performs poorly in:	Rock, coral	Soft mud	Hard-packed sand, soft mud	Soft mud
Key advantage	Easy to handle	Point penetrates bottoms that other anchors skate over	Resets itself in two shank lengths if tripped	Often holds when nothing else will
Key disadvantage	Does not reset itself once tripped	Point pulls through soft mud or fine sand	Large pieces of coral or rock can foul claw	Difficult to stow and to handle

read carefully, you'll learn that this recommendation is good up to 30 knots. For storm conditions an anchor one to two sizes larger is suggested. Thus, a 45-pound CQR should be considered the minimum for a 40-foot offshore voyager.

A similar rule should be applied to the rode. An all-chain rode wrapped around a rock or coral head with the bow pitching in a steep chop causes huge shock loads. In Pacific coral waters in these conditions, some 40-foot boats broke 5/16-inch high test chain and others stretched 3/8-inch BBB chain, even using snubbers. In waters where your chain could snag on rock or coral, you need a minimum breaking strength of about 75 percent of your boat's displacement. For most boats, that works out to one size larger than recommended. But the heaviest ground tackle in the world won't protect you if your anchor shank is twisted. Anchors with bent shanks drag because they cannot efficiently distribute the boat's pull to the flukes.

From a safety perspective, this is one area where bigger is better. Offshore boats should carry the largest anchor and rode that can be reasonably handled by the crew and safely carried by the boat.

Maximize the holding power of your rode

All-chain rode is widely considered optimal for a bluewater boat. Chain resists the chafe and abrasion that occurs as it is dragged over coral or rock. The weight of the chain keeps the pull on the anchor parallel to the bottom, which keeps the forces of wind and tide from tripping the anchor. A third advantage of an all-chain rode is less obvious: On a rock or coral bottom, chain friction significantly increases holding power.

Compare how hard it is to drag a length of chain over a rocky beach versus dragging a length of rope. The chain dissipates force every time it takes a slight bend around a rock while the rope glides over the top. We sat through a gale in Arrecife in the Canaries, a rocky harbor where several other boats had trouble getting their anchors to hold. Evans dove to check our anchor and was surprised to see that it was taking almost no strain at all. The chain dissipated the gale forces through numerous 10- to 20-degree bends around medium-sized rocks. Chain friction can also increase holding in deep, thick mud.

Most offshore voyagers find this combination of chafe resistance, weight, and increased friction irresistible. The standard rode for bluewater boats consists of 300 feet of chain. But an all-chain rode lacks elasticity. Drag-proof ground tackle also requires a good elastic snubber.

Adding elasticity to an all-chain rode prevents the anchor from being yanked out of the bottom while saving the windlass and cleats from unnecessary strain. Many motor boats with all-chain rodes and push-button windlasses don't take the time to put on a snubber at all, and many coastal sailboats use a short, thin snubber that doesn't reach the water. As the wind comes up and the forces on the anchor double and double again, the snubber becomes the most critical element of the anchoring system. In Niue, a small island between the Cook Islands and Tonga, dangerous waves can build quickly in the open roadstead anchorage. In such conditions, the 1/4-inch snubber broke on a friend's boat. The chain destroyed the bow roller, damaged the windlass and pulpit, and injured the skipper's hand as the bow crashed up and down in steep chop.

What is a proper size for an offshore snubber? When tied to a dock, the load is spread among three or more strong and elastic docklines. At anchor this load is concentrated on one line. This line should be as strong as and more elastic than your docklines. That means a relatively long nylon snubber about the same diameter as that recommended for the boat's docklines. The snubber should be long enough so if you pay out more scope, you can let out more snubber without disconnecting it from the chain. A length of 30 feet of 1/2-inch nylon is not unreasonable for a 40-foot boat.

An oversized, all-chain rode with a long, elastic snubber maximizes holding power. Unfortunately, the weight of chain, which serves the boat so well when anchored, becomes a hindrance under sail. Carrying 300 feet of 3/8-inch BBB chain in the bow is the equivalent of having two halfbacks standing on your foredeck at all times. For well-found, offshore boats over 40 feet this may not be a problem. But for smaller boats, sailing performance will be adversely affected. Pitching will increase dramatically, making it uncomfortable below and reducing windward sailing ability. Smaller boats often lack the room to move the weight aft. If this is the case with your boat, you can do one of two things—

reduce the chain size of the all-chain rode or switch to a mixed rope-and-chain rode.

When weighing your options, consider a simple engineering fact. For two rodes with the same total weight and length (assuming a frictionless bottom), the one with its weight concentrated in a shorter length of heavier chain followed by nylon will hold better than a longer all-chain rode of lighter chain. Concentrating the weight near the anchor means less leverage on the anchor as wind and wave forces try to lift or drag it. You are therefore better off using a mixed rope-and-chain rode with heavier chain. The mixed rode will be stronger and have greater holding power than an all-chain rode of smaller diameter. That's the theory.

On an actual bottom where friction is a real component, the shorter-heavier approach can only be taken so far. The benefits of concentrating the weight near the anchor have to be weighed against the benefits of increased chain friction and reduced chafe from a longer chain. The optimal mixed rode includes a length of chain that maximizes the value of chain friction while concentrating as much of the weight of the chain near the anchor as possible. For most anchorages, this translates into a minimum of 40 feet of oversized chain in a mixed rode. If the chain length is increased to 60 to 100 feet, you will be able to anchor on all chain in most anchorages while significantly reducing the weight in your bow. The mixed rode weighs 60 percent less than the original all-chain configuration, and at least 40 percent less than a downsized all-chain rode (Table 5-2). If you use high test chain instead of BBB, you can end up with a stronger and lighter rode.

Oversized rodes and anchors mean nothing if the connections between anchoring components are not sized for the same loads as the rest of the equipment. Table 5-3 summarizes the ways to connect the anchor to the rode and the chain to the line.

In most rodes, one of these connectors will be the proverbial weak link. In selecting connectors, your first concern should be strength. If the connection might go through the windlass, then your second concern should be whether or not it will do so. Connecting links and three-strand, rope-to-chain splices offer the greatest strength and should be your first choice for connecting your rode. If the chain is connected to the anchor, open and lubricate both the galvanized quick links and the screw-pin anchor shackles regularly to prevent corrosion. We purchased French-made stainless quick links that had a higher breaking strength than screw-pin anchor shackles, did not rust, and did not need to be tied with seizing wire to prevent them from opening. They made it simple to attach the anchor to the rode when we were approaching an anchorage after a passage. Stainless can suffer from pit corrosion if left underwater permanently, but these worked fine in an anchor rode where they were regularly exposed to air. Despite almost continuous use over the course of two years, they never showed any sign of corrosion.

While a 300-foot, all-chain rode is the offshore standard, that rode may prove unworkable for some boats. For those boats, the optimal solution concentrates the weight of the rode near the anchor by using a mixed rode of 40 to 100 feet of oversized chain with several hundred feet of line. The mixed rode is easier to handle

Table 5-2. The weights of five anchor rode configurations

Configuration	Chain weight per foot	Line weight per foot	Total weight	Breaking strength
300 feet of ⅜-inch BBB chain	1.7 lb.		510 lb.	11,000 lb.
300 feet of ⁵⁄₁₆-inch BBB chain	1.2 lb.		360 lb.	7,600 lb.
300 feet of ⁵⁄₁₆-inch high test chain	1.1 lb.		330 lb.	11,600 lb.
100 feet of ⅜-inch BBB chain and 200-feet of ⅝-inch line	1.7 lb.	0.13 lb.	196 lb.	11,000 lb.
100 feet of ⅜-inch high test chain and 200-feet of ⅝-inch line	1.5 lb.	0.13 lb.	176 lb.	12,200 lb.[1]

[1] In this case, the breaking strength of the rode is determined by the line; the breaking strength of the chain is 16,200 lb

Table 5-3. Comparison of ways to connect rode components

Type of connector	Description	Strength compared to equivalent sized BBB chain	Comments	Recommended use
Lap link	Open link closed by pressing edges together with a wrench	About half	Cold forged from rolled steel, no positive connection to hold closed	None
Screw-pin anchor shackle	Galvanized steel shackle closed by pin and seizing wire	About 80 percent	Do rust over time, will not go through windlass	To connect anchor to chain
Connecting link	Link of chain held closed by two rivets	The same	Will fit through windlass	For connecting a second length of chain to your primary rode
Rope-to-chain splice	Splice that connects the line to the chain in a mixed rode	About the same[1]	Thimbles often rust or break	For connecting line to chain in a mixed rode
Galvanized steel quick link	Steel oval closed by a barrel bolt	The same	Will not fit through windlass, must close barrel bolt with wrench	To connect chain to anchor or rope to chain
Mid-links or double-clevis links	Back-to-back U's with screw pins	Higher	Will not fit through windlass, not corrosion resistant	Temporary link between two chains

[1]The breaking strength of three strand is slightly reduced by a splice, but the line breaking strength is generally slightly higher than the BBB chain with which it is used. Cored line can lose up to half of its strength when spliced. Check with line manufacturers before using cored line spliced in your anchor rode.

with a windlass that can haul both line and chain. But we found that pulling the line up by hand and then using the windlass for the chain worked in most situations.

Anchoring technique

After you select the proper equipment, you need to learn the right technique. To set the anchor well and minimize your chances of dragging, select your spot carefully. That means locating a spot with wind protection and a good bottom. You then need to set your anchor securely, even if that means resetting it several times. Put out sufficient scope for the conditions, and set the boat up to minimize the peak loads on your ground tackle. If you approach anchoring one step at a time, you will enjoy a good night's rest. If you skip one step, you can have a very long night.

Select your spot

When entering the anchorage, you need to decide on the general area where you will drop your anchor. To do that, evaluate the layout of the anchorage according to the following guidelines.

■ **Wind protection.** When you select an anchorage, choose an area that is protected from the actual and predicted wind directions. Even then, wind funnels around points and down valleys to create less-protected areas within the harbor. As you enter the anchorage, watch the wind patterns on the water and note where the wind lines stop. Select a spot in the calmest area that offers good protection from the widest number of directions.

■ **Wave protection.** Wave protection matters more than wind protection. While it is possible to anchor in 30- and 40-knot winds for days at a time without dragging, it is almost impossible to remain anchored in a two- or three-foot chop for more than a few hours. Not only will you subject your ground tackle to extreme shock loads, but the pitching will make life aboard unbearable. When you decide where to drop your anchor, consider the fetch from all directions, particularly those of the prevailing and predicted winds. You are better off in a gale anchored 50 yards behind a reef that blocks the waves than anchored a half-mile off a shoreline where the wind speed is half but the chop is twice as high.

■ **Escape route.** Seasoned voyagers head out to sea if conditions become dangerous. All but the most secure anchorages can become untenable within a few hours of an unfavorable wind shift. As you consider your spot, plan how you would leave if conditions deteriorated (at night, if necessary). The ideal spot will have easy access to the harbor entrance and open water.

Having selected the general area, you need to find the best bottom conditions within that area. In June 1995, *Practical Sailor* magazine and West Marine participated in an anchor test sponsored by the Safety at Sea Committee of the Sailing Foundation of Seattle. The objective of the test was to evaluate the relative performance of anchors commonly recommended for boats in the 40- to 45-foot range. The first sentence under "Conclusions" reads: "The tests indicate that . . . a selection of suitability of bottom for anchoring may be more important than selection of an anchor." In other words, any anchor will drag in certain types of conditions and most anchors will hold given a nice sandy bottom.

In tropical waters where you can see the bottom, you want a patch of sand large enough that the boat can swing in a circle without dragging the chain through coral. Having the chain grind through coral chafes and abrades the chain and destroys the living coral. As cruisers, if we want to avoid having every anchorage filled with mooring buoys to protect the coral, then we must anchor responsibly. We failed to find a coral-free spot in only a half-dozen anchorages around the world.

Where you don't have the luxury of seeing the bottom, you have to rely on the chart. Examine the chart symbols for bottom type and then drop the anchor to see if it will set. If the chart shows a difficult bottom for your primary anchor, prepare the appropriate anchor rather than deploy one that won't set securely.

Set securely

Setting an anchor well is an art. It takes experience, but it also takes sensitivity to the boat's motion and the messages coming from your ground tackle. We use the following procedure.

When we approach an anchorage, we are both in the cockpit discussing where we want to anchor based on the depths and bottom conditions shown on the chart, the best protection from wind and swell, and the location of other boats. Once we have decided upon a general area, I go up to the bow as we motor in slowly. I attach a trip line, if necessary (see the sidebar, "Raising a fouled anchor" in this chapter), then push the anchor over the bow roller and lower it just to the water level. As we approach the spot we have picked, Evans puts the boat into neutral and we coast into the area where we want to drop the anchor while I look for the best bottom conditions. When I have found the exact spot, I signal to Evans. He puts the boat in reverse as we reach it and calls out the depth from the depth sounder. When the boat starts moving backward, evidenced by the water flow over the anchor, I throw the trip line out in front of the boat and release the anchor. Using the windlass or my hands, I control the anchor's fall to the bottom and then pay out scope as we motor backward gently.

The boat's momentum must be used to get a solid set on the anchor while giving the anchor time to dig in. Some people drop the anchor and chain in a heap, don't back down enough to straighten out the pile of chain, and then turn off the engine, believing the anchor is set. Other people back down so hard and fast that the anchor has no chance to set at all and hops and skips along the bottom. To get the anchor to set well, Evans backs up at about a half-knot of boat speed while I pay out 4-to-1 scope of chain based on the depth when we dropped the anchor. I attach the snubber to the rode, and Evans sets the anchor by gently increasing reverse until we reach about 2,000 rpm. I signal to him when the snubber is taut and the full force of the boat is on the ground tackle.

At that point, I put my foot on the snubber to feel what is happening to the rode. If the anchor is not set, the rode will be oscillating as tension comes on and off the snubber. If the anchor is set, the rode will feel solid with no underlying vibration. At the same time, Evans finds a couple of good transits and watches to make sure that they do not change. A mast against a rock or tree ashore makes an excellent transit. If both of us are satisfied, Evans turns off the engine and, in tropical waters, dives to check how well the anchor is set (and our neighbors' anchors as well; it pays to be aware that someone near you may be coming your way if the wind shifts or increases).

If either of us is dissatisfied with our position in relation to other boats or the prevailing wind and swell once the anchor is set, we reset the anchor immediately. If the anchor does not hold because it is incompatible with the bottom conditions, we switch anchors. A windlass greatly increases your willingness to retrieve the anchor and try again. If you don't have one, you must still reset the anchor as many times as necessary—or you won't get much sleep!

Sufficient scope

Once the anchor is set, we adjust the scope based on our swinging room, the weather forecast, fetch, and bottom conditions. On all-chain rode, we use 4-to-1 scope in normal conditions. In gale conditions, we let out as much as we can. With an all-nylon rode, 7-to-1 scope should be considered minimum in good conditions.

The angle of the bottom has a tremendous impact on how much scope to use. It is much harder to drag an anchor up a slope, easier to drag it down a slope. If you normally use 5-to-1 scope on a flat bottom, you would need a 10-to-1 scope to get the same angle of pull anchoring on a downhill slope pitched at 5 1/2 degrees (1 foot down for every 10 along, which is common in the Caribbean). If you were anchoring uphill, you would need only about 4-to-1 scope (Figure 5-1).

If you dive to check your anchor, look at the bottom slope and take this into account when you decide how much scope you need. Otherwise, use the chart and your depth sounder or lead line to determine the steepness of the bottom. If you are on a moderate grade and pulling downhill, or if the wind might shift so that you could end up that way, put out a generous amount of extra rode—up to twice as much is not excessive. But make sure you won't go aground if the wind shifts and swings you toward shore!

Extra scope can minimize the shock loads on the anchor. A boat that tends to yaw or "sail" at anchor is more likely to drag than a boat that rides steadily into the wind. The boat builds up momentum while "sailing" that imposes a peak load on the ground tackle when it fetches up. When you are anchored at small islands, the wind often funnels around one side of the island and then around the other. The boat will sail off in one direction and fetch up just as it is hit by a gust from

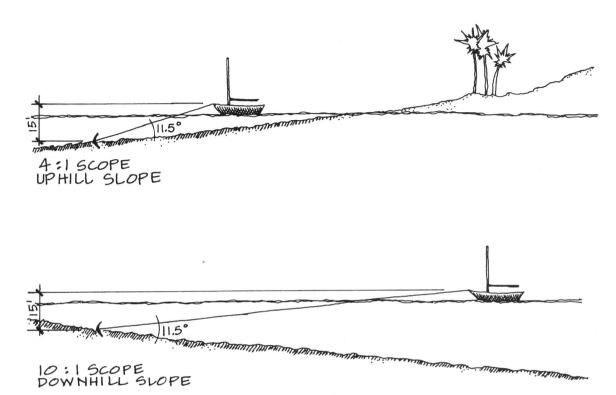

4:1 SCOPE
UPHILL SLOPE

10:1 SCOPE
DOWNHILL SLOPE

Figure 5-1. Scope required to achieve the same angle of pull on different bottom slopes

the other direction. On *Silk,* we estimated that the loads on the ground tackle are roughly twice as high when we let her sail around.

In gusty winds, rig your boat at anchor to reduce its sailing motion. This can be accomplished by putting up a riding sail or mizzen to keep the boat pointing steadily into the wind. Other options include creating a bridle by using two long snubbers, one attached to the port bow cleat, the other attached to the starboard one; or using two anchors set at a 45-degree angle to one another. Where these options are not feasible, extra scope helps to buffer the anchor and prevent it from being tripped.

REAL-WORLD ANCHORING SOLUTIONS

How do these requirements translate into a complete ground tackle and anchoring arrangement aboard an offshore boat? The equipment we carried aboard *Silk*

and the situations we encountered provide some guidelines. Rather than discuss every possible situation, this section focuses on how we managed real situations with the ground tackle we had aboard. This chapter does not address how to sit out a hurricane aboard your boat—though preparation is important, luck plays a much larger role. Even assuming your anchors hold, only luck determines whether your boat gets hit by one of the dozens of boats dragging around you. We chose not to test our luck in this way, and I would not encourage anyone else to do so.

Basic gear

A good bow platform is the basis for anchoring activities. Beyond that, offshore boats must carry a primary anchor plus a backup anchor, which can serve as a primary if necessary. You need a stern or kedge anchor and rodes for each anchor. Additional gear includes snubbers, chafe protection, trip lines, and stern lines. Finally, most boats need a good windlass to facilitate setting and retrieving the primary anchor. All this equipment costs money and uses precious stowage space, but it is not a discretionary expense. Your life could well depend on your ground tackle.

The following section details *Silk's* anchoring equipment and discusses a range of solutions on other boats.

Primary anchor and rode

Among the circumnavigators we knew, two boats used Danforths as their primary anchors. The rest used either the Bruce or the CQR, with the CQR being more common. We carried a Bruce 44 on the bow as our primary anchor (one size larger than recommended for our boat length). The Bruce performed well for us all the way around the world on all types of bottoms. No matter which type of anchor they used, voyagers trusted their primary anchors and felt comfortable in less-than-ideal conditions. That's the only anchor test that matters.

Most offshore voyagers carried 300 feet of all-chain rode for their primary anchor. Given *Silk's* sensitivity to weight in her bow, we had to modify this solution. We used 75 feet of ⅜-inch high test chain followed by 250 feet of ⅝-inch three-strand nylon. The recommended rode for *Silk* was ⁵⁄₁₆-inch BBB chain and ⁹⁄₁₆-inch three-strand nylon for winds up to 30 knots. Our rode offered 60 percent greater breaking strength than the recommended one, and its breaking strength of 12,200 lb. equaled 75 percent of *Silk's* displacement.

The 75-foot length of chain allowed us to anchor on an all-chain rode with 4-to-1 scope throughout most of the world. In deep Pacific anchorages, we attached a

Raising a fouled anchor

After spending an idyllic week anchored in a tropical paradise of coral reefs and sand beaches, it is time to leave. Everything is stowed, the dinghy is aboard, and you are ready to set sail. You start the engine and motor forward. Your partner goes to the bow and begins to bring in the chain. Suddenly, you hear an ugly crunch and the chain goes bar-tight against the bow roller. Your chain or your anchor is fouled on a coral boulder.

Immediately take the strain off the windlass—it is not designed to handle the shock loads that occur when chain is this tight. Snub off the chain on a bow cleat while you consider your options. If the direction of the chain shows the fouled area is still in front of the boat, leave the chain snubbed off and motor slowly forward until the angle of pull is back underneath the boat and the chain is once again tight. As the bow lifts and falls, the foul may pull free and let you retrieve your anchor. If not, most fouls can be freed by motoring in a small circle around the area.

If that fails, the next step is to take a swim and look at what is going on. If the water is less than 20 feet deep, you may be able to snorkel and clear the foul by hand. If you are in water over 20 feet deep (some anchorages in the Pacific are two to three times that depth), you'll need scuba gear. Many cruisers carry scuba equipment for just this situation.

If all else fails, you may have to abandon some of your ground tackle. Offshore boats must carry a second anchor capable of replacing a lost primary. They also must have at least 40 feet of extra chain for a mixed rode in the event the main rode is lost.

Preventing a fouled anchor is easier than retrieving one. We used a trip line whenever the bottom was foul, the depth was greater than 20 feet, or we had heard of problems in the anchorage. A trip line is a long, small-diameter, polypropylene line tied through the eye on the front of the anchor and buoyed by a small float. By motoring up to the float and pulling on the line, you can pull the anchor out, flukes first, and free it from most obstructions. If the chain is fouled, you can often free it once you have retrieved your anchor using the trip line. At worst, you may lose a small section of chain. A trip line also tells you where your anchor is and keeps other boats from fouling your ground tackle. In crowded anchorages, a trip line may end up in somebody's propeller. But if an anchorage is that crowded, you can get help if your anchor is fouled.

second 75-foot length of chain (for a total of 150 feet) using a connecting link. The extra chain was stored in the bilge when not in use. We attached the chain to the nylon line and the chain to the anchor using French-made ½-inch stainless steel quick links.

The rode must be secured to a part of the boat that can take the shock load of the boat fetching up against it without breaking. The bitter end of our primary rode was tied with a bowline to a pad eye through-bolted to the bulkhead in the chain locker. In the event that the snubber had broken and the chain had run out, the rode would have remained attached to the boat. An all-chain rode should be secured to the bulkhead by a length of line so that it can be cut in an emergency.

You'll need to know how much scope you have let out. Marking the rode proved less straightforward than we had assumed. Paint chips off the rode in a few weeks of daily use. The windlass mangles the anchor rode markers available in chandleries. We ended up using large wire ties. We wrapped them around the chain link, pulled them tight, and cut off the tail. These were readily visible as the chain ran out from the locker. They were cheap and easy to replace as frequently as necessary—but they lasted for a year or more without breaking or coming off the chain link. We used one wire tie to mark 25 feet, two to mark 50. When our second length of chain was attached, the connecting link marked 75 feet. On the second length of chain, we used two wire ties for 25 feet, one for 50 feet. With this pattern, we could end-for-end the chain without changing the marks. We used a similar pattern to mark the nylon rode at 25-foot intervals. On the line we used colored thread sewn into the nylon and covered with epoxy to protect it from chafe.

For a snubber, we used a 30-foot length of ½-inch nylon attached to a ⅜-inch chain hook. In most conditions, we would let out 8 to 10 feet of snubber—enough so that the chain hook was under the water even when backing down on the anchor.

We originally used a rolling hitch to attach the snubber to the chain, but this arrangement was too complicated. Never attach the snubber in a way that it cannot be removed quickly, such as with a shackle. The chain hook could be flipped off the chain before it reached the bow roller, preventing the snubber from getting fouled in the roller or wrapped around the chain. A snubber that can not be removed in an emergency will render the windlass useless. Both the chain hook and the rolling hitch would fall off the chain occasionally when we were floating over the anchor in calm conditions. But in these conditions, shock absorption is not an issue.

For chafe protection on both the snubber and the nylon rode, we used lengths of plastic hose. About a foot of ½-inch plastic hose was threaded on the snubber and could be positioned in the fairlead. The nylon rode had 4 feet of a ⅝-inch hose threaded onto the anchor rode. The hose could be slid up or down to the right position depending on the amount of scope that was out (Figure 5-2). This hose extended from just in front of the windlass all the way out over the bow roller. We used the same two pieces of plastic hose all the way around the world, and we never suffered any chafe on either the snubber or the nylon anchor rode.

Additional anchors and rodes

Our secondary anchor was a CQR 35. We originally carried this on the bow roller opposite the Bruce, but we did not use it often enough to justify the weight at the end of our five-foot-long bowsprit. We then built a set of chocks for the CQR in the cockpit locker and stowed it there when it was not in use. The rode for this anchor was 40 feet of ⅜-inch high test chain and 250 feet of ⅝-inch three-strand nylon. We stowed the rode in the bow at all times, so it was ready to run if we needed a second anchor.

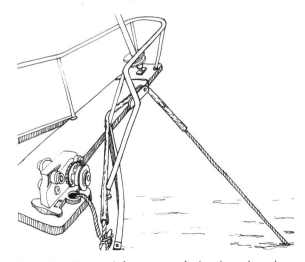

Figure 5-2. Our anti-chafe arrangement for the nylon anchor rode

Figure 5-3. A solid stainless steel bow platform that could be fabricated for most offshore boats

Figure 5-4. A smaller platform offers most of the same advantages, but it would be considerably lighter.

The secondary anchor was also attached to the rode using a ½-inch stainless steel quick link. A four-foot length of plastic hose was threaded on the nylon line for chafe protection. The chain was not marked for length, but the nylon was marked every 25 feet with thread covered with epoxy. We secured the bitter end of the rode to the chain locker in the same way as our primary rode. This was the least-used piece of ground tackle aboard, but it would have replaced our primary anchor if it was ever lost.

For a stern anchor, we used a 25-pound Danforth with 20 feet of ⅜-inch high test chain and 150 feet of ⅝-inch three-strand nylon line. This anchor could be set and retrieved easily by one person in the dinghy. We also used it as a kedge anchor to hold us off a wharf when there was surge. Both anchor and rode were stowed in our cockpit locker—the anchor in chocks and the rode in a canvas bag.

Other gear

A workable bow platform requires several features. The space must accommodate one person, a windlass, and a large anchor. It must also include details such as large cleats, functional bow rollers, and well-placed fairleads. (The general layout of the bow platform was covered in Chapter 2.) As you prepare your boat for worldwide anchoring, you can modify certain details to make anchoring safer and easier.

If your boat lacks foredeck space or the anchoring platform will not accommodate two anchors, consider adding a bowsprit. Figure 5-3 shows an elegant stain-

Figure 5-5. While the cheeks' flares could extend outward another inch or so, this represents a serviceable and inexpensive aftermarket anchor mount.

less steel bowsprit that could be retrofit to most boats. A boat that is sensitive to weight in her ends would not do well with such a large platform; the approach shown in Figure 5-4 would be more appropriate.

The following details will help facilitate your anchor handling.

■ *Bow rollers.* A poor bow roller deforms under the loads imposed by chain and anchors. A good bow roller turns easily with even a small amount of pressure, fits well in the anchor mount without binding, and is strong enough to withstand large loads.

■ *Anchor mounts.* The cheeks on either side of the roller should be well rounded and flared outward to prevent chafe when the rode is at an angle to the boat. To

Figure 5-7. Fluke-type anchors pose special stowage challenges. This arrangement will not remain secure at sea.

Figure 5-6. Good brackets make it easier to secure an anchor at sea.

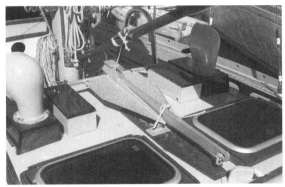

Figure 5-8. An excellent and accessible arrangement for stowing a Fortress anchor on the coach roof

keep the rode from jumping out of the mount, the cheeks need to be at least two inches higher than the top of the bow roller. Figure 5-5 shows a bow roller designed specifically for the Bruce that can be purchased at most marine stores.

■ *Anchor chocks.* Good brackets at either end of the anchor make it easier to secure at sea (Figure 5-6). If the existing chocks do not fit the anchor you have selected, modify them.

Even with a good bow platform, the lightweight fluke-type anchors can be difficult to stow (Figure 5-7). Given their light weight, you can move them more easily than their heavy counterparts. Chocks on the coach roof or foredeck offer a seamanlike solution to this

cumbersome problem (Figure 5-8).

If your boat is over 35 feet, you will need a windlass of some type. If it is over 45 feet, an electric windlass is advisable. If you or your partner has back problems, you should buy the best electric windlass you can afford—no matter what size your boat is. We used a manual windlass, which proved workable and durable. It gave us a good workout whenever we raised the anchor, though. Our windlass could haul both chain and rope, which is necessary if you use a mixed rode.

We considered a trip line an important element of our anchoring gear (see the sidebar, "Raising a fouled anchor"). Our trip line was 40 feet of $3/8$-inch polypropylene line tied to a 4-inch red buoy. When Evans dove to check the anchor after it had been deployed, he coiled up any excess on the trip line and tied it off below the float.

We dove with snorkel equipment to see how well the anchor had set and make sure it was not fouled. In cold water, some people carry a "look bucket"—a plastic bucket with a clear Lexan bottom. Some marine catalogs sell an inflatable device designed for reef viewing, which also works. This equipment allows you to view the anchor from the comfort of your dinghy, but you'll still have to get wet if the anchor is fouled!

When anchoring in the deep anchorages of French Polynesia, we often took a stern line ashore and tied it to a palm tree. Our preferred warp was 150 feet of ⅝-inch nylon braid. We also carried a 300-foot polypropylene line, which we used when the distance made the weight of the nylon difficult to manage. Polypropylene is not as strong as nylon for a given diameter, and it deteriorates in sunlight. Many cruisers still use it because it is relatively light, even when wet; it floats, so people running around in dinghies can see it; and its low-stretch quality keeps you off your neighbors when the wind comes on the beam.

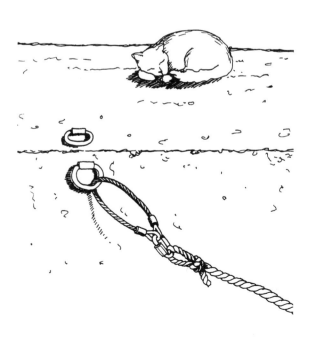

Figure 5-9. Anti-chafe arrangement for securing mooring lines ashore

When we secured a line ashore where chafe was possible, like around a boulder, we shackled the line to a 1×19 stainless wire loop (Figure 5-9). We used this mooring pendant to tie to nasty concrete wharves when clearing customs, for taking on fuel, and when were rafted off marina walls in the Azores and the Canaries.

Actual situations

The following examples cover 90 percent of the anchoring situations we found ourselves in over the course of our circumnavigation.

Normal anchoring

Eighty percent of the time, we were secure on one anchor on a good bottom in 12 to 20 feet of water with an all-chain (or close to all-chain) rode. We found sand bottoms or sand over coral or rock throughout the Caribbean, in many of the Pacific atolls, and throughout the Indian Ocean islands. We found heavy mud and silt bottoms created by runoff from the surrounding land in parts of Fiji and New Caledonia and in river anchorages in Australia and New Zealand. In all these conditions, we anchored on the Bruce with 4-to-1 scope in normal weather. For example, in 20 feet of water we would have all 75 feet of chain out and be riding to 10 feet of nylon line.

We would increase the scope if bottom conditions or weather warranted. We used 6-to-1 or 7-to-1 scope if we were pulling down a steep slope. We let out as much as the harbor allowed in a blow (14-to-1 scope in the Bermuda storm described earlier). We used at least 10 feet of nylon rode or snubber in normal conditions, and 30 feet or more in high winds or heavy chop.

In French Polynesia, many of the anchorages are 50 feet deep, with coral heads that rise from the bottom to within a few feet of the surface. There we added our second length of chain to our primary rode and looked for shallow anchorages. Our 150 feet of chain allowed us to anchor with four-to-one scope on all chain throughout French Polynesia—but not always in the most convenient place with respect to towns and villages. This was the only place where we would have preferred some additional chain.

Some cruisers recommend setting two anchors as a general rule. We found that we were almost always bet-

Pretrip preparations: beyond anchors and rodes

You will spend most of your time at anchor. But you also need to be prepared to tie up in a marina, pick up a mooring, and stow your ground tackle securely at sea. Before you leave, make sure that you have appropriate equipment to deal with each of these situations.

Most coastal cruisers spend enough time in marinas to have good docklines. However, these docklines tend to be too short to use rafted three or four boats out from a marina wall. In this situation, which is common in some of the older European harbors (Figure 5-10), you will need four normal docklines for your bow, stern, and two spring lines. Each line should be roughly the length of the boat. In addition, etiquette and seamanship require you to take a bow and stern line ashore to keep some of your boat's weight off the raft. That means two additional lines 60 to 100 feet long. We secured these lines to our

Figure 5-11. Anti-chafe protection for docklines

mooring pendants (Figure 5-9) to prevent chafe.

When tied up for long periods of time, we used plastic hose on our docklines to prevent chafe (Figure 5-11). Hose was inexpensive, lasted forever, and didn't slide out of position like canvas or rubber chafe protectors did. The hose needed to be the same diameter as the dockline.

If you transit the Panama Canal, you will need four 125-foot docklines of a diameter appropriate for your boat size. These lines should not be spliced or tied together. If your lines are not adequate, the pilot can refuse to let you transit the Canal. Some people use anchor rodes; others rent lines. Be prepared to find a solution when you reach the Canal.

For transiting, rafting up five boats off a wall, going against a fishing pier for diesel, or tying to a freighter wharf to check into customs, you will need good fenders to protect your topsides. We started with four normal marina fenders and ended up with six fenders of various sizes, including two round fenders with 18-inch diameters. We also carried a spare tire in the cockpit locker, which we covered with a garbage bag before using. We kept a fender board for several months but found we didn't use it enough to justify stowing it.

For mooring, you will need a good, solid boathook or two and a dedicated mooring line. Boathooks are useful for everything from picking up a mooring, to

Figure 5-10. The marina wall at Horta, Faial, in the Azores, about 900 miles off the coast of Portugal

(continued)

(continued)

fending off a pier, to snagging a halyard about to go up the mast. But they have a tendency to end up overboard, so carry more than one. You will want to designate one of your less attractive docklines as a mooring line. Use this line to keep the muddy, sea-weed-covered tether attached to the mooring buoy off your boat. When mooring to a buoy, attach your line to a bow cleat, thread it through the eye on the mooring line, and attach it to the other bow cleat. This creates a bridle that will keep your boat stable and is easy to release.

At sea, any anchors not left on the bow need to be stowed in chocks. Anchors that stay on the bow need to be held securely in place. Most standard pin arrangements will not hold a heavy anchor when the boat is pounding into heavy seas. We secured our an-chor with several small pieces of spare line and checked them frequently. A small line can chafe through in a few days of bad weather.

You will need to make the hawsepipe watertight at sea. Leaks through hawsers are one of the most common sources of water below on passage. We had a teak plug specially made with an eye on the bottom. After we left the anchorage and were in open water, we tied down the anchor, took off the chain, attached it to the eye on the plug, and then put the plug into the hawsepipe. Within a few hours the plug would swell and prevent any water from coming below. The hawsepipe for our second anchor was protected by a spring-loaded metal cover that was not watertight. We sealed this opening with duct tape before heading off on a passage.

ter off with one well-set anchor. In few anchorages do wind and tide hold the boat in one position all night, so setting two anchors means untangling two rodes in the morning. The entwined rodes can shorten the effective scope to the point where you start to drag, or one rode can trip the other anchor. One well-set anchor is less complicated and more effective in normal conditions.

Other situations

The majority of our anchoring situations fell into the above category. But several other anchoring and moor-ing situations occurred frequently enough to warrant discussion. These include anchorages subject to swell, anchorages with little swinging room, and tying up to a wharf with wind on the beam.

About 10 percent of the time, a swell in the anchor-age would make the area rolly and uncomfortable. A swell can be reflected around a point that offers good wind protection. Or, when anchored behind a reef, a small surge can pass over the reef at high tide. To re-duce rolling, hold the boat's bow or stern into the on-coming swell. In addition to our primary anchor off the bow, we set a stern anchor or tied a line ashore. We used the Danforth as a stern anchor because it was eas-ier to handle and retrieve than the CQR. We used our 150 feet of nylon braid for the line ashore.

About five percent of the time, we needed to hold the boat in position because swinging room was minimal. Setting a second anchor at 45 degrees to the first only decreases the size of the circle the boat moves through. We again preferred to use a stern anchor or tie to shore. But your solution will be dictated by what others are doing. In some areas, like Papeete in Tahiti, a line of 50 or 60 boats will be anchored just offshore with stern lines to palm trees. To keep from interfering with them, you will have to join the crowd.

This arrangement gets exciting when the wind comes on the beam. We were in Papeete when a line of fronts came through. Over a period of three days, we experi-enced 30- and 40-knot winds, at times directly on the beam. A second anchor oriented at 45 degrees to the primary anchor does help to hold the boat in place in these conditions with no risk of tangling the rodes (Fig-ure 5-12). We also learned to leave fenders on the wind-ward side of the boat in case our neighbor ended up snuggled against us.

In crowded harbors with strong tides or currents, someone had usually solved the problem for us. In many rivers in New Zealand and Australia, and along the south coast of England, bow and stern buoys or pil-ings hold the boat securely in place against wind and tide. Be sure that the mooring or piling can handle your boat's displacement, and use the mooring pendant to minimize chafe. Swinging room is more limited in the

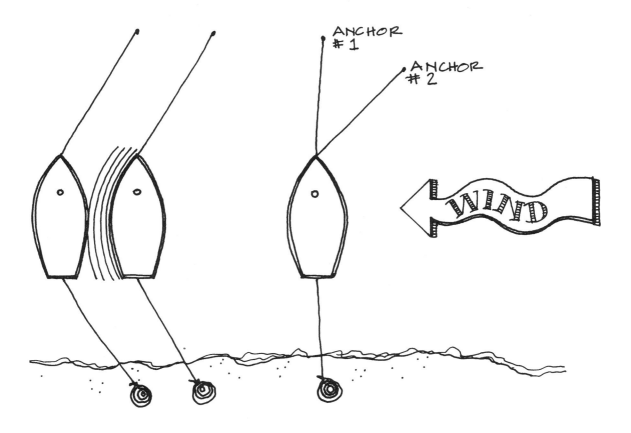

Figure 5-12. About the only time we found a second anchor off the bow useful was in Papeete when we were tied stern-to a palm tree and the wind was on the beam.

Mediterranean than in the areas we visited. The sidebar "Anchoring solutions in the Mediterranean" shares one solution.

A handful of times we had to go up against a wharf with a bad surge or wind on the beam. These were our scariest—and potentially most dangerous—anchoring and mooring situations. When we were in the Marque-sas, we had to take on diesel fuel. To do that, we had to go up against a concrete wharf despite a two-foot surge. We used the Danforth as a kedge anchor. We tied the rode to the spring cleat opposite the wharf, and this held us 2 feet away from the concrete. In another situation, strong winds on our beam threatened to pin us to a wharf. A kedge anchor helped us to get clear.

Anchoring solutions in the Mediterranean

Joe and Kathy Möeller have been cruising the Mediterranean for the last four summers aboard their Slocum 43 *Windscape*. Their primary anchor is a Bruce 66, which is one size larger than the usual recommendation for their boat. Their primary rode is 300 feet of ⅜-inch BBB chain. Their secondary anchor is a 45-pound CQR with 50 feet of ⅜-inch BBB chain and 200 feet of ⅝-inch nylon. They also carry a Fortress FX-23.

Joe and Kathy are averse to staying in marinas, and they spend as much time on the hook as possible. Contrary to cruising scuttlebutt, they have had few bad experiences anchoring in the Med, with the exception of one anchorage in Italy. Joe dove but he could not even set the anchor by hand in the soft mud. The bottom was so porous he could push his hand as far down as he wanted and watch the bubbles come up. "The only boat that didn't drag dumped two hundred feet of chain into the mud," Joe laughs.

In the Med, anchorages tend to be more crowded and swinging room is more limited. To avoid hitting others, most boats put out less scope than they would otherwise. To keep from dragging, especially in the deeper anchorages, many people use two anchors on the same chain rode.

Joe and Kathy have used the following solution. They shackle 25 feet of ¼-inch chain to the end of the ⅜-inch chain where the Bruce is shackled. When getting ready to anchor, they shackle the Fortress to the end of the ¼-inch chain and drop it first. The Bruce follows 25 feet behind. They let out about 3-to-1 scope. "When we set the anchor, we are really setting the Bruce. But the weight of the Bruce makes any pull on the Fortress parallel to the bottom. If the Bruce starts to drag, it will set the Fortress," says Joe (Figure 5-13).

When they retrieve the anchor, they pull up the chain until the Bruce is in the bow roller and then pull up the 15-pound Fortress and 25 feet of chain by hand. "The only downside," says Joe, "is controlling the weight of the combination of anchors and chain as it drops to the bottom. We wish we had a windlass that worked in both directions—that would let the chain out as well as bring it back in. . . . Other people are doing similar things with plow anchors, though the weight of the plow means that it takes some of our friends a half-hour to retrieve their ground tackle."

While trip lines are a good idea, they are a problem in the crowded Mediterranean anchorages. "Something always seems to happen to them with all the boats and dinghies running around," says Joe. "But we've never been in a situation where we really needed one."

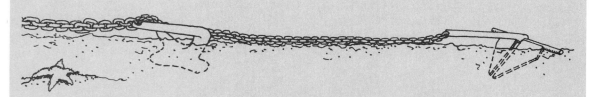

Figure 5-13. The Möellers' short scope Mediterranean solution

CHAPTER 6

OTHER ESSENTIALS: SELF-STEERING AND DINGHIES

Self-steering ■ *Wind vanes* ■ *Electric autopilots* ■ *Alternative solutions* ■ **Dinghy** ■ *Rigid vs. inflatable dinghies* ■ *Dinghy tips and tricks*

After choosing ground tackle and sails, you must add two other major items before you venture out into the world. You need some way to steer the boat when you and your crewmates are occupied changing sails, cooking, sleeping, eating, or simply relaxing. And you need some way to get ashore to explore after you drop your anchor at a tropical landfall.

A self-steering system and a dinghy for transportation to shore are essential equipment. You will depend on your self-steering every day you are at sea, and you will depend on your dinghy every day you are at anchor. As with ground tackle and sails, you need this equipment. Unlike ground tackle and sails, you have to make some difficult tradeoffs when selecting these items.

You must decide between electric or wind-driven self-steering and between a hard or inflatable dinghy. Take the time to find the right solution for your boat, then buy the best quality you can afford. If you have to make a choice, you are better off spending money on a good self-steering system and a rugged dinghy than on a refrigerator, watermaker, or generator.

SELF-STEERING

Shorthanded crews don't steer offshore. Before we got our wind vane, we had no self-steering on one passage after our electric pilot failed. That passage lasted three days—but it seemed like three weeks! While self-steering is appreciated by offshore crews of four or more, it's imperative for crews of three or fewer. For these shorthanded crews, only sails and ground tackle are more important than self-steering. Self-steering not only makes keeping watch 24 hours a day feasible for

a crew of three or fewer, it also makes boat handling safer. Extra hands to douse a spinnaker or set a pole make boat handling more controlled and may enable you to handle the unexpected. You never want to be tied to the helm while you helplessly watch a disaster unfold on the foredeck.

Self-steering gear works harder than any other piece of equipment aboard: 24 hours a day, day after day, for up to a month at sea. If it breaks, the very nature of passagemaking changes. No matter what system you choose, you will want a backup if you can possibly afford it.

Many would-be voyagers leave the decision about self-steering until the last minute. They are faced with finding a wind vane that won't interfere with their transom-mounted swim ladder or finding a below-decks autopilot that can be shoehorned into the cockpit locker. Self-steering matters too much to be treated as an afterthought. Treat your self-steering system like the uncomplaining crew member it is and design your boat around it from the very beginning.

You must first decide between an electric and a wind-driven·system. No self-steering system works in all situations and sea conditions. Wind vanes do not work without wind, and electric systems do not work without electricity. On this issue, most voyagers agree on the solution. Only 2 out of 30 circumnavigators we knew did not carry a wind vane. (One of those had a crew of 6 who hand steered.) A wind vane marks an offshore yacht more than any other piece of equipment.

After selecting your primary self-steering system, consider your backup. On this matter, no single solution dominated. We knew of boats without any backup and boats with expensive below-decks electric pilots. Your solution will reflect your financial situation.

Wind vanes

I was enthralled by our wind vane after we installed it in Madeira. I could watch it for hours, fascinated by how it seemed to anticipate the wind. It was always in motion—the vane and the oar swinging from side to side, the lines moving back and forth. I never got over the sense that a small bit of magic made the whole thing work. But the concept behind the wind vane is wonderfully straightforward, although the execution can take years to perfect. Today's wind vanes combine rugged construction with almost frictionless gears to translate the forces of wind and water into accurate, effortless steering. Once properly installed, they work flawlessly day after day using only the wind's energy.

A wind vane steers the boat at a constant angle to the wind. It needs no electrical power. Rather, it uses the force of the wind and/or the force of the water to turn the helm and bring the boat back on course.

But if the wind shifts, a wind vane may steer you into danger. A wind vane should be used with great care when near shore. More than one boat has been wrecked when the self-steering faithfully followed the wind through a major shift. About halfway between the Canaries and the Caribbean, we went through a gradual wind shift from northeast to southwest over about 20 minutes. I came up on deck to discover that the sun was in the wrong place and we were merrily sailing back the way we had come. Evans installed a compass at the head of his bunk after the first few months so he could check whether the wind had shifted whenever he woke up.

A wind vane works by aligning a light vane mounted on the boat's stern to the wind. When the boat changes its course, the force of the wind on one side of the vane will be greater than on the other side. This causes the wind vane to rotate. In the simplest of wind vanes, that movement is translated through gears and pulleys to the rudder, which turns the boat back to its original course. As the boat returns to its original orientation to the wind, the vane returns to its original position until the boat wanders off course again.

To generate adequate force to turn the rudder using only the wind on the vane requires a sizable area. Some

of the earliest vanes were several square feet in area, which is not a practical solution on the stern of most boats. To reduce the size of the vane while providing adequate force to turn the rudder, more complex vanes were developed that augmented the force from the wind with the boat's motion through the water. Over the last 30 years, three types of wind vanes have been developed: trim tab, servo-pendulum, and auxiliary rudder.

■ *Trim tab wind vanes.* These were developed for boats with outboard rudders. They attach the vane through a gear to a trim tab on the aft edge of the rudder (Figure 6-1). When the boat comes off course and the vane rotates, it turns the trim tab. The trim tab then acts like a rudder on the boat's rudder, bringing the rudder into alignment with it through the force of the water. The boat follows along, and the vane returns to its original position. Trim tab wind vanes are not very efficient, but they can still be seen on some boats with outboard rudders.

■ *Servo-pendulum wind vanes.* These are the most complicated but most efficient type of wind vane. They

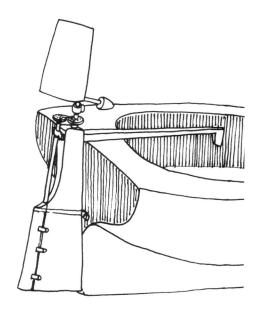

Figure 6-1. A trim tab wind vane steers through a trim tab on the outboard edge of a transom-hung rudder.

consist of a lightweight vane set on a counterweight that is attached through a complex series of gears to what appears to be a rudder but is actually called an oar (Figure 6-2). With the vane oriented into the wind and the boat moving through the water, the counterweight holds the vane vertical. The vane experiences equal pressure on both sides from the wind. Without any pressure from the vane, the oar stays vertical as well and experiences equal pressure on both sides as it moves through the water.

If the boat comes off course, the wind pressure changes on the vane. Rather than rotating, the vane swings to one side. Through the gears in the mid-section of the vane, the oar is rotated about five degrees in the vertical plane. The water now exerts a differential pressure on the two sides of the oar. This causes it to swing sideways with some force (Figure 6-3), and this movement turns the helm through a series of pulleys and lines.

■ *Auxiliary rudder wind vanes.* These bypass the boat's rudder altogether. The vane turns an auxiliary rudder, which turns the boat. These systems are used on boats with a center cockpit or high freeboard where lines cannot be led directly to the helm. They are also used on boats with hydraulic or worm gear steering that are not responsive enough for servo-pendulum wind vanes. Auxiliary rudder wind vanes offer the advantage of a backup steering system in case the boat's rudder is lost. But the auxiliary rudder is smaller and less efficient than the boat's normal rudder, and steering tends to be less precise than with the servo-pendulum wind vanes.

Most wind vanes today are the servo-pendulum type, with Aries and Monitor being the dominant brands. The original Aries has been out of business for many years,

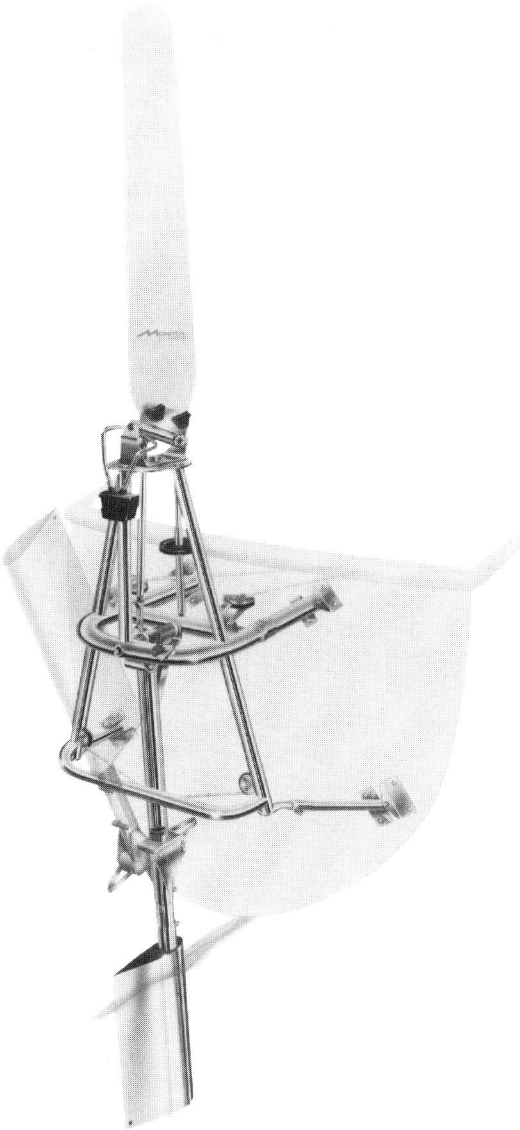

Photo courtesy of Scanmar Marine

Figure 6-2. A servo-pendulum wind vane (in this case, the Monitor) consists of a vane and an oar connected by some very clever gears.

Photo courtesy of Scanmar Marine

Figure 6-3. When the vane is forced to one side by the wind, it rotates the oar and water pressure swings it to one side.

but their vanes continue to be rebuilt, reconditioned, and resold. Used Aries vanes sell for anywhere from a couple hundred dollars to a couple thousand. A company in Denmark has recently bought the rights to build the Aries, but it remains to be seen whether or not their product will live up to the quality of the original. The Monitor wind vanes have gained an excellent reputation. Their stainless steel construction make them virtually indestructible. They cost about $3,500 new, including necessary spares kits. A number of new wind vanes have been introduced in the past two decades, including the Fleming and the Sailomat. We met cruisers who were happy with each, but neither brand is as well represented on offshore boats as the Aries and Monitor.

The common complaints against wind vanes are that they do not steer well dead downwind or under motor. Both problems reflect the one weakness of the wind vane: It needs wind to steer. Our Monitor would steer *Silk* very well dead downwind until the apparent wind fell to 4 knots or less. When motoring, if the wind was light enough that the apparent wind ended up over the bow, the vane couldn't steer. But if the apparent wind was strong enough that it remained just in front of the beam or aft, the vane could steer us while motor sailing. When the apparent wind is too light to operate the vane, you will need some sort of backup. This will occur infrequently enough, so hand steering as a backup is a viable option.

A good wind vane on a well-balanced boat will never be as accurate as an electric pilot. But it should steer the boat within 5 degrees of her course at just about any wind angle. To steer well, the wind vane needs to be correctly installed and maintained. The boat must be balanced, and the sails need to be properly trimmed. The suggestions that follow come from our experiences with a Monitor wind vane aboard *Silk*. The specific comments apply to most servo-pendulum gears, and the general principles apply to most wind vanes.

Installation

Our Monitor wind vane steered our boat through several gales. There were times when the system had to turn the helm in conditions where we would have needed both hands and some muscle. These types of conditions create significant torsional forces on the wind vane's members, and rugged construction and a

solid mount are necessary to prevent bolts from twisting or tearing out. Servo-pendulum gears need to be through-bolted into the transom, and the bracing needs to be adequate to support the large forces that will be generated.

On a servo-pendulum wind vane, the control lines translate the oar's motion into a lateral pull on the helm. They run from the vane, through a series of blocks, and directly to the tiller or to a drum attached to the wheel (Figure 6-4). These lines are in almost constant motion when they are steering, so a poor installation will result in serious chafe.

The biggest challenge is leading the lines fair from one component to another. The best installations use only a single turning block between the vane and the helm. The control lines must exit the block exactly parallel to the attachment point on the helm and enter the drum at a right angle to that point. Otherwise, the pull on the drum will not be directly sideways and some of the wind vane's motion will be lost. Our installation aboard *Silk* worked perfectly for over 30,000 nautical miles. The only difficulty we experienced was some chafe on the teak coaming where the lines exited the block.

The control lines need to be low stretch and not sensitive to UV. They also need to be kept properly tensioned: tight enough to efficiently translate the movements of the oar to the helm, but not so tight as to create friction. Optimal tension varies with wind conditions. The lighter the wind, the *looser* the lines should be. In these conditions, swells cause the vane to wave around. Loose lines prevent these random movements from steering the boat off course. The heavier the wind, the *tighter* the lines should be. The wheel needs to respond rapidly to vane movements when the boat starts to lose her course in bad conditions. We placed small turnbuckles in the two control lines between the vane and the blocks to adjust our line tension. These allowed us to adjust the control lines quickly and easily without taking them off the drum. The hitch shown in Figure 6-5, which has been used successfully by offshore singlehanded BOC racers, accomplishes the same end.

Care and feeding

Wind vanes require remarkably little attention. Check yours frequently to be sure that the control lines are

Figure 6-4. *Silk's* wind vane installation used a single turning block between the wind vane and the wheel.

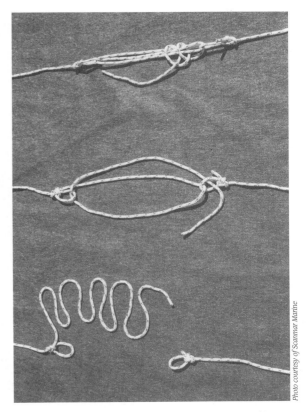

Photo courtesy of Scanmar Marine

Figure 6-5. A trucker's hitch (finished at top) allows the control lines to be tightened and loosened easily.

properly tensioned and not chafing, and wash the gear with fresh water when it is available. On passage, we rinsed the stainless steel drum attached to the wheel once a week if we had not gotten any rain. Otherwise, the pin that locks the drum would start to stick. This can make disengaging the vane difficult, which can be dangerous in heavy weather or when flying a spinnaker. We usually lubricated this pin with dish soap after we had rinsed the drum. Lubricate the blocks regularly with a water-dispersing spray. (On *Silk*, the blocks alerted us with a squeaky chorus when it was time to lubricate!) Finally, clean from the oar any gooseneck barnacles or grass that collect on a long, slow passage. To prevent unwanted growth, some cruisers put antifouling paint on their water blades.

Inspect the unit carefully at least once a month. Look for tiny cracks or seams in the welds. Check that no bolts have worked loose or lost their nuts. We developed cracks in the welds at the right-angle bends of the supporting arms of our wind vane three-quarters of the way through the 4,000-mile passage from St. Helena to Antigua. We lashed the unit to our stern with line and aluminum bracing for the last 1,000 miles. To prevent this, use bent tubes instead of welded joints, if at all possible (Figure 6-6).

Besides a failure in the welds, only two things can go wrong with the wind vane under normal conditions—the vane or the oar can be damaged.

The vane can be broken by a large wave, which happened to us, or you can lose it overboard. Carry a spare. Monitor offers a light air vane, larger than the normal plywood blade and made of Styrofoam. We had one, but we did not find it made that much difference. We would have preferred a heavy air vane about two-thirds the

Figure 6-6. This installation uses bent top tubes instead of welded right angles as we had on *Silk* (see Figure 6-4), thereby eliminating the risk of cracks around the welds at the joint.

size and heavier than the normal vane. This would have been useful in gales where the normal blade was often overpowered.

The oar can hit something and be damaged. Aries and Monitor wind vanes are designed with a tube that breaks so the rest of the components are not damaged by the impact. Attach the bottom of the oar to the wind vane so it's not lost if the tube breaks. Carry a spare tube.

Sail trim

If the vane has been installed and maintained properly, all you need to do is balance the boat for the conditions. The vane will teach you to sail the boat balanced, if you don't already do so. Most people learn that they keep too much canvas up and overtrim the sails. If the vane

is not steering well, try easing the sheets. Reef when the vane starts to steer sloppily (when it takes several seconds to correct). We knew it was time to reef *Silk* when she felt like she was doing the giant slalom. If we disengaged the vane and took the helm, we could confirm that she was overcanvassed.

Do not expect too much precision when the wind is on the beam and gusty. In these conditions, the boat will sail up to 10 degrees on either side of her course. On long passages, we found that these swings tended to average out. If you are sailing where 10 degrees off your course could put you in danger, hand steer.

The wind vane is not designed to make up for weather helm through steering motion. You need to set your system for the amount of weather helm, given the wind speed and the angle of heel. Many times when the vane seemed to be steering poorly, the wind had eased or strengthened and the boat was no longer balanced. It can be frustrating to change the vane every half-hour as the wind gusts or veers, but it beats hand steering the entire time.

Electric autopilots

Electric pilots steer by the compass and use electricity to turn the helm. To our modern eyes, they seem far less sophisticated than wind vanes. These pilots compare the boat's actual course to the course that has been programmed into the system and adjust the helm until the two come back into alignment. Autopilots lack the automatic feedback that a wind vane receives constantly from the wind. Early models understeered or oversteered, and even today's sophisticated models must be taken through a complex start-up procedure to learn how the boat reacts to the helm. Steering a boat becomes a complicated problem when variables such as the boat's displacement, keel configuration, and steering sensitivity, as well as wave conditions and weather helm, are considered.

All electric pilots consist of a few basic components:

■ **Compass.** Electric pilots don't use the ship's compass to steer. They come with their own compass—generally, the more reliable fluxgate type. This is installed in a remote location away from the rest of the unit in an area near the centerline of the boat. The compass must be protected from metal and stray electrical interference.

■ **Control head.** All electric pilots need a brain—a central processor that compares actual course to programmed course and determines how to react. Called the control head, this component varies from a box with a few dials on it to a sophisticated processor with more computing power than first-generation laptop computers.

■ **Drive unit.** Some type of motor provides the pilot's muscle. The drive unit can range from an electric motor that turns a belt attached to the wheel to a hydraulic ram that directly turns the rudder.

These components can steer a boat on a single course as long as the batteries hold up and the equipment doesn't break. For more sophistication, you can calibrate the control head to the boat's displacement and steering characteristics to increase steering efficiency. You can install feedback loops that tell the control head how much the boat is heeling and how much rudder is being applied. The unit can also be interfaced with a GPS so that it can steer course changes when you reach waypoints. All these components bring the autopilot's steering ability closer to that of a human, but they also increase complexity, cost, and the likelihood of failure.

There are two major types of electric autopilots: helm-mounted or below-decks. Helm-mounted autopilots are mounted in the cockpit, and they turn the helm using an electric motor. This motor may drive a piston arm that turns a tiller or a belt that turns a wheel. Below-decks pilots are located near the steering quadrant, and they turn the rudder shaft itself using a hydraulic ram or a direct-drive motor.

Each type of system has advantages and disadvantages. Whichever you choose, be sure that your electrical system is sized to meet the autopilot's energy demands. You will also need to bring along a locker full of spares. In surveys of owners of electric autopilots done by *Prac-*

tical Sailor, respondents reported repair rates of 50 percent and over on many of the best-selling brands. The SSCA 1996 Equipment Survey showed that electric pilots averaged 1,215 hours between breakdowns, which translates to just over 50 days of continuous use. For offshore voyagers who use an electric pilot as their primary means of self-steering, that means repairing the electric pilot at least once an ocean.

Helm-mounted pilots

The drive unit of a helm-mounted pilot is located in the cockpit. For wheel steering, some are mounted to the binnacle (see our CPT unit mounted to the binnacle in Figure 6-4) and others have compact electric motors that hang from the wheel itself (Figure 6-7A). For tiller steering, most units mount on the coaming and use a ram to push and pull the tiller.

Helm-mounted pilots cost less and require less energy than below-decks pilots (Table 6-1), in large part because they are designed for use on smaller boats with smaller steering loads. Helm-mounted pilots steer well in light wind conditions or when motoring. They do not steer well in a following sea, with moderate winds on the beam, in gusty conditions, or in large waves. They should not be relied on as the primary self-steering aboard an offshore boat, but they do make a reasonably inexpensive backup.

Electric pilots that operate a tiller are more reliable than wheel-mounted pilots. These pilots can be adapted to work with a wind vane. Several boats we encountered attached a small tiller pilot to the oar of the wind vane. As the boat came off course, the pilot turned the oar, which then turned the helm. This approach uses the water to magnify a small force and steer the boat—just as the wind vane does. It allows a much smaller electric pilot than normal to effectively drive the wheel or tiller of a large boat. These sailors used the wind vane as their primary self-steering and attached the

Table 6-1. Comparison of helm-mounted to below-decks electric pilots (U.S. dollars)

	Peak draw at 12 V	Average draw at 12 V	Estimate of maximum daily electrical usage	Estimated cost	Our repair problems
Helm-mounted pilots	~3 A	0.5–1.0 A	36 Ah	$700–$1,200	Broken belts, malfunctioning control heads
Below-decks pilots	10–30 A	2–6 A	96 Ah	$2,500–$6,000	Low voltage, malfunctioning control heads

Figure 6-7A. Some wheel-mounted pilots have both the electric motor and belt encased in plastic and suspended from the wheel.

Figure 6-7B. The control head for such units is mounted separately near the helmsman.

tiller pilot in light air or when motoring. When not in use, the tiller pilot was kept below so it was protected from sun and spray.

If you head offshore with a wheel-mounted pilot, you can avoid some common problem areas by taking the following precautions:

■ *Protect the control head.* The most delicate part of the electric pilot is the control head. Though most are described as watertight, they cannot take constant exposure to spray. The direct rays of the sun can also create condensation inside the unit. Mount the control head in a protected position, either under your dodger or down below in the navigation station.

■ *Carry spares.* If the pilot has external belts, carry at least one spare. If it has shear pins in the motor, carry several dozen spares. If it is a sealed unit like the Autohelm 4000 or the Navico Wheelpilot 300CX, about all you can do for backup is carry a second unit or resort to hand steering.

■ *Protect electrical connections.* Electrical connections between components can be a source of problems. Try to keep connections protected from spray. Where that is not possible, make sure they are watertight. Be careful to support wiring, particularly into the back of the control head. Some models have pins connecting the electrical wires to the control head; these will pull out under the weight of the wires. Our wheel-mounted pilot started steering in random directions halfway between Bermuda and the Azores. A half-dozen of the pins had pulled out and the control head had lost all sense of direction.

Below-decks pilots

A below-decks pilot's drive is located near the steering quadrant and is connected by a tiller arm directly to the rudder shaft. Drive mechanisms may be either electrical-mechanical or electrical-hydraulic systems. The first uses an electric motor to drive the reduction gears that move the tiller arm. The second uses an electric motor to drive a hydraulic pump that moves the tiller arm. Because the tiller arm is attached directly to the rudder, the autopilot can still steer a wheel-driven boat even if the steering cables break.

Below-decks pilots are much more reliable than their helm-mounted counterparts, but they are by no means trouble free offshore. They require regular maintenance, and their control heads are just as vulnerable as the helm-mounted pilots' are to sun and spray.

These units operate reliably only when supplied by a properly sized battery bank that can meet their extensive energy requirements. To regularly run a below-decks autopilot that draws an average of 4 amps for 24 hours straight without charging would require almost 400 Ah of batteries to be dedicated to the autopilot (see the Chapter 7 sidebar, "Balancing your electrical system"). While a smaller battery bank can manage the average draw for longer periods, it will not be able to meet the peak loads as the batteries become discharged. Given insufficient voltage to meet peak demands, many of these units will cease to operate.

If you opt for a below-decks pilot as your primary means of self-steering, carefully consider your backup. While these systems are more reliable than the helm-mounted pilots, they still suffer from frequent failure rates. In the SSCA 1996 Equipment Survey, most below-decks units averaged between 1,200 and 1,800 hours between breakdowns. Some of the most avid proponents of advanced below-decks electric autopilots recommend installing two identical units in parallel in the absence of another form of backup. But for these units, backup does not just mean another system to steer. Thanks to their demand for power, you will also need an alternative way to generate electricity if your engine fails.

The following guidelines will help you maximize your chance for trouble-free operation of a below-decks pilot.

■ *Use properly sized cable.* Make sure to size the cable for the amperage and the distance of the wire run in order to minimize the voltage drop from batteries to motor.

■ *Protect the control head from the elements.* After our second cockpit-installed control head failed, we purchased a hand-held control head that we could use in the cockpit and store below. If you want a control head in the cockpit, select a remote unit or mount a permanent unit under the dodger.

■ *Perform set-up procedures.* The below-decks pilots are more sophisticated than their helm-mounted cousins. After installation, you will acquaint the pilot with the boat through a series of calibration procedures. You must tell the unit whether the boat is sail or power, light or heavy, coastal or offshore. You must steer the boat through a series of S-curves so the pilot can learn how the boat responds to the rudder. If the unit is not steering well, recalibrating it will often help. Some pilots steer better in extreme conditions if the initial settings are adjusted (e.g., increasing the displacement in heavy weather). For best performance, consult the owner's manual and experiment with whatever settings you have.

Sophisticated autopilots can interface with the GPS, allowing you to steer from waypoint to waypoint with multiple course changes. By using data from the GPS, the pilot can also correct for current and leeway and steer right to your destination. This option can be a valuable safety feature when sailing coastwise in an area with hazards.

Alternative solutions

For a boat you intend to take voyaging, self-steering must be a priority. Your solution should include a primary and a backup means to steer the boat. For boats up to 50 feet, a wind vane represents the best solution for primary self-steering offshore.

There are three main advantages of a wind vane over an electric pilot. First, a wind vane uses no power. You will still be able to steer the boat even if your engine dies and you cannot charge your batteries. Second, the worse conditions are, the better it steers. In heavy weather, most electric pilots will eventually be overwhelmed by waves and wind. Without a vane you will be forced to hand steer or lash the helm. Third, a wind vane is almost bulletproof. If you do develop a problem, a little welding in the next port will almost always solve it. If used as primary self-steering, electric pilots rarely last more than an ocean between repairs. For offshore passagemaking, a wind vane is the self-steering system of choice.

Leaving with an electric pilot and no wind vane was our single biggest mistake in outfitting *Silk*. Over the course of our voyage, we tried three different popular electric autopilots (two helm-mounted pilots and one below-decks system). We used two of these pilots only for motoring or in light downwind conditions. On average, each pilot worked for less than three months before requiring repair. The wind vane, on the other hand, steered flawlessly for over 25,000 miles before needing some minor welding.

Electric pilots do have their place aboard offshore boats. For those situations when there is too little apparent wind for the vane to be used, a backup electric autopilot is ideal. When sailing coastwise, the precision of an electric pilot and its ability to steer by the compass instead of by the wind lessens your chances of a mishap with the shore. If you plan on doing extensive coastal cruising, an electric pilot is an excellent investment.

The most common steering solutions for offshore voyaging include the following:

■ **Wind vane alone.** We met many boats, mostly under 35 feet, whose only means of self-steering was a wind vane. When motoring or in light downwind conditions, their backup was hand steering. This represents the least expensive feasible solution for the short-handed crew. You can purchase a used wind vane for less than $2,000.

■ **Wind vane with helm-mounted pilot for backup.** This combination was the solution of choice for boats between 35 and 45 feet. These cruisers used the wind vane in all conditions, except motoring and light air. The demands placed on the electric pilot were minimal, and the pilot was often stored below when not in use. If the wind vane failed, the pilot would not be up to the demands of offshore steering. But few high quality wind vanes fail. The total cost for this solution varied from $3,000 to $5,000, depending on the type of equipment and whether it was new or used.

■ **Wind vane with below-decks pilot for backup.** On boats between 40 and 50 feet with an appropriate budget, a below-decks pilot provided a full backup to the wind vane. For boats planning extensive coastal cruising, this solution offers the best of both worlds. However, we met few boatowners who chose this solution: The cost starts at around $5,000 and can run double that.

■ **Below-decks pilot with spares for backup.** Current wind vanes work well on boats up to about 50 feet. Most boats larger than that have the space and electrical system to install an oversized, heavy duty, below-decks autopilot whose energy demands would overwhelm a smaller boat's battery bank. We knew a handful of boats around 50 feet in length that used an all-electric solution to self-steering. Some of these crews had installed a complete second unit as backup. Others carried an extensive array of spares—including a backup drive unit, control head, and processing unit. The total cost depends on the type of pilot, but this solution represents the most expensive alternative for most boats.

While a wind vane should be first on your list when considering self-steering for offshore voyaging, electric pilots have their place. As time goes by, these units will become even more reliable, less expensive, and less energy intensive. There may come a day when a yacht with a wind vane is as much an anachronism as a yacht without an engine is today. Until then, the wind vane on the stern will continue to be one of the hallmarks of the true offshore voyager.

DINGHY

The dinghy is the offshore voyager's packhorse. Your dinghy must be able to carry your entire crew plus a hundred pounds of groceries, water, or spare parts. It must be durable enough to land on beaches of sand, coral, or gravel; light enough so one person can haul it up the beach and out of the tide's reach; stable enough to be managed in surf and dry enough so contents won't get wet. It must be capable of traveling through a 2-foot chop and against a 2-knot current without swamping. It must stow compactly and securely, either on deck or below. If you go aground, your dinghy must be deployable in minutes. It must be capable of being rowed against wind and chop to kedge out an anchor.

It should come as no surprise that the perfect dinghy has yet to be invented. Every dinghy represents a set of compromises, and no single type suits every cruiser. The dinghy dock in any major offshore port is proof enough: You will see dainty fiberglass sailing dinghies, Avon and Zodiac inflatables, homemade wooden rowing skiffs, hard-bottom inflatables, and plastic kayaks. This is one of the most difficult gear decisions you make as a voyager, and you will live with your choice every day you are in port.

Rigid versus inflatable dinghies

Ask yourself how you plan to use a dinghy. It will be your transportation when you leave the boat—are you looking for a car or a bicycle?

A large inflatable dinghy with an outboard motor is the dinghy equivalent of a car. You can use it to travel relatively long distances. It can carry you upriver into the jungle or across the bay to a waterfall. Like a car, it does not do much without an engine. All but the most expensive inflatables are difficult to row at all, and impossible to row for any real distance in wind or chop. And like a car, an inflatable and its engine require regular preventive maintenance. Inflatables can be damaged by sand, coral, and UV radiation. The engine requires tune-ups and spark plug changes, clean fuel, and good oil.

An inflatable with an engine complicates your life. Not only do you need to stow the dinghy, but you also need to stow the outboard so it is protected from salt water. You will have to find good quality gasoline in port (not a simple task in islands like the Tuamotus, where there are no cars and the fishing fleet uses diesel) and stow it safely aboard. Like a car, inflatables are expensive and not particularly durable. A 10-foot dinghy will cost around $2,000 and the 10- to 15-horsepower outboard to go with it costs at least as much. The U.K. equivalent price is £1,200 for a new dinghy and about £800 for an outboard.

A hard dinghy without an engine is the dinghy equivalent of a bicycle. Like an old-fashioned, three-speed bike, a hard dinghy will stand up to just about anything without fuss. Even if you bounce it off piers, drag it up coral beaches, leave it full of sand, and let it live in the sun, you will never need to do much more than patch a scrape and repaint the bottom. Life is simpler too because you are not dependent on the vagaries of an engine. But like a bicycle, a hard dinghy requires muscle. While a well-designed hard dinghy rows well, it's work to go more than a half-mile or so. You will be less likely to explore upriver into the jungle or cross that bay to the waterfall. A hard dinghy is difficult to climb in and out of from the water, so it is not a good dive platform. You will also need to stow 8 feet or more of hard dinghy safely on deck.

Like an old-fashioned bicycle, a hard dinghy is inexpensive and lasts forever. You can buy or build a good rigid dinghy for a few hundred dollars, and it will stand up to a decade or more of hard use. Hard dinghies are rarely stolen, while outboards and inflatables are targets for theft.

Figure 6-8. This RIB aboard a 40-foot Valiant shows that they can be more difficult to stow than a rigid dinghy.

There are alternatives to these two extremes. You can add an outboard engine to a hard dinghy and increase your range, but you will never reach the planing speeds of an inflatable. You can buy a rigid inflatable boat (RIB), which has a molded fiberglass bottom with inflatable chambers. RIBs plane like inflatables and can be rowed moderate distances, but they are as difficult to stow as a hard dinghy (Figure 6-8) and most are too heavy to be handled by one person.

Once you decide on a hard dinghy or a type of inflatable, you must make further decisions. There is a wide range of inflatable dinghies available with different characteristics (Table 6-2).

Hard-bottom inflatables add a rigid floor made of plywood or fiberglass to a regular inflatable dinghy. The rigid bottom allows them to plane, but the floor makes it difficult to stow. To solve that problem, roll-up inflatables come equipped with a rigid bottom that is sectioned so the whole thing can be rolled up when deflated. The resulting bundle takes up more room than a regular inflatable but is far easier to stow than a hard-bottomed model. An RIB can be described as a fiberglass hard dinghy with inflation tubes around the gunwales. Even with the chambers deflated, an RIB will take up almost as much room as a hard dinghy. Most cruisers find RIBs too heavy for a shorthanded crew. While the inflatable dinghy still offers the best value, the roll-up dinghies offer the best mix of attributes as an offshore voyager's tender.

You face just as much variety if you choose a hard dinghy. At a minimum, you want a dinghy that is rugged, at least 8 feet long, fairly stable, and capable of being stowed on your boat's deck. You also want two rowing positions for different conditions, three seats for carrying three or four people, and positive flotation so the dinghy will never sink. A self-bailer simplifies life when towing the dinghy. The possibilities include a homemade fiberglass or plywood dinghy that costs $200, a foldable or nesting dinghy that takes up less space but costs $1,000 and up, and fiberglass sailing dinghies like the Trinka or the Fatty Knees that can cost up to $3,000. One of the best rigid dinghies in the U.K. is the 12-foot Tepco, about £800 new. None of these will be able to carry more than a 2- to 3-horsepower engine, but all will row well.

Much discussion revolves around the relative merits of rigid versus inflatable dinghies as primary or backup liferafts. No dinghy is built to withstand open-ocean conditions. Large waves and high winds can flip an inflatable dinghy and make it difficult or impossible to right. A rigid dinghy, even one with positive flotation, will be swamped to the gunwales in big waves. However, if you cannot afford an offshore liferaft, you must be prepared to use your dinghy in an abandon-ship situation.

If you do choose to make your dinghy act as your primary liferaft, research its characteristics carefully. Select the most stable, rugged, easy-to-right dinghy you can find. Equip it with an awning to protect you from the sun and solid rings to which you can attach tethers. You will also need several sizes of bailers and, for an inflatable dinghy, a patch kit that works under water. While a sailing rig may increase your chances of reaching shipping traffic or land, it must be accessible if it is to end up on the dinghy in an emergency.

Most boats under 30 feet cannot stow a hard dinghy on deck, so an inflatable is the only practical solution.

If you like to dive and are planning to take scuba gear along, you will want an inflatable for a dive platform. If you have children, you will prefer the stability of an inflatable and its ability to easily carry four people and gear. For these reasons, inflatables accounted for three-quarters of the dinghies among our friends who circumnavigated.

Most voyagers agree that this is one of the toughest gear decisions to make. If space and money allowed, the ideal solution would be to carry two dinghies: one hard and one inflatable. If you have children or more than three crew, two dinghies offer greater freedom and increased harmony aboard.

Dinghy tips and tricks

Managing your personal transportation takes some preparation and practice. Just as your boat needs additional equipment, your dinghy also needs certain gear to make it seaworthy and versatile. To protect the dinghy from theft and to keep her in good condition, you need to take some basic precautions. At a minimum, your dinghy should be equipped with the following items.

■ **Oars.** Always, always, always have a pair of oars in your dinghy. When we took a liveaboard cruising course in the Caribbean, our instructor got into the dinghy, untied the painter, and tried to start the outboard. The engine refused to cooperate, and our teacher was drifting off toward South America at a rapid clip. A boat boy came by, looked the situation over, and said, "Five EC to get your skipper." After some negotiation, our chastened instructor was retrieved. Don't step into the dinghy without putting the oars in first. Carry a spare set of dinghy oars, oarlocks, and chafe protection somewhere aboard.

Table 6-2. Comparison of various types of inflatable dinghies (U.S. dollars)

	Size	Approximate weight	Maximum horsepower	Estimated cost	Pros	Cons
Inflatable dinghy	9–10 ft.	40 lb.	4	$1,000–$1,500	Easy to stow, light	Not durable
Hard-bottom inflatables	9–11 ft.	70 lb.	8–15	$1,500–$2,000	Planes well, reasonably light	Hard to assemble
Roll-up inflatables	10–11 ft.	80–100 lb.	8–15	$2,500–$3,000	Planes well, stows well	Expensive, heavy
Rigid inflatable boats (RIBs)	9–11 ft.	120–150 lb.	15–25	$3,000+	Rows well, motors well, planes well	Must stow on deck, very heavy

Silk's faithful tender

Our dinghy choice was unusual. We opted for an 8-foot Trinka fiberglass dinghy without an outboard (Figure 6-9). *Silky* just barely stowed under *Silk's* boom on passage, and the proximity of her bow to the mast prohibited us from using a rigid vang. She weighed about 75 pounds; either of us could pull her a hundred yards up the beach alone. She rowed beautifully and provided exercise when we were in a port.

When we left, we brought the sailing rig. However, we found that the amount we sailed the dinghy did not justify the stowage space for the bulky rudder, tiller, centerboard, and spars. When you drop anchor after a day sail or a passage, the last thing you want to do is dig out the equipment from the bottom of a locker and go for a little sail. Only those with kids aboard felt a sailing rig

Figure 6-9. *Our trusty tender at rest in the Caribbean*

was used enough to make it a worthwhile investment.

We regretted not having an outboard in only two places. In Academy Bay in the Galapagos Islands, we faced a half-mile row against a strong tidal current and a steep chop. In Cairns, Australia, we had to row across a half-mile-wide river with a 2- to 3-knot river current on the beam. After one exhausting trip, we moved to the marina despite the expense.

In many other places, we would have done more if we had carried an outboard. We would have headed for the outer reefs to snorkel more frequently. We would have taken the dinghy up rivers rather than going in friends' dinghies or missing out altogether. Obviously, we did not feel it was a high priority, as we never bought an outboard. But we are seriously considering having one for our next trip.

■ *Dinghy painters.* Keep two painters permanently attached to the dinghy's bow, one about 6 feet long and one about 20 feet long. Use the short one to tie the dink to your boat. In tidal areas, you will also want a removable stern painter to hold the dinghy against the side of the boat. Use the long painter to tie to dinghy docks. Cruising etiquette requires that you tie your tender on as long a painter as possible, allowing others to work their way into the dock without hitting a solid mass of dinghies. You will also use the long painter for towing the dinghy when sailing coastwise and in tidal areas when tying to a wharf that may be 10 feet or more out of the water at low tide. Polypropylene makes a good tow line because it floats and is low stretch. But UV weakens this type of line, so make sure to change it every year.

■ *Bailer.* Always keep a bailer aboard. The top half of a laundry detergent bottle is ideal. To keep the bailer for

more than a few days, secure it with a lanyard to a piece of hardware in the dinghy.

■ *Lifting eyes.* Whether inflatable or rigid, your dinghy should have lifting eyes so you can easily get it aboard with a bridle and the main halyard. The best arrangement is two lifting eyes in the stern, one on each side, and a third at the bow near the centerline. When lifting our rigid dinghy, we attached only the stern lifting eye farthest from the boat. When we lifted the dinghy, it went up outboard-side first. We raised it until it was hanging from its side, level with the rail, with the interior of the dinghy facing the deck of the boat. We then used buckets of water to flush the sand out of it before bringing it on deck.

■ *Towing rings.* On a rigid dinghy, towing rings should be through-bolted and located low on the bow so the dinghy will plane when towed. On an inflatable, the towing eyes should be well reinforced, as these are always the first things to fail.

■ *Anchor.* If you want to snorkel or dive from the dinghy, you will need a dinghy anchor. You will also need one if you want to anchor just outside the surf line where the surge is so bad or the beach is so rocky that you don't want to take your dinghy ashore. A good dinghy anchor has no sharp edges to damage an inflatable. An inexpensive 5-pound mushroom anchor works well. The long dinghy painter makes an excellent rode.

Secure all this equipment to the dinghy whenever you leave it ashore or at a dock. A rigid tender can be accidentally capsized by someone crossing over to reach their own dinghy. Children also love to play in dinghies tied to town docks. In the Galapagos and the Tuamotus, dozens of kids would use the dinghies as diving boards, pretend to run the outboards, and even "borrow" a dinghy for a quick row around the harbor. Most of the time no harm is done and no one should be upset by it. But if you leave loose articles in your dinghy, at some point your anchor will end up on the bottom or your oars will head off to sea.

In major harbors or in any area where you have heard of thievery, lock your tender to the dinghy dock. We created a "leash" out of an 8-foot length of 1×19 stainless steel wire and swages. We attached it by a swage to a fitting in the bottom of the dinghy. When in use, it passed through our oarlocks, though the dock, and then locked to itself with a padlock. If you have an outboard without its own lock, your leash should include it. This could be cut with the right tool, but it will deter the casual thief.

To keep your belongings dry when underway, buy dry bags of several sizes from marine stores. These can be made almost fully watertight, and they will float if the dinghy is capsized. We used these for everything from protecting my camera when going ashore to bringing clean laundry back to the boat.

While you will master the subtleties of a hard dinghy after a few outings, the following tips for inflatables take longer to discover on your own.

■ *Marine growth.* Turning your dinghy upside down at night will keep grass from growing on it. Hauling it up on the main halyard and securing it at deck level will do the same, while also preventing theft.

■ *Rowing.* If you have to row your inflatable, there are ways to make it easier. When rowing with two people, paddle Indian-style on either side. With one person, kneel in the bow and paddle on one side and then the other. You'll be surprised at how well you can row either way, though it still is very inefficient.

■ *Wind.* Inflatables will flip over in windy anchorages, so take a few precautions to keep your dinghy grounded. Remove the engine so its weight will not flip the dinghy if wind gets under the bow. Turning the dinghy over will reduce the chances that it will try to fly. Lash the inflatable to the deck if you expect winds over 20 knots.

Regardless of the type of dinghy you choose, you should be comfortable with your tender and be able to handle it in a variety of conditions. You should be able to bring it alongside a boat or a dock without fuss, ride a wave into a beach, head out through surf back to your boat, and maneuver it with three people or a hundred pounds of groceries aboard. Your dinghy will be your lifeline when you are at anchor, and all crewmembers should have total confidence in their ability to manage it.

CHAPTER 7

ADDITIONAL EQUIPMENT: CONVENIENCE VERSUS COMPLEXITY

Other equipment: managing complexity ■ *Safety equipment* ■ *Navigation equipment* ■ *Comforts and conveniences* ■ *Engine, charging equipment, and batteries* ■ *Balancing your electrical system* ■ *Battery down exercise* ■ **Examples of three successful alternatives** ■ *Additional resources*

A bluewater-capable yacht with a sound hull, well-made sails, modern ground tackle, trustworthy dinghy, and a self-steering system is better equipped than many boats that have circumnavigated. We met a half-dozen boats whose only additional equipment were a sextant, some safety gear, and a few creature comforts. As you consider the equipment in this chapter, keep these boats in mind. In the previous three chapters, I encouraged you to buy the best equipment you can afford. As you read this chapter, think about starting by spending as little as possible.

Simplicity has its own merits. After sailing 10,000 nautical miles in five months, we arrived in South Africa with a five-page list of maintenance tasks. Over the successive weeks, we rebuilt all of our electrical pumps, replaced our engine control panel, rebedded two dozen deck fittings, replaced our autopilot control head, replaced a deck light, replaced our electronic battery bank manager, serviced our refrigerator, and rewired the navigation station. About that time, Clive Shute and Laila Stjerndrüp arrived aboard 30-foot *Isa Lei* (see the sidebar in Chapter 2). *Isa Lei* does not carry any electrical gear or refrigeration. Clive and Laila rebedded their forward hatch and were ready to go sightseeing.

The modern gear many of us have come to rely on carries a mixed blessing. Additional gear makes a boat more convenient—but also more complex. Most equipment exacts a price in terms of money, maintenance, energy, and space. If you own a boat, chances are you already have a selection of gear aboard and are considering adding more before heading off on a longer voyage. This chapter considers the tradeoffs of additional gear to help you find your own balance between convenience and complexity.

Equipment lists for simple, moderate, and complex approaches are also included, along with discussions on the cost, maintenance loads, and energy usage of each alternative.

OTHER EQUIPMENT: MANAGING COMPLEXITY

Every piece of equipment must be evaluated in terms of the voyaging lifestyle you want to support. In Chapter 1, I advised you and your crewmates to establish a shared view of life aboard. To a large extent, that vision determines what equipment you will carry. You may choose a simple boat with basic accommodations and 1950s conveniences. In return, you will have more time to explore your surroundings and live the voyaging life. Or you may choose to have 1990s conveniences and invest more time, energy, and money in equipment. At the extreme, a complex electrical system will be required to power the equipment, and you will need a boat over 40 feet to accommodate it.

If you are willing to live with 1950s amenities, you can equip a basic boat (including self-steering and a dinghy) for less than $10,000 (£6,000) if you do all installation yourself. You will be rewarded with a boat that requires a minimum amount of maintenance and attention—fewer than 10 crew hours a week with 80 crew hours at haulout time. At the other end of the spectrum, you can have fresh water and electricity on demand plus a host of gadgets to make life easier and entertain you. You will need to spend over $50,000 (£30,000) on the gear alone, not including installation, and you will also spend a great deal of time on maintenance—an average of 20 to 40 crew hours per week and about 160 crew hours at haulout time (or pay someone the equivalent). There is a wide range of alternatives between these two extremes.

A well-equipped voyaging yacht, her gear, and her crew create a balanced system. The electrical system meets the loads imposed on it. The crew manages the routine maintenance on board without outside assistance. The overall cost of the whole system falls within the crew's budget. All of the gear fits aboard and can be properly stowed. Add a major piece of additional gear, and you can shift the balance.

As you consider each piece of gear on your boat, weigh its value in terms of the following factors. To assist you in making these tradeoffs, this chapter evaluates equipment using the following guidelines:

■ *Space/weight needs.* The overall size of your boat limits how much equipment you can carry. Most boats under 40 feet do not have enough space for a high-capacity watermaker or generator. Spares also take up valuable stowage space. Crews on small or light displacement boats need to consider the weight of additional gear. *The following symbols are used throughout the chapter to denote space requirements: * means space and weight considerations are negligible; ** means the equipment takes up more than 1 cubic foot or weighs more than 50 pounds; *** means that the equipment takes up 4 cubic feet of space or more and will be difficult to carry on a boat under 40 feet.*

■ *Electrical demand.* On most boats, the balance of electrical use against charging and battery storage capacity defines how much equipment can be carried. Adding gear with a high energy demand changes the balance and requires additional charging and battery capacity. It makes little sense to carry gear that cannot be used regularly because electrical capacity is limited. Throughout this chapter, peak electrical demand at 12 volts, expected use at sea, and average daily demand are shown for each piece of equipment.

■ *Maintenance requirements.* Every piece of gear increases the crew's maintenance load. When maintenance loads reach 20 hours per crewmember each week, they interfere with the enjoyment of voyaging. The maintenance requirement for each piece of gear is

less important than the total maintenance load aboard. *The following symbols are used throughout the chapter to denote maintenance requirements: * means that while you may have one major episode of repair at some point, for the most part this gear requires almost no maintenance; ** means that the gear will require attention on a regular basis but won't change your overall maintenance load dramatically; *** means that you will face a major increase in complexity and maintenance load by adding this piece of gear.*

■ *Cost.* Apart from space considerations, initial cost quickly defines your limits. This chapter uses discount prices for new equipment. Professional installation can double the cost. Used equipment can be purchased in many cases, often for half the quoted price. Even if you can afford the original cost, your maintenance costs will increase in proportion to the time spent on maintenance. For gear with three asterisks under maintenance, you can assume that maintenance expenses will have an impact on your overall budget. This chapter uses 1997 discount prices for new equipment.

Each major category of equipment is subdivided into "basic boat" and "additional." Consider the basic boat a starting point. Remember that many boats have successfully completed circumnavigations with only that gear aboard. Make sure that additional gear will compensate you for the various costs you incur to carry it.

While this chapter covers a broad range of equipment for offshore voyaging, new equipment appears constantly. Manufacturers and brands also change quickly. This chapter covers the tradeoffs for the type of equipment available today without discussing specific brands. To decide which brand you should purchase, consult the sources listed in "Additional resources" at the end of the chapter.

Safety equipment

Safety gear proliferates faster than any other category. We are all concerned about safety, and most cruisers invest money to buy peace of mind. However, you could probably spend half your equipment budget on safety equipment and still not have safety gear for every eventuality. At some point, you have to draw the line. Your

Table 7-1. "Basic boat" safety gear (U.S. dollars)

Equipment	Peak draw at 12 volts	Expected daily use at sea	Estimate of average daily electricity usage	Estimated cost	Maintenance load	Space/ weight needs
Medical kit	—	—	—	$750+	*	**
30 GPM manual bilge pump	—	—	—	$400	*	**
Jacklines and harnesses	—	—	—	$200	*	*
Abandon-ship kit	—	—	—	$50	*	*
Fire extinguisher	—	—	—	$20	*	*

decisions in this area must reflect the attitudes you and your crewmates share toward safety.

The basic boat: essential safety equipment

In port, a well-stocked medical kit is your first line of defense against minor accidents, injuries, and illnesses. At sea, your medical kit may well be your only line of defense. You should carry as complete a kit as possible: a kit put together in cooperation with your personal physician. Every crewmember must be trained to use it at a moment's notice. The contents of our medical kit are summarized in Appendix 2. A proper offshore medical kit requires a significant amount of storage space—ours filled a small suitcase.

Crew overboard is one of the most feared emergencies at sea. Evans did a great deal of rock climbing before going voyaging. He felt falling off the boat should be just as unacceptable as falling off a rock. High quality harnesses keep you aboard. We wore ours whenever the weather was rough. We clipped them to our jacklines by double tethers so we were always attached to the boat.

If your hull is compromised, you need time. A bilge pump that moves great amounts of water quickly gives you that time. You should have a high-capacity pump that can remove at least 30 gallons per minute from the bilge. Like the medical kit, a good bilge pump requires a lot of space. Our high-capacity Edson bilge pump took up a locker of 2 cubic feet in the nav seat.

The bilge pump gives you time to patch the hull so you can get to port. Once you pump out enough water to see what needs to be done, you will need something to repair the damage. Carry spare sailcloth, underwater putty, and marine plywood. You can buy collision mats at marine stores or make your own for less money with nylon line and a square of heavy canvas 8-by-8 feet in size with a grommet in each corner and a few along each edge.

When all else fails, you have to be prepared to abandon ship. However, everyone aboard must view the liferaft as the last resort, and you should never abandon ship until you have to "step up" to get into the liferaft. In the 1979 Fastnet Race off the southern coast of England, seven lives were lost in liferafts after crews abandoned boats that were later found afloat and towed back to harbor. This supports the conclusion that survival rates are higher if you stay with your vessel.

Offshore liferafts start at about $3,000. Some voyagers choose not to carry them, arguing that the money is better spent on extra bilge pumps and good maintenance. If you decide not to carry a dedicated liferaft, you must be prepared to convert your dinghy into a lifeboat. Every crewmember must know the procedures.

At minimum, your abandon-ship kit should include a liter of water for each person aboard, some high-energy foods, fishing line and hooks, a space blanket, a small first aid kit, seasickness medicines, sun block, a mirror, a knife, a flashlight with spare batteries, and a patch kit if your lifeboat is inflatable.

Pros and cons of additional safety equipment

Many voyagers don't feel tradeoffs should be made with respect to safety equipment. They view these items the way they view insurance—as an acceptable cost to deal with an unlikely but potentially calamitous disaster.

Beyond the basic safety gear, most voyagers carry a dedicated offshore liferaft. You must inflate, inspect, maintain, and repack liferafts regularly—usually on an annual basis. Without proper care, liferafts may fail to inflate when needed, or the rubber may deteriorate to the point where it falls apart shortly after being deployed. Inspections need to be done by the original manufacturer or a qualified representative, and servicing costs often exceed $250 annually. When deciding on a liferaft, ask about the frequency and cost of the inspections and the ability to have it serviced worldwide. Also ask others who own the same raft what condition they were in when they were serviced.

A manual watermaker should go in your abandon-ship kit, if you can possibly afford it. Unlike their large capacity cousins, these watermakers can be considered vital safety equipment. The 6-gallon-per-day unit is reasonably priced and could keep several people alive indefinitely. Like the raft, a watermaker must be serviced regularly. Treat the sensitive membranes with a preservative solution once a year, or they will dry out and deteriorate.

A handheld VHF can be used to signal vessels or aircraft from the liferaft until the batteries give out. This is another good addition to the abandon-ship kit, as long as it is kept fully charged.

When activated, an EPIRB (Emergency Positioning Indicator Radio Beacon) emits a signal that satellites can triangulate on to determine the EPIRB's position. The more sophisticated 406 MHz models also emit an identification code that the EPIRB manufacturer can match to the owner registration to learn the identity of the vessel in trouble. If you are going to purchase an EPIRB for offshore use, it makes sense to pay the extra money for the 406 MHz models. The identification will aid in a search at sea, and many models automatically emit if they are submerged. Unlike an SSB, the EPIRB can go with you if you have to abandon ship, which dramatically increases your chances of being rescued.

If you purchase a 406 MHz model, make sure you register it. In 1994, singlehanded offshore racer Mike Plant failed to register his before sailing transatlantic from the United States to Europe to qualify for the BOC singlehanded round-the-world race. When his EPIRB sent out two bursts, the information was received by the U.S. Mission Control Center in Maryland and the equivalent agency in Canada. Both failed to pass the information on to the U.S. Coast Guard because they could not verify that the signal belonged to a registered EPIRB. Only when Plant's family reported him overdue nine days later was a search launched. The boat was eventually located, but Plant was never found. If the EPIRB had been registered, a search would have been initiated immediately. The boat could have been found in a fraction of the time, and Plant might have been found as well.

Table 7-2. Comparison of other safety equipment (U.S. dollars)

Equipment	Peak draw at 12 volts	Expected daily use at sea	Estimate of average daily electricity usage	Estimated cost	Maintenance load	Space/ weight needs
Offshore liferaft	—	—	—	$3,000+	***	***
35 GPD manual watermaker	—	—	—	$1,300	*	*
6 GPD manual watermaker	—	—	—	$500	*	*
406 MHz EPIRB	—	—	—	$800–$1,000	*	*
Class B EPIRB	—	—	—	$250	*	*
Collision Avoidance Radar Detector (CARD)	0.1 A	24 hours	2.4 Ah	$500	*	*
2000 GPH electric bilge pump	4.8 A	1 hour	4.8 Ah	$75	**	*
Handheld VHF	—	—	—	$300	*	*

The CARD (Collision Avoidance Radar Detector) is designed to keep you out of the liferaft. These systems warn you if there are ships in your vicinity. They sound an alarm when they detect radar in use within their range, which is similar to the range of a VHF radio. Unlike radar, their low energy consumption makes it realistic to leave them on all the time while at sea. They will not pick up vessels operating without radar, but they offer some protection from a collision at sea.

The range of crew overboard equipment defies description. Consider all of your options, based on your own boat and crew situation, and try as many as possible before deciding. Whether you carry a horseshoe buoy or a one-man liferaft attached to the stern rail, you still have to get the person back aboard the boat. To rescue a conscious crewmember, you'll need a ladder or sling that can be deployed quickly, is stable, and can be used when the boat is rolling. For an unconscious person, you'll need a block-and-tackle arrangement and a lifting harness.

Navigation equipment

Position finding has undergone a radical transformation in the last two decades. In 1988, when Scott and Kitty Kuhner left on their second circumnavigation (see the sidebar, "A tale of two cruises," in this chapter), GPS wasn't even being discussed by the offshore community. By the time we left four years later, GPS had almost completely supplanted satnav and loran. More changes are on the way. In the next decade, electronic charts will become an integrated part of an offshore voyager's navigation station, and worldwide telephone and computer communications will be an affordable reality. But these systems still need to be refined, and industry standards need to be developed. For now, GPS and SSB remain the navigation and communication tools of the trade for voyaging.

The basic boat: essential navigation gear

At minimum, an offshore boat must have a compass, a good pair of binoculars, several ways to locate the boat's position, a way to determine depth in anchorages, a way to forecast the weather, and navigation lights (Table 7-3).

Early voyagers and cruisers who lacked the money for more sophisticated systems found their position offshore with a sextant and the necessary tables. An RDF (Radio Direction Finder), a hand-bearing compass, a lead line, and charts were used for navigation near land. The lead line also served to determine depth and bottom type in an anchorage. They used a hurricane lamp for navigation lights and a barometer for weather forecasting. Today the sextant has been superseded by the GPS, the lead line by the depth sounder, and the hurricane lamp by electric navigation lights. Despite a wealth of modern equipment, the barometer remains vital in short-term weather forecasting at sea.

The GPS now offers an accurate, affordable method for finding position offshore or near land and has supplanted many of the other electronics that used to be considered essential. The GPS and accurate charts make the radar much less critical for navigating near land. Information provided by other instruments—such as speed over ground, distance logged over ground—can be obtained from the GPS, as well as a host of new values including course made good, course to be steered, distance to go, estimated time of arrival, etc. A basic handheld GPS now costs about half what a plastic sextant does, but the GPS offers more accuracy, versatility, and simplicity.

The GPS is electronic gear, and it cannot be trusted implicitly offshore. We knew several people who lost their GPS to water damage. We installed a "waterproof" handheld GPS unit in our navigation station rather than the larger, less-water-resistant model designed for permanent installation. When salt water from a leaking stanchion gate migrated throughout the navigation station, the GPS was undamaged. But during a wild thunderstorm in the doldrums, we lost our GPS to static electricity.

Every boat should carry a GPS. But every offshore boat needs a sextant for backup. Some cruisers carried two GPS units. But if the satellite system went down, batteries were unavailable, or their GPS model had a systematic failure, they would be left without position-finding capability. A sextant is the only failure-proof backup. A plastic sextant does not cost much, and taking sights and reducing them is not difficult to learn.

A sextant offers amusement and self-sufficiency, even if you never use it in lieu of your GPS. We used our sextant to learn the Southern Hemisphere stars. To reduce sights, you need a set of sight reduction tables and a ship's clock (or some way to get a time signal); your sextant sight can only be as accurate as your time piece. Celestial calculators simplify sight reduction and calculating bearings for the brightest celestial bodies.

The depth sounder provides the one bit of navigation information not supplied by a GPS. We knew many offshore voyagers who sailed thousands of miles without wind instruments or logs, but they considered a functioning depth sounder essential. The depth sounder and an accurate chart pinpoint your position when you are close to land. It can enable you to navigate along the fathom lines on the chart. It warns you if you enter shoal water. It helps you to determine how much scope must be put out when you set your anchor.

Two more pieces of navigational gear must be included in the list of basic equipment: a VHF radio and a world-band receiver. The VHF (Very High Frequency) radio has become the worldwide standard for communicating in a line-of-sight pathway between vessels at sea and between vessels and land stations. We were hailed by the U.S. Coast Guard aboard a helicopter 150 miles off the coast of Colombia, wondering if we had drugs aboard; by the Australian Coastwatch plane along Australia's Great Barrier Reef wanting to make sure we were not smuggling illegal aliens; and by the *Tanker King* 20 miles off the coast of Rhode Island politely asking if we would mind altering course. In each of these situations, not having a VHF aboard would have been problematic.

A world-band receiver offers an inexpensive alternative to carrying an SSB. With these portable units, you can eavesdrop on the short-wave bands. More expensive units receive all SSB and Ham frequencies, giving you weather forecasts worldwide. Some models can be connected to a laptop computer to receive weather faxes. A world-band receiver provides time signals for sextant sights and offers hours of entertainment from the BBC and VOA. Our Sony receiver picked up weather forecasts more clearly than some SSB units and worked well all the way around the world. Though we wired it to run off ship's power, it could use dry cells if we lost our engine or battery bank. Even if we put an SSB aboard our next boat, we will take a world-band receiver along as a backup.

Table 7-3. "Basic boat" navigation gear (U.S. dollars)

Equipment	Peak draw at 12 volts	Expected daily use at sea	Estimate of average daily electricity usage	Estimated cost	Maintenance load	Space/ weight needs
Bronze sextant	—	—	—	$2,000+	*	*
Plastic sextant	—	—	—	$300	*	*
GPS	0.3 A	24 hours	7.2 Ah	$150–$900	*	*
Depth sounder	0.1 A	24 hours	2.4 Ah	$300–$600	*	*
VHF	2.0 A	0.2 hours	0.4 Ah	$200–$700	*	*
World-band receiver	—	—	—	$150–$500	*	*
Binnacle compass with light	0.1 A	12 hours	1.2 Ah	$300–$400	*	*
Binoculars	—	—	—	$200+	*	*
Barometer	—	—	—	$200+	*	*
Steaming lights	1.0 A	12 hours	12.0 Ah	$150	**	*
Anchor light	1.0 A	12 hours	12.0 Ah	$50	**	*

Pros and cons of other navigation equipment

A host of additional gear can be used in navigation. A wide range of methods exist for plotting GPS positions on an electronic chart—all of which are expensive compared to the basic gear described above. Marine communications are undergoing a revolution, and no clear winner has yet emerged. Just as GPS supplanted sat-nav and loran, these new systems may supplant today's radar and SSB. If you want to equip a boat now, how should you decide among the items in Table 7-4?

Most offshore voyagers would rank the SSB or Ham radio as the most important item on this list. A long-distance radio is the offshore voyager's telephone. It can be used to contact rescue services or medical personnel in an emergency. But it also serves a number of more mundane functions. You can find port information, weather forecasts, and route tips in every ocean of the world on radio nets. Boats at sea report current weather conditions in daily roll calls. The SSB is the glue that binds the offshore voyaging community together, but it is not for everyone.

Long-distance radios are expensive. Aside from that, they can create a false sense of security that makes people less self-sufficient. Being able to contact an emergency service or the Coast Guard does not guarantee physical assistance. When given the opportunity, inexperienced crews have abandoned yachts that were in no serious danger. An SSB does not substitute for preparedness or mitigate your responsibility for the safety of your vessel and crew.

For some voyagers, marine-band radio compromises the isolation and adventure of voyaging. We left without an SSB, then installed one in South Africa six months before we returned. It changed the way we lived aboard—making us more competitive when we knew others were in our vicinity, spoiling some of the magic of a new island by hearing about it beforehand, and tying us to the daily radio schedule (the sched). If we did not come up as expected because we were doing a sail change, we caused unnecessary anxiety. You should carry an SSB if your primary concerns are safety and social contact or if you have children aboard. If you want to preserve your privacy and budget, you can listen without participating using the world-band receiver.

SSB and Ham dominate long-distance marine communications at this time, but new technologies portend a new world. One couple crossing the Indian Ocean and Red Sea has been corresponding with us by e-mail using their laptop computer and satellite links to the Internet.

Table 7-4. Comparison of various types of navigation equipment (U.S. dollars)

Equipment	Peak draw at 12 volts	Expected daily use at sea	Estimate of average daily electricity usage	Estimated cost	Maintenance load	Space/ weight needs
Radar with chart plotter	3–4 A	6 hours	20.0 Ah	$3,000–$4,000	*	*
LCD radar	2–3 A	6 hours	15.0 Ah	$2,000–$3,000	*	*
Chart plotters	0.5 A	24 hours	12.0 Ah	$1,000–$2,000	*	*
Laptop and software	0.5 A	24 hours	12.0 Ah	$2,000–$3,000	*	*
SSB[1]	30.0 A[2]	0.5 hours	15 Ah	$2,000–$3,000	*	*
Wind and speed instruments	0.4 A	24 hours	9.6 Ah	$1,000–$2,000	* *	*
GPS repeater	0.1 A	24 hours	2.4 Ah	$1,000	*	*
Handheld VHF	—	—	—	$300	*	*

[1] Ham radio is a less expensive alternative, but you will need a Ham license.
[2] When transmitting

Charges of up to $2 per minute make such communication prohibitive for most voyagers. But operating costs will go down. The new global cellular phone system will change the face of offshore communications even more. These technologies offer two things that Ham and SSB do not: private communications and links to family members without access to a long-distance radio. But these new technologies will have difficulty supplanting the low-cost, well-established, reliable, specialized communication system that marine-band radio represents. It seems likely that the new technologies will be used for private communications, but SSB and Ham will continue to operate as the marine party line.

Five years ago, radar was considered a necessity for offshore voyaging. A 16-mile radar could locate land after the sextant or satnav put you in range. Radar could also be used to clear an island or enter a wide reef pass. These functions have been supplanted by the GPS where chart accuracy allows, though radar still makes a valuable second aid to navigation to confirm your location.

The radar's remaining unique contribution is its ability to locate objects, such as ships or land, in low- or no-visibility situations such as in fog or at night and to warn you of their existence by visual means or with an alarm. If the radar could be left on 24 hours a day with an alarm set, it would simplify watchkeeping tremendously. While the new LCD radars have reduced their energy consumption by more than one-third over the old CRT models, the electricity demand for 24-hour use is still impractical for most boats. The radar can reasonably be used for three or four hours a day while sailing or all the time while motoring. For areas such as the Maine coast and parts of northern Europe, where fog is common and shipping traffic is heavy, you will want to carry a radar if you can afford it. On a trade wind circumnavigation, radar is desirable but by no means essential.

Electronic chart plotters have not yet reached the stage where they are viable for the offshore voyager. Today, you can do electronic chart plotting using your radar screen. But you cannot combine the two functions, and you have to toggle between a radar image and a chart of the area. You can purchase a dedicated chart plotter, which is little more than a laptop computer. Finally, you can put an electronic plotting program on your laptop computer. All of these technologies require position input from your GPS and the purchase of charts on

diskettes, the price of which is not included in the price range quoted in Table 7-4. You can buy diskettes for the United States and Europe in any number of competing formats. World coverage will remain unavailable, at least until one technology starts to dominate.

In theory, electronic charts would save space and money and offer increased accuracy compared to paper charts. But like a GPS, you cannot completely trust an electronic system at sea. You would still have to carry enough paper charts to get you into a major port in the event of electrical or equipment failure. Worldwide chart coverage needs to be available on diskette before these systems can replace paper charts. Manufacturers say the potential market may never justify the cost for more remote corners of the globe. Where accurate charts and differential GPS both exist, this technology allows you to pinpoint your location on the computer. For now, this type of electronic chart plotting is limited to the United States, Europe, and the Caribbean.

Does a laptop computer make sense aboard? A dedicated laptop will be the brains of navigation stations of the future. Today, aside from electronic chart plotting, laptops already provide weather faxes via a fax program and the SSB; worldwide e-mail through the SSB and satellite networks; and the entertainment, word processing, and record keeping functions of home computers. All that capability requires minimal electrical consumption and comes at a price comparable to dedicated electronic plotting systems. But you must protect laptops from the corrosive and concussive marine environment. We stored our laptop in a watertight briefcase on passage. While the computer held up remarkably well, it did suffer massive failure after three years. Though not indispensable, a laptop is tremendously useful. We will have one aboard our next boat.

A GPS repeater in the cockpit offers good value for the money. When standing watch, a GPS repeater keeps you informed on how you are doing against your course. It displays your latitude and longitude, your course and speed over the ground, your course to the waypoint, and your cross-track error. Cross-track error represents the boat's deviation from your planned course. By keeping your cross-track error to zero you can be confident that you have not strayed into danger.

Instruments are useful but often problematic. Logs get fouled by barnacles or grass, which means they often don't work for the first few days of a passage. Masthead wind instruments are easily damaged by birds or dirt. Instrument repeaters, even those designed for the cockpit, are often not watertight. Our cockpit repeater was located on a stainless steel arch over the binnacle and had to be replaced twice during our trip. Try to locate your repeaters where they will be protected from spray.

If you choose to have instruments, consider an instrument repeater for the navigation station. When filling out the log on passage, all of the relevant information is right in front of you. If you are sitting out a gale at anchor, you will know if the wind is increasing or decreasing. A second small compass mounted in the nav station will tell you if the wind is shifting at night or during a gale.

Comforts and conveniences

You can add a vast array of amenities below to make life simpler and more enjoyable. Like the GPS, watermakers and refrigeration have revolutionized life afloat in the last five years. But abundant water and cold beers come at a higher cost than easy position fixing. You will have to decide if they are worth it. This section focuses on a range of conveniences from lights to watermakers. In addition, you may want to add other electronics that fall into the category of entertainment, including CD players, televisions, VCRs, etc.

The basic boat: gear for the simple life

Beyond safety and navigational equipment, a few features should be considered essential on an offshore yacht. At minimum, the galley should contain a sink, a stove with at least two burners, and a well-insulated icebox (a minimum of 4 inches of insulation). We found that keeping ice as dry as possible prolonged its life significantly. The icebox should have good rubber gaskets around any openings to keep moisture out, shelves to hold the ice and other contents off the wet bottom, a drain for removing melted water, and a trap in the drain to prevent warm air from entering. The sink should be equipped with a foot pump for fresh water. A second foot pump for salt water improves water conservation, but a bucket and some discipline work just as well.

The head should contain a marine toilet. All bunk cushions should be a minimum of 4 inches thick, though 6 is better for anyone prone to muscle or back pain. And you should have a few strategically placed reading lights. These should be electric if you plan to spend much time in the tropics. (Kerosene lanterns are wonderfully romantic, but they give off far too much heat when it is already hot and sticky.)

You might decide to add more items to this list, but these can be considered the basics. We knew a half-dozen boats that circumnavigated with only these essentials aboard. Generally speaking, crews on these boats did not miss the things that other crews considered necessities.

Pros and cons of other equipment

Beyond the essentials, most people want a good marine propane stove with three burners and an oven. The best units are equipped with a crash bar, safety rails, and adjustable wire pot-holders to hold pans in place. A hot meal does more to restore one's sense of order in a gale

Table 7-5. "Basic boat" comforts and conveniences (U.S. dollars)

Equipment	Peak draw at 12 volts	Expected daily use at sea	Estimate of average daily electricity usage	Estimated cost	Maintenance load	Space/weight needs
Alcohol stove	—	—	—	$300–$500	**	**
Icebox	—	—	—	$200	*	***
Marine toilet	—	—	—	$200–$600	**	**
Reading light	2.0 A	5 hours	10.0 Ah	$20	*	*
Foot pump	—	—	—	$70	*	*

than anything else. Fresh bread is one of the luxuries of the liveaboard life. If you can afford only one additional item beyond the basics, make it a good stove.

A butane stove and butane cartridges offer an extra burner, as well as a backup in the event that something happens to your propane system. This inexpensive alternative to your main stove can be purchased from most marine stores.

After a high quality stove, most people opt for refrigeration. Don't assume refrigeration is essential. We used our engine-driven refrigeration very little once we started across the Pacific. In places where fresh dairy products and meat were available—such as New Zealand, Australia, and South Africa—ice could also be purchased. In these areas, we relied on the icebox and found it more efficient than the refrigeration. We do not plan to install refrigeration on our next boat.

For cruisers who want ice for their drinks and meat for the table, refrigeration enhances life aboard. Circumnavigator Kitty Kuhner points out that refrigeration

becomes less a luxury when you have children along (see the sidebar, "A tale of two cruises," in this chapter). Refrigeration increases your maintenance load, but the units are becoming more reliable. If you are undecided about refrigeration, read the information in Chapter 10 on living without refrigeration.

Watermakers are the most controversial equipment on this list. We met cruisers who ranked them second only to a GPS on their list of essential gear. Others wished they had never even heard of them. If not used regularly, the membranes dry out and deteriorate. They must be pickled with biocide if they are left unused for a week or more. If you fail to pickle the membrane, a replacement will cost $350 or more. The membranes can also be ruined by pollution or diesel in the water. You will therefore be unable to use a watermaker in major harbors like Papeete or Suva.

A watermaker can never replace sufficient tankage. Watermakers above all depend on the engine or batteries to meet their voracious energy demands. They

Table 7-6. Comparison of other comforts and conveniences (U.S. dollars)

Equipment	Peak draw at 12 volts	Expected daily use at sea	Estimate of average daily electricity usage	Estimated cost	Maintenance load	Space/ weight needs
500 GPD engine-driven watermaker	5.0 A	1 hour for 20 gallons	5.0 Ah	$4,500	***	***
86 GPD 12-volt watermaker	8.0 A	5 hours for 20 gallons	40.0 Ah	$3,000	***	***
35 GPD 12-volt watermaker	4.0 A	15 hours for 20 gallons	60.0 Ah	$2,000	**	**
Engine-driven refrigeration	—	—	—	$2,500	**	**
Cold plate refrigeration	40.0 A	1–1.5 hours	40.0–60.0 Ah	$3,000–$4,000	**	**
Propane stove with oven	0.5 A[1]	4 hours	2.0 Ah	$1,000	**	***
Forced air diesel heater	2.0 A	24 hours	48.0 Ah	$1,500	**	**
Bulkhead diesel heater	0.3 A	24 hours	7.0 Ah	$500	**	**
Engine-driven hot water heater	—	—	—	$400	*	**
Pressure water	6.0 A	0.25 hours	1.5 Ah	$200	**	*
Deck wash	6.0 A	0.25 hours	1.5 Ah	$200	**	*
One-burner butane stove	—	—	—	$60	*	*

[1] For propane solenoid

A tale of two cruises

Scott and Kitty Kuhner have circumnavigated twice. They were in their late 20s during their first trip, from 1971 to 1975, in a 30-foot Allied Seawind ketch called *Bebinka.* At that time, most of the boats and gear they encountered were small and simple like *Bebinka.*

"We carried a compass, a lead line, a sextant, and an RDF for navigation," Kitty said. "Swinging that RDF around looking for the strongest signal used to drive me crazy!" They had a manual windlass, a Hasler wind vane (the original type pioneered by Blondie Hasler), and an engine that powered two deep-cycle marine batteries. All of their headsails hanked on. "We knew a few people with roller furlers," Kitty said, "but [the systems] were nothing but trouble."

Below they had a kerosene stove but no oven, an icebox that they used for storage, fresh- and saltwater foot pumps, a few electric lights and kerosene lanterns, and a manual bilge pump. They were given an AM radio with a 200-mile range that they used to communicate with their friends on other boats across the Indian Ocean.

By the time they left on their second circumnavigation in 1987, many things had changed. New gear had been invented and existing gear improved. They had two sons—Alex, age 11, and Spencer, age 9 (Figure 7-1). "Many of our gear decisions for the second trip were safety decisions with respect to the kids," Kitty says. As a family of four, they sailed on a bigger boat: Valiant 40 *Tamure.* "For navigation, we had our old sextant, plus a satnav, a loran, and a radar. This was still before GPS, and the loran and satnav didn't give continuous positions. If we'd had to choose between radar and satnav, we'd have picked the radar. We could get close to land with the sextant, but we used the radar to find our way in from there."

Roller furlers had been improved and, after initial reluctance, they put one aboard *Tamure* and never regretted it. They also carried an electric windlass, an autopilot, and their trusty Hasler wind vane from the first boat. They had a full set of marine instruments. Below they had a full-size propane stove and oven and a Sea Frost engine-driven refrigerator. "With the kids we needed to be able to cook more food. The

oven was wonderful for baking. And the refrigeration was necessary to get the kids to drink powdered milk." In addition to the fresh- and saltwater foot pumps in the galley, they also had pressurized water. They carried a VHF and a modern SSB which they viewed as their lifeline in the event of a medical emergency aboard. To power their new gear, they ran the engine 30 minutes to one hour per day to charge their four deep-cycle batteries. They had two solar panels for trickle charging the rest of the time.

"There are only two things that I wish we had had on the second trip," Kitty concluded. "While we had a dodger, we never did figure out a good way to provide adequate shade on deck in the tropics for more than one person. Often we rigged bed sheets for an awning, but that was far from satisfactory. As a result, we spent too much time below, especially at sea. And with two kids aboard, I would have loved some sort of small washing machine, even something that was hand-cranked."

Scott believes, "We had two very different boats in terms of size, sailing ability, gear, and conveniences, but that didn't affect our fun or our lifestyle one iota." Kitty has a slightly different perspective. "The fact of the matter is that having kids on board is harder on the wife, and a few conveniences make everything a lot more manageable."

Figure 7-1. The Kuhners enjoy a Polynesian feast in Niuatoputapu, Tonga. From left: Spencer (9), Scott, Alex (11), and Kitty.

cannot be relied on when disaster strikes and you are at sea without an engine or electrical system. Unlike manual watermakers, engine-driven or electrical watermakers need to be viewed as a convenience, exacting a high price in terms of initial cost and energy demands.

Twelve-volt watermakers use at least 2 ampere-hours to create 1 gallon of water. To really increase your water usage, you will need an additional 150 to 200 ampere-hours of battery capacity. Engine-driven watermakers produce greater quantities more efficiently, but they are also more expensive. Weigh the benefits of almost unlimited fresh water against these disadvantages. Again, having children aboard may be the deciding factor. The information in Chapter 12 on managing water will help you determine the right solution for your situation.

With regard to television, the standards for broadcasting differ widely from country to country. An American television will not function with most foreign signals. If you want TV aboard, you have three choices. You can buy one that is compatible with the broadcast signal in the area you plan to travel to, use your existing TV strictly with your VCR, or purchase a television that is capable of receiving all types of signals. You can buy the latter at major electronics stores in metropolitan areas.

Most other items on this list have understandable tradeoffs. For example, only you can measure the value of a warm cabin when you arrive in New Zealand.

Factor your overall maintenance load into the equation. With liveaboard usage, pressure water pumps, foot pumps, and marine toilets need annual overhauls. Refrigeration systems need to be flushed with muriatic acid once a year in the tropics. An instrument transducer or oven thermostat that succumbs to salt air or water will have to be sent back via the postal service to the manufacturer. For every such replacement part, you will spend money in faxes and duties, as well as several days of your time dealing with the postal service, shipping agents, and customs.

At some point, you may feel as if you are maintaining your boat more than enjoying the places you came to visit. It does not pay to start with all the bells and whistles. Save time and money and start with a simple boat.

Engine, charging equipment, and batteries

You can calculate how much electricity you will use based on the gear and gadgets you want to take along. The needs of the "basic boat" outlined above are minimal. But if you add even one of the high-electrical-use items—such as an electric autopilot, 12-volt refrigeration, or 12-volt watermaker—you will overwhelm the electrical system of the basic boat. If you want to add more than one of these items, you will need to add significant electrical charging and storage capacity.

Configuration to run the basic boat

Many boats have completed momentous voyages without auxiliary power, and an engine is not considered essential equipment by every cruiser. As little as 15 years ago, the unreliability of marine diesels made their value questionable. However, marine diesels have become reliable and reasonably inexpensive. Almost any boat you buy today will have one aboard. Any boat that doesn't should be equipped with one. I consider those who voyage without an engine to be the last of the purists. Few of us are sailors enough to wait for days or weeks for wind in the doldrums, to sail our way into crowded marinas, or to sail upriver against wind and current to a safe anchorage.

Once you have an engine equipped with an alternator and regulator, you have a power plant that can generate electricity. By adding a marine battery, you can store that electricity for future use. Very few of the items on the "basic boat" list require ship's power. The GPS, VHF, and world-band receiver can run on batter-

Table 7-7. "Basic boat" electrical system (U.S. dollars)						
Equipment	Generation at 12 volts	Average hours per day	Estimate of average daily electricity production	Estimated cost	Maintenance load	Space/weight needs
Solar panel	4.6 A	8 hours	20–30 Ah	$500	*	**
105 Ah deep-cycle battery	—	—	—	$100	*	**

ies. Only the depth sounder, navigation lights, and reading lights rely on the boat's electrical system for a total demand of under 50 ampere-hours per day. A 200–ampere-hour battery bank charged every day by running the engine for an hour or two would meet this demand. A solar panel also falls into the category of inexpensive, trouble-free gear. In areas with good sunlight, the panel will halve the basic boat's required engine running time. For more on sizing your battery bank and charging system for your energy demand, see the sidebar, "Balancing your electrical system" in this chapter.

While Table 7-7 makes the maintenance load for these items look small, the decision to put an electrical system on even the simplest boat creates a major change aboard. Be prepared to spend an hour or so a week on the electrical system—checking battery fluid levels, fixing a switch, adjusting the alternator belt, and so on.

Electrical system to meet higher energy requirements

The electrical system on the "basic boat" is well balanced against the equipment's demands. To meet the demand from a high-consumption item like an autopilot, you would need to increase the battery bank to 400 ampere-hours, add a 125-amp alternator to increase charging capacity (Table 7-8), and add a second solar panel. You would need daily engine runs of one hour. In addition to the load of 50 ampere-hours from the "basic

boat," this system could handle the 40 to 50 additional ampere-hours required to meet the daily electrical demand of a 12-volt watermaker, a 12-volt refrigerator, or a helm-mounted electric pilot.

To operate more than one of these items, you will need to radically increase your electrical capacity. Table 7-8 summarizes the equipment that can be used to build a high-output system.

Four high-energy options follow:

■ *Alternative charging approach.* Most offshore voyagers want additional electricity, but they don't want to run their engines any more than necessary. Wind generators, tow generators, and additional solar panels can be added to increase charging capacity. Solar panels offer the most reliable and inexpensive energy. Wind and tow generators, which combine mechanical and electrical parts in a corrosive environment, produce more power but are less worry-free. Most circumnavigators we knew carried solar panels, but only a half-dozen carried wind or tow generators all the way around.

■ *Engine-driven approach.* The excess power generated by the engine when charging the batteries can be used to run other equipment. You can belt a mechanically driven watermaker and refrigerator compressor off the engine, and add a high-output alternator and "smart" regulator to charge the battery bank more efficiently. By running the engine an hour a day, the watermaker would provide up to 20 gallons of fresh water,

Table 7-8. Comparison of other electrical and charging system equipment (U.S. dollars)

Equipment	Generation at 12 volts	Average hours per day	Estimate of average daily electricity production	Estimated cost	Maintenance load	Space/ weight needs
Diesel generator[1]	50 A	2 hours	65 Ah	$2,500–$10,000	∗∗∗	∗∗∗
Large wind generator[2]	6 A	8 hours	25–50 Ah	$1,000	∗∗	∗∗∗
125-amp alternator	100 A	1 hour	75 Ah	$800	∗∗	∗∗
Inverter/charger	50 A[3]	—	—	$1,000	∗	∗
Smart regulator	—	—	—	$160	∗∗	∗
Battery bank monitor	—	—	—	$400	∗∗	∗

[1] With 50-amp alternator
[2] With 15 knots of wind
[3] Only if plugged into shore power

a well-insulated refrigerator would remain cold, and the batteries would be charged sufficiently to run a wide assortment of other equipment.

■ *DC generator approach.* A marine diesel is an inefficient way to generate electricity. Diesels prefer to be run under a load. Running the engine an hour a day under small charging loads increases engine hours and required maintenance and shortens engine life. Some voyagers with sizable energy needs have turned to generators. A 5- to 10-horsepower diesel generator belted

to a watermaker, refrigerator compressor, and a high-output alternator represents one solution. The engine is equipped with its own high-output alternator as a backup to the generator. This solution offers all the amenities of the engine-driven approach with desirable redundancy, but at much higher cost and a radical increase in complexity. From a maintenance standpoint, a generator can be viewed as a second engine.

■ *AC genset approach.* For larger boats with all the comforts of home, a 5- to 15-kW AC genset running

---

Balancing your electrical system

How much battery capacity do you need? How much charging will that system require? You can answer these questions only after you determine how much electricity you plan to use in a day. Some basic principles for sizing your system and a few rules of thumb will help you make a rough calculation of your electrical needs.

For normal "household" equipment—reading lights, navigation lights, propane solenoids, and so on—the base load is about 50 ampere-hours per day. The "basic boat" described in this chapter illustrates this daily usage. To that you should add an additional 50 ampere-hours for each major 12-volt draw: for a 12-volt watermaker, a 12-volt refrigerator, or a helm-mounted electric autopilot. If you install all three, or if you plan on a below-decks autopilot, you will qualify as a high-energy–consumption boat with an estimated 200 ampere-hours–per-day load. If you plan to carry a half-dozen other electrical devices such as TVs, VCRs, or microwaves, factor in an additional 50 ampere-hours to cover smaller items and a safety margin. The safety margin ensures sufficient voltage for peak draws and protects voltage-sensitive equipment like SSB's and autopilots. At this point, your projected daily energy consumption will be somewhere between 50 and 250 ampere-hours.

You will need four times your daily electricity demand in battery bank capacity. While this seems outrageous, electrical systems aboard boats are surprisingly inefficient. Most boats charge their batteries only once a day, so the batteries must be capable of delivering the total daily demand between charges.

Battery life depends upon how often and how deeply they are discharged. For reasonable battery life, they should not be discharged by more than 50 percent. While recharging a battery up to 70 or 80 percent of its capacity is efficient, recharging the last 20 percent of battery capacity is very inefficient. No matter what type of equipment you have, the last 20 percent will take hours. As batteries age they become even less efficient, so a safety factor needs to be included.

If you only discharge the battery by 50 percent and recharge it to 80 percent, then whatever daily demand you have calculated must be supplied by 30 percent of the battery bank's capacity plus some safety factor. For a 50 ampere-hour load, that translates to a minimum of 167 ampere-hours of capacity. If you add in a 20 percent safety margin, you need a 200 ampere-hour battery bank, or four times your daily demand, to support the minimal load of the "basic boat."

In terms of charging sources, you need to replace only those ampere-hours that you use in a day—not the full battery bank capacity. You need to be able to generate about one-quarter of the battery bank capacity per day. You could buy an alternator rated at one-quarter of your battery bank's capacity and charge for something over an hour every day (the alternators are not perfectly efficient), or you could buy several solar or wind panels whose total average output will equal one-quarter of your bank's capacity. For the "basic boat," a 50-amp alternator used for 1 1/2 to 2 hours per day or two solar panels that averaged 30 ampere-hours per day in the tropics would keep the battery bank adequately charged.

continuously can supply unlimited power to AC refrigeration, AC watermakers, AC galley appliances, and even AC air conditioning. The genset can also charge a battery bank through a charger. The engine acts as a backup for charging the batteries. This option, long used aboard large motor yachts and ships, has recently become feasible for medium-sized yachts with the introduction of more compact gensets. As with the DC generator approach, you must weigh the benefits against the high cost and increased complexity of such a system.

For any DC-based electrical system, an inverter/charger provides AC current for a laptop computer or for your non–12-volt tools. It also allows you to give the batteries a good, soaking charge on the rare occasion when you are in a marina. Not all chargers are created equal. For a charger to work outside the United States, it must accept 220 volts and 50 hertz (as opposed to the 60 hertz that is standard in this country). Battery chargers rated at 220 volts and 60 hertz do not charge effectively at the lower cycle level. Some marine chargers can be switched from 110/60 to 220/50,

Battery down exercise

No piece of electrical gear on an offshore boat can be trusted implicitly. You need to ensure that if you lost your batteries or charging capability, your boat could still function. The best way to do this is to perform a "battery down" exercise. Think the exercise through first. Then try it on your shakedown passage, while you are still within reach of chandleries and boatyards.

To perform the exercise, turn off the main battery switch for an entire day and see what problems arise. If you have a GPS hooked to ship's power, you will need to dig out the sextant or the spare GPS. If you have pressurized water, you will have to use hand pumps. Once it gets dark, you will need spare flashlights. For a day, you'll be without your SSB and Ham radio. You will also lose your VHF, unless you carry a handheld that was fully charged when you started the exercise. You won't have any instruments, radar, electronic chart plotting, GPS repeater, CD player, deck lights, navigation lights, 12-volt refrigeration, or 12-volt watermaker. What serious problems develop? What if you also lost your engine?

This exercise will show you how dependent you are on your electrical system, and you will learn how to prepare for the reality. You may miss several critical areas if you only think the exercise through in your mind.

■ *Propane solenoid.* On most boats, the propane system requires an electrical solenoid to function. This is an important safety feature. If you ever lose your batteries, you will need to bypass the solenoid switch to serve hot meals.

■ *Time signals.* To use the sextant as a backup to the GPS, you need some method of getting time signals. A world-band receiver that operates on dry cells is one option. A ship's clock and a time log are another.

■ *Electric bilge pump.* If your primary bilge pump uses electricity, you will need to check the bilge regularly for water during the exercise. No boat should leave without a manual bilge pump as a backup for the electric pump.

■ *Safety lighting.* Flashlights and plenty of spare batteries may not be enough if you have no other electricity. Consider how you will warn a large ship of your presence if you are on a collision course at night and you have no VHF or navigation lights. Floodlights will be equally useless without your battery bank. A flare will more likely bring the other vessel to your aid and endanger you—not make them steer clear. Two alternatives are a high-powered flashlight that can be reflected off the sails or a hurricane lantern that can be raised into the rigging.

■ *Batteries.* The exercise should convince you that you never want to be short of dry cell batteries. You need to know where the batteries are and be able to get them into the necessary equipment in the dark or with a flashlight. We carried a large battery bag in the front of an accessible locker.

Table 7-9. Comparison of the equipment carried by three different boats

	Simplicity	Moderation	High Life		Simplicity	Moderation	High Life
Major gear	Used Aries wind vane	New wind vane	New wind vane	Navigational gear	Compass	Compass	Compass
	Inflatable 8-foot dinghy	10-foot roll-up inflatable	10-foot roll-up inflatable		Binoculars	Binoculars	Binoculars
		3.5-hp outboard	15-hp outboard		Navigation lights	Navigation lights	Navigation lights
		Roller furler	Two roller furlers		VHF	VHF	VHF & handheld VHF
		Helm-mounted pilot	Below-decks pilot		Depth sounder	Full instruments	Full instruments with repeater below
		Manual windlass	Electric windlass		World-band receiver	SSB and world-band receiver	SSB & world-band receiver
			10-foot RIB		Barometer	Barometer	Barometer
Safety equipment	Medical kit	Medical kit	Medical kit		Plastic sextant	GPS and sextant	2 GPS units and sextant
	Jacklines & harnesses	Jacklines & harnesses	Jacklines & harnesses			LCD radar	LCD radar
	Abandon-ship kit	Abandon-ship kit	Abandon-ship kit				Laptop with navigation software & charts
	One fire extinguisher	Two fire extinguishers	Three fire extinguishers				GPS repeater in cockpit
	Manual bilge pump	Two manual bilge pumps	Two manual bilge pumps	Comforts & conveniences	8 reading lights	12 reading lights	14 reading lights
	Used liferaft	Offshore liferaft	Offshore liferaft		Marine toilet	Marine toilet	Marine toilet
		Electric bilge pump	Electric bilge pump		Icebox	Engine-driven refrigeration	Engine-driven/ 12-volt refrigeration
		Deck lights	Deck lights		Alcohol stove	Propane stove and oven	Propane stove and oven
		406 MHz EPIRB	406 MHz EPIRB		Saltwater/fresh-water foot pumps	Saltwater/fresh-water foot pumps	Saltwater/fresh-water foot pumps
		Lifesling	Lifesling & dan buoy		AM/FM radio Cassette player	AM/FM radio CD player	AM/FM radio CD player
			Manual watermaker			Pressure fresh water	Pressure fresh water
			Collision Avoidance Radar Detector (CARD)			Deck wash	Deck wash
			12-volt floodlight			Hot water heater	Hot water heater
			Handheld VHF			Bulkhead diesel heater	Forced air diesel heater
						Inverter/battery charger	Inverter/battery charger
							Engine-driven watermaker
							TV, VCR, & Microwave

or you can purchase a European automotive battery charger.

Until now, most offshore voyagers have kept it simple. They relied on a medium to large battery bank that they charged with a combination of engine running and solar, wind, or water-driven sources. But an increasing number of long distance cruisers are proving that the engine-driven and DC generator approach can work on an offshore voyaging yacht—but only at a high initial cost and with a sizable ongoing investment in maintenance.

EXAMPLES OF THREE SUCCESSFUL ALTERNATIVES

This section describes equipment configurations for three different boats. Each solution is a balanced approach with respect to cost, electrical demand, space utilization, and maintenance load. The three boats are *Simplicity, Moderation,* and *High Life.* They each carry appropriate sails and ground tackle for their boat size. The additional equipment they carry is compared in Table 7-9.

Simplicity is a 30-foot fiberglass cutter with a precareer couple aboard. They cannot afford much beyond the essentials. *Moderation* is a 37-foot ketch with a sabbatical couple aboard. They have some money to spare but have made many tradeoffs in arriving at their equipment list. *High Life* is a 47-foot aluminum cutter with a family of four aboard. They sold a business before they went

cruising and had enough money to equip the boat as they pleased. The 12-year-old daughter loves to tinker and does about half the maintenance. Some of their equipment is used primarily by the two kids: for example, the second dinghy, the VCR, and the extra lights.

As Table 7-10 shows, these three boats cover the gamut in terms of electrical requirements and the cost of the equipment aboard. These costs reflect the initial purchase price of the equipment and do not include the cost of installation or ongoing maintenance.

The difference in costs between the three boats' electrical systems reflects their different electrical demands. As Table 7-11 shows, *High Life* relies on a diesel generator for charging and running the refrigerator and watermaker. She also carries four times the battery capacity that *Simplicity* does. All three boats carry solar panels for trickle charging.

Simplicity's battery capacity of 210 ampere-hours easily meets her daily demand of 52 ampere-hours (Table 7-12). *High Life* has almost unlimited, highly efficient generating capability from either the engine or the diesel generator. She has plenty of battery capacity to store the energy generated. *Moderation's* electrical balance is the most precarious. To steer with the electric pilot 24 hours a day or operate the radar for more than 4 hours, they need to run the engine for 1 to 2 extra hours each day. To stay in balance, they need to be very energy conscious. They are also aware that any additional electrical equipment will change their balance and force them to rethink their charging and storage arrangements.

Table 7-10. Comparison of the costs and electricity needs of three different boats (U.S. dollars)

| | Simplicity | | Moderation | | High Life | |
	Estimated cost	Daily energy usage[1]	Estimated cost	Daily energy usage[1]	Estimated cost	Daily energy usage[1]
Major gear	$1,750	0 Ah	$9,500	18 Ah	$22,750	72 Ah
Safety equipment	3,000	0 Ah	5,750	0 Ah	8,000	10 Ah
Navigational gear	2,000	16 Ah	8,500	52 Ah	11,000	59 Ah
Comforts and conveniences	1,250	36 Ah	6,000	42 Ah	11,750	55 Ah
Electrical system	750	—	2,500	—	11,750	—
Total	$8,750	52 Ah	$32,250	112 Ah	$65,250	196 Ah

[1] Estimated demand based on reasonable usage on passage

The three boats spend different amounts on diesel fuel to meet their energy requirements. In theory, *Simplicity* spends about $500 per year by running her engine an hour and a half every other day. In reality, *Simplicity* can meet her minor energy needs at anchor with the solar panels and by motoring in and out of anchorages every few days. *Moderation* needs to run her engine at anchor, so she spends about $700 per year on diesel for charging. Running the diesel generator for two hours every day, *High Life* spends $1,400 per year to meet her electrical demands. Her diesel bill totals over $2,000 annually for charging, motoring, and heating.

With respect to maintenance, *Simplicity's* crew spends fewer than 10 hours per week on preventive maintenance—the majority of it on keeping her sails in good shape and varnishing a few pieces of exterior teak. At haulout time, each crewmember spends about 40 hours painting her bottom and doing other out-of-water maintenance work. This includes polishing through-hulls, cleaning and greasing winches, sanding and repainting propane tanks, buffing and waxing topsides, and rebuilding the head.

Moderation's crew averages about 15 hours per week on maintenance. Sails and teak take the most time, but there also are a host of smaller chores every week: lubricating blocks and other equipment on deck, waxing the hull, replacing corroded connections, and end-for-ending lines to combat chafe. The crew tries to complete one major chore each week: rewiring an electric light, changing the engine oil, or rebuilding a water pump. At haulout time, they spend about the same amount of time as *Simplicity's* crew, but they hire someone to do the bottom painting. Their time is spent on *Simplicity's* other chores plus servicing the windlass, servicing the diesel and water heaters, rebuilding pressure and foot pumps, and servicing the autopilot. Every few months they invest a day or more locating spares for their electric bilge pump, diesel heater, or autopilot.

High Life's crew averages almost 30 hours a week keeping the boat in shape, including the time they spend getting spares through customs, hunting down parts, and talking to manufacturers and their service representatives. They spend more absolute time on sails and teak than *Simplicity* and *Moderation* because they have a larger surface area of both. However, these chores represent only about half of their maintenance hours. The generator requires maintenance as frequently as the engine, so some gets done every week. The watermaker needs to be pickled when they enter contaminated harbors. Maintaining the electrical system averages several hours a week for everything from cleaning corrosion off the battery terminals to tightening the alternator belts. At haulout time, all four of the crew put in a 40-hour week, though they pay to have the hull painted and polished and have the teak varnished.

For all of their work, *High Life* enjoys luxuries undreamed of by *Simplicity* and *Moderation*. The crew aboard *High Life* do not have to check the voltmeter before turning on the sixth light. They have almost unlimited fresh water and cold drinks. At sea, they can afford to run the radar 24 hours per day while steering

Table 7-11. Comparison of electrical systems aboard three different boats

	Simplicity	Moderation	High Life
Charging sources	80-watt solar panel	Two 80-watt solar panels	Two 80-watt solar panels
	Standard alternator on engine	125-amp alternator on engine	200-amp alternator on engine
			200-amp alternator on diesel generator
Monitoring equipment	none	Smart regulator	Smart regulator
		Battery bank monitor	Battery bank monitor
Battery bank size	210 Ah	420 Ah	840 Ah

with the electric autopilot. The VCR entertains the kids.

Where do you fit? Today *Moderation* represents the most common configuration for an offshore voyager, with variations for individual preferences. But there are dozens of *Simplicity's* out there enjoying the world's oceans. *High Life* has traditionally been a coastal or limited offshore solution because her equipment requires frequent access to boatyards and chandleries. But by the time we finished our circumnavigation, *High Life* was proving a viable voyaging option for a mechanically adept crew.

What about us? *Silk* resembled *Moderation*. Our next boat will be even simpler, though not nearly as basic as *Simplicity*. We've learned what is really important to us, and we've decided that we like to have time to smell the roses along the way.

Table 7-12. Comparison of electricity consumption and generation aboard three boats

	Simplicity	Moderation	High Life
Charging sources	80-watt solar panel	Two 80-watt solar panels	Two 80-watt solar panels
Daily electrical requirements	52 Ah	112 Ah	196 Ah
Daily electrical generation from solar panels	25 Ah	50 Ah	50 Ah
Daily energy deficit after solar panels	27 Ah	62 Ah	164 Ah
Other charging sources	1½ hours of engine every other day	1 hour of engine per day	2 hours of generator per day
Optimal battery bank size	208 Ah	448 Ah	784 Ah
Actual battery bank size	210 Ah	420 Ah	840 Ah

Additional resources

Once you have decided what equipment you want to carry aboard, you will have to decide what brand to buy. Any piece of gear you consider for offshore voyaging should come from a company with worldwide servicing capabilities and a reputation for good customer response. Take along the manufacturer's list of recommended service providers when you leave. Beyond that, the following sources can provide information to assist you in your decision making.

■ **SSCA Equipment Survey.** Every four years, the Seven Seas Cruising Association asks its members to complete an extensive questionnaire. The resulting survey covers all types of equipment—from abandon-ship kits to wind instruments. Satisfaction ratings and breakdown rates are reported by brand. Small sample sizes make some of the data questionable, but much of it offers useful insights into prod-

uct performance (see "Additional resources" in Chapter 1 for contact information).

■ *Practical Sailor.* This publication's product tests are designed to duplicate real-world conditions. They retest equipment regularly in areas where products are changing rapidly. Recent tests have included the new LCD radars and offshore e-mail systems (see "Additional resources" in Chapter 2 for contact information).

■ **West Marine.** The West Advisors in the West Marine catalog offer generally good advice on which brands are designed to meet coastal versus offshore needs. West Marine's customer service representatives go out of their way to provide useful information on their products. While they cannot be considered an unbiased source, they can help you focus in on a few specific brands that will best meet your needs. West Marine's toll-free number is 800-538-0775.

CHAPTER 8 | MOVING ABOARD

Managing space ■ *Maximizing stowage space* ■ *Organizing space* ■ *Living within your space* ■ **To stow or not to stow**
■ *What not to bring* ■ *What to bring* ■ *Additional resources*

Some of the hardest choices about outfitting your boat come *after* you've decided on your basic gear and equipment. As an offshore voyager, you have to carry everything you need to be self-sufficient for months at a time. You have to stow far more volume than what you need for coastal cruising. When you move aboard you face hundreds of small but important decisions about what to bring and what to leave behind. You will have to weigh the tradeoffs: Do you take your laptop computer or a sewing machine, scuba gear or oil paints?

Once you narrow down your choices, you will need to find stowage space where each item is accessible yet safe enough to survive a severe knockdown.

The process doesn't end. Living in a space as small as a sailboat requires continual work. You need to actively manage your stowage by reviewing your belongings, getting rid of items not being used, and reorganizing regularly.

MANAGING SPACE

To manage space efficiently aboard an offshore sailboat, you need to use every bit of available space. Before you move on board, find or create as much stowage area as possible. Get to know your boat intimately—both the designated stowage areas and the hidden spaces that can increase your storage volume. Then organize stowage spaces so you can use them efficiently.

Maximizing stowage space

Most production boats have plenty of space for the equipment, provisions, and clothing needed for coastal cruising. When we decommissioned *Silk,* we left only the coastal equipment aboard. The offshore gear we removed weighed over 2,000 pounds; removing it raised her waterline by two inches. When you head offshore, the stowage space that was adequate for coastal cruising is quickly filled.

You can create new space and make use of otherwise inaccessible spaces. You can also look for ways to make better use of the space you do have. Modifications to improve space usage range from moderately expensive interior renovations to new approaches that cost next to nothing. If you are making modifications, flexibility matters. You do not want to redesign your boat to such an extent that your new equipment is the cause of a costly, time-consuming refit. The ideas that follow are flexible and easily reversed.

Creating space

Your boat's stowage depends on her overall size, age, depth of the bilge, and the designer's ingenuity. While boats between 35 and 40 feet can carry everything a cruising couple needs, stowing those items for offshore passagemaking requires compromises and modifications to the existing boat. With a boat smaller than 35 feet, you will have more difficult decisions to make. By trading some of the interior space for stowage, you may not have to leave anything behind. The following suggestions require some interior renovations, but they should make a small or medium-sized boat capable of carrying offshore loads.

Several spaces considered standard on a production boat may not be essential for an offshore voyager. For example, if you have a small boat with a good-sized salon area that can seat four or more, that space will get limited use for entertaining. It will be used more as your lounge and passagemaking bedroom. For that you do not need a large table. You can replace the existing table with one that seats two and folds up on a bulkhead when not in use. This will open up space for additional lockers at the ends of the settees.

The shower area is frequently wasted aboard many medium-sized boats. Most people shower in the cockpit. If your boat includes a standup shower, consider modifying it for stowage. *Silk* had a space the size of a small stall shower in front of the toilet. We installed a removable rack and collapsible milk crates where we stowed fruits and vegetables at sea (Figure 8-1). The collapsible crates offered good air circulation, which kept the produce fresh, and the location allowed me to inspect for

Figure 8-1. Collapsible milk crates installed in a rack in *Silk's* head made perfect stowage for fresh fruits and vegetables.

spoilage regularly. We cleaned the crates easily with the shower head. In port, we could remove the crates and shower below if we preferred. This solution makes good use of a second head on larger boats as well.

Most boats between 35 and 40 feet have either a quarter berth or a pilot berth. In port, that space becomes a catchall for large items that don't fit anywhere else. We stowed our spare sails, a large crate of backup medical supplies, sleeping bags, and three wool blankets in *Silk's* quarter berth. At sea, these areas are needed as sea berths. We would transfer the contents of the quarter berth to the V-berth in the forepeak. We installed pad eyes under the V-berth cushions to lash everything down. Our spare sails were stowed on the floor of the forward cabin or between our salon table and a settee.

Good sea berths should be no more than 24 inches wide, but many quarter berths are as wide as 4 feet. Fitting lockers against the hull increases your stowage space and improves the usefulness of the quarter berth at sea. Make sure these lockers have no sharp edges and put some padding on the side facing the bunk. We have seen a locker for stowing foldable bikes and one for stowing charts along the side of the quarter berth.

You can also use the space between the salon table and the settee. *Silk* had limited stowage for her size because of her shallow bilge and centerboard design. When we filled the boat for six months' cruising in a major port, we put extra food in two plastic battery boxes that fit securely on the floor in this space. After a month, these stores were depleted and the extra stowage was no longer needed. The battery boxes were then stored under the V-berth with other things inside of them.

Some boats with U-shaped galleys, like the Crealock 37 and Shannon 37, have unused space over the galley island (Figure 8-2). Crealock sells an overhead locker that fits this space, but a custom unit could easily be made for any boat with this configuration. If you add a locker over the sink, consider adding a feature common in Scandinavian homes and used by Swan—an integral dish rack and plate stowage. Washed and put away, the dishes drip-dry into the sink (Figure 8-3).

Using dead space

Seek out inaccessible dead space. Create access to it or enclose the space to make it usable.

Figure 8-2. Aboard *Silk,* the area over the sink was dead space that could have been utilized by adding overhead shelves.

Figure 8-3. The galley of this Swan 47 includes a dish stowage area that doubles as a drying rack.

Lockers may hide useful space along the hull behind wooden trim pieces. Remove the trim pieces and check. In hanging lockers, the space along the curved hull behind the hanging clothes is often wasted. By adding a bracket or a shelf, you can stow anything from shoes to a spare sextant. Going one step further, shelves are a more efficient use of space than hanging lockers. You could get along without any hanging space at all, but a foot of hanging space per person allows you to stow a few nice clothes. Convert the rest of the hanging space to shelves.

Areas under or behind drawers can be usable space. Pull out all your drawers and remove any trim pieces until you see the hull or cabin sole. The space behind a drawer along the curved hull can be used to stow a few small items. A few cans can often be stowed beneath a drawer. Drawers in a row under a bunk or settee often have 6 inches of wasted space between them. Replacing the drawers with a large locker can increase the stowage in a given area by 20 percent. Make sure that the area is dry or use the new space for items that can stand an occasional dousing.

Large stowage areas under settees or V-berths are often enclosed with trim. Remove trim pieces from the bottom or sides of any locker until you reach the hull. By cutting an access hole in the bottom of a locker like this, you can often add another cubic foot of space for long-term stowage. Make sure you know where your water and fuel tanks are before you cut! Check with the manufacturer before cutting anything that looks like a box beam or structural reinforcement.

After your stowage survey, you should be able to diagram every square inch of space in your hull. While all of this space is not created equal, you will eventually find uses for most of it. To do that, you must know it is there in the first place. On *Silk,* we "found" about 10 cubic feet of space in these types of areas. By the time we left South Africa to cross our last ocean, all of that space was full.

You can also enclose areas to create stowage space. Take a hard look at areas of your boat you see every day and reconsider them as useful stowage space. Add a spice rack in the galley or a shelf for flashlights and sun-tan lotion by the companionway. Consider adding a shelf or netting at the foot of a quarter berth or pilot berth, hammocks or lockers at the foot of a V-berth, and eye hooks for hanging ditty bags in useful places. If you use hammocks or netting, don't use cotton. Nylon ones will not mold or mildew, and they can be washed frequently without rotting.

The space under the companionway stairs can be turned into useful stowage. The options range from fully enclosed drawers under each step to Velcro strips attached to the underside of a step to hold frequently used tools. Using this space can make engine access more difficult. The weight of the stowed items will also make removing the steps more cumbersome, especially at sea. But if your steps are mounted semi-permanently and the engine is accessible without removing them, you can use the steps to create some useful stowage.

Increasing space visually

The racks and hammocks and extra lockers that increase your stowage space will reduce your visual space. But you can use visual tricks to keep the boat from feeling claustrophobic.

Light makes a boat feel bigger. White on the sides of the cabin trunk and the headliner will increase the sense of space below. Light-colored upholstery (patterned so as not to show dirt) also enhances the sense of space. Increasing visual space by removing doors also makes a boat feel larger. Doors can be replaced by removable curtains to create privacy for guests.

Mirrors extend the visual plane of an area while increasing the available light. *Silk's* new owners installed a large mirror in her head that doubled the visual space. If you put mirrors aboard, use shatterproof Lexan rather than glass for safety reasons. (You'll also like how thin you look in these mirrors!)

Organizing space

The contents of a large locker emptied on a settee can make a main salon feel chaotic. In the midst of a major repair at sea, the result can be a disaster. "A place for everything and everything in its place" is nowhere more necessary than on a boat. But how do you manage to organize everything?

Weight is your first priority in deciding what goes where. Heavy things stay low and near the center of the boat. Canned goods, spare anchors, chain, heavy tools, and spare parts all need to go in the bilge or in the bottom of lockers under settee berths. Lighter spare parts, spare sails, charts, bulky galley equipment, and other items of medium weight can be stowed higher: on top of heavier items in settee berths, behind settees against the hull, or forward in V-berths. Paper goods, spare clothing, blankets, and lightweight items including foodstuffs are best stowed under pilot berths and in the lockers just beneath the deck.

It is one thing to stow everything away, but quite another to retrieve exactly what you want when you want it. The following sections cover how to maximize efficiency and accessibility without compromising the space itself.

Bulk stowage: divide and conquer

Bulk space is the most efficient but the hardest to use. To find a sail needle and some sail tape at sea, you inevitably have to remove all of the contents of a large locker and hold them in place while the boat is heeling over and pounding. Many bulk stowage areas cannot be counted on to stay dry. To improve your bulk stowage, divide the contents into useful compartments that are as watertight as possible.

You can use large, plastic stowage containers, the heavy-duty type with clear plastic covers used to organize garages and work benches, to compartmentalize bulk stowage areas. Spares and tools stow well in these containers, especially if you separate your spares into Ziploc bags with clear labels to minimize rummaging. For smaller spaces and smaller items, use Tupperware or other types of quality food-storage containers. Square containers stow more efficiently than round ones. Battery boxes fit well in the odd spaces at the bottoms of lockers near the curved hull. These can be glassed into a platform with 2-inch sides to keep them from shifting. With their tops strapped on, they make a good bottom layer under other containers.

Heavy plastic lawn and garden bags conform to odd spaces in the bottom of lockers or along the hull. Use them to stow spare hose, electrical wire, 1×19 rigging wire, and similar items. Label them with masking tape and indelible ink markers.

Line conforms to any niche and can get wet occasionally.

For small, frequently used items that may get lost in a large container, use a plastic dishpan along the edges of the opening to bulk storage lockers or the access to the bilge (Figure 8-4). These create a watertight catch-all for zip-top or ditty bags full of batteries, bulbs, tape, sewing kits, and so on. Leave the dishpan empty in one of the bilge openings to act as a dustpan, or make one specially for the space using fiberglass.

Plastic milk crates work well for stowage on the floor of a hanging locker or under the galley sink. To make this stowage temporary, use the collapsible milk crates that fold down to an inch or so high. Milk crates can also be used to stow line and other bulky items in V-berth and settee lockers. You can also use heavy canvas carry bags in these areas, but don't expect them to last forever: Canvas molds and rots after repeated exposure to water. These bags are also surprisingly bulky to stow when not being used. Carry bags made from parachute material that fold up small enough to fit inside a purse are now sold by many camping stores. Though more expensive than canvas bags, these are less prone to rot and can be cleaned if they mold.

To avoid cockroaches, never allow cardboard or paper packaging aboard. Use a selection of Tupperware containers that fit each of your food storage lockers to stow cookies, cereal, pasta, flour, rice, crackers, and just about everything else. Indelible ink labels that are visible when the locker door is open will help you find what you need without emptying the locker. Ask your favorite restaurant to save you some 2-gallon

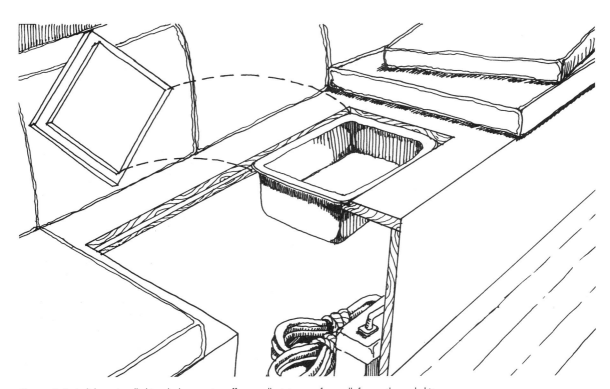

Figure 8-4. A dishpan installed in a locker opening offers excellent stowage for small, frequently needed items.

mayonnaise containers. These make wonderful stowage containers for bulk foods.

Beyond the horizontal bulk stowage areas under berths and in the bilge, most stowage is vertical. If you open a locker door or remove a fiddle, the contents of the locker will end up in your lap if the boat is rolling. All such lockers, even those with doors, should have moderately small openings equipped with fiddles that will hold

Figure 8-5. The lockers behind the settees on board *Silk* had relatively small openings that helped to hold the contents in place—even when we rummaged through them in a rolly sea.

contents while you rummage for what you need (Figure 8-5). Alternatively, canvas covers that snap over lockers can be opened a few snaps at a time (Figure 8-6).

Long shelves for CDs, cassettes, or VCR tapes with one fiddle do not work well. If one fiddle holds several dozen CDs in, they will all end up on the cabin sole when you remove the fiddle to get one out. If a shelf is not full, prop up books or CDs so they don't fall over and slide out under the fiddle. Partition shelves meant to stow large numbers of items or set them up so one item can be removed without removing the fiddle. Alternatively, create an adjustable bookend using dowels inserted into holes drilled into the shelf (Figure 8-7).

Fit hanging lockers or other lockers with large, hinged doors with means of stowage on the inside of the door. The canvas pockets used to store shoes make a good home for a variety of small items that would be lost in a large locker. However, locker ventilation has to take precedence over stowage, so be careful not to cover the caning or ventilation slots.

Zippered pillow cases meant for throw pillows can stow a variety of bulky items while providing color and comfort on bunks. You can store clothes for cold weather, including wool sweaters, thermal underwear, and foul-weather gear in pillow cases. On some boats, the bedding for each bunk is stowed in these pillow cases during the day.

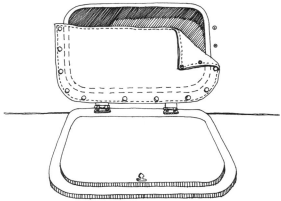

Figure 8-6. Canvas covers with snaps can be placed over locker openings to hold contents while allowing access.

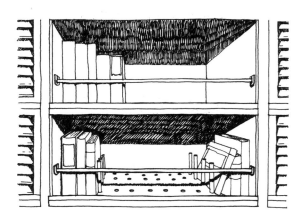

Figure 8-7. An adjustable bookend and a fiddle arrangement that allows you to remove one item in a bookshelf without losing all of them will save you many hours of frustration.

The cockpit locker: organize and prioritize

On most boats, the cockpit locker is the biggest organizational challenge. This locker holds the largest, bulkiest items—many of which must be accessible for emergency use. The batteries and engine transmission are often accessed through this locker. Some of the items stowed require special care: gasoline or diesel fuel, batteries, spare anchors, and so on. You need to be able to keep the locker open while you work. Shock cord attached to the lid of the cockpit locker with a loop that can be flipped over a winch or onto a cleat can prevent a broken finger or even a head injury.

Docklines and spare anchor lines need to be accessible at a moment's notice. But unless they are well organized, they will turn the cockpit locker into a nightmare. A board installed under the lip of the opening and fitted with shock cord for hanging lines prevents cruisers' spaghetti from forming in the bottom of the locker (Figure 8-8).

Fenders are bulky and difficult to stow. We had six large fenders aboard, and when inflated they would not fit anywhere. Still, fenders must be accessible to be useful. We compromised by carrying them on the stern pulpit (Figure 8-9), which is a fairly common solution. A dedicated area to stow fenders, lines, and perhaps sails becomes possible on boats over 40 feet. On *Emily,* a custom-built, 45-foot aluminum cutter, lines and fenders can be secured to the rod above the anchor locker or to metal hooks in the locker wells and still be accessible from the deck through a hatch (Figure 8-10).

Chocks should be installed to hold spare anchors securely in place within the cockpit locker. To stow an outboard engine or gasoline, partition off an area of the locker without electrical equipment and install an overboard drain. On most boats under 40 feet, the cockpit locker is too small to make this feasible. The outboard engine is then stowed on the stern pulpit. Gasoline is lashed on deck, preferably in a shady area. Diesel, being less volatile than gasoline, can be stowed in the bottom of the cockpit locker.

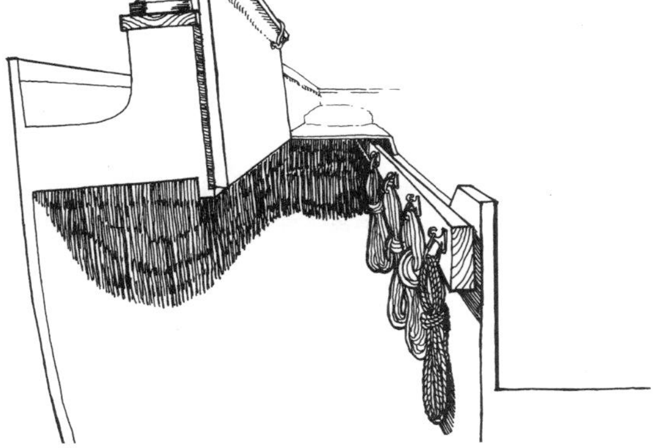

Figure 8-9. On *Silk,* we stowed our fenders on the stern pulpit. This is a less-than-perfect solution but one of the only ways to deal with large fenders on boats under 40 feet.

Figure 8-10. For boats over 40 feet, the chain locker may be modified to create excellent and accessible stowage for lines and fenders.

Figure 8-8. A good solution for storing line in a cockpit locker is a board with shock cord installed below the lip of the locker.

Electrical cords and hoses get less use offshore than they do when coastal cruising. Stow them below in the bottom of a settee or V-berth locker. Keep some sort of a drogue or warp for heavy weather readily accessible in the cockpit locker. This may be a used tire, several hundred feet of line, or a specially made series or parachute drogue.

The little things: ready at hand

The smallest items on board are often appropriated by the ship's gremlins and found months later under a cushion or in the bilge. Some of these items must be accessible (e.g., everyday tools, suntan lotion, seasickness medications), but their size makes them least likely to be found if stowed in a large locker. To keep track of these things, dedicate some space to organizing them—even at the cost of stowage efficiency.

Suntan lotion, binoculars, and flashlights should be accessible from the cockpit or the bottom of the companionway. A shelf along the bulkhead next to the companionway keeps these items in reach, or use ditty bags hung from padeyes on either side of the companionway. Stow flashlights and more delicate equipment in a drawer at the base of the companionway.

Do not leave port without a full range of seasickness medicines within reach from the bottom of the companionway. On our first offshore passage, we made the mistake of leaving our seasickness medications in our medical kit, stowed at the bottom of a hanging locker near the bow. When we got into a gale, we were too seasick to get to the medications. Thereafter we stowed our seasickness medications in a Ziploc bag in the navigation station.

Sunglasses and eyeglasses can pose a real challenge. If you have several people aboard who wear both, you will quickly end up with a half-dozen or more pairs that require an accessible but safe stowage place. Mount a labeled canvas eyeglass holder on a bulkhead near the companionway (Figure 8-11).

The canisters that hold 35-mm film are great for stowing small items like pills, coins, sewing accessories, fishing lures, keys, cotter pins, and so on. To keep track of what is inside, buy Fuji film for their clear canisters or label the opaque ones with indelible ink markers on masking tape. Stow these in a dishpan or

Tupperware, or in a dedicated rack located just under the lip of a vertical locker (Figure 8-12).

Sail ties need to be accessible, but they seem to disappear like socks in the dryer. A net bag attached to the underside of the cockpit locker hatch offers dry and accessible stowage. You can adapt similar bags or buy specialty bags to hold the tail ends of sheets and halyards. Not only can trailing lines be annoying, but they can be dangerous in heavy weather if they roll underfoot or if they loop around an ankle.

Ditty bags from camping stores offer an all-purpose solution for keeping track of small items. We ordered several dozen of these nylon bags in a variety of sizes and used them for everything from our sewing kit to spare toothbrushes. We preferred the fine-weave mesh ones; they offered ventilation in case the contents got damp, and we could see through them enough to figure out what was inside without opening them.

Finally, Ziploc bags in all available sizes are indispensable. We used Ziploc bags for everything from stowing flour and sugar within larger plastic containers to keeping sweaters smelling sweet for several months in the tropics. They are unavailable outside the United

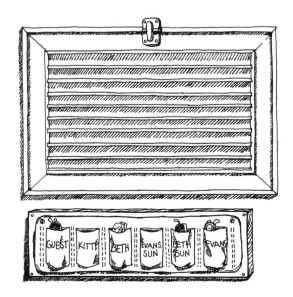

Figure 8-11. A bulkhead-mounted canvas holder is one excellent way to keep eyeglasses organized and accessible.

Figure 8-12. A small rack can be fit just inside a locker to hold 35-mm film canisters.

States and Europe. Most voyagers guard their Ziploc bags tenaciously and even wash and reuse them.

The stowage plan

Keeping track of everything aboard is a monumental task. You may be able to remember where everything is on a 35-foot boat, but on boats over 40 feet, a stowage plan will help tremendously.

Silk had many small stowage areas rather than a few large ones. We could separate things by area, so we did not feel the need for a formal stowage plan. Based on the layout shown in Figure 8-13, we always knew where to start looking for something. Most boats under 40 feet used this approach.

Larger boats require more formal stowage plans. Joe and Kathy Möeller have the most comprehensive stowage plan imaginable on their Slocum 43 *Windscape.* A number is written on each locker and on an enlarged copy of the boat layout. A spreadsheet lists every item aboard with its location by locker number. From this spreadsheet the Möellers generate two lists: a list of each locker's contents and an alphabetical list of items.

Your own plan may fall somewhere between our approach and the Möellers' and will depend on how organized you tend to be. At the very least, most cruisers agree on names for each stowage space. When asked by a crewmember where an item is, the crew can offer a specific location and avoid confusion.

Living within your space

Managing your stowage spaces is a continual process. You will refine your arrangement after you head offshore and learn which items must be most accessible. You will also acquire things as you travel: souvenirs, shells, line from replaced running rigging, spare parts stripped from broken gear, and so on.

Every few months during the first year, evaluate your stowage arrangements. You made most of these decisions before you left, and you will modify many of them as you adjust to life aboard. Carefully reconsider whether infrequently used equipment or items you use three times a day are in the best places.

After living with our stowage arrangement for six weeks, I reorganized the lockers around the galley, where the items I used most at sea were not accessible. I added a cache of flour in a galley locker with enough flour to make four loaves of bread, reorganized my condiments so I could get to a few critical ones without fully opening the sliding locker door, converted a drawer into a spice rack, and reorganized my pans into two lockers (one for daily use and one for occasional use). These changes made cooking on passage easier.

Even after you get the basics right, set aside one day every six months to review your stowage. You will always find ways to improve your arrangement.

Make an effort to get rid of unnecessary items. Gear expands to fill the usable space on board. The smaller your boat is, the more acute the situation will be. We used the following three rules on *Silk* to keep our priorities straight.

■ *An item that has not been used in six months must be sold or sent home.* With the exception of safety equipment, we got rid of anything we weren't using. Evans never wore his dressier cloths, so we shipped them home and never missed them. I hadn't used our pressure cooker in many months, so we sold it in New Zealand to another cruising couple.

■ *The stowage space for new gear must be paid for with other gear.* If we wanted to bring a new item aboard (anything larger than a book), something of equal size had to be taken off the boat. To do this, we had to make hard tradeoffs. When I bought a laptop

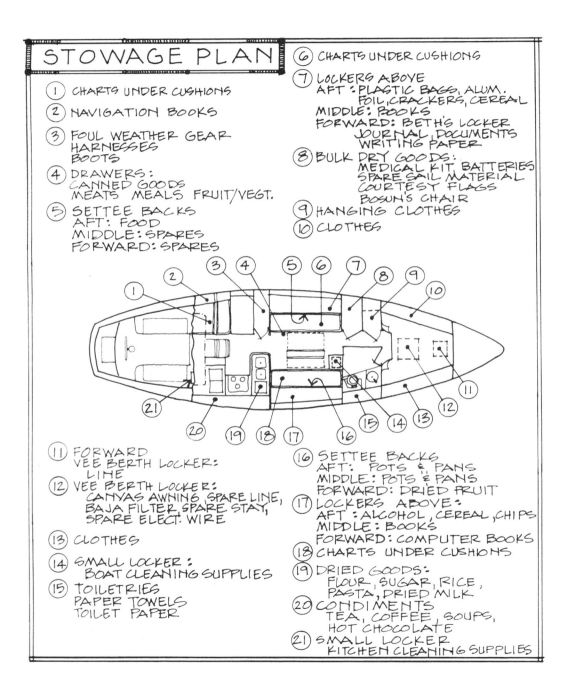

STOWAGE PLAN

1. CHARTS UNDER CUSHIONS
2. NAVIGATION BOOKS
3. FOUL WEATHER GEAR
   HARNESSES
   BOOTS
4. DRAWERS:
   CANNED GOODS
   MEATS MEALS FRUIT/VEGT.
5. SETTEE BACKS
   AFT: FOOD
   MIDDLE: SPARES
   FORWARD: SPARES

6. CHARTS UNDER CUSHIONS
7. LOCKERS ABOVE
   AFT: PLASTIC BAGS, ALUM.
      FOIL, CRACKERS, CEREAL
   MIDDLE: BOOKS
   FORWARD: BETH'S LOCKER
      JOURNAL, DOCUMENTS
      WRITING PAPER
8. BULK DRY GOODS:
   MEDICAL KIT BATTERIES
   SPARE SAIL MATERIAL
   COURTESY FLAGS
   BOSUN'S CHAIR
9. HANGING CLOTHES
10. CLOTHES

11. FORWARD
    VEE BERTH LOCKER:
       LINE
12. VEE BERTH LOCKER:
    CANVAS AWNING, SPARE LINE,
    BAJA FILTER, SPARE STAY,
    SPARE ELECT. WIRE
13. CLOTHES
14. SMALL LOCKER:
    BOAT CLEANING SUPPLIES
15. TOILETRIES
    PAPER TOWELS
    TOILET PAPER

16. SETTEE BACKS
    AFT: POTS & PANS
    MIDDLE: POTS & PANS
    FORWARD: DRIED FRUIT
17. LOCKERS ABOVE:
    AFT: ALCOHOL, CEREAL, CHIPS
    MIDDLE: BOOKS
    FORWARD: COMPUTER BOOKS
18. CHARTS UNDER CUSHIONS
19. DRIED GOODS:
    FLOUR, SUGAR, RICE,
    PASTA, DRIED MILK
20. CONDIMENTS
    TEA, COFFEE, SOUPS,
    HOT CHOCOLATE
21. SMALL LOCKER
    KITCHEN CLEANING SUPPLIES

Figure 8-13. *Silk's* stowage areas were compartmentalized so we could stow items by area and not risk losing track of things.

computer in New Zealand, I didn't mind giving up my manual typewriter. But when we added a second hank-on sail in New Zealand, we debated for a week before we agreed to give up the sailing rig for our dinghy.

■ *Souvenirs are not allowed to live aboard.* I loved buying baskets, tapa cloth, molas, and local jewelry. Aside from the space issue, most of these items are made from plant or animal products and create problems with customs. Whenever postage was inexpensive, we mailed our souvenirs to our families.

These three rules, used in conjunction with rearranging your stowage once or twice a year, will help you live comfortably within your space.

TO STOW OR NOT TO STOW

This section covers what to bring along and what to leave at home. Tips for stowing and caring for various items in a humid, salty, and damp home are included.

What not to bring

A list of the items we determined *not* useful to have on board may be more helpful than a list of those we kept aboard. When we left, we struggled to find room for some large items that we later abandoned along the way. This list reflects our choices, but the reasons why may help you make your own list.

Bicycles sound like a terrific way to reach grocery stores and sightsee on faraway islands. But bicycles do not survive well on board. Even the marine folding bikes take up a great deal of stowage space. Brake and shift components are susceptible to rust from salt air. Bikes are cumbersome to get ashore, and forks and gears pose a major hazard to inflatable dinghies. When you do get them ashore, you will often find rocky, overgrown trails suited only for high-performance mountain bikes. No one we knew who left with bicycles still had them aboard at the end of a circumnavigation. A bicycle might be worth the effort if you voyage only in developed areas in Europe, the United States, the Caribbean, New Zealand, or Australia. In these areas, you can also purchase a bike for your stay and then sell it when you leave.

Sail repair alone does not justify the stowage space for a sewing machine on boats under 40 feet. Outside the United States and Europe, sail repair was our most reasonable marine expense. We had all five of our working sails reconditioned in Antigua. Broken stitches were repaired, worn areas were reinforced, and patches were applied for just over $100. Most of the sail repairs we did ourselves were hand-stitch jobs that did not justify getting the sewing machine out of stowage for. When we left with a sewing machine, we envisioned making our own clothes and courtesy flags, repairing our sails, and doing canvas work. We sold the machine less than a year later. We had not done any of those things, and we desperately needed the space for something else. Friends of ours who used their machines for these tasks kept their machines on board.

A number of materials do not do well aboard, and you should avoid them if possible. Leather molds quickly and is best left at home. Our leather belts and boots were covered with a layer of green mold after a few months in the tropics. If you want to have leather aboard, stow it in a Ziploc bag with a mildew control product. Apply Vaseline on any buckles or snaps to prevent corrosion.

Humidity causes down to clump, reducing its insulating properties. With the new fleece materials and old-fashioned wool, down is not essential aboard. If you want to carry a down jacket or sleeping bag, stow it in heavy plastic sealed against moisture. Air it out thoroughly every few months.

All but the toughest metals corrode from salt air and occasional exposure to salt water. Mild steel is most vulnerable to corrosion, and it is used in the least obvious places. The contacts on many pieces of electrical equipment are made from mild steel. We had a hand-held tape recorder, a Sony Walkman, numerous flashlights, and a camera flash fail beyond repair due to corrosion on battery or switch contacts. While corrosion is unavoidable in electrical equipment at sea, you can minimize the likelihood of failures. Don't buy electrical equipment with contacts that look cheap and flimsy. Don't store batteries in electrical equipment that is not used on a daily basis. Clean the contacts monthly, regardless of how much the equipment is used.

You will also find mild steel in items that are mostly stainless: nail clippers, zippers, graters, poor quality silverware, belt buckles, fasteners, and can openers, to name some. The little springs in barrel bolts or flashlights are often made of mild steel. All of these items will rust, and many will fail completely. Inspect everything you bring aboard. Use a magnet to test that the metal is stainless. If it isn't, beware of nasty rust stains and store these items where they won't damage something more valuable.

Aluminum works as well as stainless steel, as long as it is not in contact with other metals. Corrosion caused by mixed metals occurred in a wide variety of seemingly indestructible items. The stainless steel blades of our Swiss Army knives were hinged with an aluminum pin, which corroded within two months to the point where the knives were locked shut and totally useless. A small, invisible component can prove to be aluminum and cause corrosion in eyeglasses, zippers, fasteners, and utensils. Even when not in contact with other metals, aluminum will oxidize. You will have to clean the white dust from the object once in a while.

The corrosive environment can damage precious metals. Leave your gold and silver jewelry, pearls, and gemstones at home. Shell jewelry provides plenty of decoration and better reflects your new lifestyle.

What to bring

After the short list of the things not worth bringing, the laundry list of what to bring seems overwhelming. Most boats over 35 feet, however, find room for all of this and more. A combination of ingenuity and persistence yields

The most personal of decisions: firearms aboard

Carrying guns is one of the most contentious issues among offshore voyagers. About one-third of the voyagers we met did carry firearms. Evans and I both enjoyed target shooting before we went sailing, but neither of us felt that guns were appropriate aboard. Before you make your own decision, consider the following points.

If you carry guns, you are supposed to declare them when you clear customs. In many countries, guns will be confiscated by customs officials and returned only when you leave. Flare guns and spear guns may be confiscated as well. If you do not declare your guns and they are found in a search, you have broken the law. At minimum, you will be warned and fined. In many countries, your boat can be impounded and you can be thrown into jail. Outside the port captain's office in Port Klang, Malaysia, a sign reads, "Mandatory death sentence for unlawful possession of firearms!"

Most cruisers who carry guns are worried about pirates. Over the course of our three-year circumnavigation, we never met anyone who had encountered pirates. We never heard of a single instance where a gun helped in a questionable situation, but we heard of two instances where unarmed bandits got control of the ship's gun and used it on the crew.

We also heard of several situations where a gun was almost used on local people who were only trying to be hospitable. When language and customs differ, intentions can be easily misinterpreted. Someone with a gun aboard might have reacted differently in the tense situation circumnavigator Scott Kuhner recounts.

"We were in Indonesia. We had just dropped anchor behind a reef after an overnight sail when we were approached by one of the local fishing boats. The men on board were dressed completely in black—long-sleeved black shirts and long trousers, with black ski masks over their heads. They steamed straight to our boat, tied their boat to ours, and jumped aboard before we could react. I started screaming at them to get off my boat, and they started screaming back in their own language. They looked menacing, and I didn't know what they wanted.

"Then Kitty appeared in the companionway. She held out three Coca-Colas and a pack of cigarettes. The tension was instantly broken. They removed their ski masks and accepted the gifts with big grins. We later found out that many of the fisherman in the area wore ski masks to protect themselves from the sun. These guys were just curious fishermen who had finished their night's fishing and stopped by to give us some of their catch."

Having a gun aboard is a personal decision. If you do decide to carry firearms, be absolutely certain before using them in fear or anger.

results. If all else fails, you too can store some of the lighter but bulkier items in the pilot berth or quarter berth and move them into the forepeak during passages.

Deck gear

Deck equipment is bulky and difficult to stow, but it needs to be accessible. In addition to the suggestions for organizing the cockpit locker, the following ideas will help you stow the items in Table 8-1.

■ *Snorkels, masks, and fins.* Aside from entertainment, snorkel gear allows you to check the anchor and free it if it gets fouled. It is prone to mold and mildew and should be rinsed with fresh water at least once a week. We initially stowed our snorkel gear in a canvas bag in the cockpit locker, but the bag rotted within six months at sea. A large polypropylene bag purchased from a company that specialized in space management solutions (Figure 8-14) worked extremely well and lasted for over two years. Others used large nylon net bags available from marine stores.

■ *Hatchboards.* When we purchased *Silk,* she came with a set of teak hatchboards. These gave us privacy but not ventilation or a visual connection with the cockpit.

In New Zealand, we had a pair of Lexan hatchboards built with a ventilation scoop and found these to be a big improvement (Figure 8-15). We continued to use the teak hatchboards when leaving the boat so that our navigation equipment wasn't visible from outside. Both sets of hatchboards must be stowed when not in use; a specially designed shelf near the companionway or a flat canvas bag that snaps to the bulkhead are two possibilities.

■ *Dinghy oars.* These are cumbersome and difficult to store. Most people end up lashing them on deck somewhere. A spare set of oars must also be stowed aboard. A set of aluminum oars that can be taken apart are much easier to stow than wooden ones.

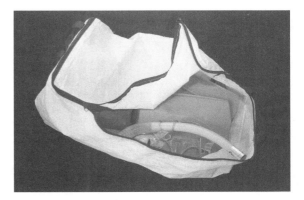

Figure 8-14. Our snorkel gear stowed well in this heavy-duty polypropylene storage bag.

Figure 8-15. Our Lexan hatchboards allowed visual contact between the off-watch and the on-watch person and permitted some ventilation, even in storm conditions. Figure 11-10, page 205, details how the ventilation scoop worked.

Table 8-1. Deck gear for the offshore voyager

Stowage challenges	Other	Special stowage requirements
Snorkels, masks, fins	Swim ladder	Outboard engine
Hatchboards	Two buckets with lanyards	Gasoline
Dinghy oars and spares	Good cockpit cushions	
Harbor awning	Wind scoops	
Large fenders	Dinghy step	
Docklines, spare halyards, etc.	Solar shower	
Spare anchors	Freshwater hose	
Stern anchor and rode	Electrical cord for shore power	
Baja filter		

■ *Harbor awnings.* A large awning that covers not only the cockpit but also the cabin trunk right to the mast will keep the boat's interior cool in the tropics. In 100-degree heat, *Silk* would stay 10 to 15 degrees cooler below when our harbor awning was shading her cabintop (Figure 8-16). With the awning up, we could keep the main hatch, companionway, and some ports open for ventilation, even when it rained. We resorted to the quarter berth to stow this large piece of canvas and its aluminum tube. Smaller awnings that cover individual hatches provide good ventilation and present less of a stowage challenge.

■ *Baja filter.* While troublesome to stow, a Baja filter protects your engine from contaminated fuel. These filters can even remove water from diesel. They are an odd shape and take up a significant amount of room. They are best stowed in the bilge, protected by a heavy plastic bag.

■ *Line.* We had well over 1,000 feet of line stowed aboard in addition to our anchor rodes. This was a bit extreme, but a 35-foot boat needs at least 500 feet: four 30-foot dock lines, one 150-foot stern line, one 100-foot spare halyard, two 30-foot spare sheets, one 30-foot spinnaker sheet, and a few spares for running rigging. If you add the four 125-foot continuous lines we used for the Panama Canal, you come to the 1,000 feet we had aboard. Storing all this line consumes a considerable amount of space. Line was a major component in three of our largest lockers.

■ *Buckets.* Buckets are used for everything from washing the deck to laundering clothes. A bucket meets offshore specifications if it can be dragged through the water behind the boat at seven knots without breaking. Plastic buckets with small wire handles do not pass this test. Black rubber horse buckets work wonderfully. Our one large and two small buckets made it all the way around the world, which may be a bucket record. They also made great laundry buckets: The water got positively hot when we left them all day in the sun. They leave black marks on fiberglass if they rub against the cabintop on passage. Stow them in a locker when not in use. Five-gallon wallboard compound buckets also live up to the rigors of life at sea.

■ *Cockpit cushions.* When we left, Evans did not want to take the cockpit cushions that came with the boat. He thought we would lose them in the first big wave. We never lost our cushions. They proved to be essential for backsides that were tired from hours of sitting on passage.

■ *Solar shower.* We had an engine-driven water heater, but a solar shower was a better solution in the tropics. Hot water was available on demand—not just when we had been running the engine. The shower nozzle provided more pressure than our handheld shower heads. We also used the solar shower to heat water for dishes when we weren't running the engine.

Tools and spares

You will need a wider range of tools and spares than the supply you would take on a coastal cruise. An exhaustive list of the items to include can be found in the next chapter. The following paragraphs offer a few stowage guidelines. Tools and spares took up almost half of our readily available stowage space in the main salon. To meet this organizational challenge, we divided these items into four categories.

■ *Basic tools and spares.* We used these almost daily in port or at sea. Most boats carry a set of frequently used tools in a navigation station drawer or in a bracket near the companionway. These include an adjustable wrench, a few of the most commonly used box wrenches, straight and Phillips-head screwdrivers, and a pair of adjustable pliers. Having these few tools available will save you dozens of trips into the main tool chest. We stored a few frequently used supplies with these basic tools, including silicone or Teflon spray, sail tape, light bulbs, spare batteries, duct tape, and electrical tape.

■ *Electrical troubleshooting kit.* You will use this kit many times each week; stowing it in an accessible place will save you time and frustration. The kit should include an electrical multimeter, a good crimper, heat-shrink tubing, and electrical connectors. We stowed these in a nylon mesh ditty bag at the front of one of our large lockers.

■ *Emergency tools and supplies.* If you experience a dismasting, you will need immediate access to a hack-

Figure 8-16. *Silk's* harbor awning provided ventilation in tropical rain storms and kept her significantly cooler below in the tropical sun.

saw and good bolt cutters (hydraulic, if you can afford them). Stow these somewhere near the companionway in a relatively dry place where you can reach them in a few seconds. We stowed ours in a locker in the navigation seat that also housed our Edson high-capacity bilge pump. You should also carry a length of 1×19 stainless steel wire the length of your longest stay. This can be difficult to stow, but it will usually fit coiled in a settee or V-berth locker. Underwater epoxy and hull repair materials should be readily accessible.

■ *Heavy-duty tool box and long-term spares.* This should include a full range of special situation tools and an extensive set of wrenches and sockets. It can be stowed in a less accessible place, but it must be low in the boat. You will need to reach the tool box on passage, in case a major repair needs to be done underway. Spare parts to be stowed as long-term items include rebuild kits for foot and pressure pumps, most engine spares, electrical wire, hoses, and additional 1×19 stain-

less steel wire for rigging repairs. Put them in Ziploc bags and stow in plastic containers low in the boat.

You will also need to stow a variety of cleaning supplies. We stowed dish detergent, laundry detergent, glass cleaner, a multipurpose cleaner, bleach, and Soft Scrub in a locker in the galley. A second small locker held all the boat-specific cleaning and maintenance supplies, including silicone caulk, 5200 sealant, solvents, fiberglass cleaner and polish, and several types of grease. Do not stow rags or paper with these materials, since many are flammable.

Navigation needs

Paper charts take up a tremendous amount of space. A stack of charts for a year of offshore voyaging may be an inch thick. They must be kept dry and, if stowed flat, they need to be kept somewhere where they will not get wrinkled or ripped. Only the largest boats have dedicated chart drawers. How do the rest of us manage?

Most offshore voyagers stow their charts under the cushions on settees or V-berths. To keep them dry, we put them in "chart slickers"—large vinyl envelopes meant to protect charts from spray when used in the cockpit, available from marine retailers. We stowed all our charts in chart slickers, even those in our navigation station. We could stow as many as a dozen charts in one slicker under a settee cushion.

Charts can also be stowed rolled in specially made lockers. We saw several innovative chart lockers built into the sides of too-wide quarter berths.

We kept enough charts aboard for one year of travel, and sold and traded the others as we went along. If you want to keep your charts, send home a stack when you finish crossing an ocean. Aside from charts, the navigation station should be equipped with plotters, dividers, pencils, pens, erasers, a log book, and a calculator. Stow your ship's papers, passports, and other official documents in a watertight envelope. Find a hiding place for these items when you leave the boat.

The sextant and your ship's library will take up a large shelf. The sextant needs to be stowed in its case for protection. The navigation shelf should include the following books:

■ **Ocean Passages for the World *or* World Cruising Routes.** You will use these books to plan your route for each passage. *Ocean Passages for the World,* issued by the British Admiralty, originally gave information and recommended routes for clipper ships. It has been updated for engine-driven vessels, which makes it less useful for sailors. *World Cruising Routes* (International Marine and Adlard Coles Nautical, 1995) by Jimmy Cornell takes the information from *Ocean Passages for the World* and adapts it to the needs of modern sailboats.

■ **Sight Reduction Tables for Air Navigation, Volumes 1–3, *and the current Almanac.*** To use your sextant, you need to carry the tables to reduce the sights and find your position. The Air Tables are the easiest. Carry something you are comfortable using, even if you carry a celestial calculator.

■ *Tide tables.* You will need tide tables for the areas you intend to visit. Ocean guides are available through the government or marine book retailers. Four books cover the world. Purchasing one book for any given year will get you across an ocean.

■ *Cruising guides and coast pilots.* Cruising guides to local areas offer detailed harbor sketches and valuable information on facilities and customs procedures. These guides change constantly. The SSCA, Royal Yachting Association (RYA), and Cruising Association bulletins often mention useful guides and give additional, up-to-date information for a given area. Coast pilots offer detailed information on coastal features. Both DMA and the British Admiralty create volumes that cover the world. They are especially useful where no cruising guides exist.

■ *General boating book.* The U.S. Coast Guard requires that you carry something that outlines the rules of the road for seagoing vessels. In addition, you will want a quick reference for light configurations at night. A general-purpose handbook, such as *Chapman Piloting* (60th edition, Hearst Marine, 1991) or *The Annapolis Book of Seamanship* (Simon & Schuster, 1989), offers valuable information while satisfying the Coast Guard requirement. In the U.K. and Europe, an annual nautical almanac, such as Macmillan's, will serve you well. Marine retailers also sell plastic-coated quick reference cards that summarize light configurations and rules of the road.

Any papers that you want to keep in good condition should be stored in plastic page protectors and kept in three-ring notebooks. Stationery stores sell plastic envelopes that can be closed with a snap. These can be used to protect important papers in the dinghy or in the navigation station.

After you enter a new country and clear customs, you must fly the country's flag from your starboard spreader for as long as you remain in the nation's waters. With the exception of France, most countries take courtesy flags very seriously. Courtesy flags are available from marine retailers and are advertised in the back of sailing magazines. They are expensive, so many people bring material and hand-paint or sew their own flags. In some cases, you can buy flag material when you arrive, hem it, and have a flag for less than a dollar. We made a Spanish flag this way in the Canaries. The small island nations tend to be most concerned about courtesy flags. Their designs are often complex ones that would be hard to paint or sew. You will probably have to buy the dozen or so complicated flags of the Caribbean nations.

Galley equipment

Galley equipment can be bulky, but it is also relatively light, so it can be stowed more easily than many of the items already considered. More always seems better, but you can carry minimum equipment and still have enough flexibility to serve up to eight people. We carried the equipment in Table 8-2 and used it for the two of us most of the time. We also used it to prepare and serve a complete Christmas dinner for eight.

The following comments offer some insight into equipment requirements for a galley.

■ *Pressure cookers.* The value of a pressure cooker depends on your diet and your galley. We started with one and did not find it useful. Other voyagers swore that it was the only piece of galley equipment they could not live without. Our diet revolved around pasta and rice, which can't be prepared in the pressure cooker because the starch clogs the vent. About half the people who loved their pressure cookers did not have ovens. They used the pressure cooker to prepare meat and bread. The other half often ate stews and other meat dishes made in a pressure cooker. If you do not have an oven, you will want a pressure cooker. If you do, consider how many meals you regularly eat ashore could be prepared in a pressure cooker before investing in one.

■ *An 8-quart soup pot.* This served as our catchall bowl and stew pot. I used it to mix bread and cookie dough, boil corn, boil lobsters, make soup, and for anything else that involved large quantities of food. The concentrated, high-heat flames of marine stoves are hard to regulate, and they are punishing to pots and pans. Good pots stand up to the abuse better than cheap ones do. All pans aboard should be made of high quality stainless steel with aluminum or copper cladding on the bottom. Teflon tends to rust quickly if washed in salt water and should be avoided.

■ *Heavy stainless steel cookie sheet.* Most high quality marine ovens come with a flat, heavy-gauge, stainless steel sheet. This spreads the heat from the small flame area in the oven to cook things more evenly. I found that bread baked on this sheet cooked from the bottom up, but the top did not get crisp without the bottom burning. Without the sheet, the top grew crisp but the bread did not cook through. I used this sheet for part of the baking period, for everything from bread to

Table 8-2. Minimal galley equipment for the offshore voyager

Pots and pans	Cooking equipment	Dishware	Utensils
Large frying pan	Cutting board that fits into sink	Three nesting stainless steel bowls	Complete silverware set
8-quart soup pot	Plastic sifter	Full dish set for eight	Assorted kitchen knives
2-quart saucepan	Stainless steel grater	Four large, stackable mugs	Assorted wooden spoons
1-quart saucepan	Lemon juicer	Eight shatterproof glasses	Perforated serving spoon
9-inch square casserole	Plastic garlic press	Folding dish rack	Measuring spoons
6-inch square casserole	Hand beater or wire whisk		Stainless steel kitchen shears
Plastic colander	Measuring cups		Bottle opener and corkscrew
Two standard bread pans	Salt and pepper shakers		Ice pick
10-inch coated aluminum pie plate	Pot holders		Manual can opener
Heavy stainless steel cookie sheet	Butane barbecue lighter		Vegetable peeler
Heavy duty large tea kettle			
Vacuum flask			

casseroles. If your oven is not equipped with such a stainless sheet and cooks unevenly, try to buy one or have one made. Even with the cookie sheet, I had to rotate things halfway through.

■ *Tea kettle.* Tea kettles get a great deal of hard use aboard. Buy one the same quality as your pans that can be opened to be cleaned. The minerals in the water from various places will create a scale. To remove it, scrub the tea kettle occasionally with vinegar.

■ *Pot holders.* Once you leave the United States, you will not see another heavy-duty, flame-retardant pot holder. Before you leave, buy the barbecue style that goes high up the arm. The wire racks in marine stoves get far hotter than those ashore. On several occasions I have burned through the material of lesser mitts when trying to pull the rack out.

■ *Plates, bowls, coffee cups, etc.* Whether you choose stoneware or marine plastic plates, you want stackable dishes that take up as little room as possible. Make sure that every piece of your dish set has some sort of nonskid on the bottom, such as a layer of dried rubber cement. Line shelves used to store glasses or dishes with nonskid fabric to reduce the likelihood of breakage. For heavy weather, you will use either a mug or bowl for everything on the menu—make sure yours are large enough to hold a dinner. For storing dishes, peg boards with dowels offer flexibility. (See Figure 8-7.)

■ *Knives.* Buy less expensive brands and replace them more often. We started out with top-of-the-line chef's knives, and within a few months large chips were coming out of the blades when we tried to sharpen them. We replaced them with the less expensive laser knives in stainless steel, and these held up remarkably well. When they lost their edge after a year or more, we threw them away and bought another set. Make sure that knife storage is enclosed to prevent flying blades during a knockdown. We tried a magnetic knife holder on the inside of a locker door. We never knew where the knives would be when we opened the locker. A drawer offers the safest solution, but put them in a rack or holder so that you don't cut yourself when searching for a wooden spoon.

■ *Silverware.* When rolling in a big sea, knives, forks, and spoons can make a racket that will wake the dead.

We fashioned simple wooden blocks that fit tightly into our drawer with slits in them. Our silverware stacked in the slits and were held firmly in place. This reduced the noise to bearable levels.

■ *Salt and pepper mills.* No perfect solution exists for dispensing salt and pepper aboard a boat at sea. After trying many alternatives, we found that a plastic shaker with a closable lid proved best for salt. With a dozen or so grains of rice mixed in, the salt remained pourable for a minimum of several weeks. After a month or so, the salt would be so damp that we had to empty out the shaker, wash it thoroughly, and dry it for a day or two before starting over again. We kept two shakers aboard and alternated them. Peppercorns keep better than ground pepper, but pepper mills are frequently made with mild steel. Buy a high quality pepper mill made with stainless and make a cover to fit over the bottom when not in use. The cover greatly extended the life of the pepper and kept ground pepper from getting all over the locker.

■ *Can opener.* Few things are standard from country to country, and can sizes are no exception. We went through three standard American can openers. All of them broke because the lips on European cans were wider than the lips on American cans. We finally found a solution in a Swiss can opener that opens the can along the lip below the top. These are called Lifter Can Openers and are now available from marine retailers.

Beyond galley equipment, consider adding other eating and drinking essentials to your boat. If you are eating in the cockpit on passage, a drink holder leaves your hands free to manage your plate. Locate your spice rack so it is not near the heat of the oven or in direct sunlight; heat and sun will greatly reduce the life of your spices. A spice rack mounted inside a drawer or cupboard is better than one mounted on a bulkhead.

Most people want to take along a coffeemaker. The stove-top percolator kind are best suited to life aboard. I am a coffee gourmet and I love drip coffee made with a Melitta cone. While this worked reasonably well in port, the three times I tried it on passage I ended up with coffee grounds all over the cabin sole, since the cone is too tipsy if the boat is moving. For coffee at sea, stick to the percolator or switch to instant. Toast presents a similar problem. The burner units to make toast quickly succumb to rust and corrosion. Prepare toast in a dry frying pan or turn on the oven and put it under the broiler. Toast will probably lose its appeal in the heat of the tropics anyway.

For provisions, you will want a range of quality, heavy-duty plastic containers that fit your lockers. Provisions took up half of our easily accessible stowage space in the main salon. When leaving a major port for an ocean crossing, we would have temporary stowage in several areas that would be used for the first three to six weeks.

For cleaning dishes, stock up on Teflon scrubbers. Steel wool rusts when used to wash dishes in salt water. A long-handled plastic scrub brush will minimize the drying effects of salt water on your hands.

Garbage creates a real challenge from a stowage perspective, particularly on passage. You can install a garbage can under the galley sink or in the countertop; use a medium-sized kitchen garbage can, not the tiny bathroom size found on many boats. You will need to stow a certain amount of garbage at sea until you get to port, and few boats have any solution to this problem. As we filled plastic bags with garbage, we stowed them in the forepeak near the chain locker. The sidebar "Managing garbage at sea" in Chapter 18 covers this in more detail.

A kerosene lantern makes for a romantic dinner, but protecting it at sea is a major challenge. To do so, take out the chimney and secure the hanging lantern to a table leg or other handy protrusion using shock cord. Wrap the chimney in bubble wrap and put it in a cloth or canvas bag. Then stow it in a protected place in a locker. Bubble wrap is handy to have aboard for anything delicate when heading out to sea.

Finally, you will want several cookbooks aboard. Most people find that they tend to eat much the same as they had ashore, so bring some of your favorite cookbooks and recipes along. I would also recommend a good all-purpose book such as *Joy of Cooking*.

Linens and bedding

Unless you use down comforters or electric blankets, take the type of bedding and linens that you are most comfortable with at home. All bedding needs to be dripdry, quick-dry, easily laundered, and colored to hide dirt.

While you will be quite warm in the tropics, you will need cold weather bedding for other locales.

A sheet was enough of a covering most of the time in the tropics. Sheets should be patterned in moderate colors that will hide dirt but not fade too badly with multiple washings. We had two full sets of sheets aboard and found that was enough. Our sheets were not specially fitted to the forepeak. We had a total of four queen-size flat sheets that could be tucked in to match the shape of any berth aboard. We added a light cotton blanket for cooler nights in the tropics. For temperate climates, we carried four wool blankets of varying weights. On occasion, we used three at once to stay warm.

Wool blankets are very bulky and hard to stow. Fleece blankets are less bulky, but they still take up a fair amount of space. You can use netting at the foot of a quarter berth or pilot berth to stow blankets, and to store the cushions used to convert a single bunk into a double.

We carried two luxury towels made of good cotton and a half-dozen beach towels. Beach towels worked better than thick cotton ones on passage because they dried more quickly. In port, we used the thick cotton towels and dried them on deck in the sun. Towels absorb the mold and mildew odors that accumulate aboard. Storing them with fabric softener sheets between them prevents this. These are unavailable in most places outside the United States, though; in that case, a mildew preventer in the locker will help.

Take along a dozen or so absorbent tea towels. When paper towels are scarce, you will rely on tea towels just like your grandmother did. We used them for cleaning spills, drying dishes, wiping hands, and a host of other tasks. A damp tea towel spread on a counter under plates and mugs keeps the dishes from sliding. On passage, I went through a tea towel every other day, so the more the better.

Personal belongings

The sailing life takes its toll on clothes. Humidity can lead to mold and mildew. Engine oil, winch grease, bottom paint, and a dozen other hazards can stain or damage fabrics. You will wash your clothes in a rubber bucket with no gentle cycle, then hang them on the lifelines in the tropical sun. The clothes you select for boat life should wear like iron, be practical for tropical heat, and be made from materials that can withstand multiple washings.

Mold and mildew are most apparent on white. Bright colors, particularly red, fade in the sunlight. Like most liveaboards, we had boat clothes and shore clothes. We kept newly purchased clothes in separate lockers, often in plastic, and used them for going ashore. After they had become faded and stained, we relegated them to boat work and wore them on passages.

Cotton and wool remain excellent options for boat life. Cotton breathes and wicks moisture away from the body. However, it does not retain heat once it is wet. Wool is one of the few materials that keeps you warm even when it is soaked through. You will need it for wet watches in higher latitudes. Wool tends to absorb odors, and keeping wool sweaters sweet smelling can be a challenge. The new synthetic fleeces definitely have their place aboard. Though not as warm as wool when wet, they do not retain odors. Finally, Lycra stretch pants add warmth when layered under foul-weather gear or when used alone in the tropics at night. They dry quickly, are almost indestructible in the ship's laundry, and are very comfortable. Polypropylene also has its place for undergarments as it is breathable, dries quickly, and keeps you warm. Clothes made of most other synthetic materials, such as polyester and nylon, have no place aboard. They tend to be overly warm and sticky in the tropics and not warm enough for higher latitudes. Silk, satin, and other fussy fabrics are equally unwelcome.

What clothes should you take along? You need to carry clothes for both warm and cold weather if you intend to leave the tropics during hurricane season. On passages in the tropics you will wear only enough to protect you from the sun. In higher latitudes, you will need clothes to keep you warm and dry in a variety of conditions. The items listed in Table 8-3 can be considered a minimum for voyaging in trade wind and temperate latitudes.

■ **Foul-weather gear.** While bulky and difficult to stow, foul-weather gear is essential. We never used ours in the tropics, but we were grateful for it when we headed north or south of 25 degrees latitude. If space and money allow, take two sets—a good quality heavy-duty offshore set for cold weather and a lighter weight,

less expensive coastal set for milder weather. If you only take one, make it the best you can afford. Stow foul-weather gear in a hanging locker with its own drain pan. Antarctic voyagers Pauline and Tim Carr on 28-foot *Curlew* stow theirs in cylindrical pillowcases.

■ **Waterproof shell.** We used our windbreakers or shells constantly. On a windy night or during a frontal passage, a lightweight shell will keep you warm and dry during a sail change. Unfortunately, the pores of many breatheable materials will get clogged by salt and lose their breatheability. We prefer good quality, nonbreatheable shells that are water resistant. They hold up well to frequent washings, are tough enough to get snagged on a cotter pin without ripping, and offer the versatility of layering as the weather gets cooler.

■ **Heavy wool sweaters.** Wool sweaters are very bulky. They stow better rolled than folded. You can store them in pillowcases and use them as pillows if you lack storage space for clothes. To keep wool sweaters smelling sweet, seal them in a plastic or polypropylene bag with some fabric softener sheets when entering the tropics. Two-gallon Ziploc bags work well. Outside the tropics, air them out after every passage.

■ **Long pants.** While everyone has a pair of jeans aboard, they get little use in the tropics. Jeans are heavy and warm and absorb moisture once exposed to salt water. Military combat pants are lighter weight, dry more quickly, and last forever. They are available in Army-Navy stores for reasonable prices and come in a variety of colors (not just camouflage).

■ **Shorts.** You will live in shorts most of the time. Good boat shorts are lightweight and long enough to protect the backs of your legs from hot decks or sticky cushions. Canvas or cotton shorts are the toughest, though some of the new materials like Supplex hold up well and dry quickly.

■ **Formal clothes for men.** Even once-formal yacht clubs have succumbed to the "dress down" mentality. But take a jacket and two pairs of slacks along just in case. If you plan to do work along the way that requires formal clothes, bring an extra jacket and one suit. Store these in hanging plastic bags with mildew preventer. Use plastic hangers, not metal. Even the coated metal hangers, if damaged, will deposit rust stains on your best clothes. Keep hanging clothes from moving—if they are not packed in tightly or otherwise held in place, the constant motion of the boat will cause the hanger to chafe right through the fabric.

■ **Formal clothes for women.** Throughout the South Pacific and in many Islamic countries, tradition dictates that women be covered from ankle to shoulder. In these countries, women should never wear shorts ashore outside of tourist areas. Instead, women can wear the local attire: a sarong, pareu, or lava-lava, depending on the country. These are names for a piece of bright-colored material about two yards long that is wrapped around the body and secured with a knot or pin. Loose, waistless, wide-sleeved cotton dresses make an acceptable alternative.

■ **Hats.** Even when we wore nothing else in the tropics, we always wore a hat. But the perfect hat is hard to find. Canvas is too hot, and it molds or rots when exposed to salt water. Many hats have mild steel buckles or snaps that quickly rust away to nothing. A good boat hat needs a wide brim all the way around to protect your forehead, nose, and the back of your neck. The hat needs to be secured to your head in windy weather, and it should be a light color to reflect the sun (but not white, which quickly becomes spotted with mildew and mold). The hat should be washable without shrinking or losing its shape.

You will need several hats because you will lose at least one overboard. We used cheap baseball caps made out of parachute material or very light cotton as "disposable" hats in windy conditions. We purchased these in volume when we first found them in Fiji. The rest of the time we wore a wide-brimmed safari hat made from nylon rather than canvas. The Ultimate Hat, which is sold through marine retailers, is the best we have ever found.

■ **Shoes.** You will spend a lot of time in bare feet. However, many situations require shoes, and each situation requires a different type. You will use sea boots and boat shoes on deck in cold or wet weather. Flip

Table 8-3. Clothing for the offshore voyager

Cold-climate clothing	Tropical clothing	Footwear
Foul-weather gear	Three to four pairs lightweight pants	Sea boots
Fleece or pile jacket	Three to four lightweight long-sleeved shirts	Deck shoes
Lightweight shell	One lightweight set of dress clothes	Flip flops
Three heavy wool sweaters	Six pairs of shorts	Good walking shoes
Lightweight wool/cotton sweater	Ten tee-shirts/short-sleeved shirts	Hiking boots
Wool watch cap	Four tank tops	Sandals
Polypropylene long underwear	Swimsuits	Reef shoes
Two pairs of Lycra stretch pants	Sarongs/pareus/lava-lavas	
Jeans	Two loose cotton dresses	
One or two pairs long pants	Six pairs of cotton ankle socks	
Four or five long-sleeved shirts	Underwear, preferably cotton	
Heavy wool and polypropylene socks	Hats	
Heavy wool or fleece mittens	Sailing gloves	

flops are handy while landing the dinghy on a sandy beach, and they will protect you from athlete's foot in communal showers. You will want good walking shoes or high quality sneakers for long walks ashore. With hiking boots—preferably the lightweight, nonleather kind—you can bushwhack up rough trails. A nice pair of sandals makes good tropical dress shoes. For exploring in coral you will want reef shoes that cover the tops and sides of your feet. Canvas tennis shoes work well, as do the French plastic sandals that cover most of the foot. The latter can be purchased just about anywhere in the South Pacific.

All these shoes take up a tremendous amount of space. Stowage options include canvas pockets on the back of a locker door, shelves at the back of a hanging locker, or a canvas bag that sits on the floor of a hanging locker.

You will want to bring sunglasses and croakies to keep them on your face. For entertainment aboard any boat, a CD or tape player is a wonderful diversion. Metal speaker grilles rust away to nothing in six months; replace them with fabric before you leave.

Safety equipment

Place fire extinguishers in accessible locations throughout the boat. At minimum, you should have one in the galley and one in the main salon. Fix these in brackets against bulkheads in recessed areas where they will be protected. Purchase the units with plastic brackets; the metal ones will rust and break within a year or so.

Emergency tillers are best stowed upright in a hanging locker where they will be quickly accessible. If yours is nicely varnished, wrap it in bubble wrap or old rags to protect it. Keep several flares near the companionway, and stow additional flares in the abandon-ship kit.

Don't underestimate how much room a properly equipped offshore medical kit requires. Figure 8-17 shows an offshore medical kit sitting on deck. Such a kit will take up a moderate-sized locker and needs to be available within seconds, even at sea.

Miscellany

Beyond the items described above, you will want to bring many small items, some of which have special requirements in the marine environment. You will miss the following items if you leave them behind.

■ *Mosquito screens.* You will need protection from mosquitoes where malaria is a problem. Most good quality portlights come with screens, or you can order screens for them from the manufacturer. For hatches and companionways, draped mosquito netting is a temporary solution. Velcro or flexible battens can be used to make more permanent coverings.

■ *Cart.* For my first birthday aboard, Evans bought me a heavy-duty, aluminum, folding hand cart that I treasured. We used it to carry water, diesel, groceries, ice, batteries, and just about everything else. Over the course of three years, it held up beautifully despite much abuse and frequent exposure to salt water. These can be expensive, but they are worth the investment.

■ *Canvas square.* A 4-foot by 4-foot canvas square with heavy-duty grommets sewn into each corner can serve a dozen purposes. We used ours as a small, movable awning, a hatch cover for rainy weather, a tool holder when working on deck, and a rain catcher. We used a second square as a drop cloth when working on the engine, cleaning winches, greasing the windlass, or painting our wind vane blade. In an emergency, this cloth could serve as a collision mat. If space allows, carry two or three of varying sizes.

■ *Flashlights.* You need flashlights that will hold up in a marine environment. Flashlight switches and battery connections corrode and break. During our first six months, we went through seven flashlights—from penlights to large household lanterns. Then we started using halogen dive lights rated submersible to 100 feet. These were bright enough to guide us into a harbor at night and small enough to tuck into the bunk when we went to sleep. And even after two years of constant use, they never corroded. They are expensive but worth every penny. You will want one for each regular member of your crew and a backup for the ship.

■ *Clothespins.* The boat gremlins love clothespins. You will lose them in the bilge and over the side. Buy several dozen and stow them in a ditty bag near the companionway. The wooden ones are more durable than the plastic variety, and, contrary to popular belief, the plastic ones do not float.

Figure 8-17. Don't overlook how much space your medical kit will require when making those all-important space decisions.

- **Watches.** High quality sport or dive watches last the longest and are the most useful. Buy a watch with two time zones to keep track of Greenwich Mean Time, a timer for cooking, an alarm for watchkeeping, and a good light for seeing the time at night. The band should be heavy-duty rubber or plastic with a stainless steel buckle. Each person aboard should have their own. If you are using a sextant, you may also want to mount one in the nav station as a ship's clock.

- **Needles.** Mild steel needles rust from the salt air alone. Stainless steel needles break when any force is applied to them. There is no perfect answer. For sails, high quality sailmakers' needles are best. For normal sewing, mild steel needles are better than stainless, but you'll have to replace them frequently. Store them in a film canister with some household or sewing machine oil to extend their life.

- **Eyeglass screws.** Everyone we knew had trouble with the screws that held their eyeglasses together. Our first stop in several major ports was the local optician's office to replace screws. The screws corrode quickly because they are often made out of mild steel or aluminum. Before you leave, purchase spare screws for each pair of glasses aboard—not just for hinges, but for nose pieces as well. Stow them in a film canister with a bit of oil. Don't forget to bring a jeweler's screwdriver. If your glasses break and you don't have the right screw, a twist of seizing wire offers a temporary fix.

- **Work light.** We made an emergency work light by attaching alligator clips to a 12-volt bulb in a plastic cage. For working on the engine, we attached the clips directly to the battery and hung the light over the engine. This light also proved handy for cockpit parties when hung from the boom.

Additional resources

If you have a great deal of inaccessible space that you can't figure out how to get at, or if you decide to radically reconfigure your interior, these two books will help you through a major modification.

■ *This Old Boat* by **Don Casey.** If you are thinking about upgrading your current boat for offshore work, Casey offers a detailed, step-by-step approach to everything from building drawers to moving structural bulkheads. (International Marine, 1991)

■ *From a Bare Hull* by **Ferenc Maté.** This book includes an excellent survey of techniques and ideas for rebuilding a boat interior, along with critical dimensions for everything from bunks to cockpit seats. (Norton, 1983)

To purchase marine books and charts, you can visit your local chandlery or West Marine outlet. However, the following companies specialize in marine publications and will be able to help with both mundane and obscure requests.

■ **Bluewater Books & Charts.** Specializes in guides, charts, and courtesy flags. They offer excellent services and a worldwide knowledge and capability. On several occasions we called and told them our itinerary; they faxed a list of recommended charts and guidebooks for our review. They always delivered our final choices within two weeks even to New Zealand and South Africa. To reach them call (954)763-6533 or fax (954)522-2278.

■ **Armchair Sailor.** While they also carry charts and guides, they focus on marine books. Their catalog includes just about every marine book currently in print. If you can't find a book I've recommended, they will have it. To reach them call (800)292-4278 or fax (401)847-1219. In Rhode Island, call (401)847-4252.

■ **Warsash Nautical Bookshop.** Wide range of new and second-hand nautical books. They will mail worldwide. To reach them call 44(0)1489-572384 or fax 44(0)1489-885756.

■ **Kelvin Hughes.** The largest stocklist of nautical books in the U.K., plus yachting charts, logbooks, etc. To reach them call 44(0)1703-223772 or fax 44(0)1703-330014.

■ **Reeds Nautical Bookshop.** Specialists in worldwide mail order of nautical books, calendars, prints, etc. To reach them call 44(0)181-941-7878 or fax 44(0)181-941-8787.

■ *Toiletry kit.* A strong, compartmentalized ditty bag for your toiletries is useful both aboard the boat and when you are heading ashore for a shower. We made our own out of canvas. Leave the fancy leather ones at home.

■ *Luggage.* You will need some luggage when you go ashore as a tourist or head home for a visit. A duffel bag and a backpack for each person aboard meets most needs. To stow well, backpacks should not have frames. Inspect all luggage for mild steel closures or mixed-metal zippers. The best zippers are the all-plastic or all-stainless ones.

PART  LIVEABOARD SKILLS

CHAPTER 9 | BETTER BOATKEEPING

Find it, fix it, maintain it ■ *Find it and fix it: day-to-day preventive maintenance* ■ *Maintain it: preventive maintenance schedules* ■ *The annual haulout* ■ *Troubleshooting: 90 percent solutions* ■ **Pretrip preparations: tools and spares** ■ *The voyager's toolbox* ■ *The spares locker* ■ *Additional resources*

As liveaboard voyagers sailing an average of 12,000 miles a year, we depended on the condition of our boat and gear for our very lives. But we didn't begin our voyage as expert boatkeepers.

When we left on our circumnavigation, we had little sailing experience and almost no experience with our boat. *Silk* had never been used for offshore voyaging. We constantly faced crises at sea that required emergency repairs, often in the worst conditions. We despaired at each new problem and ignored some in the hope they would go away. The boat's systems mystified us, gremlins lurked in every corner, and the idea of fixing things ourselves intimidated us.

After a year aboard, our attitude changed radically. Our shift in thinking began with a willingness to work on the boat ourselves—to tackle any job no matter how daunting and to make a few mistakes along the way. We began to view maintenance and troubleshooting as frustrating but not complicated, and we grew to know our boat and the intricacies of its systems.

By the end of our trip, 90 percent of our maintenance was preventive. We had found permanent solutions to early difficulties. We were always looking for trouble—because a new problem became a challenge rather than an intractable puzzle. We learned to take charge of our boat's condition and follow a rule of good seamanship: "Find it, fix it, maintain it!"

FIND IT, FIX IT, MAINTAIN IT

When you drop a sail, look for signs of chafe. When you get something out of a locker, feel whether it is damp. When you find something amiss, take the time to design

a permanent cure. The ultimate (and unrealizable) goal is to reduce maintenance that is not preventive to zero.

A permanent fix is not possible everywhere. Every boat needs a regular maintenance schedule to keep its systems operating. "Find it, fix it, forget it" won't work for the long haul.

Find it and fix it: day-to-day preventive maintenance

We developed a keen sensitivity to the condition of our boat and gear and a willingness to see things that were not quite right. Now, within 20 minutes of boarding a boat we have a good idea of the little problems aboard—many of which the owner has not yet noticed. Like these owners, we used to prefer not to know about potential problems. But the "If it's not broke, don't fix it" attitude can be dangerous offshore.

What did we look for when we wandered around the boat each day on passage and every few days at anchor? What did we do when we found it? Table 9-1 summarizes our day-to-day maintenance activities.

This inspection tour became one of our most essential daily activities, especially on passage, where wear and tear are extreme. Every day on passage we did two or three things from the right-hand column of Table 9-1. In port, we worked on some of these things every few days in addition to the major maintenance discussed below. Many crews took the approach of "a job a day" to keep their boats in offshore-capable condition.

The more you sail your boat, the more frequent these inspections need to be. Salt water and motion cause almost all of the problems listed in Table 9-1. Most

Table 9-1. Day-to-day preventive maintenance

System	Look for:	Fix it with:
Engine	Salt water in bilge	Inspect and tighten stuffing box on prop shaft or centerboard
	Poor charging of batteries	Inspect and tighten alternator belt Inspect battery terminals for corrosion or loose connections and clean thoroughly Check regulator function
Hull	Salt encrusted decks, brightwork, deck hardware, standing rigging	Rinse with fresh water as often as practical including all blocks, genoa tracks, windlass, furling drum, wind vane, chainplates, and terminal ends
	Battered, dry, worn, or scratched teak	Touch up as needed
	Damp, moldy-smelling lockers, weeping deck fittings	Rebed deck fittings
Rigging	Squeaky blocks, or blocks that are not running free	Rinse with fresh water as often as possible; spray blocks with WD-40 or other water-dispersing lubricant
	Chafed or frayed lines	End-for-end running rigging if necessary; change leads or apply chafe protection Rewhip any fraying bitter ends of lines or use vinyl rope dip as temporary solution in rough weather offshore
	Bent or damaged cotter or clevis pins	Replace cotter or clevis pins as necessary
Sails	Chafe or broken stitches on any sail	Fix any broken stitches Build chafe patches or reinforce with sail tape
Ground tackle	Chafe on anchor rode or docklines	Whip and end-for-end minor chafe on anchor rode, replace if chafe is major Whip minor chafe on docklines, replace if chafe is major
	Bent or rusty shackles anywhere in rode; seizing wire damaged	Replace seizing wire and/or shackles as necessary
Wind vane self-steering	Squeaky or stiff blocks	Rinse as often as possible with fresh water Lubricate all blocks with water-dispersing lubricant
	Spring lock on wheel stiff and hard to engage/disengage	Rinse with fresh water every few days, even on passage Lubricate spring lock on wheel with liquid soap
Safety	Loose lifelines	Inspect and tighten turnbuckles and replace cotter pins on lifelines
	Chafed, stretched, or frayed jacklines	Replace jacklines
Plumbing	"Rotten egg" odor in head	Clean out head with marine cleaner or baking soda solution
	Fresh water in bilge	Inspect and tighten hose clamps
Electrical	Burned out bulbs anywhere in boat	Replace bulbs as needed
	Any intermittent electrical problems in fixtures or equipment	Inspect wiring for corrosion or loose connections

coastal boats get very little exposure to either—perhaps a few hours a week. When offshore, however, a boat is in motion 24 hours a day and subjected to salt water for weeks on end. The following sections offer suggestions for combating the most common enemies aboard a pounding, rolling, flexing boat.

Chafe

During the first six months of passagemaking, we thought we'd never see the end of chafed-through mizzen and main boom topping lifts, broken stitches on the mainsail, and split batten pockets. Even metal can chafe: The stainless shackle holding up a spinnaker halyard block chafed right through. We kept reinforcing sails with sail tape, putting webbing on batten pockets, and trying different blocks and lines on the boom topping lift. By our third major passage, we had eliminated 90 percent of our chafe problems. A few of our lessons learned follow:

■ ***Headsail chafe.*** The foot and tack of a headsail chafe on the bow pulpit on most boats. If a sail is not full-hoist, attach the tack to a pendant to raise it above the pulpit (Figure 9-1). On a full-hoist headsail, use extra sun cover material as a sacrificial patch where the sail goes over the pulpit. Replace the patch as often as necessary. On a roller furler, regularly reinforce the stitching around the grommet where it gets twisted when the sail is furled.

■ ***Shroud chafe.*** On many boats, an eased mainsail chafes against the shrouds during downwind sailing. The resultant damage will keep you busy with the sail palm. We learned to cover all areas that touched the standing rigging with a layer of sail tape, which we replaced whenever it started to chafe through. This solution allowed us to sail over 20,000 miles on our full-battened mainsail without repairing a stitch due to rigging chafe.

■ ***Batten chafe.*** To keep partial battens from chafing through their pockets, cover the end of the batten pocket with two or three layers of sail tape or tape over the batten ends before putting them in the pocket. For full battens, sail tape may be needed along the top and bottom of the batten pockets, particularly where the battens touch the shrouds.

Figure 9-1. On *Silk,* we reduced chafe and wear on the Yankee by using a pendant to raise the sail's tack and foot above the bow pulpit.

■ ***Topping lift and running backstay chafe.*** The best way to avoid topping lift chafe is to use a rigid vang. We stowed our dinghy under the boom, which prevented us from installing a rigid vang. We taped over the block where the topping lift split as it came down to the boom. This prevented the block from chafing the sail and the pin from coming out of the block. On a cutter, consider using shock cord attached to the backstay to hold the topping lift off the sail when not in use. You can use a similar solution to keep running backstays safely out of the way of the mainsail when not in use (Figure 9-2).

Loose fasteners

One of Murphy's Laws of Offshore Voyaging states that any fastener you want to stay tight will work loose, and any fastener you want to remove will be frozen solid. Machine screws for pump covers, wood screws in trim pieces, and metal screws on the faceplates of electrical and mechanical equipment should be quick and easy to remove. Unfortunately, fasteners that join metal to metal frequently corrode, especially in water pumps and around the engine. Where access is more important than an unbreakable bond, use an anti-seizing compound when reassembling to make the job easier next time around.

We were always astonished at the ease with which seemingly immovable bolts and tightly seized nuts could loosen over the course of a passage. To keep nuts and bolts tight in areas of constant movement, you have

Figure 9-2. This arrangement pulls the lazy running backstay against the backstay to prevent chafe. You can use a similar approach to hold the topping lift away from the mainsail on a cutter.

four practical options. A lock washer and torque from a wrench offers the cheapest solution. If that fails to hold the fastener, the next step is an aircraft locking nut. Drilling and wiring the bolts in place takes the most effort. A product like Loctite or a dab of silicone caulk can work miracles. If you are going to use such a product, be sure the bonding surface is absolutely clean and the appropriate adhesive is used. Note that there are several grades of Loctite. With the strongest grade, you may need a blow torch to break the bolt loose.

Don't rely on spring rings (better known as ring-dings among sailors). These have an uncanny ability to work loose. When they tinkle onto the deck, you are left wondering what is about to fall down on your head. Replace these with cotter or clevis pins. Where that is not possible (for example, with batten cars), replace the bolts and spring rings with bolts and aircraft locking nuts.

There are four places where bolts work loose on many boats. Make sure that these bolts are properly secured before you go to sea.

■ *Engine bolts.* When we arrived in New Zealand, we had so much engine noise that we feared the engine manifold needed to be replaced. But an inspection revealed that three of the four bolts that secured the manifold were gone. Engine vibration always plays havoc with engine bolts, so use Loctite and inspect regularly.

■ *Wind vane.* The wind vane is in constant motion when in use. Its position over the stern makes it particularly vulnerable to lost fasteners. Friends with older vanes often tightened bolts several times during a passage. We never had a problem, though we frequently inspected for lost wire or loose bolts. Our Monitor came with stainless lock washers for most bolts, and drilled bolts and seizing wire for critical areas. If your wind vane is not so equipped, consider making modifications.

■ *Roller-furling gear.* In our first gale at sea, the bolts that held the roller-furling drum in place vibrated loose. Luckily, we saw what had happened when we tried to unfurl the sail. Later, after a week of headwinds between New Zealand and New Caledonia, the bolts that held the drum to the foil vibrated off. In both cases, we ended up using lock washers and Loctite and taping over the bolts to minimize motion. No matter how well secured they are, bring plenty of replacements for these bolts!

■ *Steering system.* Our Edson system used cotter pins, but others use bolts. Given the constant motion in this area, bolts should be replaced with a system using cotter pins or secured using one of the methods mentioned above.

Electrical corrosion

Corrosion is even more insidious than chafe because it occurs out of sight—behind trim pieces or at the backs of lockers. Probably 90 percent of marine electrical problems are due to corroded connections or improper wire. Whether you solder or crimp, the motion of the boat and the conductivity of the salt air will ultimately undo your best work. But you can slow down the process by using multistrand, tinned wire and proper connections. Use a proper ratchet crimper (rather than the common automotive "masher/crusher"), seal the crimp with silicone caulk and/or heat-shrink tubing and spray all connections with an anticorrosive. Secure all wires firmly with wire ties. Make sure there are no leaks or spray reaching bus bars or switch panels. Some additional thoughts for upgrading your electrical system follow.

■ *Coax wire.* The sponge-like outer braid on coax makes it susceptible to capillary action. Use marine-grade coax cable to prevent corrosion inside your mast. Inspect your VHF cable where it exits the base of the mast. If the outer braid is saturated or the wire underneath is corroded, replace it before you leave. You'll save yourself a big headache down the line.

■ *Soldering.* If you choose to solder, use quality tinned terminals. Crimp the terminal on. Solder the wire to the terminal so the solder flows into the wire and onto the terminal. Use rosin core or solid solder; never use acid core. Wire brush the outside of the barrel to remove any flux residue and leave clean, bright metal. Seal the insulation to the connector barrel with adhesive-lined heat-shrink tubing. Anchor down all wiring using properly sized wire ties to prevent vibration that could break the solder. A proper solder joint requires good soldering technique and sufficient heat. Insufficient heat makes a "cold solder" joint that is weak, resistive, and more likely to corrode than a simple crimp properly applied.

■ *Vaseline.* Vaseline is the amateur boat electrician's best friend. Used liberally on bus bar and battery terminals, it keeps out moisture and prevents corrosion for months.

Water and mold

Do not ignore water anywhere in your boat, either salt or fresh, and consider mold in lockers a solvable problem—not an inconvenience of onboard life. Fresh water in the bilge almost always means a loose hose clamp or cracked plastic fitting somewhere nearby. Salt water in the bilge rarely signals a catastrophic breach in the hull. Most often the cause can be traced to the following areas.

■ *Stuffing box.* Tighten the stuffing box if it is dripping more than one drip every six seconds when the shaft is turning. A drip a second could fill up the shallow bilge in our centerboard boat within a half-day. If you tighten the stuffing box one week and it is leaking again the next, your stuffing box needs to be repacked, your cutlass bearing needs to be replaced, or your engine needs to be realigned.

■ *Plug for chain hawser.* If you are taking green water over the bow on passage, check your chain hawsers. Almost everyone we knew forgot to plug their hawsers at least once, which leads to a stream of water traveling below with every wave. We carried a teak plug that was custom made for our hawser. But if we forgot it, or if the weather got rough on a day sail, several plastic bags stuffed into the hawser cut the water flow considerably.

■ *Deck leaks.* If the water source isn't your stuffing box or chain hawser, look for a deck leak. A damp or moldy locker could be a sign of a deck leak. Finding the leak can be a challenge, because water always seems to migrate as far as possible from the point of entry. However, leaking fittings will have rust and dirt around the edges above decks and weep dirt and water below; they need to be rebedded. We even rebedded fittings at sea when the alternative was two weeks of Chinese water torture in one of our bunks.

UV deterioration

In tropical latitudes, you will notice the sun's effects on your sails, lines, webbing, and wood. Your best defense is preventive: minimize exposure and replace important items before wear and chafe become obvious. A few tips for minimizing UV damage follow.

■ *Teak.* Make sure that whatever teak treatment you select offers excellent UV protection. Otherwise, the varnish will turn cloudy, the oil will turn black, and other treatments will peel or strip away during a single passage. The top of the companionway steps, the teak trim around large hatches, and the hand grips and trim near the companionway are all subject to UV exposure and should be considered exterior teak.

■ *Sails.* You will extend the life of your sails if you cover them when they are not in use. Roller-furling headsails must be equipped with sun covers. The sail cover should be used on the mainsail if you are running under headsails for several days (or weeks) on end. Sun protection materials lose their UV resistance before they show signs of wear. Many need to be replaced every two years in the tropics. Check with the manufacturer and follow their recommendations.

■ *Jacklines.* If your jacklines are nylon webbing, they will degrade with exposure to UV radiation and should be replaced every 12 months. We preferred webbing to wire for jacklines, because the wire rolls underfoot. Consider threading low-stretch cord (like Spectra) through the hollow webbing to increase strength and reduce stretch.

Maintain it:
preventive maintenance schedules

Preventive maintenance requires much more time on a liveaboard cruising boat than on a coastal boat. We spent about 20 hours per week and 80 hours at haulout time. In addition, we usually had one or two major repairs each year.

To be successful at both preventive maintenance and troubleshooting, you need complete manuals for every piece of gear on board. You also need separate parts manuals that list part numbers, if these are not included in the owner's manual. Survey your manuals and write for any you don't have. Most manufacturers provide replacements for free or a small fee. For the engine, the owner's manual covers only routine maintenance and troubleshooting. Contact the manufacturer and order the complete shop manual. This will be your primary resource should you ever have to rebuild your raw water pump or take apart your transmission. Buy a good do-it-yourself book for your outboard. These offer step-by-step instructions and greater detail than the shop manuals.

Equipment manuals will provide preventive maintenance schedules. Our own maintenance schedules are shown in tables 9-2 (page 155) and 9-3 (page 158). These often suggest more frequent maintenance than the manuals, reflecting both our circumspect attitudes and the rigorous demands of voyaging. Our maintenance schedules will help you develop your own approach and keep you from missing anything important.

No matter how thorough your maintenance program, at some point you will be faced with malfunctioning equipment in a deserted anchorage thousands of miles from the nearest chandlery. Even if you are not particularly mechanical, you can do a surprising amount with the shop manual and your own two hands. Our lack of confidence was often our biggest impediment to getting the job done. When you approach a serious problem, keep the following points in mind.

1. *Don't be afraid to tackle a job.* Most things are simpler than they appear. Frustration is far more likely than failure.

2. *Check the simplest things first.* The sidebar on "Troubleshooting: 90 percent solutions" in this chapter offers ideas on where to start.

3. *Take your time.* Sleep on it before you disassemble a critical piece of gear. With the exception of frozen bolts, most things come apart easily when approached the right way. If you think something needs to be forced, back off and rethink it. Consider calling the manufacturer on the high seas radio before proceeding.

4. *If you take something major apart, stay organized.* Keep all screws and parts in separate, labeled containers so you can put it back together again. If you have a video camera aboard, you may want to record the whole process.

Major repairs will come along periodically. But a regular approach of finding it, fixing it, and maintaining it will keep your boat working smoothly.

Engine

Modern marine diesels are virtually indestructible when cared for properly. A little Tender Loving Care will help maximize the life of your diesel engine.

Don't start and stop your engine without letting it warm up and letting the oil pressure come up to normal range. Don't run heavy compressor motors before the engine is warm. Don't let it run at idle for long periods (the daily two-hour charge while at anchor is one of the fastest ways to shorten engine life).

Try to run the engine under load once it is warmed up. While charging at anchor, you can run the engine in gentle reverse. Feed your diesel clean fuel and oil and change the oil frequently. The recommended timing in Table 9-2 may seem excessive. (Our Yanmar manual recommended an oil change every 150 hours.) However, frequent oil changes provide cheap insurance. Check the oil level each time you start your engine—or as near to that as possible.

Run a quick check of your engine every few days. Check belt tension, oil level, and freshwater and coolant levels. Make sure the Racor filter does not have any water or dirt in its glass bottom. Combined with the regular maintenance above, these simple precautions should forestall any major problems.

Within our circumnavigating community, the few engine problems we encountered were almost all fuel-related. The following suggestions will help to keep your fuel contaminant free and your engine happy and healthy.

■ **Put only the cleanest fuel in your tank.** We bought diesel from automotive pumps rather than fuel docks wherever possible. The fuel there tends to be cleaner because the turnover is higher and cars are fussier. We used a Baja filter when this was impractical and we were concerned about fuel quality. This large filter contains several increasingly fine screens. It will filter most particles and water out of diesel fuel. The Baja filter slows down the fueling process, but it protects the engine from bad diesel.

■ **Filter fuel between the tank and the engine.** If your fuel system does not include a prefilter between the fuel tank and the engine, add one. Install it with stop cocks on either side to keep air out of the fuel system during a filter change. Inspect the bowl for water or dirt

Table 9-2. Engine maintenance schedule	
Engine hours	Activity
Every 50 hours:	Change engine oil
	Tighten engine belts and check pulleys
	Clean raw water filter
	Check electrical connections
Every 100 hours:	Change oil and fuel filters
	Check all hoses and tighten hose clamps
	Tighten fuel lines
Every 150 hours:	Change transmission oil
	Clean air filter
	Touch up engine paint
Every 500 hours:	Check engine alignment
	Replace cooling water impeller
	Repack stuffing box [1]

[1] Generally timed to coincide with annual haulout

every time you check the oil. Change the filter regularly. Our Racor filter saved our engine from dirty fuel and also from salt water forced down the breather of the diesel tank by a wave.

■ **Drain the diesel tank sump.** If you are getting a lot of dirt or water in the prefilter, drain or pump out the sump of the fuel tank. To remove all debris, let the boat sit calmly at anchor for at least 12 hours. If you do not have a convenient stop cock attached to a drain on your diesel tank sump, you will need a hand pump and a rod or wire to tape to the hose to keep it rigid.

■ **Keep tanks topped off.** Water in the tanks can become a breeding ground for bacteria that clog up filters and damage the engine. In cooler climates, condensation can lead to water even if fuel enters your tank water-free. Full tanks reduce the likelihood of condensation. You can also discourage bacteria by draining excess water out of the sump or by using a biocide additive for your diesel. Make sure the biocide does not include alcohol, which can damage O-rings and seals.

■ *Filter fuel from drums.* If you take on diesel from a drum, use a Baja filter. Fuel from drums is often very dirty. The last few gallons can contain bottom dirt and sludge. To test how dirty the bottom is, attach a rag to a long stick and dip it into the drum.

■ *Carry at least five gallons of spare diesel in a plastic jug.* You should carry some diesel outside of your fuel tanks. You may need several quarts of clean fuel to change the fuel or Racor filter, flush the fuel lines, or bleed the engine. If the fuel in your tank becomes contaminated, you can still maneuver into harbor after a passage.

■ *Steam clean the diesel tank.* No matter how careful you are, you will build up residue in the bottom of your tank after several years. Make sure your tanks have adequate access through inspection hatches to be steam cleaned. Be prepared to steam clean every three to five years.

The regular engine-maintenance task that must be done the most frequently is an oil change. To speed the process and minimize the mess, change the oil when it is warm. Keep old oil containers to store the dirty oil. If you really want to make life simple, consider installing a dedicated electric pump to empty the oil pan. Set it up with a safety switch to prevent oil from being pumped into the bilge accidentally.

A few final hints and tips on engine maintenance follow.

■ *Air filters.* Washable filter elements for the air intake last forever. They also eliminate the need to find, buy, and stow paper cartridges.

■ *Belt wear.* Black dust or fuzz on engine accessories or pulleys signals belt wear. Check and adjust pulley alignment and belt tension. Change the belt if it is worn. Buy the highest quality belts you can find and make sure they fit perfectly. Belts that slip because they are too narrow or too thin can lead to inefficient charging or an overheated engine. Belts need to be tight but not too tight; otherwise they will wear bearings and pulleys. Follow your engine manual precisely.

■ *Engine stop.* Engine stop knobs located in the cockpit tend to freeze up from corrosion. After our original cable corroded and broke, we moved ours below. Even inside, the cables tend to stick. Check frequently to be sure the cable is moving freely and the ends show no sign of corrosion. Lubricate with a water-dispersing lubricant every few weeks.

■ *Engine mounts.* Good engine mounts reduce vibration and keep the engine in alignment. Rubber engine mounts break down under assault from oil and diesel. They should be replaced every five years.

■ *Stuffing boxes.* While dripless stuffing boxes offer a convenient alternative, the old-fashioned kind work just fine. On most boats, the stuffing box can be repacked without hauling. To seal the outside of the stern tube, dive and wrap a large piece of plastic wrap around the stern tube and shaft. Repack the stuffing and then remove the plastic wrap.

■ *Transmission.* The arrangement between the engine and the propeller differs tremendously from boat to boat. Learn your own system and be able to take it apart and take out the prop shaft. You may need special keys, a prop puller, or other dedicated tools. Find out what you need before you go and make sure they are aboard. The cutlass bearing should be replaced when you can move the prop shaft by hand more than $1/16$ inch to either side ($1/8$ inch in total). When the transmission oil needs to be changed, the transmission becomes less positive (about the 150-hour mark). Change it when it is warm.

Engines are no longer dragons lurking in the bilge like they were in the early days of offshore voyaging. Given care and attention, they will provide years of dedicated service. Even if you are mechanically challenged, you can learn to master the mysteries of engine maintenance.

Hull

Table 9-3 (page 158) shows the periodic maintenance schedule for the rest of the boat's systems. We tried to time the annual and biannual tasks to coincide with our haulout.

Clean and wax the topsides regularly. Wax protects the gelcoat from UV radiation, oil and diesel in the water, dirty rubber fenders, and a host of other hazards.

Teak's extreme oiliness protects it from the drying effects of salt water. Although it has always been the best wood for use on boats, any wood requires care at sea. With the modern materials now available, most experienced voyagers prefer to minimize a boat's exterior wood. Our next boat will have no teak on deck at all. But your boat most likely came with exterior wood, and you will need to decide how to maintain it. Those who love the traditional teak look will opt for a different solution than those who are most concerned with low maintenance.

We tried almost every option for protecting *Silk's* extensive exterior teak. Before we left, we oiled it with a high quality, UV-resistant teak oil. By the end of our second passage, the components in the oil had turned rancid and our teak had turned black. Teak oil doesn't keep and can rarely be found outside the United States. Unopened teak oil grows mold after a few months in tropical heat. Don't consider oil an option for exterior teak, though it can be a workable solution for the interior.

For the next year and a half, we scrubbed the teak with salt water, sometimes mixed with Joy dishwashing liquid. After six months, we got rid of the black oil. The silvered teak looked good when it was kept clean, but it needed to be scrubbed once a week. Such regular scrubbing does remove wood. If you have teak decks, scrub the teak across the grain to limit wood loss. After many years of scrubbing, teak will have to be replaced. If your primary concern is convenience, bare teak requires the least maintenance. If your primary concern is the aesthetics of the teak or the resale value of the boat, you will want to find a different solution.

Many people love the traditional look of varnished teak. Near the end of our trip, we varnished the teak on the coach roof and in the cockpit and left the toerail, bowsprit, and rubrail silvered. Unfortunately, perfect varnishing conditions rarely exist in the tropics. An afternoon rain shower can spoil a day's work, and varnish applied in the sun will dry wavy or cloudy. Varnish on a cruising boat rarely meets boatshow standards. Once applied, however, a limited amount of varnish is easily maintained and looks better than most other options.

Many people choose varnish if their boat has a small amount of exterior teak, or they varnish 3 or 4 square feet and leave the rest bare.

Cetol, and other products like it, had just come out when we left on our trip. Like teak oil, these products are not available outside the United States, and they won't hold up to offshore passages without constant touchup. Unlike oil, these products will not turn black, and they do protect the wood.

If we were leaving tomorrow on *Silk* for another circumnavigation, we would take a completely different approach. We would apply 8 to 10 light coats of varnish to the exterior teak and then paint the varnished teak with silver-gray paint. The varnish protects the wood and prevents it from absorbing any of the paint. The paint stands up to the sun and salt and lasts for up to five years. We would fix any damaged spots. Upon return, we would strip off the paint with a heat gun and give the varnish a touchup. This option preserves the wood and offers an acceptable look, but it won't satisfy the traditionalist's aesthetic sense.

Whatever option you select for the rest of the teak, only two solutions make sense for teak rubrails, toerails, and bowsprits on a boat where those areas are frequently submerged during upwind sailing. Sun and spray will strip off oil, varnish, or Cetol during the first long passage. Either leave these areas bare and silvered or use the varnish-and-paint approach described above.

After maintaining exterior teak, you will spend most of your time keeping deck fittings, ports, and hatches watertight. This topic is covered extensively in Chapter 11.

A few more hints and suggestions for maintaining the hull follow.

■ *Floor boards.* Wood swells in the tropics, causing problems in accessing the bilge. Before you leave, plane the edges of the floorboards down until they fit somewhat loosely. Otherwise, you'll need a crowbar to get them up. Each time we returned to the tropics from more temperate latitudes, we had to plane down the floor boards again. We never figured out how that could be possible, but it was a common experience.

■ *Zincs (anodes).* Marinas often have stray electrical charges that can destroy your zincs in no time. After an extended period in a marina, we would stop at an

Table 9-3. Periodic maintenance schedule

System	Monthly	Quarterly	Annually	Every three years or as needed
Hull	Dive and check zincs, prop, through-hulls, and bottom paint Use mild liquid abrasive to take rust off all exterior stainless Touch up any exterior varnish	Inspect and rebed deck fittings as needed Inspect prop for pitting, corrosion Grease folding prop	Polish and wax hull Paint bottom with antifouling Clean and grease winches Varnish cabin sole	
Rigging		Check rig tune, fittings, all welds and terminal ends Clean mast track and spray with silicone	Complete mast and rig inspection, retune rig Inspect every halyard and sheet over its entire length, replace or end-for-end as necessary Wash salt-encrusted halyards Remove, clean, and reseal mast boot	Pull mast and inspect mast base, mast step, and all wiring in mast
Plumbing		Inspect, open, and close all seacocks to be sure they are not frozen	Inspect all through-hulls above and below waterline Polish any seacocks that are leaking Grease all seacocks Replace seals in saltwater hand/foot pumps Rebuild head, replace all valves and seals Replace seals and rebuild electric bilge, freshwater, and deck wash pumps Inspect all hose clamps; lubricate if necessary	Clean water tanks
Electrical	Check battery fluid Clean battery terminals Check all major charging system connections, battery terminals, and bus bars for corrosion or loose wires	"Equalize" wet cells Check all navigation and deck light bulbs and connections		

(continued)

Table 9-3. Periodic maintenance schedule (continued)

System	Monthly	Quarterly	Annually	Every three years or as needed
Sails		Inspect every sail for chafe and pulled stitches, patch as needed	Wash sails in mild detergent	
Ground tackle		End-for-end chain and rope rodes	Service electric windlass Replace length markings on chain and rope rode Wash all docklines	Regalvanize anchors and chain if needed Open and relubricate manual windlass
Steering and self-steering	Check and lubricate steering controls, oil bearings in sheaves Top up autopilot oil on below-decks pilot Inspect wind vane welds, clean rust off	Tighten wind vane control lines, end-for-end if any wear	Inspect and lubricate wire rope, roller chain, and pedestal shaft bearing Remove compass from binnacle to lubricate needle bearings and lightly oil wire Inspect rudder bearings for leaking, binding	Repack rudder bearings
Refrigeration		Check refrigerant level, recharge if necessary [1]	Flush refrigerator condenser with muriatic acid in the tropics Replace refrigerator zinc	
Propane		Check all propane connections	Clean connections and refit with aluminum tape Sand and repaint propane tanks	
Safety gear	Check EPIRB battery	Replace materials in abandon-ship bag, be sure everything works properly	Have liferaft inspected and serviced Have fire extinguishers tested and serviced Test EPIRB Inspect jacklines and replace if frayed or worn or if made from webbing (not UV resistant) Repickle membranes in handheld watermaker	

[1] Some models may need to be recharged by a qualified technician. Check your operating manual for instructions.

anchorage and dive to check our zincs before heading out on passage. A spare zinc that can be hung over the side of the boat in a marina will provide additional protection. Consider one of the various AC isolation systems if you have an ongoing problem with electrolysis.

■ *Cosmetics.* Keeping stainless bright helps prevent difficult-to-remove rust marks from developing on the hull. Diluted oxalic acid applied every few months will remove all rust from stainless, and Soft Scrub or some other mild liquid abrasive can be used between major cleanings. Silicone spray on a rag also protects stainless for short periods of time.

■ *Hardware.* Machine shops will custom-build just about anything at reasonable rates. We had a 5-inch stainless steel sheave machined in Tahiti and flown into Raiatea for about $60. An equivalent sheave or pulley from a discount marine store in the United States would have been well over $100 without freight. On a half-dozen occasions we had top quality machine work done in stainless for a fraction of the chandlery price.

The annual haulout

The annual haulout offers the opportunity to put all your systems in working order. Inspect everything and fix as much as you can afford to. The only things that really have to be done on the hard are bottom paint, greasing and polishing seacocks, rebedding underwater through-hulls, repacking rudder bearings, and maintaining a below-waterline centerboard. While the boat is out of the water, you can do other chores more easily, including replacing worn zincs, rebuilding the head, repacking the stuffing box, greasing a folding prop, and so on.

Before choosing a particular yard, take a good look at their haulout equipment. Make sure belts and wires are free of chafe and pulleys look well oiled. Make sure your insurance or their insurance will cover any damage if your boat is mishandled. I know of Americans in New Zealand who spent a year litigating for damages after their boat was dropped from a Travelift.

When you are about to be hauled, check the slings on the Travelift or pads on the trolley for dirt and grime. If they look soiled, cover them with plastic garbage bags. Grit on slings or pads can scratch or damage the gelcoat; oil can be ground in and become impossible to remove. Whether the boat is being hauled on a marine railway or a Travelift, make sure the trolley or straps are properly aligned with the hull. Sling markers attached to the toerail can help you position the boat, but you should also carry a diagram of your underwater profile to show to the machine operator.

Once out of the water, have the yard pressure-wash the bottom before blocking her in place. Most grass and dirt will come off easily if it is pressure washed before it dries. When they block up the boat, be sure that the bow is well supported to prevent the hull from flexing and damaging interior bulkheads. Many yards we were in neglected to do this unless asked.

The main reason to haul the boat annually is to re-paint the bottom. Only new sails can offer greater performance improvement than a clean bottom. As our bottom became fouled, we lost a knot in boat speed, adding days on a long passage. Once a year, we pressure-washed, lightly sanded, and then painted the bottom with high quality antifouling.

Tropical water is a richer environment for marine life than more temperate seas. After trying several alternatives, we found the ablative (or soft) antifouling paints worked best when we were doing a great deal of passagemaking in a year. If anything did take hold, it would be shed along with the paint while we were sailing. We preferred one coat of a hard antifouling paint of one color (for example, red) followed by three coats of a compatible soft antifouling paint of another color (blue). When we saw red paint, we knew we needed to repaint. If you use the ablative paints, never scrub them. You'll only thin the effective layer of paint. A heavy layer of grass will be sailed off after a day on passage. If you choose to use only the hard antifouling paint without the ablative overcoats, be sure to give it a good scrub before you put to sea.

When the boat is on the hard, check the following items.

■ *Inspect and service through-hulls.* Look for cracked caulk and rebed if necessary. Remove all hoses and check the hose and the hose ends. Replace worn hoses. Replace hose clamps. Polish any leaking seacocks. Grease all seacocks.

■ *Inspect the propeller.* Make sure that the prop turns free and fair. Check that the crown nut is snug and the cotter pin is well secured and not worn. If your prop is one of the folding or feathering varieties, make sure that it changes position smoothly and lubricate it generously.

■ *Inspect the rudder.* Make sure that the rudder moves freely without binding. Repack the rudder stuffing box if necessary. Clean barnacles out from between the rudder and skeg and on the top edge of the rudder next to the boat. Use a dental pick to remove barnacles from tight crevices.

■ *Inspect and replace zincs (anodes).* Inspect all zincs. Replace any that are more than 60 percent worn away.

■ *Clean the transducer paddle wheel.* Make sure it spins freely. Use a dental tool to remove barnacles and other growth. Some antifouling paints can attack the transducer material, so use a specialty paint or leave it bare.

■ *Inspect the keel bolts.* If your boat has keel bolts, tap them with a ballpeen hammer. If you hear anything but a satisfying "chunk," you will need to investigate further.

■ *Open and inspect below-waterline centerboard areas.* If you have a centerboard, open it and inspect the pendant and pulleys for wear or chafe. Replace any zincs in the centerboard trunk.

Rigging

Passagemaking puts tremendous wear and tear on spars and standing and running rigging. The shock loads from a suddenly backed headsail or a small spinnaker filling with a crack can easily damage a weakened rig. To be sure your rig is up to offshore standards, inspect it regularly. That means a half-hour check before and after every passage and an annual inspection that lasts several hours.

Terminal ends and welds tend to fail first. The masthead crane is subject to violent and extreme shock loads. Inspect these areas closely, preferably with a magnifying glass. Look for any cracks in welds, swages, or terminal ends, and for fraying or stranding in wire rigging. Running a rag over the wire rigging will quickly locate any barbs that signal weakened wire. Each year, loosen all the stays, inspect each fitting, apply a dry lubricant, and retune the rig.

Don't forget to inspect the bobstay and its fittings when you inspect the rest of the rigging. A bobstay failure can cause damage equal to a headstay failure. We saw two boats after their bobstays had failed. One boat had been under full sail in 20 knots of wind. The pressure on the genoa pulled the 5-foot-long bowsprit right out of the deck. The other boat had been in a gale with storm sails set. They had to jury-rig a new bobstay in the middle of the gale or risk losing the mast.

Some additional tips for keeping your rig in offshore condition follow.

■ *Rinse with fresh water.* At every chance, rinse the rig, winches, and blocks with fresh water. Force high-pressure water through your blocks to remove salt crystals.

■ *Avoid rigging tape.* Avoid taping your rigging. Tape traps salt water and speeds corrosion. Where taping or covering your rigging cannot be avoided, inspect beneath the tape regularly. After we finished our trip, we found that one spreader end had badly corroded under the tape. Corrosion can result in any area where stainless steel rigging comes into contact with the aluminum mast.

■ *Reducing mast track friction.* If you are having a problem dousing the main, take a single sail slide and attach a halyard to the top and a downhaul to the bottom. Run the sail slide up and down the track to find the problem area. If the track is burred or distorted, file it down. Then fix whatever is causing the chafe.

Sails

Sails and running rigging should be inspected daily on passage to find any chafe before it becomes a serious problem. Every six months, follow each seam from leech to luff and fix any broken stitches. Use sail tape to protect areas prone to chafe. These precautions will prevent a whole seam or panel from blowing out, at least until the sail material is so weak that it can no longer hold the stitches.

Other suggestions for maximizing sail life follow.

■ *Sew in batten ends.* Batten pockets should be sewn closed so battens are not lost if the sail flogs. Carry two spare battens equal in length to your longest batten. Spares can be cut down with a hacksaw to replace any battens that break or get lost. A hollow boom makes a good stowage place for long battens.

■ *Prevent sail stretch.* Let the tension off the genoa halyard and release leech and luff lines when in port. This will prevent the sail from stretching and losing its shape prematurely.

■ *Stow sails properly.* If you use hank-on headsails, stow them securely when they are not in use. Initially, we dropped our Yankee and lashed it loosely to the bowsprit. The sail chafed on the bow pulpit and deteriorated from UV radiation. We then stowed it in a custom-made sailbag lashed to the bow pulpit. The sail was still ready to fly the moment the weather deteriorated, but it was well protected from chafe and the sun.

Plumbing

To become your own plumber, you need to know your own system. If you don't have a complete plumbing diagram, take several hours one day and create one. If you do have one, kindly supplied by the boat manufacturer or the previous owner, take a few hours and verify it. Locate all water tanks, holding tanks, and sumps. Find the valves that turn off and on every tank. Trace tank overflows from where they exit the tank to where they exit the boat. Learn the location and type of each pump aboard and their associated filters. Follow the path from each tank to each plumbing fixture. Determine the location and function of every seacock and know how to access them.

As you inspect your plumbing system, replace anything not of the highest quality. Over the course of our first year, many of the boat's cheap nylon and PVC plumbing fittings broke. In one case, a water tank fit-

ting snapped and we lost 50 gallons of fresh water into the bilge in the middle of a gale. If you find such fittings aboard, replace them with bronze or Marelon fittings.

Check valves tend to stick in pipes that carry waste water. Avoid check valves where possible. Otherwise, clean them once a year and use a rubber mallet or ballpeen hammer to break them loose when they stick. If your head hose is more than a few years old, replace it with sanitary hose designed to minimize odors. Make sure every seacock has a wooden plug of the proper diameter located within reach that can be used in an emergency.

For all of the abuse they get, marine heads have become quite reliable. A little attention will keep them functioning well for years. To keep your head in good condition, be sure that nothing goes into it other than human waste and toilet paper. If yours discharges overboard, flush the entire system with clean salt water after every use. On most boats, several feet of hose must be flushed, which means 10 to 12 strokes after the bowl looks clean. Failure to clear the exhaust hose will leave an unpleasant odor and clog the head after several successive uses. Only after the system has been thoroughly flushed should the bowl be pumped dry.

Even with liveaboard use, head parts will last three to five years. But rebuilding your head every year or so will keep you from having to do this nasty job at sea. Most spare parts kits or owner's manuals provide complete instructions. To minimize the mess, rebuild the head when you are in a marina or during your haulout. Unbolt the whole unit from its base and take it to running water so you can clean as you go. Once it is clean, smear grease liberally on all moving parts.

Most head pumps have a packing gland around the pump shaft. If this starts to leak, gently tighten the packing nut about a half a turn until the leaking stops. If it starts leaking again within a week or so, loosen the packing nut and add some waterproof grease. This will often stop the leaking for a month or more. The packing gland itself will need to be repacked every few years.

As grease gradually wears away, seacocks start to weep and become difficult to open and close. Grease them annually when the boat is hauled out.

Electrical

To become your own electrician, you need a complete

wiring diagram for your boat. If you don't have one, make one. If you do have one, trace every wire to check its accuracy. If one thing has changed aboard your boat since it was launched, it will be the wiring. Trace the charging system. Locate every bus bar. Determine whether any gear bypasses the main control panel (an electric bilge pump, for example). Make sure to locate all the little black boxes for your fancy electronic equipment. Find the fluxgate compass for your electric autopilot, the processor for your instruments, and the tuner for your SSB. Unless you know where every component is and how it is wired into the electrical system, you will spend hours trying to trace a voltage drop that turns out to be a CD player that wasn't wired into the main control panel.

Your battery maintenance will depend on whether you install gel cells or wet cells. There is great debate surrounding this issue. The gel-cell batteries can be dis-

charged more deeply and charged more rapidly. They have a lower self-discharge rate. They are sealed, which makes them safer: no possibility of corrosive fumes, explosive gases, or acid in the bilge. They require no maintenance. However, with proper charging and maintenance, wet cells can last two to three times as long as the more expensive gel cells. Within our voyaging community, people who took advantage of the deep discharge and fast recharge capabilities of the gel cells were happiest with them. These batteries make the most sense aboard boats with extensive electrical equipment including electric windlasses, SSBs, and electric autopilots. Boats with more modest electrical requirements did better with deep-cycle wet cells.

If you have wet-cell batteries, you will need to check the fluid regularly. You will also need to "equalize" them about once a month if you are away from shore power. This means highly charging the batteries to remove any

A day in the life: the demands of the sea

The following is excerpted from a letter I wrote a friend from New Zealand, November 28, 1993:

"The boat itself requires a tremendous amount of work—far more than I would have guessed. Don't trade in your house yet! We've spent the last three weeks in a boatyard refitting Silk after her first 20,000 nautical miles. Our to-do list took up three pages and included replacing cables, lights, and battery terminals that had corroded; replacing our propane tanks that had rusted; varnishing the floor and oiling the teak; buying new sails; cleaning and painting the bottom; fixing our broken diesel heater. . . . The boatyard has done some of the work, but Evans and I have invested 12 hours a day, six days a week. I find boat work to be very satisfying—work where you can stand back and admire what you have done when you are finished; work that gets you physically tired but leaves your mind clear. Hard work but good work.

"I am amazed at the destructiveness of the sea environment. Salt water and air corrode anything electrical or metal. Even high-grade stainless steel weeps rust in a matter of months. The motion works constantly on joints and seams in the boat. The rolling or pounding

in heavy waves sometimes causes the hull to flex. The pressure of the wind in sails breaks shackles rated at a breaking strength of a half-ton. In light winds (8 to 10 mph), our spinnaker got caught and ripped a metal fitting off our bowsprit—along with a piece of teak 3 inches thick and 6 inches long. Everything happens slowly but with terrific force. I have truly come to respect the potential of wind and water—respect built from painstaking experience.

"And the sea is hard on us as well. Physically demanding, yes, but also emotionally demanding. The sea teaches relentlessly—lessons about patience, about quality, about change, and about violence. You learn these lessons or you stop sailing—one way or another. You also learn how to accommodate your partner in situations that most couples cannot even begin to comprehend. Evans and I have been absolutely, totally alone together for 29 days straight in a space the size of a large living room, dealing with conditions that could conceivably kill us. It's taken time to find a balance, especially given that before we left we only saw each other for a few hours each week. As you put it, 'Marriage is not all rosebuds and moonshine.' But we've become closer lately in a way that I'm very comfortable with."

buildup of sulfur, accomplished by running the battery voltage up to 16 volts at a very low charge rate. If you have a smart regulator that is not set up for this type of charging, you will need to find a way to bypass it. While batteries are being equalized, they must be isolated from electrical equipment that could be damaged by this high voltage.

Beyond knowing your electrical system and understanding your batteries, learn how to track down a short using a multimeter. In most cases, you'll find that corrosion or a loose connection has caused the problem.

Ground tackle

Ground tackle takes a great deal of punishment and requires almost no maintenance. Inspect the rode and shackles for chafe and wear. Replace worn shackles and end-for-end rodes regularly. Make sure that the shank or flukes of the anchor are not bent. Rinse the

---

Troubleshooting: 90 percent solutions

The first time our engine wouldn't start or our batteries wouldn't charge, we were frustrated and a bit frightened. The second time, we knew where to begin looking for the problem. The third time, we were 90 percent certain how to fix the problem based on the symptoms. A major failure is always possible, but many times the problem is a basic one. If you experience any of the following symptoms, save yourself time and effort by checking the basics first.

■ *Engine won't start.* Make sure your batteries are charged and the battery switch is set to the appropriate battery bank. If your gear shift has to be in neutral, check that. Make sure the engine stop knob is not pulled out. Check to see that there is fuel in the tank and no dirt or water lurks in the glass bowl at the bottom of the Racor filter. If these are all fine and you hear the engine cranking but not starting, then you probably need to bleed the engine.

Your manual will provide specific instructions on bleeding your engine, which will include the following steps: Unscrew the air-vent bolt on top of the fuel strainer; pump the small fuel-feed pump, if your engine has one, or crank the engine until the fuel coming out around the bolt is clear and without obvious air bubbles; tighten the bolt firmly and try the engine again. Most of the time, the engine will start.

If the engine doesn't start, or if it starts and runs rough, bleed the injectors. Unscrew the nut on the first injector; crank the engine until the fuel flow is clear; tighten the nut. Repeat the process with the next injector until the engine starts and runs smoothly.

■ *Engine overheating.* Check for blockage to the raw water intake. Plastic bags are the usual culprit. Check belt tension on the water pump. Change the water pump impeller.

■ *Electrical system not charging.* Check the connections at the alternator, regulator, and batteries. Clean them if there is any sign of corrosion. If the problem is intermittent, check for loose connections. Check the alternator belt for wear and adjust the tension.

■ *Electrical equipment not functioning.* Make sure your batteries are charged and the battery switch is set to the appropriate battery bank. Use a multimeter to check if electricity is reaching the equipment. If not, check the battery terminals and the electrical connection to the equipment for corrosion. Trace the wires between the batteries and equipment and look for a loose, wet, or dirty connection. If electricity is reaching the equipment, check the on/off switch for corrosion. If all of this is working, the most likely problem is a bad circuit board. Contact the manufacturer.

■ *Electrical bilge pump with float switch running constantly or not at all.* Check the float switch—the electrical connections always get corroded. Make sure the hose isn't clogged. Clean any dirt out of the bilge pump.

■ *Pressure water system running constantly.* Look for leaking faucets, particularly the head on the cockpit shower. If those are not the problem, check for fresh water in the bilge. If you find fresh water, look for a loose hose clamp.

chain and anchor as often as possible with fresh water to protect galvanizing. Few people realize that bacteria can attack and destroy chain in tropical waters unless weed and coral are scrubbed off regularly. When anchored for a month or more, raise the anchor once every 10 days, clean it off, and inspect it. In the main anchorage at Suva in Fiji, some sort of chemical or metal in the water attacked ground tackle and destroyed most of the galvanizing. If you hear about a problem or notice one, don't let the damage get to the point where your chain could be weakened.

After hundreds of nights at anchor, the zinc galvanizing that protects the underlying steel will wear away and your chain and anchor will start to rust. You should then consider regalvanizing to extend the life of your ground tackle. Regalvanizing does not replace lost metal or restore original strength, so don't let ground tackle deteriorate for too long before taking action. Regalvanizing anchors requires far less skill than regalvanizing chain—and the price of an anchor versus the price of galvanizing makes the decision academic.

On the other hand, only regalvanize your chain if you can find a reputable metal shop that others have used with good success. When improperly done, regalvanizing can cause chain stretch or distortion. After some friends had their chain regalvanized in Venezuela, it no longer fit in their windlass gypsy. They raised the anchor by hand all the way across the Pacific. In South Africa, one shop did not remove the excess zinc before it hardened. The crew had to pick out the balls of metal from between each link.

In most countries outside the United States regalvanizing is cost-effective and worth considering. When you call for a quote, ask them how they clean the chain beforehand and how they remove the excess zinc afterwards. The price is usually quoted by weight, and many shops have a minimum weight requirement. Consider pooling the ground tackle of several boats.

PRETRIP PREPARATIONS: TOOLS AND SPARES

Voyagers enjoy being self-sufficient. But self-sufficiency takes on new meaning when it's time to do some basic maintenance in a remote anchorage hundreds of miles from the nearest chandlery or diesel mechanic. Good maintenance requires proper tools and necessary spares. We found the following items to be a base level for voyaging in remote areas.

The voyager's toolbox

Salt water and damp air easily damage tools. Only high quality tools can stand up to the constant use and abuse of life aboard. Stainless steel tools cost two to three times as much as regular tools and may break your heart when they go over the side (which they will). We bought high quality nonstainless tools and cared for them well.

After using a tool, we lightly rinsed it in fresh water, wiped it down thoroughly, and then sprayed it with water-dispersing spray. About once every six months, we went through the toolbox and cleaned off any rust or corrosion from each tool. We did not store battery packs and batteries in power tools to prevent the terminal contacts from corroding.

With this approach, our tools held up relatively well. Allen wrenches and drill bits proved most susceptible to rust. On our next voyage, we will buy one of the Allen wrench sets that look like pocket knives with a plastic body and anodized wrenches. These will not rust, and the wrenches will not end up all over the cabin sole every time we need to use one. Small drill bits can be stowed in a plastic container with a small amount of household oil.

Table 9-4 shows the basic hand tools for the voyager's toolbox—both ones you will want to keep handy for everyday use and additional tools you won't need immediate access to but that you will use often. The "special needs" column highlights areas where you may have to bring along special tools for your boat. Before you leave, make sure you have the proper tools for each situation described.

Screwdrivers need to be made from high quality materials. Bring one with a 4-inch handle and a 1/4-inch tip for tight places. This proved to be one of our most useful screwdrivers, often the only solution for unscrewing trim pieces in the far corners of lockers. The slotted screwdriver blades need to be thick enough for a number 10 screw head.

Table 9-4. Tools for the self-sufficient voyager

Equipment	Everyday	Additional	Special needs
Screwdrivers	One medium, one small slotted head One medium, one small Phillips-head	Large slotted head with grippable handle Large Phillips-head Stub-sized slotted and Phillips-head Large to extremely small jeweler's screwdrivers	Offset screwdrivers to access hose clamps
Wrenches	6- and 8-inch adjustable wrenches	Pipe wrench 10-inch adjustable wrench Set of open-end and box wrenches, metric and SAE standard Full set of metric and SAE standard Allen (hex) wrenches Chain wrench ¼- and ½-inch ratchet drive socket sets with 3- to 4-inch socket extension	Angled wrenches to access seacocks Box or open-end wrench large enough to service through-hulls Allen wrenches that fit all winches aboard Adjustable wrench large enough to fit shaft packing nut Chain wrench that can be used on oil and fuel filter if necessary Long enough extension for hard-to-reach engine bolts
Pliers	Needlenose pliers Slip joint pliers Medium locking pliers Wire cutters Small metal file	Small and large locking pliers (Vise-Grips) Large slip joint pliers Side cutting pliers End cutting pliers Set of metal files from small to large	Wire cutters that will cut through damaged rigging Metal working tools
Paint and polish tools		Putty knife Paint brushes of various sizes 3-inch scraper	Wire brush
Other	Small ballpeen hammer 6-foot tape measure in metric and English Wooden folding rule	Rubber mallet Pry bar Punches, cold chisels, wood chisels Small hand drill Set of feeler gauges Dental tools Mirror with extension handle Heavy-duty scissors	Something that can be used as lever to tighten V-belt on engine Some sort of pick or dental tool that can be used to remove flax from packing glands

You will need a complete set of both metric and SAE standard wrenches and sockets. On many American-made boats, the diesel engine will be metric and all other hardware (nuts, bolts, screws) will be standard. If you are organized enough, you can determine which sizes are actually necessary aboard and which you can leave behind. As you work on your boat, try to replace odd-sized nuts, bolts, and screws with a standard size. Few of us are that organized, so we bring them all along.

Beyond these basics, a grease gun is useful for lubrication and essential for greasing a folding prop. A professional caulk gun will see almost constant use. Try to get one in heavy-gauge steel. We went through one every few months until we bought a professional quality gun in New Zealand.

Small hand pumps serve many purposes aboard, including removing dirt and water from the sump in the diesel tank, emptying a blocked sink or head, and removing water from the bilge due to clogged limber holes. Carry three or four of various sizes.

A commercial quality drill finds a dozen uses on any boat. Bring along two sets of high quality drill bits because you will lose some over time. They will break, rust, end up over the side, or get lost in the bilge. The drill will be used on teak, fiberglass, aluminum, and stainless, so buy the most powerful drill you can afford. It needs to run on 12 volts or be rechargeable using an inverter and battery packs.

You will need a good digital multimeter for electrical troubleshooting. A proper ratchet crimper and a 12-volt or butane hotknife/soldering iron with rosin-core solder will reduce the number of times you have to redo the major electrical connections on your boat. The hotknife is also useful for line and sail work. If you do not have sealed batteries, you will need a hydrometer to test the batteries occasionally.

No boat should try to do without a good bosun's chair. We left with a climbing harness, which we intended to use as a surrogate bosun's chair. We could tolerate it for only 10 to 15 minutes, but many tasks up the mast took twice that long. We made a comfortable bosun's chair from a teak plank, some carabiners, and the remnants of an old sail and then only used the climbing harness at sea.

A hacksaw with a variety of blades (18-, 24-, and 32-tooth) will handle most cutting problems. To really cut through rigging, bolt cutters become too big to store on smaller boats—unless you can afford the hydraulic type.

You will use a good stainless steel rigging knife with marlinspike daily. A nicropress kit, taps, and dies are good for metal, wire, and rigging work. You will want taps for the most common types of machine screws: 10 to 24 and 44 to 20. If you plan to splice cored line, you will also want some hollow fids. A small wire swaging press (made by Ormiston in England) would be a useful addition.

For boats over 40 feet, you may want to add a vise and C-clamps, a riveting tool and rivets, a 4-pound sledge, and a small wheel puller. A small grinder and a small palm sander make fiberglass work much easier. You can use a Dremel tool for a variety of tasks, including the removal of recalcitrant bolts. While these are all useful, most smaller boats get along without them.

The spares locker

You really can't have too many spares when you leave the United States. In retrospect, most cruisers wish they had devoted more stowage to spares even at the expense of provisions. Table 9-5 reflects what we regularly carried after the boat had been broken in and we had learned to do most repairs ourselves.

Your spares need to reflect your emergency preparations. Ask yourself how you would construct a jury rig if you lost your mast, how you would get water out of your tanks if your pump broke, and how you would stop a leak after a collision. Make sure you have the equipment to carry out the emergency procedures you develop after reading Chapter 19.

Table 9-6 shows some additional useful supplies. Tongue depressors proved useful for everything from stirring paint, to applying epoxy, to scraping excess sealant off newly rebedded deck fittings. We used surgical gloves for cleaning and for working with epoxy and other hazardous materials. Large syringes can be used to mix two-part epoxies or to baste the turkey for Thanksgiving dinner. Bronze wool pads don't rust like steel wool.

Create a list of all batteries and bulbs used aboard. We stowed spare batteries in one large ditty bag and spare bulbs in another. Inside the ditty bag, we kept a list of the batteries used aboard, average length of time the batteries lasted, and our current inventory. We tried

Table 9-5. Spares and materials for the self-sufficient voyager

System	Recommended spares	Supplies	Other
Engine	Several oil and fuel filters	Eight quarts of engine oil	Some spare flax packing
	Cooling water pump impeller and rebuild kit	Two liters of transmission oil	A length of spare engine hose
	Starter solenoid	Engine coolant	A length of spare high pressure fuel line
	Several spare belts of all types	Biocide for diesel	
	Full manufacturer's replacement gasket set		Spare gasket material and gasket sealant
	Spare regulator		
	Thermostat and gasket		
	Alternator bearings		
	Brushes and diodes		
	Starter motor bearings and brushes		
	Injectors		
	Fuel nozzle		
Hull	Spare zincs	White gelcoat and hardener	Fiberglass rubbing compound
	Winch repair kits	Gelcoat color additive (if necessary)	Fiberglass polish and wax
	Winch ratchet springs (at least a dozen)	Epoxy putty	
		Underwater epoxy	
Rig	Assorted shackles and blocks	Teflon spray	Spare 7 x 19 wire
	Spare vang	Water-dispersing spray	Several snatch blocks
	Spare 1 x 19 wire with one piece long enough to replace a headstay	Whipping twine and vinyl rope dip	Messenger line twice the height of mast
	Spare halyard and set of sheets	Cotter and clevis pins	
	Spare turnbuckles	A half-dozen Sta-Lok fittings	
Sail	Two spare battens of longest length (store in boom)	Sail tape	A sailmaker's palm
	Spare hanks and slides	Sail twine, plain and waxed	
	Spare webbing of various sizes	Heavy thread	
	Sail cloth of various weights	Many heavy needles	

(continued)

Table 9-5. Spares and materials for the self-sufficient voyager (continued)

System	Recommended spares	Supplies	Other
Steering and self-steering	Spare wind vane wind blade (vane)		Emergency tiller
	Spare wind vane crash tube and oar		
	Spares kit for electric autopilot		
	Steering cables		
Plumbing	Rebuild kits for all pumps and the head	Teflon tape or plumber's tape	Spare hose of various sizes
	Spare float switch for electric bilge pump	Stainless hose clamps of all sizes	An assortment of hose and pipe fittings
Electrical	Spare bulbs of all types	Assorted crimp-on terminals	An assortment of fuses
	Flashlight bulbs	Electrical tape	Wire ties of several sizes
	Spare batteries	Heat-shrink tubing	Multistrand, tinned wire of various sizes
		Vaseline and other anticorrosives	
Refrigeration	Spare electronic control panel (switch, timer, light)	Refrigerant	Fitting for charging
	Spare drive belt	Pencil zincs for condenser	

Table 9-6. Additional supplies for maintenance and repair

Fluids	Supplies	Other
Light household oil	One box of wooden tongue depressors	Two or three large medical syringes
Loctite or NeverSeize	One box of surgical gloves	Duct tape, masking tape, aluminum tape
Teak oil, varnish, paint	Monel seizing wire	Super glue, rubber cement, wood glue
Lubricating sprays of all types	40- to 500-grit sandpaper, wet and dry	Shock cord in several sizes
Lithium grease	An assortment of 316 stainless bolts, locking nuts, and screws	Bronze wool pads
Solvents including acetone, rubbing alcohol, and mineral spirits	Assorted small pieces of plywood, teak, stainless, and aluminum	
Silicone and 5200 caulk	Piece of marine ply large enough to cover opening for biggest port	

to keep a six-month supply available, although we only kept one spare for the calculator, watch, and camera batteries, because they did not last well.

If your boat is energy intensive and you depend on a generator or the engine for power, you will want to add some additional engine spares. These include a spare starter motor, alternator, and saltwater pump. After a certain point, you will start to feel like you should be towing a sistership so you can scavenge parts as you go. When you decide you have enough spares for all but the most improbable scenarios, you're ready to head off to sea.

Our ability to keep the boat going in the most remote parts of the world with only the tools and equipment that we had on hand represented one measure of our independence. Over time, ingenuity became more important than having exactly the right part. When we reached places with chandleries and marine professionals, we gradually switched from looking for the largest chandlery to looking for the best hardware store.

Additional resources

Owner's manuals provide the best information for your particular systems. Beyond that, Nigel Calder's *Boatowner's Mechanical and Electrical Manual* (International Marine, 1996) offers comprehensive and understandable information on almost every aspect of maintenance aboard. His extensive discussion of gel cells versus wet cells meshes well with our experiences. Calder's *Marine Diesel Engines* (International Marine, 1992) is also excellent.

CHAPTER 10 | GALLEYWISE

Foresight ▪ *Provisioning ports* ▪ *Strategic provisioning* ▪ **Filling up** ▪ *Starting from an empty boat—the mechanics of stowing and tracking* ▪ *Provisioning tips and tricks* ▪ *Additional resources*

The need for self-sufficiency aboard becomes obvious when it comes to provisioning. When you are coastal cruising, provisioning means menu-planning for a few days at a time. If you misjudge, you can step ashore and buy some milk. When you prepare for short offshore passages, more precision and a greater safety margin are required. Otherwise, you might have to make do without the milk for a day or two. But when you cross an ocean, provisioning means stocking the boat with everything you will need for a period of months. If you have underestimated, you will have to live without or substitute. Provisioning for an extended period in tropical islands cannot be done meal by meal. Once we left the Atlantic, we were basically provisioning ocean by ocean.

Deciding what you must take along can seem overwhelming, but information makes the process manageable. You need to know what goods are available in paradise—and what goods aren't. You also need to know the mechanics of filling up—how to select, stow, and preserve everything, from canned goods to toilet paper.

FORESIGHT

What you need to bring depends on what you will find along the way. Every place has its own local foods and products, but ports tend to fall into one of three categories. Village markets provide basic produce and a few staples at good prices. Major island ports offer a much broader selection at a price premium. Mainland ports provide the best opportunity to stock the boat inexpensively with a full range of provisions.

You also need to know where to limit your provisioning. Some countries will confiscate produce and even canned and packaged goods. Prudent provisioning means limiting the amount of food you lose when you reach these places.

Provisioning ports

When you leave the Atlantic or the Mediterranean to head off across the Pacific or Indian Oceans, the three types of ports will define your provisioning routine. Almost every island has a village where the local people gather to sell their produce—from coconuts to exotic fruits and vegetables. We supplemented our ship's stores with fresh fruits and vegetables and wonderful bakery bread from these markets. Every few months, we arrived at a major port city with a wider range of goods; here we could buy basic foods for reasonable prices. But luxuries such as exotic spices, prepared meals, sweets, and snacks were unavailable or expensive. Most voyagers spend hurricane season in developed regions—New Zealand, South Africa, Australia, Thailand, or the Mediterranean. In these places, we filled the boat with everything we wouldn't see again for another six months.

Table 10-1 summarizes what is available in the different types of ports.

My approach to provisioning depended on where we were sailing. When we were cruising along the coast of New Zealand or South Africa, I menu-planned for a week, just as I would do when coastal cruising in the United States or Europe. Ice was plentiful and the water was cool, so we used the icebox, and my provisioning

Table 10-1. Provisions available in different types of ports

Category	Products	Village market basics	Island port provisions [1]	Mainland provisions [1]
Dairy products	Shelf-stable products	Margarine Kraft processed cheese Canned parmesan cheese	UHT milk, dried milk Tinned butter, processed cheese	Full variety
Meat and eggs	Canned	Corned beef Spam Tuna in oil	Tuna and other fish (in oil) Seafood (smoked mussels, oysters, etc.)–$$ Ham–$$ Other meats–mutton, beef	Tuna in water Chicken or turkey
	Fresh	Eggs–$$	Eggs Full range of fresh and frozen meat	
	Dried		Pepperoni, sausage, etc.	Beef jerky
Prepared meals	Canned		Soups, baked beans, spaghetti	Stews, chili, ravioli, etc.
	Freeze-dried			Pasta or rice packet meals
Cereal and grains	Cereals	Rice	Breakfast cereals–$$ Oatmeal, Cream of Wheat	Full variety
	Flour	White flour	Whole wheat flour	Rye flour Corn meal
	Pasta	Spaghetti Ramen noodles	Macaroni, fettucini, linguini, etc.	
Vegetables	Fresh	Carrots, onions, potatoes Tomatoes, lettuce	Cassava, taro Cucumbers, green peppers	
	Canned	Beans	Asparagus, water chestnuts–$$	Full variety
Fruits	Fresh	Bananas, coconuts Pineapples Lemons, ginger	Apples, oranges Breadfruit, mangoes, papayas Pamplemousse, watermelon	
	Canned	Peaches, pears–$$ (sweet syrup)	Fruit cocktail (sweet syrup)	Full variety, canned in natural juices
	Dried		Raisins Figs or dates–$$	Almost any other dried fruit

[1] The items shown are in addition to those listed in the previous columns. $$ = expensive

(continued)

Table 10-1. Provisions available in different types of ports (continued)

Category	Products	Village market basics	Island port provisions[1]	Mainland provisions[1]
Baking supplies	Basics	Flour, yeast	Olive oil	Exotic spices—cumin, coriander, nutmeg, etc.
		Corn oil	Baking powder, baking soda	
			Basic spices	Prepared mixes—cakes, cookies, breads, muffins, etc.
	Sweeteners	Sugar	Cocoa	Baking chocolate, chocolate chips
			Honey	Molasses, maple syrup
Snacks	Munchies		Popcorn	Other chips
			Potato or corn chips	
			Peanuts, other nuts	
	Crackers/cookies	Digestive biscuits	Fancy crackers	Saltines, graham crackers
			Packaged cookies	Pop-tarts, granola bars
	Candy		Hard candy	M&Ms
			Cadbury candy bars	American candy bars
Other foods	Garnishes		Mustard, mayonnaise, catsup	Relish
			Pickles, olives	Applesauce
	Sandwich makings		Jelly or jam	Peanut butter
Beverages	Soft drinks		Soda, drink mixes, juice	UHT juice
	Hot drinks	Black tea	Herbal tea, coffee	Hot chocolate mix
	Alcohol		Beer, wine–$$ unless duty free	High quality wine
			Hard liquor–$$ unless duty free	Brand name liquors
Nonfood items	Batteries and bulbs		Alkaline batteries–AAA to D	Flashlight bulbs
			Calculator, watch, camera batteries–$$	
	Toiletries		Suntan lotion	Deodorant
			Toothpaste, dental floss	
			Feminine products	
	Paper goods		Paper towels (poor quality)	Veggie storage bags
			Toilet paper (poor quality)	Zip-top bags
			Garbage bags, plastic bags	Heavy-duty tin foil

[1]The items shown are in addition to those listed in the previous columns. $$ = expensive

list included fresh milk and meat. When we were anchored off a major island port such as Suva in Fiji, I could buy fresh food every day. Even without the icebox, we could eat pretty much as we wanted. But for the months that we spent in small islands, the icebox was not much use. Ice was unavailable and the water was often the same temperature as the air. No fresh dairy or meat products were available ashore. For these periods, we would live off ship's stores without refrigeration. We purchased fresh food to supplement our diet of pasta, rice, and canned goods.

Market village basics

The hearty (or desperate) can always find enough food to survive until the next major port. Only in a few places—such as Suvarov atoll in the Cook Islands, tiny Minerva and Beveridge reefs in the Pacific, and Chagos archipelago in the Indian Ocean—will you find no population and nothing ashore except coconuts and crabs. Everywhere else, there are villages with people who survive on what the island provides and what the supply ships bring.

Almost every island we visited had a main town with a market where all the islanders brought their produce. If we arrived very early on market day, we could get coconuts, bananas, tomatoes, carrots, lettuce, and fresh ginger. If the island had an average amount of rainfall we would find cassava, taro, cucumbers, green peppers, pineapples, and watermelons. We often bought succulent lemons that looked like small limes and were orange inside. Occasionally, we found pamplemousse—the cabbage-sized, green, delicious grapefruit of the Pacific islands.

In general, we found less fruit in less variety than we had envisioned. On desert islands like the Tuamotus, even bananas cannot grow. Much of what is available elsewhere is seasonal. We often ended up relying on canned fruit.

In addition to the market, look for the village bakery. As you travel from the Azores to the Caribbean, from the Tuamotus to Fiji, from Mauritius to St. Helena, just about every village has a bakery that supplies fresh bread six days a week. Most villages also have a store, though it often resembles a carnival booth more than a supermarket. Most stores are a corrugated tin shed, one side of which has a waist-high counter (Figure 10-1). A smiling, corpulent shopkeeper produces what is asked for from the dim and dusty shelves. Almost everything on those shelves is expected to last for years, and most of it has.

In the store you can find corned beef, tuna fish, canned fruit, and canned vegetables. However, the corned beef contains large amounts of fat and gristle, the tuna fish is canned in heavy oil and salt, and the fruit is covered with sweet syrup. But you can buy potatoes and onions, eggs, rice, pasta (usually spaghetti), ramen noodles, crackers, corn oil, tea, sugar, and shelf-stable, imitation dairy products (a Velveeta-like processed cheese and fluorescent orange margarine). Most of these staples are subsidized, so they are quite inexpensive. Dishwashing soap and laundry detergent are also available, but the dish soap does not clean well in salt water and the detergent costs up to $10 for the smallest box.

The store also has yeast and flour. Since everyone buys their bread from the bakery, the flour is often weevily or moldy and the yeast so old it will not prove. When we could, we bought flour and yeast from the bakery. Otherwise, we bought small quantities from the store, inspected them carefully before bringing them aboard, and used them up quickly.

If a supply ship has recently come in, you may find any number of other items. We found imitation rice crispies or corn flakes, cookies, UHT (ultra–heat treated) milk, tinned butter, and poor quality paper towels in these grocery stores. When available, such things are expensive (two to three times U.S. prices).

Don't expect to find fresh meat in these small villages, unless the local chief slaughters one of his pigs for a feast. Domestic dogs and cats are unheard of; and dogs are still considered a delicacy on many islands. In the more remote Pacific islands, eggs are so expensive because feral cats carry off the chickens. In the Marquesas, wild goats and horses abound. But don't take your own meat unless you are hunting with the local chieftain who "owns" the animals. In Tonga, pigs wander everywhere, but they are considered semi-sacred and owned by chieftains. If you do find meat in these villages, it won't be labeled and wrapped in plastic.

Using the provisions available in any market village, you can make basic, nutritious meals. Fresh fish and shellfish, when you are lucky enough to catch or trade for it, will spoil you forever. Rice, pasta, and potatoes

Figure 10-1. Most supermarkets in the Pacific islands looked more like a carnival booth.

cooked with canned tuna or corned beef and flavored by a good dose of spices can provide enough variety for many weeks. With bakery bread, homemade bread, and eggs you can concoct a half-dozen breakfast variations. Fresh fruits and vegetables add some interest and variety. Where fresh is not available, you can almost always purchase canned. The meals you serve made from basic island foods will not put you on the cover of *Gourmet* magazine, but they will provide a healthy diet for you and your crew.

Island port provisioning

Almost every island group has one large port, usually where yachts must clear customs: Suva in Fiji, Nuku'alofa in Tonga, Papeete in Tahiti, Las Palmas in the Canaries, Horta in the Azores. These ports offer an array of goods beyond what is available in smaller island ports (Table 10-2). Though we could find most things on our provisioning list in these places, imported goods cost at least 30 percent more than in a mainland port. To keep food costs under control, we limited our provisioning to reasonably priced local items.

All of the small island villages bring their best produce to the big market in the major port city. In these ports, therefore, you will find much greater variety and much higher quality than in the villages. Suva, on the big island of Viti Levu in Fiji, and Papeete on Tahiti boast fabulous markets offering mangoes, papayas, breadfruit, lemons, limes, oranges, watermelons, pineapples, coconuts, bananas, pamplemousse, guavas, apples, kiwis, and a full assortment of vegetables (depending on the season). Exploring these markets is a real adventure. You are expected to deliberate over every fruit and haggle over every purchase.

Near the market, you will find a street lined with small bakeries, butchers, pastry makers, and other specialty stores. The butchers offer a surprising array of relatively inexpensive, high quality fresh meat. Western-style supermarkets are increasingly common in many of these ports. But the best prices and highest quality are still to be found in the market and the small specialty stores.

On most islands, you won't have any problem filling propane tanks. People in more developed areas of the Pacific and Indian Oceans rely on propane for cooking.

We had two 10-pound tanks aboard; each lasted for six to eight weeks cooking two meals a day and baking bread every few days. We never had a problem refilling our tanks, and we never had an issue with fittings. If your tanks are rusty, repaint them. Some places will refuse to refill rusting tanks for fear that they are structurally unsound.

In major ports like Papeete and Port des Galets in Réunion, we took our tanks to the natural gas facility in the port where gas was offloaded from tankers. They filled them for free or for a small fee. In many places, butane is substituted for propane. We noticed no difference in cooking. Butane burned a bit dirtier and left black marks on our pots and pans. We cleaned them off with Soft Scrub.

Throughout the world, the French islands offer a fantastic selection of imported French products. The prices will quickly break most voyagers' budgets. Yet many staples are subsidized, such as bread, pasta, dried milk, flour, and rice. By stocking only these staples and locally grown produce, you can cruise quite frugally throughout French Polynesia and in other French territories in the Indian Ocean and the Caribbean. Table 10-2 summarizes the best island provisioning ports by area.

Mainland provisioning

Many of the luxuries in Table 10-1 can be found in places where voyagers spend hurricane season: New Zealand, Australia, Singapore, the Mediterranean, South Africa, and Venezuela, and of course the United States. Even in these mainland ports, however, you will not find some staples of the American diet. Only in the United States can you find all those fat-free, sugar-free, cholesterol-free products. For those who are diabetic or have other dietary restrictions, these items must be provisioned in the States. Other things you won't often find include peanut butter, maple syrup, applesauce, molasses, chicken breast canned in water, zip-top bags, and vegetable storage bags. We learned to do without these items, or we filled our luggage with them on visits home.

Table 10-2. Island provisioning ports

Area	Port	Selection	Prices	Comments
North Atlantic	Las Palmas, Canary Islands	Excellent	Moderate	Top up boat for Atlantic crossing
Caribbean	Puerto Rico	Excellent	Inexpensive	U.S. goods at U.S. prices
	U.S. Virgins	Excellent	Moderate	
	Grenada	Good	Moderate	If not stopping in Venezuela, can use to provision to Panama
Pacific	Pago Pago, American Samoa	Excellent	Inexpensive	Located halfway across Pacific, good stop for small boats that must provision between Panama and NZ/Australia
	Guam	Excellent	Inexpensive	U.S. goods at U.S. prices
	Suva, Fiji	Excellent	Moderate	Spot provision before heading to NZ/Australia
	Papeete, Tahiti	Excellent	Very expensive	French island—stick to subsidized staples for best buys
	Raratonga, Cook Islands	Good	Expensive	
	Nuku'alofa, Tonga	Good	Expensive	
Indian Ocean	Galle, Sri Lanka	Good	Moderate	
	Port Louis, Mauritius	Excellent	Moderate	Best provisioning port in southern Indian Ocean
	Saint Denis, Réunion	Excellent	Very expensive	French island—stick to subsidized staples for best buys
South Atlantic	St. Helena	Good	Moderate	

Any major port in the United States offers a full range of provisions at some of the best prices in the world. European prices vary a great deal, from country to country and from village to city. European prices are generally somewhat higher than U.S. prices, with southern Europe being less expensive than northern Europe. Scandinavian prices are the highest. We lived in Sweden for a year before setting sail, and I paid triple U.S. prices for most groceries. Small villages often have lower prices than major port cities. Spain and Portugal offer

A day in the life—visiting an Indian market

The following is my journal entry from Durban, South Africa, November 12, 1994:

"Laila and I went to the Indian market after the day turned gloomy instead of weepy. We walked our normal route to the supermarket, then continued a few blocks beyond to where the streets got seedy and the buildings wore primary colors. We turned down a side alley and found ourselves in the small byways of an old market square. Shops lined either side of a ten-foot wide alley, their wares sprawling out their open doors. Hawkers grabbed our sleeves and named their prices, dropping them by half as we turned to walk away. Hawkers and shoppers alike were Indian—dusky Indian men with gold necklaces and slicked back hair, elegant Indian women in multicolored saris.

"The alley twisted and turned, leading us by jewelry stores selling rhinestones and paste and others selling real gold and diamonds, cooking stores with parts for primus stoves next to pots and pans of every description, and clothing stores full of saris and skirts. It ended at the Victoria Market, a two-story building composed of arches broken by expanses of violet, pink, purple, and blue.

"We went into the fish market where men pushed prawns and crabs under our noses and snapped out a price, only to have the vendor next door offer a lower one. A crush of people milled around—mostly Indian, but there were many blacks as well. As far as I could tell, we were the only whites, and we attracted considerable attention. 'Where you from? Germany?' 'For you two girls, I give you a real deal . . . ' 'Watch your backpack girls. Many bad people here.'

"Repelled by the overwhelming smell of fish spoiling in the 85-degree heat, we crossed the street to the spice market. This turned out to be another major curio center, carrying all of the souvenirs that we have seen throughout South Africa. Soapstone elephants and rhinos, verdite busts of wise witch doctors, gemstones of every description, baskets and more baskets, rugs, mats, table settings—Africa in a box, ready to ship home.

"Vendors with shelf after shelf of Indian spices—beyranis and curries and masalas—were forced into the back corner of the market by this wealth of Africana. There Indian women in saris held out spoons of spices, 'Chicken spice mix—just try it.' 'Mother-in-law Exterminator: This will make her go back to where she came from.' 'This is Honeymoon Barbecue—just shake and bake for a match made in heaven!' We bought a few things, and found that two or three rand (about $1) satisfied the shop owners. They would quickly lose interest in us and turn to the next group strolling by.

"Finally, Laila and I had had enough—too many people, too much humidity, too little space. We fled with our purchases. On the way back to the yacht club, just on the outskirts of the Indian area, Laila stopped and peered into a window full of herbs and spices. Still searching for nutmeg and cinnamon, we entered. Inside, we were greeted by gruesome sights. Hanging from the ceiling were animal parts of every description—antlers from several different kinds of antelopes with large pieces of flesh still attached, desiccated cats' heads suspended by an ear staring down at us with hostility, the dried haunches of what looked like a mongoose. One wall was covered with branches from every obscure tree in Africa, another decorated with pickled animal parts ranging from testicles to ears and tails.

"It was only after an awed perusal of the entire room that we looked closely at the proprietor. Then we noticed the animal bones on the counter in front of him and the wooden stick decorated with the hair of several animals in his hand. I'm not sure who was more surprised—him, to find two blonde, blue-eyed white women staring at him, or us, to realize we had entered a witch doctor's store. We were clearly not welcome, so we fled back to the suddenly mundane Durban streets, hoping we had not attracted the magician's enmity."

the least expensive provisioning, and duty-free Gibraltar remains the best place to fill the boat for the Atlantic crossing.

Table 10-3 summarizes mainland provisioning outside of the U.S. and Europe.

Strategic provisioning

Strategic provisioning means buying food where it is least expensive and not arriving in port with food that might be confiscated. The least expensive mainland and island ports at the time of our circumnavigation are summarized below. For up-to-date information, follow the Seven Seas Cruising Association bulletins. But the overall situation changes slowly. Our best provisioning ports were much the same as Scott and Kitty Kuhner's on their first circumnavigation over 20 years ago.

Problem ports—ports where provisions will be confiscated—change more rapidly. The SSCA bulletins provide updated information. Most times, the quarantine inspection consists of a cursory check. But in a few places, quarantine is a serious business. If you arrive

with problem provisions, you could lose stores intended to get you across an ocean.

Almost all countries confiscate fresh produce and anything that can sprout—beans, seeds, and so on. Australia and New Zealand go far beyond this. They take honey, eggs, fresh milk, and other dairy products. In some cases, frozen meat is confiscated. Meats canned in South America and any home-canned foods are taken. Other canned food, as long as it does not contain meat, is rarely touched. They will even ask if you have hiking boots aboard that might carry dirt from another country.

At Christmas Island and Cocos Keeling, the same restrictions apply. If you leave Australia, visit Indonesia, and return to Christmas Island, be prepared to go through the whole process again.

While these stringent procedures are annoying, they are justified. Australia and New Zealand are still free of rabies and many cattle diseases. All cattle are quarantined on Cocos Keeling island before they can be imported into Australia. Contaminated honey has all but destroyed wild honey bees in the United States, a fate that Australia and New Zealand have so far avoided.

Table 10-3. Mainland provisioning

Area	Country	Selection	Prices	Comments
Caribbean	Venezuela	Excellent	Inexpensive	Getting more expensive, but less costly than Caribbean
	Panama	Excellent	Moderate	Imports somewhat pricey, a good place to provision for Pacific
Pacific	New Zealand	Excellent	Inexpensive	Bulk stores offer great prices and no packaging
	Southern Australia (Sydney, Brisbane, Fremantle)	Excellent	Inexpensive	
	Northern Australia (Cairns to Darwin)	Good	Moderate	Most produce (including eggs) has been refrigerated and shipped—spoils quickly
Indian Ocean	Singapore	Excellent	Inexpensive	Best provisioning stop before heading to the Red Sea
	Phuket, Thailand	Good	Moderate	
	Salalah, Oman	Excellent	Moderate	Good stop before the Red Sea
	Durban, South Africa	Excellent	Inexpensive	
South Atlantic	Cape Town, South Africa	Excellent	Inexpensive	
	Brazil	Good	Moderate	Used to be least expensive place in the world; prices now comparable to U.S.

Painful as it is, comply with the regulations and help these countries protect their fragile ecosystems.

On most islands, quarantine officers focus on alcohol. In Fiji, anything over one bottle per person was taken and returned at check-out. In other countries, alcohol was sealed into a locker. Cruising scuttlebutt and the SSCA bulletins provide current information.

FILLING UP

So where do you start when the boat is empty and an ocean awaits? Everyone develops their own methods over time. This section walks you through our provisioning process—how we shopped, how we prepared food to be stowed, and what we did to keep foods fresh for as long as possible.

Starting from an empty boat— the mechanics of stowing and tracking

We are in New Zealand after having crossed the Pacific. We have been here for several months, but in a month we will be leaving for Fiji. While in New Zealand, we have enjoyed well-stocked supermarkets. We no longer wander the aisles with our mouths open, but we still appreciate being able to get anything in several sizes and colors. We shop week by week, and we have been enjoying fresh meat and dairy products. The time has come to fill the boat for the six-month run to South Africa.

We start by taking inventory of everything left on the boat—not just food items but also batteries, light bulbs, cleaning supplies, toiletries, paper goods, and plastic bags. We go through every locker and examine every can and package. We discard any cans that are dented or look rusty, especially along the seams. We check the dates on the pharmaceuticals in our medical kit and decide if they must be replaced. We look at the expiration dates on all batteries and test any that are suspect. We throw away all spices older than three months.

We dig into the dark recesses of every locker and get rid of anything questionable: ravioli bought in Venezuela that tasted too sweet, packaged soup mixes that tasted like straw, a can of green beans with rust on the seam. We assume that what we haven't used in the last six months won't get used in the next six months. To free up stowage space, we eat those still-edible leftovers or give the food away.

During our inventory, we make two lists. The items we need to buy, with rough amounts, make up our master provisioning list. The meals we can cook from the goods in our lockers and those we plan to buy make up our master menu guide. This menu guide offers instant ideas when nothing comes to mind for dinner. It lets us know what is available without tearing apart our lockers. But most importantly, this list forms the basis for the next round of provisioning: When we eat the last can of clams, linguini and clam sauce gets crossed off the list so we'll know to buy more when we reach a major provisioning port.

With our lists in hand, we take the next few weeks to try various prepared foods. We sample canned foods such as baked beans and corned beef. We also try freeze-dried pasta, rice meals, canned and packaged soups. We eliminate brands we find too sweet or too salty. By the time we are ready to begin provisioning, we know what prepared foods we want to have aboard.

We talk to local butchers about vacuum-packing meats for the refrigerator. We look for a farmer's market where we can buy fresh eggs, fruits, and vegetables that have never been washed or refrigerated. We locate batteries for the celestial calculator and light bulbs for the interior lights, contact a physician to restock our supply of antibiotics, and fill our propane tanks.

A week or so before we expect to leave, we wash all our dry goods storage containers, including spice jars, and let them air out for a day. Then we head to the supermarket with our master provisioning list and buy canned goods, dried foods, beverages, snacks, and non-food items. We do not purchase any dairy or fresh food. We buy about 20 percent less of the bulk items than we think we will need, such as flour, sugar, rice, pasta, and dried milk, and we choose small containers, enough to be used up immediately once opened. The cost savings of buying large sizes are wasted in leftovers that spoil. We check expiration dates on everything and buy the packages with the most current dates.

Many of our buying decisions revolve around packaging. Cardboard is never allowed on board: It harbors cockroach eggs, clogs the refrigerator drainage system, and disintegrates in the humidity. We buy goods with cardboard outer packaging only if they are also packaged in cellophane or wax paper inside.

Metal containers are unwelcome aboard, though cans are unavoidable. Baking powder, yeast, hot chocolate mix, crackers, and cookies sometimes come in cheap metal containers. These leave rust marks in lockers and make a gooey mess when they rust through. We can often find the same items in plastic packaging, or we transfer the contents to plastic containers. Soda cans are easily punctured or crushed; we buy soda in large plastic bottles, available throughout the world.

When goods come in either plastic or glass, we generally choose plastic. While Tupperware can stand up to almost anything, light plastic packaging can break. Plastic bottles of corn oil can split their seams in a gale and create chaos in the galley locker. We buy plastic, unless it feels flimsy (flimsy enough to be crushed with our bare hands). We have never had a glass container break aboard, but we worry about the dangers inherent in glass. If we have to buy the product in glass, we store it in an old sock for cushioning.

Eggs create special packaging problems. Cardboard egg cartons are particularly attractive to cockroaches. Plastic egg carriers from camping stores proved too small and regular for farm fresh eggs. In the islands, you will be handed eggs wrapped in newspapers. We used Styrofoam egg cartons, which we found in most mainland ports. We washed and reused them for months. Our egg cartons occasionally got confiscated by quarantine officers, but only where we could replace them.

We take a taxi back to the boat and unload the goods onto the dinghy dock. Then the real work begins. We bring our plastic containers ashore and transfer the contents of cardboard, metal, or light plastic packaging into them. When transferring dried goods such as pasta, rice, or flour to plastic containers, we divide them into half-pound or one-pound portions, transfer to separate Ziploc bags, and put the filled bags in the plastic containers. We stow small amounts in the galley and larger amounts in several places around the boat. (We started doing this after water got into one of our large plastic containers and ruined our entire store of flour.) The plastic bags also keep the containers clean: When flour and dried milk get wet, they dry into a cementlike substance that is very difficult to get out of containers.

We dispose of all discarded packaging and take the provisions out to the boat in the dinghy. Once aboard, we stow everything we have purchased and see how much room is left for more. Though we bought 20 percent less than our master list called for, the boat seems full to overflowing. We've completed our first round of provisioning.

Based on how much money and space we have left, we reprioritize our master list into essentials and luxuries. A few days later, we take one more look around, rearrange the stowage spaces, and make a final provisioning list for the nonperishable items. We go through one more round much the same way as the first. We've got it just about right if we feel we have enough food for a decade.

We will leave within the next few days, weather permitting. We decide exactly how much more money we are going to spend on provisioning. We set aside $100 or so for perishable foods and go back to the store with whatever is left. This time, we wander up and down the aisles and look for things we might have forgotten and for treats, snacks, or specialty items. By the time we get back to the boat, we know we cannot stow another non-perishable item.

Whether they look dirty or not, we clean out our refrigerator and our vegetable and fruit stowage areas with bleach (about 1 ounce in 1 gallon of water). A small amount of bacteria or fungus in a plastic crate filled with onions or apples can cause them all to go bad within a few weeks. Once our storage areas are clean and dry, we do our first round of perishable provisioning. We buy onions, potatoes, garlic, apples, oranges, and other heavy items that will keep for a month or more. We inspect them to make sure they are clean, then stow them in our storage areas.

The weather looks perfect. We decide to leave as soon as we clear customs. First, off we go to the local market, the farm stand, or wherever the food is the freshest. We buy eggs and the rest of our fruits and vegetables, including the short-lived ones for the first few days at sea. Then we get our dairy products and bread. We stop at the butcher and pick up our vacuum-packed meat. Back at the boat, we inspect the fruits and vegetables to be sure they are clean. Then we load everything aboard, clear customs, and set sail. We've provisioned for the next six months.

Provisioning tips and tricks

Before our first few major passages, I wandered the aisles of supermarkets convinced I had forgotten something essential. I racked my brain: If we ran out of anything while we were thousands of miles from the nearest supply, I knew it would be critical. I eventually realized that you can substitute for almost anything. And what can't be substituted for, you can do without. Appendix 1 provides a list of useful substitutes and equivalents for voyaging. If you forget something, it is unlikely to prove a major disaster.

To give you some idea of what we stocked, this section details our mainland provisioning list by category. The quantities reflect our limited stowage and our diet. We did not use our refrigerator much, preferred pasta and rice to meat, and did a great deal of baking (bread every two to three days at sea). Your own list will depend on your diet. Tables 10-4 through 10-7 are offered as rough guidelines you can use as a starting point. This section also offers tips on keeping food for as long as possible, even without refrigeration, and for stowing items.

Canned goods and dried foods

These items took up the bulk of our stowage space and were the foundation of most meals once we had been offshore for 10 days. If necessary, we could have survived for three months on these provisions alone. We supplemented with locally purchased flour, sugar, rice, vegetable oil, spaghetti, dried milk, and other shelf-stable dairy products. We assumed we could buy or trade for fresh fruits, vegetables, and seafood. We didn't plan on finding meat along the way.

Dairy products

While none of the shelf-stable dairy products can satisfy a fresh-milk drinker, many come close, especially if served cold. For cooking, no one can tell the difference.

■ *UHT milk* is widely available outside of the United States. It does not taste as good as fresh, especially when it's warm. However, it tastes better than dried milk and will last up to two months unopened, even in the tropics. UHT milk has been known to explode in lockers after it passes its expiration date. Check the dates when you buy it and stow the boxes in plastic

bags. Use them up a week or so before they expire. Once opened, UHT milk lasts about 24 hours unrefrigerated in the tropics.

■ *Dried milk* is available in any major island port. Use it for cooking, even if you don't like the taste for drinking. We either purchased the boxes with a dozen foil envelopes inside and stowed those in Ziploc bags or bought 1-pound boxes and transferred the contents to plastic bags in a plastic container. When mixing dried milk, cold water keeps it from lumping. If possible, refrigerate it overnight for a taste and texture closest to fresh. Even if you drink skim milk, buy some whole dried milk for cooking, especially to make substitutes for cream. Anchor's whole cream milk, a New Zealand brand sold throughout the Pacific, comes the closest to fresh. Most kids drank it willingly.

■ *Tinned butter* is widely available throughout the tropical islands. It tastes surprisingly good and works well for cooking. Check the expiration dates: Some of the cans in Pacific villages have been there forever. Once opened, the butter will keep for a week or two unrefrigerated, so plan your baking accordingly.

Meats

We never acquired a taste for corned beef or Spam, but canned meats played an important role in our diets. We ate canned tuna for lunch, canned clams or shrimp in a white sauce over pasta for dinner, and canned chicken in packet pasta meals or curry dishes. Danish canned ham (the real thing, not the pressed variety) adorned our pizza and livened up our macaroni and cheese. Mutton stew and corned mutton from New Zealand proved much more appetizing than corned beef. You can buy high quality canned beef, pork, chicken, and turkey by the case before you leave (see "Additional resources" in this chapter). Don't buy canned ham from the refrigerator case unless you plan to keep it refrigerated; look for the tins on the shelves.

■ *Smoked seafood* makes a wonderful treat when you crave the taste and texture of fresh meat. It comes in small cans like sardines and is widely available throughout the Pacific islands, though quite expensive. If you provision it in the United States or New Zealand, it is considerably less expensive and lasts forever.

Table 10-4. Major provisioning—canned goods and dried foods

Category	Products	Specific items	Approximate quantities
Dairy products	Shelf-stable products	UHT milk	8–12 1-liter boxes
		Dried milk—whole and skim	3 16-oz. boxes
		Tinned butter	4–5 16-oz. tins
		Parmesan cheese	5–6 16-oz. plastic containers
		Condensed milk	3–4 14-oz. cans
Meat	Canned meats	Tuna in water	3 dozen 6-oz. cans
		Chicken/turkey breast in water	1 dozen 6-oz. cans
		Canned clams or shrimp	6–8 6-oz. cans
		Smoked mussels, oysters, etc.	1 dozen 12-oz. tins
		Ham	4–5 1-pound tins
		Corned mutton, corned beef	6 1-pound cans
	Dried meats	Pepperoni, sausage, etc.	5–6 individual meats
		Beef jerky	Small packages to make ~ 2 lbs.
Prepared meals	Canned	Soups—condensed for cooking	1 dozen 12-oz. cans
		Soups—hearty for heavy weather	8–10 19-oz. cans
		Baked beans, stews, chili, etc.	8–10 1-pound cans
		Spaghetti, ravioli, etc.	5–6 1-pound cans
	Freeze-dried	Pasta or rice packet meals	15–20 packages
		Cup-a-Soup	1 dozen packets
		Ramen noodles	1 dozen packages
Fruits	Canned	Fruit cocktail, peaches, etc.	1–2 dozen cans
	Dried	Raisins	Small packages to make ~ 5 lbs.
		Figs or dates	Small packages to make ~ 2 lbs.
		Apricots, apples, pears, etc.	Small packages to make ~ 5 lbs.
		Banana chips	As money allowed
Vegetables	Canned	Green beans, wax beans, corn	1 dozen cans
		Exotic vegetables to eat cold	1 dozen cans
		Mushrooms	1 dozen smallest cans available

(continued)

Table 10-4. Major provisioning—canned goods and dried foods (continued)

Category	Products	Specific items	Approximate quantities
Vegetables (continued)		Canned puréed tomatoes	1 dozen small cans
		Tomato paste	6–8 small cans
Cereal and grains	Cereals	Breakfast cereals	6 large boxes
		Oatmeal (for baking/breakfast)	Small packages to make ~ 4 lbs.
		Cream of Wheat	2 1-pound packages
	Flours	White flour	10–12 1-pound packages
		Whole wheat flour	2–3 1-pound packages
		Rye flour	1–2 1-pound packages
		Corn meal	1 1-pound package
	Grains	Rice	Small packages to make ~ 5 lbs.
		Bulgur	Small packages to make ~ 2 lbs.
	Pasta	Spaghetti, linguini	4–5 1-pound packages
		Macaroni, bows, etc.	4–5 1-pound packages
Baking supplies	Basics	Vegetable oil	3–4 small, strong bottles
		Olive oil	5–6 small, strong bottles
		Wine or herbed vinegar	4–5 small bottles
		Cider vinegar	1 large bottle
		Soy sauce	1 large bottle
		Tabasco sauce	1 small bottle
		Other sauces	1 small bottle of each
		Yeast	Small packages to make ~ 1lb.
		Baking powder	2–3 10-oz. packages
		Baking soda	1 1-pound package
		Pepper	1 large bottle of peppercorns
		Salt	1 12-oz. package
		Vanilla	2 large bottles
		Basic spices	2 bottles of each
		Exotic spices	1 bottle of each

(continued)

Table 10-4. Major provisioning—canned goods and dried foods (continued)

Category	Products	Specific items	Approximate quantities
Baking supplies (continued)	Sweeteners	Sugar	10 1-pound packages
		Honey	3 1-pound bottles
		Cocoa	3 12-oz. plastic containers
		Chocolate chips	6–8 8-oz. packages
		Molasses	1 16-oz. bottle
		Maple syrup	3–4 8-oz. bottles
Other foods	Garnishes	Mustard	4 small jars
		Mayonnaise	6 small jars
		Catsup	1 large plastic bottle
		Relish	5–6 small jars
	Spreads	Jelly or jam	5–6 small jars
		Peanut butter	5–6 small jars

■ **Corned beef.** Buy it even if you don't like it. You'll be amazed what you can trade it for across the Pacific. I traded two cans of corned beef in Tonga for a gorgeous 3-foot by 10-foot piece of tapa cloth that the owner wanted $50 for.

■ **Pepperoni, sausage, other dried meats.** Unrefrigerated, commercially packaged brands or the type that hangs above the deli counter keep almost indefinitely. If they do mold, scrape off the white dust from the outside and use as normal.

Prepared meals

Cans need to be stowed in a dry place or they will rust. Even then, they will develop small rust marks around the seams. We had three drawers under one of the settees in the main salon where we stowed our cans. We never had a problem with labels coming off, and the drawers were dry enough that we never had a major rust problem. If you think labels might come off, use an indelible ink pen to mark the cans with a two-letter code and a date. If you must stow them in the bilge, protect them with plastic or wax. I don't recommend var-

nish because it may end up in the food when you open it. To wax cans, melt a small candle and dip the can's bottom, top, and side seam. Some people used a vacuum sealer to protect their cans (see "Additional resources," page 192, for more information).

We never tried freeze-dried camping meals because they were so expensive and unavailable outside the United States. The freeze-dried soup and stew mixes that come in a cuplike container were also expensive and difficult to stow. We did use the packet pasta and rice meals available in most supermarkets. We found these in all our mainland provisioning ports, though some were very sweet or salty. Try them before you buy.

Keep at least one month of canned goods as emergency rations. Replace them once a year or so. Thick stews or soups that can be heated in one over-sized pan provide quick nutrition in heavy weather. These can double as emergency rations.

Our three can drawers measured 18 inches by 18 inches by 12 inches. We stowed cans on their sides so we could see the labels and put about three dozen cans in each drawer. We used one drawer for canned meats, one for canned soups and meals, and one for canned fruits and vegetables. Even if you don't have drawers, set up a compartmentalized arrangement so you can find things. If only can tops are visible, mark them with indelible ink so you don't have to remove the cans to check the labels.

Fruits and vegetables

We used canned fruits and vegetables on passage and in remote islands where fresh food wasn't available. After the fresh vegetables had run out on passage, we enjoyed the taste and texture of exotic vegetables like asparagus, baby corn, water chestnuts, artichokes, and so on. These offered much needed variety and were worth the premium price.

Dried fruit lasts for months if the bag is well sealed. Even a pinhole rupture will let in enough air to cause the fruit to ferment, so double-bag in zip-top bags and check often. If a bag puffs up, eat the contents immediately if they taste normal. Figs, raisins, and dates never fermented, but apples, apricots, pears, and prunes did.

Drying your own fruits and vegetables using a dehydrator offers a lightweight alternative to carrying cans. Dried fruits and vegetables retain more of their nutritional value than canned ones, and they require less stowage space. Once opened, they do not need to be used immediately to prevent spoilage. Dehydrators take a large amount of electricity, so you will need a good battery bank and an inverter or shore power (see "Additional resources" in this chapter for more information).

Cereals and grains

Few countries share the American penchant for breakfast. If available, cereal is quite expensive. Pancake mix, maple syrup, Pop-tarts, and American bacon are all difficult to find. Bisquick is widely available, and canned American bacon can be purchased in American Samoa, Australia, and New Zealand. Most of the time, we relied on hot cereal, bread variations, and an occasional egg. For special brunches, we stowed maple syrup and made our own pancake batter or French toast.

Cereal needs to be stowed so it won't get crushed. We removed the waxed paper liner and discarded the box. Then we sealed the liner into a large Ziploc bag. We stowed these with bags of chips or cookies in a dedicated locker or crate. We also stowed cereal on top of fruits and vegetables in our stowage crates.

Select flour carefully. We often bought one bag and inspected it before we stocked up. We discarded any flour that had colored specks or strings or otherwise looked suspicious. Smell the flour as well—this is the best way to detect mold. We transferred the flour to zip-top bags that we stowed in airtight plastic containers. We used one or two bay leaves for each large zip-top bag of flour and never had weevils. Perhaps that is because we were so careful about selecting our flour in the first place, but who wants to argue with success?

Baking supplies

We didn't worry too much about widely available items like flour, sugar, and vegetable oil. We would buy these as we went and keep a reserve for use if an island hadn't gotten a recent shipment.

Fresh spices turn basic ingredients into palatable fare, but spices are sensitive to light and heat. They keep longest when stowed in a cool, dark place. Even so, we needed to replace our spices completely once a year.

- **Basic spices** include thyme, basil, oregano, parsley, mixed Italian spices, bay leaves, cinnamon, cloves, garlic, and paprika. Just about everything else can be considered exotic and will only be available in mainland ports.

- **Exotic spices** we carried include dry mustard, cumin, chili powder, ginger, coriander, nutmeg, allspice, rosemary, tarragon, marjoram, and dill seed or weed.

- **Honey** sometimes crystallizes. If that happens, put the container in hot water for 10 to 15 minutes.

- **Molasses and maple syrup** are almost nonexistent outside of the United States. Honey can substitute for either with only a minor change in flavor. Buy maple syrup in small containers because it will mold after a month or so once opened.

- **Cocoa** is available in major island ports. Unsweetened baking chocolate tends to melt in the tropics.

- **Vegetable shortening** is hard to find and doesn't keep well unrefrigerated. Substitute margarine or butter.

Other foods

Heavy-duty squeeze bottles for mustard and catsup are ideal when the boat is rolling and you only have one hand to spare. You can buy these in the States and refill them as you go along. All these items do fine unrefrigerated. Jellies and jams may ferment after several weeks, so use them up quickly once opened.

Even mayonnaise will keep indefinitely without refrigeration if you always use a clean spoon to serve it. We kept mayonnaise for months in tropical temperatures. But if you suspect a contaminated spoon has touched your mayonnaise, throw it away. Most marine refrigerators do not maintain the temperature as well as a home refrigerator, so keeping mayonnaise in them may be less safe than using the clean spoon approach. If you are uncomfortable with this solution, buy a box of the restaurant-size single servings.

Salad dressings are quite expensive and do not keep well once opened. We made small amounts of vinaigrette using herbed vinegar, olive oil, garlic, spices, and a bit of mustard, or we made Russian dressing using mayonnaise, catsup, and relish. The vinaigrette was also used on canned vegetables, pasta, and potato salads.

Beverages

Dehydration can be debilitating. When running downwind with light breezes and a hot sun, we would each drink close to a half-gallon of liquid per day. Having a variety of beverages onboard keeps the crew drinking throughout the day.

Good water and fresh lemonade comprised our beverage basics. We also drank iced tea, made from herbal tea or black tea with spices. We allowed ourselves one box of UHT juice per week after we used up the bottled juice.

We don't drink carbonated soft drinks. For those who do, Coke, Pepsi, and other soft drinks can be found in any mainland or major island port. These are the easiest beverages to find and stow, and the large plastic bottles hold up well offshore. For those who don't like soda, the choices are more limited. We would take along a few bottles of ginger ale or Orangina. Ginger ale is soothing for a slightly seasick stomach, and Orangina is more like real juice than most sodas.

Table 10-5. Major provisioning—beverages

Category	Products	Specific items	Approximate quantities
Beverages	Soft drinks	Ginger ale/Orangina	6–8 1-liter bottles
		Drink mixes	Enough to make 15–20 gallons
		Juice	5–6 medium-sized bottles
		UHT juice	8–10 1-liter boxes
		Bottled water	2 dozen 1.5-liter bottles
		Tonic	Two six-packs of small bottles
	Hot drinks	Herbal tea	5–6 boxes
		Regular tea	1 large box
		Coffee	Small packages to make ~ 3 lbs.
		Hot chocolate mix	2–3 dozen individual packets
	Alcohol	Beer	2 six-packs
		Wine	4–5 bottles
		Hard liquor	1 bottle each of rum and gin
		Other	1 bottle each of sherry and port

We were always trying drink mixes. When we found ones we liked, we stocked up. Our personal favorite is "Sunquick," a concentrated liquid that comes in wonderful flavors like pamplemousse and tangerine. This French product is available in the French islands worldwide, and in New Zealand and Australia. Many boats carry Tang and use that for breakfast. Regular and sugar-free Kool-aide and similar products are also available.

We drank coffee only in port (after several mishaps at sea with coffee grounds on the cabin sole), even though I am a dedicated coffee drinker. At sea, our hot drinks were regular tea, herbal tea, and just-add-water hot chocolate. Above 25 degrees in either hemisphere, we drank several cups a day. In the tropics, we rarely wanted hot beverages.

Our alcohol purchases depended on the price of al-cohol and the quarantine practices of neighboring countries. In general, we didn't carry much alcohol and never drank at sea. The table shows the most we carried upon leaving a port. We often had no alcohol aboard.

Snacks

Our snacks depended upon what was available and what we could afford. Your body needs salt to absorb the water you drink and to prevent dehydration, and we craved salt at sea. Most snacks are expensive, take up a surprising amount of space, and are easily crushed. They do, however, last well.

Our base level of snacks included popcorn, lightly salted peanuts, small packages of olives, hard candy, and saltines. All are inexpensive and stow well. We considered the rest discretionary and only bought them after the basic provisioning was completed.

Table 10-6. Major provisioning—snacks

Category	Products	Specific items	Approximate quantities
Snacks	Munchies	Popcorn	Small packages to make ~ 3 lbs.
		Potato, corn, or other chips	10–12 packages
		Peanuts	Small packages to make ~ 5 lbs.
		Other nuts	As money allowed
	Crackers/cookies	Saltines	3 1-pound boxes
		Graham crackers	3 1-pound boxes
		Triscuits, Cheez-its, etc.	5–6 boxes
		Packaged cookies	1 dozen packages
		Pop-tarts, granola bars	As money allowed
	Other	Pickles	6–8 large jars
		Black olives	One dozen small containers
		Green olives	5–6 small jars
		Applesauce	8–10 small containers
	Candy	Hard candy	5–6 one-pound bags
		Candy bars	1–2 "fun size" bags
		M&M's	6 8-oz. bags

After a week or so at sea, we craved textures, not specific foods. Pickles, olives, and crackers offered fun combinations of salt and texture. Canned asparagus and other exotic vegetables provided a refreshing and crunchy treat weeks after the last cabbage had become cole slaw. Pop-tarts and granola bars made great breakfast substitutes when we were tired of bread, but they were very expensive and hard to find. M&M's are the only candy that survives unrefrigerated in the tropics, but they do "melt in the hand" when eating them in 90+-degree heat, and the food coloring stains clothes and fingers.

A few hints for stowing these snacks follow:

■ **Popcorn.** To keep it fresh, keep it airtight. Tightly sealed plastic containers are the best answer. Good quality popcorn lasts for several months at sea, though old popcorn takes longer to pop than fresh.

■ **Cookies and crackers.** We looked for cookies and crackers packaged in waxed paper, tin foil, or cellophane. We would discard the cardboard and fit the separate packages into a large plastic container. We would also put several packages together into large ditty bags and store them in the locker dedicated to cereal and chips.

■ **Olives.** In many places, small portions (10 to 15) of black and green olives are sold in heavy plastic bags. The small size allows you a quick snack without forcing you to eat a pound of olives before they spoil. This packaging is not completely rupture proof, so store a half-dozen in a heavy zip-top bag.

■ **Applesauce.** Generally, applesauce comes in glass jars. Buy small ones because the applesauce will mold in two to three days if not refrigerated. When available, the plastic trays with individual servings save spoilage.

Nonfood items—paper goods, cleaning supplies, and toiletries

Many of these items you won't see between mainland ports. While you can always get by with local foods or clever substitutes, you will have to do without if you run out of most of the things on this list. When available, they will be dated and expensive. So stock up before you go, even if it means carrying less food.

Buy only the highest quality alkaline batteries as they last twice as long at sea. Check expiration dates carefully, especially when buying batteries in the islands.

Batteries for flashlights, radios, a Walkman, tape recorders, and handheld GPS units often lasted less than a month at sea, and good quality alkaline batteries were unavailable on many islands. We stowed at least four sets of spare batteries for these gadgets when leaving a mainland port.

While our toiletries list reflects our individual preferences, it also reflects the reality of life at sea. The reasons behind some of our specific choices follow:

■ **Suntan lotion** was available in any major island port. We carried SPF (Sun Protection Factor) 8, 15, 24, and a complete block. Whenever we returned to the tropics from temperate latitudes, we had to reacclimate to the sun, even though we were still tanned. A complete sun block on nose and ears for the first week protected these sensitive areas from repeatedly burning. We also used lip balm with SPF 15 several times a day.

■ **Facial cream with sun protection** was less oily than suntan lotion and protected our faces. Even Evans used Oil of Olay in preference to suntan lotion on his face. He also used the facial wash for shaving when we were making landfall.

■ **High quality facial soaps** such as Dove or Caress are hard to come by. If your skin requires a mild soap, take it along. Bacterial soaps are easy to find. If you are prone to eruptions or sores if your skin is not kept clean, you will want to wash regularly with a good bacterial soap.

■ **Feminine products** are widely available, though often of poor quality. A small stock aboard will allow you to purchase only where the quality is acceptable.

■ **Deodorant** can be hard to find, especially if you have a favorite brand. Unfortunately, it does not last well aboard. Cake deodorants break apart after a few months, aerosol deodorant cans rust, and liquid deodorants get runny in tropical heat.

Toiletries do best stowed in a cool place, not directly under the deck in a medicine cabinet. Soap and deodorant run if they get too hot; suntan lotion and liquid soaps turn soupy. Install a drawer or plastic dishpan in a cool place for these items.

Joy dishwashing liquid remains one of the few soaps that will lather in salt water. If you can't find Joy, test the

Table 10-7. Major provisioning—nonfood items

Category	Products	Specific items	Approximate quantities
Nonfood items	Batteries and bulbs	Alkaline batteries—AAA to D	Battery inventory x 2–4
		Calculator, camera batteries	Battery inventory x 2
		Flashlight bulbs	2 spares for each flashlight
	Toiletries	Suntan lotion	At least 1 spare of each type carried
		SPF 15 lip balm	2–3 tubes
		Oil of Olay SPF 15	3–4 bottles
		Oil of Olay Face Wash	2–3 tubes
		Facial soap	8–10 bars
		Bacterial soap	2–3 bars
		Razor blades	1–2 dozen
		Toothpaste	3–4 tubes
		Dental floss	5–6 packages
		Toothbrushes	2–3 spares for each person
		Feminine products	2–3 packages
		Deodorant	6+ packages
		Mosquito repellent	3–4 small bottles
	Cleaning supplies	Joy dishwashing liquid	5–6 bottles
		Soft Scrub	5–6 bottles
		Laundry detergent	2 large containers
		Liquid fabric softener	1 medium bottle
		Fabric softener sheets	1 large box
		Clorox	1 1-gallon bottle
		Scrub brushes	3–4 plastic brushes
		Windex	1 large bottle
		Bug spray	1–2 large cans
		Cockroach spray	1 large can
	Paper goods	Paper towels	6–8 rolls or more as stowage allowed
		Toilet paper	8–10 rolls or more as stowage allowed
		Garbage bags	2 large packages
		Sandwich bags	1 large package
		Large storage bags	1 large package
		Zip-top bags—all sizes	4–5 large packages
		Veggie storage bags	2 large packages
		Heavy-duty tin foil	1 large package

type you want to buy. Those that don't lather do not clean greasy dishes, especially in lukewarm saltwater. You can also use Joy to wash your hair in salt water.

Laundry detergent has many uses aboard and is very expensive outside of the mainland ports. Liquid detergent dissolves better in cold water and cuts grease in the bilge. If powder is the only alternative, stow it in a plastic container or it will quickly become a soggy mess.

While paper towels and toilet paper are generally available, they are expensive and of poor quality, and they lack strength and absorbency. We would stow as much as we had room for, then rely on rags and tea towels before using precious paper towels. While you will find garbage bags and low quality aluminum foil in major island ports, you won't see most of the other things until you reach another mainland port. Stow your aluminum foil in plastic: When exposed to salt water and sometimes salt air, it welds itself into a solid round mass. Zip-top bags and vegetable storage bags are available only in the United States and Europe. Freezer bags last longer than regular ones. Take a full range of sizes (1-pint to 2-gallon) and reuse them.

Perishable foods— living without refrigeration

Americans assume many items require refrigeration that really do not. Most fruits and vegetables, eggs, and some dairy products last for a reasonable time unrefrigerated, even in the tropics. Fresh dairy and meat products do require refrigeration, but both are scarce in all but the largest island ports. This section offers tips and suggestions for living without refrigeration that will be useful for anyone venturing offshore. If you do refrigerate, dairy products and vegetables will last up to twice what is indicated in Table 10-8.

Dairy products

Even for those with refrigeration, fresh milk will only last for a week or so. At that point, your choices will be UHT or dried milk, though the refrigerator will make either more palatable. Cheese survives surprisingly well unrefrigerated. We bought commercially packaged cheeses in small quantities and kept them for up to a month unrefrigerated. The harder the cheese, the longer it lasts. Fatty cheeses like mozzarella will get very soft, but they usually won't spoil or mold until opened. The hard

cheeses packaged in wax for holiday gift boxes keep indefinitely—ask for some in a care package. Or make up your own—wrap cheese in vinegar moistened cheesecloth and dip in melted paraffin to seal. If the only thing available is unpackaged cheese, coat it lightly in vinegar, wrap it in aluminum foil, and store it in a plastic bag. This retards mold on hard cheese for several weeks.

Margarine and butter also keep unrefrigerated. After a month or so, margarine will mold, but that can be scraped off and the rest can be used. Buy high quality margarine, otherwise it turns soupy. Fresh butter will go rancid given enough time, but we only had it happen once after over three weeks in tropical heat. Tinned butter goes off more quickly than regular butter once opened, so be sure to use it up within 10 days. For both butter and margarine, plastic tubs make the best packaging. Oil leaches through other packaging and makes a mess.

Eggs

Fresh eggs that have never been refrigerated or washed will keep up to two months if turned every other day. This was easier and worked just as well as covering the eggs with Vaseline or flash-boiling them. Stow as many as possible when you leave a major port. Where chickens are scarce, eggs are outrageously expensive. We spent $9 for a dozen eggs on Makemo in the Tuamotus.

In Gove, Australia, all eggs arrive refrigerated from Queensland. The eggs we purchased there rotted within a week. If you are forced to buy refrigerated eggs, coat them with Vaseline. If they are not refrigerated when you buy them, you can be fairly certain that they never have been or they would quickly spoil. To get the freshest eggs, go to a farmer or a farmer's market.

When cooking with older eggs, crack them into a measuring cup to protect your other ingredients from a bad one. If you are in doubt, put it into a pan of water. If it floats and you know you didn't hard-boil it, toss it overboard. As eggs get old, they get runny. It becomes difficult to separate the yolk from the white, but they still taste fine.

Bread

Bread makes a wonderful mid-day treat or a great basic breakfast food, but it does not keep well aboard. Bread baked with salt absorbs moisture from the air and starts

Table 10-8. Major provisioning—perishable items

Category	Specific items	Expected life	Approximate quantities
Dairy products	Hard cheeses, small packages	2–3 weeks	6–8 8-oz. packages
	Margarine	4–5 weeks	2–3 16-oz. plastic tubs
	Butter	2–3 weeks	1–2 16-oz. packages
Eggs	Farm fresh eggs	6–8 weeks	4–5 dozen
Bread	Fresh bakery bread	7–10 days	Two loaves
	Commercially packaged dark bread	10–14 days	One loaf
Fruits	Apples	4–5 weeks	2–3 dozen
	Oranges	4–5 weeks	1–2 dozen
	Lemons/limes (for lemonade)	3–4 weeks	1–2 dozen
	Pineapples	2–3 weeks	3–4 small
	Bananas	10 days	1–2 large hands
	Melons	1 week	3–4
	Peaches, pears, apricots, grapes, etc.	About 1 week, slightly more if green	Small quantities for early use
Vegetables	Cabbage	4–5 weeks	3–4 small heads
	Winter squash	4–6 weeks	1–2 small if available
	English cucumbers	2 weeks	2–3
	Tomatoes (firm and green)	2–3 weeks	10–12
	Carrots	1–2 weeks	2–3 pounds
	Onions (cooking)	1–2 months	5–10 pounds
	Potatoes	1–2 months	20–30 medium-sized
	Garlic	2–3 months	5–6 heads
	Green beans, peas, broccoli, cauliflower, corn, lettuce, etc.	About 1 week	Small quantities for early use

to mold after a few days. You can coat the bread with vinegar, cover it with foil, and stow it in plastic. Even then, bread won't last more than 10 days. Good bread disappears quickly, so the best solution is to bake it every few days.

When leaving on passage, I never assumed that I would be up to bread baking the first days out. Just before we left, we would buy a loaf or two of fresh bakery bread and a loaf of industrial-strength dark bread—thin sliced pumpernickel or Jewish rye. The latter would last up to two weeks, thanks to the preservatives. Check that the label doesn't recommend refrigerating once it is opened.

Fruits and vegetables

Fruits and vegetables need air circulating around them to keep for long periods of time unrefrigerated. You must also prevent mold growth and bruising. To protect from mold, put them in sanitized stowage areas and keep them dry. Our collapsible milk crates, which provided great air flow and could be thoroughly sanitized with bleach, worked well. We padded them with towels and rags to keep the fruit from bruising. We didn't use hanging mesh bags because we never figured out how to keep them from swinging into a bulkhead and bruising the contents.

No matter how well they have been stowed, fruits and vegetables will develop mold or start to rot after many weeks at sea. Inspect them daily, and remove and use suspect individuals. The adage "One bad apple can spoil the whole barrel" is true for more than apples. If left unattended, mold from one orange will spread to the rest of the citrus, one rotten onion will start the oth-

ers fermenting, and one sprouted potato will have the rest full of eyes in a few days.

Our fruit choices depended on availability. Unrefrigerated, Granny Smith apples and citrus fruits keep the longest (up to five weeks in tropical conditions). New Zealand Granny Smiths were available throughout the Pacific and lasted twice as the long as red apples. Don't store apples and citrus in the same locker, bin, or milk crate. The citrus will cause the apples to ripen rapidly, bruise, and turn brown.

We bought bananas as green as possible and kept them covered. In theory, ripening can be promoted by dunking them in salt water or exposing them to light. In fact, bananas tend to ripen all at the same time, so we did not take large quantities. Pineapples, coconuts, and bananas harbor spiders, ants, and cockroaches. Get

Additional resources

I still find that the two best marine books for complete information on storing fruits and vegetables are *The Care and Feeding of the Sailing Crew* by Lin Pardey (Norton, 1995) and *The Cruising Chef Cookbook* by Michael Greenwaeld (The Cruising Chef, 1984). Many of the recipes don't reflect the nutritional revolution, but they can be easily modified.

While not specifically for the marine market, Janet Bailey's *Keeping Food Fresh* (Harper & Row Publishers, 1989) offers great advice on storing and keeping every type of food. It covers many tropical fruits and vegetables. The book assumes you have refrigeration, but it contains many ideas that don't require its use.

Besides an almost infinite number of recipes, *Joy of Cooking* (Macmillan/Dutton, various editions) or a similar general purpose reference gives a wide range of substitutes and equivalents beyond the ones discussed in Appendix 1. It also covers everything from bread baking to carving a roast.

Vacuum sealers provide a versatile alternative to all those Ziploc bags. They can be used for preserving dozens of food items and for keeping everything dry, from electronic spares to sweaters. Prices range from $50 to over $150. Make sure to get a high quality unit with a wide sealing bar. Temperature control is es-

sential—too hot and the bags melt, too cool and they won't seal. You can find vacuum sealers in specialty kitchen catalogs and stores.

Both American Harvest and Mr. Coffee make dehydrators for less than $50. They can be purchased in discount stores like Service Merchandise.

High quality canned turkey, beef, and chicken (with or without salt) can be purchased in 3-, 6-, or 12-can (28 ounces per can) cases from Brinkman Turkey Farms, Inc. in Findlay, Ohio (phone 419-365-5127). They also offer pork, ground beef, turkey, and chicken broth, as well as several types of prepared meals. In the U.K., there are many game and specialist delicatessen-type canners, but home-potted meat also keeps well.

If you will be buying fresh meat, you won't find the meat cuts you are used to. You can muddle through when buying chops or steaks in small quantities. Stew meats, roasts, shoulder, and rib cuts are hard to sort out, especially with respect to quality. When I shopped for items like these, I asked lots of questions or went with an Australian or British cruiser. If meat is central to your diet, purchase a European cookbook that shows meat cuts and compare it to your American cookbook.

rid of them by completely submerging the fruit in the ocean until the critters flee the sinking ship.

Potatoes and onions keep indefinitely. We inspected potatoes when we purchased them to be sure there were no eyes and covered them with a towel to keep out the light and slow sprouting. Onions sprout if covered, so leave them in the light. Cabbage lasts two to three weeks unrefrigerated, which is the longest of the green vegetables. Green tomatoes wrapped in newspaper last several weeks. Use them once they start to ripen.

American cucumbers become soft and squishy after about five days. You can purchase English cucumbers in most Commonwealth countries and throughout the Caribbean; they are thinner and longer than the American variety, and they come wrapped in cellophane.

They keep up to two weeks unrefrigerated. Carrots keep a week to 10 days if the greens are removed. If they become rubbery, peel off skin and soak them in water overnight. They won't taste quite like fresh, but they will be crisp and have good flavor. Vegetable storage bags work best when used in the refrigerator, but they extend the life of greens by several days even out in the open.

We normally did not treat fruits and vegetables with a fruit dip. Most fruits and vegetables keep best when left unwashed. But if any of the citrus fruits developed mold, we rinsed all of them in a mild chlorine solution. We washed all fruits and vegetables thoroughly in fresh water before using them. If we were concerned about bacteria, we would remove the skin before eating them.

CHAPTER 11 | WATER, WATER, EVERYWHERE

Find and fix deck leaks ■ *Finding the leaks* ■ *Stopping the leaks* ■ **Fight dampness, mold, and mildew** ■ *Fine-tune your ventilation* ■ *Pretrip preparations: rebed and reseal* ■ *Minimize dampness* ■ *Prevent mold and mildew*

Offshore voyagers are continually trying to keep *salt water* out of the boat and *fresh water* in it. Life would be so simple if the sea were not salt! Keeping a boat dry while minimizing mold, mildew, and odors requires time and effort.

Most fiberglass boats aren't absolutely watertight all of the time, but some stay more dry than others. A "wet" boat with low freeboard that traps water on deck is going to leak more than a "dry" boat with high freeboard and open toerails. But all fiberglass boats leak after crossing a couple of oceans—the question is simply how much.

Some simple steps will keep water out of your boat most of the time. First, you need to find and fix any deck leaks and maintain the boat so they do not reappear. Second, you need to fight dampness, mold, and mildew. That process starts with good ventilation. On most boats, the process never really ends. It simply becomes part of life afloat.

FIND AND FIX DECK LEAKS

Boatbuilders start with a hull that is watertight and then drill holes through it. No fiberglass hull is ever quite the same. To keep your boat dry, you need to make those small holes and the major openings watertight.

Even if your boat has never leaked, don't underestimate the rigors of ocean voyaging. With only one exception, every fiberglass boat we knew that had crossed more than one ocean had leaks somewhere. Fiberglass flexes constantly at sea. The sealant used to connect the hull to the rigid bolts and deck hardware will fail sooner or later. A cubic yard of water weighs over one ton, and a breaking wave moves at a speed of 20 to 30 knots. Those forces on a hatch or companionway will push some amount of water through any gasket system. The heat of the tropics also takes its toll on the boat's watertight integrity. Caulk and gaskets dry up and crack from constant exposure to heat and UV radiation.

If you want a leak-proof boat, avoid holes through the hull. Deck fittings can be welded onto metal boats. Some fiberglass boatbuilders are molding chainplates and stanchion bases from fiberglass; often these are reinforced with carbon fiber (Figure 11-1).

But most of us can't afford a new boat built to minimize deck leaks. Take heart: Much can be done on an older boat. You can get rid of most of your leaks by investing some time to find and fix problem areas. But

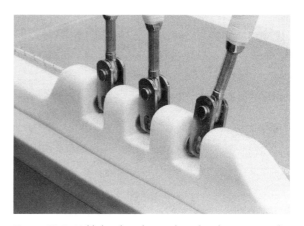

Figure 11-1. Molded-in chainplates and stanchion bases promise dry fiberglass boats someday.

don't assume this is a one-time project. Keeping an offshore boat watertight requires continual maintenance and occasional innovation.

If you start with the assumption that your boat will be watertight only if you make it that way, you will deal constructively with leaks when they appear. No fiberglass boat is absolutely watertight—even straight from the factory. And most never need to be. But the rigors of offshore voyaging will show you the limits of your boat's ability to keep salt water where it belongs.

Finding the leaks

Locating leaks is often harder than fixing them. Another one of Murphy's Laws of Offshore Voyaging states that water will migrate as far as possible from its point of entry just to prevent you from finding the leak. A piecemeal approach will only frustrate you. Just when you think you've cured that drip into your galley lockers, a little rough weather will show that you cured something but not that leak. A systematic approach will locate all problem areas and prevent frustration in the long run.

Start by inspecting the inside and outside of the boat thoroughly. The following are the areas you should look at.

■ **Deck fittings and chainplates.** On the exterior, look for small rust spots weeping from bolts, rusty bolt heads, and worn caulking. While stainless is stain*less,* not stain*free,* we found a high correlation between localized rust around a specific bolt head and a leaking deck fitting. If you scrape at caulking around the base of a deck fitting and it comes up black, you have a leak. On the interior, inspect the fitting for rust on the underside, rust marks or weeping from underneath, and water trails below. Salt water leaves visible marks on most surfaces, even after it dries. If you see any of these things, rebed the fitting. On deck fills and scupper fittings, check for a loose hose clamp before you assume the fitting is leaking.

■ **Hatches.** If your hatches are the older, wood and Plexiglas or Lexan type, look for rust or dirt around screw heads. Examine the wood-to-plastic and wood-to-wood seams for any signs of dirt or dampness. On newer aluminum hatches, look for any misalignment between the hatch and its base. On all hatches, inspect

the gasket for deterioration. Look for signs of weeping on the surfaces below the hatch.

■ **Ports.** Look for water marks or dirt on the cabin trunk below the port. Scrape out a little caulking from around the port on both the inside and the outside. Any dirt or visible gaps in the caulk mean the port should be rebedded. It's a messy job, but don't ignore it. Water entering along portlights can get into unsealed edges of cored decks and cause rot. Water can also migrate along hull liners to far corners of the boat. Most of our "mystery leaks" turned out to be portlights in need of rebedding.

■ **Mast boot and mast collar.** Mast boots need to be resealed regularly to keep both salt water and rain water out. Check the mast where it enters the boat for signs of weeping, rust, or dirt. If the mast boot has not been resealed in a year or more, assume you will need to do so before setting off. Bolts in mast collars may leak as well, especially if the collar is not designed to distribute the load correctly. Check the interior side of the bolts for signs of weeping, rust, or dirt.

If the first three or four fittings you examine show signs of leaking on an older boat, don't complete the watertight inspection. You will need to rebed most deck hardware using the suggestions in the next section, which will take several days to a week of hard work. If few of the fittings show signs of leakage on a newer or recently refit boat, you may only need a couple of hours to rebed problem areas.

If you have a "mystery leak" that you can't find after rebedding all the problem areas, or if you want to check your boat's watertight integrity, pressure-test it. You will need your tool kit, some heavy plastic garbage bags, a roll of duct tape, a freshwater hose, some soap that lathers well, a leaf blower or a shop vacuum cleaner that can be run to exhaust air, and a free day. In this test, you pressurize the inside of the boat and use soapy water to locate where air is leaking out.

Close the boat up and seal all openings, except for two Dorade vents. Close all the seacocks. Dog the hatches and ports. Plug your hawsers. Screw storm plates into the Dorade vents. Tape off the engine exhaust and bilge pump openings. Put the hatch boards in and seal them with duct tape. Tape around the cockpit locker openings.

Tape plastic bags over the two Dorade vents you left unsealed. Cut a hole in one the size of the hose on the shop vacuum or blower. Feed the hose through and seal the bag to the hose with duct tape. Turn on the shop vacuum or leaf blower and pressurize the interior of the boat. When the bag on the second ventilator stands up, you've pressurized the boat. Mix up a 50/50 solution of soap and water and sponge it over all deck fittings, the toerail, hatches, and ports. Watch for soap bubbles from air being forced through small openings in hatches, around deck fittings, or alongside portlights.

Only a watertight boat can pass this test. If you seal all the leaks that show up this way, you will come as close as possible to a dry offshore boat. A breaking wave may still force water through a gasket and motion may create new leaks. But, for the most part, you will be snug and dry.

Stopping the leaks

Single-minded attention to detail determines your success rate for keeping salt water out. For each deck fit-

ting, a few tricks increase the likelihood of a lasting solution. However, unless you get the basics right, no trick will stop the leak. The basics mean using the right sealant and applying it properly.

Three types of sealants are commonly used in the marine industry. Each has its strengths and its best use. Table 11-1 compares the three major sealants.

For bedding ABS (acrylonitrile/butadione/styrene) or Lexan plastic, use silicone. For the rest of your bedding needs, polyurethane offers the highest adhesion and a faster cure rate while polysulfide will create a longer lasting, more flexible bond. Don't use polyurethane if you think you may ever want to remove the fitting. For most metal deck fittings, polysulfide works well.

Once you have determined the appropriate sealant, follow these seven steps for a watertight seal.

1. *Remove hardware.* Whether you are about to rebed a cleat, a stanchion base, or a portlight, you have to remove it first. If the head of a recalcitrant bolt or screw becomes mangled, use a Dremel tool to turn the bolt head into a hex or to create a new slot to facilitate removal by a wrench or a large screwdriver. A heat gun

Table 11-1. Comparison of marine sealants

Sealant	Uses	Properties	Best used	Limitations
Silicone	To form a flexible gasket	Lowest adhesion Most flexible 20-year life Cures completely in 24 hours	With plastic, even ABS and Lexan Where flexibility is key	Not for underwater use
Polysulfide	For bedding everything except plastic	Medium adhesion 20-year life Most chemical-resistant Cures to sandable hardness in 24 to 48 hours, takes longest to cure completely	With teak Where bonded surface needs to be sanded, painted, or chemical-resistant	Incompatible with all plastics
Polyurethane	To form a permanent bond	Highest adhesion 10-year life Tack-free in 24 to 48 hours, cures completely in 3 to 7 days	On hull-to-deck joints On through-hull fittings	Incompatible with ABS and Lexan plastic

will release polyurethane. But often the motion of the boat causes the bolt holes to enlarge, and the hardware comes off easily.

2. *Sand all surfaces and clean thoroughly with solvent.* Even the best caulks do not bond to surfaces that have dirt or leftover sealant on them. After you have removed the hardware, sand off any dirt, old sealant, corrosion, or rust until the metal surface is bright and shiny. Scrape away the old caulking on deck and sand with fine-grit sandpaper. Wipe down the hardware and the deck with acetone. Do the same with the backing plate, bolts, and the underside of the deck where the backing plate is attached. Replace any bolts that are bent, stripped, or otherwise compromised.

3. *Drill out holes and the core around the holes.* Drill out the bolt holes to get rid of any dirt or old caulking. Remove enough core from around the bolt hole to create a barrier to the passage of moisture; an area ½ inch around the hole will create a tube of epoxy that will resist bending and compression. Use a nail bent at a right angle and attached to a drill to clear the core from the area around the bolt holes.

4. *Seal the core and fill the hole with thickened epoxy.* Tape the bottom of the hole. Fill to deck level with epoxy and allow it to sit for a few minutes, then remove the tape and allow it to drain into a cup. This coats the far reaches of the drilled holes with a thin layer of epoxy. Retape the bottom of the hole, thicken the epoxy, and then fill to deck level once again. This creates a new surface into which to sink the bolt. For portlights on cored hulls, sand the edge of the cut-out, clean it with acetone, and seal it with thickened epoxy to prevent water from migrating into the core.

5. *Once the epoxy has hardened, drill and tap new bolt holes.* Tapped bolt holes will increase the surface area for bonding the bolt to the boat.

6. *Dry-fit fitting and tape.* Trace around the fitting, and then tape along your traced lines. Put tape on the top of the fitting. This makes cleanup easier.

7. *Apply sealant liberally to create gasket.* This is no place to economize. Apply sealant to the fitting and the deck. Spread evenly with a putty knife. Apply sealant liberally around the head of each bolt. Do not overtighten!

While some sealant should be forced out from all sides, enough should remain to form a gasket between the fitting and the deck.

Don't apply sealant to the backing plate. If the fitting does leak, you don't want to trap water in the deck where it could find its way into the core.

Once the sealant dries, remove the tape and use solvent to remove any sealant that remains on the deck. Be careful to keep the solvent away from your newly sealed fitting. For silicone use acetone, for polyurethane use rubbing alcohol, and for polysulfide use mineral spirits (paint thinner). For rebedding ports, use a wooden wedge to remove extra caulk before it dries: It is inexpensive, reusable, and does not scratch the gel coat.

If you gradually rebed all deck hardware using these principles and rebed a few fittings every few months as part of your preventive maintenance, you should not be troubled by leaks. We discovered a few useful tricks for different types of hardware and fittings. None of these ideas are difficult to implement, but a few can almost eliminate the potential for deck leaks through certain types of fittings.

Ports and hatches

If your portlights are not watertight, you will need to rebed or replace them. For opening ports, the source of the leak determines how you fix it. The port can be leaking through the gasket, water can be migrating along the frame, or both. To determine if water is coming through the gasket, coat it with talcum powder, close and dog the port, and flood the area with a high pressure hose. If the talcum powder still makes an unbroken ring around the gasket when you open the port, water is coming in around the frame and you need to rebed the whole portlight. If the talcum powder ring is broken, you need to replace the gasket and see if it still leaks.

If you have to rebed the whole portlight, regardless of whether the port is opening or nonopening, investigate the possibility of through-bolting the inside and outside of the frame together. Stainless steel bolts and aircraft locking nuts are much stronger than screws, and they facilitate future removal for rebedding. You will have to decide if a few extra holes are justified by the increased strength of the port.

Even a small leak through a hatch can let in a significant amount of water, often onto a settee or bunk. If

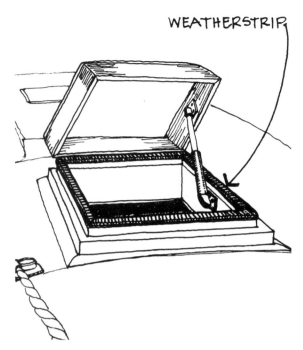

WEATHERSTRIP

Figure 11-2. Weather stripping applied to the top of the lip on our hatches made them almost watertight.

Figure 11-3. On the aluminum boat that we are in the process of building, the builder welded a breakwater around the base of the hatch. This will keep the force of a breaking wave from reaching the gasket.

your boat is over 15 years old, consider replacing leaking hatches with new, high quality aluminum hatches, available from several manufacturers. If you cannot afford to do that, or your boat is not that old, several modifications can reduce leaking substantially.

On wood and fiberglass hatches, most leaks occur along the coaming lip even when the hatch is well dogged. To test this, run a high pressure hose along the bottom edge of your hatch and see if you can force water up and over the lip. To fix this problem, replace the gasket material to revitalize the hatch seal. Gasket material should be hollow or 10- to 12-pound neoprene. On many older hatch designs, even new gasket material won't stop water under high pressure from forcing its way through. If that is the case, a second gasket along the top edge of the hatch coaming may help. We installed professional quality, neoprene weather stripping made by 3M on our main salon hatch (Figure 11-2). To compress the gasket after that, one of us stood on the hatch so the other could dog it. With the exception of one breaking wave, we never had water through that hatch again. High quality weather stripping also keeps water out of cockpit lockers and reduces leaks in companionway hatches.

If the weather stripping does not eliminate leaks in heavy weather, you'll need to protect the hatch from taking the full force of breaking waves. A dam or breakwater can channel the force of the wave away from the hatch (Figure 11-3). Small canvas hatch covers and spray hoods (Figure 11-4) can often break enough of the force of a wave to keep an otherwise sealed hatch from leaking.

Mast boots, chain plates, and deck fittings

Proper bedding of deck fittings such as water and diesel fills, scuppers, above-waterline through-hulls, and others that have little force exerted on them will seal these fittings for several years. An initial investment and some ongoing maintenance will keep mast boots and collars watertight. Stanchion bases, chainplate covers, and cleats are more difficult to keep free from leaks. The most difficult of all are lifeline stanchion gates.

To keep the hole through which the mast enters the boat from letting water in as well, start by removing the mast boot and whatever seal is underneath it and carefully examining the mast collar. In some cases, the collar is not designed to distribute the load correctly, or mast wedges have caused unequal loading. If your mast collar shows signs of leaking from such stresses, you will want to re-engineer it to eliminate these stresses before rebedding the collar. Once you have dealt with leaks through the collar, reseal the mast boot itself. A technique that has worked well for many voyagers is a piece of neoprene or a truck tire inner tube attached to the mast with tape or a hose clamp 3 inches above the deck, then folded down over itself and sealed to the deck. The fold protects the clamp or tape from chafe and creates a good seal against the mast.

If this area proves problematic on your boat, a product called Spartite creates a flexible seal around the mast and eliminates the need for wedges and a mast boot. To use it, you build a dam around the bottom of the mast collar and pour in the material. The substance can take four days to fully cure, during which time the mast needs to be secured against movement, usually by means of lines. When the mast is removed from the boat, this flexible gasket goes with it. The mast can be reinstalled using the same gasket.

We found a permanent solution to deck leaks through our chainplate covers. When we rebedded our chainplate covers for the first time, we inserted a piece of neoprene between the deck and the chainplate cover. This created a flexible gasket that eliminated chainplate leaks for the remainder of our voyage.

On some boats, this solution eliminates deck leaks around cleats and stanchion bases as well. The neoprene gasket solution, however, never worked for us on cleats or stanchion bases. On *Silk,* these deck fittings were subjected to too much torque and movement. After a few months, bolt holes enlarged, sealants broke down, and water started to migrate around or through the gasket to the interior of the boat. In addition to the procedure outlined above, a little extra care and a few extra steps are required to make these deck fittings watertight.

Many boats use oversized washers in lieu of real backing plates. For hardware that never takes any strain, washers may be adequate. But they are inadequate for cleats, stanchion bases, blocks, and other hardware that may be shock-loaded. For these items, use a real, metal backing plate larger than the deck fit-

Figure 11-4. A small canvas spray hood can break the force of the water and divert some of it away from the hatch seals.

ting (of stainless steel if you plan to use stainless bolts). The backing plate spreads shock loads over a wider area and reduces the chance that the fitting will be pulled out of the deck. It also increases the rigidity of the fitting and the bolts that hold it, reducing motion and the likelihood of leaks.

To make stanchion bases and cleats watertight, replace oversized washers with stainless steel backing plates drilled and tapped for the bolts from the deck fitting. When bedding the fitting, create an extra gasket around each bolt. Countersink a small hole in the deck about a 1/2-inch wide and 1/4-inch deep for a 1/4-inch bolt (Figure 11-5). This depression forms a well into which sealant is forced when the bolt is tightened. Done properly, this creates a gasket around each bolt that seals water out.

You have now created a relatively rigid unit from backing plate to deck fitting, with enough of a flexible gasket to absorb the motion of the boat. To give your newly rebedded fittings a fighting chance of being watertight, you also need to minimize the shock loads they receive. For cleats, use good, elastic docklines and spread the load across as many lines as possible. Make sure the boat does not continually fetch up against one cleat (for example, when it "sails" at anchor).

To minimize the shock load on stanchion bases, avoid securing things to your lifelines. We have seen everything from fender boards to sailboards tied to lifelines. When hit by a breaking wave, these items can place a tremendous force on stanchion bases. Fenders tied to lifelines can also exert large forces on the stanchion bases if the fenders are dragged along a pier. Tie

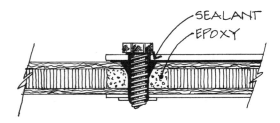

Figure 11-5. A small countersunk hole around the head of the bolt will create a gasket to keep water from coming in through the bolt hole itself.

your fenders to cleats or to the toerail where possible. In the interests of good seamanship and a dry boat, leave your lifelines unencumbered.

Even with all these precautions, we still had problems with our lifeline gate stanchion bases. When getting on and off the boat, most people pull on these stanchions; the constant shock loads will loosen even well-bedded bolts. Lifeline gates may also be the least well-engineered piece of equipment on the average boat. Whatever bracing exists on most gates does not offset the relevant shock loads (Figure 11-6). Most lifeline gate stanchion bases are located in an area of the deck that traps water, so they are often submerged in a heavy sea or a hard rain. On many boats, these bases leak into critical areas like the navigation station, the pilot berth, or the galley.

To reduce the likelihood of leaks through lifeline gate stanchion bases, you can eliminate the shock loads and/or improve the engineering.

You can try to forbid your crew from touching the stanchion gates as they climb aboard, but don't expect that to work. It is better to reduce the need to use the gates to get aboard. Many boats use the swim ladder on the stern as their "front door" rather than the lifeline gate. A proper swim ladder kept over the side while you are anchored allows guests to climb aboard without grabbing the gates.

Our swim ladder interfered with bringing our rigid dinghy fully alongside, so we had to step even further to get to the deck. Evans built a small teak

step that we clipped to padeyes on the toerail (Figure 11-7). The back of the step was cushioned with nonskid. One step was all it took to climb aboard without touching the stanchion gates. People with open toerails can clip on a dinghy step even more easily.

If any of your stanchion base sits in water much of the time, improve your deck drainage by cutting an additional hole in the toerail next to the stanchion base. Consider mounting the stanchion to the toerail (see Figure 2-11, page 30) or mounting it on a fiberglass pad to raise the screw heads above the water. If your stanchion base is poorly engineered, add additional bracing to increase its rigidity. Install an angled brace from the top of the gate to the top of the toerail or braces that bolt into the side of the toerail (Figure 11-8).

On most boats, a thorough rebedding will make the majority of your deck fittings watertight. For some, the combination of the boat's design and your own activities will increase the likelihood of leaks. The ideas in this section can be adapted to reduce leaks in whatever fittings give you the most problems.

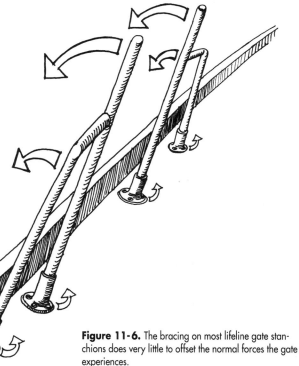

Figure 11-6. The bracing on most lifeline gate stanchions does very little to offset the normal forces the gate experiences.

Figure 11-7. Our dinghy step was easy to stow, quick to install, and minimized the forces on lifeline gate stanchions.

Toerails, rubrails, and bowsprits

If you try the pressure test described previously, you may find extensive leaks through toerails and rubrails and around the bowsprit. Many boatbuilders use polyurethane to bed these areas because it has the highest adhesion. But it only has a 10-year life, so leaks are common in these areas on older boats. If you have to tackle this job, rebed your toerail and rubrail in a good boatyard before you leave. If your hull-to-deck joint is leaking, glassing over the entire joint can eliminate problems down the line on boats where the joint is accessible.

FIGHT DAMPNESS, MOLD, AND MILDEW

Having a dry, mildew-free boat below requires more than keeping the salt water out. Water that does get in needs to find its way back out again. Outside of the trop-

ics, your hull must be adequately insulated to prevent yet another source of water aboard: condensation. Ventilation reduces condensation and minimizes mold in the tropics. Adequate ventilation for temperate latitudes will not provide enough air circulation closer to the equator. You must keep salt water *and* salt outside of the boat and away from your clothes, bedding, and body to minimize dampness.

Water that gets aboard must find its way overboard quickly and efficiently. (This topic was discussed in Chapter 2 in "Bilge drainage and access.") No area of the bilge should trap water. It should flow from the chain locker to the bilge sump without pooling under the cabin sole in hidden areas. Once water reaches the sump, a bilge pump should return it overboard quickly and efficiently.

If you intend to voyage outside the tropics, ensure that your hull is adequately insulated. We were in temperatures below freezing a half-dozen times. We arrived in New Zealand in November, which is the equivalent of early spring in the temperate latitudes of the Northern Hemisphere. In such temperatures, condensation forms on poorly insulated hulls; the amount of water can be astonishing. In South Africa, friends of ours on an older boat with a solid fiberglass hull had streams of water trickling down the cabin sides in 30-degree temperatures. In cored fiberglass hulls, the core acts as insulation. We had almost no condensation problems on *Silk*. If your boat is uninsulated metal or solid fiberglass, add insulation to your list if you are planning a major rebuild. Otherwise, be ready to deal with a fair amount of condensation a few times during the course of your trip. If you are dreaming about voyaging in high latitudes, add lots of insulation (3 inches for a metal boat) or get a different boat.

Without good ventilation, mold and mildew will be rampant. But even good ventilation is not enough. To rid your boat of a musty odor and damp feel and achieve a dry, comfortable home, you must keep salt itself outside and keep the boat free of mold and mildew. I'm a fanatic on this, since I'm allergic to mold.

Fine-tune your ventilation

Your ventilation options at sea depend on the conditions. Rod Stephens's wondrous Dorade vents, named for the first boat to carry them, has yet to be improved upon in rough weather. It meets the dual requirements of ventilators at sea—it lets air in and keeps water out. A variety of alternatives have been developed since *Dorade,* including low-profile vents equipped with solar-powered fans. To make a real difference in onboard ventilation, the units need to be large enough to move a significant volume of air and rugged enough to handle offshore conditions. We never saw a solar vent that

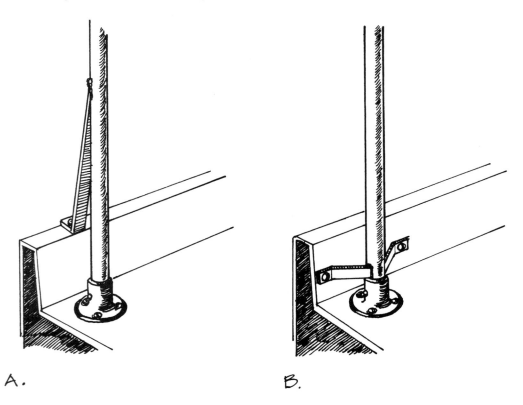

A.

B.

Figure 11-8. To improve the engineering of lifeline gate stanchions, install bracing from the stanchion to the toerail.

Pretrip preparations: rebed and reseal

If you're starting with an older used boat that has not had more than a passing acquaintance with a caulk gun, you will have your work cut out for you. The following table summarizes what you need to do to make your boat watertight.

By the time you are done, your boat should be snug and dry. To keep her that way, start a cycle of rebedding your fittings six months after you finish.

Table 11-2. Pre-departure checklist for a watertight boat

Fitting	Activities	Comments
Hatches	Replace any warped, cracked, or broken hatches	
	Replace acrylic or Plexiglas on other hatches as needed, replace gaskets	
	Add weather stripping around hatches and cockpit lockers and anchor locker openings	
Companionway	Add sea hood if the boat does not have one	See Figure 2-12, page 30, for an example of a sea hood
	Seal with weather stripping	
Ports	Rebed all ports whether nonopening or opening	
	Replace gaskets in opening ports	
	Through-bolt frames if possible	
Chainplates	Make accessible from below so that leaks are easily detected	Leaks inside hull linings or behind wood trim will go unnoticed for longer and be harder to locate
	Rebed using neoprene gaskets	
Deck fittings	Make as accessible as possible to ease maintenance	If you can't get at it, you will put off maintenance and end up with more of a problem
	Improve engineering of stanchion gates	
	Replace washers with proper backing plates	
	Rebed all deck fittings	
	Replace tops or seals on deck fills for diesel and water	
Toerail, rubrail, and bowsprit	Remove and rebed if leaking	If hull-to-deck joint is leaking, see if you can glass over seam
Other	Rebed mast collar, reseal mast boot	
	Find a leak-proof solution to closing off the chain hawser	

stood up to the rigors of voyaging. The mechanical and electrical components are prone to failure and the vents themselves tend to leak. If you are going to put an additional hole through your deck for ventilation, add another Dorade ventilator and use a separate fan below to move the air.

The airflow through even the largest Dorades is a fraction of the airflow through a small hatch. In calmer conditions, open hatches at sea greatly improve ventilation. But sooner or later, you will take a wave through the opening. Small hatches and ports located where a little salt water won't do any damage make ideal sea ports.

For most conditions at sea, we had three sources for basic ventilation. *Silk's* four Dorades offered good circulation into the major living areas of the boat. We kept the portlight in the head open almost all the time. If a wave splashed water through this port, it was contained and easily cleaned up. We also left the top hatchboard out of the companionway. To keep out sun and salt water without a dodger, the lower hatchboard was kept in the companionway and the hatch was kept closed. In most conditions, our four Dorades, the open port in the head, and the open top half of the companionway provided good ventilation throughout the boat. The port in the head and the open companionway reduced odors that could cause seasickness in the head, galley, and around the engine.

Sailing downwind in light air, we left a variety of ports and hatches open including the forward hatch, the ports in the forepeak, and the ports in the galley. But when the wind went over 15 knots apparent or shifted forward of the stern quarter, we started to batten down. By the time we were getting water on deck, we would be back to our basic ventilation.

In heavy weather, Dorade vents are the only source of ventilation on most boats. To provide good airflow, Dorades need to be properly placed and adequately sized. To be watertight, they must be properly constructed. While most racing sailors know that wind velocity at the masthead is greater than at deck level, many don't consider the implications for ventilation. To illustrate the point, bluewater sailor and author Donald Street suggests a "ribbon test." Take several pieces of yarn or ribbon and tie them at 3-inch, 6-inch, 12-inch, and 18-inch heights above the deck, and then go sailing. Only a few minutes are necessary to see that ventilator openings need to be 12 inches or higher off the deck.

The airflow through a Dorade vent increases with the square of half the diameter of the through-deck pipe. For example, a 4-inch diameter pipe has a cross-sectional area of 12.5 square inches, but a 5-inch diameter pipe increases that area by over 50 percent to 19.6 square inches. The airflow increases proportionally with the change in the area. To be most effective, through-deck pipes need to be as large as possible. A 4-inch size should be considered minimum, but 5 or 6 inches is preferable.

To be watertight, Dorades need to be well engineered. The through-deck pipe should be a minimum of 3 inches off the deck (Figure 11-9). There should be at least 2 inches between the top of the pipe and the top of the Dorade box. The bottom of the intake pipe and the top of the exhaust pipe should be at the same level. There should be at least two inches between the two pipes. A baffle placed between the pipes and extending down from the top of the box to a level just below the pipe openings keeps water from entering the through-deck pipe. The cowls need to be as large as possible. You should be able to rotate them in any direction to take advantage of the smallest breeze on passage or in port. One-inch-square drainage holes should be cut into each of the corners. The vent should be equipped with a removable screen for use in mosquito infested ports.

How many Dorade vents do you need? At minimum, you need one large vent in the head and one in the galley. Two in each area would improve airflow even more by providing intake and exhaust ventilation. Ideally, your boat should also have two or three Dorade vents into the main salon and one into each sleeping cabin.

In storm conditions with large breaking waves, even Dorade ventilators won't keep water out. A wave breaking into the cowl of a Dorade ventilator will fill the box and force water through the deck pipe before the box can drain. Ventilation then becomes secondary to keeping the boat watertight. For this situation, each Dorade needs a threaded metal plate that can be screwed into the bottom of the deck pipe or into the top of the Dorade box after the cowl is removed. For most gales, orienting the Dorade vents away from the prevailing wind was sufficient. We resorted to closing off the Dorade ventilators in only one storm.

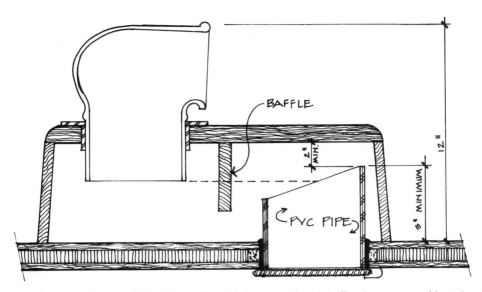

Figure 11-9. A well-constructed Dorade includes the largest through-deck pipe possible and a baffle to keep water out of the intake pipe.

For heavy weather conditions, we had one other ventilation source. Between our first and second Lexan hatchboards, we designed an overlapping lip that acted as an air scoop (Figure 11-10). This offered some additional circulation when we were depending strictly on the Dorade vents. This small opening improved galley air circulation. For those with hard dodgers, you can install a larger scoop. The increase in air circulation could mean the difference between a hot or a cold meal for the crew in rough conditions.

Poor air circulation contributes to debilitating seasickness. If your boat's Dorade vents are inadequate in size, poorly engineered, or insufficient in number, improve them before you head off to sea.

Ventilation in port requires different solutions than at sea. Most coastal sailors have extensive experience with this. Take along your wind scoops, fans, and whatever else has worked on those hot, windless, humid summer nights. Screens decrease ventilation by as much as 75 percent, so don't use them unless you really need to.

Most coastal sailors are less used to maintaining adequate ventilation during heavy downpours. In temperate climates, downpours usually bring a significant drop in temperature and an increase in wind. In the tropics, many downpours are not accompanied by wind or

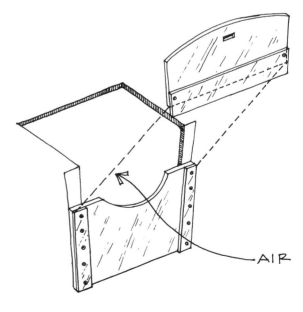

Figure 11-10. A small wind scoop designed into our Lexan hatchboards increased ventilation in the galley during heavy weather.

cooler temperatures. Closing up the boat creates stifling conditions that breed mold and mildew. Several solutions work in these conditions.

If the rain brings little wind, canvas is the answer. Spray hoods over hatches, a dodger over a companionway, or a harbor awning over the main hatch all let air in and keep rain out. When the rain is accompanied by strong winds, the canvas solution becomes less attractive. Harbor awnings make the boat sail at anchor and "jig" at a dock, putting unnecessary strain on ground tackle or mooring lines. Spray hoods still offer some protection at anchor where boats can swing with the wind. But in a marina, rain will blow into some openings.

Hatches that can be opened just a few inches and protected with a spray hood or a canvas square are the most practical solution. Most modern production hatches can be adjusted to any height. On many older boats, hatches are either open or closed. A notched piece of wood that can be used to open the hatch 1 inch, 3 inches, or 6 inches makes a simple hatch holder. It can be kept on a bracket near the hatch. A 1- or 2-inch opening protected by canvas will provide adequate ventilation and keep rain out in a torrential downpour.

Minimize dampness

In wet conditions, water and salt will travel below on you and your clothes. Salt is insidious: Constant moisture from salt can lead to open sores and rashes; salt in clothes and bedding absorbs moisture from the air and makes fabrics clammy and leaves you chilled; salt from bedding can be absorbed into cushions, which renders them perpetually damp. Airing out the offending clothes and bedding will help for only as long as they are in the sun and wind. When back below, they become damp again within a few hours. Once a passage gets off to a wet and salty start, it will be uncomfortable until everything can be rinsed out thoroughly in port.

But don't despair. A well-managed, fairly watertight boat won't get into this situation in the first place. After a few damp, uncomfortable passages, we developed four simple rules that improved life aboard. Managing clothes and foul-weather gear in a limited space is always awkward. But dry, comfortable, and welcoming quarters below make the effort worthwhile.

■ *Protect the companionway.* An open companionway is like a magnet for waves. After several unpleasant experiences, we made a rule that both hatchboards went in and the hatch was closed the minute the first wave left visible splash marks in the cockpit. That rule saved us many times when conditions seemed benign. If you have a dodger, you may be able to leave the companionway open a bit longer, but an appropriate rule will help to prevent a major dousing.

■ *Minimize clothes.* On our first long, wet passage, we made the mistake of repeatedly changing into dry clothes. We kept thinking we wouldn't get wet the next time we went out on deck, but we went through a half-dozen changes of clothes in two days. Salty clothes are difficult to stow and impossible to clean on passage. Try to keep your salty clothes to a minimum.

In the tropics, we were better off stripping and going on deck naked in wet weather. In slightly cooler temperatures, we took off whatever we had on below and put on a windbreaker and quick-dry lightweight shorts or pants. In temperate latitudes, we pulled on our foul-weather gear with nothing underneath. In chilly spring and fall weather in New Zealand and South Africa, we wore polypropylene underwear or stretch pants and a light shirt beneath our foul-weather gear. For real winter weather, you will have to add several more layers.

■ *Strip and rinse at the foot of the companionway.* After coming below from a wet and salty deck, we were often soaked. We would strip at the bottom of the companionway and wipe ourselves down with a freshwater washcloth. Then we would towel off with a dry towel. (Simply toweling off left salt on our skin, which caused chapping and chafing.) We also wiped ourselves down with a washcloth to remove dried salt from light spray or humidity. Otherwise, salt would accumulate in the cushions where we sat most frequently, leaving them damp after a few days at sea. After wiping ourselves down, we would put back on the dry clothes we had taken off when we went on deck.

■ *Keep salty clothes by the companionway.* Salty clothes were not allowed anywhere in the boat except by the companionway. When we came below and stripped, we hung our wet clothes on hangers from the handrail in the galley or just forward of the nav station, or dropped them over the oven safety bar. When we went back out, we got back into our wet clothes. They warmed up quickly enough once we got moving, as long as they weren't cotton.

A head at the bottom of the companionway steps equipped with a hanging locker helps you adhere to these rules *and* maintain privacy. A curtain at the foot of the companionway also provides privacy and helps isolate the on-watch activity from below. If these arrangements are not feasible on your boat, the choice comes down to modesty or a salt-free home. The choice was easy for us, but we never took on extra crew.

Our rule of no salt water below also applied in port when we went swimming. After a swim, we rinsed off in the cockpit to remove any residual salt. This kept our home dry and our cushions free of salt, and it reinforced good habits for our time at sea.

No matter how careful you are, salt will find its way into your bedding over the course of a long passage. Bedding takes the most fresh water to get clean. Large washing machines are the only way to remove salt from bulky blankets and sleeping bags. To make laundering as painless as possible, stick to cotton sheets and light blankets in the tropics. We used light bedding for about two weeks at sea before it became uninhabitable. When you use heavy blankets or sleeping bags, put several layers between your body and the heavier bedding. This minimizes the chance of salt getting into heavier bedding and keeps it clean, even when you haven't had a shower in a few days. Using this strategy, we managed to get away with laundering our heavy bedding once a year.

Prevent mold and mildew

Despite your best efforts, the boat will still be vulnerable to mold and mildew in areas with poor ventilation. As discussed in Chapter 2, good ventilation in all lockers will prevent mold, mildew, and the odors that accompany them. A number of additional suggestions follow.

■ *Cushions.* Mold and mildew flourish in cushions, especially between the cushion's bottom and the bunk. Cushions should be aired frequently, even if they are just propped up in the cabin for an hour or so every few days. If your cushions can be flipped over, do so regu-

larly. Marine retailers sell an absorbent material called "Dry Bunk" for use between the cushion and the bunk. We found that it drew moisture away from the cushion and decreased mold and mildew.

■ *Clothes.* Keeping clothes free from mildew, even in well-ventilated lockers, takes practice. We gradually developed a routine for passagemaking that greatly extended the life of our clothes. We had three lockers over each side of the forepeak V-berth. Before leaving port, we would stow in the aftmost locker any clothing we might need during the passage. We stowed the rest of our clothes in the two forward lockers in dry bags (polypropylene bags that fit the dimensions of the locker and could be zippered closed to be watertight). Other people we knew used 2-gallon Ziploc bags. Even if water found its way into these lockers, the clothes would still be fresh and sweet smelling. Only store clothes that are absolutely dry in sealed plastic bags, otherwise condensation will form and mold will follow.

■ *Other items.* Don't pack lockers too full with little or no space between items. This restricts air circulation and promotes mold and mildew, even in lockers with louvered doors. Clothes and books packed tightly are particularly susceptible. If you need to stow things tightly, bag them in Ziploc bags or stow them with fabric softener sheets or mildew preventer.

For items that are particularly sensitive to damage from moisture, such as cameras and laptop computers, marine retailers sell waterproof safety cases with foam inserts for reasonable prices. Put desiccant in these watertight cases to help protect your equipment. Marine retailers sell a number of such desiccant products; you can also use silica gel, used in flower drying and available at craft stores. If you cannot afford these cases or don't have the room to stow them, keep equipment in dry bags. These are available from marine suppliers and are practically watertight when sealed. Wrap equipment in several layers of soft cloth and stow it in these bags with desiccant. As a last resort, you can put the components in large Ziploc bags with desiccant and stow them in their normal carry bag, but they will be less protected this way, from both moisture and concussion.

The last piece of the puzzle when dealing with all that water everywhere is to keep surfaces clean where mold might grow. Diluting vinegar in water and rubbing the solution over almost any surface discourages mold. Clean the inside of Dorade vents with a vinegar or Clorox solution every month. Otherwise, they will harbor mold and make the entire boat smell musty. The "ceiling" of the icebox is another area that is easy to overlook.

Never ignore a musty or moldy odor. Find the cause and remedy it. No boat should ever smell sour under normal passagemaking conditions. If it does, take it as a challenge. Look for leaks, improve the ventilation, and find ways to discourage the growth of mold and mildew. The boat is your home, and it should be held to the same standard.

CHAPTER 12 | NOR ANY DROP TO DRINK

Freshwater management—the basics ▪ *Assessing requirements* ▪ *Stowage* ▪ *Keeping it potable* ▪ **Freshwater sources—getting it aboard** ▪ *Refilling* ▪ *Rain catching* ▪ *Watermaking* ▪ **Freshwater uses—using it wisely** ▪ *Laundry* ▪ *Cooking and dish washing* ▪ *Showers* ▪ *Cleaning*

Voyaging wealth can be measured in terms of fresh water. One of the major differences between a 30-footer and a 50-footer is the amount of water they carry, which to some extent determines the quality of life aboard. Most cruisers miss having unlimited fresh water. But much of that "unlimited" fresh water ashore ends up quickly down the drain. Voyaging teaches you that a little water goes a long way: To be happy, healthy, and wealthy aboard, you need very little water by shoreside standards.

We met a family of four on a 25-foot boat that carried only 25 gallons of water tankage. Plastic containers held an additional 10 gallons. On passage they used fresh water for one thing only—drinking. When there was no alternative, they used salt water to bathe and shower, wash dishes, and do laundry. They lived with dampness and salt in conditions that many would have found unacceptable.

On the other end of the spectrum, some boats carry 200 hundred gallons of water plus an engine-driven watermaker. Families aboard these boats use fresh water for everything. Although they use less water than they would ashore, they don't put a great deal of effort into conservation.

Being able to carry extra water makes life at sea more comfortable, but the real advantage comes when you are cruising dry tropical islands. We went six to eight weeks between high quality water supplies on three occasions. Over the 4,000 nautical miles between Panama and Tahiti, Daniel's Bay on Nuku Hiva in the Marquesas was the only place where we found sufficient quality fresh water to fill our tanks. To visit the Galapagos or the dozens of gorgeous atolls in the Tuamotus east of Tahiti, you must be self-sufficient with respect to water

for one to two months. As with provisioning, plan on refilling your water tanks from shore only a few times while island-hopping across an ocean.

Even with a watermaker, you and your crew will cut consumption by three-quarters from shoreside levels. To do that, you need to practice the art of water management until it becomes second nature. That means knowing how much water you will need, how to stow it, and how to manage freshwater sources and uses to stretch your supply as far as possible.

FRESHWATER MANAGEMENT— THE BASICS

When we moved aboard *Silk,* I had no idea how much water I drank every day, let alone how much I used to do the dishes, cook, or shower. Even if I had known how much I used ashore, I couldn't have translated that to life aboard. I didn't know if *Silk's* 100 gallons of tankage was a lot or a little, or how long we would be able to go without filling our tanks.

A few guidelines provide minimum and average levels of water usage for various activities. You can decide how much water you will need to carry based on your boat size and your voyaging "standard of living." Then you can decide how you will stow that water and keep it fresh for the weeks and months between major ports.

Assessing requirements

The average American uses 70 gallons of water a day ashore. On a boat, therefore, water consumption will expand to whatever supply is available. Don't ask how much you will want—the answer is as much as you can carry. Assess your minimal requirements without compromising your standards for hygiene and health, and ask how much you will *need*.

To stay healthy, high quality drinking water must be freely available. This defines the absolute minimum amount of fresh water that any boat must carry.

Doctors recommend drinking 6 to 8 pints (3 to 4 quarts) of water per day to prevent even mild symptoms of dehydration like headache or nausea. We each averaged between 4 and 6 pints of beverages per day, not all of which was water. In extreme heat, our consumption increased to 8 pints each a day, about 6 pints of which would be water. An offshore boat should carry at least ½ gallon of fresh water per person per day for as many days as the boat may be away from good water. (Note: A U.S. gallon is 3.8 litres whereas an Imperial gallon is 4.5 litres.) Therefore, a couple on a trade wind circumnavigation will need to carry a minimum of fifty gallons for drinking. We knew people who carried less, but they planned on catching rain and they carried other beverages besides water. This 50-gallon estimate provides an adequate safety margin and does not assume rain water or other beverages will be available.

How much water you use beyond this minimum depends on the size of your boat and the levels of comfort and convenience you want on board. It will also depend on whether you are cruising where fresh water is freely available ashore.

On passage and cruising remote areas

When water was unavailable, the crews whose boats carried 50 gallons or less reserved their water for drinking, washing, brushing teeth, and cooking where salt water cannot be used. Salt water was used for almost everything else, including laundry, boat cleaning, dish washing, and showering. This represents the least luxurious end of the spectrum.

The situation aboard most boats is more civilized. *Silk* carried 100 gallons of water in two 50-gallon tanks, a typical arrangement for an offshore boat. In addition, we carried an extra 20 gallons in a flexible tank and a number of smaller containers. With that much water aboard, we used about 1 gallon per day per person. We used 1½ quarts for drinking (some of it as lemonade or iced tea) and 2 quarts for showering (we each used

2 quarts every other day). An additional quart would be used for everything else—from brushing our teeth to rinsing dishes. We washed dishes in salt water and lightly rinsed them in fresh. When it rained, we topped up our tanks first and used extra water for additional showers and laundry.

Based on our capacity and usage, we never went through more than one of our 50-gallon main tanks between watering stops. We never felt that we lacked for water. Once we got past our shoreside mindset, using water sparingly became automatic. To help us conserve water, we had a manual freshwater system and a saltwater pump in the galley. Though we had pressure water aboard, we used it only in port where water was plentiful.

At the luxurious end of the spectrum, consumption varies from 5 to 10 gallons per day per person aboard boats with several hundred gallons of tankage plus a watermaker. Showers are taken as often as desired. Though water is turned off while lathering up, the amount used per shower is measured in gallons, not quarts. Dishes are washed in fresh water. Though laundry is done as needed, a minimum amount of water is used. The last two items make the biggest difference in overall consumption.

Where will you be along this spectrum? If your boat is under 30 feet, assume you will fall into the minimal usage category. If your boat is between 30 and 50 feet, you will probably be in the average category—although if you carry a watermaker, you'll have some additional capacity. If your boat is over 50 feet, you'll be able to carry enough water to live luxuriously.

In the end, we never felt deprived aboard *Silk,* nor did most people we knew. We might have enjoyed more water, but we certainly didn't *need* it.

In port

When fresh water was readily available, we took advantage of it. We used fresh water freely for showers, cleaning the boat, or washing dishes. In port, we more than doubled our usage aboard as well as using a fair amount ashore. If showers were available on shore, we used all the water we wanted rather than shower on the boat. We took our dirty clothes to laundromats or used the local laundry service. If we had to do it ourselves, we used tank water for the initial wash and soak, but rinsed it ashore. Overall, we averaged between 2 and 3 gallons per day per person from our boat tankage and 5 and 10 gallons ashore per day for showers and laundry. Our water usage would be about the same while cruising coastwise or doing limited offshore passages in New Zealand, Australia, and South Africa. Those times seemed very luxurious after spending months conserving every drop of water aboard. In port, we almost never felt we needed or wanted more water.

Stowage

You should now have an idea of how much water you will need to carry. If you are considering a watermaker, don't assume it will let you carry less water. Electric and engine-driven watermakers should be used to supplement your tankage—not replace it. If your engine dies or your generator fails, you will have to make do with the water stowed in your tanks. Again, fifty gallons should be considered a minimum for a voyaging couple. If that is all you have aboard, you would be forced to reserve it for drinking water if your watermaker failed. Before you rip out that spare water tank to put in a watermaker, make sure that you and your crew have evaluated the trade-offs. In no case should you end up with less than 25 to 30 gallons of tankage per person aboard.

You will store the bulk of your water in your boat's main tanks. Ideally, this stowage will be divided into more than one tank. Stowing water in multiple tanks ensures that you do not lose all your water if a tank ruptures or becomes contaminated. If your boat has only one main storage tank, add an additional tank somewhere or carry plastic jugs with extra water for use in an emergency.

Track your usage so you can learn from the past and plan for the future. Develop a system for measuring the water left in each tank. Fancy gauges are easy to use, but an old-fashioned dipstick inserted into the inspection hatch works just as well and will never break.

If your boat has multiple tanks, you will want an easy way to switch between tanks, tell which is in use, and equalize the tanks. The system on *Silk* was accessible and simple. The outlet pipes from our two main tanks met at a tee under the galley sink. Two faucets controlled which tank fed the water pumps. We could work from one tank or both.

All tanks must be well supported and properly baffled, with removable inspection hatches for cleaning. If stainless tanks are strapped in, make sure the strapping is not aluminum. Galvanic corrosion could cause a tank to break loose in heavy weather. Also check to see that tank outlets are not corroded with age or mounted so that they could shear off on a bulkhead in severe pounding.

Before you leave, empty your tanks and then fill them with 5-gallon jugs to determine your usable tank capacity. On many boats, the last few gallons are below the level of the outflow fitting. At the same time, you may want to mark a dipstick at each five gallon increment. Once you determine how much water you really have available, you can decide if you need additional capacity. You can add tanks in low areas of the boat. Table 12-1 suggests other water stowage areas.

We used our main tank's water as the primary source for the galley. We used it for cooking, for rinsing dishes, cleaning, and wiping down our bodies when we were salty. We also used our main tanks as backup for other water aboard. When we ran out of drinking water in the icebox or shower water in the cockpit, we used the water from our main tanks.

Table 12-1. Additional stowage areas and their uses aboard *Silk*

Location	Amount	Would last	Use	Comments
Icebox	Two 3-gallon jugs and two dozen quart bottles	Three weeks	Drinking	Purchased bottled water or excellent tap water
Flexible tank in forepeak	10 gallons	Several weeks	Washing, shaving in head	Did not use at sea
Plastic jugs on deck	Two 5-gallon jugs	Three weeks	Shower water	Not for drinking—algae grew in jugs stowed on deck, even with chlorine

Keeping it potable

To get good water out of the tanks, you have to put good water into them. Once contaminated water gets into your tanks, you will have to thoroughly disinfect them. In many areas, that will not be possible for weeks or even months. No matter where you get your water from or how fresh it is, algae and bacteria will grow once you stow it in a tank and leave it for weeks. Water needs to be treated to keep it pure. Over time dust, dirt, and other residue will collect on the bottom of the tanks. That residue needs to be cleaned out periodically to keep the water potable.

Deciding whether or not to take it aboard

The quality of local water is well known. In Vava'u in Tonga, every new boat was warned that, though potable, the water from the fuel dock smelled and tasted like sulfur. In Cocos Keeling, word passed from boat to boat that the cistern that stored rain water was full of mosquito larvae. Upon entering a new harbor, we weren't referring to swimming when we asked other voyagers, "How's the water?"

The Seven Seas Cruising Association bulletins and local cruising guides offer warnings where water is suspect. But check with people who are there. You don't want to take on contaminated water or get sick from drinking it.

In the few places where information is scarce, ask where the water comes from. If it is from a desalination plant, a deep water well, or a deep spring, you should have little concern over its quality. If it is coming from a cistern or island runoff, avoid it. On most islands, streams and rivers serve as laundromats and bathrooms. They are often contaminated by human and animal waste. Even if the locals have no problem with the water, you probably will. Water in cisterns tends to be untreated and harbors small critters that will play havoc with your digestion.

Smell and taste the water before putting it in your tanks. In some places, potable water carries strong odors that can create a horrible stench difficult to remove from the freshwater system. In other places, the water tasted so good we filled every available container. If you are the least bit concerned about water quality, put it in your secondary stowage areas and avoid filling your main tanks. We would use just about any water in

---

Emergency water—abandon-ship kit

A person can survive for up to three weeks without food but for only three days without water. If you have to abandon ship, water must be your first concern. A person can stay fit on a pint of water a day for 10 to 14 days and survive on a half-pint a day for many weeks as evidenced by Steve Callahan's ordeal in the book *Adrift*.

Our abandon-ship plan called for one of us to grab the abandon-ship kit and at least one of the 3-gallon water containers from the icebox. The icebox was located by the companionway, and the jug was always accessible. We carried 6 quarts of bottled water in the panic kit. Our plan also called for me to cut the line that lashed the shower water to the mizzen mast. This water was not good quality, but we could have survived on it. The jugs were never full after the first few days of a passage, so they would float. If we

couldn't take them with us, we hoped to retrieve them after we had abandoned ship.

If we were successful, we would have had somewhere between 5 and 10 gallons of fresh water, enough for 40 to 80 days. If we managed only to get the panic kit, we would have had enough water to keep us alive for about two weeks. We also carried a thermal blanket, which we would have experimented with to create a solar still, though we would have preferred a more certain solution for making water.

When we left on our trip, handheld watermakers were relatively new and we could not afford one. Now, we would definitely buy one for our panic kit and would recommend that others do the same. The 6-gallon-per-day watermakers used a few hours per day could keep you alive indefinitely. For that, the price of $500 has to be considered cheap.

our shower jerry cans, and any potable water, regardless of the taste, in our forepeak flexible tank.

You need to be cautious even when catching rain water, unless you are far offshore. Within a hundred miles or so downwind of land, catch some rain in a bucket and take a good look before you fill your tanks. Many islanders raise sugarcane and burn the cane stalks to clear the fields. Rain can carry ash that will contaminate your tanks. In the Canary Islands and the Red Sea, rain often carries red dust from the nearby desert. Downwind of large urban centers, the rain may smell or taste questionable. We caught all the rain we could at sea or in remote islands, but we were careful elsewhere.

Treating water

The only water we did not treat for purity was bottled water or the tap water we used to refill our bottles. The bottles stowed water for only a few weeks at a time and were thoroughly disinfected between uses. Rain water and watermaker water both need to be treated. Rain water is fairly pure and the reverse osmosis process removes all bacteria and algae. But once the water is in a tank, microbes will grow again within a few weeks.

Almost everybody treats their water with Clorox bleach. But people disagree over exactly how much bleach to use. Various sources recommend anywhere from 2 to 24 ounces of 4- to 6-percent chlorine solution (Clorox is 5.5 percent) per 100 gallons of water. Anything over 8 ounces left a strong chlorine taste, which did not dissipate for up to a week. We used between 4 and 5 ounces per 100 gallons. This did not leave any residual taste or smell after a day or two, and it kept the water algae-free for months. For water stored on deck for showering, we used 1 ounce per 5-gallon container. Otherwise, algae grew within a period of days.

Do not use bleach products with perfumes or deodorizers, and be careful of the different strengths of chlorine products available. Half a teaspoon of swimming pool chlorine to 100 gallons of water is the equivalent of 7 ounces of Clorox.

Like many chemicals, chlorine attacks aluminum. Don't treat your water with chlorine if you have aluminum tanks. Prefilter the water and use water purification tablets. You can purchase these from marine supply stores. Stock up: They can be hard to find outside the United States.

Filtering water

An activated charcoal filter between the tank and the tap will remove any residual chlorine or tank taste. Unfortunately, the filters for these systems are hard to stow and can be difficult to locate in foreign countries. Our unfiltered tank water didn't satisfy my overly sensitive palate, but we preferred stowing separate drinking water to installing a filter. Our next boat will be larger and stowage will be less of an issue, so we will carry filters. Whether or not we install one between the tanks and the tap, we will use them to filter water as it enters the tanks (see "Rain catching" on page 214).

Many boats used the activated charcoal filters that can be purchased at a hardware store. These are much cheaper than the marine equivalent. They last only a few months as opposed to the year or so for the marine version, but the overall cost is still lower. Make sure to stock plenty of extra cartridges, O-rings, and a wrench that fits the filter. Install the filter in an accessible place. You'll need to change it regularly to realize the benefits.

More expensive filters like the Seagull Drinking Water System remove more contaminants and offer great-tasting water. If you choose to install one, install a separate faucet and use it only for drinking water. Not only will that preserve the filter, it will also keep the slow flow rate through the filter from frustrating you when you're doing dishes. The filters can be installed with a manual pump supplied by the manufacturer if you don't have pressure water, but that doubles the cost.

Keeping tanks clean

No matter how clean the water appears, suspended particles will work their way out of the water and down to the bottom of your tank. A sludgy residue will slowly develop there that must be cleaned out every few years.

Between major cleanings, we would shock treat our tanks to minimize the amount of sludge that accumulated. We only did this where we had plenty of water available. When both of our 50-gallon tanks were down to the last 10 to 15 gallons, we put 6 or 8 ounces of Clorox in each tank. This would kill everything inside. We let the water sit for a few hours, then emptied the tank as completely as possible. We refilled the tank and pumped it out again. After flushing the tank three or four times, the water coming out no longer smelled like a laundry. We then refilled the tanks with clean water without adding any bleach. The residual amount kept the water clean until we filled our tanks again. The bleach smell dissipated within the next day or so. If it didn't, we did one final flush.

In addition to these occasional shock treatments and system flushes, you will need to clean the inside of your tank every few years. To do this, drain the water from the tank, open the inspection hatch, and detach the outlet hose (the highly chlorinated water from cleaning will destroy water pump membranes). Set up the water tank so it can be drained into a bucket or siphoned into a sink. Wipe down the interior with straight Clorox on a rag. Do not use any soap, detergents, or solvents. Rinse repeatedly. While the tank is open, look for cracks, corrosion, or blisters. Fix any problems before resealing the inspection hatch.

If the inspection hatches do not allow adequate access to the tank interior, you will have to have your tanks professionally steam cleaned. Such services can only be found in major yachting centers. If you make sure that your tank has adequate access before you leave, you will have a choice.

With shock treatments once or twice a year and a thorough cleaning every few years, your tanks will stay reasonably clean, unless you take on contaminated water. If that happens, you will need to clean the tanks as soon as you have sufficient fresh water to do so.

FRESHWATER SOURCES— GETTING IT ABOARD

When you are coastal cruising and your tanks start to get low, you pull out the cruising guide and look for a fuel dock or a nearby marina. After tying up, you set up your own hose or use the dock's, turn on the spigot, and wait for that satisfying boom. You will not have the same convenience when offshore voyaging. When we traveled 8,000 nautical miles in eight months from Panama to New Zealand, we never pulled up to a dock and took on water. In a handful of places, there were fuel docks where we could have gotten water. But given the condition of the dock, we preferred to use other sources.

This again illustrates the need to carry sufficient tankage for offshore voyaging and cruising in remote islands. But when you can't go that long without refilling your tanks, what are your alternatives?

Refilling

We used our dinghy to ferry water out to the boat. In places such as the Marquesas in the Pacific, Christmas Island in the Indian Ocean, and St. Helena in the South Atlantic, we put all of our plastic jerry jugs in the dinghy, took them ashore to a spigot, filled them, and rowed them back out to the boat. We often topped our tanks up this way when coastal cruising rather than going into a fuel dock. We could fill our water tanks and all of our other stowage areas in about an hour and a half.

Voyagers carry lots of plastic jerry jugs for just this purpose. To fill our tanks, we used the two 5-gallon jerry jugs we stowed on deck and the two 3-gallon jugs we stowed in the icebox. We emptied them, rinsed them lightly with a mild Clorox solution, and let them air out for a few hours. In a harbor with other yachts, pooling plastic containers speeds up refilling. However, be sure that the jugs you borrow are clean before using them to fill your tanks.

When selecting the size of your jerry jugs, consider the strength of each crewmember. Five-gallon containers reduce the number of trips, but they are too heavy for many people. Three-gallon plastic jugs are easier to carry, handle, and stow, but you will have to make a few more trips. Collapsible jugs are easy to stow, but they are harder to carry and they can rip. We stowed all available containers full of water, so collapsible jugs offered us no real advantage.

Rain catching

Catching free water from the sky is like getting free power from the sun. Unfortunately, it happens less frequently—we were surprised by how seldom it rained at sea. Outside of the doldrums, we often went weeks without rain. We filled our tanks this way less often than we filled them using jerry cans and the dinghy or a hose at the dock.

Rain is more frequent near a high island. The slight change in altitude and the temperature differential between land and water generate precipitation from the humid air. In the desert island–like atolls, the late-afternoon cloud formations that form over the islets generally disperse by evening without bringing any real moisture.

Whatever system you use for rain catching, it must be efficient, self-tending, workable at sea and in port, and able to stand up to windy conditions. Ideally, it will also keep you from getting wet. You will find the best way to catch rain on your boat through trial and error. But most boats eventually come to one or a couple of the following solutions. When a real downpour does come, make an effort to catch it in any available container. Make use of buckets, the dinghy, and large pots. You'll enjoy the benefits of extra water for days afterwards.

Trapping rain on the side decks

The most efficient way to capture the largest volume of water is to use the entire surface area of the boat. While this seems obvious, making it work may require some minor modifications.

Silk's deck fills were mounted flush on the side decks which is ideal for efficient rain catching. At sea or in remote ports, we kept the decks clean with frequent salt-water scrubs. The first five minutes of heavy rain would rinse off the salt. Then we dammed off the decks with towels just aft of the deck fills and opened the top. In the doldrums between St. Helena and the Caribbean, we caught 40 gallons of water in about 15 minutes of heavy downpour.

There were two drawbacks with this method. If the boat was heeled over or if waves were reaching the deck, we risked getting salt water into our tanks. In these conditions, we relied on canvas, as discussed below. Unless the decks were really clean, small amounts of dirt got into the water tanks. To solve this problem, plumb Y-valves into the hoses that drain the deck scuppers; the valve diverts the scupper water through charcoal filters into the water tanks. This system works even if deck fills are not flush mounted on the side decks. Rather than going out in the rain and opening the deck fills, turn the valve from below and fill your tanks with filtered rain water.

Some boats do not have their deck fills flush mounted in the side deck, and a retrofit using the scuppers is impractical. An alternative method works well for these boats, but it requires you to get wet. Plug the scupper through-hulls with a bung and allow the water to accumulate on the side decks. Take one of your hand pumps (not the one you change the oil with!), put the exhaust hose into your deck fill, and pump the water from the side decks into your tanks. Alternatively, lash a bucket under the scupper through-hull and catch the water as it exits the boat. This last option is the least efficient. Use it for gathering water for showers or laundry rather than tank water.

Capturing rain in canvas

We used canvas at sea when rain water was likely to be contaminated with salt water (almost any time the wind was forward of the beam, and downwind when it was very windy or wavy). We used canvas in port when our tanks were full, and we wanted some extra water for laundry or cleaning the boat. Most boats with teak decks used canvas to avoid contaminating their tanks with teak, oil, and dirt.

If we were unable to use our deck fills at sea, then the wind would be too strong for a large awning. We experimented with a variety of solutions, only to find that the canvas of the main or mizzen sail provided the largest surface area for catching rain. We then hung a canvas catcher under the boom to trap water coming off the sail (Figure 12-1).

Our catcher consisted of a 4-foot by 4-foot square of canvas with grommets along two edges. We reinforced one end with a vinyl patch through which we installed a

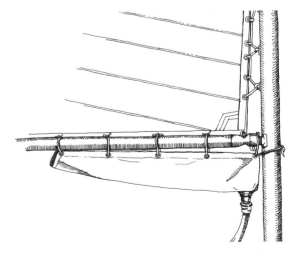

Figure 12-1. When the side decks were too salty for rain catching, our solution was a canvas catcher positioned under the main boom.

nylon through-hull fitting. When we wanted to catch rain, we tied the canvas under the boom so that water was directed into the through-hull. Raising the boom with the topping lift facilitated water collection. We either filled jerry cans directly from the through-hull or attached a length of hose that connected the through-hull to our deck fills.

In port, we rigged our canvas catcher so it covered the cockpit (Figure 12-2). We led the hose down through the companionway where I could fill buckets, jerry cans, and pots and pans without getting wet. This option did not provide the surface area of most of our water-catching solutions, but we could collect 10 to 15 gallons of extra water in a downpour.

Many cruisers have success using a large harbor awning for rain catching. But we found this method difficult to rig so that more than a small section could catch water. Our 4-foot by 4-foot square did as good a job as our harbor awning, and we could use the square even in heavy winds. You can never have too many ways to catch water, so equip your harbor awning with a removable through-hull and experiment.

Watermaking

Watermakers represent a revolution in the offshore voyaging community. These marvels of modern technology work by forcing salt water through a microscopically fine membrane that removes not only the salt but also bacteria and viruses. Watermakers depend upon two things to operate properly—an energy source that can generate the tremendous pressures needed (around 800 psi) and a membrane that is free of contamination by any number of substances. Both are difficult requirements to meet on an offshore boat. But if water is a high enough priority, they can be managed.

As discussed in Chapter 7, the advantages of additional water must be traded off against a watermaker's stowage requirements, cost, maintenance load, and power consumption. If possible, try to live without a watermaker for a few months before installing one. Most voyagers we knew with tankage of 100 gallons or more did not want to add a watermaker. You won't know if you can get along without one unless you try it. If you can do without, you will greatly simplify your life aboard.

If you are considering adding a watermaker, research the available brands, which change rapidly. Make sure to ask about warranty information. Ask if they have repair facilities worldwide, or if the local dealer simply ships the unit back to the manufacturer. Find out how complete the documentation is that comes with the system: You'll want all the information you can get when it packs up in the South Pacific. Ask

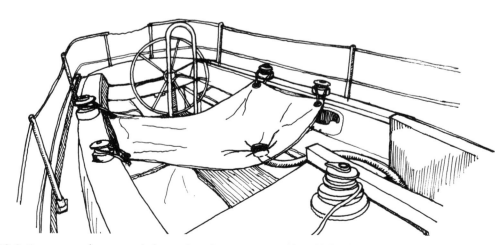

Figure 12-2. Our canvas catcher was stretched across the cockpit in port, so I could stand below decks and gather water from the skies.

how the system is flushed and cleaned and how the membranes are preserved. Try to get some history on the repair record of each of the components. Talk to cruisers who have them aboard and review *Practical Sailor* and the Seven Seas Cruising Association Equipment Survey for unbiased information on different brands.

Again, if you do decide to add a watermaker, don't substitute the watermaker for tankage. Also take mineral supplements along, because a watermaker strains minerals out of the water.

Consider three questions to minimize the complexity of the system and maximize your enjoyment of the water it produces: How large a system should you install, how will you meet its power demands, and how will you protect the membranes from contamination?

Sizing the system

You should already have some sense of how much water you will need to produce. As mentioned before, most cruisers we knew with watermakers aboard used between 5 and 10 gallons of water per day per person. If you plan on washing dishes in fresh water and doing laundry aboard, you will be at the top of that range. Bear in mind that you will need enough tankage to stow the water you make, especially if you want to maintain your standard of living in a port where you can't run the unit for a week or two.

Given the amount you want to be able to produce in a day, you can't make the logical leap to watermaker capacity without considering some of the realities of how the reverse osmosis process actually works aboard a boat. Manufacturers' rated capacities are generally given in gallons per day, but few watermakers are made to operate around the clock. As a first step, think in terms of gallons per hour and look for a watermaker that can produce the water you want in an hour or two of operation per day.

No watermaker performs up to its rated capacity in all conditions. Your actual capacity will be determined by the following:

■ *Feed water temperature.* Most manufacturers' rated capacities are based on a feed water temperature of 77 degrees Fahrenheit. If the actual temperature is 56 degrees, capacity will be reduced by about 25 percent. You will encounter temperatures in this range in New Zealand, around South Africa, and in parts of the North Atlantic. Don't boost the temperature of the feed water by passing it through an engine heat exchanger. Even a pin hole in the exchanger will allow enough antifreeze to reach the watermaker membrane to destroy it.

■ *Membrane condition.* Membranes become less efficient with age. An older membrane can reduce capacity in the system by 20 to 25 percent, but not be old enough to justify replacement.

■ *Salinity.* The watermaker is less efficient in saltier water. The salinity of sea water varies tremendously, even over the course of a passage. In some places we sailed, the water was so salty that the morning dew would leave a crust of salt on the mast and deck. In other places, the water almost tasted fresh.

These factors can combine to cause a 50-percent variance in your watermaker's actual performance compared to its rated capacity. Your per-day average usage does not take into account peak loads. You will want to be able to meet the extra demand if you have guests aboard. Once you make the decision to carry a watermaker, select one that is oversized relative to your normal requirements.

Take, for example, a couple on a 45-foot boat who want to make an average of 5 gallons per day for each person aboard. With two guests on board, their peak demand will be 20 gallons per day. They are considering a 200-gallon-per-day, engine-driven watermaker. In optimal conditions, this will make about 8 gallons per hour. At full efficiency, the watermaker could meet their normal demand in a little over 1 hour. This matches the amount of time they run their engine each day to charge their batteries and cool their refrigerator. If the watermaker's production declined by 50 percent due to colder feed water and an aging membrane, the running time would increase to 2½ hours, which is not ideal but feasible. But at the 50-percent performance rate with two guests onboard, their running time would increase to 5 hours a day. As long as they do not plan to have guests very often, and they will be in tropical waters, the 200-gallon-per-day system will meet their needs. Otherwise, they should go one size larger.

Whatever size you determine is appropriate for you, monitor the actual rate of freshwater production. If it is too high, the membranes can blow out and do permanent damage to the unit. If it is too low, bacterial growth will be facilitated. Your owner's manual should state the optimal range. If not, contact the manufacturer and find out.

Powering the system

Generating the force necessary to get water to pass through the tiny pores in the watermaker's membrane requires a large amount of energy. Some watermakers use electricity from your batteries; others are driven directly off an engine or generator.

Most 12-volt models use between 2.5 and 3.5 amp-hours per gallon of water produced. The average demand for our couple on the 45-footer, described above, would require 25 to 35 amp-hours, or 100 to 140 amp-hours of dedicated battery capacity. To service this kind of additional load on a daily basis requires an excellent charging system with a high-output alternator and a "smart" regulator and battery bank manager. If our couple does not already have such a system aboard, they will need to consider the cost when evaluating the watermaker tradeoff. In addition, if they want to be able to service their peak load in degraded conditions, they may find themselves using over 400 amp-hours just to make water, an amount that will tax a large battery bank and a high capacity charging system.

While the engine- or generator-driven units are more efficient, the longevity of the watermaking equipment is a function of how well the equipment is installed. Among other issues, the reverse-osmosis pressure pump must be run only at specified rpms, or you risk exploding a high pressure line. These pumps are sensitive to vibration and will wear excessively if not installed properly. Even a mechanically adept person will need a minimum of 30 hours to install one of these units. It pays to get some professional advice before beginning the installation.

Maintaining the system

The complex membranes are the heart and soul of any watermaker. They can be destroyed by trace amounts of fuel, chlorine, oil, and even bacteria—all of which are often present in sea water close to land. The system must prevent contaminants from reaching the membrane, and it must be routinely flushed to remove any impurities.

To keep contaminants away from the membrane, the system should include one or more prefilters. Install the intake as far below the waterline as possible. Do not use the watermaker in any harbor where diesel is visible on the surface of the water or where there is any sign of oil. Oil droplets can be churned under in harbors. And if the boat is rolling, contaminants on the surface can reach the intake. Do not use the system in harbors with freighter traffic, large numbers of other boats, or a sewage discharge.

If you will be in such an area for a week or more, you will have to pickle the watermaker with a biocide solution to keep the membrane moist and free of contaminants. Upon heading back out to sea, flush the entire unit with fresh water thoroughly before use. The best systems automatically perform freshwater flushes after every cycle. You must run the watermaker at least once every two weeks if it has not been pickled. And you will have to change the prefilters every 50 hours or so, so bring plenty of spares.

Watermakers are a mixed blessing. Their reliability is improving, and in a few years the tradeoffs may not be so dramatic. Until then, investigate watermakers thoroughly before installing one aboard. If you feel you need additional water capacity, you should adequately size the system, think through the power requirements, and commit yourself to a rigorous maintenance schedule.

Finally, a bit of advice from a woman who sells and services watermakers: Leave your boat keys near the bottle of biocide. Every time you pick up your keys to lock the boat, ask yourself if there is *any* chance you won't be back in a week. If so, pickle your watermaker. A membrane destroyed by a lack of foresight will cause a great deal more aggravation than maintaining the machine.

FRESHWATER USES— USING IT WISELY

Drinking water should never be limited. But there are many painless ways to conserve water for other uses aboard. Beyond drinking, there are four major uses for water: laundry, cooking and dishes, showers, and boat cleaning. At one end of the spectrum, all these needs could be met with salt water. At the other end, they could all be done with fresh water. We eventually found optimal solutions that we felt conserved our fresh water without greatly reducing our quality of life.

Laundry

Laundry consumes the largest amount of water. Even done as frugally as possible, laundry water usage is measured in gallons, not quarts. After an initial attempt that failed miserably, we never used salt water again for laundry. Even the most diehard saltwater users did not use it on jeans, towels, or heavy cotton garments. It took more fresh water to rinse out the salt than to wash *and* rinse in fresh water.

· Conserving water starts by minimizing the amount of laundry you need to do. Most of your tropical wardrobe makes for easy laundry. But no matter how little you wear, sheets and towels, the worst of the laundry, still remain. These require the most fresh water, take up the most space, and take the longest to dry.

We never did laundry on passage. We stowed laundry aboard until we got into port. When we arrived, one of our first priorities was to figure out how to manage laundry in that destination. Where possible, we preferred laundromats. When they were reputable, we used the local laundress. But if prices were extreme, if no one did laundry in the local village, or if there was no local village, then we did the laundry ourselves. This was the case about one-third of the time. I came to enjoy the rituals that went with getting laundry done.

While I entertained fantasies of taking the laundry ashore and pounding away on a rock, this never worked out in practice. Instead, we did laundry on the boat using as little water as possible. You will develop your own solution for doing laundry with limited water. The following describes how we managed it, and it may help you avoid some of our early mistakes.

We did not wash towels and heavy cotton items unless we had a source of fresh water ashore. Without adequate rinse water, they ended up stiff, rough, and uncomfortable. Most of the time we could find a source of water, though often it was not potable. Assuming this was the case, our laundry ritual went like this:

1. *Sort laundry.* Categories include sheets, towels, whites, colored garments, and too-dirty-to-consider-washing-with-other-things.

2. *Pretreat stains.* To conserve detergent and limit rinsing, pretreat major stains. WD-40 or a grease cleaner for hands removes oil or greasy dirt. For mildew, try rubbing the stain with lemon juice or a paste of baking soda and leave it in the sun for an hour or so. Bleach works but is hard on fabrics. A paste of vinegar and baking soda will remove shirt collar stains or general grime.

3. *Assemble laundry buckets.* We had two large (4-gallon) and two small (2-gallon) black rubber buckets. If necessary, rinse the buckets with an inch of fresh water in the bottom.

4. *Prepare wash water.* Fill each bucket about half full with fresh water and add laundry detergent. Don't use too much! The amount of rinse water required is directly proportional to how much detergent goes in the bucket. For our 2-gallon buckets, one fistful of powdered detergent or one-quarter of the measuring cap of liquid was plenty. For the 4-gallon buckets, I used about twice that (less with towels, which are generally not as soiled and hold soap tenaciously). Beware of concentrated detergent brands. They are easier to stow, but they are harder to use without overdoing it. Stir the water well until the detergent is dissolved.

5. *Fill buckets three-quarters full with clothes, add water, and let soak.* Put separated piles into the buckets. Our small buckets held about three pairs of shorts and three tee-shirts. Our large buckets held three bath towels or two sheets and two pillowcases plus some clothes. Whoosh the dirty clothes around until most of the water has been absorbed. Now fill the bucket to the rim with additional fresh water and give it another stir. Let the clothes soak for a few hours. This is where our black rubber buckets came in handy: They absorbed heat. Thus our soak cycle was done with hot water.

6. *Scrub as needed.* After the clothes had soaked for a few hours in hot water, I checked to see if the stains had been lifted. If not, I scrubbed with a toothbrush or rubbed the material against itself. This process takes some patience but most pretreated stains come out with a little elbow grease. Teak oil and rust are the exceptions. Once the stain came out (or I gave up), the clothes went back in the bucket for another hour or so of soaking.

7. For towels, jeans, and heavy cotton, perform a rinse cycle. For heavy cotton items, empty the water out of the bucket after several hours of soaking. Refill the bucket with fresh water without adding any additional soap. Add about a quarter cup of liquid fabric softener if available. The softener makes towels and jeans feel softer, facilitates rinsing the detergent out, and helps keep the clothes from drying stiff. After this "rinse," leave the clothes to soak for another hour or so. Don't let the dirty water go to waste: Evans used it to give the decks a good scrub.

8. Take everything ashore for rinsing. You are finally ready to go ashore. Empty as much of the water out of the buckets as possible, then load the buckets into the dinghy. Add a canvas tarp, plastic sheet, or several plastic garbage bags. Once ashore, carry everything to the freshwater tap and empty the clothes out on the plastic bags or canvas tarp.

9. Rinse and wring clothes. Rinse the soap out of all the buckets and fill two with water. Rinse the clothes one at a time under the tap. To check if all of the soap is out, drop them into one of the buckets and swirl them around. If the water goes murky in a few seconds, keep rinsing. When things seem to be soap free, wring them out and drop them into one of the two empty buckets. This whole process can take up to an hour for four buckets of laundry.

10. Load everything back into the dinghy, return to the boat, and hang the laundry out to dry. When hanging clothes to dry, be very careful not to hang them so they are in contact with stanchions or stays. Otherwise, small, difficult-to-remove rust spots will appear on your favorite clothes. To be sure that things stay put, use plenty of clothespins. For towels, keep the wind from getting inside by pinning them to the top and bottom lifeline. For sheets, string a line from the roller furler to the main mast and pin them closed under the line to keep the wind out.

Several of our friends preferred baby baths to buckets. Laila Stjerndrüp from *Isa Lei* advises, "Fill the baby bath with water, soap, and laundry. Take off your shoes and take a walk in the bath. Clean feet, clean laundry, and no sore back."

Try to avoid washing woolens using the method described above. They do not like to be soaked, especially in hot water. They will take even more water to rinse than towels. To avoid washing them in a bucket, launder them every six months or so when you are in a developed country. Keep them clean, and air them out in the sunshine regularly to prevent musty odors.

If there is no fresh water ashore, don't try to do the towels and sheets. Stick to the shorts and tee-shirts you need to be presentable. Do everything as above until you come to the rinse step. To get the soap out with the minimum of water, fill each of your buckets one-quarter full. Take each garment and rinse it in the first bucket and then the second, third, and fourth. By the time it gets to the fourth it should be rinsing clean. When the first bucket is too cloudy to be doing any good, empty it, move all the buckets up one in the line, and continue with three buckets. You can rinse a small load of laundry using this method, although the clothes may be a little stiff.

To speed drying, some cruisers like to use a wringer, although they can be hard to find and are prone to rust. The rigging works just as well—loop the clothes around and twist. When ashore look for a sturdy branch or use the standpipe of the faucet.

If your clothes come out stiff—if your jeans stand on their own and your towels feel spiky—you are using too much detergent, not rinsing well enough, or both. Properly washed and rinsed, clothes come out as if they were washed in the machine at home without fabric softener.

This sounds like a long, drawn-out process—and it is. On the other hand, very little of it actually requires any work. It took three to four hours to do two buckets of lightweight clothes, but I was actually *doing* something for only an hour of that. We often left clothes soaking overnight, which meant less work. When you are anchored and there is fresh water ashore, do a little at a time.

You may want to invest in a few things to make laundry easier. If you have arthritis in your hands, buy a clothes wringer. Lake City Industries in Lake City, Pennsylvania (814-774-9616), manufactures a sturdy brand,

and they have distributors all over the country. These are not plastic and will rust over time, but many cruisers find them worthwhile. A second helpmate is a Tumble Tub, a hand-crank washing machine that uses 3 gallons of water to wash and the same to rinse. This requires some elbow grease to spin, but it uses pressure to get the clothes clean. You can find these at discount stores like K-Mart for about $50.

Cooking and dish washing

There are several options for minimizing water usage while cooking or cleaning up. You can substitute salt water for fresh, better control your use of fresh water, and recycle fresh water.

The largest savings comes from substituting salt water for fresh, particularly for doing dishes. To realize this savings, invest in a saltwater hand or foot pump in the galley. While we could always go up on deck and grab a bucket of sea water, our good intentions rarely translated into actions. Our average water usage decreased by well over a gallon per day once we installed our saltwater pump.

When installing the saltwater pump, try to avoid putting another hole in your boat for the through-hull. We used the seacock that had served as the saltwater intake for the 110-volt refrigeration, a piece of equipment that had proven completely worthless once we left U.S. waters. With a little thought, some plumbing fittings, and some hose, you should be able to come up with an option on your boat.

Some people complain that their saltwater galley pump smells of sulfur. To avoid odors in the intake line, use it frequently. Salt water that sits in a hose for several days or weeks turns putrid. As long as we used the saltwater pump daily, we had no problems. If we left the boat for several days or more, we closed the seacock and pumped all of the water out of the line. If we returned to a foul odor, a few days of use generally took care of it. If not, we would close the seacock, remove the hose, stick the end into a jug of vinegar and pump a quart or so through. That would end the odors until the next time we left the boat for a long period.

Using salt water for washing dishes does cause rust problems. Sink drains are often made of mild steel, even if the rest of the sink is stainless. Ours eventually rusted through and had to be replaced, so carry spares or replace a mild steel drain with plastic. Rinsing the sink with a small amount of fresh water after use will extend the life of your sink drains.

For those who have decided that they draw the limit at washing their dishes in salt water, the best way to facilitate water conservation is to install a manual pump. Most pressure pumps do not offer adequate control, so you end up using a pint of fresh water to rinse off your eyeglasses. With a hand or foot pump, you can fine-tune the amount of water you use down to the level of drops. Given that kind of control and an incentive to conserve, you will decrease your water usage.

Cooking

Use salt water to cook potatoes and hard-boil eggs. But use fresh water for pasta, or it comes out tough. To make 3 cups of rice, use 1 cup of salt water and 1 cup of fresh to 1 cup of uncooked rice. You'll use even less water if you cook rice risotto style: Fry the raw rice in a skillet and then add water, a little at a time, until done. To cook potatoes in a pressure cooker, use about ½ cup of salt water.

To recycle cooking water, plan ahead. After cooking pasta, use the water to hard-boil a few eggs for later. When making potato salad, boil the potatoes and then use the same water to boil the eggs (put the eggs in last since they are usually not clean; this saves you from having to rinse them with fresh water). When the boiling water had served all possible cooking uses on *Silk,* I added a dollop of soap and used it to remove major residue from really dirty dishes. When making bread, I used it to clean up the bread bowl and the counter.

Another way to conserve water by planning ahead is to make double quantities. Extra pasta became pasta salad the next day. Extra rice became rice pudding, one of our favorite breakfast treats. Extra potatoes became potato salad or potato bread.

You can cook many things in less water than you use ashore. Soft-boiled eggs will cook in a few inches of water if the pot is tightly covered—and so will hard-boiled eggs, given enough time. Potatoes will cook in a small amount of water if they are cut up (in this case, you won't want to substitute salt water). Even pasta does not need much water. For two cups of uncooked pasta I used one quart of water, which meant that the pasta had a couple of inches of water over it. To keep pasta from sticking, add a splash of vegetable oil or margarine.

Dish washing

Like laundry, dish washing requires a surprising amount of water when compared to most other uses. To reduce water usage, minimize the number of dishes to be washed. At sea, I served everything we ate and drank in a designated drinking cup, coffee mug, and bowl. If more than one thing was being served, we either mixed it all together or did a quick freshwater rinse between courses using a 1/4-cup of water. One-pot meals and containers that could be used to stow, reheat, and serve meals reduced the number of dishes that had to be washed every day.

When the time came to clean up, we washed not-so-dirty dishes, bowls, cups, and mugs in salt water. The less soap you use, the less rinse water you will need. Joy liquid lathers well in cold salt water, and a quick squeeze is plenty. With concentrated soaps, you often use too much for the job at hand. To get the space savings without losing the ability to control the quantity, stow the soap in its concentrated form and dilute it in an old liquid soap bottle for daily use. Dilute nonconcentrated dishwashing soaps if you find you are using too much fresh water for rinsing.

We stacked washed dishes in our second sink: plates and bowls at the bottom, silverware on them, and cups and mugs standing upright on the top. We took one cup, filled it with fresh water, and dribbled the water over everything else. We dried that cup, put it away, and picked up the next cup. This would be half-full with fresh water. We'd add a tiny bit if necessary, swish it around, and dribble the water over the remaining dishes. By the time we got to the silverware and the plates, they had been pretty thoroughly rinsed. Depending upon how many dishes were involved, we used between a half-quart and a quart of water this way.

For really dirty dishes, we rinsed them with salt water to remove the major grime. There would often be a greasy residue left that wouldn't come off with salt water. We boiled fresh water in the teakettle and put two to three inches in the bottom of one of the sinks along with a small amount of soap. A quick scrub with a brush or nylon scrubber removed the grease, and we then stacked them in the second sink and rinsed as before.

The worst cleanup job was after baking bread, especially the bowl and the cutting board (or countertop) covered with sticky bread dough. Don't use scrubbers or brushes. The dough will adhere to your cleaning implement, and the only way to get it off is with copious amounts of soap and hot, fresh water. If not cleaned thoroughly, your scrub brush will start to smell within a few hours.

Instead of ruining your scrub brush, when you start your bread dough also start heating some water in the teakettle. The water will boil right about when you turn the dough out on the cutting board to knead it. Put the empty bowl in the sink and pour one or two inches of boiling water into the bottom, then add a couple of drops of soap. By the time your dough is ready to return to the bowl, the water will have dissolved most of the stickiest residue. Now use your hand (which is already covered with bread dough anyway) as a scrubber to get the rest of the dough off the bowl. By the time the bowl is clean, your hands will be as well, and you will have saved not only your scrubber but about a half-gallon of fresh water. Clean the cutting board with a light rinse of the boiling water, a drop of soap, and some more elbow grease. This technique works on most tough cleanup jobs in the galley.

Another good technique for cleanup is to use salt without water on hands, bowls, pans, and so on. Just don't wet anything!

By using salt water and making judicious use of cooking water, your water consumption for dish washing should be around a quart a day for two people. If you choose not to use salt water, the approach outlined above can consume about a gallon a day. It is difficult to do much better without resorting to paper or plastic, which makes little sense on an offshore boat.

Showers

We did not use salt water for showering, though I would often wash my hair while swimming and rinse it off with fresh water. If we did not regularly rinse off with fresh water, we were prone to saltwater rashes, often in very uncomfortable places. Others we knew suffered from saltwater boils that festered and took a long time to heal. Good hygiene is the best way to avoid these maladies, and that means washing in fresh water.

At sea, we allowed ourselves one 2-quart teakettle of water every other day for showering. While this sounds woefully inadequate, we found it was plenty to get us clean and even to wash my shoulder-length hair.

Our shower water was stowed on deck in dark jerry jugs, so it was generally warm. I showered standing up so the water would cover as much area as possible before ending up in the scuppers. I started by emptying about a third of the teakettle on my head, making sure to thoroughly soak my hair. Then I would lather my hair up with shampoo and use a small amount of soap on my underarms. To limit rinse water, don't use much soap or shampoo. Even with my long hair, a tablespoon of shampoo was about right.

When water is limited, you need to get rid of dead skin, which normally washes away in the shower. Rubbing our damp skin hard with our hands got the dead skin to peel off. About once a week, I used a small amount of a defoliant facial soap on areas that always seemed to be the worst—between my toes, around my ankles, on the sides of my knees, and on my upper arms.

Then I used another third of the teakettle to rinse off. This got rid of most of the shampoo and the dead skin. If my hair did not feel squeaky clean, I used a bit more. Then I dried myself lightly with a towel. Generally this is the time you discover the skin you didn't get in your scrubbing. I used the last third of the teakettle to dampen any problem areas and rinse off the dead skin after a thorough scrub, and to rinse between my legs.

Women have to pay particular attention to keeping their private parts clean. Bladder and yeast infections are very common at sea due to the heat, humidity, and lack of hygiene. Also common are rashes that cause external itching and burning around the genitals and make life miserable. After a few months of discomfort, I learned that a thorough rinsing (soap only seemed to aggravate matters, perhaps because it was difficult to rinse it all away) every other day pretty much eliminated any problems.

My hair likes conditioner. If we were doing well on water, I would use a half-quart for that. Otherwise, we carried a spray-on, comb-in conditioner, which kept my hair healthy and manageable.

While this regimen sounds Spartan, it did get us

clean. But if a black cloud came along we were both out in the cockpit, soap in hand. No high pressure shower head can begin to compare with the invigorating thrill of a real squall at sea. The pelting rain stings your skin and causes it to tingle the way rubbing alcohol does. The pressure feels like the needlepoint fingers of a masseuse. Those are moments when life itself fills you to overflowing!

Common alternatives to the teakettle are solar showers and garden sprayers, both of which feel more like a shower. If you absolutely have to have more water, one alternative is to use buckets of salt water to clean yourself and wash your hair, followed by a teakettle of fresh water for an all-over rinse. While this got me clean, my skin did not appreciate the salt water every other day.

Evans shaved about once a week at sea. He found that his skin was very sensitive after not being shaved for days. Any sunburn could make the whole experience quite painful. He had always preferred bar soap to shaving cream, but on the boat he started using a liquid face soap that was easier on his skin. The plastic container did not rust the way shaving cream cans do, and it was readily available in most major ports. A foot pump in the head facilitated shaving by leaving Evans' hands free to manage himself and the razor in the rolling boat.

Making landfall was the only time we used pressure water on passage. If we still had lots of water in our tanks (which we always did), and we were motoring in (which it seemed like we always were), we treated ourselves to hot, pressure-water showers. Even then, we were not profligate with the water. We turned the shower head on over a bucket and caught any cold water before the hot came through the hoses. We wet ourselves down, turned off the water, lathered up, turned on the water, and rinsed off. No matter how careful we were, we still went through a couple gallons of water, which was why we stuck to the teakettle at sea.

Cleaning

The water used to keep the boat clean can be substantial. Much of it needs to be fresh water. While you can scrub the decks with salt water, you have to use fresh water for interior cleaning. Otherwise, you risk mold and mildew blooms. To minimize water usage

Table 12-2. Some universal cleaning solutions

Cleaner	Uses	Comments
Joy dish liquid	Clean the decks, clean vinyl cushions	Use with salt water and a good scrub brush
Soft Scrub	Clean and whiten lifelines, hull, interior surfaces	Use nylon scrubber and wipe down with damp cloth to remove residue
	Remove grime from fenders, rust from stanchions, rust stains from hull	
	Remove stains from toilet bowl	
Non-phosphorous laundry detergent	Remove mildew stains from fiberglass	Let sit 30 minutes, then rub off
	Minimize odors; break down oil and grease in bilge	Put a capful in the bilge every few weeks
Clorox	Disinfect and deodorize refrigerator, control mold and mildew	Once a month or so, clean out completely with mild bleach solution, let dry thoroughly before closing up again
	Clean white surfaces and prevent mildew; prevent mold in Dorades	One-quarter cup in a gallon of water wiped over surfaces
Spray-on, vacuum-off rug cleaner	Clean settee and bunk cushion covers	Use about every three months
Glass cleaner	Remove carpet or cushion mildew	Removes mildew without leaving residues that attract dirt
Vinegar	Remove dust from oxidation on fiberglass	3 tablespoons to 1 gallon of water
	Control mineral deposits and remove waterline marks in toilets	Pump 2 to 3 cups through toilet every few weeks; soak bowl overnight to remove stains
Lemon juice	Remove stains from fabrics, gelcoat	Apply and let sit in sun for several hours before scrubbing
Baking soda	Clean white dust off holding plate to increase refrigeration efficiency	Wipe down with solution of baking soda
	Reduce odors from drains	Flush solution down drain
	Eliminate odors in cushions and cushion covers	Sprinkle on, allow to sit for an hour, vacuum off
Vegetable oil	Lubricate seals and pump mechanism	Pump a quarter cup through head weekly, also useful on saltwater pumps

while keeping the boat clean, you need the right cleaner for the job.

Yes, you can buy an incredible number of specialized cleaning products, and yes, some of them work very well. But you won't be able to find them once you leave the United States, and it is not worth storing a five-year supply. The cleaning power in most of those specialized products comes from strong acids and bases, and they require large amounts of water to rinse off. What you really want are a few simple and fairly universal cleaning solutions that are environmentally friendly, require little water to rinse away, can be found just about everywhere, and will do the job well though perhaps not to the 120 percent level that some of the "made for" products do. In addition, you want one or two potent cleaners you can use for a wide range of uses.

Table 12-2 summarizes cleaning supplies with low freshwater requirements and the jobs they can be used for. Most of these cleaning solutions rely on basic household items like baking soda and vinegar. You will also want a few tools to assist you, including sponges, rags, a scrub brush with a handle, a children's broom (much easier to stow than a full-size broom), and a 12-volt car vacuum. A few pieces of indoor/outdoor carpet make good welcome mats in marinas or on the hard.

The fiberglass cleaning product FSR is diluted oxalic acid suspended in a paste. It removes rust from stainless steel and fiberglass, can clean almost any stain off fiberglass, and removes black marks from pots and oven racks. It does require quantities of fresh water to rinse it off after use, and you do need to rewax your hull after applying it. Oven cleaner is another water-intensive solution for stubborn deck stains and for galley cleanup challenges. Allow it to sit, then rinse thoroughly with fresh water.

CHAPTER 13

STAYING HEALTHY: BEING YOUR OWN DOCTOR

Preparation—before you leave ■ *Know thyself* ■ *Know the basics* ■ *Know thy medical kit*
■ *Prevention—managing day-to-day health* ■ *Seasickness* ■ *Additional resources* ■ *Infections* ■ *Allergic reactions*
■ *Emergencies and traumatic injuries* ■ *Protection—ensuring long-term health* ■ *Sun protection and skin care*
■ *Exercise* ■ *Managing major health concerns*

If you are going to face the isolation of being at sea, you need to make your own medical skill a primary concern. Every offshore cruiser must be prepared to handle medical emergencies without outside assistance. Our medical log reveals that we suffered only minor ailments. But even minor infections and allergic reactions can become medical emergencies if they are not treated quickly and effectively. We found voyaging to be a healthy way of life, but voyagers must deal with some long-term health issues specific to cruising. Our medical experiences offer insights into the necessary equipment and training you will need to be self reliant for long periods of time.

Successful medical care aboard comes down to three things: preparation, prevention, and protection. Before you leave, you need to equip your boat and prepare yourself for medical issues that may arise. Once you are voyaging, you need to take steps to prevent day-to-day health problems. Finally, you need to protect yourself from the long-term effects of sun exposure, limited exercise, and occasional poor nutrition.

PREPARATION—BEFORE YOU LEAVE

Evans and I believe that you can learn most offshore voyaging skills as you go. If you don't know anything about diesel mechanics, provisioning, rain catching, or even sailing your boat, you will learn if you want to continue voyaging. The one exception is medical skill and preparation. If you are skilled but poorly equipped or if you take a sophisticated medical kit but lack basic first aid skills, you won't figure it out once you're out there—and your health or the health of your crew may be seriously jeopardized.

How do you go about learning medicine in months instead of years? Obviously you can't learn everything. You have to use the medical history of the crew to focus your efforts. With the help of a doctor, you will put together a complete medical kit that reflects those health requirements. You must master some basic skills and be certain that every crewmember is prepared to deal with a medical emergency.

Know thyself

When we left on our voyage, we had tremendous faith in the medical system and little knowledge of our own bodies. We now know that medicine is a developing science, and for some ailments, there are no easy answers. We learned that our bodies were like the boat: No one knew them as well as we did. We became less reliant on getting ourselves "fixed" and more aware of how to avoid getting "broken" in the first place. Our faith in medicine declined, but our faith in our abilities to help our bodies heal increased.

Evaluate your health

Before you become serious about leaving civilization behind, consider your medical history and its implications for life aboard. If you are young and healthy, this takes about five minutes. But if you are older, or if you have even minor health problems, consult your doctor early in the planning process. Talk to others who have been voyaging and share your health profile. Doctors who sail offshore can also offer a perspective. Don't assume you will be healthier voyaging. Most ailments improve, but a few are aggravated.

We did not go through this process, and it came back to haunt us throughout the trip. When we left, Evans was 33, in excellent physical condition, and had no history of even minor ailments. If we had gone through this process, we would have rightly concluded that his health was not an issue.

I had a long history of complaints, none of which seemed relevant. I suffered from severe ear infections, which had become chronic because of the flying I was doing for my job. I had been allergic to mold as a child, but after weekly allergy shots for several years I seemed to outgrow this sensitivity. I had dislocated my kneecap twice and had a history of joint problems. Evans and I discussed how sailing would improve all of these conditions: I wouldn't be flying, we'd be living in the open air, and I would be exercising a great deal. The reality was that my ears were aggravated by swimming in bacteria-rich coral waters, my allergies flared until we learned to control mold and mildew aboard, and my knees suffered from the lack of exercise on passages.

Your health needs will impact every aspect of planning your trip. You likely haven't thought much about health issues if you've only had a few minor ailments. But if you prepare now, you can make sure the minor problems don't jeopardize your trip. The following ailments may be aggravated by life aboard.

■ **Sun sensitivity.** If you have any history of abnormal sensitivity to the sun, whether mild rashes or major lesions, you will need to protect yourself at all times.

■ **Allergies.** As I found out, allergies to mold and mildew can be a major problem. On tropical islands with plenty of rainfall, the wealth of vegetation can make hay fever sufferers miserable. Insects abound, and a sensitivity to bites or stings requires proper preparation. Consider any drug allergies when putting together the medical kit.

■ **Arthritis or joint pain.** If you suffer from arthritis or joint pain, the inactivity of passagemaking followed by vigorous exercise in port will aggravate the situation.

■ **Ear infections.** If you have a history of chronic ear infections, even as a youth, assume that you could have a recurrence when you start swimming and snorkeling in coral water. If you have children aboard, prepare for ear infections.

■ **Inner ear problems.** If you have ever had inner ear problems, the motion at sea can cause severe and debilitating dizziness. This can be treated only with drugs that reduce motion sensation in the inner ear.

■ **Hemorrhoids.** Sitting at sea for days will aggravate any tendency toward hemorrhoids.

■ **Yeast and bladder infections.** The moist, humid environment and sometimes less-than-hygienic conditions make vaginal yeast infections and bladder infections common among women.

A healthy diet, outdoor living, and exercise make most voyagers feel healthier. Most believe that they have reduced their long-term health risks for heart disease, high blood pressure, and even cancer. Against these benefits, the list above represents small risks. By paying attention to these minor ailments, you can ensure that your new lifestyle will be as disease-free and healthy as possible.

Get a major physical and inoculations

In those last hectic months before you head off to sea, get a full physical and dental examination. Talk to your doctor and dentist about your plans. Ask them to assume that you will not have access to high quality care for six months. Based on your history and your current physical condition, have them put together a list of specific medications you should bring along. If you have any complications in your medical history, get them to be as specific as possible about early symptoms and possible treatments. Have your dentist fill even the smallest cavities. Take care of any major dental work you've been putting off. By the time you leave, you should feel fit and be sure that no medical surprises await.

Some physicians are uncomfortable with equipping you to doctor yourself. If necessary, spend money outside of your health-care plan. Find someone who understands your situation and is committed enough to invest time and energy in your dream. Many doctors do sail, and they will be sympathetic to your needs. If you are a member of a yacht club, you probably know several sailing doctors. Otherwise, taking an offshore medical training course (see "Additional resources" in this chapter) will put you in touch with a sympathetic physician who can help you find a sailing doctor in your area.

Plan on spending two or three sessions lasting an hour or more with your doctor covering the basics in the next section. If you have children or a complex medical problem, the time invested will double. To be sure that you are properly prepared, start early. Unless you are under 35 and completely healthy, your first visit to your family doctor should be at least six months before your planned departure date.

Right before you go, get a complete copy of the medical records for every person aboard along with a written summary of their medical history. Enter them into the ship's medical log. Include baseline data from blood work, an EKG, a mammogram (for female crewmembers), dental X-rays, and records of medical conditions and medications. The baseline data provides valuable information for diagnosing ailments, and the other records will allow a doctor to offer immediate assistance.

You need to get inoculations against the major diseases you might encounter. The Centers for Disease Control (CDC) publishes *Health Information for International Travel* (see "Additional resources" in this chapter), which specifies health risks throughout the world. The International Association for Medical Assistance to Travellers (IAMAT) produces a World Immunization Chart (see "Additional resources") that recommends inoculations by country. These will help you decide what immunizations to get and understand how long they will protect you.

Of the dozens of immunizations available, very few are appropriate for everyone. IAMAT recommends the tetanus-diphtheria booster for all travelers over age seven and the poliomyelitis booster for all travelers regardless of age. Measles, mumps, rubella, influenza, and pneumococcal vaccinations are recommended for different groups depending on age, sex, and immunization history. Yellow fever is endemic in parts of Africa and much of South America. Most doctors agree the vaccine is necessary for travel to those areas. The vaccine for yellow fever cannot be administered to children under one year of age, so don't plan on visiting an infected area with an infant. The litany of other possible vaccinations includes typhoid, cholera, hepatitis, meningococcal meningitis, plague, and encephalitis. Each of these vaccines has risks and benefits, and a few are effective only for periods of six months to a year.

After reviewing the CDC and IAMAT material, you should discuss the vaccinations you are considering with your doctor. Ask how long they last, special health issues you should consider, and the pros and cons of inoculation for older or younger crewmembers.

To get immunized, contact your county health department. They will administer the vaccines and provide you with the World Health Organization's International Certificate of Vaccination (see Figure 20-4). This yellow booklet documents the vaccinations you have received and proves you meet the entry requirements for a specific country.

Vaccinations must be spread out over several weeks to minimize the chances of a severe reaction. After an immunization you will probably feel lethargic for 12 to 24 hours and you may experience a low-grade fever.

Know the basics

Understanding your specific needs is not enough. You also need basic knowledge of medical treatments and emergency procedures. Unfortunately, basic first aid courses and references appropriate ashore are not designed to meet the needs of a ship's crew at sea. Most first aid courses and books aim to stabilize, not treat, the patient. Instructions for handling injuries or illnesses usually end with, "Call 911 or contact your physician." Many books and courses designed for use at sea focus on emergency situations. These are long on treatment procedures and short on diagnosis. Given a series of nebulous symptoms, you won't know where to begin. To be prepared for the variety of roles the ship's surgeon must fill, take a variety of courses and carry a number of information resources.

Every crewmember should take a basic first aid course and a cardiopulmonary resuscitation (CPR) course during the year before heading offshore. While the basic first aid course ends where the real treatment begins, everyone on board needs to know how to stop bleeding, prevent shock, and stabilize a patient. CPR teaches you how to resuscitate someone in the event of a near-drowning—a skill anyone who lives on the water should possess.

At least one member of the crew should take an advanced medical training course designed specifically for sailors. There are several excellent courses available (some are cited in "Additional resources" in this chap-

Children and older voyagers—special considerations

Children and older voyagers have special medical needs that you should take into account as you prepare your medical kit.

The children we met seemed healthier than their shoreside counterparts. They spent most of their time outdoors. The sterile sea environment means less exposure to germs, at least on passage. Kids were in frequent contact with local children ashore, so they did contract some ailments. Dr. Pat LaFrate, a pediatrician and sailor we consulted with before leaving, points out that most children's infections are viral, self-limited fevers that run their course without causing great harm.

You will want to bring a quantity of antibiotics and cold remedies in children's dosages. If your children are not yet swallowing pills, make sure you have an emergency water supply in your medical kit to mix up antibiotic dosages from powders. If your children suffer from ear infections ashore, prepare to deal with them in the tropics. Whenever they come out of the water, flush out their ears with an over-the-counter product designed to prevent swimmer's ear or a solution of 50 percent vinegar and 50 percent rubbing alcohol.

Beyond individual ailments, arthritis and joint pain seemed to be the major medical complaint for older voyagers. Their boats need to be set up to minimize strains. Before leaving, equip the boat with oversized winches, electric windlasses, outboard motors, sail-handling systems, and an easy and effective block and tackle arrangement for getting things on and off the boat. Once out there, always use these systems. Strategically placed handholds and a good swim ladder or dinghy step can reduce the strain on hips and knees as you travel up and down the companionway and on and off the boat. The medical kit should include a variety of over-the-counter pain relievers including aspirin and ibuprofen. Several dozen chemical ice packs will relieve joint swelling after a strain or injury. Hot-water bottles for cold night watches will keep a problematic joint limber.

For those on medications, you need to understand drug interactions. Ask your doctor about possible interactions with each drug you plan to carry. Find out what symptoms will result from each interaction. If certain crewmembers can't use certain drugs, mark the jar itself. Keep a separate list of all drugs each person takes in an accessible place in case you have to pass the information over the radio in an emergency.

ter). You can find others in the classified ads of national sailing magazines. Make sure the course is designed for offshore sailing where you could be out of SSB or Ham radio contact for weeks. Ask if the course covers suturing, splinting, dehydration, shock, severe infections, and allergic reactions. Find out what offshore experience the instructor has and make sure that he or she is a qualified doctor.

If you have a friend who is doctor and a serious sailor, you may be able to arrange a private course tailored to your needs. A cardiologist friend of ours ran a clinic for a half-dozen offshore sailors that included suturing a chicken leg and injecting an orange. If your first offshore experience is going to be a cruiser's rally, check with the organizers to see if they have scheduled a seminar with a doctor to cover these topics.

These courses deal primarily with major trauma and life-threatening illnesses. You also need to know how to handle more mundane situations. If you have a rash or need antibiotics at home, you make a quick phone call or schedule a short office visit with your family physician. At sea and in many remote ports, you have to manage these situations yourself. No course covers all this ground. To prepare for this role, you need to sit down with your sympathetic doctor and talk through the range of symptoms and possible treatments for common ailments.

We did this with Dr. LaFrate. We spent several hours reviewing notes he had made. Then Evans and I put together a reference notebook from our discussion. We went over this notebook with Dr. LaFrate, and he corrected and amplified where necessary. We ended up with 20 pages of notes on ailments, symptoms, treatments, and the uses and dosages of the drugs in our medical kit. Unlike any reference we could have purchased, our notes reflected our medical history and were organized in a way that we understood.

When putting together this reference, focus on your special needs. If you have children, concentrate on the ailments they might experience. If you are older, explore drug interactions and side effects. The result should be a useful information source that is organized the way you think. Our 20 pages went into our medical log and were the most helpful resource we had aboard. We referred to them constantly.

Take along a variety of other medical references. An unexplained ailment can be terrifying, and a lack of information to resolve the problem can be traumatic. We purchased the usual medical references recommended for the ship's library including *The Ship's Medicine Chest and Medical Aid at Sea* (Gordon Press, 1994), the standard text used by the U.S. Merchant Marine. While these books offered excellent advice on treating illnesses and injuries, they did not help in diagnosing some of the more exotic symptoms associated with infections or allergic reactions.

Wilderness survival guides are often recommended for voyagers. While useful, they can be too basic. Many assume you do not have access to antibiotics or prescription drugs. Therefore, in addition to the standard litany of shipboard medical texts and do-it-yourself wilderness medicine guides, carry one of each of the following.

■ *General reference book on symptoms.* These affordable consumer books are meant to educate patients on their treatments and diagnose ailments from general symptoms. Texts such as the *AMA Guide to Your Family's Symptoms* (Random House, 1992) or *Complete Guide to Symptoms, Illnesses, and Surgery* by H. Winter Griffith, MD (The Body Press, 1995), provide flow charts and diagrams organized by symptom to aid in diagnosis. The flow chart will identify the most likely ailment, but it generally ends with, "See your family physician." Given some idea of the ailment, you can turn to other references for treatments.

■ *An excellent first aid reference with diagrams.* Some of the shipboard first aid books are simply too specialized and describe only typical shipboard injuries. For cruisers traveling in remote areas far from medical help, even when they are ashore, a general first aid reference with step-by-step instructions and diagrams is useful. *First Aid Handbook* by the National Safety Council (Jones and Bartlett Publishers, 1995) is one example of an easy-to-use, well-organized text. Another is the St. John's Ambulance *First Aid Manual* (published by Dorling Kindersley Ltd), which has a superb reputation. These books aim to stabilize the patient and await the paramedics, but your offshore medical course should take over where these books end.

■ **Health Information for International Travel.** This booklet published by the Centers for Disease Control (HHS Publication #CDC 95-8280) highlights health risks of various regions, necessary vaccinations and precautions, and recommended treatments for malaria where it is endemic. You can order it through the Superintendent of Documents at the U.S. Government Printing Office (phone 202-512-1800). Up-to-date information by country is available on the CDC's International Travelers' Hotline (phone 404-332-4559). *A Traveller's Guide to Health,* published by Sphere in the U.K. in association with the National Geographic Association, is regularly updated and makes excellent reading.

If you have children aboard or you have a medical condition that could prove life threatening, an SSB or a Ham radio will help you contact medical aid while at sea. Assuming that you have a well-equipped medical kit and some basic knowledge, a doctor on the other end of the radio can talk you through even extreme emergencies. But, while the radio can offer life-saving advice, it does not reduce your responsibility to be self-sufficient. In a serious emergency, the ship's batteries may be down, the antenna gone, or the radio not working (for more on assistance services via radio, see "Additional resources" in this chapter).

Know thy medical kit

An offshore medical kit must include prescriptions for a variety of drugs from antibiotics to analgesics. Without a sympathetic doctor, you will find this the most difficult part of preparation. Beyond knowing what to include, you also need to know how to make use of it. From your previous discussions and the reference you created, you should know the correct uses and dosages for everything in the kit. But you also need to be able to find what you need in an emergency. Organizing the medical kit well means you can find needed supplies in less than a minute.

Appendix 2 shows the contents and quantities of our medical kit when we left. We never used most of what is listed, but we were still grateful to have it aboard. We took too much of the more common medical supplies such as cotton swabs and gauze, which can be re-stocked annually in any developed country. We did not take enough variety of antibiotics and antihistamines, our most frequently used prescription drugs. Unfortunately, the shelf life of most prescription drugs is relatively short (a year or so), so we should have started with smaller quantities and restocked each year when I went home for Christmas.

Our medical kit reflects the needs of two healthy 30-year-olds with fairly high medical competence. While it can serve as a starting point, you'll need to modify your kit with your physician's advice to reflect your situation and training. Some medicines can *only* be carried on board; contact the Port Medical Officer for advice and permission to carry drugs prior to leaving.

A few months before you leave, start buying medical supplies and organizing your medical kit. It took several tries to find a solution for stowing things so we could get to them quickly. We kept day-to-day supplies such as Band-Aids, nonprescription pain relievers, cold medicines, skin creams, antibiotic ointments, and antibacterial soaps in a storage area in the head. In our medical kit we organized supplies for more serious conditions by ailment—lacerations, gastrointestinal problems, severe burns, eye problems, and orthopedic problems. We stored prescription drugs in a bag in a separate locked briefcase to prevent an intruder from finding them.

The Medical Sea Paks available from marine suppliers offer a well-organized, simple alternative, but they are expensive. These come in a large canvas bag with smaller bags inside labeled and organized by ailment. They include a booklet that is color-coded to match the labels and coloration of the smaller bags. If someone cuts himself in the galley, you grab the book and bag marked "Major lacerations" and you are in business. These cost significantly more than if you put the kit to-gether yourself. But if you can't organize your own sup-plies, the money saved is meaningless. These kits do not include any prescription medications, so you will still need to arrange those through your own doctor.

Make sure that everyone aboard is familiar with the location of all medicines and supplies. Keep a master list of all supplies and their locations in the medical log.

As you put your kit together, pay particular attention to medications and prescriptions. Many drugs have a short shelf life, so check expiration dates and buy the freshest available. Tell your pharmacist that the drugs are not for immediate use but for long-term storage, and allow some extra time in filling the prescriptions to obtain fresher drugs. Drug names change from country to country. Ask your doctor or pharmacist to give you the generic name and the common brand names for all drugs you are taking aboard.

Keep a copy of each prescription with your doctor's signature in your medical log. You may be required to show these to customs when clearing in. We were al-most always asked if we had drugs aboard. The answer "Only in our medical kit" was usually sufficient. On a few occasions we had to describe what drugs we had, and once we had to show the prescriptions. The cus-toms officials often wanted to know if the drugs were stored in a locked area. They didn't want the drugs to be stolen and sold on the streets.

On each prescription, highlight the expiration date of the drugs. This helps you manage your drug inven-tory and replace prescriptions as needed. Track the use of prescription drugs in the medical log. Note the crew-member's name, dosage, number of days that the drug was used, and any side effects or reactions. This will help you track which drugs work for each crewmember and note any sensitivities that develop. The record could assist a doctor in determining how to treat a more complex problem. Particularly if you carry nonfamily members as crew, your records could protect you from liability in your role as ship's surgeon.

By now you should feel well prepared to manage just about any emergency aboard. You cannot eliminate the risk, but you can manage it. You cannot foresee every-thing—strange accidents happen just as they do ashore. But once you have prepared yourself, a medical emer-gency that you cannot handle becomes a calculated risk—like hitting a container or slipping in the bathtub. In all likelihood, you'll never use even a fraction of what you have learned—and you'll be glad for that.

PREVENTION—
MANAGING DAY-TO-DAY HEALTH

While we always worried about a major medical mishap, most of what we dealt with was more mundane and, in retrospect, fairly predictable. We both suffered from seasickness to varying degrees. Exposure to strange insects and foods caused allergic reactions, and the humid environment fostered frequent infections. We had our share of minor traumas, with galley-related injuries being the most common.

Seasickness

The sailor's most common malady is *mal de mer.* Seasickness is caused by conflict between visual perception and inner ear balance perception, and it results in a range of symptoms—from lethargy and queasiness to headache and vomiting. Like most of our friends, we experienced listlessness, drowsiness, mild queasiness, yawning, and increased salivation the first few days of every passage. During that period we were susceptible to more extreme seasickness. Once acclimated, we felt fine for the rest of the passage unless we encountered severe weather.

When seasickness progresses to vomiting, dry heaves, dizziness, and eventually total apathy, it ceases to be a minor annoyance and becomes a serious health risk. The classic quip "No one ever dies of seasickness: They only wish they would" is not true at the extreme. In our first gale at sea, we were both so seasick we could not even keep water down for over 60 hours. At the end of the gale, we were so weak from dehydration and hunger that I could not coil a line without stopping to rest. If the gale had continued for another 24 hours, we could have been too weak and apathetic to respond to an emergency.

Prevention

To prevent seasickness, avoid crossing the line from mild discomfort to full-blown symptoms. Once vomiting has started, your options are more limited for restoring normalcy. We took several precautions to limit our chances of getting sick the first few days at sea.

We avoided seasickness medications because we learned that they only delayed the symptoms. Most of our cruising friends agreed that unless you spent the entire passage drugged, you still had to acclimate when you stopped the medication. Rather than take pills, we tried to adjust as quickly as possible. Sometimes we managed to adjust before the passage even started. If we had been in a marina for more than a week, we would leave a few days before the passage and anchor in the rolliest anchorage we could find. We would actually get seasick at anchor, but we eliminated all symptoms at sea on a few passages.

We did everything possible to limit time spent below the first few days at sea. Before leaving port, we made up all sea berths, put extra clothes at the foot of each bunk, premade meals and left them in a handy spot in the galley, and put a bucket on deck to substitute for the head. Once at sea, we stayed on deck as much as possible. We avoided extremes in temperature, strong odors, and poor ventilation. If we could make it through the first night when the sun went down and we lost the horizon, we were usually fine for the rest of the trip. Leaving on a full moon almost always meant a faster adjustment to sea conditions.

Close eye work increases the likelihood of getting ill. No matter how good we felt, we didn't read for the first two or three days of a passage. We limited time spent navigating or writing to 10 or 15 minutes. If we started to feel early symptoms, an hour at the helm or an hour's nap would often take care of the problem.

We found that it was important to keep our stomachs busy, for we would sometimes mistake hunger for the first feelings of queasiness. Everyone has their favorite foods for staving off seasickness. We liked bread, saltines, pickles, hard candy, and dried fruit. Ginger has been medically proven to help prevent mild seasickness, and we both found it effective. I would often make ginger snaps right before we left, and we would keep ginger ale aboard for those first few sensitive days.

Treatment

There are a wide variety of seasickness medications, but it is impossible to generalize about their efficacy. Seasickness is an individual ailment. Specific symptoms and their severity differ from person to person, along with the usefulness and side effects of medications. Anyone who suffers from severe seasickness will have to experiment to find a cure that works. Try po-

Additional resources

The following organizations offer specific medical services to travelers and sailors.

■ **Centers for Disease Control (CDC).** Located in Atlanta, Georgia, the CDC offers a range of services for Americans traveling abroad. Beyond the *Health Information for International Travel* publication described in the main text, they also sponsor a malaria hotline (phone 404-488-4046) and a disease hotline (phone 404-332-4555).

■ **International Association of Medical Assistance to Travellers (IAMAT).** This organization of English-speaking doctors of all nationalities provides services to travelers. Anyone can join IAMAT, and there is no charge for membership, although a small donation is requested. Membership entitles you to a worldwide directory of English-speaking physicians, a world immunization chart, and a world malaria risk chart and protection guide. For a $25 donation, you will also receive world climate charts that include information on the sanitary conditions of water, milk, and food by country. (IAMAT, 417 Center Street, Lewiston, NY 14092; phone 716-754-4883.)

■ **Ocean Voyages.** This worldwide charter company offers hands-on medical training programs aboard sailboats on the U.S. West Coast. The course takes place while cruising and covers preparation of your medical kit, suturing, splinting, and the treatment and prevention of seasickness, among other topics (phone 415-332-4681).

■ **Medical Advisory Services.** This subscription service provides physician consultation 24 hours a day. They also offer marine medical training courses and will help you put your medical kit together. (Medical Advisory Services, Box 193, Pennsylvania Avenue Extension, Owings, MD 20736; phone 410-257-9505.)

■ **Maritime Health Services.** This subscription service also offers a two- to three-day medical training course called SALTS (Save a Life at Sea). They will not refuse a call from anyone. (Maritime Health Services, 4050 Columbia Seafirst Center, 701 5th Avenue, Seattle, WA 98104; phone 206-781-8770.)

■ **Foreign consulates and embassies.** No one knows more about the health conditions in a given country than that country's consulate or embassy. If you talk to the consulates of Vanuatu and the Solomon Islands before leaving Fiji, you will be better prepared to manage the malaria risk in those countries. Some countries are not forthcoming about health conditions because they are afraid of damaging tourism. Check their data against the information available from the CDC, IAMAT, and the voyaging grapevine.

---

tential cures on land first to check for side effects.

Evans and I illustrate how different symptoms and reactions to medications can be. Evans succumbs in heavy weather with the wind on the beam or forward. He will feel fine for several hours, suddenly feel sick, vomit within an hour or so, and then be fine again for several hours. Medications make him feel drugged, so he won't take any. I get sick when the wind is over the stern and light and we have a long, slow ocean swell on the quarter. I feel queasy and headachy. I get more lethargic and miserable with each hour. I rarely vomit, although I often wish I would. Dramamine and other mild medications don't help, but a stronger medicine eliminates all symptoms for as long as I take it.

Before turning to drugs to treat seasickness, experiment with some of the less traditional cures. A sailing friend of ours who suffered from seasickness on passages tried TENS (transcutaneous electrical nerve stimulator) devices. The bands are worn on the inside of the forearm, and the device uses electrical stimulation that cannot be felt. She recently crossed the Atlantic with no symptoms. Others we knew found acupressure wrist bands to be effective. It is worthwhile finding out if these cures work for you. The obvious advantage is the lack of side effects.

For mild seasickness, most people used Bonine (meclizine) or Dramamine. Stugeron is well regarded throughout the cruising community but has never been available in the United States. Enthusiasts report total elimination of symptoms with no side effects. Many cruisers stock up when they are in Europe, Australia, or Bermuda. All of these medications must be taken before the onset of symptoms.

After being taken off the market due to reports of hallucinations and irrational behavior, an updated scopolamine patch is available again with a doctor's prescription. A gel form is also available. If you use the gel, wash your hands thoroughly after applying it.

The few times when I was seriously ill, I used a combination of one 50-mg tablet of ephedrine (promethazine) and one 25-mg tablet of Phenergan. I could take this even after the onset of vomiting. As long as I could keep it down for an hour, all symptoms would disappear. This combination is called the "Navy cocktail," because the Navy (and astronauts) use these drugs to prevent seasickness. The effects lasted for 12 hours without making me feel drugged.

Once seasickness moves into the phase of repeated vomiting, suppositories are the only way to get medication into the person. Phenergan or Dramamine both work well. If someone reaches this stage, your treatment has to focus on preventing dehydration. Enemas of electrolyte solutions (or even chicken bouillon) will provide needed nutrients and water if no other treatment is effective.

Infections

Along with *mal de mer,* we frequently experienced various types of infections; we controlled them with proper treatment. While not all infections are bacterial, most of the ones we encountered in the tropics were. Microbes flourish in the warm, moist climate of the tropics. Coral waters harbor a wealth of bacteria, some quite toxic. Infections in the tropics are much more virulent than in colder climates. Severe infections can develop from minor scrapes, posing a serious health risk to a crewmember. Higher dosages of antibiotics are required to treat infections effectively.

Table 13-1 summarizes the major medical situations we faced involving infections.

Two schools of thought exist on the use of salt water on wounds. Many sailors advocate immediately immersing any wounds in salt water to disinfect them,

while others claim that this increases the likelihood of infection. While the immersion might remove the strep and staph bacteria always present on the skin, many sinister types of bacteria often exist in tropical waters. In some areas, the water may be free of these bacteria and may facilitate healing. But after seeing a number of infections caused or exacerbated by coral waters, we found it safer to assume that salt water promoted infections.

To avoid problems, treat every cut as if it is already infected and assume coral water is hostile. The following precautions and practices became routine aboard *Silk:*

- **Treat cuts and scrapes.** Clean open cuts or scrapes thoroughly when they occur and after swimming with a good disinfectant such as Betadine. Apply an antibiotic ointment or powder several times per day to open cuts. Try to avoid covering scrapes to encourage them to dry out. If going ashore where there are flies, cover open cuts with fabric Band-Aids (plastic bandages fall off when repeatedly exposed to salt water).

- **Fight waterborne bacteria.** Avoid swimming in major ports, even if the water seems clean. Dose your ears with an over-the-counter product designed to prevent swimmer's ear or a solution of half vinegar and half rubbing alcohol after snorkeling or diving to prevent ear infections. Don't use ear plugs, which trap bacteria in the ear. Lamb's wool works much better. Cuts from coral, fish hooks, or other fishing equipment and stings from venomous marine life are highly susceptible to infection. If the cut is deep or redness and swelling develop, a course of antibiotics should be administered as early as possible.

- **Disinfect skin irritations.** Acne, pustules, shaving nicks, and other skin irritations can foster staph infections. Scrub them with bacterial soap whenever showering. Minor eruptions on Evans' neck and back lead to his staph infection in the Marquesas. After that we scrubbed his back whenever he came out of the water. This prevented infection and reduced the skin irritations so common at sea.

- **Use effective dosage and type of antibiotic.** No one antibiotic works for every person or against every bacteria. Carry antibiotics of several varieties. If in port,

Table 13-1. Infections

Date/Location	Description	Treatment
5/93 to 7/93 French Polynesia	Beth suffers from a series of ear infections that are the result of snorkeling in coral waters. Symptoms begin enroute between the Galapagos and Marquesas on a 29-day passage, recur three times over the next two months. Doctors prescribe increasing dosages of antibiotics. Massive dosages finally end infections.	1. Self-treats with 250-mg amoxycillin three times per day for 10 days enroute to Tahiti (June). 2. In Tahiti (June), infection results in 104° fever; doctor administers injectable antibiotic and prescribes 500 mg Augmentin twice a day for 6 days. 3. In Raiatea (July) symptoms recur, doctor prescribes 900 mg Bactrim Fort twice a day for 10 days.
5/93 Marquesas, French Polynesia	Evans develops staph infection after swimming in Taiohae Baie.	Self-treats with 250 mg Augmentin three times per day for 10 days.
11/94 Durban, South Africa	When trying to haul out the boat in Durban's polluted harbor, Evans has to dive to check if the keel is sitting on the cradle properly. Twenty-four hours later, Evans develops severe fever and diarrhea that lasts for two days.	Viral infection. Bed rest, aspirin, water to prevent dehydration, bland foods as he recovers.

see a local doctor conversant with tropical infections. I used too little antibiotic when I got an ear infection, and I managed only to make the infection more resistant. In the tropics, a dosage two to four times the normal amount may be required. We carried a potent injectable antibiotic (Cephtriaxone) as a last resort in case of a severe infection where the patient would be too ill for oral administration.

Aside from bacterial infections, fungal infections occur frequently. Among women, yeast infections resulted from less-than-perfect hygiene on passage. Many women develop yeast infections after taking antibiotics. Bring a good supply of cream or suppositories and start treatment at the first sign of an infection.

Allergic reactions

We both suffered a number of allergic reactions. Oftentimes, we were not certain of the cause.

Besides the normal travel hazards of unusual foods and different water, cruisers also face venomous ma-

rine life and stinging insects. Table 13-2 summarizes our experiences with major allergic reactions. Though rarely life threatening and generally treatable with over-the-counter antihistamines, some symptoms are so unusual that they can be quite alarming. To manage allergic reactions, you need to recognize them and then treat them with antihistamines (systemic reactions) and skin ointments (localized itchy rashes).

It can sometimes be difficult to distinguish between an allergic reaction and an infection. Infections are characterized by heat and painful swellings under the skin, but the same symptoms can appear with severe but localized allergic reactions. If in doubt, rub the area with cortisone cream. If symptoms diminish, you are having an allergic reaction and should dose yourself with antihistamine. Assume that any type of inexplicable redness on the skin is caused by an allergic reaction. You cannot have too many antihistamines aboard—including adrenaline, which is useful in the event of a life-threatening reaction. If anyone aboard suffers from particular allergies, discuss the range of possible symptoms with your physician. If anyone suf-

Table 13-2. Allergic reactions

Date/Location	Description	Treatment
3/93 Panama	Beth wakes covered with hives and experiencing shortness of breath—possibly a reaction to medication.	Self-treats with two 10-mg tablets of Hismanal (antihistamine) to start and one every 4 hours for a day after.
5/93 Marquesas, French Polynesia	Evans attacked by "no-no's," small biting insects that are found near fresh water, when he is refilling our water tanks. His entire back is red, swollen, itchy.	Self-treats with 10-mg tablets of Hismanal every 4 hours for several days until redness and swelling disappear.
7/94 Mauritius Island in the Indian Ocean	Evans develops itchy rash and hives as we are preparing to leave on passage for Reunion Island. Cause unknown.	Self-treats with 25-mg tablets of Benadryl (antihistamine) every 4 hours for 12 hours. We delay passage until symptoms disappear.
9/94 On passage to Durban, South Africa	Beth develops painful, red, hot, swollen area over right hip. Gradually red "fingers" radiate outward from it, spreading across back. Doctor in Durban diagnoses as allergic reaction possibly to spider bite or jellyfish sting.	Doctor prescribes four times daily application of cortisone cream and 25-mg tablets of Benadryl every 4 hours for almost two weeks before symptoms disappear completely.

Table 13-3. Emergencies and traumatic injuries

Date/Location	Description	Treatment
7/92 On passage to Azores	While serving dinner in the galley, the boat rolls through 30 degrees. Beth is thrown across the boat, lands on the edge of the nav table, and cracks a rib.	For the next week on passage, Beth controls the pain with Tylenol with Codeine. Once we reach port, the injury requires two weeks of total rest and six weeks to heal completely.
3/93 On passage to Galapagos	While taking a pill at sea, Beth starts to choke when the boat rolls and the pill lodges in her windpipe.	Beth cannot speak or cough and is gesturing for help. Evans administers the Heimlich maneuver and dislodges pill.
2/94 On passage in South Atlantic	While serving pizza, Beth drops a slice on her leg. The hot cheese causes a deep second-degree burn.	Applies Silvadene cream and sterile bandage for several weeks, then leaves uncovered for short periods to dry out.

fers from insect allergies, carry an emergency kit with you at all times.

Emergencies and traumatic injuries

We carried a full range of emergency and first aid equipment that we were fortunate enough not to have to use. This included air splints and fiberglass cast materials, suturing supplies, and an airway resuscitation kit. Our emergencies and injuries, summarized in Table 13-3, were quite minor. But one situation could have been disastrous had we not had knowledge of medical technique.

Pain relief plays a central role in effective trauma management. Carry a variety of pain relievers, including injectables. When at sea, many treatments can be simplified with the proper equipment. Steri-strips function as well as stitches in most cases. Air casts or fiberglass casts can be used to set a broken bone until port is reached. Adjustable finger and wrist splints and knee and ankle braces offer a quick response to a trauma. Discuss all this equipment with your doctor and practice using it where appropriate.

PROTECTION— ENSURING LONG-TERM HEALTH

While the overall lifestyle is a healthy one, voyaging does increase certain types of health risks. Our voyaging diet was normally well balanced, but we occasionally experienced a lack of certain nutrients. While the basic food pyramid offers the best guidelines to achieving a well-balanced diet, supplements can make up for short-term deficiencies. If a good portion of your water is coming from a watermaker, all minerals will be filtered out of your water along with the salt. Stock up on a general mineral supplement and take it regularly.

Women may need to take an iron supplement if they are not eating much red meat and a calcium supplement if they are not consuming enough milk or dairy products. A lack of vitamin C can cause gum problems, and scurvy still occurs. You will not be able to eat many fresh fruits and vegetables on passage, and you may want to take a daily vitamin supplement. Nutritional supplements can be hard to find in less developed countries, and they can be expensive—even in developed countries. You may want to buy in bulk before you leave. Make sure to check the expiration dates and get bottles that will last for several years.

Beyond managing nutrition with a diet that is occasionally limited, voyagers must also learn to manage sun exposure and exercise, particularly on long passages.

Sun protection and skin care

The greatest risk the offshore voyager faces may well be the long-term effects of overexposure to the sun and the possibility of cancer. In the beginning, we thought less about sun protection than we did about getting struck by lightning. We were sun worshipers. But by the time we returned, we actively avoided the sun and protected ourselves against its harmful rays. While we both had deep tans, we always wore hats. We used sun block every day on our faces and often on the rest of our bodies.

Sun protection tops the list for our next trip. Our future boat will have a hard dodger as much to provide shade as shelter.

To protect yourself from the sun, dress for success. Light, long-sleeved cotton shirts and pants block the sun and keep you cool. Surgical scrubs are ideal. A good hat that you will wear in the tropics comes next (the perfect hat is described in Chapter 8). We wore a hat at all times when we were not below, even when we skipped the other clothes. Buy a good pair of sunglasses equipped with side flaps for glare protection. The side flaps can be hot, but they reduce the risk of cataracts and other growths from prolonged exposure to the sun. Good sun block is the last ingredient for the perfect tropical wardrobe.

Suntan lotions are rated by their sun protection factor (SPF). An SPF of 15 allows you a maximum limit of exposure that is 15 times longer than what would be safe for bare skin. But sun block can only protect you from the sun if you put it on. Left unprotected, our faces burned no matter how deep our tans were.

Initially, our facial skin reacted to many sun products, and waterproof lotions did not last well. After a few months at sea, my complexion was constantly irritated by the oil in the suntan lotions. The skin on my face had also become dry and chapped. Wrinkles were forming around my eyes from the wind, salt spray, and sun. Evans, who refused to use the oily lotions, had repeatedly burned his ears and nose to the point of blistering.

At that point, facial moisturizers such as Oil of Olay started to become available with a sun protection factor. I started applying Oil of Olay lotion with SPF 15 to my face several times a day. This kept me from burning and kept my skin moist. Evans even came to like Oil of Olay as a facial sun block solution. We kept it by the companionway and applied it three or four times a day. Keeping salt off my face also kept it from drying out. I would rinse my face several times a day with a small amount of fresh water, each time reapplying the Oil of Olay. Any good facial moisturizer with sun protection will work, so take along your favorite and use it.

We applied normal suntan lotion to the rest of our bodies as needed. When we had been in the tropics for many weeks, we rarely put on any lotion, especially if we were wearing light cotton clothes. We did use lip balm with sunscreen several times a day. Sunburned lips can be accompanied by an allergic reaction that causes them to swell to several times their normal size. Protect your lips as carefully as you protect the rest of your face.

The ozone layer is thickest over the tropical latitudes. We therefore had the most protection when we were wearing the least clothing, on our trade wind passages. New Zealand and Australia, on the other hand, have been experiencing intensified UV radiation due to the hole in the ozone layer. The incidence of skin cancer is higher in southern Australia than anywhere else in the world. While in those countries, we used a minimum of SPF 15 sun block at all times, and we often upgraded to an SPF 30 product or a complete sun block—especially on sensitive areas like ears and lips.

A bimini or dodger provides shade, the last ingredient in good sun protection. Find a canvas or hard dodger solution that offers two people adequate protection in most sun angles. If you are particularly sensitive to the sun, use side curtains to protect you from reflected sun glare. Make sure any such arrangement is removable for heavy weather, then leave them on as much as possible in other conditions.

Sometimes you will burn. The very best treatment for a minor sunburn is pure aloe vera gel. This takes the heat and sting out within a few minutes and will often turn a burn into a tan overnight. If you don't have any aloe on board, wet tea bags, dab them on the burn, and allow the liquid to evaporate. A paste of baking soda and water will also relieve the pain.

The sun poses dangers beyond the long-term damage from UV radiation. Dehydration can be debilitating. Recognize and react to early symptoms: headache, general listlessness, or slight queasiness in conditions where you should not be seasick. For me, dehydration started with a pain over one eye like a sinus headache. Immediately get out of the sun and force yourself to drink water. You may not want water at first, so monitor your intake and drink at least a quart of water within the first hour. Take a salt tablet or eat something salty. Your body cannot absorb water unless it has the proper amount of salt. No matter how much you drink, if you are salt-starved you will not feel any relief. If you experience these symptoms frequently and water helps, you should consider adding a couple of salt tablets to your daily diet.

Treat sunstroke or heat stroke as a medical emergency. The victim loses the ability to sweat or dilate blood vessels under the skin and cannot dissipate heat. Along with the symptoms for dehydration, an elevated body temperature and warm, dry skin signal heat stroke. The patient must be cooled to avoid death. Apply ice packs on the groin, armpits, neck, and chest.

After a few months aboard, protecting yourself from the sun becomes automatic. But when friends visit and spend hours sunning on deck, be prepared with the aloe and the tea bags. After a day or so, they will realize why you're always protected from the sun's rays.

Exercise

In port we got plenty of exercise, especially since we didn't have an outboard for our dinghy. On passage, we continued to get a good workout for our upper bodies, but we both lost muscle tone and condition in our legs. After several weeks at sea with almost no leg exercise at all, we would arrive in port and walk four or five miles the first day to clear customs, go shopping, get water, and so on. After losing muscle conditioning at sea, the sudden exercise caused me to have joint pain and inflammation.

Anyone with orthopedic problems should wear high quality, supportive boat shoes at all times. Going barefoot all the time causes your feet to spread and aggravates orthopedic problems.

Anyone with joint pain or arthritis in their legs should have a plan for maintaining their muscle conditioning and joint flexibility at sea. I eventually developed a stretching and weight routine that kept my muscles toned up and prevented joint problems when we made landfall.

Pulls and strains are very common, even for those without a history of joint problems. When you need to do something on a boat at sea, it often comes after many hours of inactivity and is accompanied by a burst of adrenaline and sudden muscular loads. Muscles that are not warmed up or kept flexible can rip and tear. This can also cause a sprain or strain in a joint. But finding exercise you can do on a pitching, rolling boat takes ingenuity and preparation.

You need to be able to do your onboard exercise routine even if the boat is rolling through 30 or 40 degrees. Videotapes of Jane Fonda won't work. Exercises that can be done sitting down, lying down, or standing braced against something can work. The following alternatives worked for us or for people we knew:

■ **Stretching or yoga.** Twenty minutes or so a day of stretching will help your muscles adjust to sudden demands. Hamstring stretches (runner's stretch), quadricep stretches, and straddle stretches work major muscle groups and help you stay limber. Unlike stretching, yoga maintains muscle strength as well as tone. But don't try it on your own or from a book. Many of the positions are extremely difficult. If not done correctly, they can damage muscles and joints.

■ **Isometric exercises.** Exercises where you contract a muscle group and hold it are called isometric exercises. These maintain muscle strength and endurance and keep you limber. For example, put your back against a bulkhead or the mast and slide down until your thighs are parallel to the deck or sole. Hold this position for 30 seconds and repeat the exercise three times. Work up to holding the position for several minutes and performing the move five times. You can buy exercise books that cover isometric exercises or develop a customized plan with an aerobics instructor or personal trainer. Most isometric exercises can be done sitting or lying down.

■ **Stretch bands and Bullworkers.** For a more intense workout, add resistance to the exercises in order to push specific muscle groups. Many health clubs use stretch bands with handles on either end or small circular bands that look like oversized rubber bands. These work major muscle groups like triceps, biceps, quadriceps, calves, and hip flexors with exercises that can be done seated or lying down. For example, lie on your side and put the band around both ankles. Perform leg raises with the top leg against the resistance of the band.

Bullworkers are spring-loaded devices that are often advertised in weightlifting magazines. These offer more resistance than the bands and can be used to work major muscle groups in much the same way. When you buy either type of equipment from a sporting goods store, they come with a booklet that describes exercises for specific muscle groups.

■ **Free weights.** Ankle or wrist weights constructed of heavy nylon pockets that hold from one to four small weights offer the most flexible arrangement for working specific muscle groups. You can vary the resistance to match your needs for each exercise, and the exercises themselves do not depend on opposing the motion with another part of your body. I used these weights and an exercise book entitled *The Twelve-Minute Total-Body Workout* (Warner Books, 1993) by Joyce Vedral. This routine was designed for business people who travel and can be done in a hotel room without special equipment. It exercises every major muscle group twice (the abdominal muscles three times) each week. I could do all but three or four of the exercises in the worst sea conditions. If I took 40 minutes each day to do two days' worth of workouts and stretch thoroughly, my muscles lost very little conditioning between ports.

When considering an exercise routine for use at sea, focus on maintaining muscle tone and strength; don't worry too much about aerobic conditioning. If you have problems with your joints, work on a program with your doctor, a physical therapist, a personal trainer, or an aerobics instructor. Picture how you will manage each exercise with the boat rolling through 30 degrees. Ask your advisor to recommend several different exercises that work the same muscle group so you can always find one that will work in the conditions. Commit to maintaining your conditioning. For those with muscle and joint problems, the exercise may help you stretch your voyaging years.

Managing major health concerns

A range of additional health risks peculiar to voyaging can be serious, although their actual incidence is low among offshore sailors. For most of these, prevention means protection.

■ *Appendicitis.* We knew voyagers who had their appendixes removed to eliminate the risk of appendicitis at sea. But a person with appendicitis can be stabilized for many days using injectable, high-potency antibiotics. Many hospitals now treat appendicitis this way rather than performing surgery. Carry such antibiotics aboard and avoid the unnecessary surgery.

■ *AIDS.* In many parts of the world, including much of Africa, AIDS is an epidemic. In these areas, up to half of the population can be HIV positive. Besides the normal precautions against AIDS, carry your own hypodermic needles aboard and ask a doctor to use them if you need an injection.

■ *Malaria.* Malaria is not present in the majority of trade wind destinations. However, the Solomon Islands, Vanuatu, and parts of Indonesia have serious malaria problems with strains that are resistant to quinine. We knew of two cruisers who died because they were taking prophylactics that masked the malarial symptoms. In one year, more than half the voyagers who visited the Solomon Islands contracted malaria. Factor the malaria risk into your decision to visit these areas. Don't rely solely on prophylactics. To prevent malaria, make sure you are not bitten by the Anopheles mosquito. That means not being ashore at dusk when they feed, anchoring away from villages, and using screens and repellent from mid-afternoon until well after dark. The publication issued by IAMAT called "How to Protect Yourself Against Malaria" is the best summary I have seen on preventive practices.

■ *Ciguatera.* This nerve disorder can occur after eating reef fish. It is caused by a toxin that accumulates in fish that live and feed off infected reefs. Different fish species exhibit varying toxicity in different areas. We knew several people who experienced symptoms including upset stomach, numb lips, and tingling limbs. The effects are cumulative and can be fatal. The best way to avoid ciguatera is not to eat reef fish at all—pelagic fish caught in the open ocean are free of the toxin. If you catch a reef fish that you want to eat, show it to the local fishermen and ask their opinion. Don't eat any reef fish that are "ugly" (an exotic-looking fish covered with spines, for instance) or over a foot in length.

■ *Dengue fever.* Also known as "break bone fever" because of the intense joint pain that characterizes it, dengue fever is caused by a virus carried by mosquitoes. Symptoms include a very high fever for several days accompanied by a rash, muscle and joint ache, and a headache that lasts two to three days. It can take several weeks to get over, though the reduced energy level may last for several months. We knew people who contracted the disease in relatively "civilized" places like St. Martin and Tahiti. One woman who contracted it in uninhabited Suvarov atoll could have died if she hadn't been evacuated. Those suffering from dengue fever should not take aspirin, since it can cause internal bleeding. The mosquitoes that carry the fever feed during the day, so wear repellent, pants, and long-sleeved shirts where it has been reported. Bed rest is the only cure, but seek medical help if any symptoms of internal bleeding develop (black or bloody stools).

■ *Cholera and typhoid.* While there are vaccinations for both of these ailments, they are short-lived and offer only moderate protection. Both of these ailments are transmitted through human waste. If in an area where you are at risk, do not take on water, do not swim in the harbors, and peel all fruits and vegetables before eating them. Be particularly careful ashore about ice in drinks, salads, and food made with water (e.g., ice cream).

On a final note, voyagers need to be careful about birth control. Birth control pills have to stay in your body to work. We knew of at least five couples who got pregnant during the course of a passage thanks to a few pills that ended up "feeding the fish" during a bout with seasickness. In most cases, they didn't discover the fact for many weeks. Morning sickness was mistaken for seasickness, and a skipped period was attributed to changes in food, water, and surroundings.

If unplanned, getting pregnant can radically alter your cruising dream. I switched from the pill to the Norplant implant, a birth control device that is implanted just under the skin and works for five years. I had no problem with this and loved the simplicity and convenience. Some cruising couples opt for a vasectomy or tubal ligation.

CHAPTER 14

STAYING CHALLENGED: FOLLOWING YOUR HEART

No matter how old you are when you set off, going voyaging is like retiring. The day-to-day activities that once defined your life are gone. You have to create a new routine based on who you are and what you really want to do. Many people find the adjustment to retirement difficult. They lose their sense of self-worth and their orientation within society. This can happen to new voyagers, too. To avoid it, prepare yourself mentally for free time and consider how you want to use it.

This problem is exacerbated by our society's increasing need to be entertained. Even a decade ago, individuals and families spent more time entertaining themselves. Whether it was horseshoes or charades in the living room, people knew how to amuse themselves. Today, we turn to the television, the VCR, the Internet, or the movies for entertainment. We have become passive observers instead of active participants.

Most younger voyagers will have to learn how to entertain themselves at sea. They will also need to learn that it is not necessary to *do* every minute of every day. With our backgrounds in business, we had learned that time was a precious commodity and that we always had to be *productive* and *focused*. In our previous lives, there had been no room for sitting and contemplating. One of the major changes we went through was learning to love just being out there. When we first started, I found a two-hour watch too long. In the end, I found that I could sit on deck and lose myself in the sea and the sun, only to discover that four or five hours had slipped away.

These quiet spaces between times allow you to meet yourself. To prepare, take the time before you go to consider what you really want to do when you retire. What have you always said you would do if you had the time?

In the final press to get the boat ready to head offshore, you can lose sight of the fact that this is a huge lifestyle change and one you need to prepare for—at least a bit.

ACTIVITIES THAT LEND THEMSELVES TO SHIPBOARD LIFE

A wide variety of activities are a natural outgrowth of living aboard. For most of these you need very little in the way of extra equipment or special planning. The activities that follow are many of the pursuits that are common to offshore voyagers. Raising children aboard can be considered an activity unto itself, well suited to voyaging. The time you spend together and the experiences you share will make your family life rich and intense. If you have children aboard, consider the following ideas a grab bag from which to select the day's entertainment.

Early on, you will probably find yourself spending much of your free time doing something from this list of activities. But as the months pass and living aboard becomes your life, you will feel more like you do in your own home on a Sunday afternoon. Your extracurricular activities will be less a way to find amusement and more a way to seek stimulation and enrichment. At that point, you may find yourself becoming less interested in snorkeling and shell collecting and more interested in developing a new skill or pursuing a long-time passion.

Remember that what has become your life represents a vacation to your visitors. We found that even the most experienced sailors were to some extent expecting to be entertained. Turn your guests loose and let them enjoy snorkeling and sailboarding while you relax or do what you would normally do.

Water time

If you are going voyaging, you presumably like the water. When you are anchored in a remote lagoon, water-related activities are an obvious form of entertainment. While people often worry about sharks and venomous marine animals, a bit of common sense and a healthy respect for local knowledge will ensure that you can safely enjoy the water that is all around you.

Fishing

There are two kinds of fishing that voyagers engage in, and the goals, methods, and satisfactions from each are quite different. There are those for whom fishing is a sport, with fair struggle under specific rules being far more important than catching a fish. These people must be descended from Hemingway and his "old man." There are those for whom fishing has one and only one purpose: a means of catching some of the most delicious food on the entire planet. No words can describe the flavor of a thick steak cut off a fresh tuna. No restaurant in the world can match this delicacy, at any price.

If you are an aficionado of sportfishing, you will want to buy the heaviest, highest quality ocean fishing rod you can find. When trolling on passage, you will need the full advantage of your rules of engagement or you will lose the fish that strikes before you even get to the fair fight part. If you are after food and nothing else, dispense with the rod altogether.

Most offshore voyagers use 100-pound–test line led directly to a winch. They tie together several of the largest hooks they can find, attach brightly colored plastic for a lure (plastic garbage bags seem to be most common), and some large washers for sinkers. There is no fair fight here. You want to hook the monster and get it aboard as painlessly as possible. Many crews rig a bell on the line to sound the alarm when they get a strike.

Once the fish is caught, there are two schools of thought on what to do next. One school advocates towing the fish along behind until it drowns, then bringing it in to filet for dinner. But the catch could be lost to sharks before it gets on board the boat. The other school recommends pulling your catch alongside the boat and pouring a generous dose of alcohol (cheap gin, rum, or whiskey) into its gills. This sedates

the fish and allows you to bring it aboard with very little fuss, bother, and bloodshed.

Some crews catch fish no matter what they do. Others never make a catch, even after towing a fishing line all the way around the world. I have sat through discussions between these two groups. Though they used the same techniques and sailed the same passages at about the same time, the fish always gravitated toward one boat and not the other. Such mysteries have always surrounded fishing. If you go an ocean or two without a bite, give it up.

Whether you are fishing for sport or for food, view the following tips as generally accepted wisdom—although there are never any guarantees.

- **When to fish.** Pelagic fish generally feed at dusk and dawn, so that is the best time to try to catch them. At those times, they are cruising near the surface and looking for small, shiny things to eat. At other times, they are in deep water sleeping or otherwise entertaining themselves.

- **Where to fish** Most species of pelagic fish feed near land. The best fishing is generally when you are approaching or leaving land. Fish favor currents where they find other critters to feed on, so you have a better chance of catching something wherever a current flows. This includes reef passes and river entrances, as well as the great ocean currents like the Gulf Stream and the Agulhas Current off South Africa.

- **Be careful of sea birds.** In the crystal clear waters offshore, you need to weight your lures so you do not attract sea birds. Pelagic birds will normally gravitate to a boat at sea, often hoping for a little ride. If you are towing a lure and it is flashing on the surface of the water, a bird will mistake it for a small fish and try for it. There is nothing fun or funny about a very frightened, angry wild bird with a hook in its gullet. If you can see your lure in your wake or you notice a bird repeatedly flying over the area where your hook is, haul your line back in and put more washers on it.

Snorkeling and swimming

Anyone who hasn't snorkeled in tropical waters will find their first time a life-changing experience. Swimming slowly over a reef teeming with technicolored fish changes your perspective on the ocean. Snorkeling can be enjoyed by young and old, fit and not-so-fit, sailors and nonsailors. A face mask, flippers, and a snorkel are your passport to a new world.

Every crewmember should have high quality gear that fits properly. The fins should be broad with good ribs to provide maximum power from your kick. Get fins that fit your foot without binding around the ankle (blisters are very uncomfortable in salt water and can become infected). Everyone's face is shaped differently, and your enjoyment will be directly related to how much water is seeping in around your mask. It took Evans and me two tries each to find masks that suited our faces, but the rejects formed the basis of our spare snorkel gear for visitors. Carry several extra pairs of fins and snorkels for guests as well.

Snorkel gear is prone to mold and mildew. Within a month or so, mold will form in the snorkel tubes and mouthpieces. Keep a toothbrush with your snorkel gear, and scrub these parts with baking soda before and after use. Every once in a while, soak the mouthpieces in a mild vinegar solution and rinse them thoroughly. That keeps them mold-free for several weeks.

Before you don your gear and head into the water, ask the local fishermen about any hazards—sharks, moray eels, stone fish, and so on. In our travels, sharks posed a serious threat in only two places—the Great Barrier Reef from Australia up into Papua New Guinea, and along the eastern and southern coast of South Africa from Richard's Bay to Mosselbaie. In the Pacific, we frequently saw small (2- to 4-feet) nurse sharks, which had no interest in us. If locals mention any problems with sharks, keep a person posted on deck as a lookout.

Three other hazards should keep you out of the water, and all are found along the Australian coastline. Box jellyfish are an extremely poisonous type of jellyfish whose sting is often fatal. Though summer temperatures soar well above 100 degrees Fahrenheit along the northern coast of Australia, no one swims during the annual box jellyfish migration. Saltwater crocodiles also prowl the Australian coast. These ferocious beasts can reach lengths of 12 feet or more, and they are quite common in the brackish water where rivers meet the sea along the Barrier Reef. Though large, they can be tremendously fast, even on land. The tracks themselves should be enough to send you back to your boat. They do not usu-

ally reach the small islets on the outer reaches of the Great Barrier Reef, but ask to be certain before you go into the water. Sea snakes along the Barrier Reef are very large and very poisonous. They are usually seen offshore, but you may run across one while snorkeling. Get out of the water immediately. We were told that touching one could prove fatal. After seeing one half the length of the boat, we had no desire to find out.

Most other marine hazards can be managed by a simple rule: Look, don't touch. Many denizens of a coral reef are poisonous, but they are not aggressive. Even the coral itself, if you are scratched by it, can cause serious infections. Cruise quietly over the top of the world you are viewing, but keep your hands to yourself and everyone will be happy.

Don't assume that because you are in the water, you are protected from the sun. In clear water, the sun's rays seem to be magnified, and many people have been quite seriously burned while swimming or snorkeling for an hour or so in the heat of the day. A tee-shirt over your swimsuit offers some protection, especially for guests who do not have a deep tan. Wear waterproof sun block. Be particularly careful to cover the backs of your knees and the backs of your upper arms when you apply it.

Drift diving through a reef pass is exciting and magical. Coral atolls, like the ones that make up the Tuamotus Archipelago in the South Pacific, consist of a barrier reef of coral with small, sandy islets linked by reefs on the leeward sides of the atolls. The inner lagoon enclosed by the reef and islets may be 20 or 30 miles long and half as wide. On the windward side of the atoll, the barrier reef breaks down under the constant assault of the sea, so it is often awash. Most atolls have a constant flow of water coming in over the windward side and flowing out of one or more passes on the leeward side. In the Society Islands of French Polynesia, barrier reefs surround high volcanic islands. The same pattern of an inflow over the windward reef and an outflow through one or several passes exists. This current through the pass is rich in nutrients from the surrounding coral, and it attracts all manner of sea creatures. When you drift dive, you allow the current to carry you through the reef pass and you watch the wildlife that has gathered there to feed.

Be sure that the current is not so strong that you cannot return when you reach the other side. In some areas, outflows can be up to 7 knots at certain tidal states, so figure out the tidal flow before you go. A "chaser" in a dinghy can recover anyone who seems to be having trouble with the current.

Spearfishing is a wonderful way to get dinner, but ask before you do it. In Cocos Keeling, Christmas Island, and many other places, your spear gun (or at least the rubbers) will be confiscated when you clear customs. This protects their underwater wildlife, especially in areas where they are creating marine parks. In other places, like Fiji and parts of Tonga, the fish in the lagoon are considered the property of the local people, as are the coconuts on the trees and the shells on the beach. Taking fish without permission is a serious breach of local custom and common courtesy. Some of these reef areas are becoming so overfished that local people are forced to buy high priced canned tuna and corned beef to supplement their protein intake.

Scuba

Everything that was said about snorkeling applies equally to scuba diving. In addition, scuba requires special gear and certification. Certification is mandatory, not only legally but for your own safety. Most places will ask you to show proof of certification before they will fill your tanks. We knew of a woman who died in French Polynesia drift scuba diving through a pass. She was a guest on a cruising boat and she was not certified. She panicked halfway through the pass and somehow drowned. If you want to dive, get the proper training and don't let anyone who has not been certified use your equipment.

The gear, particularly the tanks, must be stowed so that it cannot break loose. A special rack in a large locker is a good idea. You can have tanks refilled at dive shops and resorts the world over. Even on the remote atolls, many of the locals dive for pearls or fish, so there is a compressor somewhere. Tank fills cost between $5 and $10 throughout most of the world.

Scuba provides more than just recreation; it can help you free a fouled anchor or work on the bottom of the boat. If your primary goal is to use scuba for boat maintenance, you probably need only one tank (a tank lasts about an hour). If you are planning scuba as recreation, you will want two tanks per person. If you have a large crew and scuba is likely to be one of your key activi-

ties, you may want to consider putting a compressor on board to reduce the cost of tank fills. You'll need to consider the space and electrical requirements before making a final decision.

Dinghy sailing and sailboarding

If you have children aboard, these two activities are guaranteed to keep them occupied for many hours. A small sailing dinghy or sailboard can be a link between your children and the children of a Polynesian village. Kitty Kuhner from *Tamure* said that her sons, Alex and Spencer, made more friends by teaching local children how to sail than any other way.

A sailing dinghy or sailboard does take up precious stowage space. We didn't think it was worth it. But if you have a child aboard or if you expect to have guests frequently, explore the feasibility of a small sailboard or a sailing rig for your hard dinghy.

Learning time

Traveling means always learning. Whether you are researching the history of your next landfall or searching the night sky to find the Southern Cross for the first time, every day offers numerous opportunities to expand your horizons and your mind. Learning time comes in many different guises aboard, and none of them require much preparation. If you are blessed with an open mind and abundant curiosity, you are as prepared as you need to be to use the time aboard effectively.

Decide if there is a specific skill you want to develop. Have you always wished for enough time to learn a language, play a musical instrument, read the classics, or learn to sketch? Whatever your desire, plan on making it a focus for your learning aboard. For many activities, this will take no more than a little forethought and a few supplies. If there is a subject you have always wanted to study formally, set up your own self-study course or take a correspondence course. If you have a general thirst for knowledge and a desire to learn, you will be quite happy learning about the things you come across during your voyage.

We spent much of our time trying to learn about the places we were visiting before we arrived and while we were there. One of the joys of traveling is to make an intimate connection with a place, to discover where it stands in relation to history, culture, anthropology, geopolitics, and local politics. This understanding made personal interactions deeper and more meaningful for us, and our appreciation of the culture more complete. This learning covered many different aspects—from reading history and literature to learning the language. It was extremely fulfilling, and it made each place more real and more special.

Cultural literacy

I am a firm believer that cultural literacy must start with linguistic literacy. Anyone who has mastered a language to a basic conversational level knows that language is the personality of a culture—that the culture's idiosyncrasies, fears, logic, and history are embedded in its language. While you can never completely understand a culture you weren't born into, you will not even come to a superficial understanding without insights gained from the language.

Of course, you cannot learn a dozen languages as you cross the face of the globe. But you can learn a key language to a level where you can converse—not flawlessly and not in a written form, but to the point where you can exchange ideas with someone who is patient. You can also learn a few key words whenever you approach a new culture. For a Pacific circle or a trade wind circumnavigation, French in addition to your native English will allow you to communicate almost everywhere. Acquiring a basic knowledge of Polynesian is not difficult, and a similar vocabulary is used from the Marquesas to Fiji, New Zealand, and Hawaii. For travel in South America, Spanish should be your first choice.

If you do not have any basis in the language, your instruction should start before you head off to sea. But good intentions seldom lead to actions on this front, so arm yourself with a comprehensive self-teaching course on cassette, CD, videotape, or computer software. The best way to learn any language is immersion, and the best way to improve your language skills is to have to survive using them. If you can learn basic phrases, sentence structure, and a vocabulary of several hundred words, you will improve rapidly once you are in a place and using the language.

Look for a course that emphasizes living in the culture rather than being a tourist or a business traveler. The kind of vocabulary you will need is comprehensive.

Knowing how to ask a cab driver to take you to the airport is not going to be very useful. Develop a broad vocabulary and rely on intuition and sign language to make up the gap in grammar and sentence structure. The Capretz method for French developed by Yale University and called *French in Action* can get you understanding and speaking basic conversational French in eight weeks. *Destinos* uses a similar method to teach Spanish. Though expensive, both programs are well worth the investment. Call the Annanberg/CPB Project at 800-LEARNER, or write PO Box 2345, South Burlington, VT 05407.

Beyond understanding some of the language, we wanted to know about the country's history, culture, and traditions. Travel guides provide much of this information. The Lonely Planet series and other backpacking guides met our needs better than tourist-oriented guidebooks. These give good, up-to-date information on the culture, history, current political situation, medical and other hazards, and the local traditions that you will be expected to respect. One boat always had a guidebook to the next island or country. Everyone tended to borrow them, take notes, and return them before leaving for that destination. *The South Pacific Handbook* offered a broad array of information on each of the South Pacific islands (see "Additional resources" in Chapter 22).

The information in guidebooks can be a bit superficial. For most places we visited, we also looked for a history of the country and any related literature we could find. We read books on Darwin as we approached the Galapagos, Melville's *Typee* when we were on passage to the Marquesas, Robert Louis Stevenson's short stories (re-released as *In the South Seas,* by KPI, Limited, 1986) while traveling through the South Pacific, and *Cry, the Beloved Country* by Alan Patton when we approached South Africa. A quick search at a library will turn up relevant titles. These books make wonderful gifts from loved ones for birthdays and Christmas.

By the time you get there, you will be ready to explore the culture. Spend as much time as you can interacting with the people themselves. While this seems axiomatic, it is astonishing how easy it is for the voyaging community to become insular. It takes a special effort to meet and really get to know local people, but you are rewarded with a new way of viewing the world.

You can make connections through the local markets. When you buy fruits and vegetables, ask lots of questions. Those selling the produce will be delighted, and you will learn all about exotic fruits and vegetables and how to prepare them. Get recipes, try them, and return to the market to tell the recipe giver how they worked out. In most countries we visited, the market is the social hub anyway, so it is a natural place to interact where you will be accepted quickly and easily.

Once you find a doorway into a village, you can become involved in an infinite number of activities. You will be invited to visit the local plantation where they grow cash crops for selling in the main market. Women will be asked if they want to learn how to weave baskets from coconut palm fronds or how to smoke fish in the village smoke house. Men may be invited on a late night fishing expedition or to village ceremonies. We found that when we were anchored off a village where we had become accepted, we had no spare time to worry about how to stay occupied. We were doing what we had set out to do in the first place—learning about new cultures and making new friends.

Arts and crafts

You can pursue an endless range of hobbies at sea. With some colored paper, scissors, and felt-tip pens, you and your kids can stay busy for hours. One woman made wall hangings using paper cutouts of contrasting colors layered together to create images, seascapes, and wildlife. Her creations were exceptional enough to sell in tourist ports and to other cruisers.

As we crossed the Indian Ocean, we became friends with a couple on a 37-foot steel boat named *Skerryvore*. They were both artists: Spider in oil paints and Kim in a variety of media. They each kept a sketchbook of their trip just as I kept a journal, and the images they recorded of sunsets and stormy seas are most certainly worth a thousand words. If you have ever had an interest in sketching, bring along a basic how-to book and give it a try. Store your paper in multiple layers of plastic bags. Pencils, felt-tip pens, and colored pencils are most easily managed aboard. Pastels can be very messy. Watercolors and oils are best left to those with experience.

Acrylic paints are more forgiving. They mix well, clean up with water, and dry quickly. One cruising friend painted courtesy flags and sold them to other boats. She also painted on shells, sand dollars, and on tee-shirts. She did specialized voyaging tee-shirts with your boat's name and insignia on the front and your route shown on a globe on the back. For someone with some artistic talent, the possibilities are endless.

Learning a musical instrument is another favorite pastime. Once you have mastered some basic tunes on the guitar, fiddle, harmonica, or flute, you will be a welcome addition to any party. Not many other instruments do particularly well on a boat, and even those mentioned must be protected from humidity. Our musical friends recommended leaving your best instrument at home and buying an inexpensive model that you would worry about less and enjoy more at sea.

Small needlepoint, knitting, or quilting projects pass the time when you are tired of reading on a long passage, and they don't take up much space. Both sewing and knitting needles tend to rust over time. I had done about two-thirds of an intricate needlepoint on our passage to the Marquesas, then left it for a few weeks after we made landfall. When I returned to it, the needle I had inserted in the middle had rusted away to nothing, and the horrible rust stain had ruined the needlepoint. Keep your needle separate from your work and make sure it is not rusty before you resume.

Making bead jewelry can be fun, but don't try managing the small beads on passage. In many parts of the world, beadwork is a treasured art. If you have an interest, you will find immediate entree into the local culture and a variety of skill-building opportunities.

Shells collected from the beach offer almost unlimited possibilities for creativity. We saw wind chimes, bookends, plant holders, bowls, and potpourri containers made from shells. Small shells can decorate cards to family and friends. Larger shells can be strung on a chain to make a necklace or a bracelet. But please, don't collect live shells. Not only are many of the creatures that live inside quite capable of defending themselves, but the coral reef habitat is also a fragile one. The collection of shells and the killing of their inhabitants have damaged reefs in many places.

Finally, the traditional crafts done by sailors through the ages offer modern sailors entertainment and satisfaction. If you ever wanted to learn how to carve, get a few how-to books in woodworker specialty shops and bring along a few carving knives and a small set of chisels. Traditional knotwork keeps the hands busy while the mind wanders where it will. *The Marlinspike Sailor* by Hervey Garrett Smith (International Marine, 1993) is the bible of knotwork. You will have plenty of chafed bits of line to turn into fine art. Macramé is also popular and wrist and ankle bracelets are traditional tokens of friendship between sailors, especially children.

Nature watching

If you love nature and your tastes run toward identifying and cataloging species, you will find much to keep you busy. Many of the pelagic birds' life cycles and behaviors are poorly understood because they are so seldom observed in their natural habitat. The same can be said for many species of dolphins and whales. Identifying tropical fish, different corals, and various types of mollusks can heighten the wonder of snorkeling. Ashore, learning to recognize frangipani and bougainvillea as well as lemon and breadfruit trees offers practical as well as aesthetic rewards. Stargazing and constellation identification were passions on several boats we knew. Even those who think they have no interest in such things suddenly want to know more when a whale is looking them in the eye.

Take along a good field guide for whatever your particular passion is—shells, whales and dolphins, sea birds, land birds, flora, tropical fish, corals, and so on. The best guide to sea birds we found was *Seabirds* by Peter Harrison (Houghton Mifflin, 1983). The best sea

---

A day in the life: introduction to a Polynesian village

The following is a journal entry written from Garuma village on Raroia atoll in the Tuamotu Archipelago, March 17, 1993:

"After setting the anchor, we have just gotten the boat to a livable state after our three-day passage. We are both on deck viewing the amazing colors in the lagoon waters and the strange huts ashore. A motorboat comes alongside, and its owner steps aboard Silk. *Gaston introduces himself, and we begin a long conversation in French. He lives in the village of 150 people. He and his family have recently become part of a pearl cooperative. The Japanese started the pearling operation last year. The only other crop is Copra from the bountiful coconut palms—about ten tons per year. The atoll is too dry to grow anything else. Water comes from cachement.*

"Gaston tells us that he has lived here all of his life except for going to school in Papeete. He has two children, ages six and ten. He explains that children go to school here until age eight, then to Makemo (a nearby atoll with a larger village) until 14, then to Papeete until 18. While on Makemo and Papeete, children come home only for summer and Christmas vacations. The children learn French and Tahitian before they leave Raroia.

"Gaston talks of the independence movement in Tahiti. They want 'moitié-moitié' he says—half and half, the best of both worlds. In the Taumotus, they all know that they could not live on the atolls without French investment and subsidies. He claims that the Tahitians want the benefits of French investment without French rule—c'est impossible—an impossibility.

"All supplies come aboard an inter-island freighter that docks at the quay every other Sunday. There is no local store—everyone goes aboard the freighter and buys what they want. Besides food, the supply ship brings culture in the form of video cassettes. Tahitian television is transmitted from Papeete via satellite. The whole village watches the video tapes and the French network on the single communal television located in the community center.

"Gaston asks if we have any video cassettes—obviously the prized item for barter nowadays. He seems disappointed when we say no. Then he reaches into his pocket and pulls out a magnificent black pearl, the size of small marble. 'The Japanese tell us that Americans will pay $100 for this,' he says. 'We don't know whether or not to believe them. Why would anyone pay so much for such a small thing?' He seems genuinely puzzled. We reassure him solemnly that Americans will pay that much for a pearl but find we cannot explain why.

"We ask Gaston if he ever thinks about leaving the atoll. He smiles. 'Everyone here has seen Tahiti. You can't do anything there without money in your pocket. To get the money you have to work all the time. We chose to come back here where you can catch fish on the reef and get coconuts from the trees.'"

mammal guide was *The Sierra Club Handbook of Whales and Dolphins* by Leatherwood and Reeves (Sierra Club Books, 1983). The field guides will help you identify particular species, but they typically do not go into too much detail on life cycle and animal behavior. If these areas interest you, find some good naturalist's books to accompany the guides.

While we were out, several researchers were using voyagers' sightings to gather information on dolphin and whale populations. They asked voyagers to note the following information from any sighting: species, size and color of individuals, number of young, location, weather information, and water temperature. Greenpeace had a formal program, and a naturalist in French Polynesia was collecting information less formally. In the Pacific, John Anderson (Ham call signal VK95A) gathers information for Pacific Wildlife Watch (PO Box 19, Norfolk Island, Australia, L899). If you are interested, contact organizations that study marine mammals—such as the Woods Hole Oceanographic Institution, Greenpeace, and the World Wildlife Fund—to see if you can be of help.

If you are interested in stars and constellations, you may want to buy a star finder, a cylindrical tube that illustrates the night sky at different latitudes and times and labels the stars and constellations. I have seen these only for the Northern Hemisphere, but they can be lots of fun as you are sailing along at night. If you are a serious aficionado, you may want to consider taking along a spy glass. The boat is not stable enough for very high magnification, but the clarity of the sky and the utter darkness of a moonless night will permit you to see many things not visible from land.

No matter what interests you, observe it in nature, photograph it, study it—but don't interfere with it. As mentioned above, even shells should never be taken alive. Do not touch plants unless you have the owner's permission. Respect the beauty, record it, then leave it for those who follow to enjoy.

Celestial navigation

If you haven't already learned celestial navigation, you'll never have a better opportunity. It makes a wonderful diversion when on passage and offers an easy way to learn the southern stars when you cross into the Southern Hemisphere and the night sky changes in ways you've never seen before. On night watch, you naturally orient yourself by the stars. Knowing how the Southern Cross will move while you are on watch lets you keep track of your course without having to get up and look at the compass.

If someone on board knows how to do celestial navigation, that person should become the instructor to the rest of the crew. Otherwise, take along a good celestial navigation book. Practice makes perfect. You will take many sights before you experience the thrill of that perfect cocked hat around your current position.

Quiet time

Before you head off, you may picture yourself flitting from anchorage to anchorage, eagerly embracing every culture and new experience, and always being challenged and active. But most cruisers find they learn to treasure the quiet that the sea offers in abundance—to pause and reflect, to breathe and to be. This is time we did not allow ourselves during our hectic shore-based lives. When not contemplating the endless expanse of the ocean, most voyagers fill their quiet times with a few simple activities. Sailors have been avid readers as long as the average seaman knew how to read. They have also been avid scribblers—writing letters, keeping notes and journals, chronicling their own sea changes and experiences with different cultures. These things still entertain us at sea. At least one person keeps a diary on most boats, and every crewmember devours books.

ACTIVITIES THAT REQUIRE SPECIAL EQUIPMENT AND FORETHOUGHT

Both Evans and I came to voyaging as overachievers who had been "doing things" all our lives. Over the course of our first year aboard, we had to learn to slow down and live life—not just skate over it. If you have been raised with the work ethic, it will take time for you to find the serenity and contentment that comes from simply being.

Over the course of our second year aboard, both of us came to understand the value of *not* doing anything and embraced it for perhaps the first time in our lives. But by the third year, we realized that if we were to continue indefinitely, we would need some sort of intellectual stimulation. We found ourselves hungering for a mental challenge to accompany the physical and emotional challenges of voyaging.

Some people are content with the activities described above, and we envied them their inner peace. But we, and others who came from similar backgrounds, started looking for a way to find mental stimulation, focus our energy, and grow in a different plane after a few years of living aboard. Ways to earn money while voyaging were discussed in Chapter 3. Any of these could fall into the category of entertainment.

If you have an interest you wish to pursue, you can probably find a way to do so with a bit of ingenuity and a few compromises. We saw the following ideas in practice on different boats. Some of them may even earn you some money, but don't count on it.

Writing professionally

As discussed in Chapter 3, many sailors dream of being writers. But writing professionally takes access to editors and publishers as well as good writing skills. This can be difficult to manage when you are actually out there. Like many others, I had a few articles published during our trip, but writing really started to work when I was back ashore and a phone call away. A few tips for getting published follow:

■ *Focus on how-to.* Anyone with ambitions of some-day writing for a living will naturally be drawn to the poetry and romanticism of voyaging as their subject. But publishers are inundated with beautifully written narrative prose about faraway islands and stunning personal changes. They are seeking hands-on, well researched, clearly presented articles and books on how to do what you have done—break away from the rat race and make your dream a reality. Everything from maintaining watermakers to rebuilding the head is fair game and will be well received if it is well executed. Don't limit yourself to the sailing magazines. Travel magazines need material from exotic places, and many encourage unpublished authors to send short, fact-based pieces on the unique aspects of a given location.

■ *Illustrations.* Magazines always need illustrations, and good line art or photos can turn an otherwise average article into a published piece. If you are a good enough photographer or illustrator, you could focus on this and forget the writing. But few of us have the professional training and equipment to do more than competently illustrate the how-to pieces that publishers love. As discussed in Chapter 3, to create good photographs you will need to take along the proper equipment and use slide film for the marine magazines. For line art, you will need sketch materials or you will have to take lots of photos from which you can later create illustrations.

■ *Know your magazines.* Name recognition and personal relationships do count when an editor is looking at a pile of a dozen newly arrived manuscripts. Breaking in can be very difficult, but once you are known as someone who writes well and delivers what has been promised, your manuscript will be the one the editor reaches for first. To get to that stage, read the magazines you want to write for and send for their submission guidelines. This will give you a big edge in targeting your article to the right magazine and presenting it in the right way. Don't give up. You will get rejections, but find out why and try to improve. Often the magazine has already purchased an article on your topic, which has not yet been published. If you keep at it, you will reach the point where you can call and ask if they want an article on a specific topic before you invest your time in writing.

■ *Submit professional-looking manuscripts.* The days are long gone when you could get away with submitting a manuscript that was salt-stained, hand-written, and difficult to read. If you are serious about writing as a profession, equip yourself with the tools to give your manuscript a fighting chance. While a computer is ideal, a $300 manual typewriter works just as well. Make sure to keep it well lubricated with a water-dispersing spray.

If this all sounds cold-blooded, it is. Writing is a profession like any other. Even if you have talent, it takes focus, energy, and hard work. But if you have some ability and truly enjoy it, writing offers many rewards.

Photography

As discussed in Chapter 3, photography is an expensive hobby to pursue aboard a voyaging boat. But capturing even a few of those "Kodak moments" means capturing the essence of voyaging.

To give yourself the best chance of getting those breathtaking photos, outfit yourself with good camera equipment and keep it protected and in good working order. To minimize damage from salt water and humid air, keep your camera in a waterproof safety case with desiccant whenever it is not in use. Use a dry bag or inflatable zip-top sport bag for transporting the camera ashore in the dinghy. If the dinghy is swamped, your gear should stay protected for several minutes—with luck, long enough for you to get it ashore.

To protect your lenses, put a sky or haze filter on each one. If the filter gets scratched, it will cost you a tiny fraction of what a new lens costs. Take a good camera cleaning kit, which includes a puff brush, lint-free lens paper, a chamois cloth, and cleaning fluid. Clean your lenses every few days of use to keep them free from the sticky residue that develops from salt air. As discussed in Chapter 3, you will need to have the lenses professionally cleaned once a year or risk damage from mold and mildew in the lens body.

An underwater camera lets you take those action-packed heavy weather shots. The Nikonos is the top of the line. If you cannot afford a second camera, use a watertight bag that protects your camera body and lens. These are sold in camera stores for professional photographers. I would not trust them underwater (though some claim to be capable of that), but I would use them on deck when there is spray about.

Capturing heavy weather takes practice. The largest seas flatten out when photographed and end up looking tame. You need a 200-mm lens with a frame of reference. Take breaking seas looking astern from the bow, with a dodger or a person in the foreground. For those lovely tropical water photos, use a polarizing filter. The best photos in the tropics are always taken at dawn and dusk. At midday, the bright sun washes out the colors, even with a polarizing filter. When taking photographs of people, ask their permission. If you think you may ever use the photos professionally, get a signed release. (I, however, never figured out how to do that in practice.)

Keep your film in the coolest place on the boat (in the refrigerator, if you have one). Allow it to warm up before you load it or it may break. Once the film is exposed, it is even more sensitive to heat. Keep it in a cool place, and develop it as soon as possible. Don't keep developed slides on board. The humid environment will cause a celluloid-eating fungus to take hold. Instead, send them home and see them when you get there. A stack of prints will turn into a single sticky mass, so keep them in some kind of an album.

Photography is a wonderful skill to develop aboard. Be sure to have a plan for managing the basic incompatibility between photographic equipment and the marine environment.

Other arts

Beyond the arts and crafts described above, many of our friends pursued a number of more complex artistic activities that are fulfilling, challenging, and rewarding. All of them take some special equipment, but the materials can usually be scavenged as you go along.

■ *Woodworking.* A small lathe does not take up much space aboard and can turn out a variety of wooden curios, from paper towel holders to Christmas ornaments. You might scavenge interesting wood from the beach or find small quantities of high quality wood in the refuse pile at the local boatyard. Though it takes up more space, a router can be used to make name boards for boats.

■ *Metal working.* You can use a small metal punch to make wind chimes, wall hangings, ornaments, and other small trinkets. Exotic metals are harder to come by than wood, but for inspiration look at what Caribbean artisans make from the steel drums after they are retired from the local band (Figure 14-1).

■ *Jewelry making.* You can collect objects from the beach to create high quality jewelry. One couple we knew carried small quantities of precious metals and bartered for the black pearls found in the South Pacific islands. She designed the jewelry and created exotic and beautiful art, and he executed the design with great skill. This requires some investment in specialized tools. However, space requirements are small and returns are high if you have an artistic sense and a craftsman's quality.

Few activities are totally incompatible with life aboard. One man even exercised his passion for golf. He carried a set of clubs aboard, and whenever he

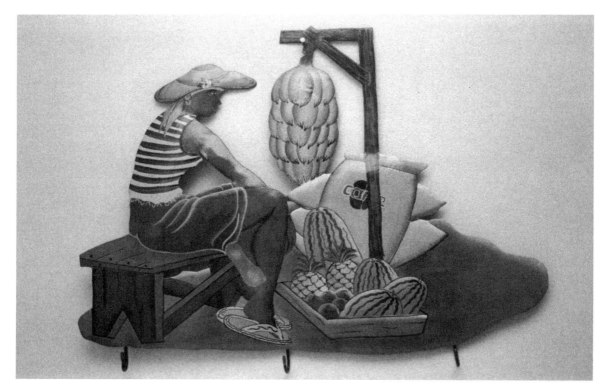

Figure 14-1. This wall hanging was made in the Caribbean from an oil drum. Does it give you any ideas?

arrived at a resort destination with a golf course, he loaded his clubs into the dinghy and off he went. He played on excellent courses at five-star resorts in Bermuda, the Caribbean, and Fiji—places he would never have traveled to just for the sake of playing golf. So think flexibly about what you want to do with your free time when you become a voyager, and you'll be challenged and energized by your new life.

Fear and voyaging ■ *Safety on and near land* ■ Using modern navigation wisely ■ Protecting the boat in port
■ Fire aboard ■ Managing local risks

When the word *safety* comes up in a discussion about sailing, we automatically tag on the words *at sea.* Yet most of the serious incidents we were involved in or heard about occurred near land. As sailors, we respect the sea and tend to be better prepared for its dangers than for perils on or near land. This chapter covers a key liveaboard skill: keeping yourself and your boat safe when you are *not* on passage.

Getting sea room applies to more than just bad weather. You will be most at risk of a collision in the heavier shipping traffic surrounding major ports. In countries that are politically unstable, you may need sea room to get away from a riot or a civil war. When your first instinct is to head to sea at any sign of danger, you have become a sailor.

Safety is one of those topics often asked about by would-be cruisers, but it is difficult to discuss in the abstract. The discussion is far more meaningful when specific situations and their outcomes are examined in detail—as Adlard Coles did in his classic book, *Heavy Weather Sailing.* Rather than talk theoretically about everything that could possibly happen, this chapter focuses on what did happen to us and others we knew. After examining some of the more unusual and unexpected incidents, you will be better prepared to handle the situations you might encounter.

FEAR AND VOYAGING

Fear can be the most destructive of shipmates. It can reduce morale aboard and erode trust between crewmembers. In the extreme, it can endanger the yacht and her crew by causing someone to freeze at a critical moment. To deal with fear head-on, the threat must have a name. Shapeless fears cannot be dealt with constructively, and this chapter will help you give some definition to the vague fears you and your crew may be struggling with.

Voyaging clarifies the difference between a minor incident and a truly dangerous situation. Going aground on a sandbar on a rising tide or having a dinghy stolen in a foreign port are minor inconveniences that can be solved by time or money. Running the boat up on the reef of a deserted atoll or being hit by a barge when you are at anchor in a crowded harbor could result in the loss of your boat, the end of your trip, or personal injury.

When discussing fear with crewmembers, always make the distinction between these two types of risks. Skippers who respond with the same intensity to every threat create crews whose anxiety level is unhealthy and whose reaction to serious emergencies may be panic. The following ideas will help you minimize fear and maximize the likelihood of an organized, calm reaction to an emergency:

■ *Designate a captain with ultimate responsibility.* In some situations, decision making must be instantaneous. In most emergencies, doing something is infinitely preferable to doing nothing. If there is disagreement aboard, there has to be one person whose authority is absolute. If all crewmembers have agreed to this beforehand, there should be no recriminations if that person makes the wrong decision in an emergency.

■ *Use veto power where the decision does not need to be instantaneous.* As discussed briefly in Chapter 1, when decisions can be made jointly, one person should be able to veto the riskier course. If you are making landfall at night and one crewmember is uncomfortable with entering the anchorage, that person has the right to insist on heaving-to until morning light. If all crewmembers agree to the riskier course, it should be a safe one to pursue.

■ *Develop explicit plans and procedures for managing emergencies.* Left with nothing else to do, the mind becomes vulnerable to the insistent voice of fear. To prevent this, you need a plan for each event that could reasonably occur. You and your shipmates have probably detailed individual responsibilities for a rigging failure, a major leak, abandoning ship, or other disasters that can occur at sea. You also need to consider how you would handle a grounding on a coral reef, a fouled prop, or a dragging anchor. You are more likely to have to deal with several of these realities than with the at-sea scenarios you have probably already thought through. On most boats, these procedures are agreed to verbally and reviewed several times during the first year at sea. For larger crews or where crewmembers change over time, these procedures are written in full detail; new arrivals are asked to read the procedures and are told what their role would be.

■ *Don't get complacent.* Many situations we either saw or experienced resulted from complacency. You can get too comfortable with the sea and the benign conditions that prevail so much of the time. This is more true near land than on passage. You need to think ahead, whether you are putting your boat against the fuel dock or entering a reef pass. When everything is new and strange, you will be more cautious than you will be once these activities become mundane. The safety factor you give up may mean the difference between a close call and a serious incident.

Don't let your preparation become paranoia. Once you have done everything you can to prepare for emergencies, fear should no longer be a part of your crew. If you are still plagued by a particular anxiety, you need to either do more planning or find a way to let it go. I was particularly fearful of lightning at sea. Even after talking to the boatbuilder about the grounding system aboard, I faced a black terror whenever we were in a storm. Then we met a couple who had been hit by light

ning and I realized that they hadn't been vaporized off the face of the globe. The damage was serious but fixable. After that, being struck by lightning became one of those uncontrollable risks we could prepare for but never eliminate. I never really got over the fear, but I accepted it and learned to enjoy the wild and awesome beauty of a thunderstorm at sea.

When danger came along, my mind focused on the bare essentials and I did what was necessary. This seems to be the case with most people. The world somehow slows down to accommodate your thought process, and in that sudden clarity you act rather than react. When the tension is gone and the situation is resolved, the reaction sets in. I talked to dozens of people about this; they all agreed that after the fact, they might have been astonished at what they did. But at the time, their actions seemed nothing more than natural.

Managing fear requires a balance. While you want to prepare for as many situations as you can, you also have to maintain your perspective. Assuming you are prudent, you will experience only a handful of potentially life- or boat-threatening incidents. As you read this chapter, keep in mind that the rewards vastly outweigh the risks; for every frightening experience, we had hundreds of peaceful nights and idyllic days.

SAFETY ON AND NEAR LAND

Health risks top the list of voyaging dangers. Of the handful of deaths we heard of, more than half were caused by malaria contracted in the western Pacific. Because it is an important topic, staying healthy is discussed separately in Chapter 13.

Beyond major health risks, the litany of horrors is reasonably brief and personal injuries or fatalities are uncommon. Near land, the boat is endangered more often than the crew. Navigating near land has always been one of the most hazardous of shipboard activities. The GPS has not eliminated the risk; it has simply redefined it. Anyone who thinks otherwise will run into problems. In port, your boat can be endangered when entering a harbor, during changing weather conditions, and when your are maneuvering near other boats in restricted areas. Of the boats we knew that were seriously damaged while voyaging, 90 percent of the incidents occurred in port or when entering a port. Some dangers come from the people and politics of the places you visit. While thievery is much less a concern than most people imagine, risks associated with political instability should not be underestimated.

Using modern navigation wisely

The GPS has revolutionized both offshore passagemaking and coastal cruising. In any book on offshore sailing from the mid-1980s or earlier, one-third to one-half the chapters are devoted to various aspects of navigation. Nowadays, most of what is covered in those chapters is accomplished with the press of a button.

Yet the GPS could be considered "too much of a good thing." Its precision lulls sailors into a false sense of security that can be confounded by inaccurate charts, a malfunctioning electrical system, or any number of navigational shortcuts. While every sailor knows that leaving port without a backup to the GPS is not prudent, many choose to do so anyway. The key to using modern navigation wisely lies in understanding its very real limitations. The gift of push-button positions does not come free.

We had several serious incidents involving the GPS. Most of these were the result of our placing too much faith in the technology and putting too little thought into our navigation. The following incident illustrates how *not* to navigate with the GPS.

After a week spent cruising around the southern tip of New Caledonia within the 12-mile-wide lagoon, we were on our way back to the capital, Nouméa. We had planned on a relaxing coastal sail, including a lunch and photo stop at the Amédée lighthouse that marks the entrance through the lagoon to Nouméa. We had entered through that pass three weeks earlier after a passage from New Zealand, and at that time we had been too tired to appreciate the lovely white lighthouse that graced the small islet just inside the reef entrance. Our relaxing daysail had turned into a four-hour close reach in 30 knots as the leading edge of a strong high drove the barometer up rapidly. The seas inside the lagoon were short and steep, and the sailing was wet and uncomfortable.

We reached the lighthouse, took a few quick pictures, abandoned the idea of lunch in the choppy anchorage, and turned toward Nouméa. We were now sailing close

to the track we had followed when we had made landfall three weeks earlier. Evans, thinking that we were on our original track through the reef, suggested I put a route in the GPS and give him a course to steer. He told me to use the stored waypoint for the reef channel (rfchan) we had passed through to reach the entrance to Nouméa harbor. I went below, found the waypoint he had given me, and created a route that started from our current position and went to the waypoint. I glanced at the chart, noted the waypoint Evans had plotted when we arrived three weeks before, and eye-balled the route from our position to the waypoint (Figure 15-1). Satisfied that the course was clear of danger, I read out the bearing and distance to Evans. He started sailing toward the second waypoint. A few minutes later the depth alarm went off and our depth dropped, reading 20 feet, 15, 12 . . .

As had been the case all week, the water was cloudy with sediment from strip-mining, the island's biggest in-

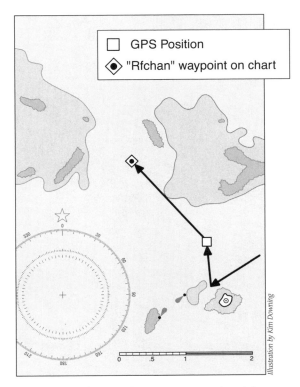

Figure 15-1. When I gave Evans a course to steer through the reef, this is how the chart of the area appeared to me.

dustry. We were surrounded by choppy seas and white-caps from the windy conditions. We could not see any changes in water color that would indicate shoal water or the deep-water channel. There was an islet about a half-mile to starboard and a stake to port, the kind commonly used in the Pacific islands to indicate shoal water, that was not shown on the chart. I raced below and checked our GPS position on the French chart only to find that it showed us still in deep water. The depth was continuing to drop, and Evans was calling for me to tell him which way to turn. Between us, we had just made four major navigational errors, any one of which could have cost us the boat (Figure 15-2).

After our New Caledonia misadventure, Evans and I created 10 best navigational practices to ensure that we used the GPS wisely and prudently.

1. *Know how accurate your GPS fix is.* When you push that small position button on your GPS and look at the screen that precisely declares "You are exactly . . . here!" keep in mind that a GPS fix is not a statement of fact. Just as a sextant sight gives you a line of position and three sights give you a "cocked hat" within which you *most likely* are, the GPS fix is a statement of probability.

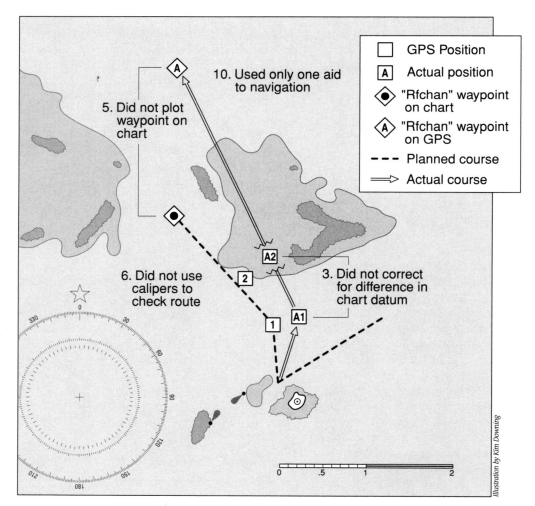

Figure 15-2. This is the actual situation when we were between Amédée lighthouse and Nouméa. The four major navigational errors are highlighted.

For the GPS, unlike the sextant, the degree of accuracy of any given fix is known with some certainty. GPS technology is capable of providing a position accurate to within 10 or 15 meters 95 percent of the time—but *your* GPS does not offer such accuracy. It doesn't because the Department of Defense purposely degrades the signal for nonmilitary use under a system called *selective availability* (SA). Thanks to SA, the position your GPS shows so absolutely is correct to 100 meters 95 percent of the time and to 300 meters for the remaining 5 percent of the time. That means that *any* fix that your GPS receiver shows you *might* be off by as much as two-tenths of a mile. And don't expect it to tell you that it's not sure!

To remove selective availability and to make GPS more accurate for coastal sailing, the Coast Guard has been installing land-based differential stations for U.S. waters over the last few years. These stations broadcast a correction factor to the GPS by comparing their known position to the position the satellites provide. For a GPS that is set up to receive differential signals, position accuracy should approach 6 to 10 meters 95 percent of the time. If you have been sailing in U.S. waters using differential GPS, you have most likely gotten used to things being pretty much exactly where you expected them to be. Once you leave differential GPS areas, be prepared for the margin of error on your fixes to be an order of magnitude higher.

There has been discussion of "turning off" selective availability and allowing everyone access to the higher quality fixes. Yet even after allowing for the issue of SA and the availability of differential GPS, not all GPS fixes are created equal. For a two-dimensional fix, your GPS receiver determines its position by triangulating on the signals received from 3 or more of the 24 satellites in the U.S. Department of Defense's (DOD) Navstar Positioning System. The best satellite geometry results when these satellites are located in different quadrants of the sky. As with a sextant, a GPS's margin of error increases if the "celestial bodies" are grouped in one part of the sky. While your GPS will select the most favorable satellite geometry, the most desirable satellites may not be available and the result will be a less accurate fix. Questionable fixes can occur in areas of the world that are not as well covered by satellites or where the angles to the satellites are poor, such as in the higher latitudes.

Even with perfect satellite geometry, signal degradation can still occur between the satellite and the GPS receiver due to a variety of atmospheric and equipment-related conditions. This degradation reduces the accuracy of the fix. Good GPS receivers monitor and display the quality of the signal. Some provide information on both satellite geometry and signal strength. When total quality falls below a certain level, many GPS models display an icon and/or sound an alarm. When rounding South Africa and sailing in remote areas, it was not unusual when the signal was degraded for us to see this icon every 15 or 20 minutes for a few minutes or more. It was also not unusual for the GPS to show us doing 20 knots over the bottom or to change the reported position by several miles within a few minutes.

Sailors in American waters who have a GPS that can receive differential signals can use the GPS to sail to a buoy or navigate through a channel 95 percent of the time. This level of reliance on the GPS can result in disaster in other parts of the world. When sailing in foreign waters, GPS accuracy will be significantly lower than it is in American waters. You must use other aids to navigation to verify your position near land.

2. *Know how accurate your charts are.* The best fix in the world means nothing if it's plotted on an inaccurate chart. Charts for many parts of the world are based on surveys taken when the area was first discovered, and they have been sporadically updated since. When we left in 1992, we purchased the most up-to-date charts available. But many charts informed us that the information was "Based on original survey of 1878." Further investigation often revealed a comment like the one we found on our chart for the Marquesas Islands: "Charted positions cannot be corrected for electronic navigation." On Nuku Hiva in the Marquesas, our charted position was one mile south of our GPS position in Taiohae Bay. Just a few miles down the coast in Daniel's Bay, it was one mile north of our GPS position. Our DMA chart for the Pacific—the most up-to-date available when we left in 1992—included several comments like the one for Palmerston Island: "Rep[orted] to lie 3 miles SE."

Some charts contain correction factors for electronic navigation. When you are working with such a chart, make sure you adjust all the waypoints before entering them in the GPS. Also make sure you adjust your GPS position when you plot it on the chart. In many places, correction factors are a few seconds. In some areas of the Pacific and Indian oceans, correction factors were several minutes, which translates to several nautical miles.

Until you know with certainty the accuracy of the chart you are using, do not trust it in conjunction with your GPS. If you have any question regarding the accuracy of your chart when you are close to land at night, heave-to at least 10 miles offshore and wait for daylight. Almost all of the boats that were lost during the course of our circumnavigation were lost closing with land at night. Some were trying to enter reef passes in the dark—something they would never have considered had they not had a GPS aboard. No matter how good your GPS position is, it cannot make up for an inaccurate chart.

3. *Set GPS to match chart datum.* Different charts make different assumptions about the shape of the world. These assumptions are captured in the chart datum on which the chart is based. Using French charts in New Caledonia, we found that the difference in chart datum created up to a 0.2-nautical mile difference between our GPS and our charted position. This is something I failed to take into account in the above incident, both when I set up the route and when I went below to check our position.

Correction factors may be given for adjusting chart datum to match your GPS configuration. For example, the DMA chart for Martha's Vineyard to Block Island reads, "The horizontal reference datum of this chart is North American Datum 1983 (NAD 83) and for charting purposes is considered equivalent to the World Geodetic System 1984 (WGS 84). Geographic positions referred to the North American Datum of 1927 must be corrected an average of 0.376" northward and 1.838" eastward to agree with this chart." Most GPS models can be set to accept different chart datum and should be adjusted when switching to charts that use different datum. If the GPS does not have this feature or you choose not to change the chart datum, waypoints and positions must be adjusted by the correction, if it is specified. Otherwise, factor in an additional safety margin and rely on alternative aids to navigation.

4. *Place waypoints in clear water.* After spending three blissful weeks in the Tuamotus, we were on our way to Tahiti and civilization. We left Tahanea atoll and skirted its northern edge before turning to go through the pass between it and neighboring Faaite. I put in a waypoint to indicate the easternmost edge of Faaite's outlying reef. I then plotted our position on the chart to be sure we were staying off the reef. The day was blisteringly hot, and the wind vane was steering. I was plotting our position below and checking above every 10 minutes as we worked our way through the channel. When I came on deck for my third check I was horrified to see breaking water and the emerald green of Faaite's inner lagoon not more than 100 yards off our bow. The current in the pass had swept us to the west. That combined with some chart error and some changes in the reef itself meant that we were now approaching my waypoint by way of the reef! (See Figure 15-3.)

While the first lesson from this experience is the importance of a proper watch, the second lesson is to place your waypoint where you want the boat to go—not on the buoy or reef you wish to steer around. Your selection of a waypoint should reflect the visibility and your chart's accuracy, as well as the current and tidal conditions. Be particularly careful about selecting waypoints near reefs. These living organisms grow and change, and charts cannot be expected to be totally accurate.

5. *Double-check all waypoints and plot them on the chart.* Unless you are working with an electronic chart plotter, creating routes in your GPS involves entering waypoints. This tedious and time-consuming process demands complete accuracy. On passage from the Canaries to the Caribbean, we were on what we considered to be the final countdown for a long passage—the point when the distance to go had dropped below four digits. Yet as we got closer, the distance to go did not seem to match the chart. I reviewed the GPS waypoints to find that the longitude for Antigua was off by two degrees, which meant another day of sailing. In that case, the result was minor disappointment. The result could have been significantly worse if we had been off by two minutes going up the Great Barrier Reef.

After this incident, we always had a second person review each waypoint to be sure that a simple inputting error had not occurred. Be just as careful with waypoints you get from other boats or from guides. It pays to plot the waypoint on your chart and make sure it looks like it is where it should be. Even then, proceed with caution. Given the issues with accuracy already discussed, your GPS and theirs will not give the exact same reading in the same place.

In the New Caledonia incident, one of my biggest mistakes was using a stored waypoint without double-checking that the waypoint was at the spot marked on the chart. It turned out that Evans had changed the position of the waypoint, which he called "rfchan." One of his mistakes was not updating the chart to reflect that change or warning me that the chart was no longer accurate. When I took our current position and checked the route to the waypoint, I was in fact using the wrong waypoint. If I had simply glanced at the waypoint's coordinates on the GPS, I would have realized that it was several miles away from the position shown on the chart.

6. Plot every route between two waypoints using calipers. When I set up the route between our current position and what I thought was the waypoint that Evans wanted me to use, I used my fingers to find our current position on the chart and then "eye-balled" the course to the marked waypoint. Later, when I went below to try to figure out where we were, I again used my fingers to locate our position. Given the scale of most charts and the width of a finger, the error from such sloppy navigation can easily be several tenths of a mile—much too near land. When creating a route on the GPS, plot all waypoints using calipers and draw in the route with a straight edge. Make absolutely sure that the proposed route keeps you clear of all dangers after factoring in the accuracy of the chart.

7. Use cross-track error to judge your position. Like many cruisers, we had a GPS repeater in the cockpit that we used frequently. The repeater allows a crewmember to maintain a proper watch while having access to the GPS information normally available only in the nav station. But we soon found that navigating with bearing and distance could be dangerous. Cross-track error offers greater accuracy when navigating from the cockpit.

We rarely manage to steer the exact course the navigator gives us. Even the best helmsman cannot steer a perfect course if current or leeway cause the track through the water to vary significantly from the compass course. If the course to steer to the waypoint

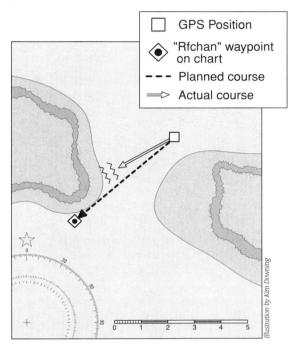

Figure 15-3. By putting my waypoint on the reef, I left us no safety margin for leeway from wind or current.

changes by a few degrees, a change that might not even be noticed by the helmsman, a grounding can result. Given a route through reef- or rock-strewn waters, the key issue becomes the width of the track you can steer and still avoid all major dangers (Figure 15-4). When sailing a course, keeping cross-track error to zero ensures the boat is in safe water.

8. Don't forget the reality checks. Electronic chart plotters have several advantages over GPS and chart navigation. They remove the errors from entering waypoints discussed above, and they plot your course more accurately than you can do using calipers and a straight edge. But they further insulate you from the sense that an electronic position is *virtual* reality, not reality.

Pilots can get so fixated on their instruments that they forget to look around to verify their actual position. With electronic chart plotting interfaced to the GPS, you can start to believe you have more information inside than out. As navigator, don't be seduced into believing that accuracy is 100 percent. These systems are subject to

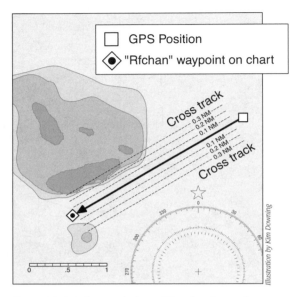

Figure 15-4. In this case, the boat will be safe as long as the cross-track stays below 0.1 nautical miles.

the same limitations as GPS and paper charts. Your helmsman cannot see the chart, and it is very difficult to communicate subtleties of waypoints or landmarks. Don't forget that the only reality check is *reality*. Go out into the cockpit and visually confirm each waypoint.

9. *Always have a backup.* Two days to go to our landfall on our first offshore passage from Newport to Bermuda, we saw a sail ahead traveling at a right angle to our course and watched as the boat hove-to to wait for us. On the VHF, the skipper's first question was, "Do you know where you are?" He had lost his GPS a day out of Montauk and had been "sort of dead reckoning" to Bermuda ever since. While he had a sextant aboard, he had no idea how to use it.

This was not the last time that we were asked for a position at sea by someone who had chosen to rely on GPS alone. In some cases, the unit itself had failed. More frequently, the yacht's electrical system had been compromised. We lost our GPS between St. Helena and Antigua in a lightning storm. Static electricity had shorted out the antennae and damaged the electronics in the GPS. While we had a handheld backup, we chose to navigate with our sextant for the 3,500 nautical miles to Antigua, confirming our position with the GPS once every few days.

If some of the navigation satellites were ever compromised or if the entire system went down, your GPS would be useless. A systematic failure in a particular model of GPS sounds far-fetched, but it has happened. While we were out, a major manufacturer's GPS units failed simultaneously from a software programming error. Voyagers were sending them back to the factory for months afterwards. The millennium effect (in which programs using only two digits to designate the year will cause software problems when the year changes from '99 to '00) may also create problems on some units. Don't be left without any backup in these situations.

For extended coastal cruising, a handheld GPS is sufficient for backup. For offshore passagemaking, it is not prudent to make your handheld your only backup due to the battery life on a handheld, the possibility that the unit has corroded while you have relied on your primary GPS, and the potential for a systemic failure. Good seamanship (and common sense) dictate that you have a sextant and know how to use it!

10. *Don't rely on only one aid to navigation.* This age-old rule is repeated on every chart and in every sailing book, and it is just as valid today as when the first mariners set sail! When entering harbors on volcanic islands, our GPS sometimes lost one or more satellites when they were blocked by the high cliffs. When the GPS switched between satellites, we sometimes lost our signal for five minutes or more. You should always have more than one way to ascertain where you are, and you should exercise this alternate method when you are navigating anywhere near land.

In the case of our New Caledonia incident, I could have taken a bearing on the lighthouse and another on the end of the island to get a rough fix. I could have also used the depthsounder readings to determine where we were. But I was so focused on getting the answer from the GPS that I didn't even consider the obvious alternatives. This incident taught us how dependent we had both become on the GPS and forced us to rethink our navigational practices. Afterwards, we regularly took bearings to confirm our position—both to foster independence from push-button positions and to practice our coastal navigation skills.

Not relying on one aid to navigation also includes not depending on someone else's instructions and anchor light to enter a harbor at night. If we did decide to enter a harbor in poor visibility, we did so only if we had multiple aids to navigation in addition to the GPS: good leading lights, the radar, and the depth sounder. In most situations, the last piece of equipment we trusted was the GPS. By the end of our trip, our relationship with that marvel of modern technology was based on wary skepticism that had been reinforced by many incidents where we had grown overconfident in its prognostications. The GPS is a wondrous aid to navigation, but it is only an aid. It can never replace the navigator who is using it.

Protecting the boat in port

There is an old saying that sailing is easy as long as you don't hit anything. The chances of hitting something (or being hit by something) increase radically as you approach land. You are often entering a strange harbor when you are at your lowest ebb—tired from many days of little sleep, anxious about the accuracy of your charts, and overwhelmed by freighter and ship traffic in the vicinity. Once in port, your boat can be damaged maneuvering in restricted areas or while anchored in a variety of weather conditions.

To protect your boat, consider in advance the risks and how you can minimize them. Don't assume that port represents a refuge and an end to all dangers. View every port with a sailor's suspicion of land. Have an escape hatch ready in the event of unfavorable weather and a game plan for managing contingencies when you are moving around in port.

Reef pass entry

We made landfall on New Caledonia on a moonless night after an unpleasant eight days hard on the wind from New Zealand. We were tired, the boat needed to be aired out, and we wanted nothing more than to be in port with all of the motion and noise behind us. When we had left New Zealand, everyone had assured us that there were excellent leading lights through the barrier reef and right into the main anchorage at Nouméa. Given that information, we had planned on making a night entry, if necessary. When we saw the loom of the Amédée lighthouse at dusk, we thought that we would be anchored and sleeping soundly well before daybreak.

As we approached, we started to distinguish the leading lights. Yet things were not as we thought they should be. The flash pattern on the lighthouse did not match the pattern described on the most recent charts, and we couldn't locate the third light, which should have been visible. Though the leading lights lined up on the correct bearing, we felt uneasy. According to the GPS, we had closed to within five miles of the reef. Still, things did not resolve themselves. We discussed our options—though not very logically given how tired we were and how much we wanted to get into port. Very reluctantly, we decided that we were not willing to close with land under the circumstances.

We headed out on a reciprocal course to the bearing for the pass entrance until the GPS indicated that we were about eight miles offshore. There, we hove-to and stood watches until daylight. When we went in the next day, we were exactly where we thought we had been. We could see nothing amiss and attributed our concerns of the night before to being overtired. "Next time we'll trust the lights," we decided. When we arrived in Cairns, Australia, after a 10-day passage from New Caledonia, we heard about another cruising boat who sailed from New Zealand and tried to go into Nouméa at night. They ended up on the reef; the mother and daughter made it into the liferaft, and the father was lost. We never questioned our judgment after that incident.

One of Murphy's Laws of Offshore Voyaging states that landfall always seems to be made in the middle of the night with no moon. Though the odds are against it, we really did make about 60 percent of our landfalls at night, two-thirds of them without any moonlight because of weather or the phase of the moon. On any passage of a few days or longer, chance decides when you arrive.

While you can enter well-charted harbors with good leading lights at night if you have properly functioning radar, it is almost always more prudent to wait for daylight. But don't heave-to in shipping lanes or areas with freighter traffic. The restricted space and slower speeds of a channel entrance make freighters less maneuverable. The clutter of buoys and big ships near the entrance to most major ports will make it difficult to pick up your radar image. Enter the harbor or get further offshore and out of the shipping traffic.

Never enter reef passes on deserted atolls at night. One couple who had been voyaging for 12 years and were in the midst of their second circumnavigation lost their boat trying to enter one of the Tuamotus atolls at night. No matter how much experience you have, the combination of living reef and changing currents can render the most up-to-date chart useless. Use caution and common sense: Get plenty of sea room, heave-to, and wait for daylight.

During the day, coral visibility depends on good sunlight. In addition to a clear sky, the sun needs to be as close to directly overhead as possible. In the tropics, that means arranging your schedule so you navigate coral waters between 10 A.M. and 4 P.M. In the coral waters of the Pacific, you will learn to read the water color with great accuracy. In many areas, you will be able to see coral heads near the surface from a quarter-mile away because the water is so clear. Deep blue water signifies safety no matter how deep your draft. Where the water takes on its first green hues, expect 15 to 20 feet. Any trace of yellow or brown means danger for any boat. You will learn exactly what shade to expect at your favorite anchoring depth.

The following tips and tricks make reading coral water easier:

■ *Polarizing sunglasses.* Unless you have tried them, you can't imagine how much they improve your ability to pick out the color changes associated with coral. Even in less-than-perfect light, you can detect shading in the water not visible to the naked eye. It pays to invest in a good pair. In the almost uncharted interior of many atolls, they are your best, and in some cases your only, protection against a close encounter of the reef kind.

■ *Elevation.* To best see coral, you need to be looking straight down through the water, not across the surface. Getting above deck level improves visibility, even when the sun isn't at the perfect angle. While a few boats used ratlines, we found that standing on our bow pulpit gave us enough height to see about 100 yards farther than we could see from deck level.

■ *Surface indications.* In light winds, you can navigate by the small wavelets that form over the shallow coral. In windy conditions with bad light (for example, if you are trying to leave a coral atoll before an approaching front hits), you can detect shallow water by a break in the wave pattern. This often takes the form of an area that appears calmer than the surrounding water, as if oil had been spilled on the waves. We have successfully navigated 10 miles out of a coral lagoon using these signs. But practice before you try this in earnest—and don't do it if you don't have to.

Untenable anchorages

When we went through the Tuamotu Archipelago on our way to Tahiti from the Marquesas, we took a more southerly route than most people take. Most of our "class," as the group of boats crossing the Pacific each year is called, took the normal northerly route that skirts most of the Tuamotus and visited the largest and most accessible atoll, Rangiroa. As in many of these reef-encircled lagoons, the primary anchorage offers wind and wave protection from one direction only. If the wind shifts when a front comes through, anchored yachts are subject to the full fetch of the inner lagoon, which in the case of Rangiroa can be up to 40 miles.

About the time we arrived in Tahiti, such a front came through. The weather services that cover the area had not predicted it, and the winds on the leading edge were severe and gusting well over 50 knots. About a dozen boats were anchored in the atoll at Rangiroa when the front came through just after dark one night. We knew three of them quite well and talked to them after to find out what had happened.

None of the boats could make for open water with the change in weather. The atolls must be navigated in good light when the uncharted reef patches are visible. The passes are unmarked except for a few stakes hardly visible during the day. Most of the boats had been closely monitoring the weather and planned on making for sea when a front was forecast, but they got no warning.

One 40-foot German boat, its bow pitching up and down in the 4-foot chop, snapped their 5/16-inch high test chain after their snubber broke. They spent the rest of the night motoring against the wind and waves to hold their position. A 30-foot boat started to drag. In the process of trying to retrieve their anchor, they fouled their prop with the anchor line. As they were slowly being forced back onto the reef, friends of theirs on a 40-foot boat nearby let out enough scope to fall back and tie them alongside, then winched both boats away from the reef using the anchor windlass. The only boat that didn't make it through the night was a 22-meter steel Jongert that dragged onto the reef at the height of the storm. The boat was hauled off the reef by local villagers and yachties over the course of the next week, and the dents were pounded out in Tahiti a few weeks later.

Any time you anchor in an unprotected anchorage with navigational hazards you run a risk if the weather deteriorates. Both situations occur together infrequently. If an anchorage does not offer protection from frontal winds, it is usually open enough so you can plan a course that will take you safely out of the harbor to open water. In a handful of the most wonderful places along the milk-run route, places like the Tuamotus atolls and Cocos Keeling, you will be at risk in an unforecast frontal passage. You will have to decide if you are comfortable taking that risk.

In-port collisions

We spent almost our entire stay in Bermuda on the hard repairing the damage to our centerboard from a storm we had encountered on our passage. While we were there, a series of two- and three-day gales assaulted the island, one after the other. On our third day in St. George's harbor, we had the VHF on and tuned in to Bermuda Harbour Radio. We heard an exchange between the traffic controllers and a cruise ship. The cruise ship had been pinned down by weather for two days and was late departing for New York. Bermuda Harbour Radio asked the ship to stay in the harbor for another few hours, at which time they expected the wind to drop. As they explained to the cruise ship, large vessels were not supposed to navigate the narrow cut leading out of St. George's harbor in anything over 15 knots of wind. In the cut, vessels would be beam-on to the wind and could become very hard to maneuver. The wind was a steady 25 knots with higher gusts.

We were surprised to hear the captain of the cruise ship insist that he was going to leave. Less than an hour later, we heard distress calls on the VHF. The cruise ship had attempted to leave the anchorage, and when they got into the narrow cut with the full force of the wind on their beam, they were swept sideways— right down on the yacht anchorage just to the north of the cut. Their thrusters were on full blast in an attempt

to maneuver back into the channel. The first yacht they hit was a 32-foot steel cruising boat with an experienced couple aboard.

The couple heard the commotion and came on deck to see the cruise ship bearing down on them. They tried to let go of their anchor and motor to safety, but the cruise ship's powerful thrusters were pulling their boat under the ship. Their chain was bar tight; they could not get enough slack to free the anchor from the windlass, even under full throttle. They were pinned against the side of the ship for 45 agonizing minutes during which their topsides, masthead, and stanchions were damaged. Two tug boats finally maneuvered the cruise ship away from the yacht anchorage. After their ordeal, the couple brought their boat to the boatyard where *Silk* was on the hard. The wife said tearfully, "You expect storms at sea, but this situation was so much more terrifying because we were helpless."

I wish this were an isolated incident, the likes of which we never heard of again. But we heard of similar situations far more frequently than I would ever have guessed. In Raratonga in the Cook Islands, about a dozen cruising boats were med-moored to a wall in two layers. An out-of-control barge almost careened into some of the outermost boats. Only the fast thinking and heroic actions of a couple of yachties saved several boats from losing the first 6 feet of their bows. In Phuket, Thailand, while at anchor in the designated yacht anchorage, some good friends of ours on a Hallberg-Rassy were rammed by a fishing boat. The repairs took many months, and the battle to get compensation from the fishermen took even longer.

As the number of yachts increases, designated anchorages are often filled to overflowing. Many shipping lanes that once included a large margin of error now run right along the edge of these anchorages. Cruise ships are becoming more common in remote destinations, and their space requirements for maneuvering further restrict areas where yachts are safe. Most island nations now have ferries to outer islands, and these also require space for turning around and maneuvering up to the dock. As harbors become more crowded, these types of accidents are likely to increase.

So what can be done? Being aware of the problem is half the battle. Our friends on the steel boat in Bermuda never thought twice about anchoring along the deep water channel. While the following suggestions cannot absolutely guarantee the safety of your boat, they should reduce the odds of a serious incident.

■ *Avoid large shipping ports.* Try not to spend any more time than you have to in ports where fishing boats and freighters congregate, unless there is a designated area for yachts isolated from traffic. In most places, you must clear customs in the same anchorage and sometimes on the same wharf as the big ships, so you cannot avoid this situation altogether. But once you are official, find another harbor without big-ship traffic to hole up in—even if it means a walk or a cab ride back into town.

■ *Don't anchor along big-boat channels.* If you can't avoid being in the vicinity of big ships, at least avoid anchoring along the big-ship channels. In most harbors, the channels used by ships, fishing boats, and ferries are clearly marked on the chart. If you come into a harbor where there is an obvious area clear of anchored boats with a dock at the end of it, assume that a local ferry will be coming in and out at some point and anchor as far away as possible. If in doubt, ask someone who is already anchored to suggest a quiet area.

■ *Use anchor lights if boats may be maneuvering around you at night.* If there could be activity in the harbor at night (for instance, if there is a large fleet of local fishing boats or a channel for a ferry), leave your anchor light on, even in a designated anchorage. A little light goes a long way toward protecting you against the possibility of a nighttime collision.

Marina maneuvering

New Caledonia was one disaster after another for us. Another incident that occurred in our eventful three weeks there involved maneuvering in a marina.

Most cruising boats do not maneuver particularly well in tight quarters. The skeg-hung rudder and fully protected aperture on many traditional cruising boats create a tremendous amount of turbulence that makes these boats sluggish and difficult to steer at slow speeds. We had our share of excitement aboard *Silk,* but for the most part, the incidents were not in the serious category. A layer or two of fiberglass from our boat or someone else's was all that was ever at risk. But in some situations, as demonstrated by this incident in

New Caledonia, the lack of maneuverability can be truly dangerous.

We had to take on fuel in Nouméa, so we went to have a look at the fuel dock the day before we fueled up. The fuel dock was located in a tight area at the end of the marina, surrounded by rip-rap breakwalls, and oriented perpendicular to the prevailing winds. We decided to get to the fuel dock as early as possible the next morning and be gone before the winds came up.

We got to the dock and tied up by the 8:00 A.M. opening time. Someone showed up at 9:30, and we weren't fueled until after 10:00. The wind had come up in the meantime, and it was blowing 25 knots on our beam, pinning us to the dock. We used a springline to try to swing the bow out into the wind as we motored off the dock. We thought we had gotten the bow through the wind, but as soon as the springline was released, the wind pushed us right back down on the dock. I was on the bow desperately trying to fend us off, and Evans was at the helm trying to swing the bow back into the wind. We bounced along the dock for a minute, and then we were out of dock and *Silk* was blowing down on the curving rip-rap breakwater of the marina. As I stood on the bow and watched concrete slabs coming up to meet us, I felt the same utter helplessness I'd felt once before on someone else's boat as we drifted down onto rocks and ended up aground. Using a full throttle and every one of our 44 horsepower, Evans just managed to pivot *Silk* away from the breakwall with less than a foot to spare.

A few months later in Gove, Australia, we found ourselves in exactly the same situation. This time, we put out a bow anchor at a 60-degree angle as we came into the dock. When the time came to leave, we used our windlass to help get our bow through the wind and get ourselves off the dock without incident.

If your boat performs sluggishly at slow speeds, take a good look at what you need to do on land before you approach from the water. Avoid maneuvering in windy conditions. Learn how to force your boat through the wind within her length plus a little before you head off to sea. Pick a day when the wind is 25 knots or so and find a place where the water is relatively flat and you have some room. Figure out if your boat travels more easily in a bow-first or stern-first direction and find out what techniques work best. You will probably be using all your engine's

Fire aboard

Fire is one of the most serious risks any sailor faces. Though most of us no longer sail aboard wooden boats, the flammability of fiberglass almost equals that of wood, and the noxious gases can kill almost as quickly as the flames. Fires are among the most preventable onboard emergency. An electrical short caused all three of the fires that we heard about, as well as the one that we experienced.

Our fire happened at sea, but it could have happened just as easily while we were tied up in a marina. We were on passage from the Canaries to the Caribbean at approximately 18°N and 50°W with a little over 500 miles to go to Antigua. It was the 21st day of a light-air passage. The wind had died completely, leaving us to roll in a big swell. We decided to run the engine for a few hours to charge up the batteries and look for some more wind. After the engine had been running for an hour or so, I went below and smelled a faint chemical smell. I called Evans below but he couldn't smell anything. Still bothered, I tried to find the cause. I opened up the engine compartment, searched the galley area around the stove, and explored around the navigation station. Finally, I went out into the cockpit and opened up the cockpit locker. An acrid white smoke came pouring out. Evans turned off the engine immediately while I grabbed the fire extinguisher from the galley. An inspection revealed that the solar panel had shorted out. The boatyard that had installed the panel had led the wires directly to the battery bus bar without the protection of a fuse. The short had started a smoldering electrical fire.

The full magnitude of the danger did not sink in until after it was all over. The physical damage was slight. We were saved from a major fire by the fact that we did not carry gasoline in the cockpit locker.

We both had nightmares afterwards about a serious fire aboard—something that had seemed a remote possibility until I opened the cockpit locker that day. When we reached Antigua, we went over every inch of our electrical system looking for shorts and adding extra fuses.

In St. Thomas, we were docked across from a boat that suffered a serious electrical fire when their battery charger shorted out. The fire could have spread to other boats at the dock, except the owners were eating in a restaurant that overlooked the harbor and saw the fire as it caught on the sail covers. But by the time the owners and others got the fire out with extinguishers, the boat was a total loss and smoke damage had ruined most of the couple's possessions.

To minimize the risk of a fire aboard, check that *all* wiring is fused, no matter who has installed it. Do not store gasoline anywhere near electrical wires, motors, or batteries. Install a normal smoke alarm in the engine compartment and near the galley. Many boats don't take this simple precaution. An alarm may give you enough warning so you can react before the fire gets out of control. In our case, it almost certainly would have warned us before my nose did.

Fires can also occur in the galley or around the exhaust system of the engine or generator. We didn't know anyone who had fires in these areas, but it pays to be prepared. Water will not extinguish fires fueled by grease, oil, diesel, or even fiberglass (once it starts to melt the resin). Carry several dry-type fire extinguishers and make sure they are properly maintained. Boats under 40 feet should carry at least two—one near the engine, one in the galley (unless the engine one is within reach), and one more near a forward bulkhead. Larger boats should carry three or more.

capacity to get the bow through the wind, alternating between forward and reverse at full power.

Managing local risks

Since our return, we have been asked hundreds of times about theft, piracy, bribery, and so on. When we were approached by people with their hands out, they were trying to give, not take. I can count the exceptions on one hand. After five years in the business world, our three years of voyaging restored our faith in humanity. This was one of the greatest joys of the cruising life, and one that changed us both dramatically.

But to suggest that anyone should approach the world with total trust and naiveté would be as much of a disservice as overstressing the less generous side of human nature. Like most things, interactions with others over the course of your trip will be a balance of good and bad. We found the balance far more to the good than we expected. That doesn't mean we didn't use common sense and avoid areas where there were problems. Use the cruising grapevine to identify and define local risks. Then make an informed decision about whether to visit a given area or not and know how to behave when you get there.

Of the topics that fall under local risks, no one ever asks us about the only real threat we faced. We encountered a volatile political situation in several countries. In one case, we could have been at significant risk. Part of your pretrip planning should be to educate yourself about the political situation in a country before you arrive. Deciding to leave if things get crazy is as valid as leaving because the weather deteriorates.

Volatile political situations

New Caledonia, one of many French colonies in the Pacific, was in many ways our nemesis. If we hadn't already been cruising for two years, the incidents that we went through there might have made us quit. The last, and perhaps the most serious, occurred after all the others described in this chapter.

After cruising around the island for several weeks, we returned to Nouméa. We tied up in the marina and went to bed early. We were awakened close to midnight by someone knocking loudly on the hull.

I put on a bathrobe and stumbled out to find the skip-per of the boat across the dock from us. "I thought you'd want to know that all of the other boats have left," he said. While Evans and I had slept peacefully, a huge group of dump trucks and their drivers had congregated in the open area near the market. They had started to vandalize a government building just behind the marina office, barely 200 yards off the dock to which we were tied. A full-scale riot was in the making. As we talked, several other boats left.

I went below and Evans and I talked over our options. Evans's solution was simple—"Let's have a glass of sherry." Neither of us wanted to anchor out, and we both were convinced that the men would stay with their trucks. So we sat and sipped sherry while the sounds of a decent-sized riot grew outside.

For the next several hours, one or the other of us watched the goings on. We finally slept again for a few hours near dawn. By 7:30 A.M., boats were returning to the marina. We went ashore and saw the damage—a half-dozen downed light poles, concrete fence supports and the fence itself bashed to the ground, a corner off the guard house, piles of gravel and dirt on the lawn of the building, and a few smashed cars in the street. More frightening, in a sense, were the black-clothed riot police now stationed discreetly around the square.

We learned that the government had decided to make the mines more competitive by breaking the trucking union. The truck drivers owned their own trucks, bought at government instigation, and now they had huge debts to pay on them. They were understandably upset: no jobs, no way to pay for the worthless trucks. That Friday morning, they agreed to wait until Monday to begin negotiations. Over the weekend that followed that wild night, more and more French troops arrived along with a battleship from Tahiti. By Monday afternoon, the lines were drawn. That was when we decided to get out of there. I made the mistake of a last run to the post office and barely got back to the boat through the police cordon. We anchored off for the night—a night punctuated by gunshots and helicopters flying overhead—and left at first light.

In our experience, limited though it is, the administrations of the French islands are very good at keeping such situations contained and out of the media's eye. But that means you won't have much warning before the fact. We became aware of the significant tensions against the government only after we arrived in New Caledonia. After we left, we could find no mention of any of this in the press. We scanned the airwaves and bought newspapers in Cairns when we made landfall, but we came up with nothing.

To determine if there are political problems in areas along your route, talk to others who have been there, follow the SSCA's bulletins, and talk to the U.S. consulate wherever you are about the area you wish to visit. Outside of the French colonies, general news reports offer good insights—although we found that any violence was often overstated. If the political situation looks unstable, think long and hard about whether or not the visit is worth the risk. If you arrive and find that things are not as they should be, get the boat ready to leave again at a moment's notice.

Theft

Theft was a problem for us in only a handful of places. These locations were well known within the cruising community, right down to specific harbors or beaches where repeated thefts had occurred. For the most part, theft was limited to stealing outboards and dinghies. Along with money and some electronic gear, these are the only items voyagers have local thieves might really value. Keeping dinghies and outboards locked and secured, even to the extent of taking them on board at night, was the major precaution in areas where dinghy theft was common.

Many of us did not even bother to lock our boats throughout much of the world. If anchored off a village in Tonga or Fiji, the entire village would view it as a disgrace if anything were taken. But the relative wealth of yachties can itself create a problem. We were asked several times by local people how long they would have to work on their taro or cassava plantation to be able to buy a boat like ours. The answer, or the inability to answer, reflected an unbridgeable gulf between our cultures. While we were building friendships, there were times when we were aware that we were also raising uncomfortable questions for those who shared their lives with us. Thus, the problem of theft is likely to increase as voyaging becomes more popular and island villages become less remote.

To avoid theft, avoid situations where you could be a victim. That starts by not visiting areas where theft is a real problem, where actual incidents have been reported by several reliable sources. Beyond that, we did lock the boat and often locked our dinghy at the dinghy dock in crowded harbors. Our other precautions, all more or less common sense, included the following:

■ **Use wooden hatchboards when leaving the boat.** When leaving the boat for any period of time or when leaving it in an area where we needed to lock it, we would use our wooden hatchboards instead of our Lexan ones so the electronic goodies in the nav station were not visible from outside.

■ **Strive for a conservative appearance.** Larger, flashier boats are far more likely to be the target of theft than small, unassuming ones. Wearing jewelry or openly carrying cameras ashore will draw attention and can make you a target. The more understated your dress, behavior, and boat, the less likely it is that something will be stolen. Even large boats can be set up so they look workmanlike but not ostentatious. This is another argument for simplicity—our rowing tender without outboard became an unlikely target when surrounded by fancy inflatables with outboards.

■ **Ask port officials for advice on safety and security issues.** In most ports where theft was an issue, we were warned by officials. If you have heard rumors, ask whether there are any problems and what precautions you should take. They will often give the best advice about where to anchor, what areas to avoid ashore, and what items have been targets of recent thefts in the area.

■ **Anchor off if possible.** Unless there is controlled access to the quays or docks, anchoring off is always safer than being tied up alongside. Get to know those anchored near you. If there is a problem with theft in the area, set up a neighborhood watch and agree to challenge anyone who approaches the boats nearby when the owners are ashore.

■ **Leave a dinghy tied off the stern when you are ashore.** A dinghy tied off the stern means someone is home—both to voyaging friends and to would-be thieves. We had friends who kept their dinghy when it wore out and tied that off the stern when they were leaving the boat. Short of keeping a watchdog aboard, this is one of the most effective, least expensive theft prevention measures.

■ *Ask someone to watch the boat for a fee.* In some places, the best way to safeguard your belongings is to pay someone to watch it for you. In the Caribbean, that might mean hiring another yachtie to run your engine and check your batteries while you travel home for a few weeks. If only away for the day, you might pay one of the local "boat boys" a couple of dollars to watch your boat. Consider this as a last resort where boats are common and theft has been reported. Don't offer to pay for safety in a Pacific village where you have been accepted as a guest. You will greatly offend the people who have already promised to protect you and your property.

While most theft occurs in large ports and areas with many cruising boats, there are a few exceptions. Again, these incidents are usually well known in the cruising community. In Madagascar, several yachts were stripped while their owners were ashore. The poverty is so extreme in this country that absolutely anything has value. In Venezuela and Brazil, theft is becoming more serious. But throughout most of the Pacific and Indian Oceans, theft will be the least likely misfortune to befall you as long as you exercise a bit of common sense.

PART IV

SHORTHANDED PASSAGE-MAKING SKILLS

CHAPTER 16 | WEATHER WISDOM

We left on our voyage believing short-term weather forecasting was a science. We returned believing it was an uncertain art. We thought we could get a reliable and accurate forecast for the next 48 hours in any civilized country, but we found that, even where extensive weather services are available, forecasts are not terribly accurate. On shore, a poor forecast will go unnoticed unless it causes you to get wet. Not so at sea!

Weather defines every aspect of life aboard. You do not observe it through a window—you live it. Yet the hands-on understanding of weather has changed remarkably little since shorthanded voyaging boats first set off to sea. Eric Hiscock wrote in *Cruising Under Sail,* "Meteorology is a complex subject and far from being an exact science, and even the experts at meteorological offices with a wealth of information at their disposal frequently make inaccurate forecasts. So the yachtsman, whose observations are limited to the small area of sky within his view and to readings of only one barometer, can hardly expect to be a very reliable weather prophet."

While voyagers now have access to a wealth of data through weather fax or weather reports via SSB, the most accurate and reliable short-term forecasting still comes from observations of wind speed and wind direction, sea state, cloud cover, and barometric pressure. The longer we sailed, the more we realized this.

When we were sailing between the Canaries and the Caribbean, the daily forecast was for Force 4 to 5 from the east for weeks on end. At that time, we were actually experiencing Force 3 or less from every direction but east. At times, weather faxes were not much better. Three friends who were trying to pick a weather

window when leaving Bora Bora got faxes with 24-hour forecasts from three different places (Guam, Australia, and New Zealand). Each fax showed three completely different weather pictures that implied three contradictory strategies (see the sidebar "A tropics example—South Pacific passage" in this chapter).

When forecasting offshore conditions, meteorologists work at a serious disadvantage. There is a paucity of information about actual barometric pressure, wind speed, and wind direction at sea, information that is necessary for interpreting satellite data. By the time a forecast is actually prepared and broadcast, a typical forecast for the next 12 hours can be 6 hours old. In more remote waters, forecasts rebroadcast over a cruising net are received once a day. There, the forecast for the next 12 hours may actually be for the 12 hours just gone by. Even information from weather faxes takes 5 hours or more to prepare and broadcast. Intense low pressure weather systems, however, can develop in 12 to 24 hours. You could already be *in* such a system before you even receive the forecast that predicts it, assuming its presence is detected at all.

In theory, the offshore voyager can make use of weather information in the following ways:

▪ *Voyage planning.* The prudent mariner uses historic information regarding prevailing winds, currents, and the timing of tropical revolving storms to determine the most favorable routes. Understanding global weather patterns doesn't involve forecasting, but it does allow mariners to predict general weather patterns with great accuracy. Weather and voyage planning are considered in the first section of this chapter.

■ *Departure weather window.* When setting off on a passage, sailors try to pick a good weather window. That means favorable winds that will give them a good start toward their destination and moderate conditions that will allow them to acclimate quickly. Given reasonably accurate forecasting corroborated by observed weather signs, picking a departure weather window is easily mastered. This is discussed in the next chapter.

■ *Weather routing.* Voyagers can use weather forecasts to put their boat in a favorable position in relation to the moving weather systems. Ideally, forecasts could help voyagers avoid intense lows and take advantage of strong, favorable winds. Yet, the timeliness and inaccuracy of most forecasts makes them less than useful for the average voyager. Given timely information, offshore racing boats sailing 300+ miles per day and tankers or freighters averaging 500 miles per day can maneuver relative to a system that is moving 600 miles per day. A boat sailing 150 miles per day that receives information that is six hours old cannot position itself with respect to a fast moving low. For these reasons, weather routing is not discussed in this chapter. However, references on reading and interpreting weather charts are included in "Additional resources" in this chapter for those who are interested. Once you have mastered these skills, you'll know enough to try your own weather routing.

■ *Sail-handling decisions.* Sailors want to know how much sail to carry for the next 6 to 12 hours. Most importantly, they want several hours' warning of an impending gale so they can prepare. Given the delay in receiving forecasts at sea, outside information may not be very useful. But barometric pressure, sea state, cloud formations, and wind direction provide all the information necessary for accurate short-term forecasting. This topic is covered extensively in the second section of this chapter.

WORLD WEATHER PATTERNS AND VOYAGE PLANNING

When Evans and I were preparing for our trip, we took a sailing course along the Cornish coast of England. There were three couples and one instructor aboard, and each day one person was the designated "Day Skipper." That person acted as captain and could only be overruled by the instructor, who allowed each of us to make our own mistakes if we were not endangering ourselves or the boat. Our route took us by a peninsula (or a "head" as it is called in England) where the tide ran close to 5 knots for all but a few hours each day. Our Day Skipper plotted our course, made his calculations, and told us that we would have to be ready to leave at 3:30 A.M. His wife protested bitterly, so he delayed our departure until morning light at 5:00 A.M.

The next day, we spent five hours trying to tack around that point. I will never forget the lovely old Cornish lighthouse that stood proudly on the high cliff—the one I grew to hate each time we closed with land and found it on exactly the same bearing! The sea made its point. As sailors, we are at the mercy of the elements. The best we can do is work with the elements and use them to our advantage rather than fight against them.

It is easy to think of the ocean as a trackless wilderness where you can chart your own course and let whim dictate which of the many islands you set your sails for next. In practice, sailing routes are dictated by the temperature differentials across the earth's surface and the earth's rotation. Together these create a natural air circulation that defines the prevailing ocean winds. Deviating from these traditional routes means bucking the prevailing winds and the currents they generate. For those who rely on sail power, the time-honored trade wind routes are still the easiest and fastest way to get from point to point, though not always the shortest.

These routes have their own rhythms—seasonal weather disturbances determine the safest times to be in certain areas—and each ocean has its own cycle of voyaging activity. For example, typhoons or tropical cyclones (as hurricanes are called in the Pacific) form in the southwest Pacific from December to April. Boats tend to leave from the Panama Canal, the U.S. West Coast, or the western coast of Mexico as early as February and as late as April or May to sail 7,000 to 8,000 nautical miles across the belly of the South Pacific and arrive in New Zealand or Australia by November or December. There they wait out the tropical storm season. Then they either return to the Pacific islands or head into the Indian Ocean the following April or May.

Voyage planning begins with an understanding of the winds, currents, and seasonal weather disturbances of each ocean. These factors limit your options. You need to plan the general outline of your route before your voyage even begins. As each new season approaches, you can revisit that general plan to determine the specific route you will follow.

Prevailing winds

Voyage planning starts with a basic understanding of prevailing winds around the globe. At its simplest, air rises at the equator where it receives the most heat from the sun, cools and subsides as it moves northward or southward, and travels back to the equator along the earth's surface (Figure 16-1). This air circulation is altered by the earth's rotation from west to east, which bends the airflow along the planet's surface. While these air movements sound complicated, they resolve themselves into five bands of prevailing

winds whose direction, strength, and consistency vary widely.

■ *Doldrums.* The doldrums lie in a band within 5 to 10 degrees of the equator. You must cross this area if you travel from the Northern Hemisphere to the Southern Hemisphere, or vice versa. This area sits at the convergence of the northern and southern trade wind belts and is properly called the Intertropical Convergence Zone (ITCZ).

The sun's heat on the equator causes the air to rise, creating a predominantly upward airflow and a low pressure trough at the surface. The warm, moist air cools as it rises, creating clouds and squalls. Typical weather in this region includes light and variable winds, frequent squalls with heavy rain, and violent thunderstorms.

The extent and position of the doldrums varies with the season. In February and March, it is just north of the

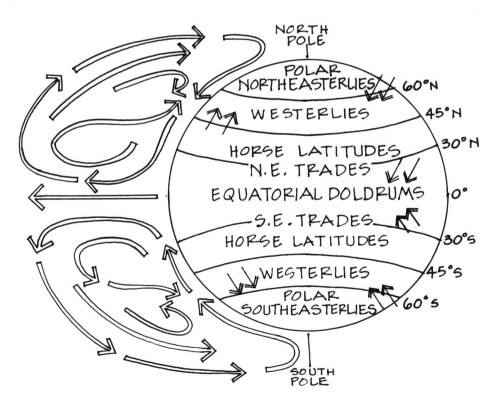

Figure 16-1. The basic circulation of air around the globe determines the prevailing winds at different latitudes.

equator and often only a few miles wide. In July and August, the doldrums can be several hundred miles wide and extend as far as 20 degrees north. In both the South Atlantic and South Pacific Oceans, the doldrums are much narrower in the west than in the east. In the South Atlantic, where there are not tropical revolving storms, sailors therefore prefer to cross the doldrums at their western end and to do so in February or March, when the area is at its narrowest.

■ *Trade winds.* The low pressure in the doldrums created by the constant air circulation upward and outward to the poles pulls air in from the high pressure systems located at about 30 degrees north and south. The rotation of the earth causes this air flow to bend as it crosses the region between the high and the doldrums, giving these winds an easterly component. This creates the fabled northeast and southeast trade winds found in the band from about 10 degrees to 30 degrees north and south. Wind direction is 80 percent constant in this area, though the trades do blow more strongly in winter than in summer.

While low pressure systems from the higher latitudes do not often move into this area, this is the region where hurricanes and typhoons form. The consistent winds and lack of low pressure systems make this the ideal area for voyaging, except during the tropical storm season. The milk run that most circumnavigators sail is situated largely in these latitudes with forays into the higher latitudes to escape the threat of hurricanes or typhoons.

■ *Horse latitudes.* When ships made runs from the Old World to the New World, they often got becalmed in the dead area of the large stationary highs that exist in every ocean. They sometimes had to throw the horses in their cargo overboard as they ran out of water, hence the name. Like the doldrums, this band of high pressure extending from 30 degrees to about 45 degrees north and south is characterized by weak pressure gradients and light, variable winds. In this region—unlike the doldrums, where the air flows upward and condenses—cool air descends and becomes less humid as it warms at lower altitudes. As a result, squalls and thunderstorms occur infrequently and the air is usually fresh and clear. Most of the traditional sailing routes avoid these large areas of light air by traveling from east to west in the

trades and returning from west to east through the band of westerlies north of the horse latitudes.

■ *Westerlies.* North and south of the horse latitudes, the air flows outward from the high pressure toward the low pressure at the poles. The rotation of the earth imparts a westerly set to these winds, resulting in a 20-degree-wide band of prevailing westerly winds. They blow northwest in the Southern Hemisphere and southwest in the Northern Hemisphere. These are the Roaring Forties and Furious Fifties of Southern Ocean fame, where winds are almost as consistent in direction as they are in the trades. In the Northern Hemisphere, large landmasses distort the pattern significantly, so the overall effect is less pronounced. For most voyaging sailors, the westerlies are of most interest when crossing the North Atlantic to Europe.

■ *Polar southeasterlies.* At the poles, the air that rose and headed outward from the equator cools and flows back toward the earth's center. This airflow is again deflected by the earth's rotation so the prevailing winds run easterly and toward the equator from each pole. For most sailors, these are not winds that are of interest!

Trade wind circumnavigations are undertaken from east to west running downwind in the band of prevailing easterlies. The routes of round-the-world races, in an effort to minimize distance by sailing in higher latitudes, travel from west to east in the westerlies. Prevailing winds have long defined the sailor's rules of engagement with the sea. Working with them, instead of against them, will make your voyage more pleasurable.

Ocean currents

The easterly trade winds and the prevailing westerlies in the higher latitudes are defined by the circulation of air around the planet. These bands of air movement in turn define the circulation of water around each ocean. Generally speaking, a weak westerly setting current exists in the trade wind belts and a weak easterly setting current exists in the zone of the prevailing westerlies. These are linked by north-south currents along the landmasses that border each ocean. The actual strength and day-to-day location of these currents varies, depending on the underwater topography, interference from landmasses, and other factors that scientists are only beginning to understand.

Taking the North Atlantic as an example, the northeast trade winds push the water before them in the region from 10 degrees to 30 degrees north, thereby creating the westward flowing North Equatorial Current (Figure 16-2). This is a fairly weak current, generally less than a knot. But when it reaches the shallow Caribbean sea and fetches up against Latin America, it is forced back out through the narrow channel between Cuba and Florida. This is the beginning of the Gulf Stream, one of the strongest ocean currents in the world, which runs along the U.S. East Coast at a 2- to 4-knot rate. The warm water of the tropics that channels through the Gulf Stream makes the Scilly Islands, located some 30 miles southwest of Land's End in England, temperate enough to grow palm trees and orchids.

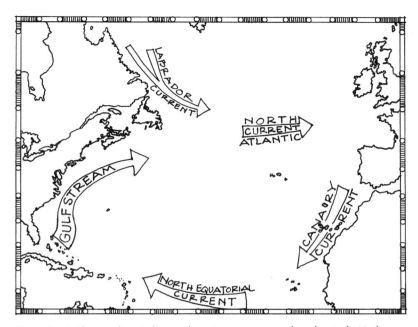

Figure 16-2. The prevailing winds create the major ocean currents, shown here in the North Atlantic.

To the north, the Labrador Current is chased southward by the polar northeasterlies. It divides when it encounters the Gulf Stream. Part of it flows down between the Gulf Stream and the coast. The other part merges with the much-weakened Gulf Stream, gets reinforced by the prevailing westerlies, and becomes the eastward flowing North Atlantic Current. The current's strength is now about a knot or so. Most of this current is deflected southward by the European landmass to become (in succession) the Azores, Portugal, and Canary Currents, each around a knot in strength. The current reaches the trades and turns westward near the Cape Verde Islands, and there the cycle is closed. Apart from some minor countercurrents and meanders, this route defines the general pattern of circulation in the North Atlantic. Similar patterns exist in every ocean of the world. The circulation between the northern and southern portions of the oceans is kept separate by the doldrums.

These ocean currents offer mariners a free gift of extra miles-made-good toward a destination. For example, a 1-knot current will add close to 20 percent to an average day's run on a 30-foot waterline. Choosing to buck that same current means losing 20 percent from the day's run, so going with the current versus going against it makes a 40 percent difference overall. The traditional sailing routes pay almost as much attention to the strongest ocean currents as to the prevailing winds. Since the prevailing winds drive the major ocean currents, there is rarely a conflict between them.

However, ocean currents do have their downside. Where strong currents exist—like the Gulf Stream or the Agulhas Current along the east coast of Africa—local weather patterns can create gale-force winds that blow contrary to the underlying flow of water. In that situation, the wind-driven waves that are created on top of and in opposition to the mass of water being driven by the current are more dangerous than in most offshore gales: They are steeper, larger, and more likely to be breaking. These waves can be more violent than those formed in significantly higher wind speeds where there is no underlying current. In addition, current-

Putting it all together: typical routes and timing

When all these constraints are put together, the seemingly limitless possibilities of the open ocean are narrowed down. In a typical trade wind circumnavigation, boats travel from east to west in the tropical latitudes to take advantage of the prevailing winds and currents. Most major passagemaking takes place in the trade wind belts of the tropics during the winter months when tropical storms are not a threat. That means May to November in the Southern Hemisphere, and November to May in the Northern Hemisphere. The rest of the year is spent either in the opposite hemisphere or outside the tropics.

The timing of our circumnavigation was typical and reflected the timing constraints illustrated in Figure 16-3. We passed through the Panama Canal in March. By September, we had reached New Zealand, where we spent the cyclone season. We left New Zealand in May, passed by the Torres Straits in June, and reached South Africa by October to avoid the southern Indian Ocean cyclone season. We left Cape

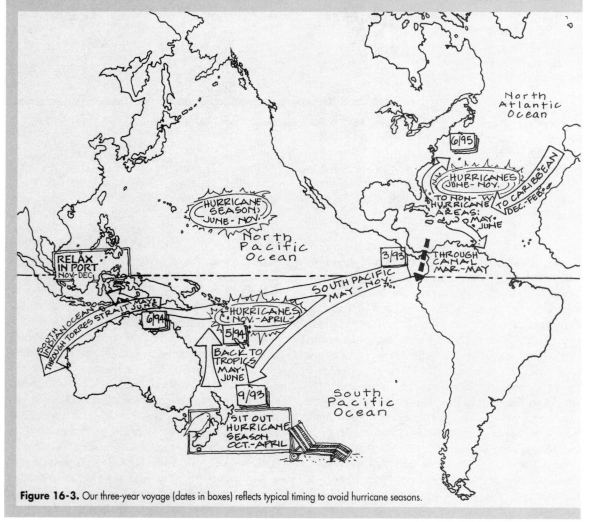

Figure 16-3. Our three-year voyage (dates in boxes) reflects typical timing to avoid hurricane seasons.

Town, South Africa, in January because the South Atlantic does not have a tropical storm season. We reached the Caribbean by late February and were back in Newport by June, just before the hurricane season began in the North Atlantic.

If we'd had an extra year, we would have circumnavigated Australia and timed the route to keep us south of the tropics during cyclone season. Many people spend a second year in the Pacific by returning to Fiji or Tonga to visit the island groups to the west, including Vanuatu, the Solomon Islands, New Caledonia, and Papua New Guinea. These cruisers would spend the next cyclone season in subtropical Australia, Singapore, or Phuket, Thailand.

To cross the northern Indian Ocean, voyagers leave Singapore in January or February to time their arrival in the Mediterranean with the spring. They head up the Red Sea in March or April. Many people spend an extra year or two cruising in the Mediterranean. They then head back across the North Atlantic to the Caribbean, usually leaving the Canaries in January or February to take advantage of the strongest trade winds.

The fastest a circumnavigation can be accomplished from the United States or Europe without sailing during hurricane season is eighteen months. In a boat with a 40-foot waterline, you will spend more than a third of your time at sea. You won't be able to experience much of what makes voyaging worthwhile. We spent one-quarter of our time passagemaking over the first two years. We found that percentage of passagemaking to be high, but it was acceptable. In the last year, we spent over a third of our time on passage and traveling the 14,500 miles from New Zealand back to the United States. We would have enjoyed that more if we had spent another leisurely year in the Pacific or a year in the Caribbean before returning home. If you only have two years, you might want to consider an Atlantic or Pacific circle.

If you are unconcerned about comfort, you have a boat that sails well to windward, and you are not worried by the possibility of sitting through a hurricane, then almost anything goes. Otherwise take advantage of the prevailing winds and currents in planning your route.

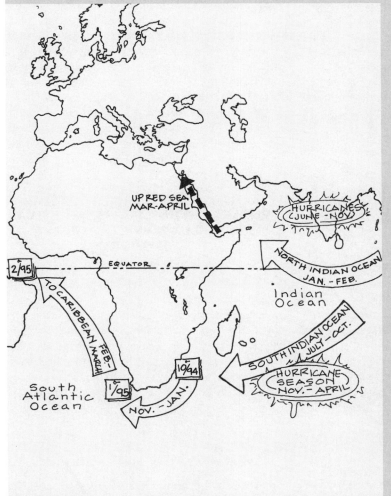

driven crosswaves can develop in the trough of the wind-driven waves. This is the situation we encountered on our first offshore passage between Newport and Bermuda when a small tropical depression caught us in the middle of the Gulf Stream. The wind-driven waves were over the top of our mizzen mast (35 feet high), and the cross waves running in the troughs were 10 or 12 feet high. The motion was like being on a demented roller coaster. We never again experienced anything close to these conditions, even in winds of 50+ knots off the coast of South Africa.

For the most part, favorable ocean currents will simply be another incentive to sail with the prevailing winds. Where ocean currents are unusually strong (3 to 4 knots), your passage planning should include some options for leaving the current in the event of contrary winds. Besides the Gulf Stream and the Agulhas Current, major ocean currents of 2 knots or more are found along the normal trade wind routes near the coast of Brazil, over the top of Australia in the Arufura Sea, and on the west coast of South Africa.

Weather disturbances

Tropical cyclone or hurricane season also determines your overall voyage plan. These fearsome storms occur in all tropical oceans *except* for the South Atlantic. The Northern Hemisphere season is generally considered to be from July through October; the Southern Hemisphere season runs from December to April. But "seasons" refer to those months with the highest historical incidence of tropical cyclones. In the North Atlantic, hurricanes have occurred in June and November. In the western North Pacific, typhoons have occurred in every month of the year, though 90 percent occur between early June and late December.

While not as devastating as tropical cyclones, winter gales can be quite severe outside of the tropics. They should be avoided if possible. The Nor'easters that can wreak havoc along the U.S. East Coast between November and March are examples of these powerful storms. Severe winter gales also occur around New Zealand, South Africa, northern Europe, and the Mediterranean. The period between tropical storm season and the winter gales generally defines the window for traveling between the tropics and the temperate latitudes. For example, most boats arrive in New Zealand after October when the frequency of the winter gales has decreased to nearly zero. They leave the following fall in April or May when the risk of tropical cyclones has subsided and before the winter gales begin.

In the Indian Ocean, monsoons further complicate the seasonal weather picture. From May to September, the Intertropical Convergence Zone (ITCZ) moves northward and becomes a large, low pressure, almost stationary air mass over Central Asia. There it produces southwest winds, frequent rain squalls, and occasional violent thunderstorms. In addition to the risk of tropical cyclones, westabout voyagers will face headwinds and very unpleasant conditions. From October to April, the ITCZ and its associated low pressure shifts southward and is replaced by a large high over the Asian landmass. The air circulation around these two systems strengthens the northeast trades. Westabout voyagers can head across the Indian Ocean to the Red Sea in favorable winds with little risk of tropical storms.

The islands of the South Pacific, southern Indian Ocean, and the Caribbean are prone to tropical revolving storms. If you want to avoid sitting out a hurricane, you'll need to spend four to six months outside of the tropics every year.

UNDERSTANDING WEATHER BASICS: TROPICS VERSUS TEMPERATE LATITUDES

I have already discussed the wind patterns formed by air circulation around the globe. If the weather picture ended there, things would be simple. But a variety of weather disturbances alter the general pattern of air circulation. We understand far less about how these dynamic weather systems develop, build, and dissipate. When experienced from deck level, meteorological theory seems to have little to do with reality. But a basic understanding of the theory can greatly aid the mariner whose primary goal is to forecast the next 6 to 12 hours of weather at sea.

Temperate and higher latitudes

In the temperate and higher latitudes, what we call "weather" is actually the visible manifestation of interactions along the edges of huge air masses many thousands of miles across. These interactions create pressure gradients and temperature differentials that cause air to flow in different ways than it would otherwise. This constant interaction along the interfaces of these air masses creates weather systems with their associated clouds, winds, and precipitation. Forecasting begins with an understanding of how these weather systems develop and move and what characteristics define them—including cloud cover, precipitation, and barometric pressure. The mariner can then translate the "bird's eye-view" to the "deck-level view" to forecast short-term weather at sea without outside assistance.

Creation of weather disturbances

The circulation of air around the planet that creates the prevailing winds also creates large masses of relatively stable air, composed of horizontal layers of air whose temperature and humidity reflect the origin of the air mass. For example, the continental arctic air mass develops over the ice fields of the planet's poles, and this air mass is characterized by cold temperatures and low humidity. A maritime tropical air mass develops over tropical oceans, and it is defined by high temperatures and high humidity. While these air masses are remarkably stable and the air within them is extremely homogenous, the air in different air masses that border one another can be sharply different. These boundary zones are called *fronts,* and the sharp change in the weather that can accompany them is familiar to anyone who has experienced a sudden 30-degree drop in temperature with the passage of a cold front.

Air from one air mass gradually replaces the air from another along a front line. Yet almost no mixing of air occurs, so fronts can be viewed as zones of transition from one air mass to another that range from 5 to 60 miles in width. The general weather picture consists of successive disturbances along these frontal zones as two conflicting air masses clash at their borders. These clashes and the fronts they create take place in three dimensions, for the exact characteristics of the horizontal layers within each air mass will differ, and their interactions across the front will also differ. This is part of the reason why weather is such a complex subject. What happens many thousands of feet above the earth's surface can be quite different from what is happening at

the surface. This activity far above the earth's surface will modify the weather experienced on the ground.

Most fronts separate air masses of different temperatures. This discontinuity in temperature implies a discontinuity in density (cold air is more dense, or heavier, than warm air). This further implies a discontinuity in pressure, with the colder air column exhibiting a higher atmospheric pressure at its base than the warmer air column. Differences in pressure cause the movement of air and, hence, the creation of wind. Air flows from areas of higher pressure toward areas of lower pressure. Another characteristic of all fronts are predictable wind shifts.

Meteorologists capture information about relative pressure visually by plotting the observed pressure from reporting stations all over the forecasting region and then connecting points of equal pressure. The lines created by this process are called *isobars* and are generally plotted at intervals of four millibars. The resulting weather map is called a *surface analysis chart* or *synoptic chart* (Figure 16-4).

There is a well-defined relationship between the isobars on a synoptic chart and the actual wind speed and direction. Rather than blowing perpendicular to the isobars from an area of high to low pressure, the wind direction is deflected by the rotation of the earth and by the force of friction from the ground. Over water, the wind blows at an angle of about 15 degrees to the isobars from the area of high pressure toward the area of low pressure (Figure 16-5). At ground level over land, where there is more friction, the wind actually blows at about a 30-degree angle to the isobars. In terms of wind speed, the closer together the isobars, the greater the pressure gradient and the stronger the wind.

In a frontal system, the difference in temperature and hence pressure between the two air masses means that the isobars cannot remain parallel. A sudden shift has to take place at the front line when the air temperature changes. This is captured on a synoptic chart by the fact that the isobars in a frontal system are "kinked." Where the 1008 millibar crosses the frontal line in Figure 16-6, the pressure must increase with the movement from warm air to cold. Indeed, if you extend that isobar in a straight line after crossing the front you will intersect with the 1012 millibar line on the other side. These kinked isobars point from lower pressure to higher

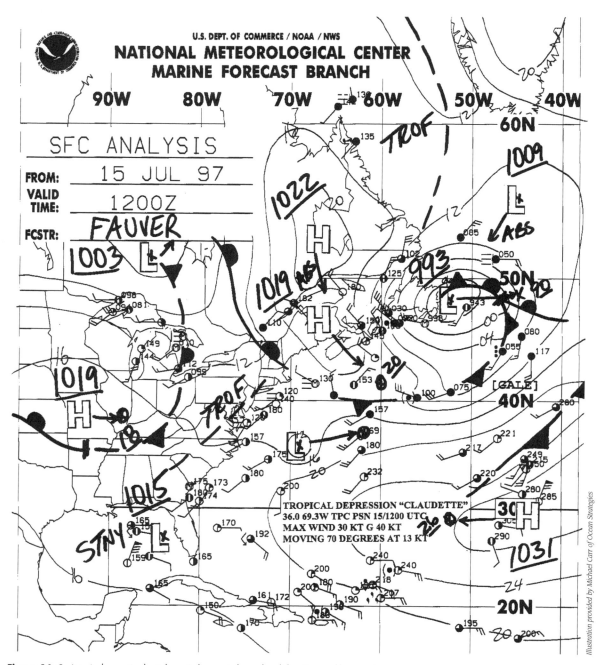

Figure 16-4. A typical synoptic chart shows isobars, wind speed and direction, and barometric pressures.

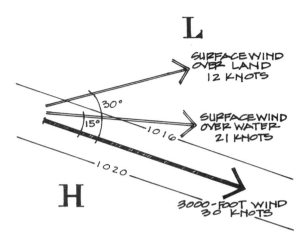

Figure 16-5. The relationship between wind angle and wind speed to the isobars reflects the amount of friction between the air and the ground.

pressure and are accompanied by a wind shift, as shown in Figure 16-6. If you stand facing the wind before the front arrives in a Northern Hemisphere frontal system, you can expect a wind shift to the *right* (clockwise) on the other side of the front line. In the Southern Hemisphere, the shift will be to the *left* (counterclockwise).

The passage of a front—marked by such sudden changes in temperature, pressure, and wind direction—is often accompanied by gusty winds and squalls. The violence of a frontal passage depends on the steepness of the pressure gradient, the stability or instability of the two air masses, and the interactions between the air masses across the vertical cross section of their overlap.

Under certain conditions, two air masses can have a more dynamic interaction across a front line. The fronts begin to differentiate, the pressure gradients become more pronounced, and eventually a low pressure system is spawned. While the process is not completely understood, the basic steps leading to the forma-

tion of a low pressure system are well described. These offer many insights into what can be expected at sea when a low and its associated fronts pass over.

The process starts with a *stationary front* along the boundary between two air masses (as shown on "day 1" in Figure 16-7). Stationary fronts are the least well understood of all frontal types. Unlike other fronts, one air mass is not replacing another. Therefore, the wind blows parallel to the frontal surface but in opposite directions on either side of the front. The weather associated with these fronts is generally mild, though clouds and light precipitation are not uncommon. As their name implies, these fronts may not move at all. Or they may oscillate back and forth over the same area many times. But they are very unstable—especially if they are characterized by hot and humid air on one side of the front and cool and dry air on the other side. Stationary fronts may remain in place for days on end, or they may start to change quite rapidly and create a new low pressure system in less than a day. Forecasters watch these fronts carefully for characteristic signs of a developing low.

In our stationary front located in the Northern Hemisphere, the winds consist of a cold easterly wind to the

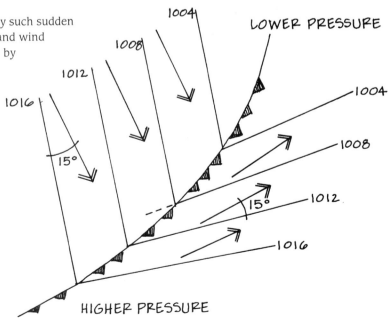

Figure 16-6. The temperature change across a front line also creates a pressure change and a wind shift.

north of the front line and a warm westerly wind to the south. The vertical surface of the front line slopes in the direction of the cold air (northward) since the cold air is heavier than the warm (Figure 16-8). In essence, the cold air is burrowing under the warm. All along the surface of the front there is a strong and almost instantaneous wind shift from east to west, which is called wind shear. This causes waves to form on the frontal surface in much the same way as they do where wind is blowing against water. This wave action creates oscillations on the vertical surface of the front. At "day 2" in Figure 16-7, a bulge has formed at ground level that is somewhat more stable than the stationary front itself.

By "day 3," the system has fundamentally altered. Air is being replaced across the frontal surface, and two different types of fronts are the result. To the west of the kink or bulge, the cold air from the north is replacing the warm air to the south along a *cold front*. To the east of the kink, the warm air from the south is replacing the cold air to the north along a *warm front*. The wind pattern has fundamentally altered as well, and the characteristic wind shifts that normally accompany front lines have become established. An area of slightly lower pressure along the front line has been created at the kink where the cold front meets the warm front.

At this point, if the wave length of the developing frontal wave is between 400 and 1,800 miles, the wave is unstable and it will continue to grow in amplitude and to steepen. At the same time, the pressure gradient becomes more compressed so the system intensifies. The winds establish a circular airflow around the low pressure kink: The airflow becomes cyclonic. The low pressure area then becomes a fully formed *extra-tropical cyclone,* also known as a *depression* or a *low*.

Cold fronts and warm fronts differ along a variety of dimensions, but the most critical for the next phase of development is that cold fronts always move faster than warm fronts. On "day 4," the cold front overtakes the warm front and the warm air is forced aloft. This creates the fourth and final type of front, called an *occluded front*. The low pressure area is said to be filling. Over the next 24 hours or so, the occluded front will dissipate and leave only the low pressure area—a mass of whirling homogenous air. The energy from differences in temperature and humidity that created the system has been depleted. The pressure gradient and its associated winds will dissipate fairly rapidly unless a new energy source is found, as could be the case if it traveled over an area of water that was considerably warmer than its own air. By the end of "day 5," the stationary front will have been re-established, and the area of low pressure

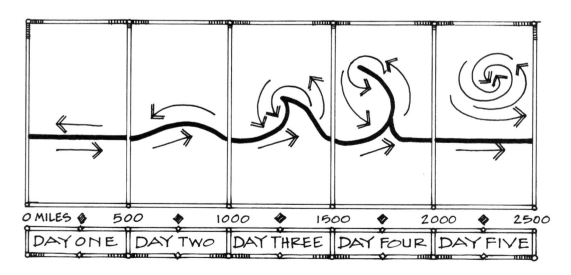

Figure 16-7. Along a stationary front, conditions can lead to the development of a low pressure system.

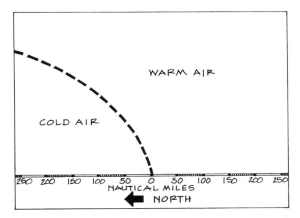

Figure 16-8. Along a stationary front line, the vertical surface of the front slopes in the direction of the cold air.

and cyclonic winds will be rapidly dissipating. As shown in Figure 16-7, the entire system may have moved several thousand miles during this process.

A low pressure system and its associated fronts, therefore, comprise an area of mixing between two air masses where differences in temperature and humidity cause a complex circulation and great instability. The opposite of this is a *high pressure system (high* or *anticyclone)*. A high is an area of generalized circulation within an air mass characterized by great stability and higher pressure relative to surrounding air. Highs are much less complex than lows, yet our understanding of exactly how they form is even more rudimentary. Generally speaking, anticyclones develop when cool, compressed, high-altitude air sinks to the earth's surface.

For this information to be useful at sea, we need to translate this general understanding of how weather patterns form and disperse into a way to predict the next 6 to 12 hours of weather. To accomplish this, we must profile these systems in terms of barometric pressure, wind speeds and directions, associated cloud cover, and precipitation.

General characteristics of weather systems

Frontal systems, highs, and lows are defined by specific atmospheric conditions. These can help the mariner identify weather patterns when synoptic charts have

vanished over the horizon. Well developed highs and lows directly or indirectly create most of the weather experienced in the temperate latitudes.

As can be seen from Figure 16-7, the forces that create a low pressure system dictate a counterclockwise air circulation in the Northern Hemisphere. Since wind blows across the isobars at an angle of 15 degrees from high pressure to low pressure, the wind toes inward. In a Northern Hemisphere high, the wind blows outward from the center in a clockwise direction. In the Southern Hemisphere, wind directions are reversed: A high is characterized by counterclockwise circulation and a low by clockwise circulation. Table 16-1 summarizes other characteristics of highs and lows.

Unlike the semipermanent lows and highs discussed in the first section, low and high pressure systems can move at considerable speed across the surface of the earth depending on surface winds and the upper air jet stream. From a stationary point on the ground, observed conditions reflect the speed and direction of movement of the entire weather pattern. Weather on the ground, then, can be viewed as a series of snapshots that must be strung together in order to identify the weather system and predict future weather.

Above about 30 degrees north or 30 degrees south, weather systems move from the west to the east with the prevailing high-altitude westerly winds of the jet stream. Thus, highs, lows, and fronts form a parade of weather patterns moving one after the other from west to east. Their movement will be affected by other weather systems around them, by high-altitude winds and pressure gradients, by changes in the temperature over the land or water, and by encounters with the semi-permanent highs and lows, among other things. These dynamic factors make accurate and timely forecasting a challenge, even with modern forecasting tools.

Given their well-defined air circulation and pressure gradients, highs and lows show characteristic patterns of barometric pressure changes and wind shifts. What you observe at sea will depend on whether the high or low is moving to the north or south of you and in which hemisphere you are located. Figure 16-9 summarizes the pressure changes and wind shifts to be expected in these different situations.

From the standpoint of forecasting at sea, there are several important points to be made about Figure 16-9.

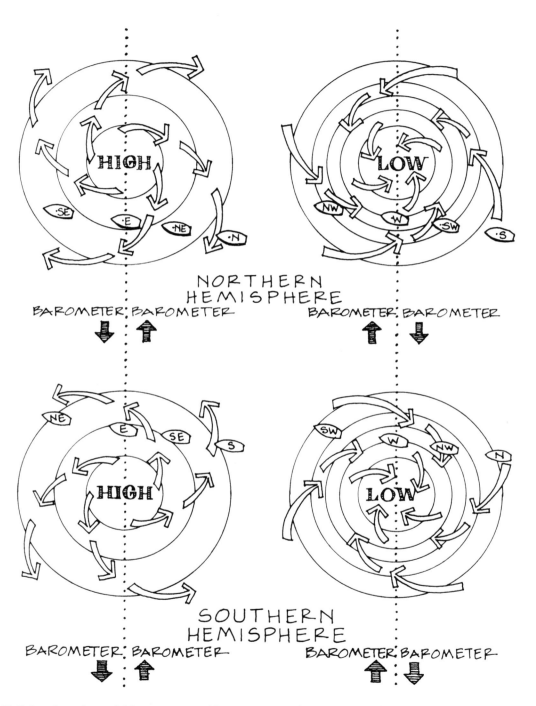

Figure 16-9. By understanding wind shifts in conjunction with barometric pressure changes, you can predict what wind shifts you will experience in the next 24 hours.

■ *Barometer change without wind shift.* If the barometer changes rapidly (more than a millibar an hour) without an accompanying wind shift, then the center of the system is coming directly toward you. A rising barometer signals a high; a falling barometer indicates a low.

■ *Similarity in conditions.* The wind direction and pressure changes in a dispersing high can resemble those in a building low. A falling barometer and a southwest wind in the Northern Hemisphere could mean that a high pressure system is retreating (*A* on Figure 16-9) or that a low pressure system is approaching (*B* on Figure 16-9). In the absence of a weather forecast or weather map, you can distinguish between the two based on the rate of change in the barometer and the next wind shift. A rapidly falling barometer or lowering and thickening clouds signal an approaching low.

■ *Locating low pressure.* Given the fact that the wind blows across the isobars at a 15-degree angle toward low pressure at sea, you can locate the low pressure system by using Buys Ballot's Law. If you stand facing

the wind with your right arm outstretched, the center of the low will be located to your right. As the wind crosses the isobars at a slight angle, the low is actually positioned about 15 degrees aft of your arm. In the Southern Hemisphere, *low* pressure sits 15 degrees aft of your *left* arm.

■ *Remembering circulation patterns.* It can be quite confusing to remember in what direction each system rotates in which hemisphere. A simple rule of thumb helps: High pressure systems in both hemispheres reinforce the trade winds. Given that the trades are easterly winds and highs interact with the trades along their southern edge in the Northern Hemisphere and their northern edge in the Southern Hemisphere, the rotation of a high can be deduced for each hemisphere (Figure 16-10). A low is always the opposite.

■ *Crossing systems.* Unfortunately, many things can complicate the diagrams in Figure 16-9. Sailing north or south instead of east or west, you may move through an advancing low into a retreating high. The wind shifts that would accompany your progress are shown in Fig-

Table 16-1. Weather characteristics of highs and lows

Weather characteristics	Highs	Lows
Overall weather	Generally fair—clear skies, light winds, and good weather	Stormy—dense cloud cover, strong winds, precipitation
Range of sizes	200 to 2,000 miles, most often in the upper half of the range	200 to 2,000 miles, most often in the lower third of the range
Average speed	Winter: 565 NM per day, Summer: 390 NM per day	Winter: 600 NM per day, Summer: 430 NM per day
Northern Hemisphere circulation	Downward, outward, clockwise	Inward, upward, counterclockwise
Southern Hemisphere circulation	Downward, outward, counterclockwise	Inward, upward, clockwise
Barometric pressure	High—most often a rapid rise on approach and slow fall on retreat	Low—most often a rapid fall on approach and slow rise on retreat
Winds	May be strong at outside edge, light for hundreds of miles across center	Increasingly strong as center of low approaches; may be small lull at center
Clouds	Usually only in the periphery	A wide variety over all altitudes
Temperature	Stable for long periods of time	Cold or warm changing to cold
Risk to mariners	Very little; strong winds may exist in leading edge	Strong winds and high seas

ure 16-11. *Cols,* areas of light and shifty winds between low and high pressure systems, can also create confusing conditions at sea. Table 16-9 is useful when clear pressure changes are accompanied by specific wind shifts, but you cannot expect to know exactly what pattern is affecting you at all times—nor do you need to. You will know if the wind is likely to become stronger or reach gale force, which is what really matters.

Even more so than highs and lows, frontal systems are marked by distinct changes in the major weather indicators as the front approaches, passes over, and then retreats. These weather characteristics are summarized in Table 16-2 for warm fronts and cold fronts.

Cold fronts are characterized by a very short zone of transition, which makes them more dynamic and volatile than warm fronts. Along the leading edge where cold air is replacing warm, the warm air is forced to rise. If the warm air is unstable, it will condense and create a broad band of squalls and thundershowers on the leading edge of the front line (Figure 16-12). Even if

the warm air is fairly stable, some shower and squall activity will occur at the front line when the warm air moves upward.

The most dangerous aspect of cold fronts, however, is the line squalls that can precede their passage by anywhere from a few hours to half a day. These zones of extreme instability form when the winds above the cold frontal surface are moving in the same direction but at a faster speed than the cold front. This cold air prevents the warm air from rising in advance of the front and traps the layer of warm, unstable air between the two cold air layers. A band of violent weather oriented parallel to the cold front and moving eastward at about the same speed develops. This band is characterized by extreme gustiness and torrential downpours. Line squalls appear as rapidly advancing bands of boiling black clouds on the horizon. Sail should be shortened immediately.

In a warm front, warm air replaces cold. Since warm air is less dense than cold air, the colder air must be receding. The warm air ascends over the top of the reced-

Figure 16-10. The winds in a high reinforce the prevailing winds in the trades.

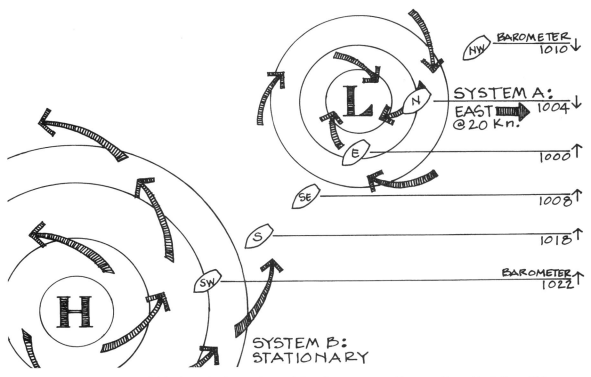

Figure 16-11. The wind shifts when sailing from north to south through two systems would not resemble anything in Figure 16-9.

Table 16-2. Weather characteristics of cold fronts and warm fronts

Weather characteristics	Warm fronts	Cold fronts
Clouds	Lowering and thickening over course of 24 to 48 hours before front, lifting rapidly after, clearing more slowly	Lowering and thickening within a few hours before front, clearing quickly afterwards
Overall weather	Heavy precipitation preceding front, light drizzle or fine rain after	Heavy rain, thunder and squalls at front line, clearing quickly after front line
Winds	Increasing before, sudden shift at front line, steady after	Increasing and squally before, sudden shift and squally at front line, gusty after
Pressure	Steady fall, level at front line, little change after	Moderate to rapid fall, sudden rise at front line, slow rise after
Temperature	Slow, steady rise throughout	Sudden drop at front line
Average speed	360 NM per day in winter, more slowly in summer	600 NM per day in winter, more slowly in summer
Risk to mariners	If warm air is unstable, thunderstorms may develop along front line	Extremely dangerous line squalls can develop 50 to 300 miles in advance of cold front

ing cold air, and the interaction between the two creates an extensive cloud system that extends up to 1,200 nautical miles in front of the front line. This translates into a much broader zone of transition, so the entire system is considerably less violent than in the case of the cold front. The cloud system and associated precipitation are diagrammed in Figure 16-13. High-level clouds that lower and thicken gradually announce an approaching warm front as much as two days prior to its arrival. Passage of a warm front means several days of cloudy, wet weather with breezy conditions. Thunderstorms in the vicinity of the front line pose the most serious hazard from a warm front.

As discussed above, air is not being replaced across a stationary front. They are characterized by clouds and light precipitation reminiscent of a warm front, but milder. Stationary fronts pose little danger to the mariner as long as they remain stationary. They can

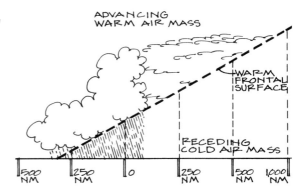

Figure 16-13. In a warm front, the frontal system is much wider. The first clouds may be sighted up to two days in advance of the system.

become a hazard if a low pressure system develops suddenly along the front line. Even if you have access to good forecasts, you will probably experience its effects before you receive the gale warning.

As discussed previously, occluded fronts result when a cold front overtakes a warm front and the warm air is forced aloft. Occluded fronts are highly unstable, since the warm air and cold air fight for position within the front line. They are characterized by precipitation on both sides of the front and by a broad band of clouds like those associated with warm fronts. An occluded front will look and act much like an unusually violent warm front when approaching and passing over, but the temperature drop and rapid clearing afterwards will resemble a cold front.

You will encounter just about every type of weather when passing through the frontal systems associated with a low. The weather changes reflect the passage of the warm and cold front, reinforced by the low pressure system (Figure 16-14). Passage through the non-frontal section of the low (the top edge in Figure 16-14) would be the same as if passing through a low without associated fronts (Figure 16-9).

Given the characteristics of the various weather systems, the forecasting horizon of 6 to 12 hours at sea should begin to make sense. With cold fronts and concentrated lows, the cloud formations will only extend a hundred miles or so in front of the system. The forecasting horizon can stretch to 18 hours with warm fronts and some lows, where cloud cover extends up to 1,000

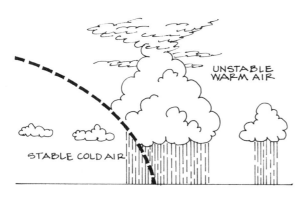

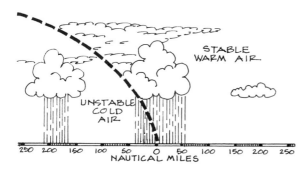

Figure 16-12. In a cold front, the frontal system is relatively narrow with clouds building only 100 miles or so in front of the line.

miles in front of the system. Though most sailboats will not have enough time to position themselves with respect to an approaching storm, they will have enough warning to prepare their boat for gale conditions.

As our understanding of weather increases, the complex picture drawn over the last few pages does not get any simpler. You should take advantage of available forecasting, described in the sidebar titled "Using outside assistance—forecasting tools." However, even if you have all the forecaster's tools at your disposal and you are expert enough to make use of them, you will still face the problem of the lack of data and its timeli-

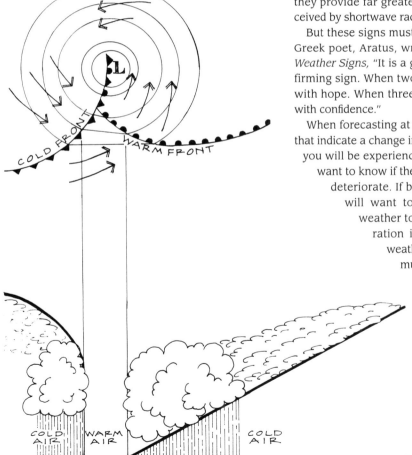

ness at sea. For this reason, understanding the language of wind, water, and sky will continue to be a mariner's key skill.

Deck-level forecasting

So how do you turn all this information into useful short-term forecasts at sea? You need to combine good observation with cautious interpretation. Be aware of the small signals you receive from the surrounding elements. You will be amazed at the variety of faces that the sea can wear—the seemingly infinite combinations of wind, cloud, wave, and sky that make each passage day different in character and mood. These small differences inform the practiced observer. Taken together, they provide far greater accuracy than a forecast received by shortwave radio or weather fax.

But these signs must be interpreted with care. The Greek poet, Aratus, wrote 2,300 years ago in his *On Weather Signs,* "It is a good rule to look for sign confirming sign. When two point the same way, forecast with hope. When three point the same way, forecast with confidence."

When forecasting at sea, you want to identify signs that indicate a change in the weather. Most of the time, you will be experiencing fine weather, and you will want to know if the good weather will continue or deteriorate. If bad weather is on the way, you will want to know exactly what type of weather to expect and how much preparation is required. If you are in bad weather, you will want to know how much longer it will last and when you will be able to make sail once again.

Table 16-3 (page 293) summarizes the signs of continuing stable weather and the early signs of an approaching change seen 24 to 48 hours ahead of the actual deterioration. Most of the signs of a change indicate an approaching warm front or low, since

Figure 16-14. Passing through the frontal system of a low creates a more complex series of weather changes that are still predictable.

Using outside assistance—forecasting tools

The outside assistance available to you at sea will be a function of the gear you choose to purchase. A wide range of weather charts offer different information to the knowledgeable user. You can receive most of these via weather fax or through an SSB connected to a laptop computer. Some of the different types of charts and their uses follow:

■ *Surface analysis chart.* The basic marine weather chart depicts conditions at the earth's surface (Figure 16-15). The information shown on a synoptic chart includes: isobars; the location of lows, highs, and fronts; wind speed and direction; and the barometric pressure of highs and lows. These charts are produced for current conditions and for prognoses of the next 12, 24, 36, 48, and 96 hours.

■ *Satellite weather images.* Satellite images may be either visible or infrared. We have all seen visible

satellite images on the nightly news, with clouds pictured swirling forward across the country (Figure 16-16). Satellite photos can also be taken with an infrared camera and color enhanced for ease of use (Figure 16-17). Used together, visible and infrared satellite images allow forecasters to analyze cloud temperature, shape, and density. You can also use infrared data to detect warm fronts, warm air flows, tropical cyclones, and the location of warm currents like the Gulf Stream.

■ *500-millibar chart.* While the surface analysis shows the pressure at the earth's surface using isobars, the 500-millibar chart shows the height and temperature contours of various weather features at 500 millibars of pressure, which is roughly the level of the jet stream (Figure 16-18). Height contours are shown as continuous lines and labeled in meters

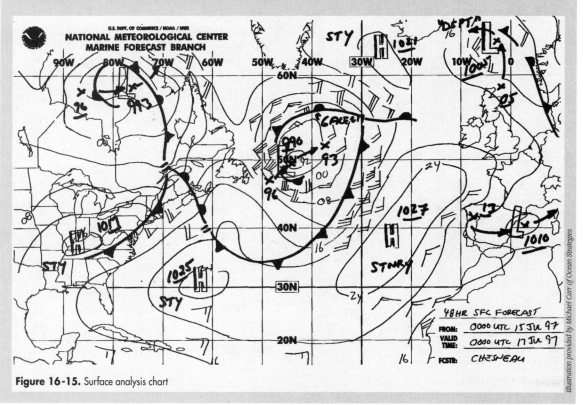

Figure 16-15. Surface analysis chart

above sea level. Arrows show wind direction and speed at this level. The understanding of the interaction between upper level weather features and surface weather has been improving. From these charts, a knowledgeable user can detect the early formation of lows and determine the likely direction of movement of surface weather disturbances.

From a forecasting point of view, these tools provide all the elements that have been discussed in this chapter. The surface analysis provides barometric readings and wind speeds and directions. The satellite imagery provides temperature and cloud cover information. The 500-millibar charts provide information on upper level winds, which the mariner surmises

(continued)

Figure 16-16. Visible satellite weather image

Figure 16-17. Infrared satellite image

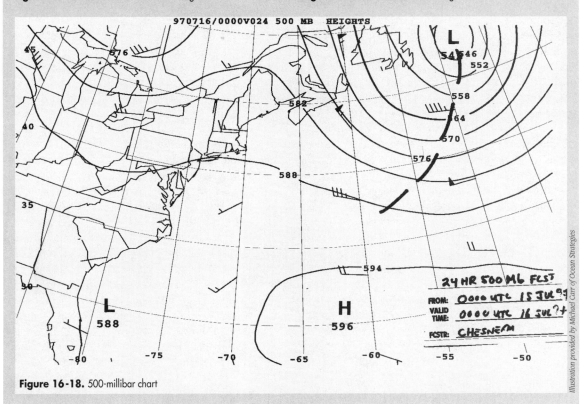

Figure 16-18. 500-millibar chart

(continued)

from observing cloud shapes and sky clarity. These tools can also be used to make predictions beyond the next 6 to 12 hours. For sources to help you read and interpret these charts, see "Additional resources" in this chapter.

But relying on all of this technology for the day after tomorrow's weather is still a risky business. Lows will suddenly appear and then move quickly or stall. Fronts will lengthen or shorten or disappear altogether. The SSB radio remains the most useful tool to supplement the barometer and what you can readily observe. Almost all of the maritime SSB nets include a weather forecast and a daily roll call of all boats in the broadcast area, an area that generally covers half of an ocean. During the roll call, each boat reports current conditions including position, barometric pressure, wind speed, wind direction, percent cloud cover, and sea state. If there are enough boats reporting, you can create your own surface analysis from actual data. You can use this information to verify the high seas synopsis and weather forecast, assess its timeliness, and update it to reflect the current situation. You can then forecast the future with a bit more confidence.

these give you more warning than an approaching cold front. Find three or more signs that point to the same change and forecast with confidence.

Clouds provide a wealth of information to the experienced mariner, but they can be terribly confusing to the neophyte. It helps to remember these basic rules: Low, puffy clouds moving with the prevailing wind indicate stable conditions; high, flat clouds moving rapidly or in a direction opposite to the prevailing wind signal a change in the higher altitude winds, which will eventually bring a change in the weather. If those clouds lower and thicken over a 6- to 12-hour period, get ready for a blow.

Given several signs of an impending change, you will want to know exactly what is coming. Over the next 12 hours, the indicators in Table 16-4 will help you identify the approaching system and judge its severity.

In frontal systems, the wind will not shift until the front line passes over. But in a low, the wind will start increasing and shifting as soon as the leading edge reaches you (unless the center of the low is coming straight for you). For any system, but especially for a low, the speed of the barometric change provides the best indication of its intensity. Intense extra-tropical cyclones are accompanied by a drop of 10 millibars in three hours. Anything over 1 millibar in three hours indicates that some bad weather is approaching, with 2 millibars in three hours often considered the benchmark for gale-force winds (35 knots), and 5 millibars in three hours considered indicative of storm-force winds (45+ knots).

While the change in the barometric pressure is always more important than the actual pressure reading itself, anything in the vicinity of 1000 millibars can be considered the "danger zone." While severe extra-tropical cyclones may drop to 950 or below, depressions of average intensity range from 988 to 1004 millibars at their center. A barometric reading below 1010 accompanied by a fall of more than 1 millibar in three hours signaled us to prepare for strong winds. Before relying on an absolute figure, compare your barometer to official pressure readings to make sure that it is properly calibrated.

On the frontal side of a low, early indicators can be difficult to distinguish from a warm front. A sharp drop in the barometer indicates that the front is likely to be accompanied by a low. The narrow zone of transition makes the cold front the most difficult to forecast: You will only get a few hours' notice from changes in the cloud cover or the barometer. The dangerous line squalls that can precede a cold front cannot be forecast with any certainty.

If you see a large swell whose crests are gradually getting closer together moving at an angle to the prevailing wind, then a very large system is approaching and you need to be fully prepared. Such a swell may reach you 48 hours in advance of the depression and can be an excellent warning sign. With smaller systems, you won't notice the swell until the system is closer, and it will take several hours to determine if the period is increasing or decreasing. If it is increasing, breathe a sigh of relief. You have managed to avoid a major storm front.

Table 16-3. Indicators of continuing good weather or of a possible change

Indicators	Continuing good weather	Possible change
Barometer	Steady, rising slowly	Falling slowly
Clouds	Clear sky or a few puffy cumulus clouds	High clouds in long, harsh streaks (mare's tails)
	Very thin high clouds that seem to evaporate	Sky covered with whitish film
	High clouds without cohesion—wild, torn look	Clouds with sharp edges or blown off tops
	Soft, delicate looking clouds	Clouds move in different directions at different heights
Temperature	Stable	Rises or falls markedly
	Heavy dew or frost at night	Humidity increases
Sea state	Settled	Confused
	Swell and waves from same direction	Swell not from same direction as waves
Wind speed	Generally steady, slight rise and fall over course of day	Strong winds in early morning
	Very slowly increasing or decreasing	
Skies	Sky is clear and light blue to dark blue	Sky becomes hazy
	Moon shines brightly	Large halo circling moon or sun
	Jet contrail disappears immediately or not visible at all	Jet contrail lingers thickly before falling apart
Sunset	Setting sun looks like a "ball of fire"	Setting sun is purplish or bruised looking
	Sun sets on a clear horizon	Sun sets high above horizon which is obscured by clouds
	Green flash	Bright yellow or pale yellow sunset
Sunrise	Sun rises from clear horizon	Sun rises high above horizon because of cloud cover
	Gray sky at dawn	

No matter what system is approaching, your preparations will be much the same when the clouds start to change and the barometer starts to drop. (This is discussed in the sidebar "Storm preparations," page 352.) It is always better to overprepare than to shrug off the early warning signs.

Once you are in the midst of gale-force winds and heavy seas, your only concern will be when you can expect the weather to improve. The faster the system develops, the more intense it will be and the more quickly it will dissipate. An old saying captures this concept best, "Long foretold, long past; short warning, soon past."

Table 16-5 summarizes the major indicators that relief is in sight.

When the storm system first shows signs of moving off, you are actually at your most vulnerable. Mentally, you are ready for the storm to be over and glad of any decrease in wind speed. Yet a lull in a storm with a period of diminished winds is often followed by a resumption of the gale in all its fury.

In two cases you should not set full sail again, even if the lull lasts for an hour or more. First, if you have been in a low and the wind dies with a rapidly rising barometer, then you have passed into the center of the low. You can expect winds in excess of those you have already encountered when you enter the other side of the system. Second, after passing through the warm front on the frontal side of a low pressure system (see Figure 16-14), the wind will shift and the barometer will level off. If the clouds do not lift or if they lift and descend again while the barometer drops, then you will soon be in the cold front with its gusty winds and squally conditions.

Even if the weather system is really moving off, the sea takes four to eight hours to moderate. If you have been employing storm tactics during the gale, don't set sail until the waves have lost some of their power. Trying to sail in gale-like waves without adequate wind can break gear and endanger crew. When the waves start to break over their backs instead of down their fronts, you are safe in assuming the gale is over and in making sail once again.

Some of the old weather proverbs will help you remember certain weather signs. These sayings only describe one sign, so don't trust them implicitly. Look for a

couple of other indicators that point in the same direction. Table 16-6 contains a number of proverbs that work equally well in both hemispheres.

Before you leave, create your own short-term forecasts from your porch using the combination of barometric changes and observations of wind, sea, and sky to forecast the next 6 to 12 hours of weather. You will soon become more accurate than the local weather forecasters.

Tropical latitudes

Most of the time, the weather in the tropics lacks the dynamism found in the temperate and higher latitudes. No borders between large air masses of different temperatures and humidity exist, so fronts are generally not found within the tropical latitudes. No constant parade of highs and lows marches steadily eastward. Yet the tropics spawn the most violent and destructive storms known to mankind—hurricanes or tropical cyclones.

Table 16-4. Indicators of approaching weather systems

Indicators	Low pressure system	Warm front	Cold front
Barometer	2 mb to 10 mb fall in three hours	Slow but steady fall	Moderate to rapid fall
Clouds	Clouds lower and thicken gradually	Clouds lower and thicken over the course of 24 to 48 hours	Clouds appear, lower and thicken within a few hours
Temperature	Slow fall	Slow rise	Unchanged
Winds	Increasing steadily and shifting (see Figure 16-9)	Increasing steadily without shifting	Increasing and becoming squally without shifting
Sea state	Large swell with decreasing period		

Table 16-5. Indicators that weather is improving

Indicators	Low pressure system	Warm front	Cold front
Barometer	Levels off, then starts to rise	Levels off	Sudden rise in pressure
Clouds	Clouds lift gradually	Clouds lift gradually	Clouds lift rapidly
Temperature	Steady	Slow rise	Sudden drop followed by slower drop
Winds	Decreasing steadily	Steady to decreasing	Gusty, no longer squally
Sea state	Waves start to break down backs instead of down fronts		

The endless cycle of energy in the higher latitudes seems to get compressed into a few spectacular displays of nature's strength in the tropical latitudes.

Much more than in the higher latitudes, global air circulation dictates tropical winds. Yet "weather" still occurs in the form of disturbances that enter the tropics from the higher latitudes and in the interactions between the northeast and southeast trade winds. While tropical weather should be more straightforward than higher latitude weather, less time has been spent studying it and many questions remain unresolved. From a sailor's perspective, wind speeds are more moderate and more consistent in direction than in the higher latitudes. This makes sailing more manageable and weather forecasting more straightforward most of the time.

Weather disturbances within the tropics

Aside from tropical revolving storms, two types of weather disturbances exist that are peculiar to the tropics: the Intertropical Convergence Zone (ITCZ) and easterly waves. Easterly waves spawn tropical cyclones when conditions are favorable. Frontal systems and even an occasional low from the temperate latitudes may invade the tropics from time to time. These systems are generally not as severe as they would be if experienced in the higher latitudes. High pressure systems may interact with the trade winds to create "reinforced trades" with winds in excess of 30 knots for many days.

■ **Intertropical Convergence Zone.** The area where the northeast trades meet the southeast trades along the equator is called the ITCZ or the doldrums. The movements of the ITCZ create tropical rainy and dry seasons that replace the four seasons of the temperate latitudes. The ITCZ migrates north and then south over the course of the year, lagging behind the seasonal movements of the sun by about two months. Many areas in the tropics experience two rainy seasons as the ITCZ migrates over them and then two dry seasons after it has passed.

The presence of the ITCZ is associated with the formation of tropical cyclones, and voyagers do not tend to be in the same hemisphere as the ITCZ. However, voyagers will have to cross the ITCZ when moving from one hemisphere to the other. They will also encounter

Table 16-6. Weather proverbs

Weather sayings	Explanation
"Quick rise after low Foretells a stronger blow," and "While rise begins after low, squalls expect after a blow."	A rapidly rising barometer does not indicate fair weather. Only when the rise has slowed can you expect the weather to moderate.
"Mackerel skies and mare's tails, Make lofty ships carry low sails," and "If clouds look as though scratched by a hen, Get ready to reef your topsails then."	These two sayings both refer to well-organized, coherent high clouds that mark the leading edge of a warm front or a low. If the clouds are disorganized, soft looking, and not oriented in the same direction, the weather will continue fair.
"When clouds appear like rocks and towers, The earth's refreshed by frequent showers."	A developed thunderhead looks like a tower, and the surrounding clouds at the base are often rounded like rocks.
"If the rain's before the wind, Then your sheets and halyards tend. If the wind's before the rain, All will soon be fine again."	This applies both to squalls and lows. In a low, the rain will reach you first on the leading edge of the warm front with the body of the low still behind it. If the wind reaches you first, it is probably caused by the depression. Rain will come with the cold front, signaling the low's passage. For a squall, this saying predicted with great accuracy whether we needed to reef.
"Rainbow to windward, foul fall the day. Rainbow to leeward, rain runs away."	This ditty is used to predict if a nearby squall will rain on you. It assumes squalls are moving with the prevailing wind, which is not always the case.

A temperate latitude example—North Atlantic passage

The day before we left Bermuda, the barometer had fallen sharply and the Bermuda Harbour Radio forecast called for a low to pass close by during the night. The wind shifted into the southwest, and we spent the night sitting anchor watches through a gale of 40+ knots passing to the north of us. The forecast then called for a strong high to fill in behind the low, which would give us several days of boisterous but favorable winds. By mid-afternoon, the barometer had started to rise and the wind had shifted into the west, which would indicate that we were now on the "back side" of the low. The following is a day-by-day chronicle of the weather conditions we experienced on that North Atlantic passage.

■ *Days 1–5: Riding the back side of a low into a strong high.* We left St. George's Harbor on July 2 at 1630 hours. Table 16-7 summarizes the first five days of weather we experienced.

For the first 18 hours, the wind veered to the west and the northwest, the barometer climbed steadily, and the clouds lifted as the low retreated. By noon on the second day, we were enjoying clear weather and close-hauled conditions. The rising barometer and northeast winds suggested that a strong high

was filling in from the north, as predicted.

As is often the case, the leading edge of the high had tightly packed isobars, which can be seen in the overnight barometric change. This pressure gradient brought strong winds and clear conditions. We hove-to for a few hours in the early morning of July 4 when the northeast winds of 25 knots made progress along our course of 60 degrees very uncomfortable. By the morning of July 4, the wind had shifted to the point where we were sailing quickly almost on our course. The barometric pressure of 1020 indicated that we were fully under the influence of the high, and the east-northeast wind indicated that the high was positioned slightly west and north of us. We have since gotten copies of the surface charts for this period, and the chart from July 4 confirms our deck-level synopsis and shows a large high pressure system extending from our position north to Labrador.

This was a large and well-developed high that offered us three days of fast sailing as the wind shifted from northeast, to east, and to southeast. At this point, we assumed that the high had passed over us and was now located to the north and east of us. On July 6, the wind shifted to the south and started to build. The barometer was still very high and holding

Table 16-7. July 2 to July 7—Receding low, high filling in

Date/time	Position	Barometer	Three hour Δ	Wind	Cloud cover
7/2, 1630	32.5°N 64.5°W	1001	+ 2 mb	W at 12 knots	Lifting
7/3, 0800	33°N 63.5°W	1007	+1 mb	NNW at 18 knots	Clouds breaking up
7/3, 1500	33.5°N 62.5°W	1010	+1 mb	NNE at 20 knots	Clear, high cirrus
7/4, 0845	34°N 62°W	1020	Steady	ENE at 15 knots	
7/5, 0500	35°N 61°W	1021	Steady	E at 12 knots	
7/5, 1200	36°N 60.5°W	1020	Steady	SE at 18 knots	
7/6, 0600	37°N 59°W	1022	Steady	SSE at 12 knots	
7/6, 1000	37.3°N 58.5°W	1023	Steady	S at 10 knots	High cirrus
7/7, 0430	38°N 57°W	1024	Steady	S at 30 knots	

Table 16-8. July 7 to July 10—Running the edge of the Azores high

Date/time	Position	Barometer	Three hour Δ	Wind	Cloud cover
7/7, 1400	38°N 56.5°W	1022	Steady	SSW at 25 knots	Clear
7/8, 1330	39°N 53°W	1024	Steady	SSW at 25 knots	
7/9, 1145	39°N 51.5°W	1025	Steady	SSW at 20 knots	
7/10, 1100	39°N 47.5°W	1021	−1 mb	SW at 10 knots	
7/10, 1600	39°N 47°W	1018	−1 mb	SW at 15 knots	
7/10, 2330	39°N 46°W	1017	−1 mb	SSW at 18 knots	High cloud cover

steady, and the only cloud cover was high cirrus. The weather felt stable. But the southerly shift and strong winds indicated that we were nearing the outer fringe at the back of this particular high. We waited to see which way the barometer would go over the next 24 hours.

■ *Days 5–8: Running the edge of the Azores high.* The barometer remained steady (Table 16-8). When the wind shifted into the southwest, we assumed that we were now coming under the influence of the large, semipermanent Azores high, which is normally stationary to the south and east of our position. The synoptic chart from July 7 confirms this and shows that the Azores high was particularly strong and widespread with a central pressure of 1038. We were running along the outer edge of the Azores high in the dense isobars between the high and the low pressure systems moving to the north of it.

We spent the next three days under a double-reefed main and staysail, making good 7 knots of boatspeed. On July 10, the barometer began a slow but steady drop. Either the high was receding, which was unlikely given its semipermanent nature, or a low was approaching slowly. We spent some time the night of July 11 making sure everything was adequately stowed, just in case.

■ *Days 9–13: Passage through frontal systems of a low.* The barometer continued to fall overnight, and the southwest wind now indicated that bad weather was on the way. We assumed a low had pushed its way over the top of the Azores high to the west and north of us and was now approaching. Over the next

Table 16-9. July 11 to July 13—Passage through the frontal systems of a low

Date/time	Position	Barometer	Three hour Δ	Wind	Cloud cover
7/11, 0840	39°N 45°W	1012	−1 mb	SW at 25 knots	Overcast
7/11, 1730	39°N 44°W	1009	−1 mb	SW at 35 knots	
7/12, 0630	39°N 42.5°W	1009	Steady	W at 20 knots	
7/12, 1800	39°N 41°W	1008	−1 mb	W at 30 knots	
7/12, 2300	39°N 40°W	1007	Steady	W at 35 knots	
7/13, 0600	39°N 40°W	1010	+2 mb	W at 15 knots	
7/13, 2300	39°N 39°W	1016	+2 mb	NW at 5 knots	Lifting

(continued)

(continued)

day, the barometer dropped farther and the wind increased (Table 16-9). The wind shifts and barometric changes were consistent with passing through the frontal systems of a low, and the low pressure of 1007 suggested that the center of the depression was fairly far to the north of us. In fact, the synoptic chart shows a complex series of interconnected lows and fronts.

We hove-to most of the night of July 12 when the winds hit gale force. Our electric autopilot could not steer in the waves, and we had been hand steering for eight hours. Twelve hours later, the weather had cleared, the barometer had ticked upward, and the wind had shifted into the northwest as the low moved away.

its effects in the northern Indian Ocean in the form of the seasonal monsoons. The edge of the ITCZ is often characterized by violent squalls and severe thunderstorms. When it is located near trade wind routes, its position is often reported in the high seas forecast.

■ *Easterly or tropical waves.* These are the fronts of the tropics. Unlike higher latitude fronts, they do not occur along the boundary between two air masses. These wavelike troughs of low pressure result from an oscillation in the easterly air current as it interacts with the stationary high pressure located in the horse latitudes. Also unlike higher latitude fronts, easterly waves move from east to west with the trade winds (Figure 16-19A).

The air across the front is relatively homogenous in terms of humidity and temperature, so these waves are not characterized by pressure changes. They are characterized by a gradual wind shift from the northeast to the southeast in the Northern Hemisphere. Clouds and bad weather often occur *after* the front line has passed, with rain and wind for several hours to half a day. Easterly waves become tropical cyclones when upper level winds and water temperatures are favorable to the formation of cyclonic circulation. Easterly waves are most common during the tropical cyclone season when voyagers are unlikely to be in the tropics. Figure 16-19B shows an easterly wave chart prepared by the National Hurricane Center.

■ *Tropical cyclones.* These differ from extra-tropical cyclones in several ways. First, they develop out of easterly waves and not along a front line between two air masses. Second, they have a core of warm, moist air through which they draw energy from the tropical waters. Extra-tropical cyclones have a cold core, and they quickly die out when they become separated from the energy of the front line that spawned them. Tropical

cyclones are not accompanied by fronts, and their sustained winds can reach 120 to 150 knots—more than double the wind speeds that extra-tropical cyclones normally attain. Tropical cyclones are relatively small. They average only 400 to 500 miles in diameter, which is half to a third the size of a well-developed extra-tropical cyclone. Tropical cyclones often follow erratic paths, sometimes recrossing their own tracks. Extra-tropical cyclones always travel to the east. The combination of the small size, changing direction, and destructive wind speeds means that tropical cyclones are often life threatening and always represent a great risk to the mariner. The only certain way to avoid them is to leave the tropics during cyclone season.

■ *Frontal systems and lows.* Frontal passages in the South Pacific are marked by light winds that shift to the east or northeast and may die altogether as the front approaches. After the front line crosses your position, the wind shifts to the southwest where it blows strongly for 6 to 12 hours before gradually moving back into the southeast. When the southeast winds return, they can be gale force as the high fills in behind the front.

On the western end of the South Pacific, the weather picture is complicated by the high pressure systems that regularly move off the hot, dry landmass of northern Australia. Between these highs, a low pressure trough sometimes develops in the tropical latitudes above 20 degrees south. These lows do not stay in the tropics long but tend to head southward to the temperate latitudes. Occasionally, this trough will become a low pressure system moving from west to east through the area between 22.5° and 30°S—the "subtropics." The low's northernmost edge may then be experienced in the area from Fiji to Tahiti, though generally the winds do not reach storm force. This phenomenon occurs most fre-

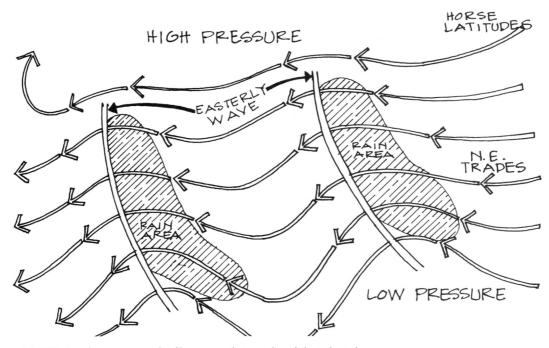

Figure 16-19A. Easterly waves are troughs of low pressure that move through the trade winds.

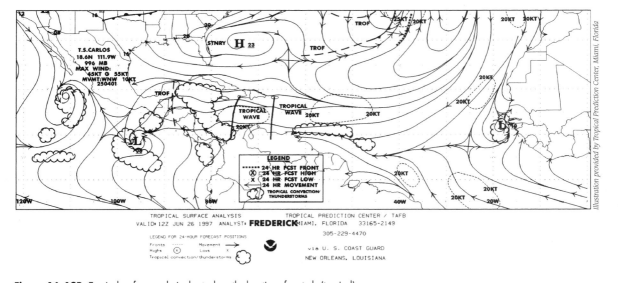

Figure 16-19B. Tropical surface analysis charts show the location of easterly (tropical) waves.

quently in May and June, the beginning of the South Pacific cruising season when boats are heading northward from New Zealand.

It was just such a low pressure system that caused the Queen's Birthday Storm, also referred to as the Pacific Fastnet, in June of 1994. About 20 boats in a cruising rally from New Zealand to Tonga were caught out in hurricane-force winds. The low pressure system involved had moved south out of the tropics in the vicinity of Fiji and then deepened rapidly, dropping by 15 millibars in 24 hours. Such a system is described as a *rapidly intensifying low* or *meteorological bomb* and is rarely detected before it has reached storm force. This particular low was further intensified by a strong high over New Zealand. The circulation of the low and the high intermeshed like cogs right over the place where most of the rally boats were located. Seven boats and two people were lost.

The many factors that must combine to create a weather pattern of this intensity make the likelihood of a repeat performance extremely low. The risk of encountering storm-force winds exists every time you head out of the tropics and occasionally exists in the tropics themselves. The western Pacific near Australia is one of the least stable areas of tropical weather, particularly in May and June—a point worth remembering when you are leaving New Zealand to head back north to the tropics.

■ *Reinforced trades.* While low pressure bombs are unusual, highs often move through the temperate or subtropical latitudes. Their airflow reinforces that of the trade winds to create gale-force winds that can last for days or even weeks. This phenomenon occurs most frequently in the middle of the winter season (July and August in the southern latitudes). A similar phenomenon creates the Caribbean Christmas winds, which generally occur between Christmas and New Year.

Weather forecasting in the tropics

The barometer offers much less assistance when forecasting in the tropics. Weather disturbances in the tropics are generally not characterized by large pressure changes. In the tropical latitudes, the barometric pressure undergoes a diurnal variation that may be as much as 2 to 3 millibars. Actual pressure changes can easily be masked by this variation.

Wind directions are also much more consistent in the tropics. An occasional front will bring a temporary shift, but in most cases the winds will be back into the eastern quarter within 6 to 12 hours. Large swells of constant period are another common feature of tropics sailing. These generally do not foretell bad weather, except in cyclone season. Crossing the western half of the southern Indian Ocean, we were assaulted by a continuous large swell on our beam that was in conflict with the wind and waves on our quarter. This came from the Southern Ocean storms and reached us because there were no landmasses south of us. The result was rolly, wet, frustrating—but extremely fast—sailing.

Without the barometer and wind shifts, you must depend on sea state and cloud conditions to forecast the next 12 hours. Table 16-3 offers the best framework for forecasting in the tropics. In settled tropical weather, you will wake to a gray dawn that will gradually lighten to blue. When you walk the decks, you will leave footprints in the dew. By noon, puffy cumulus clouds will wander by overhead against a dark blue sky. The sun will drop into the sea like a ball of fire, and then the moon and stars will shine bright and clear.

You won't be faced with frontal systems often, but you will have to manage tropical squalls. Individual squalls develop even when the weather is fair. Bands of squalls may form during the day as the heat from the sun warms the humid air. Squalls are as individual as people. Some have wind in them, and some only have rain. Some will move against the prevailing wind and chase you down, and you will have to chase some when you want to fill your water tanks. Some cause a distinct wind shift, and some just increase the wind speed. In most squalls, the wind will be about twice the strength of the prevailing winds. Occasionally they pack more wind. The fastest we ever went on *Silk* was 9.4 knots when we got hit by a 40-knot squall with double headsails up. Some useful tips for managing squalls follow:

■ *Rain versus wind.* The ditty about rain before wind in Table 16-6 applies equally to squalls. If the rain hits first, the wind—when it comes—will be strong. But if the wind increases before the rain arrives, the rain heralds the end of the wind.

■ *Reading the rain.* If the black wisps under the squall that mark the rainfall are straight down, there is little wind within the squall. If they are swept off to one side, beware!

■ *Reading the water.* If the water underneath the squall looks like fog or smoke, expect a heavy downpour and a great deal of wind. If the water looks white and churned up, then there is a hard rain without too much wind. If the water turns a darker color than the water in front of the squall, the squall carries a lot of wind and little rain.

■ *Reading direction.* You can be quite certain that a squall is going to hit you when a black cloud band arches from it to you. Measure the gap between the horizon and the cloud line with your fingers and see if the distance increases. If so, the squall is "lifting its skirts" and you will soon be under them. Don't assume that the squall will move with the prevailing wind—they sometimes have a mysterious motive force of their own. Finally, if the temperature drops suddenly when a squall

A tropics example—South Pacific passage

Leaving Bora Bora for Tonga, we read three weather faxes with three conflicting forecasts for the 24-hour prognosis. One report forecast the passage of an intense low passing through the subtropics with storm-force winds. Another forecast a frontal passage. The third forecast the development of a strong high to the south of us. The winds—though strong—were favorable, and the weather appeared settled, so we decided to leave. Within a few hours of leaving, we received a weather report that was consistent with what we were experiencing—a very strong high to the south of us was reinforcing the trades, creating 20- to 30-knot winds. Table 16-10 summarizes our weather for the first week. Note that the log entries have all been taken at noon so that barometric readings will not show any diurnal variation.

For the first few days, we ran along in the reinforced trades and made good miles every day toward Tonga. On the third day, we encountered first a warm front and then a cold front from a small subtropical low. (Note the wind shifts are opposite those in the Northern Hemisphere!) Though the wind speeds were not all that high, when the wind shifted to the southwest with the passage of the cold front they were right on our nose. We hove-to for about 12 hours and got caught up on our sleep after the hard running of the first few days.

After the fronts passed by, the high reasserted itself. We returned to running downwind in the 25-knot breeze. This continued for another three days to Tonga. From a weather perspective, this pattern was much simpler than our North Atlantic passage and fairly typical of passagemaking in the trades.

Table 16-10. First week of passage from Bora Bora to Tonga

Date/time	Position	Barometer	Three hour Δ	Wind	Cloud cover
7/14, 1200	16°S 152°W	1020	Steady	SE at 25 knots	Clear
7/15, 1200	17°S 155°W	1020	Steady	SE at 25 knots	Clear
7/16, 1200	17°S 157°W	1020	Steady	SE at 25 knots	Clouds lowering
7/17, 1200	17°S 159°W	1015	−1 mb	NW at 20 knots	Overcast
7/18, 1200	18°S 159°W	1015	Steady	SW at 20 knots	Clearing
7/19, 1200	18°S 161°W	1025	Steady	SE at 25 knots	Clear
7/20, 1200	18°S 164°W	1025	Steady	SE at 25 knots	Clear
7/21, 1200	18°S 166°W	1030	Steady	SE at 25 knots	Clear

is visible on the horizon, you can be fairly certain you will rendezvous. Get out the soap!

■ *Line squalls.* If you see a black band of billowing clouds on the horizon, reef down and prepare for a violent encounter. Though line squalls are unusual in the tropics, they can happen. We encountered line squalls in the doldrums as we were crossing back into the Northern Hemisphere from the South Atlantic. They lasted for several hours and were characterized by violent lightning and thunder, a terrific downpour, and gusty, shifty winds that went from 5 to 30 knots in seconds.

There are also some false squall signs that can be confusing. When cloud bands cross the sky, they some- times look as if they converge at the horizon. This is actually a trick of perspective: The cloud bands are actually parallel. Many fluffy cumulus clouds float by often in the tropics. The convergence can make these appear as a large mass of clouds on the horizon, which can easily be mistaken for an approaching squall. If the clouds ahead appear to part as you approach, don't worry. If the cloud mass on the horizon is white and fluffy with no blackness or bruising, the chances of squall activity are slight.

When the sun rises behind one of these cloud masses, the backlighting can make the clouds look black—a massive line squall appears to be approaching. While squall activity is not unusual in the first few hours after

Additional resources

Most offshore voyagers understand weather at the level that it is presented in this chapter and rely on forecasts and weather faxes to give them longer lead time. A few voyagers develop into weather experts; we were almost always within radio range of someone who collected all of the available weather information and provided daily forecasts to the rest of us. If you might have an interest in going the next step and learning about the intricacies of 500-mb charts and rapidly intensifying lows, the following resources offer a place to begin your education.

■ *Weather Maps: How To Read and Interpret All the Basic Weather Charts,* 2nd edition, by Peter Chaston. This book offers a good introduction to the basics of reading, interpreting, and understanding weather charts. The book can be purchased from Chaston Scientific, Inc. (P.O. Box 758, Kearney, MO 64060; phone 816-628-4770).

■ *An Introduction to Satellite Image Interpretation,* by Eric D. Conway and the Maryland Space Grant Consortium. This over-sized book offers thorough coverage of all aspects of understanding satellite imagery, including identifying cloud types, determining wind direction, understanding jet streams, and forecasting thunderstorms and severe weather. (The Johns Hopkins University Press, 1997.)

■ **Maritime Institute of Technology and Graduate Studies.** This organization offers a five-day course called "Heavy Weather Avoidance" intended for masters, mates, and pilots of offshore merchant ships. The course emphasizes the use of the 500-mb upper air charts to determine primary and secondary storm tracks. For more information, contact the Institute (5700 Hammonds Ferry Road, Linthicum Heights, MD 21090; phone 410-859-5700).

■ *Ocean Navigator* **magazine marine weather seminars.** The national maritime magazine *Ocean Navigator* offers one- and two-day seminars on marine weather in various locations throughout the United States during the fall. They also hold shorter weather-related forums at many of the boat shows. For more information, contact the magazine (P.O. Box 569, Portland, ME 04112; phone 207-772-2466).

■ **Ocean Strategies.** This organization specializes in marine weather forecasting and route planning. They offer seminars and onboard training programs for groups or individuals. Contact Michael Carr (P.O. Box 24, Peaks Island, ME 04108; phone 207-766-4430).

■ **Weather charts on the Internet.** NOAA provides weather charts of all types, which are updated several times a day at their website:
http://www.nws.noaa.gov/fax/nwsfax.shtml

the sun has risen in the tropics, the squalls will appear to be much closer to the boat when the sun comes up. If there are fluffy cumulus clouds overhead but no clearly developed squalls, most likely what you see is not a squall and will not come and get you.

Weather forecasting in the tropics is more straight-forward than in the higher latitudes. You will encounter fewer wind shifts and confused sea states. You will still need to be prepared to manage fronts and lows, though not nearly as often as in the temperate latitudes.

CHAPTER 17 | PREPARING FOR PASSAGE

Passage planning ■ *Wind strengths* ■ *Ocean currents* ■ *Other hazards* ■ *Additional resources* ■ **Passage preparations**
■ *Picking your weather window* ■ *Final shoreside preparations* ■ *The last few hours: readying the boat*

When we left Newport to head for Bermuda on our maiden voyage aboard *Silk,* we were proud of how we had prepared the boat. We thought we had done everything right. No, more than right. We had spent weeks finding a place to stow everything aboard: securing books on shelves, setting up shock cord to hold our sails in the quarter berth, building wooden spacers to keep the silverware quiet in the galley drawers. We had studied the charts and read the books on crossing the Gulf Stream. We had watched the weather and picked what we thought was the best weather window possible.

Within three days, we were in the worst storm of our entire circumnavigation. The bilge pump was clogged with sawdust and wooden plugs. Water slopped over the cabin sole with every roll. Books floated in the water. Wet clothes were scattered throughout the main cabin. The sink was full of safety harnesses and tethers. The stove was covered with clothes we hoped would dry. Seasickness prevented us from tackling the hopeless mess below. Clearly, many of our preparations were not up to the demands of the sea.

Many voyagers find their first passage a humbling experience. No benchmarks exist to judge what happens, and inexperience makes everything seem more vivid and extreme. If we had been more experienced on our shakedown cruise to Bermuda, we would never have gotten into that storm. But we learned more in that first 500 miles than we did in the next 5,000. In our first five days of voyaging, we set our benchmark for extreme conditions. We learned early what *Silk* could handle and what we could take. For the rest of our trip we were always able to say, "We've been in worse."

The most important lesson we learned on our shake-down cruise served us well throughout the rest of our voyage: *For offshore conditions, if it seems "good enough" it isn't; if it seems bulletproof, it just might do.* Before each passage, we measured our preparations against the demands of that first storm. Once we got out to sea and knew what the conditions were, we were a bit more relaxed—though we were always ready to batten down the boat in less than 20 minutes.

Preparation, by necessity, focuses on prevention, and shorthanded crews need to prepare more thoroughly than fully crewed boats to ensure an adequate margin of safety. Our prepassage routine developed from that first experience with a storm at sea and it reflected the fact that we were both prone to seasickness over the first few days. Our preparations were designed to keep us safe until we found our sea legs.

Those preparations started with passage planning weeks before we left. A few days before we wanted to leave, we would complete our final shoreside preparations while we looked for a good weather window. In the last few hours, we concentrated on preparing the boat. We sought to minimize our activities the first day or so out and prepare for as many contingencies as possible. Thorough preparation left us free to enjoy the wonders of passagemaking.

PASSAGE PLANNING

Your overall voyage plan will have taken into account the ocean currents and prevailing winds discussed in the last chapter. You now want to find the specific route that will allow you to sail as efficiently and safely as possible. But you can never know exactly what conditions you will encounter under way. Before you leave, develop a game plan that reflects average or expected conditions. Once under way, you can modify this based on what you actually experience.

Several tools will assist you in developing this plan. *Ocean Passages for the World* published by the British Admiralty or *World Cruising Routes* by Jimmy Cornell (see "Navigation needs," Chapter 8) offer route-planning advice for every major passage around the globe. The DMA or Admiralty passage chart provides information on hazards that may be encountered.

While not essential, the British Admiralty *Routing Charts* or the American *Pilot Charts* can be useful. These show historical wind speeds, directions, and currents over an entire ocean by month. The information is reported by quadrant, with each quadrant being 5 degrees on an edge (Figure 17-1). These charts are based upon reports from merchant ships, weather stations, and naval units, and the data has been averaged over a long period.

These charts can help you determine a route with the least likelihood of gales and the greatest likelihood of

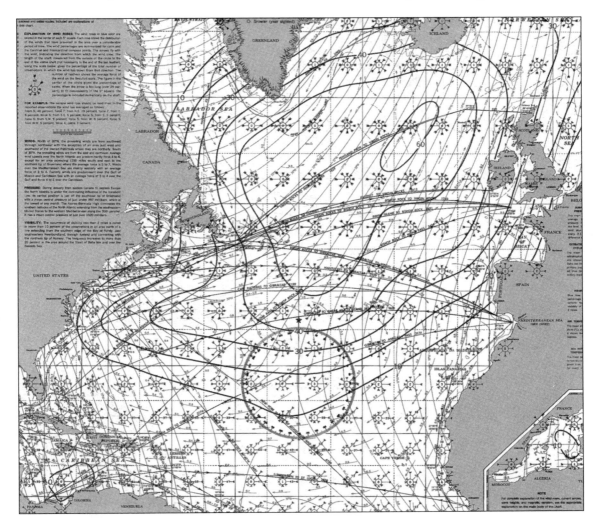

Figure 17-1. A pilot chart for the North Atlantic

favorable currents. However, all this data represents only averages and summaries of past conditions—it is no guarantee of the future. While they may be useful, an entire set of routing charts costs a great deal. Rather than paying for and carrying all the charts for a trade wind circumnavigation, we were often able to borrow the relevant chart from another boat or look at it in a chandlery.

To determine your route, you need to know the ports of entry at your destination. In most countries, you can only make landfall at ports with customs and immigration offices. These ports are listed in pilots or guidebooks to the area and are well known within the voyaging community. Your course should take you along the most direct path to a port of entry.

The rhumb line defines the shortest distance between where you are and where you want to go. This course takes into account the curvature of the earth's surface to minimize the distance. Calculating a rhumb line used to be part of the navigator's art, but the GPS now provides a rhumb line course between two points at the push of a button. Even if the route is in open water throughout, you may want to modify your course based on the wind strengths, ocean currents, and specific hazards.

Wind strengths

Passage planning books offer specific advice for each route. However, two general points underlie much of

their advice. First, the width and wind direction of the trade wind belt varies from east to west in the Atlantic and Pacific Oceans. Second, the average wind strength increases over the course of the trade wind season.

The trade wind belt narrows significantly from east to west in the Atlantic and Pacific Oceans. The winds in the eastern part have more of a northerly or southerly component to them. North-northeast and south-southeast winds commonly occur in the Northern and Southern Hemispheres respectively. In the western part of the Atlantic and Pacific Oceans, the easterly component dominates. By adding a few hundred miles to the rhumb line route to take advantage of these two factors, you can get into port a few days earlier. In general, on a westabout circumnavigation, sail north or south outside the trades and sail west in the trades.

The advice for a Canaries-to-Caribbean passage, "Sail south until the butter melts then head due west," takes advantage of both of these factors. By sailing straight into the trade winds on their eastern edge, boats enter where the trade wind band reaches farthest north. They sail south while the prevailing wind direction is more northerly (Figure 17-2). These directions mean you will sail the legs of a right triangle rather than the hypotenuse. Long experience has proven this route faster than heading directly for the Caribbean across the relatively windless horse latitudes.

This strategy works for most passages that enter or leave the trade winds and for crossing the doldrums.

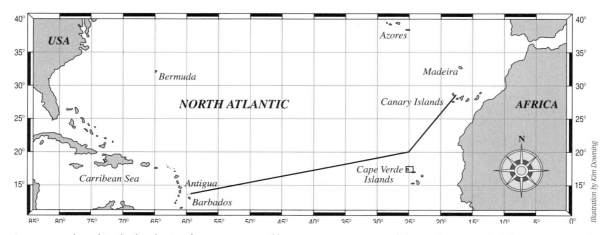

Figure 17-2. The traditional sailing directions for a Canaries-to-Caribbean passage instruct you to sail almost to the Cape Verdes before turning westward.

From the higher latitudes, sail north or south into the trades and then turn west toward your destination as shown in Figure 17-2. Leaving the trades, sail as far west as possible and then run north or south toward the higher latitudes (Figure 17-3). When crossing the doldrums, enter them at their narrowest point and then turn due north or south to cross them (Figure 17-4).

The trade winds also vary significantly in strength depending on the season. We left the Canary Islands for the Caribbean in late October. While we knew that the trade winds did not really establish themselves until after Christmas, we underestimated what that would mean for our passage. What winds we had were light and fluky with frequent violent squalls characteristic of the doldrums. We took 26 days to sail the 2,600 nautical miles—one of the slowest and longest passages of our entire trip. We were not impressed with our first experience in the trade winds: The average wind speed was about 10 knots.

Friends of ours on similar-sized boats who waited and left in mid-December or early January had twice the wind and took a third less time. For the fastest and least frustrating trip, wait for the trade winds to fill in before you set off. The trades blow more strongly in the winter months than in the summer, when the ITCZ is at its furthest reach in the opposite hemisphere. The strongest winds are in January and February in the Northern Hemisphere and July and August in the Southern Hemisphere.

In those months, the trade winds can get quite boisterous, especially when an abnormally large and intense high pressure system exists in the horse latitudes. As discussed in the last chapter, this combination results in "reinforced trade winds." We experienced reinforced trades during the Bora Bora-to-Tonga passage (described in the sidebar "A tropics example—South Pacific passage," Chapter 16). Exactly one year later, reinforced trade wind conditions in the southern Indian Ocean helped us sail almost 2,000 nautical miles from Cocos Keeling to Rodrigues in 13 days.

Once you have taken into account the normal location and strength of the trades to establish your theoretical best route, be prepared to modify your plan based on actual conditions. When we crossed the North Atlantic from Bermuda to the Azores, we planned to follow the traditional route: northeast from Bermuda to 40° N, then due east to within a couple hundred miles

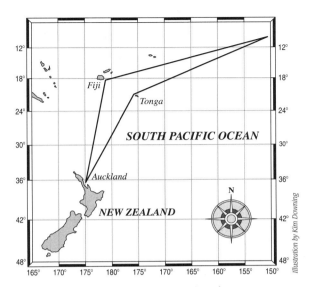

Figure 17-3. Typical routes to New Zealand leave from Tonga or Fiji.

of the Azores, then southeast. As we approached 40° N, we were listening to the daily SSB roll call. Boats were getting hit by gale after gale north of 39°. Boats were becalmed south of 38°. We modified our plan and stayed just south of 39° N. We had strong winds with one small low for the 16-day passage (see the sidebar "Example—North Atlantic passage," Chapter 16). When we headed south to New Zealand from Fiji, the daily roll call included a boat that was just over 100 miles in front of us. Twice they got into intense lows with gale-force winds, and both times we slowed down a bit to let the system pass to the south of us. Through a combination of forewarning and good luck, we had idyllic weather all the way to New Zealand.

Ocean currents

You also want to find the strongest favorable current possible. Ocean currents tend to be fickle, hard to find, and harder to keep track of once found. When we least expected it, we would suddenly realize that we were getting a 2-knot boost from somewhere. Then it would disappear, often where our charts and references said it should be strongest. While charts and routing books may get you into the area, actually finding weak currents often depends on luck or the reports of other boats.

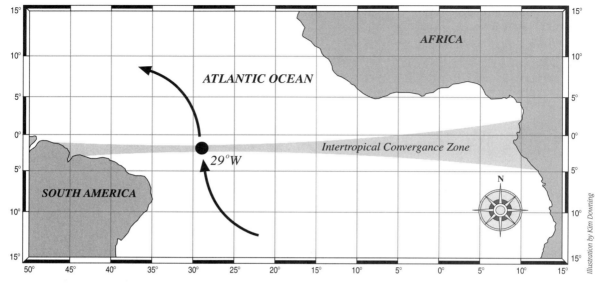

Figure 17-4. In the South Atlantic, the doldrums are crossed near Brazil where they are at their narrowest.

Strong and potentially dangerous currents such as the Gulf Stream and Agulhas Current require more planning. Low pressure systems that would normally pose little hazard can create dangerous breaking waves where wind and current conflict. The exact location of these major ocean currents varies day by day, and the information available to assist mariners can only *report* the current situation—not *predict* the future location. In only a few places, such as leaving from Florida to head to the Bahamas, can you get a reliable weather forecast for the entire period you will be in the current. When approaching the east coast of the United States or South Africa, the current is crossed at the end of a passage with weather moving off the coast toward you. You cannot time your arrival at the current with any certainty or know what weather will greet you when you get there. When heading up the U.S. East Coast or down the eastern coast of South Africa, voyagers want to take advantage of the 3- or 4-knot boost from the current without finding themselves in the dangerous waves a low can bring.

While luck plays a role in avoiding bad weather in these currents, you can control some of the risk. First you need to know when you have entered the current. Instruments make locating the current straightforward. When traveling with the current, you will see a large dif-ference between your boat speed over the ground and through the water. If crossing the current, you will notice a difference between your compass course and your GPS course. Even without instruments, the following signs indicate that you have reached the current:

■ *Bird life and wildlife.* These currents carry with them a wealth of aquatic life that feed larger marine creatures. Flocks of birds overhead, pods of dolphins around the boat, whale sightings, and large schools of fish indicate that you have entered the current.

■ *Water color and temperature.* When approaching these warm-water currents from colder water, you can often see a clear demarcation between the gray-green water of the temperate latitudes and the cobalt blue water of the tropics that is carried by the current. Water temperature will change dramatically as well, rising by 10 to 20 degrees even in the summer months. Many voyagers carry a thermometer aboard to help them locate both warm and cold currents.

■ *Cloud formations.* The churning mixture of warm and cold water at the edge of the current often results in a relatively low cloud bank. Near the center of the current, the scattered cumulus "cotton balls" of the trade wind skies often predominate in good weather.

Once you have located the current, your next step depends on whether you want to cross it or use it for some free miles toward your destination. If you want to get across as painlessly as possible, the next 24 hours of weather becomes critical. If a serious low is on the way, consider heaving-to and waiting for it to pass before entering the current. If the weather looks clear and you decide to cross, don't underestimate how much you will be set by the current. Make sure to establish a compass course that will leave you upwind and up-current of your destination.

If your goal is to hitch a ride, set your course about 10 to 15 miles inside the edge of the current closer to land. Both the Agulhas and the Gulf Stream currents run most strongly there. If the weather starts to deteriorate, you can leave the current and reach waters where the waves will be more manageable. When sailing along the east coast of South Africa, the traditional approach is to make for the 100-fathom line when the barometer starts to drop. Just be careful not to get too close to land and end up on a lee shore in a gale.

Thanks to the biennial Newport-to-Bermuda race, entire books have been written on locating and navigating the Gulf Stream. Gulf Stream maps are readily available from both private weather routers and from the Navy on the Internet (see "Additional resources" in this chapter). For your first crossing of a major current, use whatever resources are available in route planning. But don't rely too much on this preponderance of fact. Focus on crossing safely without too much regard for speed or style. Once you've mastered the basics, you can try to get that extra knot by navigating the eddies.

Other hazards

Once you have planned a route based on prevailing winds and currents, you need to make sure that no hazards exist in your path that you need to alter course for. Review the chart, the pilots, and the books and consider the following types of hazards before finalizing your route.

■ **Small islands.** As discussed in Chapter 15, small islands in midocean can be incorrectly charted by several miles. To be safe, we allowed a minimum of 10 miles between us and any small islands or reefs along our route. If your planned route takes you closer than

Additional resources

Gulf Stream charts provide valuable information for locating and crossing the Gulf Stream safely. They are posted on the Internet several times a week by the U.S. Navy at www.navo.navy.mil. These charts are based upon satellite imagery and generated by a computer. They show the location of the north wall of the Gulf Stream, surface temperatures, and approximations of the warm and cold eddies. NOAA also posts infrared charts to the Internet at www.rsmas.miami.edu. You can access either of these for free. However, they do not provide any analysis or advice on interpreting the data.

As one part of their services, many private weather routers analyze these charts and offer specific recommendations for crossing the Gulf Stream. Jennifer Clark's Gulfstream specializes in Gulf Stream routing. Jennifer Clark spent 25 years charting the Gulf Stream for NOAA until her position was cut in 1995. Now she offers charts that show the north wall of the Gulf Stream, warm and cold eddies, shelf water, continental slope water, and so on. The charts are issued three times a week. Black and white charts are $20 and color are $25. This fee includes a consultation with Jennifer via SSB while at sea. For an additional fee, you can obtain prognoses for the next several days. She can be reached at phone 301-952-0930, or at gulfstrm@erols.com.

Contact The Cruising Association in the U.K. for more advice. (Phone 44(0)171-537-2828.)

that, decide whether or not you need to adjust it. For high islands or at night, establish visual contact to be sure you have passed the island safely.

■ **Reef and shoal waters.** In the Pacific in particular, extensive reefs and shoals exist that are unbuoyed and unlit. Between Tonga and Fiji and in the Coral Sea between New Caledonia and Australia, routes are complicated by these reef systems that are uncharted or for which several positions have been reported. In other areas, free-standing reefs enclose a lagoon 10 miles or more long with nothing but a tiny sand islet above water level. Minerva Reef south of Tonga and Beveridge Reef between Niue and Tonga are two examples in the Pacific that are favored voyaging stops in settled weather. Unless you plan to stop in one of these areas, give them a very wide berth and don't try to establish visual contact.

■ *Sea mounts.* Underwater mountain ranges exist on the ocean floor in many parts of the world. In a few places, these mountains rise to within less than 100 feet of the sea's surface. When a wave form traveling just under the surface of the water hits the mountain, it can rise up out of the water and become a freak wave. We believe that is what happened to us between Cape Town and St. Helena (see the sidebar "Our most costly minute" in this chapter). Two other boats we knew had similar experiences within a few miles of underwater mountains, one between Australia and Indonesia in the Arufura Sea and one south of Madagascar. Adjust your route to allow 10 miles between you and any sea mounts that come within 100 meters of the surface.

■ *Fog-prone areas.* While you are unlikely to encounter fog in the tropics, you may have to deal with it in parts of New Zealand, the west coast of South Africa, England, and parts of the eastern and western coasts of the United States and Canada. If your route includes fog-prone areas, be sure that you have a bell and an air horn aboard and that you know how to signal and understand the signals of others. If you intend to do much voyaging in these areas, invest in a radar. Review the rules for navigating in fog, and check the chart for some alternate ports where entry would be relatively risk free in low visibility.

If you encounter ice—the other major hazard—on a trade wind voyage, you should probably check your navigation. After modifying your course to reflect these hazards, you are ready to depart. You have your game plan, and you are ready to modify it based on the winds and currents you experience.

PASSAGE PREPARATIONS

You have completed your passage planning, and in a few days you will depart. You have started to look for good weather. You now begin to prepare the boat to head offshore. After living aboard and doing no sailing

for several weeks or months, this entails far more than simply closing the ports and heading off to sea. Leaving for a passage always involves a whirl of last-minute activities, including topping up supplies, stowing belongings, and finding places for new treasures. You will also need to go over the boat thoroughly to make sure she is in passagemaking condition. When you find the right weather window, you'll make one last run ashore to clear customs and to buy perishable items. After another few hours of final preparations aboard the boat, you will be ready to head off to sea.

Picking your weather window

Once you are at sea, you have to make the best of whatever weather comes your way. Before you leave, you have access to sophisticated weather forecasting and the luxury of selecting your weather. Even then, the best you can hope for in a weather window is two to three days of favorable winds and five days with a small likelihood of bad weather.

When you start looking for your weather window, you are looking for a favorable forecast confirmed by your own short-term forecasting and consistent with weather patterns in the area. Broadly speaking, systems move from west to east outside the tropics. But every major landmass has a weather pattern that varies with the season. Nor'easters often wreak havoc along the U.S. East Coast; southerly busters may greet you near South Africa; mariners have named each of the Mediterranean's myriad winds that result from topography and the seasons. These patterns cannot be readily intuited; they must be learned. The following three sources can assist you in mastering local weather patterns:

■ *Pilots and sailing directions.* Your first introduction to the weather patterns of an area will come from your voyage planning and route planning. Pilots and guides can provide an overview of regional weather patterns and offer some local weather lore.

■ *Synoptic charts, satellite photos, and general forecasts.* Even where forecasts are inaccurate, they can help you become familiar with local weather patterns. We always followed daily weather in the newspapers, on television, or in weather faxes posted in the local yacht club.

A day in the life—our most costly minute

We were five days out of Cape Town enroute to St. Helena, and things had just settled down after a three-day gale. We were running with 20-knot winds and 10- to 12-foot seas. I was just getting out of my bunk after an hour of light sleep when I heard the sibilant sound that a breaking wave makes just before it hits the boat. The sound seemed to go on for several minutes, but it was probably no more than 10 seconds. It ended with a terrific crash, and *Silk* rolled farther than she ever had in any gale.

Water poured into my bunk from the hatch over the main salon, a hatch that was double-sealed and dogged down so tight that we had to stand on it to release it. We came back upright so suddenly and with such force that the frying pan on the gimbaled stove flew across the galley and clattered to the floor in the nav station. Our panic kit, which had never moved in 25,000 miles of open-ocean voyaging, was thrown across the cabin. The boat came back upright, but she wasn't sailing. With flogging sails and shuddering motion, she was head to wind. Evans and I scrambled out of our bunks and looked out into the cockpit.

Seawater filled the cockpit to the tops of the coamings. The plywood blade for our wind vane had disappeared. Evans headed to the forepeak to dig out our spare blade. I stepped into hip-deep water and waded back to the helm to turn *Silk* back on course. I grabbed cushions, sponges, and buckets before they floated out of the cockpit. Evans brought out the spare wind vane blade, and we set *Silk* up to sail once again.

While I cleaned up below, Evans put things back together above. Then we decided to start the engine to charge our batteries. Less than 10 minutes later, the engine slowed as if an invisible hand were pulling back the throttle. Then it died altogether. A quick look in the engine compartment revealed that the Racor filter was full of water. I suddenly pictured the seawater filling the cockpit and thought of our diesel breather located about a foot below the level of the coamings. We soon confirmed that salt water had siphoned through the diesel breather and into the fuel tank.

The next few hours were some of the worst we spent aboard *Silk*. We opened the diesel tank and pumped it out using a hand pump. Each time we rolled, fuel would pulse out of the small opening. Diesel soon covered us, the quarter berth, and the cabin sole. But we had no choice. With even a trace of salt water in the cylinders, the engine would not survive five days to St. Helena. We pumped over a liter of seawater out of the fuel tank. We reinstalled the Racor and bled the engine. We had almost given up hope when I turned the key one last time. One more long crank and it fired up.

We had saved our engine, but the freak wave that had hit us beam on had done a great deal of damage. The wind vane blade had been sheared off at the base. (We were fortunate to be able to get another spare on St. Helena, where plywood is scarce.) Our cockpit instrument repeater and the autopilot control head were destroyed. Several months later we discovered that the diesel heater had also been damaged. In that second when the wave hit us, we had suffered some $5,000 worth of damage. If we had lost the engine as well, the figure would have been more than triple that.

After things calmed down, we went to the chart and looked at the two sea mounts we were between, one of which rose from 2,000 meters below the water's surface to 23. We had intended to sail around them and had been trying to set a course to do so. But the gale had set us a bit farther north than we had planned. The night before, we had decided that the storm was abating and there was no real danger. Based on our friends' experiences with sea mounts in the Indian Ocean, we should have altered course.

We will never know how big the wave that hit us was. We are both grateful that neither of us was on deck at the time. Given the relatively calm conditions, we would have been unlikely to be wearing our safety harnesses. Our hard-won lessons from our first gale also paid off: We suffered no damage below because everything was so well stowed. Learn from our experience. Keep the boat well stowed at all times while on passage and avoid sea mounts!

■ *High seas forecasts and roll calls.* Even before you reach an area, listening to the forecasts will help you get a feel for the weather patterns. You can get insights into the accuracy of the local forecasting by comparing forecasts to the conditions actually reported in the roll call. Weeks before we got to South Africa, we knew that the weather forecasting was particularly inaccurate. A low moved off or around the African continent and into the Indian Ocean every three to four days, whether forecast or not.

Just as weather differs between the tropics and the temperate latitudes, so does departure strategy. In the tropics, we were mainly concerned with avoiding fronts and their associated westerly winds. In the temperate latitudes, we learned to time our departure to take advantage of strong but favorable winds in a low.

Temperate latitudes

Only experience can teach you the balancing act of waiting for a good weather window with leaving and dealing with whatever is out there. For longer passages, you will have to accept what you are dealt in terms of gales or calms after the first two or three days. We experienced an average of one small gale (winds of 35 knots) on each of our passages from, into, or through the higher latitudes.

When we selected a weather window, we looked for three things:

■ *Favorable forecast.* Obviously, we wanted a forecast for good weather. That meant a favorable wind direction and strong wind. Light winds often signaled a high moving in and would leave us becalmed after a few days at sea. We did not mind gale-force winds, so long as they were from behind. Like most offshore boats, *Silk* liked to run downwind in strong winds, and we were generally quite comfortable, as long as the seas were manageable.

■ *Weather signs that substantiated the forecast.* We learned not to trust a favorable forecast that we couldn't confirm with our own observations of sky, clouds, wind directions, and barometric pressure. We were more comfortable believing the long-term forecast when the short-term forecast agreed with our own predictions.

■ *No known lows along our early route.* While there was no guarantee that a low wouldn't develop after we had set off, we didn't like to leave knowing we were likely to intersect an existing low. If a low was on the weather charts and moving toward our route, we were inclined to wait another day or so for it to pass.

This approach points to a specific weather pattern. We preferred to leave after the front half of a low had passed over our position. Once the wind shifted so that we had a favorable wind direction, we would leave on the "back" of a gale that was forecast to be followed by a strong high (see "A temperate latitude example—North Atlantic passage," page 296). A strong low and a strong high are both dominant enough weather features that they are unlikely to be mistaken or to allow anything else to develop spontaneously. We would have favorable winds through the second half of the low, and then winds from much the same direction as the leading edge of the high came over us. With this weather pattern, we were almost guaranteed fast, downwind sailing for up to four days after leaving port.

Many people prefer leaving on the leading edge of a rapidly filling high. This makes the first few days less boisterous, with calmer sailing within a day or so of leaving. They find the risk of being becalmed in the high preferable to the possibility of being beaten up in a low. However, the high may be too weak to prevent the sudden formation of a low. When we left New Zealand, the synoptic chart showed a continuous weak high across the entire Tasman Sea. We left as soon as the wind shift indicated that it had reached us. Less than 12 hours later, the forecasters had "found" a little low and 24 hours later there were three little lows. Within 36 hours we were beating toward New Caledonia in gale-force winds. This strategy is best used where the high is well developed and strong, as indicated by its center pressure and by closely spaced isobars that extend several hundred miles inward from its edges.

Tropics

When leaving from one tropical destination for another, we rarely had to wait for a weather window. Settled trade wind conditions offered the best guarantee of good weather for the first few days. On the few occasions when the forecast or our own observations indicated unsettled weather, we would wait until the front or low had passed before setting off. A high moving through the temperate latitudes creates boisterous conditions, but it reduces the chances of encountering a frontal system for up to a week (see the sidebar "A tropics example—South Pacific passage," Chapter 16).

When you leave from a tropical port to sail into higher latitudes, luck plays a large role in determining your weather. If you are sailing from Fiji to New Zealand or from Réunion to South Africa, the weather window you select to leave on only carries you through the first few days in tropical latitudes. You cannot predict what weather will await you by the time you reach the temperate latitudes. The best assistance on these passages comes from a boat that is sailing a day ahead of you and reporting their weather on the roll call—plus a bit of good luck.

Final shoreside preparations

Once offshore, it always took a few days to figure out where we had stowed our sea legs. Until then, we both felt as if we were drunk. Our feet never ended up quite where we tried to put them, we were often lethargic and dull-witted, and everything from sail changes to cooking took twice as long as expected. During this period, the simple was always difficult, and the difficult was often impossible. We were at our most vulnerable those first few days—not just to seasickness, but also to mistakes in judgment that could affect our safety. Our prepassage preparations were designed to keep us safe and make life easier while we reacclimated to being offshore.

Aside from topping off all supplies, we had to convert our shoreside bungalow back into a shipshape vessel. That meant setting up the boat to minimize the likelihood of seasickness, stowing everything securely for offshore work, and performing some prepassage boatkeeping. Most of our friends followed similar prepassage routines, though some relaxed their preparations as they gained experience. We maintained a rigorous discipline in passage preparations, largely because of the lessons we learned from our first passage. Our fanaticism stood us in good stead on several occasions when the sea was unruly.

Topping off

Except where clean sources were unavailable, we topped off our fuel and water before leaving. After topping off the tanks, we put some Vaseline on the seals of the deck fills and tightened them down to prevent contamination from salt water or dirt. We filled all our extra jugs and filled our propane tanks if they needed it.

By this time, the major provisioning was done. The next phase was cleaning the icebox and the crates we used for produce storage with a Clorox solution and purchasing perishables. We started with the heavy items that were least perishable—potatoes, onions, and apples. If ice was available, we purchased 50 to 75 pounds and cooled the icebox down. If we had room to stow anything more, or if we needed to top off things like drink mixes or flour, we bought a few additional supplies.

Arranging stowage

After being in port for weeks or months, part of the process of getting our sea legs back was getting our sea eyes back—the second sense that automatically notices anything that isn't stowed well. If we had been sitting in a marina or harbor for several weeks, we always tried to take a short sail to a bay where we could anchor and sort ourselves out before we actually left. That sail was typically punctuated by at least one minor crisis, from a poorly stowed shelf to renegade dish soap. Once you have cleared customs you are technically supposed to leave the country, so in many places you cannot stop to get acclimated. In those cases we sailed to a nearby anchorage for lunch or an overnight a day before clearing customs. We returned and cleared out, confident we were shipshape.

Paying particular attention to the following areas will make the first few days at sea less eventful and more enjoyable:

■ *Restock galley containers.* I kept small amounts of most baking and cooking ingredients within easy reach of the strapped-in position in the galley. Extra quantities were stowed in less accessible areas that I considered my onboard "market." Before a passage, I would always go "shopping" and refill the galley containers with flour, sugar, salt, pasta, rice, and so on. With my galley fully stocked, I didn't need to get anything out of stowage before I had regained my sea legs.

■ *Premake meals.* Over the first few days, more than a few minutes in the galley with gas fumes and cooking odors could make either of us seasick. But we were also likely to get seasick if we did not keep our stomachs busy with nourishing food. I premade meals for the first few days of the passage—sandwiches and salads for cold meals, and leftovers or casseroles for hot meals. Boiled potatoes and hard-boiled eggs provided several alternatives for the first few days at sea.

■ *Stow clothes.* We stored our shore clothes in sealed dry bags in the forward-most forepeak lockers (see "Prevent mold and mildew," Chapter 11). Before leaving, we sorted out the clothes that we wanted accessible on passage, made sure the rest were absolutely dry and clean, and put them into "dry stowage" in the forward lockers. We left passage clothes unprotected in the easily accessible aft locker.

■ *Restow heavy things as low as possible.* In light or heavy weather, sailing performance will be adversely affected by weight high in the boat or in the ends. If you have been cruising with two anchors on the bow, restow one low in the boat along with extra chain. Tools, cans, spares, and other heavy items should be returned to their normal homes.

■ *Prepare emergency equipment.* Check emergency equipment before heading off. We took apart the abandon-ship kit, checked everything over to make sure it was still in working order, replaced the water with fresh, changed whatever food we kept in it, repacked the kit, and stowed it in its place near the companionway. We tested the EPIRB battery to make sure it was in working order (406 MHz EPIRB's come with a test switch that checks battery condition, signal burst, and strobe operation). We inventoried the medical kit, restocked the seasick medications kept in the nav station, and replenished day-to-day supplies such as Band-Aids and cold remedies kept in the head.

These preparations were all designed to make the first few days at sea as trouble free and efficient as possible. Aside from preventing seasickness, they allowed us to concentrate on sailing the boat until our passage routines were re-established.

Prepassage boatkeeping

A little boatkeeping before departure goes a long way toward making sure the first few days are trouble free. Before we left, we always did a quick inspection from the bottom of the keel to the top of the mast. After our mini-shakedown sail to a nearby anchorage, Evans would dive and take a good look at the bottom, checking the rudder, prop, zincs, and the condition of the bottom paint.

The rudder and prop must turn freely without binding. Remove any barnacles growing on the prop blades or between the rudder and the boat's underbody. Barnacles make the prop unbalanced and damage the cutlass bearing. After several weeks or months in tropical water, at least one barnacle would have decided to call our prop home. A dental probe removes small barnacles quickly and easily.

Stray electrical charges in marinas or busy anchorages can destroy zincs in a short period. Inspect them and replace them if necessary.

The difference between a clean bottom and a dirty bottom can mean a knot or more of boat speed on a light-air passage. Those using hard bottom paint can scrub off any grass or barnacles that have taken hold. Soft bottom paint should never be scrubbed, but it will benefit from the sail to a nearby anchorage.

After the underwater inspection, we put a generous coat of wax on the hull. Wax protects the gelcoat and keeps barnacles from growing above the waterline when you are heeled over day after day on passage. You can easily apply wax from a dinghy. On a long passage the action of the salt water will scrub off a light coat in a week—so go for coverage, not cosmetics.

Above decks, we cleaned the mast track and lubricated it with soap. While up the mast, we did a cursory inspection of spreaders, tangs, fittings, and the masthead crane. We checked that all lights on the mast and on deck were functioning. On the first passage of the season, we thoroughly inspected the mast and all its fittings (as described in Chapter 9). We checked all the running rigging and end-for-ended any that showed minor chafe or wear; looked for any cracks in the welds of the wind vane and inspected the control lines for chafe; lubricated the wind vane blocks and the steering drum; and tightened the lifelines and inspected the lifeline fittings.

While you can never prevent or foresee every eventuality, these preparations minimize the chances that you will find yourself dealing with a minor emergency in the first day or so at sea. Like picking a weather window, they give you confidence that you won't have to deal with any nasty surprises before you are acclimated.

The last few hours: readying the boat

The day has come. The weather window looks perfect, and your other preparations are finished. You need to clear customs, throw away any garbage, and buy those last few perishable groceries. Then you need to stow everything securely, set sail, and leave land behind. The time required to clear out of the country varies, and you can't control the timing of this task. Clearing out sometimes took an entire day, sometimes a half-hour. Most often, it took two to three hours.

We needed about two hours after we returned to the boat from our last trip ashore. We brought the dinghy aboard together. Then I worked below decks and Evans worked above decks. Once we had each completed our respective tasks, we switched and inspected each other's work. After weeks or months of not sailing the boat, Evans would often find that I had missed securing the fiddle that held 100 CDs, or I would find a sheet that had been led the wrong way through the lifelines. Right before we started the engine, one of us would do a quick once over to be sure the engine oil was topped off and filters and fittings were ready to go.

The very last thing that we did was to plug the main chain hawser. We never wanted to be maneuvering around port without the ability to drop an anchor. We left our main anchor attached to the chain and ready to run until we had actually left the port and were in open water with our sails up and drawing. Then one of us went forward, lashed the anchor down, unhooked the chain and attached it to the teak plug, and wedged the plug into the hawser. On the way back to the cockpit, we lowered the courtesy flag of the country that we were leaving. From that moment we considered ourselves offshore, and our passage routines took over.

On Deck

Sails need to be set up for the first day at sea based on the forecast and your own observations of the current conditions. We preferred to set up several potential sail combinations to meet changing conditions for the first 24 hours or so. For moderate to strong winds, we pre-set a reef in the main and hanked on the Yankee with sheets attached. The genoa was furled and the drum locked. The genoa sheets were flaked and lashed to the bow pulpit.

In calmer conditions where we planned on using the furling genoa, the Yankee was hanked on and lashed to the bow pulpit in its bag. The Yankee sheets were led through the appropriate genoa track blocks and tied off to the farthest forward handhold on the coach roof. If the weather deteriorated and we had to reduce sail, we wouldn't have to carry the Yankee forward and hank it on. By having the main, mizzen, genoa, Yankee, and staysail readily available, we could manage any winds over 10 knots without having to set up another sail.

We rarely set up the spinnaker pole before leaving. Land effects meant that it often took a day before we reached the prevailing winds and could fly our double headsails. If the weather deteriorated in the meantime, we would only have had to take the pole down. If the winds sorted themselves out more quickly, the weather was calm enough to set up the pole.

Beyond setting up the appropriate sail combinations for the expected winds, the following things need to be done before leaving port:

■ *Dinghy.* Stow your dinghy securely. Deflate inflatable dinghies and stow them below. Lash rigid dinghies to good dinghy chocks. You can tie oars inside a rigid dinghy or store them below. Don't lash oars to handholds on the cabin trunk where they could interfere with your grip. Stow your outboard below or cover it and attach it to the stern rail. Stow gasoline on deck or in a sealed locker that drains overboard.

■ *Wind vane.* Set up the oar, vane, and control lines. Adjust control line tension based on expected wind conditions.

■ *Spare hawser.* While you should plug the main hawser only after leaving port, you can plug the spare

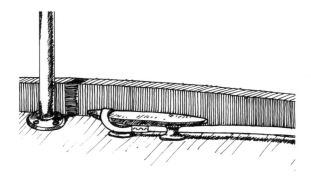

Figure 17-5. Detail of how we attached our jacklines to the bow cleat

hawser any time. Our hawser did not have a specially made plug, so we stuffed a plastic bag into it and sealed it with a couple of layers of duct tape. While this wasn't foolproof, in bad conditions water came through only in drips.

■ *Jacklines.* If these are not permanently on deck, you'll need to set them up. We used two 40-foot lengths of 1-inch tubular nylon webbing with loops sewn on one end. We hooked the loops over the forward prong of the bow cleats, led them back through the middle of the cleat (Figure 17-5), and then led them aft and tied them tightly in several layers of figure eight's to the aft cleats. Attach jacklines only to pad eyes or deck cleats. Other deck hardware is unlikely to survive a roll.

■ *Storm sails.* On passage, storm sails should not be tucked into an inaccessible locker. As a cutter-rigged

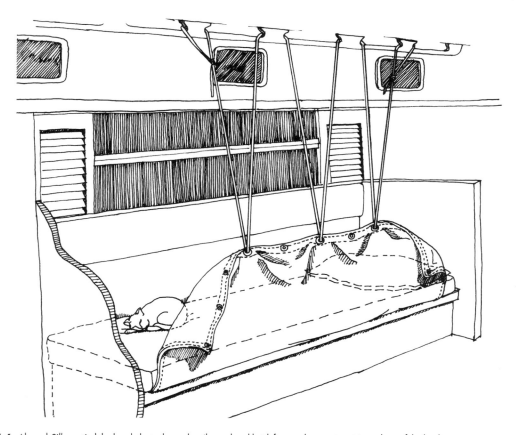

Figure 17-6. Aboard *Silk,* we tied the lee cloths to the grab rails overhead but left enough room to get in and out of the bunk.

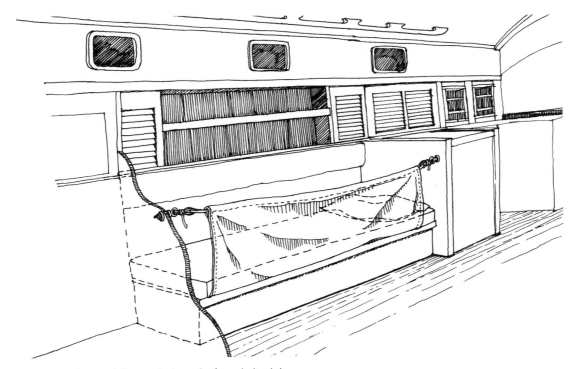

Figure 17-7. Pad eyes and clips can also be used to fasten the lee cloths.

ketch, *Silk's* storm sails—the mizzen and the staysail—were always set to fly. On a cutter, we would set up a storm trysail on its separate track and a storm jib on the staysail stay, and bag both to protect them from the sun.

Below

If your quarter berth or pilot berths are used to stow items in port, you will need to rearrange stowage for passagemaking. I started preparations below by moving all the items we normally kept in the quarter berth and stowing them securely in the forepeak. Lines and pad eyes under the forepeak cushions were used to lash everything down.

The rest of my preparations were designed to minimize our time below. These included the following:

■ *Sea berths.* I made up both settee berths and the quarterberth so I wouldn't have to make up a different bunk the first night out. The settees had lee clothes with lines that were attached to the bunk under the cushions. The line was looped through the grab rail and back

through the eyes in the cloth (Figure 17-6). We stopped about three eyes short before each end of the cloth to allow for good air circulation. We preferred this solution to snapping the lee cloth to pad eyes (Figure 17-7) because we found it easier to get in and out of the bunk. I stowed clothes for the first day or two at the foot of our respective bunks.

■ *Stowage.* Beyond making sure that all fiddles and shock cords are in place, inspect the stowage areas to make sure nothing will break or keep you awake in a rolly sea. I made a noise inspection of each locker and drawer by opening and closing them several times or by trying to shift the contents with my hands. I stuffed towels, socks, and rags between items to keep them quiet and prevent them from shifting. Make sure that each drawer and locker latches firmly when closed for the last time so they don't pop open on the first tack.

■ *Seacocks.* We closed head and galley seacocks before leaving on passage and opened them only when they were in use. This prevented any unpleasant back-filling of water into sinks or the head. If we did get water in the bilge, we could isolate the problem more quickly.

■ *Hatches and ports.* We made it a rule to leave with all ports and hatches closed just to be sure that we didn't miss any. We applied a bit of Vaseline to the black rubber gaskets on our ports before dogging them down securely. This created a watertight seal and kept the gaskets from drying out in hot, dry tropical weather.

■ *Hatchboards.* If the weather starts to deteriorate, you may need to put the hatchboards in quickly. We normally left with the lower one in place and the upper one stowed within reach of the companionway. If the weather looked boisterous, we put both in place.

■ *Emergency preparations.* Make sure all emergency gear is in place. I checked that our safety harnesses and tethers were in their proper place and easily accessible. I also checked that a Cyalume light stick was taped to each harness. We used the light sticks because both flashlights and batteries have such a marginal life span at sea. The light sticks are small and light and can be attached to the harnesses so that they are hardly noticeable.

Preparing for the worst before we left port allowed us to relax and enjoy our first few days at sea. Even if we encountered bad weather, we needed no more than 20 minutes to batten down the boat and set our storm sails. Most of the time we left confident that we were overprepared and had minimized the chances of seasickness or injury while we found our sea legs.

Taking care of the boat—watchkeeping ▪ *Watchkeeping systems* ▪ *Duties of the watchkeeper* ▪ **Taking care of the crew**
▪ *Cooking* ▪ *Sleeping* ▪ *Diversions* ▪ *Managing garbage at sea* ▪ *Safety* ▪ *Morale* ▪ **Making a successful landfall**

We always experienced a thrill when land slipped under the horizon and Evans and I were alone again with *Silk* on an empty ocean. At that moment my emotions included a mix of apprehension and excitement. After weeks in port, the sea seemed overwhelming. Yet I had felt a tremendous sense of relief as shoreside cares were replaced by the immediacy of sail combinations and weather patterns.

After three or four days, we were completely under the spell of the sea. Sunrise and sunset marked the beginning and end of each day, and the little crosses on the chart marked our progress across the vast ocean. Taking care of the boat and keeping her moving toward our destination occupied most of our attention and almost all our energy. With whatever time was left, we took care of ourselves—sleeping, eating, and socializing. After a week or so, these routines merged into a seamless round of sleeping, eating, navigating, and watchkeeping, interrupted only by sail changes, emergency repairs, and unusual sightings—rare meetings with other vessels, moments of breathtaking natural beauty, and exciting visits by marine life. When we approached landfall, the rhythm started to dissolve. A safe landfall required as much care and forethought as our first few days of passagemaking had.

TAKING CARE OF THE BOAT— WATCHKEEPING

At sea, the boat is your world and her needs must be your first concern. Taking care of a boat on passage means keeping her moving well in the right direction, navigating to avoid any hazards, changing sails in re-

sponse to actual or expected wind changes, repairing any damage and doing preventive maintenance, and watching out for other vessels operating in the area. On some days, these activities fill 24 hours for a crew of four or more. On other days, a crew of two can become bored at sea.

I have already discussed most of the things you do to take care of the boat: sail handling, using self-steering, finding and fixing potential maintenance problems, navigating, and weather forecasting. On most boats, the watchkeeping system defines how all this gets done. A person or group of people are designated as "on watch" and responsible for the vessel while another group are "off watch" and able to see to their own needs. The off watch is always available to assist if necessary.

Watchkeeping systems are as individual as the boats out there voyaging. Some boats employ a system more formal than the British Admiralty, but watchkeeping is more relaxed for many shorthanded crews. In the case of singlehanded boats, a watchkeeping system cannot be said to exist at all. For shorthanded vessels, a real conflict exists between good watchkeeping and debilitating exhaustion. But keeping a proper watch is essential. Every shorthanded crew must find a way to do it while staying alert enough to handle the unexpected.

Watchkeeping systems

Those on watch must keep the boat sailing well while keeping a proper lookout for other vessels. A freighter and a sailboat on a head-on collision course will be closing at a minimum of 25 to 30 knots. The freighter will be in visual range for less than 20 minutes during the day and only a bit longer at night. Nowadays, some supertankers and larger freighters rely on radar alarms to alert them to traffic in their area. Yet the radar profile of a small sailing boat can easily be lost in the clutter from waves or squalls. Some freighters do not even seem to monitor VHF regularly (although our success rate in getting an answer to our hail was considerably higher if I tried than if Evans did).

The risk of a collision at sea exists at all times and in all conditions. A proper watchkeeping system implies that someone is actively scanning the horizon 24 hours a day, with the length of each watch determined by how long a person can remain alert and observant. Most boats do not live up to this reality. While most people accept that singlehanded boats cannot keep a proper lookout 24 hours a day, few people are willing to admit that doublehanded boats might face a similar difficulty.

While collision is a concern, the vastness of the ocean renders it unlikely. For us, spotting another vessel at sea caused a minor uproar because it happened so seldom. As far as I know, the chances of a midocean collision between a sailboat and a freighter outside of major shipping lanes have never been calculated. But the chances seem slim indeed. Despite that, a proper watch should always be the goal—on any vessel, in any situation.

A healthy and competent crew of three or more can and should maintain a good watch at all times. And all crews, no matter how small, must maintain a proper watch within 150 miles of land where the shipping traffic increases and coastal hazards exist. That includes situations where the vessel is hove-to near land, whether in bad weather or waiting for enough light to enter port. Smaller crews on longer passages away from known shipping lanes must balance the demands of watchkeeping against the need for sleep.

Two general rules will help you develop a workable watch system. Initially, unless conditions are very mild and the crew is well adapted, watches should not exceed 4 hours at night. Very few people can maintain concentration beyond that. In heavy weather or if the crew is hand steering, shorten watches to 2 hours. Second, the smaller the crew, the more the watch system will need to reflect the sleep patterns of the individuals aboard. To get 24 hours per day out of two people, the watch system should take advantage of their natural cycles.

Beyond these general principles, the key is to find a watchkeeping system that works for you. There are some standard solutions for various crew sizes, all of which have their pros and cons. Experiment with some of these as you search for your own solution.

Crews of four or more

A crew of more than four people makes watchkeeping easy. With so many people, a formal schedule allows everyone to get into a routine and avoids confusion over who is responsible. While rigid watch schedules ignore individual sleep patterns, most people can rest fully on the long off-watch periods.

If the four crewmembers are of unequal sailing skill or if they are unused to watchkeeping, they should be combined into two watches of two people. The two standing watch can help keep one another awake. They are also less likely to need help from the off watch. Some basic schedules are shown in Table 18-1.

The shading shows that these watch schedules provide at least four full hours off twice a day. The basic watch schedule lets each watch team develop a set pattern of sleeping and waking for the entire passage. However, many people prefer to vary the watch schedule because they find one watch particularly difficult—usually the midnight to 4 A.M. "graveyard" shift. For this reason, the Royal Navy and Merchant Marine use "dog watches" in the late afternoon to stagger the schedule from day to day. If the weather is cold or stormy, or if the crew is forced to hand steer due to a mechanical failure, the 12 hours from 2000 to 0800 can be broken up into four 3-hour or six 2-hour watches.

During daylight hours, staying alert does not conflict with natural rhythms, and someone else is almost always awake and able to assist. Some boats therefore split the daylight hours into two long watches of six hours each. Other boats keep two people on each night watch but have only one designated watchkeeper during the daylight hours. This gives an inexperienced watchkeeper the opportunity to manage alone for short periods of time. When children are old enough to assist in the watchkeeping, they can be given a short daylight watch until they gain confidence and competence.

In practice, when crews get comfortable with each other and with being at sea, the daylight hours often become less formal and a watch schedule is maintained only at night. This works well for many crews, and everyone will enjoy the freedom of the days in contrast to the structure of the nights. For some crews, such an informal system can be dangerous if the burden of the daylight watchkeeping falls on one or two more diligent crewmembers. The skipper should consider the personalities involved before moving to a less structured watch system. Once informality sets in, discipline can be difficult to reassert.

Crews of three

With three people (or four people and a designated cook or floater), one person will be on watch at any given time. A standby person is designated for each watch, and that person is called first when extra assistance is needed. The cook never stands a watch in most traditional watchkeeping systems. If one person is responsible for all galley chores, this still makes good sense. If the skipper wants to be woken for any course changes or sail changes, then he or she can act as standby on all watches. The Basic and Royal Navy watch systems described above can be modified for three watches or three people (see Table 18-2).

If there is no skipper or cook, the standby person for the first half of the watch is the one who has just come off watch. The standby person for the second half of the watch is the one about to come on watch. The shaded areas in Table 18-2 show A Watch's standby schedule. With any luck, everyone gets at least four hours of uninterrupted sleep during the night. With a skipper or cook acting as standby, each watchkeeper gets a full eight hours off every night in settled weather.

When only one person is on deck at a time, many consider shorter watches desirable. Three-hour watches naturally stagger the schedule without resorting to dog watches. Again, some arrangement to designate one person on call will maximize everyone's sleep. Table 18-3 shows a standard three-hour watch system for three crewmembers.

Table 18-1. Alternative watch schedules with two watch teams of two people each

	0000 to 0200	0200 to 0400	0400 to 0600	0600 to 0800	0800 to 1000	1000 to 1200	1200 to 1400	1400 to 1600	1600 to 1800	1800 to 2000	2000 to 2200	2200 to 2400
Basic (Four on/off)	A	A	B	B	A	A	B	B	A	A	B	B
Royal Navy	A	A	B	B	A	A	B	B	A	B	A	A
Day 2	B	B	A	A	B	B	A	A	B	A	B	B
Long watch	A	A	B	B	A	A	A	B	B	B	A	A
Day 2	B	B	A	A	B	B	B	A	A	A	B	B

Table 18-2. Alternative watch schedules for three watches (Shaded areas indicate A Watch's standby schedule)

	0000 to 0200	0200 to 0400	0400 to 0600	0600 to 0800	0800 to 1000	1000 to 1200	1200 to 1400	1400 to 1600	1600 to 1800	1800 to 2000	2000 to 2200	2200 to 2400
Basic (Four on/off)	A	A	B	B	C	C	A	A	B	B	C	C
Royal Navy	A	A	B	B	C	C	A	A	B	C	A	A
Day 2	B	B	C	C	A	A	B	B	C	A	B	B
Day 3	C	C	A	A	B	B	C	C	A	B	C	C

Joe and Kathy Möeller aboard *Windscape* use a slightly different watch schedule when on passage with one additional crewmember. They break the 8 hours between 2200 and 0600 into four watches of 2 hours and the 16 daylight hours into four watches of 4 hours (Table 18-4). This automatically staggers the watches, allows everyone to get 8 hours off watch during the day, and makes the night watches shorter and more manageable.

Crews of two

As long as there are three or more competent crewmembers aboard, none of whom is incapacitated by seasickness or injury, keeping 24-hour watches is a matter of logistics. Once the crew size falls below three, the situation changes. While it is still desirable to keep a proper watch at all times, it takes more than logistics.

For the doublehanded crew, the dangers of fatigue from sleep deprivation are rarely discussed, but they are every bit as important as the risk of not keeping a proper watch. We knew of one boat that had a close brush with a freighter at sea. But we knew of a half-dozen that made serious mistakes upon landfall when the skipper exercised poor judgment because of fatigue or the crew failed to respond quickly enough because of exhaustion. When we left, these contradictions troubled

us, as did the apparent impossibility of maintaining an adequate 24-hour watch on passages longer than a few days. We found very few couples who would talk honestly about their watchkeeping routines.

As we gained more experience and got to know other voyagers, we learned that many doublehanded crews do not keep a "proper" watch. The two-person crews who kept 24-hour watches from the minute they headed offshore until they dropped their anchor at their destination were unusual. Unfortunately, crews who slept through the night at sea were more common. When hove-to in a gale, very few skippers—even the most fanatical—maintain a watch. When waiting for daylight to make landfall, many couples who kept fairly good watches would both go below and sleep, and this would typically be in an area where they were likely to encounter shipping and fishing traffic. Given the general low quality of watchkeeping, the infrequency of collisions attests to the emptiness of the oceans. But it does not justify poor watchkeeping.

Between 24-hour watches from anchor up to anchor down and going to sleep every night at 2200, many possibilities exist. The risks associated with less-than-perfect watchkeeping can be balanced against the risks associated with exhaustion. Some people can manage 2

Table 18-3. Basic three watch schedule

	0000 to 0300	0300 to 0600	0600 to 0900	0900 to 1200	1200 to 1500	1500 to 1800	1800 to 2100	2100 to 2400
Day 1	A	B	C	A	B	C	A	B
Day 2	C	A	B	C	A	B	C	A
Day 3	B	C	A	B	C	A	B	C

Table 18-4. *Windscape's* watch schedule

	0000 to 0200	0200 to 0400	0400 to 0600	0600 to 0800	0800 to 1000	1000 to 1200	1200 to 1400	1400 to 1600	1600 to 1800	1800 to 2000	2000 to 2200	2200 to 2400
Day 1	A	B	C	A	A	B	B	C	C	A	A	B
Day 2	C	A	B	C	C	A	A	B	B	C	C	A
Day 3	B	C	A	B	B	C	C	A	A	B	B	C

Table 18-5. Three-two-one system

0000 to 0300	0300 to 0500	0500 to 0600	0600 to 0700	0700 to 0900	0900 to 1200	1200 to 1500	1500 to 1700	1700 to 1800	1800 to 1900	1900 to 2100	2100 to 2400
A	B	A	B	A	B	A	B	A	B	A	B

hours on and 2 hours off forever without showing any ill effects. Others need at least 8 hours of sleep a night to function at close to a normal level.

Flexibility became the central tenet of our watchkeeping system. We strove to maintain a proper watch at all times and under all conditions. But that goal was tempered by the length of the passage, the weather conditions, and the amount of shipping traffic in the vicinity.

For an overnight hop from one island to another, we would not even bother with a formal watch schedule. For one night we could do whatever needed to be done and catch up on our sleep the next day. We found passages from two to five days to be the most problematic. It took us about a week to really get into passage rhythm, after which it didn't matter how long we were out. For shorter passages, we tried different watch schedules, such as those outlined above, but we soon learned to work with our own natural rhythms rather than forcing ourselves into an artificial schedule.

Evans needed more sleep than I did, a total of 9 or 10 hours in 24. I could function on 5 or 6 hours of sleep a night for weeks at a time, but I needed to get it all at once rather than in short naps. I would take an evening watch and stay up as late as I was able, usually until 2300 or midnight. I would wake Evans up and he would take a 5- or 6-hour-long watch, usually waking me an hour or so before dawn when he would go to bed and sleep until midmorning. If either of us needed more sleep, we would take short naps during the day. While a 4-hour night watch initially seemed interminable, we found that we both enjoyed longer watches after we had been out for a year or so. Many of our friends preferred to break the night up into four 3-hour watches or three 4-hour watches.

Like almost all couples we knew, we kept informal watches during the day. We generally ate our meals in the cockpit. If I was working in the galley, Evans would be "on watch." If he was not reading in the cockpit, he would be on deck every 15 minutes to make sure all was well. If Evans was napping, I would often be reading or exercising on deck. In the morning and evening when it was cool, we would both be in the cockpit for several hours.

For those who prefer more formal watch schedules, the watch systems outlined in Table 18-1 for two watch teams of two people each can be used for two watches of one person each. If you prefer short watches, those we met who used the three-two-one system outlined in Table 18-5 were devoted to it.

No matter what watch schedule you use, if there are only two people aboard there will be nights when neither of you gets any sleep. In squally conditions or in heavy weather, you learn to live with the fatigue and get energy from short naps. When the weather settles and you can sleep for all your off-watch hours, you will catch up. Sleep at sea is a feast-or-famine business, and most experienced voyagers will advise you to rest whenever you can to be sure that you have sufficient energy to deal with anything that comes along.

For passages over a week, especially in remote areas of the tropics where freighter and fishing traffic are unusual, our routine differed from our four- or five-day passages. In the first few days, Evans often could not sleep at all. During that period, I got as much sleep as possible. When Evans reached a level of exhaustion where he could sleep, I stood in for a night. After that we would both be in passage rhythm. We generally followed a schedule similar to the one we used for shorter passages, though we varied it depending on who felt more awake. We always kept 24-hour watches within 150 miles of land, when we were in known shipping lanes or fishing areas, or when we had seen freighter or fishing traffic in the previous 24 hours.

If we were several hundred miles from land or from shipping channels, had not seen other vessels for several days, and were both feeling fatigued after days of squally weather and little sleep, we would get less formal in our watchkeeping. The person on watch would doze in the bunk, set an alarm for every 30 minutes, and go on deck at those half-hour intervals to make sure that nothing was visible. While there was some risk that a freighter could come over the horizon and collide with us during that period, we felt that the risk was acceptably small.

We occasionally used the radar to ease watchkeeping in shipping areas. In poor weather, we would sit watches below and go on deck every hour or so to verify what the radar was showing us. When we had to get some sleep, we would set a "contact alarm" at six to eight miles that would warn us if anything came within that radius. While not foolproof, the radar proved reliable. It did consume a large amount of electricity, which limited how much we could use it without charging our batteries.

The day before a landfall, we would both be so excited that we were usually up the whole night with one of us resting for an hour or so as needed. The last few hours we would both be on deck, watching the land rise out of the sea and savoring the transition from sea back to shore.

Some of the ideas in this section should help you find your own balance between the risk of collision and the reality of fatigue. Your balance may not resemble anything that I have described in this section, but it should reflect your sleep patterns and preferences and your assessment of the risks. You need to agree on the level of watchkeeping you will maintain in various situations, so set the ground rules before you head off to sea.

Duties of the watchkeeper

Keeping a proper watch means more than drowsing on deck. It means regularly scanning the entire horizon for other vessels, taking bearings if another vessel is crossing your course, strolling the deck to look for chafe and wear, maintaining sail trim and course steered, and watching the weather. Proper watchkeeping also means knowing when additional crew are required on deck and calling them in time to reduce sail *before* the squall hits. Letting the off watch sleep is laudable, up to a point. Most crewmembers would rather be woken by a friendly hand on their shoulder than by being bounced out of their bunk.

Over time, you will learn your boat's language. You will grow sensitive to small changes in the boat's motion or sounds that surround you. Evans would wake if the wind increased by more than 2 knots. But sound and motion often seemed amplified once the sun went down and we lost our visual cues during our first night at sea. The boat felt like she was charging along too quickly. A quick check of the instruments would show that nothing had really changed and that the boat was still moving at the same speed with the same wind. If you find yourself uncomfortable in this situation, go ahead and reef. Slowing the boat down will mean a better first night's sleep for the off watch and won't change your passage time by more than a few hours.

While ship's lights will help you pick out other vessels more easily at night, vision won't help much with sailing the boat in the dark unless you keep your eyes adapted to low light. Eyes need a half-hour or more to adjust to the low light of nighttime watchkeeping, and a single flash from a cabin light can destroy your light adaptation. Red lights in the compass, galley, and nav station and red filters on flashlights will protect your night vision. We came to prefer using no light at all most of the time. On a dark night, the sound and feel of the boat tell you how well she is sailing and whether anything has changed.

While watches can be boring in settled conditions offshore, watches near shipping channels or land are often exciting. In a formal watchkeeping situation, the on-watch crew are responsible for the following.

■ *Change of watch.* At the change of the watch, the new on-watch crew should come on deck about five minutes before the changeover. Before coming up, they should take a look at the chart to determine the current position and review the log to see what has happened since their last watch. The about-to-go-off-watch crew should explain the current situation including position, course, wind speed and direction, recent sail changes, weather observations, and any trends that might be useful for the next watch. Telling the oncoming watch that the wind has been veering 15 degrees whenever a squall comes along will help them adapt more quickly. Everyone should agree on who is responsible for waking the next watch. Will the current watch wake the off-watch crew or will the off watch set alarms and come on deck themselves?

■ *Sail trim.* Most doublehanded boats require that both crewmembers be on deck for any major sail changes. The crewmember on watch trims the sails. But when the boat starts to feel undercanvassed or over-canvassed, the on-watch crew is responsible for getting the other crewmember up and managing the sail change. We both preferred to be told what to do when we were half asleep, not asked for advice. If the situation demanded deliberation, then we would confer (once we were awake enough to do so).

■ *Staying on course.* Being on watch does not mean being at the helm. If it did, we could never have managed six-hour watches alone. Staying on course generally means tweaking the wind vane or adjusting the electric pilot. Wind vane steering is not as precise as steering by hand or with an electric pilot, so don't expect your compass to read the proper course at all times. As long as you average within a few degrees of your desired course, leave the wind vane to itself. If you find yourself constantly tweaking the steering controls on the vane when the wind seems constant, make sure your sails are well balanced for the conditions.

■ *Navigation.* If you are equipped with GPS, navigation means pushing a button and writing down a position. But that shouldn't stop you from practicing with the sextant. It can take a dozen sights to recapture the skill of bringing the celestial body to the horizon from the deck of a pitching boat. Navigation also includes keeping the ship's log and plotting your position on the chart. The ship's log should include the date, time, course, speed, wind speed, wind direction, barometric reading, pressure change, position, and any comments on sail combinations, cloud cover, or swell. We updated the log every four hours during the day and less frequently at night to preserve our night vision. We plotted an X on the chart to mark our position every other day on long passages.

■ *Preventive maintenance.* Chapter 9 includes a thorough discussion of what you should look for to prevent maintenance problems. Every half-hour or so, take a stroll around deck. Check for chafe, squeaky blocks, slapping halyards, loose lifelines, and so on. Make sure everything appears normal and tend to the little problems before they become big problems.

■ *Weather watching.* Every time you step on deck, scan the horizon with your weather eye and note any changes in wind speed, wind direction, swell size, swell direction, cloud cover, cloud movements, and temperature. Whenever you make a log entry, you should automatically note the rate of change of the barometric pressure. Using the information in Chapter 16, you should be constantly updating your own short-term forecast. If enough signs point to deteriorating weather, wake the off watch and prepare the boat.

■ *Respecting the off watch.* The crew who are on watch must respect the off-watch crew's need to get as much sleep as possible. That means keeping the noise down, not making sail changes just to stay awake, and checking to be sure that unnecessary noises are eliminated. Take a stroll below and stuff a sock between the clinking bottles or reorganize the can drawer.

■ *Calling the off watch to assist.* The watchkeeper needs to call for assistance immediately when it is required. That may be for a sail change, a sudden equipment failure, a potential collision situation, or to confirm the watch's judgment. Part of learning to trust your partners is believing that they will call you if the situation warrants it; part of learning to trust yourself is distinguishing between a crisis of confidence and a crisis in reality. When in doubt, double check.

■ *Preparing to hand over the watch.* The on-watch crew should have hot water available and replenish the snacks 10 minutes or so before the off-watch crew gets out of their bunks.

On a doublehanded boat crewed by a couple, the changeover may be less formal, but the activities remain the same. As the passage takes on its own rhythm and develops its own pattern, much can be done to limit the number of disturbances experienced each night.

Many settled passages follow a daily cycle of wind increases and decreases based on local sea and air temperatures and humidity. We became most fatigued on the passages characterized by frequent and unpredictable squalls. On many of our tropical passages, the wind increased by 5 to 10 knots at night. To make our nights more relaxing, we took in a reef as the sun set and shook it out as the sun rose. On passages in or near the doldrums, the wind often went light as dusk approached and did not fill in again until the next morning. By anticipating these wind speed changes, you'll end up with fewer sail changes and more sleep.

During those times when sleep seems an impossible luxury, remember that fatigue leads to low morale and to errors. Whether you are reducing a sight, plotting a position, setting up a spinnaker pole, or end-for-ending a chafed line, double check everything. Ask your partner to look at what you've done before you put away the tools or raise the halyard. Two heads are better than one, especially when both are operating at less than 100 percent.

TAKING CARE OF THE CREW

At sea, the boat comes first. Her rhythm dictates yours, her needs dictate your priorities. But once the boat is rolling along happily in the trade wind swell, your time is yours until the boat demands your attention again. You can eat, sleep, wash, exercise, and relax.

People respond differently to unstructured time at sea. The lack of routine aboard and the need to be ready to respond to the boat's demands day or night creates a sense of limbo in which normal standards and activities seem inconsequential. Time measured by the clock gets confusing when you are losing or gaining an hour every few days that you sail. Time as we know it ashore, marked by a steady progression of meals and activities and sleep, can become irrelevant in the flow of sail changes and watches. When that happens, a certain kind of discipline can seem irrelevant as well. When day flows into day, little things like brushing your teeth, washing, or taking medications can get lost in the confusion. I believe this is one reason why the world's navies have always maintained an iron discipline.

Aboard your own boat at sea, the discipline need not be enforced with the cat-o'-nine-tails. However, for many voyagers some sort of routine does need to be superimposed on the rhythm of nature to keep a sense of order and civilization. A routine that sensibly includes hygiene, food, and sleep within the context of the boat's demands keeps crew morale and energy up. You will understand what I mean when you realize it has been five days since your last shower and nobody has noticed. As a crew, you will find a sense of structure that suits your sea style. You may encounter some rough spots as you determine how much civilization you want to impose on one another.

Cooking

We had been in the grip of a strong high with winds over 30 knots in the southern Indian Ocean for seven days straight. The combination of the normal trade wind swell over our stern and a large swell out of the Southern Ocean on our beam made being below like living in a front-loading washing machine. I was trying to make bread, and the yeast went flying off the top of the gyrating gimbaled stove three times. I was so tired of it—of the noise and the motion, but mostly of the planning required to execute even the simplest maneuver. I yelled, "I want five minutes of calm! Just five minutes when I can set something down without it going into orbit! Five minutes of peace!"

Usually you need not worry about your sanity when cooking at sea. However, avoiding injuries and preventing seasickness may require some planning when the galley is regularly moving 3 or 4 feet in different dimensions. You do want to end up with a meal that is on your plate and not on the cabin sole. Tips for coping with cooking in a seaway fall into three categories: setting up a sea-smart galley, planning meals for all sea conditions, and using sea-safe techniques to minimize risks.

Sea-smart galley

Suggestions for setting up a safe and efficient galley appear in Chapter 2. No matter how simple or luxurious your galley is, finding useable work surfaces when the boat is in a constant state of flux between flat and heeling will prove challenging. You need at least two surfaces for kneading bread, cutting up vegetables, or mixing cakes.

On most boats, the gimbaled stovetop offers the only useful surface in a rolling sea. This will often be the only surface on which you can leave things unattended for short periods of time. Install padeyes on either side of the stove and a strong safety belt so the cook can work hands free. From the belted in position, the cook needs to be able to move around enough to reach most lockers and the refrigerator. We kept several extra carabiners clipped to the padeyes to allow us to lengthen the strap when conditions were less boisterous or for washing dishes and putting things away. The ideal gimbaled stove is one that you can lock in place. In a confused sea, we often chose to leave the stove locked rather than to deal with unpredictable motions—particularly when retrieving freshly baked items from the oven.

Deep sinks offer one of the few spill-proof spots to put things while mixing ingredients or balancing hot pans. The sinks become the catchall for dirty dishes, for fruits and vegetables before and after you cut them up, and for greased bread pans while you roll the dough into loaves. Sinks can be a great place to set a bowl, add ingredients, and then mix everything up. Keep a few towels or rags within easy reach to wedge into the sink and keep things from sliding back and forth.

Hinged counters that can be locked in an angled position are less useful in rolling downwind conditions than when close-hauled. A cutting board that you can solidly wedge in place makes the most useful surface for slicing and dicing in a rolling sea. We had a wooden cutting board designed to fit securely into the top of one of the double sinks. The wood did warp and needed to be sanded down from time to time. Look for a second place where the cutting board will sit securely to give you flexibility when washing dishes. Ours just happened to fit on the engine compartment wedged in next to the companionway steps.

With a gimbaled stovetop, two deep sinks, and a good cutting board, you can create almost anything in your seagoing kitchen. If you lack one of these, you will have to simplify your meal planning. Even in the most basic galley, you can produce nutritious food at sea in most conditions. The difference is the range and variety of meals you will be able to produce.

Sea-wise meal planning

When we first headed offshore, I tried to recreate shoreside meals without regard to current conditions. I often ended up frustrated and seasick. Over time, I learned to be flexible and plan a range of possible meals for different sea states. I also evaluated the galley stability and crew appetites before deciding what to make. On a long passage (10 days or more), a few days' worth of meals from the following categories combined with normal offshore fare covers almost any eventuality.

■ *Light-air, hot weather meals.* We did not have large appetites in the tropics, especially when the wind was light, the boat rolling, and the temperatures in the high 90s. In those conditions, we preferred lots of small meals as opposed to one big one. In preparing those meals, we wanted to minimize the heat generated from cooking. We cooked when it was coolest—early in the morning or just after dark. We prepared meals that could be eaten cold later, such as macaroni and potato salad, rice salad, and bread. We supplemented this fare early on in the passage with fresh fruit and vegetables, later with dried fruit, olives, pickles, peanuts, and salad made from canned vegetables.

■ *Heavy weather meals.* In the worst of conditions, the only way to cope is to minimize the cooking. To give the crew hot, substantial, easy-to-eat food, you need meals that can be made in one pan with minimal preparation and eaten with a spoon out of a bowl or mug. Hearty soups and stews are best, either canned or freeze-dried. Take enough along to keep everybody well fed over the course of a three-day blow.

■ *Celebratory meals.* You can use special foods to celebrate passage milestones. I always planned something special for any "event"—from birthdays to equator crossings. I tried to include a few favorite dishes for each of us. I also included three or four extravagant meals to combat low morale or celebrate whale sightings. Every passage has its meaningful moments, and food allows you to mark those events at sea.

You may eventually be able to cook a three-course dinner while under way in a gale, but start with more modest goals. Avoid any menu item that involves more than a tablespoon or so of hot oil or grease during the days when you are getting your galley legs. Be realistic about the conditions and your own level of expertise in managing them. In a short time, you will be able to turn out basic, nutritious meals without compromising your health or sanity.

Sea-safe techniques

The two most difficult conditions for coping with cooking at sea are heavy weather and heavy rolling. In heavy weather, minimize the cooking with simple one-pot main courses. On most passages you will have to cope with these conditions for only a couple meals. Trade wind sailing will often involve managing a galley when rolling through 30 or 40 degrees. You will want to master this skill as quickly as possible. The techniques that follow will make cooking at sea easier in all conditions but are particularly useful in rolly, trade wind conditions.

■ *Prepare fresh food in a seated position.* If the recipe calls for peeling, slicing, and dicing fresh fruits and vegetables, your most secure position has your bottom in contact with a solid surface. Find a dishpan or a large pot and locate the necessary produce. Put the produce in the pot or pan and take it—along with a cutting board and a knife or two—somewhere where you can work while seated. Take everything out into the cockpit on a nice day. Once you have finished with the fresh food, put it in your pot or pan and set it on the gimbaled stove or wedge it into the sink with some spare towels so it doesn't slide around.

■ *Gather necessary ingredients.* Most offshore cruisers keep small quantities of baking and cooking ingredients in containers in the galley. Extra quantities are stowed in less accessible areas. Refill any containers that are low before you get started. Gather any additional ingredients, bowls, measuring cups, or pans not stowed in the galley. Put everything on the gimbaled stove or wedge them into the sink.

■ *Determine your work area.* Depending on what you are making, the best work area might be your cutting board or a large bowl or pot wedged into one of the sinks, or the frying pan or a large pot on top of the gimbaled stove. Make sure your container will stay put even if you have to let go of it from time to time. Once you have set up your work area and are satisfied that it is secure, strap yourself in and get ready to start cooking!

■ *Work with one ingredient at a time.* To keep your hands free as much as possible, get out one ingredient at a time, do what you need to do with it, and then put it away. If using measuring spoons, cups, or small utensils, rinse them off with a bit of fresh water, wipe them down, and put them back. This conserves water by minimizing the dishes to be done later and keeps the work area and sinks from getting cluttered.

Once the ingredients are mixed together and the meal is simmering happily on the stove or cooking in the oven, put away any of the ingredients that are not stowed in the galley and wash the dishes while strapped in and put them away. If you are feeling seasick, take a stroll on deck. If you are tired of the low impact aerobics, take a seat on the companionway while you wait for the watched pot to boil.

When the meal is ready, you are faced with the most hazardous part of the entire proceeding: getting the food onto a plate without injuring yourself. This is one area where "one hand for the ship and one hand for yourself" simply doesn't work. A few suggestions follow for making sure the food ends up where you want it:

■ *Pasta.* When cooking pasta or anything else in a large amount of boiling water, use a slotted spoon to transfer the cooked food to a bowl rather than trying to pour the boiling water into the sink in a moving galley. I let the water cool while we ate, then used it instead of the normal salt water to wash our dishes.

■ *Hot liquids.* Strap yourself in when pouring hot liquids, then use two hands: one for the kettle and one for the mug. You cannot pour accurately from one container to the other if you are not holding both. Never try to pour hot liquids into a container set on the gimbaled stove. The slight delay in response of the stove means that you are always trying to hit a moving target not synchronized with your own motions.

■ *Baked goods.* The balance of most gimbaled stoves changes when the door is opened, and you run the risk of having the hot food rendezvous with the galley sole or with your body unless you are quick on the draw. If you can retrieve whatever is in the oven using one hand, use the other hand to control the motion of the stove and use footholds to brace yourself in place. If you need two hands, lock the oven in place, brace yourself securely, and then time the opening of the door to correspond with the boat's roll.

While these ideas will help prevent injuries and keep the cook from getting seasick, they cannot be guaranteed to keep the cook sane. Cooking in a seaway teaches you patience and maturity—you learn to think about where you are putting things, plan before you act, and not pout when things don't stay put through a 30-degree roll (Figure 18-1). Still, there are times when the only thing that helps is to stomp around and yell at things. Indulge yourself on those occasions. A little swearing from down below will probably fit right in with what's going on above decks.

Sleeping

My recollections of passages are all sound and motion. The motion on a small boat at sea translates into a va-

riety of sounds that work their way deep into the subconscious. As I was trying to go to sleep in my bunk, my mind would sort through the litany of sounds surrounding me: the creak of wood on wood over the quarter berth, the waves gurgling by the hull next to my ear, the fresh water sloshing around in the tank under my berth, the wind rattling a halyard against the mast, the snap of

Figure 18-1. Cooking in a bouncing boat is a bit like doing low-impact aerobics.

A day in the life—pizza at sea

We were enjoying a beautiful trade wind sailing day halfway through a slow passage between the Canaries and the Caribbean when I had a sudden, inexplicable, uncontrollable urge: *Pizza!* We still had one 8-ounce package of mozzarella cheese and a stick of Italian pepperoni from Las Palmas.

I had made pizza from scratch ashore hundreds of times. I had made pizza at anchor on *Silk* a dozen times. I had made pizza on passage once, when we had been totally becalmed. I had never made pizza on passage when we were actually moving.

And we were moving! We were running almost dead downwind with double headsails up and an impressive swell from astern. *Silk* was into her hip-swaying, butt-rolling swagger—the kind that makes standing on deck feel like you are doing moguls. Swoosh, swish, swoosh!

I headed down below and strapped myself into the galley. With my body swaying in rhythm with the boat, I wedged one foot into the niche on the sole between the counter and the engine compartment, pulled out my stainless steel bread-making bowl, and set it on the wildly gyrating gimbaled stove. I then realized that I couldn't get to the yeast in the lower drawer without undoing the belt.

So, I released the galley strap, kept one hand on the stove bar, crouched down on the galley floor, and stretched with the other hand toward the drawer. Just then, *Silk* caught a big wave right on her quarter. She rolled hard to port, and for a split second I was a chimpanzee dangling by one hand from the stove bar, both feet off the floor, and looking down at the nav station directly below me. A split second later the stove crashed into my hand, and I let go of the bar with a yelp just as *Silk* rolled back upright. I ended up in a heap under the nav station, muttering to myself.

About that time, Evans looked down and said, "What are you doing?"

"Making pizza."

"Under the nav station?"

About two hours and five or six bruises later, my appetite for pizza was only slightly dimmed. By now a wonderful aroma was wafting up to us on deck and even Evans was getting enthusiastic. It was time to get the pizza out of the oven. This is always the trickiest part of cooking. Unstrap yourself from the galley belt (I've never seen a galley belt that was truly functional *and* would allow you to fully open the stove door), wedge your backside against the engine compartment, and open the stove door. This causes the swinging stove to tip toward your waiting arms. Then when the boat rolls, catch the hot food with both hands as it slides off the oven rack. The both hands is the tricky part. But one hand is usually not strong enough or swift enough to capture renegade pizza on a rendezvous with the cabin sole.

That day, I went down below and received the pizza pass flawlessly. I stood and eased the pizza

Figure 18-2. Making pizza is easy—at anchor!

onto the top of the gimbaled stove. Then I strapped myself in with the galley belt, and proceeded to wash up a few dishes while the pizza cooled the proper 15 minutes to achieve perfection.

Now I made my fatal mistake. The boat was still rolling from side to side, sashaying along like a Southern belle touring a garden party. The pizza pan was taking up the majority of my stove top, and I needed to cut and serve the pizza. Without investing a great deal of thought, I transferred the pizza to my cutting board, which fit snugly in the top of the second sink. I cut two pieces, put them on a plate, and turned to hand them to Evans. Just as he took the plate from me, the boat rolled hard and the vast majority of my prized pizza slid sideways—right into the dirty salt water that I had just used to wash the dishes. I heard one faint call for help from a drowning pepperoni, and then silence.

This was one of the most traumatic moments of our entire trip.

Of course, I've picked an extreme example to make my point. You have to be crazy to try to make something like pizza in those conditions. But it's all part of the adventure!

a sail as it filled. Gradually, my mind would accept each noise, and I would be lulled to sleep by this strange chorus (Figure 18-3). But let even one of these sounds change, and I would be up on deck within seconds.

This constant awareness means that on a double-handed boat, you rarely fall into a sound sleep. A sleep deficit—of which you may be unaware—can result. This gradual fatigue and dulling of the senses saps energy and lowers morale. To avoid it, crewmembers need to get enough rest—even if they are not falling into a deep sleep. But the excitement of departure or of landfall can make sleep difficult. Inexperienced watchkeepers will often be on deck for both watches, too excited to get into their bunks. On fully crewed boats, the skipper needs to insist that off watch means off the deck to ensure that no one crashes a few days out and throws off the whole watch schedule.

Doublehanded crews can afford to be more flexible. Once we had agreed on a watch schedule, the on-watch person could extend the watch if he or she was wide awake and let the off-watch person sleep peacefully. If the off-watch person insisted on being on deck, the on-watch person was free to go below and try to sleep. One of us could almost always get some useful rest, even if it wasn't real sleep. That meant that at least one of us had some reserve to deal with the unforeseen.

Another one of Murphy's Laws of Offshore Voyaging states that even if you struggle to keep your eyes open through the last hour of your watch, the minute you hit your bunk you will be wide awake. The following ideas might help as you adjust to sleeping offshore:

■ *Comfortable bunk.* Solid-feeling sea berths offer a sense of security and make sleep more likely. Bunks that are too wide (over 24 inches) will leave you with sore muscles and little sleep. Lee cloths or lee boards should support your weight without sagging. Otherwise, you will wake thinking you are about to fall out of bed whenever you roll into them. Bunks should not slide in or out, not even by an inch. The less stable the boat, the more stable your platform needs to be if you are to get any real rest.

■ *Well-ventilated bunks.* Stuffy bunks, especially in the tropics, will make you feel damp and short of breath. Lee cloths or lee boards need to allow air circulation. Good ventilation using Dorades or fans, oriented so the airflow is *into* the bunk and not over it, will keep air circulating.

■ *Preparations for bed.* Even if you have only a few hours before your next watch, normal bedtime routines will convince your body to go to sleep. Change out of your watch clothes. Wash your face and brush your teeth. These little rituals help your body relax into its own sleep cycle. Falling into bed with your watch clothes on will make you restless for the first half-hour and leave you feeling groggy on your next watch.

■ *Time management.* As you travel from east to west in the trade winds, you will need to turn your clock back an hour every few hundred miles. We found that changing our reference time every few days threw off our sleep cycles. But if we allowed our clocks to get too far out of line with nature, we lost track of basic routines aboard. Changing the clocks in three-hour increments balanced what nature was saying against the cycles our bodies were used to. You will need to experiment to find your own solution.

If all else fails, warm milk or herbal tea often helped us relax and get to sleep. Once we were in our passage rhythm, neither of us had much trouble sleeping in settled conditions.

Diversions

Once the boat and your most basic of needs have been taken care of, you will have time to enjoy a few diversions. Especially with children aboard, special activi-

Figure 18-3. Sleep on passage is never as deep when you are surrounded by sound and motion.

ties and celebrations can help you recognize the major milestones of a passage.

Nature provides the greatest diversions free of charge. A pod of dolphins may stay with you for several hours, giving you more entertainment than a blockbuster movie. Sea birds will try to land on your rigging and will generally not succeed, accompanying their efforts with much squawking and flying feathers. Sunsets may be breathtaking and fill the whole sky or they might be sublime and end in a green flash. Even gales and squalls have their own beauty, and rainbows at sea seem bigger and more vibrant than those on land.

Managing garbage at sea

Like so many other things, managing garbage at sea requires balancing what is possible against what is desirable. We would prefer not to throw anything overboard. But in the real world, two problems exist. First, sequestering several weeks' worth of potato peels will start a compost heap in your forepeak. That might be useful for growing sprouts aboard, but the odor will drive you from the boat. Second, and more distressing, when you arrive at many islands and dutifully drop your garbage in the rubbish bin, it is often dumped on the beach to be removed by the tide. On the most remote and pristine of islands, the islanders have always disposed of their wastes on the beach. When the waste was coconut shells and human excrement, that was not much of problem. Now that it is Coke bottles and plastic bags, it is a tragedy.

Environmentally conscientious voyagers are faced with the dilemma of disposing some waste at sea or waiting and disposing of it ashore with no assurance that it will be properly handled. We opted for a compromise that we felt minimized the adverse affects on the environment. The process started when we removed packaging from our provisions before we stowed them. Because we did major provisioning in developed countries, we were reasonably comfortable that what we were leaving behind would be properly managed. Once we set off on passage, we handled each type of garbage differently, as described below:

■ *Cooking scraps.* We threw organic waste—from carrot peelings to spoiled leftovers—overboard without much thought once we were a half a day from land. Every once in a while, such scraps would be greeted with delight by fish in the vicinity. Generally, they would float or sink out of sight.

■ *Paper.* We didn't have much paper aboard, since we discarded paper packaging when we provisioned. We rarely used paper towels at sea; tea towels were more practical and could be laundered. Still, we had to dispose of the odd piece of paper from writing or making calculations. We usually shredded these before dropping them overboard. We did use toilet paper and discharged it overboard with the waste from the head once we were offshore.

■ *Glass.* We preferred heavy plastic and reusable containers and did not carry much glass. When we did have to dispose of glass, we filled empty bottles with salt water and dropped them overboard. They would quickly sink out of sight.

■ *Cans.* We did not carry soda in cans, but we did provision canned foods. We filled the cans with salt water so they would sink to the bottom. Cans were probably our most common form of garbage after kitchen scraps, and I always regretted leaving a trail of cans behind us on the ocean floor. But it was worse to envision the cans dumped just offshore or left on a beach for the tide to take, so we buried them at sea where they could do the least harm.

■ *Plastic.* Plastic, or anything with plastic in it, never went over the side. We stowed all our UHT containers, plastic bags, bottles, tabs, rings, and fasteners in the forepeak until we made landfall in a developed port. Plastic is deadly to marine life: It can be eaten or it can get caught in blowholes or lungs. We never threw plastic away in small villages for fear it would end up on a beach. We couldn't carry it for an entire ocean—though sometimes we were inclined to try. We normally disposed of it in a major port where we had to clear customs, and we hoped that it wouldn't end up in the sea anyway.

When nature is being less than entertaining, the range of activities is necessarily limited by the boat's constant motion. The following diversions work well on passage and constitute most of what occupied us and our friends while at sea:

■ **SSB or World-band Receiver.** The ubiquitous cruising nets and chat shows provide great entertainment while on passage. Most of our friends spent an hour or more a day conversing on the SSB or Ham. When not transmitting to friends or receiving weather forecasts, the radio was often tuned to the BBC—the primary source of news, information, and entertainment for offshore sailors. There can come a point where you wonder if the whole world has stopped while you've been at sea, and the BBC offers proof that life goes on. Like the soap operas, the news changes remarkably little when listened to from a distant enough perspective. Even that is reassuring at sea.

■ **Reading.** Books offer prime entertainment at sea. Evans often read a book a day on passage (Figure 18-4). We had to make sure to stock up sufficiently before a long voyage.

■ **Games.** Some card games work well at sea, including cribbage and rummy. Travel games designed for cars work too, as long as the pieces are not so tiny that they are likely to end up in the bilge.

■ **Music or videos.** A Walkman allows you to enjoy music without disturbing others. It makes a wonderful watch companion. You may want to bring more than one, especially if you have children aboard. Video offers kids the ultimate entertainment, but most of our friends preferred diversions using paper, pencil, wood, crayons, and anything else that came to hand.

■ **Physical activity.** As discussed in Chapter 13, physical activity is difficult on passage but worth trying to keep up. Free weights, stretching, and exercise bands provide workable exercise solutions at sea. Several turns around the deck every few hours will keep your muscles from stiffening up.

■ **Social time.** When keeping strict watches, you will see little of your off-watch crewmates. Surprising as it sounds, the boat can so dominate your life at sea that you lose track of those around you. To make sure that everyone remains in touch, many boats have a daily "cocktail hour," usually in the late afternoon. Whether it involved alcohol or not, the cocktail hour provided interaction and sharing. It gave the skipper the opportunity to assess crew morale and address any problems developing between crewmembers.

While some handicrafts can be done easily at sea, close hand-eye work is more likely to cause seasickness than just about any other activity. It took me three offshore passages before I got to the point where I could write for an hour or more at a time. Make sure you are fully acclimated before trying these types of activities.

If you are becalmed, you may want to go for a swim. A surprising number of people were agoraphobic or acrophobic with respect to all that open space between them and the ocean floor thousands of meters below. We swam once when we were becalmed. The gentle swell felt like a tidal wave from the surface of the water. I was more aware than I had ever been of how my life at sea depended on *Silk*. Everyone should experience the sensation of flying far above solid ground, suspended over nothing. If you do so, make sure to take all sails down, trail a long line from the stern, and leave someone on deck. Don't swim where there is an ocean current. You may not be able to keep up with the boat, and the marine life may find you of interest!

Plan some surprises, especially if you have kids aboard. No matter what your age, when land is several hundred miles away you will appreciate a new toy or game, some candy, or a book you have wanted to read. If everyone aboard brings one surprise for everyone else, you will be sure to have a few special events along the way that will bolster crew morale and keep the crew working as a team.

Safety

All crewmembers must agree on how they are going to manage safety on a passage and faithfully follow the agreed-upon rules. Actual practices on offshore boats run the gamut from requiring harnesses and tethers at all times in all conditions to never using them at all. In the beginning, the exact approach will depend on the

Figure 18-4. Evans enjoys a book during his watch.

relative experience of the crewmembers. In the end, the crew's attitude toward safety and their assessment of the relative risks will determine how they manage safety issues at sea.

Above all other emergencies at sea, most cruisers fear a crew-overboard situation most. Getting permanently separated from the boat at sea leaves you with no options, and the chances of rescue are close to zero on a shorthanded vessel in normal trade wind conditions. When we took a sailing course along the south coast of England with a crusty old salt who had been the navigator for the Royal Yacht *Britannia,* we asked about the crew-overboard procedure. He said, "Here's my man-overboard drill," and he waved good-bye over the stern. While this seems harsh, it is accurate. One person cannot stop the boat, throw flotation devices, hit a crew-overboard button on the GPS, and keep sight of the vic-

tim all at the same time. A boat moving at 6 knots will have traveled almost a quarter-mile in two minutes—much too far for a head to be visible in a large swell.

For people who have coastal sailed for many years, raced around the buoys, and always had other boats in the vicinity, this idea can be hard to internalize. But for a crew-overboard situation offshore with a shorthanded crew, prevention is *the* priority.

You should practice crew-overboard drills, but pay at least as much attention to prevention. Tethers, harnesses, strong attachment points, and a discipline of being attached to the boat are worth more than 20 well-executed practice retrievals. We found that our close calls came not when we were clawing our way to the bow in a gale, but when we were going forward in settled conditions to free a sheet. Crewmembers are at their most vulnerable when they are relaxed. (Offshore sailors joke that if a man does go overboard, he will be found with his fly open.) Constant vigilance is the only solution.

If you do face a crew-overboard situation short-handed, the only method that makes sense is the crash stop. When you are the only one left on the boat, you have to stop as quickly as possible to keep the person in sight. Bring the boat through the wind without releasing the sheets until she is hove-to. Then start throwing things to the person in the water while you consider your options.

When you practice crew-overboard drills, tie a buoy to a bucket to represent the victim. The weight of the bucket full of water will make you realize how much strength is required to get anything back aboard. As part of your crew-overboard preparations, determine how you will get an unconscious person back on the boat.

The following questions will help you and your crew focus your discussion on safety:

■ *When and under what circumstances will harnesses be required?* When you wear life jackets? Survival gear?

■ *Under what circumstances can people leave the cockpit when they are on deck alone?* During the daytime only? Good weather only? At night only if wearing harnesses?

■ *Will two people always be required on deck for sail changes?* If not, under what conditions will two people be required?

■ *In what situations should the off watch or skipper be called on deck?* During sail changes? Crossing another vessel? At waypoints when a course change is required? Anytime anything unusual is sighted?

Morale

With self-steering, good sail combinations, and GPS, keeping the boat moving in the right direction in good conditions doesn't take that much effort. For many cruisers, the most difficult part of passagemaking can be the psychological effects from the lack of privacy, lack of exercise, lack of sleep, boredom, and underlying stress. Each crewmember needs to find a way to deal constructively with the situation.

I found the tedium of a long, light-air passage boring unless I created some structure for myself. I would exercise and bake early in the morning when it was cool, read and rest during the hottest part of the day, and write and listen to the BBC in the late afternoon. Evans, on the other hand, went into a sort of hibernation, conserving his energy until events on the boat required his attention. A couple of times a day he would take a tour of inspection from bow to stern. If anything needed fixing, we immediately set about doing it.

The difference in our respective approaches caused conflict from time to time. I would get lonely on passage and want some serious conversation or light-hearted interaction. This was not uncommon among the couples we knew. Throughout our trip, skippers commiserated on the loneliness of command, while the first mates commiserated on the loneliness of being commanded. Skippers need to make an effort to include their crews, and crewmembers need to tell their skippers if they are uncomfortable with any aspect of passagemaking. To keep up morale, everyone needs to respect the attitudes and approaches of the others.

When the urge strikes to be truly alone, you can't go for a walk. Given the lack of physical space, psychological space becomes very important. I had a favorite place on the foredeck I retreated to whenever I needed to be alone. Evans used the quarter berth as his private place. We respected each other's privacy in these do-not-disturb areas.

Be sensitive to your moods and try to be aware if your morale or your partner's is low. Little things can boost morale a great deal. A shower can change your whole outlook. A surprise celebration with a meal and some new toys lifts the spirits. Noticing the beauty of wind and water can renew your sense of wonder. For the most part, morale is attitude—and you can choose to change your attitude.

We fell under the spell of the sea after the first few days of a passage. Our rhythms matched the sea's. We celebrated the simple pleasures of nature and the satisfaction of a good day's mileage. Shoreside cares and concerns were left behind. We felt clean and tranquil,

A day in the life—passage memories

Life at sea has its own fascinations and rewards. A few of these are captured in the following journal entries made on different passages.

One day after leaving the Galapagos bound for the Marquesas: *"Last night while ghosting along at 2.5 to 3 knots in the 6-knot breeze, I was treated to a visit by a large group of dolphins. It was very dark as the sliver of new moon was obscured by the cloud bank over Isabela Island, and the dolphins' racing forms were shrouded in the most magnificent phosphorescence. The bow wave was a gleaming arc that appeared suspended in midair, below which the dolphins created blazing trails through the pitch darkness of the water. As the dolphins weaved back and forth in groups of three or four, their forms threw off a shower of sparks, like shooting stars, bright enough that I could easily see both form and color of individuals. At times, they would dive deeper and hurtle forward under the bow at awesome speeds, their forms marked only by a milky trail of incandescence.*

"These joyful creatures stayed with the boat for well over an hour. I lay on the bowsprit awed by the combination of light and dark, the feel of an alien intelligence so close at hand, and the high-pitched chatter just barely audible to my ears. I feel a camaraderie with the dolphins that I could never feel with a fish or a reptile. Instinct alone tells me that these creatures are like me—curious, intelligent, and interested in communicating."

Two hundred miles north of New Zealand on passage from Fiji: *"After a night of beating our way south against 20 knots of wind, I've just woken to find the front moving off to the east—a long, black bruise of turbulent clouds touched with yellow under the rising sun. To the west, the first clouds of the high are approaching. Light cirrus are daintily sketched against a deep, dawn-blue sky with the full moon a virginal white wafer floating eerily against the blue. And overhead, blue with cirrus meets black, roiling cloud cover—the trailing edge of the front.*

"Yesterday was a good day. I'm finally far enough, detached enough to let go of all of the turmoil of the shore and move back to my center. I'm happy and fulfilled, singing with the full-throated roar of sea and sky, thrumming with life. Like a refreshing taste of childhood euphoria, this moment has come with or without my acquiescence when I was in a fit state to receive it—scrubbed clean by stinging salt sea of the baggage I gathered ashore. Whether it lasts five minutes or five days, I revel in it and love it now, with every fiber of my being. And I know, in temporary but blinding clarity, the truth is always simple. It is I who make it otherwise."

Ten days out from St. Helena in the South Atlantic on passage to the Caribbean: *"With a slow inevitability, the days are starting to flow into one another, to merge into an almost seamless whole. For 10 days now we've flown only the gennaker, with Silk following it obediently through the water day and night. Evans has described this ocean as featureless, and indeed it seems so. No changes of weather or wind direction, no wildlife to define the days and separate them one from another. Not even flying fish dead on deck in the morning to herald the passing of another day.*

"Our days are broken only by the noon SSB chat and marking the chart. A series of asterisks now stretches like an accusing finger pointing away from St. Helena. But we've passed the one-third point of the journey. We still have a long way to go, but the number starts to look reasonable, or at least comprehensible. We can say that we have less distance to travel than between the Canaries and the Caribbean or between the Galapagos and the Marquesas. The number of miles left can now be put into a context and compared. We have direct references to understand how much further we have to go, and hence, how much more time it will take. I start to really believe that we'll complete the circle, arrive in Antigua, row ashore at Nelson's dockyard, and I'll pick up the phone and call home. The whole idea gets less abstract every day.

"But, of course, all of that is certainly 20 days away, maybe more. But even 20 sounds like a manageable number. I guess that's the difference. The equator is getting closer every day!"

and life had a clear and simple meaning. Most people come to love these aspects of passagemaking while still respecting the demands of being alone with the sea.

MAKING A SUCCESSFUL LANDFALL

On any passage, the moment when the cry of "Land ho!" echoes around the boat is a moment of intense pride and overwhelming personal accomplishment. However, just as when we left port, I always struggled with conflicting emotions. On the one hand, I was eager for a shower, a meal ashore, a walk, some privacy. On the other hand, I was often strangely reluctant to trade the clean simplicity of the ocean for the insistent complications of shore life. Like Moitessier, the Frenchman who chose to sail on rather than complete and win the first singlehanded round-the-world race, I was often tempted to sail right by this island and head onward toward the next, as long as water and food held out.

But the sight of land was usually enough to break our passage routine completely. We would both be as excited as children with five minutes before reaching Grandma's house. Rather than waste all that energy, we put it to work in preparing the boat for landfall. Over time we came to take tremendous pride in bringing *Silk* into a new port in Bristol condition.

I worked below and Evans worked on deck. My tasks included gathering all of the laundry together, including the sheets from our sea berths; putting the sea berths back to their normal state; unpacking the forepeak; stowing passage gear like harnesses and tethers; jettisoning any not-so-fresh produce; gathering all garbage for disposal ashore; cleaning the head; doing a quick cleanup of any other areas that were dirty.

Evans' tasks on deck included bagging any sails that were not in use; untying the dinghy and getting out the oars; taking the teak plug out of the hawser; setting up the anchor so it would be ready to run. We learned that the motion of passagemaking often jumbled the chain up so much that it would not run free. He flaked the chain out on the deck and then dropped it back down the hawser. If we thought we were going to go into a marina or alongside a customs dock, Evans would dig out mooring lines and fenders.

After a passage, *Silk* was usually at her cleanest—salt-scrubbed and shining. We were rarely in quite so exalted a state, so before we reached civilization we both needed a good wash. Evans shaved in the head, and we both took a hot shower with almost as much water as we wanted in the cockpit. Then we broke out some of the clean clothes from the dry bags in the forepeak lockers, and we were ready to face people once again.

By this time we would be approaching the harbor. We both reviewed the harbor chart and the state of the tide. We agreed on our likely anchoring spot if no quarantine anchorage or customs wharf was indicated. We turned on the VHF and tuned to Channel 16 to find out if we needed to call the harbormaster for instructions or if big ships were maneuvering in the area. We turned on the depthsounder and compared our soundings to the chart, and we raised the yellow Q flag to the starboard spreader to signal our request for quarantine clearance. When entering a large port, we called the harbormaster and asked how to proceed.

Once in the harbor, our only rule was to take our time. We knew that we were more tired than we felt, so we checked and double checked. We circled as many times as necessary to understand the layout of the anchorage and to pick our berth or anchoring spot. When we entered a harbor and dropped the anchor, when *Silk* settled back and sat quietly for the first time in weeks, when the motion stopped and all was still, the spell of the ocean would be broken. We eagerly dropped the dinghy over the side and headed ashore to our next adventure.

CHAPTER 19 | TOWARD SEAMANSHIP

Keeping the boat moving safely and well ▪ *Light air* ▪ *Pretrip preparations for shorthanded sailing* ▪ *Heavy weather*
▪ *Managing emergencies* ▪ *Taking on water* ▪ *Storm preparations* ▪ *Steering failures* ▪ *Rigging failures* ▪ *Piracy*

Over the course of our three-year circumnavigation, we spent a total of 266 days on passage. We completed over 20 passages of 5 days or longer and two passages of 29 days each. Over that time we learned that for a shorthanded crew, the boat and crew's condition at landfall were far more important than fast passage times.

Our per-day averages over the course of our trip reflect that we learned to sail faster—from 108 nautical miles-made-good toward our destination during the 12,000 passagemaking miles of our first year, to 133 nautical miles-made-good over the 14,500 passagemaking miles of our last year. We learned to set the boat up better for doublehanded sailing, to push the boat harder but not too hard, and to keep the boat moving longer in a wider variety of conditions.

Our passage times and per-day averages improved as a byproduct of sailing the boat more safely and efficiently. Over time, we learned how to minimize the wear and tear on the boat and on us. After the first few passages, it took us weeks to repair broken gear and get over lack of sleep and occasional crew injury. By the end of the trip, we took care of major gear repairs once an ocean and had the boat and crew back to normal a few days after arriving in port.

Once you master basic passagemaking skills, you need to develop offshore boat-handling skills. These skills will allow you to keep the boat moving well in a variety of conditions and enable you to handle emergencies with confidence—marking the difference between sailing and seamanship. You'll find that about 95 percent of the time you will be concentrating on sailing, and seamanship will be an abstraction. In fact, many

people complete circumnavigations without ever needing to use these skills. But preparing your crew and your boat for that 5 percent possibility will make your entire voyage all that much more relaxed and enjoyable.

KEEPING THE BOAT MOVING SAFELY AND WELL

There is a big difference between a daysail with a full crew and day 10 of a shorthanded passage when you have another 10 days to go. Sailing *Silk* in protected coastal waters with a crew of four and 15 knots of wind over the stern, we would be flying an asymmetrical spinnaker and charging along at our hull speed of 7+ knots. At sea with just the two of us aboard and a big sea running on our quarter, we would be flying our 135 percent genoa to leeward and our 88 percent Yankee poled out to windward and be traveling at 6 to 6.5 knots. For us, the increased safety margin was ample compensation for the reduced speed. It represented good seamanship.

Learning to sail a boat comfortably on passage while making good daily averages toward your destination takes practice. Wind speed is not the only factor when determining what sails to use; you also must consider the sea state and the crew's condition. Coastal sailing can help you understand how your boat responds to different wind speeds, but it cannot totally prepare you for passage sailing, especially with a small crew. Passagemaking on another boat can help you understand the differences between coastal and offshore sailing, but it will tell you little about how your own boat will respond to offshore conditions. The only way to learn how your boat will respond to true offshore conditions is to head off on a passage and find out.

Every boat will let you know when you are pushing too hard or not keeping enough way on for the sea conditions. Every boat is different, and you will need to pay careful attention to your boat during your first few passages to understand what she is telling you. But after a few passages, her voice will be as clear to you as your companion's. While I cannot describe exactly how your boat will feel when she wants more sail or less, the following signs should help you to understand what your boat is trying to communicate.

When the boat is pounding violently going to windward, you need to reduce sail. In certain conditions the hull form and sea state interact to create pounding. You cannot do anything—the boat would pound if you hove-to. But pounding generally suggests that the boat is overcanvassed and would sail better with reefed sails. We avoided pounding regardless of the cost in boat speed to prevent damage to *Silk's* gear and crew.

A boat can start to hobbyhorse when going to windward in waves. All her motion seems to be in an up-and-down direction without any headway. If the boat speed drops to 50 percent of your hull speed, then the boat is undercanvassed and needs more power to drive through the waves. These can be very trying conditions. When we crossed the equator on our way back to the Caribbean from the South Atlantic, we found ourselves close reaching in 25 to 30 knots with steep, uncomfortable seas. Given the wind, we would have preferred to sail under mizzen and Yankee, but we made no headway under that sail combination. Instead, we used a full main and Yankee. We sailed with the lee rail well underwater for five days and made good 150 to 170 nautical miles each day. We were not choosing between comfort and speed; being uncomfortable was unavoidable in the sea conditions.

Downwind, the situation is a bit more subtle. We knew *Silk* was overcanvassed when she started to slalom downwind. She would start to surge off in one direction and the wind vane would have a difficult time getting her back on course. If we took the helm, only brute force would stop her from surging off course. While offshore racers would have hand steered to keep her on course without reducing speed, most double-handed crews don't view that as an option. Reefing

would almost always settle her along her proper course with the wind vane steering happily.

Deciding that the boat is undercanvassed going downwind can be less obvious. *Silk's* roll increased as the wind decreased and the sails stabilized her less against the trade wind swell. This often happened when the wind died after a period of reinforced trades.

Beyond gaining an intuitive sense of how your boat feels, you also need to manage light air and heavy weather, situations that are difficult to prepare for by going coastal sailing.

Light air

Many sailors prefer the outright fury of a gale to the utter frustration of being becalmed (see the sidebar "A day in the life—Becalmed!" in this chapter). As discussed in Chapter 4, you need light-air sail combinations tough enough to stand up to squally conditions. Without effective light-air sails, you will be forced to choose between motoring and drifting. With good light-air sails and good sailing technique, you can continue to make miles toward your destination without depleting your diesel supply. Aboard *Silk,* we could make some progress right down to about 4 knots of apparent wind.

Even with good light-air sails, the time will come on some passages when you won't have enough wind to keep the boat moving. You will then have to decide whether you are going to wait for wind or try to find it. If you decide to go looking, you will also have to decide in which direction to turn your bow when you crank up the "iron genny." These decisions take experience and judgment, but some rules of thumb are helpful.

Light-air tips and tricks

Even with the right sail combinations, keeping the boat moving in light air is truly an art. The lighter the wind and the larger the swell, the more difficult it is to make forward progress. But if the light air is widespread, there will often be little swell and you can make progress with patience and attention to details. Learning to sail your boat well in light air will sharpen your sailing skills in all conditions. It will also minimize your fuel bill and enable you to keep the engine off in oppressive weather.

When the air goes light, take a quick tour around the boat and make sure all the weight is stowed as low and close to the centerline as possible. If the trip has been calm, many things may have found their way out of stowage. If you think you may be facing several days of light air, consider taking another anchor off the bow or moving more chain into the bilge. Weight in the ends causes the boat to pitch, which slows the boat down when you have the least speed to spare. Equalizing the water tanks may also help boat speed. Extra weight on the leeward side helps heel the boat, which improves the angle of the sails to the wind and reduces wetted surface. Even on a heavy cruising boat, moving water can make a difference.

Light wind accompanied by a heavy swell can be particularly frustrating. These conditions are unstable and unlikely to last for more than a day or so—except in the doldrums. An asymmetrical spinnaker can keep the boat moving. But the forces created when the boat rolls and the sail collapses and then fills again can create tremendous strains on the rigging and gear. We were flying our asymmetrical spinnaker in these conditions in a low between New Zealand and Fiji. The spinnaker's tack pendant got caught on our spare anchor when the sail collapsed. When the sail filled again, it ripped the anchor, bow roller, and a piece of teak 3 inches thick and 6 inches long off our bowsprit. Don't underestimate the forces involved in these types of conditions. Light wind can damage your boat as easily as heavy wind can.

In a large swell, reducing sail area and keeping the sails flatter will often allow you to keep the sails full despite the roll. A mainsail or mizzen sheeted in flat on the centerline may steady the boat. Stabilizing the sails so they are less likely to collapse also helps. To keep the sails drawing instead of collapsing, you can use the vang and traveler to limit the slatting of the mainsail or pole out the tack of the spinnaker on the main boom (as discussed in Chapter 4). Experiment with your boat to see what stabilizes her. On some centerboard boats, having the board down will reduce the rolling. But if the slat-

Pretrip preparations for shorthanded sailing

If you are used to sailing with a racing crew, you may need to modify your boat to make it easy for two people to handle offshore. Aside from adding reliable self-steering so the crew can tend the sails, you may need to upgrade some of the sail-handling hardware. Try managing the boat with two people on board on a windy day and consider the following:

■ *Primary winches.* To allow an extra margin of safety, primaries should be at least one size larger than normal, equipped with self-tailers, and preferably two-speed. Winches are expensive, but you will use your primaries to pull yourself in against a dock, control a flogging sail, reef your headsail in dangerous conditions, and go up the mast.

■ *Furling drum.* Your furler should be oversized for the boat. You will often need to reef in a sudden squall where you cannot turn into the wind because you have a sail poled out to leeward. You want to be able to reduce or totally furl the sail in 15 knots without having to rely on a winch.

■ *Furling line.* If your headsail furling winch is small and not self-tailing, you can replace it or set up a furling line long enough to be led to a primary winch. If you ever have to furl it in a lot of wind where you cannot round up, you will need a good sized winch for the first few turns of the furling drum. Reduce the friction in the furling line as much as possible. On most boats, the lead from the drum to the deck creates a great deal of friction.

■ *Mainsail reefing winch.* Conditions will not always be perfect when you have to reef the main. Any boat over 35 feet should be equipped with an oversized reefing winch. Even smaller boats can benefit from adding one. If your reefing winch is on the boom, move it to the deck or the front of the mast. Using a winch on the boom can put you in an unstable position in a heavy sea. Also, after the first reef it is hard to reach underneath the sail to use the winch for the second reef.

■ *Snuffers.* If you have a spinnaker or an asymmetrical spinnaker aboard, you will need a good snuffer to manage it with two people.

ting and banging start to endanger either the gear or your sanity, decide whether to start the motor or take down all your sails and wait patiently for more wind.

When light wind is not accompanied by a heavy swell, you will be able to keep the boat moving for much longer. But chances are that you will also be in light air for longer. As the swell dies, the boat and sails can be allowed to "breathe." That means using the controls to shape the sails for light winds.

On the mainsail, loosening the outhaul, easing the vang, easing the halyard until wrinkles are just about to appear on the front edge of the sail, and pulling the traveler above the boat's centerline and easing the sheet slightly will create a fuller sail shape with more twist that will be more efficient in light air. For the headsail, easing the halyard to the same point as on the main, moving the sheet leads slightly forward, and easing the sheet will accomplish the same thing. On both sails, use the telltales to make sure that the sail is breaking evenly once you have made these adjustments. For a spinnaker (asymmetrical or otherwise), raise the clew to allow the spinnaker to take on a fuller, bellied-out shape. Center the sail higher than normal in front of the boat to take advantage of the slight differential between the wind speed at the water's surface and halfway up the mast. Changing to lighter sheets on a headsail will stop the clew from dragging down and spilling the wind.

Letting the boat breathe also extends to the course that you steer. When going to windward, sailing too close to the wind will cause the sails to stall. The angle where your boat stalls will be farther off the wind than at higher wind speeds. Polar diagrams for your boat will help you find the most efficient angle to the wind in light airs. Tacking downwind may give you enough apparent wind to continue sailing. But additional speed compensates for steering off your course only up to a point. Don't be like the inexperienced Newport-to-Bermuda Race crew who ended up beam reaching at 90 degrees to their course because the boat "was going so much faster!"

Let the boat settle down and sail. The boat will never find her groove if you change sails every half-hour. In light conditions, it can take 20 minutes for the boat to work her way into sailing. During that time, minimize activity below and on deck and don't tweak.

Set her up as well as you can for the conditions and then leave her alone for at least a half-hour. After all, you do have all day.

To maximize performance, you also need to reduce underbody drag. Set the sails so the boat is balanced. If that is not possible, at least avoid lee helm (the helm has to be held to leeward rather than to windward to keep the boat moving in a straight line) when sailing to windward. The braking effect of the rudder will offset most of your boat speed in 6 or 8 knots of apparent wind. If you are experiencing lee helm, try adding more mainsail or reducing the headsail.

Minimizing steering motions also reduces underbody drag. If the winds are really light and there is no swell, the boat may do better with the helm lashed rather than being steered by a wind vane, an autopilot, or even a person. The less movement in the rudder, the less underwater turbulence there is to slow the boat down. We used to sit at the helmsman's seat with the wheel locked and move it in one smooth motion a few degrees every 10 or 15 minutes as *Silk* drifted off her course.

If you have been moving slowly for a week or so in tropical waters and the winds are predicted to stay light, consider going over the side to give the bottom a quick scrub. Pay particular attention to the prop. But don't try to remove the gooseneck barnacles. They will die of their own accord when the boat stops moving completely, and they are virtually impossible to remove before that. They will slow your boat, but you will have to live with them until you get to port.

As the wind dies and your boat speed drops, current becomes more and more important to your overall speed. In the sidebar titled "A day in the life—Becalmed!," more than half of the 200 miles-made-good in five days came from the 1-knot westerly setting current around the Galapagos Islands. Seek out any current in your area if it does not take you farther from where the wind might be.

When there truly is no wind and you don't want to or can't motor, try patience. Take all the sails down or leave up a small riding sail to reduce the rolling, and then wait. You will get some wind eventually.

When canvas fails—minimizing motoring

While experienced voyagers varied a great deal in their willingness to motor, most agreed that motoring was appropriate in three situations—when becalmed in a major ocean current, when crossing the doldrums, or when crossing the horse latitudes.

Being becalmed in the Gulf Stream or the Agulhas Current almost always means bad weather is on the way. Use the motor to cross the current before the bad weather arrives. If you are crossing the doldrums at a narrow point in the right season and you are becalmed, motor due north or south until you hit the trade wind belt. We should have done this when we were becalmed near the Galapagos. We would have reached reasonable winds with a day of motoring.

Most experienced voyagers would also motor when crossing one of the semipermanent highs in the horse latitudes, such as the one in the South Atlantic that is usually centered somewhere near St. Helena Island. The old clipper ship routes avoided this area of light air by sailing a backward S course around the Atlantic—from the U.S. East Coast, to northern Europe, south to the Cape Verde Islands, west to Brazil, south to the Roaring Forties, and across the Southern Ocean to Cape Town and beyond. Traveling back to the United States and Europe from the Cape of Good Hope, there is no good way to avoid this high. Most boats end up motoring the last day or so to St. Helena rather than sitting becalmed.

Beyond these situations where most voyagers agree that motoring makes sense, the decision to motor varies from boat to boat. Some voyagers start to motor when boat speed falls below a certain point, while others base their decision on how much fuel they have left. We never liked running the engine. If the barometer, wind, and sea state indicated that we would get wind in the next 12 hours, we would sit and wait for it. In a generalized band of light, variable winds and squally conditions, we discovered there were always pockets of wind. If squalls promising wind were on the horizon, we would motor to reach them. We remain inclined to sail our way out of light air. But we have come to accept that in certain situations, the engine offers a safer and more comfortable alternative to sitting still.

Heavy weather

Everyone who spends any time offshore will eventually encounter light air. But with a bit of planning and good luck, many boats avoid serious heavy weather. As discussed in Chapter 4, gale-force winds accounted for less than 5 percent of our time at sea. Only a few people we knew had experienced storm conditions (over 48 knots) with breaking waves and dangerous seas that required the use of ultimate storm tactics. Most people had successfully managed gales at sea, though we knew a few who completed circumnavigations without ever having to employ any heavy weather tactics. So don't be put off by the following descriptions, but do be prepared.

Even more so than in light air, no one answer works for all boats in heavy weather. Every boat differs in seakeeping ability, and every skipper differs in heavy weather experience. Even more important, every storm differs in its wind and wave characteristics. How a skipper handles a particular vessel in a particular gale may be quite different from how that skipper handles the next gale in the same boat. No "magic bullet" exists that will keep any boat safe in all conditions.

To prepare for heavy weather, learn about as many experiences of as many different boats as you can. Talk to skippers who have been out in storm conditions and try to understand their techniques. Read K. Adlard Coles's *Heavy Weather Sailing* (4th edition, International Marine, 1992) and try to absorb the range of possible solutions. Managing heavy weather is like anchoring: Successful skippers keep trying solutions until the boat feels safe, stable, and comfortable.

Take your boat out in gale conditions and try as many heavy weather techniques as possible. Heave-to and see how your boat lies and how much leeway she makes under various sail combinations in various wind speeds. Run before the wind and see how little sail you can carry and still keep moving comfortably. While you cannot replicate offshore conditions, you can start to get a feel for how your boat will respond.

When it comes to heavy weather tactics, there are two main theories. One school of thought says that you want to keep the boat moving forward, since the loss of momentum means a loss of stability and a greater chance of being rolled. Another school of thought argues that stopping the boat is almost always the best solution, since the greatest danger comes when the boat starts to surf down the wave fronts.

Not too surprisingly, these two theories have evolved from racing and cruising. They reflect the different priorities and boat designs of the two groups. Cruisers value safety above speed and view stopping as a viable option when things get uncomfortable. Traditional cruising designs with their full keels reflect this philosophy, and most cruising boats stop quite happily in all but ultimate storm conditions. Racers want to keep racing if possible. Modern racing underbodies with their fin keels are designed to be driven forward in storm conditions, and most modern racing boats seem to want to keep going just as much as the crews who

race them. Both theories have been proven: There are hundreds of voyagers who have hove-to in storm conditions and many successful BOC and Whitbread racers who keep moving in rugged Southern Ocean conditions. Much can be learned from both camps. Prudent voyagers should have many tricks up their sleeves when Neptune comes calling.

The difference in tactics also reflects the different situations of voyagers and racers. Fully crewed race boats have a competent watch ready to assist in the event of

A day in the life—Becalmed!

The following is an excerpt from my journal, written at 8:30 A.M., on March 30, 1993, approximately 100 miles south of Isabela Island in the Galapagos at ~1°30' S 93°30' W.

"After five days, we've only managed something over 200 miles. We have discussed motoring. But since we couldn't take on diesel in the Galapagos, we don't want to start off by using a lot of diesel with 2,500 miles to go to the Marquesas. We're not even sure we'll be able to get diesel there. It may be Tahiti before we can take on more fuel. We aren't certain in which direction we might find wind, because we can't yet get Arnold's weather forecasts from the Cook Islands. So we are flying blind, and we would rather wait for the winds to fill than end up short of diesel.

"I find my reactions to our slow progress interesting. I know that we have plenty of everything aboard to last us, even if the trip takes two months. But a less rational part of me seems to be quietly panicking—a little voice is arguing that at our current pace it will take us four months to get to the Marquesas. At least our water tanks are full after a squall this morning. Unfortunately, it doesn't rain diesel. Ev figures that we have enough diesel for another 40 days of daily charging. At the rate we are going, that's not going to be enough. We are low on other things too, but nothing we can't live without. It would help if we could start ticking off the miles.

"I find myself grumpy and irritable much of the time. I've been trying to keep busy with French, reading, cooking—I've even done about half the needlepoint

from Grandma. But the beastly heat day and night combined with the very high humidity undisturbed by the usual ocean breeze make me constantly lethargic. Ev and I have been eating simply, neither of us having much appetite.

"Against all this is the feeling that we haven't really started yet. That being becalmed for five days has simply delayed our departure. The trip still looms ahead, in its entirety. The reassuring countdown of 100+ miles with each day traveled is missing.

"Despite all that, I really have enjoyed experiencing the sea in a calm mood. It has been stifling hot during the day—so hot that when I went on deck at noon yesterday I blistered the soles of my feet. But at dusk as it cools off, we get treated to the sea life feeding. From 5:00 until about 7:00 every night, we've seen masses of tuna and other fish feeding in schools with sea birds spiraling overhead. Small fish leap out of the water in a rain of silver, chased by larger fish below and bombed by the waiting sea birds above. The entire surface of the ocean churns like a river with a strong current. We've also been surrounded by large pods of dolphins and whales. The last two nights, we've seen the lights from fishing boats plying their trade several miles away.

"At least this morning we are making some progress with the gennaker—two and a half knots of boat speed. The wind seems a bit more serious, less of the cat's paw that just touches the boat and withdraws chuckling across the water. I understand now why mutinies so often occurred when ships were becalmed. The heat, the uncertainty, the idleness, the lethargy: It could make one either murderous or insane."

an emergency and a container of spares and shore crew to do repairs when the boat pulls into port. Voyagers have to maintain their own reserve to deal with the unexpected and use their own resources to fix any damages. Voyagers need to know when to take a break rather than break a piece of gear. When the wind was contrary or the waves were causing us to pound badly, we often hove-to and waited for more favorable conditions. The gear that didn't break more than compensated us for a 6- to 12-hour delay.

Keeping the boat moving toward your destination

Sea state matters far more than wind speed in determining appropriate storm tactics. In protected waters, you can continue sailing in almost any wind strength by reducing sail. Even in 50 knots, you can make progress with a storm jib. As you move out of protected waters and encounter larger, steeper waves, the situation changes dramatically. The incredible forces of breaking waves destabilize the boat and can put her and her crew in serious danger.

To get some idea of the magnitude of these forces, consider that every cubic yard of water weighs more than one ton. A breaking wave may contain several hundred tons. This weight can literally fall on top of your boat. Or it can race down the face of the wave and curl over in a crest at speeds of up to 30 knots. The twisting motion and weight in the top of a breaking wave can bend stanchions and pulpits, stave in coach roofs, break portlights, and crash through weatherboards. As the waves move from large and well-behaved to steep and breaking, you have successively fewer options for ensuring the vessel's safety.

When the wind starts to build and the barometer, sea, and clouds indicate a storm is approaching, the first thing to do is to batten down the hatches (described in the sidebar "Storm preparations," page 352). As the wind builds, you successively reef until you are sailing under your storm sails. If the waves are not steep or breaking and the wind is aft of the beam, you *may* be able to comfortably continue along your course for the duration of the storm. We have run downwind with just the staysail up in winds over 50 knots with large—but not steep or breaking—seas. This tactic works if you find yourself on one side or the other of a low and your destination is compatible with the wind direction.

In many storm situations, the strongest winds will be contrary to your course and running off will not be the best option. If conditions are not too bad and you are trying to make headway to windward, you can make forward progress by *forereaching*. This means setting up the boat so that she jogs along slowly to weather. Aboard *Silk,* we would drop down to our mizzen and staysail, sheet both in tight, and lash the wheel on the centerline. *Silk* would track 50 to 60 degrees off the wind, as long as the waves were not steep or breaking and the wind was under 40 knots. If the waves stayed manageable but the wind increased, we would drop the mizzen and jog along under staysail alone in up to 50 knots. Set up this way, *Silk* made about 3 knots or so along her course. On a cutter, a trysail and storm jib (or a storm jib alone) accomplish the same thing. We kept some way on by forereaching, which meant that we made less leeway and still had rudder control.

Forereaching is safe as long as the waves remain well behaved. We used the tactic most often during the first few hours of a gale before the seas had built up. We also used it in short but intense line squalls where the sea state was not greatly affected by the gale-force winds.

In most storm situations, the waves become bigger and more confused as the wind increases and shifts. A boat will start to pound or her bow will be thrown off course by the waves, which exposes her beam to the seas. At what wind speed and what wave conditions this happens will depend on the underbody of the boat. When the pounding starts, most voyagers choose between running off and losing miles toward their destination or stopping the boat to wait for better weather. Three alternatives exist for stopping the boat: lie ahull, heave-to, or lie to a sea anchor or drogue.

The traditional solutions: heaving-to and lying ahull

Heaving-to and lying ahull are two ways to stop the boat so she rides the wind and waves without losing too much ground toward an upwind destination. Both have the advantage of simplicity: The vessel is stopped without the deployment of any gear, and she is free to respond to sudden changes in wind or waves. However, heaving-to offers all the advantages of lying ahull without the major disadvantages. For that reason, I see few situations where lying ahull is preferable.

Lying ahull means taking all sail down and allowing the boat to skid slowly sideways before the wind and the waves (Figure 19-1). On most boats, the helm must be lashed so the rudder keeps the boat's head from falling off. Most full-keeled boats will assume a position 90 degrees to the wind with the seas broad on the beam. In theory, the slick created to windward by the boat's motion through the water will cause the seas to slide past without breaking.

Lying ahull has three disadvantages. First, when lying beam-on the rolling can be terrible, and crew injury, seasickness, or gear damage are more likely compared to other storm tactics. Second, if conditions intensify and the seas reach the height of the boat's freeboard and start to break, damage to the leeward side of the vessel is likely—including bent pulpits, ripped off dodgers, stove-in coach roofs, and so on. Third, when the waves get to be roughly the same height as the

beam of the boat and are frequently breaking, a large surface area of the boat is exposed to the twisting forces in the breaking wave crest and the vessel faces a serious risk of being knocked down or rolled.

Heaving-to means setting up the sails and the rudder so they oppose one another, causing the boat to stop making headway (Figure 19-2). The boat will ride with the wind and waves 40 or 50 degrees off her bow and slide slowly to leeward. Her speed of drift will depend on the proportion of the boat exposed to water versus that exposed to the wind. Therefore, a traditional full-keel cruising boat will drift more slowly than other hull forms. In contrast to lying ahull, heaving-to exposes a smaller area of the strongest part of the boat to the forces of wind and waves and rolling is greatly reduced. Psychologically, the crew feels like the boat is dealing with the storm rather than being at its mercy.

Heaving-to is one of the simplest maneuvers that can be done aboard a boat and one of the first things neophyte sailors should learn. Heaving-to can be likened

Figure 19-1. When lying ahull, a boat will sit with her beam to the waves and slip to leeward.

to applying a hand brake. It can be used to enjoy a lovely picnic lunch on a summer afternoon a few miles offshore or to make an easy repair to a sail on passage. To heave-to on a cutter, the boat is tacked through the wind without releasing the headsail sheet and the helm is lashed to leeward. This combination of sails and rudder will cause the boat to jog up to windward, then fall off, then jog up again. The boat makes little headway and a fair amount of leeway. In storm conditions, the motion to leeward is supposed to create a slick on the surface of the ocean that helps to calm the seas reaching the boat. After trying to head to weather in winds over 30 knots, heaving-to is a sudden and surprising oasis of calm amidst the sound and fury of a gale at sea.

Perfect your technique for heaving-to before heading to sea. Try it in all wind and sea states and learn what your boat likes and what she doesn't. Again, boats differ significantly. The longer the keel, the more it will "grip" the water and the less leeway the boat will make. A traditional full-keeled boat will normally make a half-

knot to a knot of leeway, while fin keels may make over 3 knots. A fin keel is also likely to make significant headway when the boat sails up to windward before she falls off. Trying to get a real racing boat to heave-to may mean that you only succeed in cutting her speed in half.

Silk, like many ketches, hove-to on the mizzen alone without a backed headsail. We lashed the helm on the centerline and adjusted the mizzen sheet so she sat 45 to 50 degrees off the wind. We then fixed the mizzen boom in this position with a vang from the end of the boom to a stanchion base. She would drift at about a knot at a right angle to the wind. She would also heave-to with a main and the backed Yankee, but the Yankee chafed where it crossed the staysail stay. This would not be a problem on a cutter heaving-to using a staysail.

As a storm tactic and even as an offshore tool used for a wide variety of purposes, heaving-to is exceedingly effective and versatile. We met a few offshore voyagers who never even had to heave-to, and many who

Figure 19-2. When hove-to, a boat presents a much smaller surface area to wind and waves.

never had to do anything beyond heaving-to. Heaving-to proved effective for us in all but one storm situation. The leeway means that you do need sea room (most boats will drift between 20 and 50 miles to leeward every 24 hours). Assuming that the nearest land is hundreds of miles away, heaving-to is the most comfortable way to manage most storm conditions if your boat's keel configuration allows it. For a traditional full-keeled boat on a trade wind circumnavigation that travels out of the tropics during the hurricane season, heaving-to will prove a safe and effective tactic in almost all of the heavy weather she encounters.

Heaving-to does become unsafe in a "survival storm" situation. When steep, breaking waves reach a height equal to the boat's waterline length, a large wave may push the bow off so far that the side of the boat is exposed to the full fury of the sea. In that case, the boat is at risk of being rolled or tumbled, and another storm tactic needs to be employed. The seas may also reach a height where the boat is becalmed in the trough, which will cause the boat to fall off before the next wave arrives.

You are reaching the limits of heaving-to as a storm tactic when the boat begins to labor—for example, if waves are knocking her bow off repeatedly and interrupting the regular pattern of jogging up to windward and falling off to leeward. In a dangerously confused sea, a wave may strike the opposite bow and force the boat to tack through. She will also tack if the wind speed increases enough that the small sail area overpowers the rudder and brings her head through the wind. If you cannot reduce sail further, heaving-to is no longer a safe tactic. The time has come to prepare the boat for the next level of storm tactics: running downwind or lying to a drogue or sea anchor.

Other alternatives:
lying to a drogue or sea anchor

If the wind and waves have become so violent that the boat can no longer keep her bow to weather when hove-to, one alternative is to use the friction of the water itself to hold the boat in position. Drogues and sea anchors both accomplish this. Each holds a different end of the boat to weather: A sea anchor is streamed from the bow to hold the bow facing the wind and seas; a drogue is streamed from the stern to hold the stern into the storm. A sea anchor may be used in conjunction with a small riding sail to help hold the bow into the wind, but a drogue is generally employed without any sail up. In both cases, the idea is to present as small a target to the storm as possible without giving up distance if your desired course is to weather.

Drogues and sea anchors range from used parachutes, to specially designed anchors (Figure 19-3), to tires and chains, to the new series-type drogues (Figure 19-4, page 350). Parachute devices are streamed 100 feet or more from the boat with a tripping line attached. The tripping line is used to retrieve the parachute or to control the rate of drift by partially collapsing the device. Series drogues are hundreds of small cones of sail material strung together on a long line that generally is streamed from the stern. Whatever device is used, the drag created must be large enough to offset the forces on the boat, and the warp must have some give so the boat can surge forward or backward in the face of a large breaking wave.

Much controversy surrounds both techniques, and indeed there are drawbacks. It can be very difficult to deploy these devices properly from a heaving, wave-lashed deck without fouling it. If the device needs to be retrieved during the storm, considerable strength is required to get it back aboard. The warp is prone to tremendous chafe where it crosses the deck; a good fairlead and chafe protection along with frequent visual checks are required throughout the storm. Finally, if a sea anchor does not offer enough drag, the boat can be forced around broadside by the waves. If a drogue does not have enough drag or if the warp is too short, it will be carried forward with the waves and end up alongside the boat. In both cases, the forces exerted on the boat when she fetches up against the device and comes to a sudden halt can be every bit as dangerous as the forces from the wind and waves.

Still, these devices have been used successfully by fishing boats off the gale-ridden coasts of Newfoundland and Maine for decades. Many multihulls have successfully employed parachutes in severe weather. These devices do offer the valuable advantage of limiting leeway: In a situation where there is danger to leeward, they may represent the best option. We never met anyone who had actually used one, but we knew several people who carried them aboard just to have an option in heavy weather.

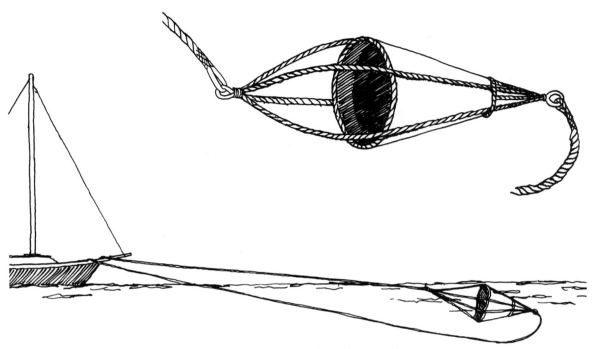

Figure 19-3. Parachute sea anchors (detail, above right) are streamed off the bow with a tripping line.

Extreme solutions: running downwind with or without warps

Assuming you have sea room, running off represents a last resort if your course is to windward. *Running downwind* means steering the boat so the wind and waves are on her stern quarter. You may carry a small amount of sail to stabilize the boat or set her to run under bare poles with no sail at all. The resistance of the mast, hull, and rigging will drive most boats at 4 to 5 knots in true storm conditions. The obvious reduction in apparent wind speed eases the strain on the boat's equipment. Because the boat is kept moving, steerageway is maintained so the helmsman can avoid a particularly vicious wave. If crewmembers are exhausted or seasick, the boat is likely to manage on her own when running off. A wind vane usually steers well, but it cannot anticipate a big sea the way a human helmsman can.

Running off only works if there is adequate sea room. Most depressions are fast-moving, and they usually calm down after 24 to 48 hours. Running off at an average speed of 4 knots means that you will need at least 100 nautical miles of sea room. That should pose no problem two to three days after setting out on a major passage. Presumably, your weather window will allow you that much fair weather at the outset of your passage. When closing with most islands, you can run off to one side or the other, but you might not have adequate sea room when you are closing with a large landmass or a reef-strewn archipelago. The chances that a storm of such severity will catch you out in this position are slight. But if it looks like a possibility based on the barometer, the sea state, and the weather reports, consider heading back out to sea rather than trying to dash for port before the storm hits.

If the vessel has been hove-to and conditions have deteriorated to the point where running off is necessary, you will have to turn your boat so her quarter is positioned to the waves. This will bring you beam-on to the seas for a brief period. When you are getting ready to turn and run off, watch the waves and wait for four or five smaller waves that are not breaking.

You then need to decide what speed to maintain. If running off is a last resort because your course is to windward, you will obviously want to keep the boat moving as slowly as possible. If you run too slowly, your boat will lose steerageway and start to wallow. The force of a breaking wave on the quarter can push the stern down the wave face faster than the bow, which exposes the boat's beam to the breaking sea and can result in a knockdown or rollover. But you also don't want to surf down the front of the wave, since the boat can bury her bow in the trough or in the wave ahead. In a worst case scenario, the combination of a breaking wave on the stern and burying the bow can cause a boat to pitchpole, or flip stern over bow.

The optimal speed will be determined by the speed of the waves and two objectives: The boat needs to go fast enough so steerageway is maintained, but slow enough so she doesn't start surfing down the wave fronts. The vessel is moving too fast if she seems to float on or near the crest and you have to fight the helm to keep her from rounding up. The boat's stern will lift to the crest and she'll try to broach (round up and turn broadside to the wind and sea). If she's not moving fast enough, you'll lose steerage in the troughs. The one time that we had to run off aboard *Silk* the optimal speed was about 4 knots. But that will vary with the boat's hull form and the wave conditions.

In order to slow the boat more, deploy warps off the stern. A warp is a heavy line that trails off the stern to a distance of 150 to 300 feet behind the boat. The warp might be tied in a large bight and doubled back to the boat. In the Southern Ocean, Robin Knox-Johnson used 100 fathoms of ⅝-inch polypropylene line tied in a bight aboard his 32-foot wooden ketch. The warp may also be weighted at one end and attached to the boat's quarter. On *Silk,* we used a 150-foot anchor line with 20 feet of chain on one end. Other solutions include tires and even anchors chained to the end of the warp to further increase the drag on the boat. Besides slowing the boat down, the warps also serve to stabilize her direction and prevent the stern from being "chased" down the wave front by a breaking wave.

The specifics of boat, wind speed, and waves will determine how much drag the boat requires to slow her

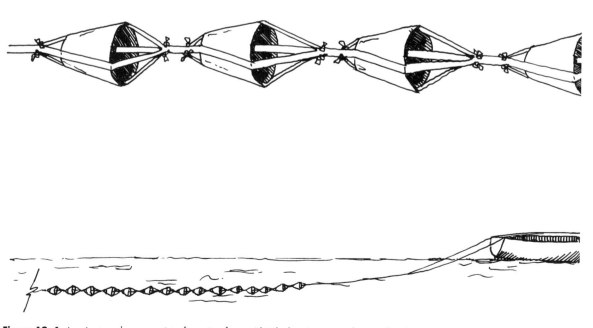

Figure 19-4. A series-type drogue consists of a series of cones (detail, above) sewn together on a long line.

down. In some cases, you may have to deploy three or four warps before there is a noticeable change in the boat's behavior. But the difference is dramatic. The vessel will go from feeling like an out-of-control freight train surging down the wave fronts to a well-mannered steamer calmly plodding along. Both the boat's speed and direction will stabilize, and a lashed helm or the wind vane should be able to hold the boat on course.

The worst part about trailing warps is assembling and deploying them. When it is time to deploy warps, you could be in foul-weather gear, at night, on a pitching boat, and possibly seasick. The warp must not be too heavy or cumbersome, and it must be readily accessible. The warp will require chafe protection, which must be checked frequently once deployed.

Some controversy does exist over trailing warps. Some well-respected offshore sailors have cut them away in the midst of a gale and found that the boat sailed better. Recent theories suggest that waves tend to be steep and breaking early in a storm. This is because the underlying water is not yet moving at speed with the wind. During that period, warps stabilize the boat. After the winds have been blowing at storm force for many hours, the waves become less steep but their velocity increases dramatically. The warps may then slow the boat too much in front of the rapidly moving waves. Few voyagers will ever have to test this theory. The incidents where cutting away warps were reported to be helpful occurred in the Southern Ocean during gales that lasted several days.

While controversy exists over stopping the boat or keeping it going in moderate gales, in ultimate storm conditions most experienced sailors view running off as the best tactic. It has been well proven on many kinds of boats. When preparing for offshore conditions, consider what you will use for warps. Then make sure they are accessible and can be deployed by one crewmember.

MANAGING EMERGENCIES

Potential misfortunes voyagers face near land are discussed in Chapter 15. Many of these can occur on passage. But the way of preventing and managing these emergencies depends little on whether you are in port or thousands of miles away from land. On the other hand, there are several emergency situations that are

dangerous because you are at sea and hundreds of miles from assistance. These situations have to do with the integrity of your vessel and her ability to get you to your destination. Survival rates in liferafts are abysmally low. The boat is your lifeline, and her safety is almost synonymous with yours. Being prepared for the worst that can happen does not start with "safety" gear. Good seamanship means never having to use that type of equipment.

Every voyager dreads the situations that follow. We knew of a few boats that suffered rigging failures, one that lost its rudder, and one that sank. We knew of twice as many boats that were damaged by poor navigation and fire than by all the situations described below. The odds predict you will never have to face these situations. Prevention improves the odds even more, and it starts with an offshore-capable boat that is worthy of your trust. But it cannot remove all of the risks of voyaging. So when prevention fails, preparation needs to take over. Resolving the situation satisfactorily hinges on your ability to do things one step at a time in a logical fashion.

There is no magic in what follows. With a bit of time to consider the problem, any reasonably intelligent person could come up with these solutions. This section succeeds if it gets you to think about the procedure before the emergency hits—before your response becomes instantaneous, before you realize that the repair would be easy if you had thought to put a certain item aboard. You need to address the realities of boat construction and crew strength in theory before you have to address these issues in fact. If the time comes, you may not have time to reason. You and your crew need to do your thinking beforehand.

Taking on water

Taking on water does not necessarily mean sinking, and you and your crew must understand the distinction. Too many vessels have been abandoned when their crews believed they were sinking, only to be found floating days or weeks later. When an existing hull opening starts to leak, the crew should be able to do a repair that will get the boat safely to port. Failures of ports or hatches only become a serious threat in severe storm conditions when the boat could be rolled. A life-threatening situation exists if hull damage from a collision allows in more water than can be pumped out in a given period of time. Even so, many boats have been kept afloat long enough for their crews to be rescued.

You must accomplish four steps when facing any breach through the hull. First, operate the bilge pumps as often as necessary to stay ahead of the leak. With a serious hole, this may mean that one crewmember is fully occupied pumping the bilge until you reach port. Second, quickly locate the leak and make it accessible. Third, install a temporary "patch" to slow the rate of seawater flowing in. Finally, put in place a more permanent solution that will allow the boat to be sailed to port.

Failure of structural openings

Any place where the structural integrity of the hull is breached to create an opening—such as seacocks, ports, hatches, hatchboards, and even cockpit locker and anchor locker lids—the potential exists for the structure that seals the opening to fail completely. For each of these openings, you need some way to reseal them to maintain the integrity of the hull. The following ideas offer some guidance when you outfit your boat.

■ *Seacocks.* As underwater fittings, a failed seacock poses a serious danger in any sea conditions. Locating the leak can be the most difficult step. Everyone on board should know the location of every seacock and how to access it. A bilge full of salt water should start an all-out search. Once you find the culprit, insert a tapered wooden plug of an appropriate diameter into the seacock to stop the flow of water. While this sounds easy, the pressure of the water coming through an opening the diameter of a seacock will require you to use some force to get the plug inserted and hold it in place. Keep one of these plugs within reach of every seacock. You can buy them at most marine supply stores or make your own.

■ *Ports.* Ports are unlikely to fail except in extreme storm conditions when hit by a breaking wave. In that situation, the boat may be vulnerable if the port is a large one and the boat is rolled. To make a patch, stuff a cushion or a life preserver into the port and secure it with duct tape, battens, or some sort of a strut. You can then consider a better remedy. Carry a piece of marine ply the size of your largest port to use for a more complete repair. You can mount it over the port with underwater epoxy and screws.

■ *Hatches, hatchboards, and locker lids.* A failure in one of these large openings poses a serious danger to the boat, especially since it is only likely in storm conditions. A large sail in its bag (like a spinnaker) stuffed into a cockpit locker after the lid has been lost makes an

---

Storm preparations

You are sailing merrily at 40° N, about halfway between Bermuda and the Azores. Over the last day the wind has gradually died, and now you have full sail up in 12 knots of southerly breeze. During the day, you have seen cirrus and then cirrostratus building high above. By 0400, when you make your log entry, the sky has lowered further and is covered with altostratus. The barometer has dropped from 1012 to 1006 since your last log entry at 1200, and you also note a fairly large swell from the southwest underlying the wind-driven waves. A low is west of you and closing quickly. What should you do in the four to six hours before the storm arrives?

1. *Take seasick medications, if necessary.* Those prone to seasickness should take the medication while they are still feeling fine. A full range of seasickness medications, from pills to suppositories, should be stowed in an accessible location.

2. *Top up your batteries.* You may not be able to charge your batteries during the next 24 to 48 hours. Your solar panels are unlikely to see any sun, and your wind generator should have the brake firmly set throughout the gale. You will not want to run the engine in large waves where the prop might freewheel. If you have refrigeration or a watermaker, run these at the same time.

3. *Restow everything.* Go through the boat and stow everything securely. Put away extra clothing, books, notebooks, cooking utensils, and so on. Check all drawers and lockers to make sure they are latched well and will not come open if the contents shift. Make sure floorboards are locked in place. Secure the covers to the icebox.

4. *Lash everything down on deck.* Remove anything that does not need to be on deck and put it below. That includes spare sails, solar panels, boat hooks, plastic jugs, cockpit cushions, and odds and ends stowed in the coamings. If you have roller furling, wrap the sheets around the sail three or four times, lash it if necessary, cleat off the furling line, and secure the drum so the sail cannot come unwrapped. Remove anything lashed to the lifelines and stow it below. Add lashings as necessary to dinghies, liferafts, spinnaker poles, and so on. Make sure extra sail ties are accessible. Three times the normal number of sail ties can be required to secure a sail in gale-force winds. Put some spare line in a handy place for lashing the helm or tying down anything that comes loose.

5. *Prepare storm devices.* Put warps, tires, chain, drogues, sea anchors, chafing gear, or other devices for storm tactics in the top of the cockpit locker where they can be easily reached. If the barometer has fallen 8 millibars or more in the last three hours, assemble lines, tires, and chain into a warp and stow it so it can be easily deployed.

6. *Make the boat watertight.* Secure all hatches and ports. Orient Dorades so that they are pointing aft. Locate the Dorade plates, put them in a convenient place, and make sure everyone knows where they are. Put in the hatchboards. Consider sealing them in place with a layer of silicone adhesive. Check the main bilge pump and emergency pumps. Pump the bilge dry.

7. *Arrange necessary equipment.* Put one dry change of clothes near each bunk. Set up harnesses, tethers, foul-weather gear, flashlights, and towels near the companionway. Check to be sure that harnesses

and tethers show no signs of chafe and lubricate clips on tethers if necessary. Check that the jacklines are properly set and secured and show no signs of chafe.

8. *Fortify the crew.* Make a hot meal to be eaten immediately and make sure that everyone (who is not already seasick) eats. Get out a few cans of hearty stews or soups and put them and a small saucepan in a secure but accessible place in the galley for a one-pot meal during the gale. Boil water and stow it in a thermos for making tea, cocoa, or hot soup. Set up an accessible stock of high-energy foods, including dried fruits, nuts, crackers, chocolate, and hard candy.

9. *Prepare the galley.* Put away all dishes, pots, pans, and so on. Leave nothing on the gimbaled stove. Make sure all knives are in an enclosed drawer. Close the seacocks on the galley sinks and notify the crew that you have done so. Leave the stove gimbaled, but if it can swing far enough to hit the safety bar in front of it, wrap the bar with a towel to protect the glass in the oven door.

10. *Discuss the plan of action.* By now you should have a good idea of exactly where the gale is and how severe it is likely to be based on the swell, the wind shifts, the cloud cover, and the change in the barometer. Sit down and discuss exactly what your plan of action will be and what alternatives you might need to employ. To minimize confusion, everyone needs to know what role they will play in each procedure. At the same time, the crew needs to understand that the captain will not know the exact course of action until the time comes to make the decision. Crew morale hinges on knowing the skipper is prepared for any eventuality.

If you can complete all 10 of these steps before the gale hits, your vessel and your crew will be well prepared. Waiting for weather can be worse than getting through it once it starts. A crew that is kept busy helping themselves before the gale arrives will be in a more confident and upbeat mood when the storm actually hits. That bit of extra energy is often all it takes to keep things from looking dire.

excellent temporary "patch." Smaller sails, sleeping bags, blankets, duffel bags full of clothes, and life preservers will temporarily seal smaller openings. But you will need a more permanent fix as quickly as possible, for water entering through such a large opening could overwhelm the boat if it were rolled. To find a piece of wood large enough to make a permanent repair, rip apart a bulkhead or the cabin sole. Secure the wood with underwater epoxy and screws or bolts.

Collision

Of all the situations discussed in this section, a collision at sea poses the most immediate and serious threat. After a collision that results in a major breach of the hull, you can do little more than deploy the liferaft and get safely off the boat. Many newer yachts are being fitted with collision bulkheads that break the boat up into separate watertight compartments. A few older boats are being fitted with positive flotation in the form carbon dioxide canisters and bags that inflate when in contact with water. Consider these structural systems when selecting and outfitting your yacht.

We knew of no voyaging boats that suffered hull damage from a collision while we were out voyaging. Of course, stories like Steve Callahan's *Adrift* and the Butlers' *Our Last Chance* prove that collisions do occur, though they seem to be mercifully rare.

If after the crash you are left wondering what happened, ensure that everyone is still aboard and unharmed. A violent collision can easily throw an untethered crewmember off the boat or cause serious injury to someone moving around below. Once you are sure that no one is missing or injured, go below and pull up the floorboards to determine if you are taking on water. If so, get all of the bilge pumps available pumping. Next, locate the damage to the hull. This might require a crowbar or a hacksaw. The area must be cleared so you can assess and possibly repair the damage. Water will be flowing in under pressure, so none of this will be as easy as it sounds. Once you locate and can reach the area, start stuffing into the hole anything you can get your hands on that might slow the flow of water: sails, clothes, duffels, sleeping bags, blankets, and so on. Use oars, boat hooks, battens, and any other rigid objects to hold this gear in place. If the hole is small enough that you have gotten this

far, eventually you should be able to lessen the flow.

Once things are controlled enough to consider the situation, two approaches may help—and you should probably try both. First, position a collision mat over the outside of the hull to cover the area. A large tarp with grommets in the corner or a sail can be used. Slide the mat across the hull using lines attached to the corners until the hole is covered and the pressure of the water holds the mat in place. Once you have sealed the hole from the outside, you can attempt a more complete repair from the inside. As described above for the hatch or locker lid, some combination of wood, screws, underwater epoxy, and ingenuity will create a patch that reduces the inflow of water to a level that can be dealt with by a high-capacity bilge pump.

Steering failures

Steering failures at sea are likely to be more frustrating than life threatening. Even at the height of a gale, you can run off trailing warps that will stabilize your course as long as you have sea room. You usually have the benefit of time with a steering failure, unless the loss of the rudder creates a hole in the hull. In that case, the lack of steering will not be your first concern. Assuming that the rudder is still attached to the boat, you need to stop the boat and secure the rudder to prevent it from being damaged since it will be thrown from side to side by the boat's motion and the waves.

Steering failures fall into three categories. A complete loss of the rudder will force you to jury rig a steering system of some sort. A failure in the mechanism that attaches the tiller or wheel to the rudder—a broken steering cable, for instance—can generally be bypassed using the emergency tiller or repaired with the spares carried aboard. A broken rudder stock, where the rudder is still present but no longer connected to the helm, used to be possible with a wooden rudder stock. With modern materials, you are unlikely to face this steering failure.

If the rudder and rudder stock are still intact and need only to be reconnected to the tiller or wheel, you will have to rely on your spares locker. Carry complete service manuals for your steering system, an emergency tiller, and spares for most of the major steering components: steering cables, clips, sheaves, and so on. Given time and these materials, you will find a way to repair the steering.

The other two situations cannot be readily fixed at sea and require some forethought. In the unlikely case of a broken rudder stock, try to find a way to attach lines to the rudder to create a rudimentary steering system. The lines can be led through blocks at the toe rail to the primary winches.

If the entire rudder has been lost, some boats will be able to stay on a certain point of sail if the sails are trimmed properly. Long-keeled, ketch-rigged boats have the greatest likelihood of being able to stay on course without a rudder over a variety of wind angles. A cutter with a more modern underbody, especially a fin keel, probably won't steer by sail trim using her normal sail combinations. Setting a storm sail or jib on the backstay as a riding sail in conjunction with a small headsail may provide some control over the boat's course. Sheeting the riding sail in should bring the boat closer to the wind; easing it should cause the boat to bear off.

The standard jury rig is to attach a large board to the end of a spinnaker pole, lash the spinnaker pole to the backstay in such a way that the backstay acts as a pivot, and then steer using lines led through a second pole, boat hook, or whisker pole to the cockpit from either side of the board (Figure 19-5). Compared to a real rudder, such a solution offers very limited steering control. You may be able to alter the boat's course by 20 degrees or so. When used in conjunction with sail trim, you should be able to hold a course that will get you somewhere near land and assistance.

Rigging failures

Of the emergencies discussed in this section, rigging failures actually happen with some regularity. We knew of a half-dozen boats that suffered failures of a single rigging member—a headstay, a shroud, or a bobstay—and the rest of the rig remained intact. We knew two boats that were dismasted. Both dismastings occurred in what has to be considered extreme

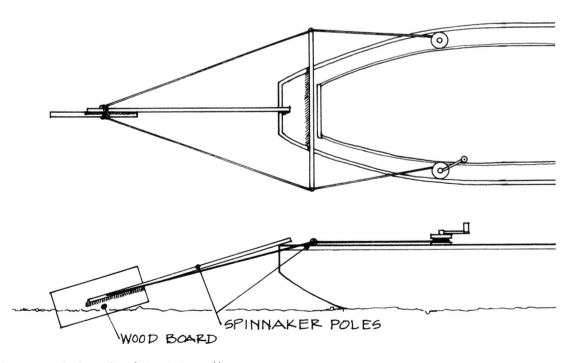

SPINNAKER POLES

WOOD BOARD

Figure 19-5. The classic solution for jury-rigging a rudder

conditions. The first was a Tayana 37 racing offshore with a spinnaker up in 25 to 30 knots apparent wind; the boat broached and the pole went into the water. The second was a Contessa 32 that got rolled sailing in the Southern Ocean in heavy weather. Our experience suggests that a complete dismasting is unlikely on a well-found offshore boat that has been adequately shaken down and that is sailed with even a modicum of prudence.

Rigging failures can be prevented by careful inspection of the rig before passage, by a thorough annual inspection by you or by a qualified rigger, and by replacing rigging after five years or so of hard offshore use. But like the other emergencies discussed in this section, when prevention isn't enough, preparation becomes essential.

Broken shroud

The half-dozen boats we knew of that suffered a broken piece of standing rigging fell into two categories.

In the first category, the cause of the failure involved a sudden shock loading and was the result of another problem aboard. In one case, this was a jammed roller furler that prevented a headsail from being reefed in a gale; the strain from the headsail caused a lower shroud to part.

In the second category, the failure was due to fatigue, either because of the age of the boat or from constant pressure on one piece of rigging over an extended period of time. Topper Hermanson's *Frog's Leap,* a steel cutter that sailed around Cape Horn, falls into this category. Topper had specified half-inch, 1 × 19 stainless lower shrouds for this trip, but he allowed himself to be talked into $7/16$-inch stainless by the riggers. He sailed from Florida to the Bay of Fundy and back, and then went through the Panama Canal and sailed around the Horn via Easter Island—almost all on port tack. The lower port shroud parted about 1 inch above the terminal end in relatively mild conditions. Subsequent investigation determined that the shroud had simply fatigued and given way.

We knew of two boats that experienced a major rigging failure when their bobstay broke. As a piece of rigging, the bobstay is often overlooked. But if it breaks when the boat is under sail with a large genoa up, the genoa can pull the bowsprit right out of the deck. Un-

less another headstay is supporting the mast, the entire rig can be lost. Bobstays are often shock loaded. They are frequently run into docks or subjected to strains from anchor rodes. They need to be inspected and replaced just as often as the rest of the rigging.

When a piece of standing rigging breaks, the strain must be taken off the affected portion of the rig to minimize the chances of additional failure. For a broken shroud that means tacking or jibing quickly while keeping the forces to a minimum. For a broken headstay that means running downwind. As soon as the strain is off the damaged rigging, you need to reduce sail and/or use a halyard to supplement the rigging. With a broken headstay, a spare spinnaker halyard shackled to the stemhead and cranked in tight can temporarily stabilize the rig.

Once the strain is off the rig, the sail has been reduced, and the boat has been slowed or stopped, lash the broken rigging or clear it out of the way. A piece of rigging wire swinging across the deck is bound to injure someone or damage something. Then get out the spare stay and fittings and jury rig a replacement for the broken rigging. At some point you will need to go up the mast to clear the fittings from the old stay and install the new one. Stabilize the mast with spare halyards before you trust yourself to it.

Total dismasting

The greatest danger from a dismasting comes not from losing the mast itself but from the possibility of a serious breach of the hull. The remains of an aluminum mast pounding against the side of a vessel in heavy waves can puncture the hull. A mast lost in a rollover may take a section of the deck with it. The priority, therefore, has to be to protect the boat from the mast, even if that means cutting the mast away completely. Until the mast and other wreckage are cleared, do not start the engine. You will almost certainly foul the prop and complicate the situation.

After a dismasting, make sure everyone is accounted for and unhurt. Before you even start evaluating the wreckage, turn off all power to the masthead. Next, size up the situation. If the wreckage is battering the hull, the sea is running, and there is little chance of calm weather in the next few hours, cut the wreckage free and let it go. Don't start thinking about a jury rig when the possibility exists of serious damage to the hull. Use fenders, life preservers, or other padding to minimize the pounding the hull takes while you get rid of the mast.

People who have been on dismasted boats say the quickness of motion makes everything more difficult. Without a mast, the boat will be a very unstable platform to work on, and much of what the crew tends to rely on for handholds will be missing or under wreckage. Before starting to work on the mast, you may want to don safety harnesses and tethers and set up alternate jackstays so you can move about easily.

If the mast has buckled and broken, there will be a lower section still standing and an upper section hanging by shrouds, mast track, cables, running rigging, and some twisted pieces of metal from the mast itself. Leave any shrouds still attached to the lower section in place to stabilize it. You will have to remove the standing rigging holding the upper section. Wherever possible, remove the clevis pins from the turnbuckles near the deck to free stays and shrouds. Where that is not possible, you will need heavy leather gloves, hydraulic cable cutters (if available), and a hacksaw. You will also want

heavy-duty pliers to remove cotter pins and heavy wire cutters or pliers to work smaller pieces of metal back and forth until they fatigue and break. The two people we know who went through this both said that removing the mast was exhausting.

Once the standing rigging, mast track, and pieces of the mast have been removed, you can use the running rigging to lower the mast section to the water. Try to salvage as much of the mainsail as possible. But if this becomes dangerous, the mainsail should also be cut free. Cut all the running rigging, except one halyard and the topping lift. The mast section should now be parallel to the boat and held fore and aft. Cut the PVC tubing and wiring, then cut the halyard and topping lift at the same time. The mast section should quickly sink out of sight. If the entire mast has come down or has been sheared off at deck level, the process is the same—except that you will need to unpin or cut all the standing rigging. The boom and spinnaker pole should be kept aboard for an eventual jury rig.

Once the wreckage is cleared, you are faced with "what next?" Even if motoring to port is a possibility, a

Piracy

We get asked about piracy so frequently that I have to say a few words about it. Piracy is defined as robbery at sea and as such is distinct from thievery near shore, which was discussed in Chapter 15. A few isolated incidents in recent years involved attempted theft near shore that turned violent—one incident in Barbuda in the Caribbean and one in the Las Perlas Islands in Panama. Both of these situations were labeled piracy, but they were instances of thievery. In both cases, unusual circumstances ended in bloodshed. Some of the precautions discussed in Chapter 15 may have prevented these situations from arising.

Most people fear piracy because of the isolation at sea. But we know no one aboard a small sailing boat who has ever been involved in piracy. We have, however, heard of a few instances where cruisers felt threatened by another boat at sea, and the cruisers made a show of force to drive the other boats off. We cannot know if those situations were really attempts

at piracy or were more like the situation in Indonesia described by circumnavigator Scott Kuhner in Chapter 8 (see "The most personal of decisions: firearms aboard").

When we were in Australia, there were several well-documented cases of piracy in the South China Sea. These were directed at freighters, and the perpetrators were equipped with high-speed Zodiacs with AK-47's mounted on the bow. They were after the cargo aboard the freighters, and it seems unlikely they would have the slightest interest in a yacht.

I am not saying that piracy never occurs, only that in the time we were out we never heard of a confirmed report directed at a yacht. Any actual incidents are likely to be widely reported in the press, through the cruising grapevine, and in the SSCA bulletins. If you pay attention to those sources, you should know what areas pose a potential risk. If you decide to travel there, do so only in company with other yachts.

jury rig will steady the motion of the boat and speed your approach to shore. If you have a portion of the mast left, then you have a firm foundation for a jury rig. If you don't, you will be left trying to create something from the boom, spinnaker poles, and boat hooks. Jury rigs come in all shapes and sizes depending on what is available for their construction. Once the mast is over the side and the boat is no longer in danger, you will have time to consider your options. With ingenuity, lots of line, spare rigging wire, a boom, and a spinnaker pole, you will find a solution.

PART V

FOREIGN SAVVY

CHAPTER 20 | DEALING WITH BUREAUCRACY

Unwinding the red tape ■ *Pretrip preparations* ■ *Patience and politeness* ■ **Managing bureaucratic hassles**
■ *Unavoidable hassles* ■ *Avoidable hassles* ■ **Burgeoning bureaucracy**

When you arrive in a country by plane, at any time of day or night, you usually whisk through customs and immigration in a scant half-hour. Ninety minutes after entering the country, you can be frolicking on the beach or sipping a tropical drink by the pool. When you arrive by boat, you will spend an average of half a day filling out forms meant for freighters and answering questions about how many stowaways you discovered enroute. You may be subject to a search, and you will almost certainly have some of your stores confiscated or bonded. If you arrive on a weekend or after hours, you will have to pay overtime fees to be cleared in or you will have to anchor off without going ashore until the officials are on duty. You may have to wait as long as a few days for your frolic on the beach.

While we had read enough to expect more red tape than plane passengers face, we hadn't expected to spend quite so much time dealing with bureaucracy— on the order of several days every month. On the other hand, we were pleasantly surprised by the professionalism and courtesy of the officials.

Bureaucracy is simply one facet of the voyaging life. Though the process is rarely efficient, it is inevitable and unavoidable. To successfully unwind the red tape, there are several things you can do: Have your key documents in order before you leave your home port; research and comply with any additional requirements, such as visas or cruising permits, as you travel; understand how to avoid bureaucratic hassles or learn how to manage them as efficiently as possible; finally, arm yourself with patience and politeness. Throughout everything, maintain your sense of humor. After all, you are in paradise.

UNWINDING THE RED TAPE

During the course of our three-year circumnavigation, we cleared in and out of 35 countries. Throughout the world, we found that there were two simple keys to clearing bureaucratic hurdles: careful preparation before leaving home waters, and patience and politeness throughout the paper-pushing process.

Pretrip preparations

Before leaving the United States, we carefully researched the subject of ship's documents. We were soon confounded by all the forms we thought we needed for different places. In fact, the many countries we visited wanted only a few simple documents. Ship's papers and passports were *always* required. In most countries, these were the *only* documents required. You may also choose to carry a number of other documents that can sometimes make life easier. Before leaving home, acquire any documents covered here that you think might be useful.

Ship's papers

The boat's documentation, registration, or ship's papers legally establish your ownership. The original document must be aboard whenever the vessel is in operation— photocopies are not acceptable. Without these papers, you may well end up in a Brazilian jail counting flies. Americans have two options for ship's papers—a state registration certificate or U.S. Coast Guard certificate of documentation (Figure 20-1). The federally issued Coast Guard papers cost a bit more to obtain, but they are more respected and accepted internationally. In 1996, there were a few incidents in the Caribbean where U.S. vessels with legal state registrations were fined hundreds of dollars for being "undocumented." Although such fines are almost certainly illegal, you can avoid the hassle altogether with federal documentation. Whether you are state registered or federally documented, you must renew your registration annually. You can renew through the mail; be sure to make the necessary arrangements before you leave.

Be very wary about turning your ship's papers over to anyone. In our only serious incidence of bribery, the harbormaster in the Galapagos took our ship's papers and refused to return them until we paid him a certain amount of money. After that incident, we carried a double-sided, color photocopy on card stock of our ship's papers that we handed to officials; we secreted the original aboard the boat in case anyone insisted upon it. In almost all cases, the duplicate was accepted without comment.

If the vessel is registered in only one name and the owner is incapacitated or dies, the boat's legal status may be tied up pending execution of a will. In such a situation, a distraught crew will be in no condition to deal with the mountain of bureaucracy in a foreign country. Ship's papers should designate a co-owner who has legal authority in the event of the death or absence of the owner. If you would prefer not to register the boat in more than one name, carry a legal document designating another crewmember as the captain. The document we carried is shown in Figure 20-2.

If you are acting as delivery skipper of a boat you don't own, you will need documents to satisfy port authorities that you have not stolen the vessel. A letter written by the owner that states who the skipper is and the approximate route and duration of the voyage usually suffices. The letter is accompanied by the original ship's papers. While generally acceptable, the owner should be prepared to receive a phone call if you run into problems.

Passports

Don't leave home without them! If traveling with children, get individual passports rather than a family passport. These will allow you to travel separately. For example, some family members may have to fly home for medical treatment while the others stay with the boat.

Before you leave, make sure the passport is valid for the period you plan to be out of the country. You can get new passports issued at U.S. embassies (often the same day) in major countries. But the consulate on most small island nations will take many weeks to replace a passport. As with your ship's papers, keep a good quality copy on board, which will be useful when replacing a lost or stolen passport. Assuming the officials are sympathetic, the copy might let you enter a country with a U.S. consulate or embassy.

Make sure you have enough pages for all the stamps and visas you will acquire (Figure 20-3). An inverse relationship seems to exist between the size of the na-

Illustration courtesy of Scott and Kitty Kuhner

Figure 20-1. U.S. Coast Guard documentation is accepted worldwide and is the standard type of registration for offshore voyagers.

POWER OF ATTORNEY

To whom it may concern:

I, Evans Starzinger, owner of the vessel SILK, USA registration number NO928512 (Hull Identification number NHN37109G787), do request that in the event of my absence, death or incapacitation due to illness, my first mate, Beth Ann Leonard be afforded all rights as captain of said vessel. She shall have the right to operate and sail said vessel, make arrangements for its trans-shipment, storage or hire another competent captain if necessary. Her name shall in this event serve as a replacement for mine on any legal documents pertaining to this vessel and its operation.

Signed this _____2ND_____ day of __March__ 1992.

Evans Starzinger

Witnessed by:

Marie Johansson
Marie Johansson

Figure 20-2. A Power of Attorney like the one shown here will ensure that your boat can be cleared in at a safe harbor if the owner is incapacitated.

tion and the size of their stamp, and on the normal milk run, or even in the Caribbean, you will be visiting many small nations. Allow one page per country you plan to visit. A consulate or embassy can insert new pages in an existing passport. If you are having a new passport issued, you can request the "businessman's special," which is extra-thick. Passports, especially U.S. passports, are a valuable and desirable commodity everywhere in the world. If your passport is up to date and has adequate pages before you depart, you'll minimize the amount of time it is on your person or in a stranger's hands in a foreign country.

Other documents

With ship's papers and your passports, you can go almost anywhere in the world today. Unfortunately, the footloose and fancy-free days may be near their end. Some countries now require proof of financial resources to be sure they don't end up with destitute yachties. The European Economic Community continues to discuss li-

Figure 20-3. A voyager's passport needs enough pages for many stamps and visas.

censing requirements for offshore sailors. For the time being, the following documents are rarely required. However, we found them helpful as levers for moving the bureaucratic mountain.

■ *International Certificate of Vaccination.* We were never asked to show our International Certificates of Vaccination from the World Health Organization, even after visiting parts of Africa (see "Know thyself" in Chapter 13). However, the card and the vaccines that go with it are cheap insurance (Figure 20-4).

■ *Insurance certificate.* We were asked to show proof of insurance for our boat in many countries to ob-

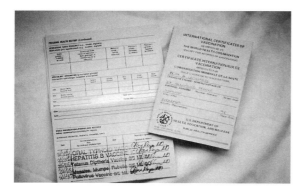

Figure 20-4. The International Certificate of Vaccination documents all the vaccinations you have received. Keep it with your passport.

Figure 20-5. Our ship's stamp was basic, but it seemed to impress recalcitrant customs and immigration officials.

tain a visa for three to six months. Those without insurance were required to show proof of additional financial resources.

■ *Radio license.* Even if the boat carries only a VHF, you will be asked for your call sign. The radio license proves that the call sign has been legally assigned to you.

■ *Ship's stamp.* We got our stamp on a lark when we were leaving, never dreaming how helpful it would be. Officials the world over were thrilled when Evans stamped and signed their half-dozen pieces of paper. The stamp seemed to make everything legal, from receipts for bonded goods to visa applications. For a couple of dollars, our stamp proved to be a finely honed blade for slashing through red tape (Figure 20-5).

■ *Crew lists.* Printed crew lists including the name, position, birth dates, nationalities, and passport information (passport number, issue date, expiration date, and place of issue) for each person on the vessel are sometimes useful. You won't need them very often (bureaucrats generally like their own forms), but about a quarter of the time they would accept ours. They were particularly impressed if we decorated it with our ship's stamp beforehand and signed it with a flourish when they came on board.

You'll need passport photos when applying for visas, so you may want to bring along a dozen or so for each crew member. We were rarely asked to show prescriptions for the drugs in our medical kit, though we had them aboard just in case. We never needed a De-ratification Certificate. Of course, we've been fortunate enough never to have seen a rat within a hundred paces of the boat. Luckily, no one requires a De-roachification Certificate . . .

Finally, prepare a will before you go. Leave it in the hands of a lawyer or a family member. The chances of its being needed are slight. But if the situation arises, things will be difficult enough in a foreign country without adding the complexity of dying intestate. Be responsible and be prepared—even for the least palatable of contingencies.

Patience and politeness

You can obtain the paperwork described in the last section before you set off, and it is good for the duration of your voyage, assuming that you faithfully renew your ship's papers. But there will be plenty of further bureaucracy that you cannot deal with until you are approaching or have arrived at the country itself.

For those countries that require visas before you arrive, your introduction to their bureaucracy will begin before you set foot on their shores. After that, you will have to clear in on arrival and clear out on leaving. Throughout our voyage, we spent a minimum of a half-day clearing in and a half-day clearing out in most countries, plus a day or more arranging visas where those were required. Most of that was "hurry up and wait" time. We learned to accept the inevitable and be patient about the delays, then to be polite when our turn came to deal with the officials. This was the most efficient way to put the paper behind us.

Visas

You will need a visa to enter many countries. Venezuela, Brazil, French Polynesia, New Zealand, and Australia, for example, all require visas for U.S. citizens. Some of these countries will issue a temporary visa upon arrival. However, it often pays to plan ahead and get a three- to six-month visa from a consulate or embassy of the country prior to landfall, especially where language might be an issue. Cornell's *World Cruising Handbook* (2nd edition, International Marine, 1996) specifies visa requirements by country and indicates which embassies and consulates can be found along your route. Cruising scuttlebutt also provides insights on where to apply for specific visas. When we crossed the Pacific, many cruisers were experiencing delays and difficulties getting visas for New Zealand from the consulate in Nuku'alofa, Tonga. We waited until Fiji and had our visas hassle free in 48 hours.

When you apply for the visa at a consulate, you will be required to provide passport photos and passports, show your ship's papers, and—for many countries—show proof of financial resources sufficient to maintain you while you are in the country. That usually means copies of bank statements proving that you have a specified sum of money per person per month for the duration of your visit. In some cases, a credit card with a high credit limit ($5,000 to $10,000) meets the requirement.

You may also be required to show proof of boat insurance. A few countries worry about having to repatriate indigent, shipwrecked sailors. Proof of additional financial resources may be accepted in lieu of insurance. French Polynesia is more obvious about their intent. They require that yachts post a bond for each person aboard equal in amount to the return airfare from Tahiti to their home country. The bond is reimbursed only when the yacht is clearing out of French waters. While many voyagers objected to this, very few found a way around it. French Polynesia wants to limit the number of freeloaders trying to make their permanent home in paradise—a problem they have had to deal with since the days of Christian Fletcher and the *Bounty*.

Obtain your visa as close to when you set sail for the country as possible. This way, you can be sure that it will still be valid when you arrive. That means getting the visa in the country you visit before setting sail for the visa-requiring country. For example, you can get visas for New Zealand in Tonga or Fiji and for Venezuela in Grenada. Request the longest time possible before expiration to give you the greatest flexibility. Specify a multiple-entry visa so that you can fly home and return without having a new visa issued. In a country like Australia, a multiple-entry visa is required to visit some of the offshore islands. While we were on Christmas Island, a French singlehander arrived from Darwin with a single-entry visa for Australia. The authorities allowed him to take on water and then insisted he leave, even though his visa had not expired.

Certificate of clearance

The visa, if required, is not the only piece of paperwork that you need before you set sail for your next destination. Before you can clear in to a new nation, you must have cleared out from somewhere else. No universal rules exist for clearing out. The brass ring is a certificate of clearance, which will be required for you to clear in anyplace else (Figure 20-6). You'll go as many times around the merry-go-round as necessary to get that one piece of paper. In St. Helena, a tiny dot in the South Atlantic, that meant one five-minute visit to customs. In Durban, that meant multiple visits to immigration, customs, the port authority, the yacht club, and the police. All that just to clear out to another South African port! They know you need the certificate of clearance, and in some places they make you work awfully hard to get it.

Figure 20-6. Our clearance certificate from Cape Town, South Africa—complete with wax seal and official signature.

Paradoxically, one of the most difficult countries to clear out of is the United States. If you call and ask the Coast Guard, you will be told that you do not need clearance to leave. While that is correct, you do need to clear out before you can clear in somewhere else. While Bermuda has learned to live without clearance forms from Americans, most countries will not allow you to clear in without a proper customs clearance from your departure port. When leaving U.S. waters, obtain Customs Form 1378, "Clearance of Vessel to a Foreign Port."

Clearing in

The stereotype of the petty bureaucrat with beady eyes and sweaty palms whose only concern is the size of the bribe turns out to be almost baseless. Out of the hundreds of officials we dealt with, only three acted in any way dishonestly. Most officials pride themselves on their thoroughness, friendliness, and professionalism. Outside of the Caribbean, the customs and immigration officers generally deal with big ships, not with yachts, and their paperwork is designed for freighters. They are as frustrated as you at having to fill out a dozen forms on cargo, bonded stores, and crew lost at sea. To make the process efficient and trouble free, be prepared, patient, and polite. They will appreciate your businesslike approach.

That approach starts with your appearance. Whenever dealing with officials, dress respectfully. If coming in from a passage, take the time for a shower, a shave, and a trim. If they are coming aboard, make the boat as pre-sentable as possible. Be ready to offer a hot or cold drink. Have all your papers handy and in order. Make sure there is somewhere for two or three people to sit and a table for one person to write on. Landfall preparations stand you in good stead. By the time you are tied up to the customs wharf or anchored in the quarantine area, the boat is ready to receive official guests.

Unlike clearing out, clearing in generally involves the same officials at every port. Outside the Caribbean, they will usually come to you. In most countries you will be asked to tie up to a customs dock—often a monstrous concrete affair festooned with stanchion-eating tractor tires and nasty re-bar poking out at odd angles. Once you are over the trauma of tying up to a dock like that, the tension only builds—as the tide comes in (or goes out), as the fishing fleet returns and ties up on either side of you, as a big ship maneuvers around you while you sit and wait for the last customs official. This is where patience is most essential.

Each official who comes calling is looking for something in particular. The sooner you provide it, the faster they will be on their way.

■ **Quarantine officer.** A local physician who acts as quarantine officer should arrive first. This person establishes whether or not your vessel is free of contagion that could infect the local population. If all is well aboard, then the doctor will issue a *practique,* or clean bill of health. Once you have been granted practique, then you can lower your quarantine flag and await the rest of the officials.

■ **Customs officer.** Customs is concerned about contraband. This officer will want to be certain that you have no drugs, guns, controlled substances, merchandise for resale, or items subject to duty aboard. Any items found aboard in any of these categories may be bonded or confiscated until you clear out. You may also be requested to submit a list of all electronics aboard including make, model, and serial numbers. We had to do this in two or three ports, supposedly to help in recovering the merchandise in the event it was stolen. We suspected that they also wanted to make sure we were not smuggling in electronics for sale on the black market.

■ **Immigration officer.** Immigration looks for illegal aliens. The immigration officer will want to see all passports, issue temporary visas if you did not get one ahead of time, and review any visa that you did get before arriving. Immigration will also be the most concerned about your movements within the country. This official will inform you if you need a cruising permit to leave the port of entry and explain how to obtain one.

■ *Agriculture officer.* This official will confiscate your unused produce and other things that are deemed to pose a hazard to local flora and fauna. This may include such diverse items as garbage, spear guns, shells, and even the dirt from hiking boots and tent stakes. In some countries, agriculture officers are on the lookout for contraband from endangered species such as sea turtle shells and ivory.

On small islands, one person will wear all of these hats. In the largest ports, a group of three or four people will crowd aboard for each of these functions. You will have to complete from one to a half-dozen forms and answer a number of questions for each official. While you are talking to them, ask whether or not you need to see them to clear out and find out exactly where their offices are located. This will save time when you're preparing to leave. When you think you've reached the last official, ask whether you need to see anyone else. Occasionally you'll be surprised to find that you are supposed to check in with the harbormaster, the Coast Guard, or the local police before you are legal. Failure to do so bruises delicate egos and makes your life uncomfortable farther down the line.

Before you are officially cleared in, only the skipper is allowed to leave the vessel. If you have arrived on a weekend or late on an afternoon weekday, you may be charged overtime fees to clear in right away or you may not be allowed to clear in until business hours. If you have to wait until Monday, you are technically not allowed to leave the boat, and in most countries you should not do so. On the other hand, when making landfall on small islands, you will probably have to go ashore to find the officials. If you haven't made radio contact and they do not show up after an hour or so, head ashore with your papers and ask.

Once you are cleared in, you will be instructed where you can anchor or berth. At long last, you can raise the courtesy flag to the starboard spreader and consider yourself official. But you may not be quite finished with the bureaucracy. In a few countries like Fiji, Australia, and Panama, yachts are required to obtain a cruising permit. To do this, you must visit the relevant officials ashore before leaving the port of entry. The immigration officials will tell you the exact procedure when you clear in. You'll need your ship's papers and a detailed itinerary. As you approach these countries, decide which islands you wish to visit and when.

Unless you have to deal with any of the bureaucratic hassles discussed in the next section, in most countries you are finished with bureaucracy until you clear out. In a few places, however, you are required to clear in and out of every port you visit. In the Azores in the North Atlantic, you have to clear in and out with three officials every time you drop your anchor. Throughout French Polynesia, you are required to clear in and out of each island. In South Africa, you must clear in and out of every port. In Australia, your cruising permit means you don't have to check in and out, but you will be contacted daily by a low flying plane as you make your way up the Barrier Reef and out through the Torres Strait. In parts of Fiji, you are required to check in with the headman of every village who will examine your cruising permit before inviting you to stay in the anchorage.

Don't try to avoid these additional procedures by keeping a low profile. Though it may be hard to believe living in the United States or Europe, yachts are few and far between in most of these areas. News of a yacht off the beaten path travels quickly. When you are the only yacht in the anchorage, the officials are waiting for you to come ashore and talk to them if they don't come out to meet you. Customs and immigration officers will tell you the exact procedures when you clear in. Follow them carefully and avoid even bigger hassles.

MANAGING BUREAUCRATIC HASSLES

Most of your interactions with officials will be limited to checking in and checking out, and you will find the people you deal with professional and courteous. But sometimes you will have to deal with officials for other things. In some cases you cannot avoid these interactions; for example, you may need to clear packages through customs. Other complications can arise from the choices you make, as in the choice to carry firearms aboard. In both situations, manage the resulting bureaucratic hassles and delays the same way as before: Be prepared, and then be patient and polite.

Unavoidable hassles

Bureaucratic interactions outside the normal clearance procedures tend to be less well structured and are more likely to bring you into contact with dishonest officials. You may encounter frustrating bureaucracy if you need to have something shipped to you, if you choose to keep your boat in the country for more than six months or so, or if you choose to leave your boat and explore the interior. In all cases, navigating the bureaucracy hinges on understanding how the system is supposed to work. Other voyagers are your greatest allies in figuring out how to minimize the hassles involved.

Getting yacht spares

Whenever I hear someone new to voyaging say, "If it breaks we'll just have a new one shipped in overnight," I have to stifle a chuckle. We have all been inundated with advertising saying "anywhere in the world in a day" so we naturally believe it. Yet in the real world, it simply doesn't work like that for anything except documents. Large, bulky packages that go "clink" when you tap on them take longer—often much longer. The overnight guarantees are based on the assumption that the package can make it through customs without assistance. Most of the things that voyagers ship can't and don't.

Our first attempt at shipping yacht supplies internationally illustrates our experiences in most countries. We were in Madeira, a Portuguese island, after crossing the North Atlantic. We wanted to put everything right that we had done wrong in outfitting the boat before leaving the United States. We ordered a wind vane, a solar panel, an autopilot, and a cockpit instrument repeater. All boxes were shipped from the United States by various methods, and all were prominently labeled, "Spare parts for yacht in transit."

The cockpit instrument repeater was shipped via UPS. We were told it would arrive in three to four days. Ten days later, we were informed that it was being held hostage in Lisbon and we would have to hire an agent and pay 50 percent VAT (value-added tax) plus an importation fee and duty. We sent off copies of our ship's documents, copies of our documents from clearing in to Madeira, notarized records of our voyage to date, and letters assuring them we would leave Madeira as soon as they released the box. When that failed, we hired an agent who told us he could get the box through customs without paying the taxes and duties. After another week, we gave up and paid the ransom. It had been 22 days since the package had been shipped, and the duties and taxes on the cockpit repeater almost equaled the purchase price.

The wind vane and solar panel were shipped by different air freight companies, both of whom promised 3-day deliveries. Both companies "lost" the packages. We traced the wind vane from airline to airline, and it was finally located in a store room in Kennedy Airport in New York City a week after it had been shipped. It arrived on Madeira 2 days later, and we spent an entire day at the airport filling out forms and running from office to office to clear it through customs. In this case, the "yacht in transit" was respected, and a customs officer accompanied us to the boat where he watched us put it aboard and would not leave until we used our trusty ship's stamp to make his documents official. After a total of 13 days, we had our wind vane and we hadn't had to pay any additional duty, bribes, or taxes.

The solar panel was located in Lisbon a week after it was shipped; the Portuguese airline had failed to pass it on to the puddle jumper to Madeira. Once it arrived, we again spent a day at the airport and ended up with a different customs officer. When we got to the point where we thought we would be heading off in a taxi back to the boat with this official, he told us that it was really his discretion whether or not to make us pay duty. "Some days I feel like making people pay one hundred percent duty, and some days I let it come in for nothing," he explained in broken English. We were helpless and he knew it. We bartered and agreed that we would pay 25 percent of the value of the solar panel, for which he did not want to give us a receipt. You are supposed to insist, but to what end when there is no obvious higher authority and you do not speak the language? After 12 days, we had our solar panel at a 25-percent premium.

When we ordered the autopilot, the company insisted that they shipped abroad regularly and that the best way was first class mail. We argued with them, but they convinced us to try it and told us to start looking for it in 7 to 10 days. The autopilot arrived 13 days later, and we cleared it through customs in the main post office downtown without having to go to the airport. The "yacht in transit" was respected, and no one even suggested we pay taxes or fees.

On successive occasions we tried most of the major overnight couriers and air express companies. The lessons that we learned on Madeira turned out to be broadly applicable. A friend or relative who is joining you for a time on the boat makes for the safest and most efficient delivery. Whenever possible, we waited for those opportunities rather than shipping parts by normal methods. When that won't work, the following steps will increase the likelihood of a trouble-free delivery. Be surprised and pleased when it happens, but don't expect it!

■ *Ask others what works.* When you find someone who has already shipped parts into the country, ask them what service they used, what the procedure was, and whether or not they had any problem with the authorities. In Madeira, we were new to voyaging and shy of asking strangers questions. After the fact, we learned that others had already been down the same path. Their advice could have saved us weeks of worry and hundreds of dollars.

■ *Have the shipper put an invoice on the outside of the package and label it "Spare parts for yacht in transit."* If "yacht in transit" is not visibly displayed on the outside of the box, you can forget getting it into the country without paying taxes and duties. If it is there, you have a fighting chance. The invoice also needs to be packed on the outside of the box so that the customs officer can determine the legal value of the package.

■ *Use U.S. Postal Service air mail outside of U.S. territories (Guam, American Samoa, U.S. Virgin Islands) and a few other parts of the Caribbean.* Within the United States or in U.S. territories, your shipping options include the full range of services you would expect, and they all work reasonably well. Outside these areas, the post office proved most reliable for packages they would accept. Customs clearance creates less hassles at the post office, perhaps because they assume the package is for personal use and not for resale. The post office won't accept a package large enough for a sail or a solar panel.

■ *If using air freight, obtain all shipping information from the shipper and track the package.* For many larger packages, air freight will be the only option. We found that we had to keep track of the process or the package got sidetracked somewhere, even when shipping to New Zealand. Ask the shipper for the manifest number and all flight numbers and dates. If the package does not arrive on the day it should, immediately start chasing it down. The longer it sits in an airport somewhere, the more likely it is to be stolen along the way.

■ *If you have to use a shipping agent, use the cruising network to find a reliable one.* You will often be told you need to hire a shipping agent for $100 and up. Before doing so, ask other voyagers who have shipped things into the country whether you really need one or not. In many cases, you can clear things yourself if you are willing to go to the airport and take the package through its rounds. In a few countries, an agent is the only way to clear a package; if you try to do it yourself, you will be stymied at every turn. Ask around to find a reputable agent. Agent's fees are easy to inflate and hard to debate. Information is your only ally.

In an ideal world, your boat would function perfectly and you would never need to ship anything. But in the real world, things break aboard and parts must be obtained. Remember that a simple boat will create fewer hassles. And when you do have to ship something to a foreign country, don't assume it will be trouble free.

VAT and import duties

Many countries require you to pay import duty or value-added tax (VAT) on your boat after you have been there for a certain period of time. In most cases you are considered a visitor and not subject to the tax for a period of six months to a year. After that time you are considered to be residing in the country, and your boat must be officially imported under the local laws. In practice, that means a payment of from 15 to 50 percent of the value of the boat—an amount few voyagers are willing to pay or able to afford. To avoid the tax, leave the country for a specified period of time (usually a month or more), and then return for another tax-free period. In most countries, the tax-free period coincides with the time your visa is valid, so everything normally works well.

The countries that make up the European Economic Community (EEC) are not in complete agreement on these regulations. They haven't yet decided how to treat foreign boats that stay in the Community for a period of years but spend less than six months in any one country. Some boats have been fined, particularly in France—the country that seems most zealous about enforcing the letter of the law. As of mid-1997, the official position allows boats to leave EEC territorial waters for 24 hours once a year to avoid VAT and import tax. Stowing the boat on the hard while the owners return to the States also qualifies it for another 12 tax-free months. Before traveling to the EEC, review the regulations and track the experiences of others in the SSCA *Commodore's Bulletin* (see "Additional resources," Chapter 1).

In many countries that have VAT, the tax is intended only for goods that are going to be used within the country. In those countries, you don't have to pay the tax on equipment that becomes a permanent part of your vessel. Bureaucratically, this can be handled in one of two ways.

In some countries or for some types of purchases, you must pay the VAT and keep records of how much you pay. When you check out, customs will inspect the boat to be sure that everything on the list is leaving the country with you. You will be refunded the money on the spot or in the form of a check issued a few weeks later. Most of the major equipment that we purchased in New Zealand was handled this way.

Alternatively, you may be able to avoid paying the tax in the first place and get the equipment at a healthy discount off local prices. In that case, someone must keep the records for you and report to the government. They will need copies of your ship's papers and passports. In South Africa, the chandleries that would handle this paperwork got the bulk of the foreign yachts' business. In New Zealand, the work we had done in a boatyard was handled this way.

In most countries VAT is included in the quoted purchase price, so it helps to know how much it is and on what types of products it is charged. The tax is often on the order of 20 percent of the value of the equipment or materials, so it pays to find out if tax relief is available. In some cases, we could even get VAT refunded on grocery purchases made as we were leaving the country.

Leaving the boat

Having traveled so far, you will want to see the country you have sailed to. In a few countries, you will need to jump through a few more bureaucratic hoops before you can do so legally—even if you have been properly cleared into the country aboard your boat. The only place we ran into a problem was South Africa. Once cleared in, we were treated like ship's crew and were not technically free to leave the port of entry. Many of our friends went sightseeing into the interior without a problem. But our plans included a visit to Swaziland, which is an autonomous country within South Africa. To cross this border—and to cross back again—we needed a tourist visa to allow us to leave the boat. This took several visits to immigration to arrange.

If you have obtained a visa before entering the country or upon arrival, then you can safely assume that you are free to do as much sightseeing as you like. But if you do not actually have a tourist visa in your passport, check with the immigration authorities when you enter the country. You could save yourself a lot of hassle: It is better to find out you haven't officially entered *before* you try to leave.

Avoidable hassles

Some of the decisions you make will determine whether you run into additional bureaucratic headaches or not. This section points out problem areas so you can make an informed decision. In some cases—as in the case of carrying pets aboard—your choice may cause you to change your itinerary. Most situations involve issues of personal comfort or convenience. In either case, every crewmember should agree to the decision after understanding the resulting hassles and the risks of not complying with all bureaucratic requirements.

Bribery

For the most part, bribery can be avoided. Problem areas are well known throughout the cruising community and often discussed in the SSCA bulletins.

Bribery is far less common than we had expected. We knew very few people who had experienced bribery firsthand when clearing in or out. We even knew of several who never paid a single bribe in Indonesia (which has a reputation for requiring bribes to accomplish just about anything) and never felt they had been asked for one when they were there. Our one experience in the Galapagos stands out because the situation was so unusual.

Of the hundreds of officials we dealt with in the more than 30 countries we visited, only one person even hinted at a bribe when we were clearing in or out. On Rodrigues Island in the southern Indian Ocean, we had been cleared by two officials when the last officer came aboard. We filled out the normal forms and went through the usual chitchat. Then he said, "So, do you have something for me?" while he rubbed his thumb and fingers together. I said, "Of course," and went and rummaged around in a drawer. I handed him a photograph of Silk, a little memento we carried for friends we met along the way. He looked at it as if it would bite before taking it. After a strangled, "Thank you," he left the boat. Other friends had similar experiences. When asked for a bribe, don't become incensed or assume that you have to play along. In some cases, the officials see no reason not to give it a try. They are easily discouraged by someone who doesn't appear to understand—especially if the confusion is accompanied by an excess of good cheer.

Firearms

The issues around carrying firearms were discussed in Chapter 8 (see "The most personal of decisions: firearms aboard"). If you choose to carry firearms (and in many countries that includes spear guns and flare guns), you will need to declare them in every port. The authorities may be less forgiving and less friendly once they know you have guns aboard. Some cruisers don't declare their arms, knowingly breaking the laws of the country they are visiting. If the weapons are discovered, their boat could be impounded. Officials found undeclared arms on two boats we knew. In one case, the couple got off with a night in jail, a fine, and a warning. In another, the skipper worked for six months to pay off the fine and free his boat from impoundment.

If you have a lockable stowage area, customs may be willing to seal the locker and leave the weapons aboard. In most countries, however, any weapons will be held by customs until you clear out. Before you can leave, you will have to return to your port of entry to get your guns. In many places, this will entail an uncomfortable windward sail. When considering having guns aboard, factor in the bureaucratic hassles involved.

Pets

We knew several people who traveled with pets aboard, and we often thought about getting a ship's cat. Some of our friends were forced to change their voyaging plans because of their furry friends. Having left without an animal aboard, we decided not to complicate our lives. If you want to bring a pet along, be prepared for the harsh bureaucratic realities that will result.

New Zealand and Australia require lengthy quarantine periods (usually several months) before the animal can be brought ashore. In those countries, you will be required to keep the animal aboard and to pay for regular inspections by a quarantine officer to prove that it has not gotten ashore. If you go alongside for fuel, you will have to keep the pet locked below. If the animal gets sick, you will have to pay the quarantine officer to accompany you to the veterinarian. If you violate any of the regulations, the animal may be put down.

Rather than submit to these harsh regulations, some of our friends chose to skip both New Zealand and Australia and head north of the equator to Guam, the Philippines, and then on to Thailand. Others purchased animals and had few problems the rest of the way around the world. Either way, you will need a Certificate of Rabies Vaccination that is no more than six months old, and you may need a Veterinary Health Certificate issued within 10 days of the date when you cleared out of your last port. Check with the local embassy or consulate with respect to the exact rules, regulations, and requirements for each country along your proposed route.

Changing crewmembers

As skipper, you are personally responsible for your crewmembers—whether they are your relatives or not. If you arrive in a country with a crewmember aboard, you are physically and financially responsible for making sure the crewmember leaves once again—on your boat or otherwise. This is one of the biggest reasons why family and couple crews are so common and why so few boats take on additional crew.

If you are taking on a crewmember, make absolutely certain the person's passport is valid. If a visa is required, agree with the crewmember beforehand how financial requirements will be handled. Decide if you are going to pay for the cost of obtaining the visa or, in French Polynesia, to post the bond. You also need to have a clear agreement regarding the duration of stay and the financial arrangements. Do you pay the crewmember or does the crewmember contribute to your costs?

When the person leaves the boat, you will need to be officially released from your responsibility. If you try to check out without all the crewmembers you arrived with, you will not be allowed to leave. Before you even go to check out, make immigration aware of any crew changes. If the crewmember is flying home, go to the immigration office with the crewmember and show them the ticket. If the crewmember has signed on aboard another boat, go to immigration with the other skipper and inform them of the change. In both cases, immigration should remove the person from your crew list.

When taking on crew, arrange everything ahead of time. Make sure the crewmember has a valid passport and learn as much as you can about the person before you sign them aboard. You don't want to end up in jail for smuggling in an illegal alien, and you don't want to end up a hostage to a crewmember who can't or won't leave your boat.

BURGEONING BUREAUCRACY

Every group has their sacred cows, but they also have their great grouses. For world voyagers, bureaucracy tops the list of complaints. Most voyagers believe a foreign country cannot impose its regulations on foreign-flag vessels. But a close look at the reality does not support that contention. Countries have the right to impose restrictions on the voyaging community. As the number of yachts in foreign waters increases, we can fully expect more regulation.

Cruising has traditionally been very inexpensive—in large part because cruisers were exempt from most so-

cial costs while they lived aboard. If someone was injured, they used the local health-care system (which is socialized in most other countries around the world) and paid nothing for the service. There were no harbor fees, no pumpout fees, no water or electricity charges. In the past, countries were willing to tolerate a handful of yachties "freeloading" on local resources because the problem was too small to warrant the cost of a solution. With the explosion of cruising yachts and the increasing demands on national budgets, countries are no longer willing to subsidize foreign cruisers. Where the problem becomes visible enough and expensive enough, they will impose a fee on foreign yachts to offset the cost of their presence.

New regulations introduced by New Zealand require yachts clearing out to have specific safety equipment aboard, including an EPIRB. Some voyagers we knew could not afford such expensive electronics. Offshore voyagers have reacted with outrage. The New Zealand regulations represent the most recent in a series of restrictions. The cruising community singled out New Zealand's new rules because they were offended at being forced to spend money on safety after reaching New Zealand safely in the first place. Voyagers are also upset that such an inexpensive, yacht-friendly country betrayed them.

But the issue at stake is not safety, but the fact that foreign yachts are "freeloading" on the rescue infrastructure of New Zealand. Other regulations, taxes, and fees have already been imposed on yachties to ensure that they do not "freeload." In the Galapagos, the outrageous per-day charges and the (until recent) "ban" on pleasure yachts were designed to protect the wildlife and the local tourism industry. In French Polynesia, the bond provisions were implemented in reaction to foreigners who arrived in Polynesia and tried to stay in the country by claiming they lacked the money to return home. On Ascension Island, yachties are required to pay a stiff daily fee; if they are treated at the local clinic, this fee offsets the cost of care. Even in the United States, foreign vessels are not supposed to discharge overboard within the three-mile limit, implying that foreign vessels must have holding tanks installed.

Cruising is becoming more expensive and more regulated because the large number of cruising boats taxes limited local resources. New Zealand's regulations are the most recent example of the trend toward forcing yachties to pay their own way. Most of the fees and restrictions that have been imposed are not inequitable. The real problem comes if countries start to impose fees to extract money from a voyaging community that has no voice or representation. Our own mobility offers the only defense against that possibility. In the meantime, you will hear a great deal of incensed discussion about bureaucracy. Sit back and enjoy it.

CHAPTER 21 | GETTING YOUR BEARINGS

Returning the boat to normal ■ *Airing out and cleaning up* ■ *The post-passage inspection* ■ *Managing the repair list*
■ **When in Rome . . .** ■ *Local money management* ■ *Local services* ■ *Avoiding pests and plagues* ■ *Local supplies*
■ **Managing the home front** ■ *Mail* ■ *Money matters*

Our first day in a new port was usually devoted to checking in, a first foray ashore, enjoying our mail and a good night's sleep. On the second day we found the energy to put the passage behind us and begin to get our bearings ashore. We wanted to air out and clean up the boat, start boat repairs, do laundry, dispose of garbage, trade books, fill our water and fuel tanks, go exploring ashore, and find the local market. The list sometimes seemed endless. Like many voyagers, we preferred to put the boat back into voyaging shape before we relaxed and enjoyed our destination. The faster we could acclimate to the new culture, learn the area, and work our way through our to-do list, the sooner we could head off and explore this strange new land.

Our first few days ashore were always a blur of activity after the solitude of life at sea. While the exact order of activities might vary, we had three major objectives during our first week ashore in a large port. First, we wanted to get the boat as close to seagoing shape as we could. In addition to cleaning up and airing out, that effort included ordering any spare parts that had to come in through customs and initiating any repairs that might take more than a few days. Second, as strangers in a strange land, we had to learn how things worked—from the local currency to the local laundress. Without tour guides and tourist hotels, we had to teach ourselves to become comfortable in the new culture as quickly as possible. Finally, we were always eager to reestablish communication with friends and family, and we often had to manage some things on the home front from thousands of miles away.

We rarely arrived in a port where we didn't have some information on what to expect. Whatever cruising guide we had for the area offered advice on water, diesel, provisions, and services. If we had managed to buy or borrow a tour book, we had a rough idea of the general layout of the town and where we might find the post office and tourist information. The SSCA bulletins offered advice on all aspects of a new port—from where to dock to where to get provisions.

But our best information came from other voyagers. Folks from New Zealand and Australia cruise throughout the Pacific and are eager to offer suggestions about their home ports and the places they have visited. You will find Americans and Europeans in almost every anchorage, and many have a wealth of experience cruising not just in their home waters but also throughout nearby countries. You'll see the South African flag frequently once you reach the Indian Ocean and throughout the Caribbean. If you see the flag of a country you think you might like to visit down the road, knock on the hull and introduce yourself. That's the way the voyaging world works.

RETURNING THE BOAT TO NORMAL

After our second passage, we were enjoying cocktails aboard another boat with a group of several yachties, most of whom were new to passagemaking. We were exchanging early impressions of the voyaging life when a woman singlehander said, "I'm still afraid to look in my lockers. Every time I open one, there's some sort of a surprise waiting. And it's never a pleasant one." We all laughed, but not wholeheartedly. I realized I had been subconsciously avoiding a number of areas on the boat for fear of what might be lurking there. One of the few experienced passagemakers in the group, an angular man who had been voyaging for a dozen years, said gruffly, "And what makes you think whatever is in there is going to go away without a little sunshine and some fresh air?"

Like our attitude toward maintenance, our attitude toward post-passagemaking tasks underwent a radical change during our first year of voyaging. By the time we reached the Pacific, we had a set routine to clean up the boat within 24 hours of arrival in a new port and to return the boat to passage-ready condition as quickly as possible. We applied our maintenance attitude of "find it, fix it" to the entire boat after a passage, finding anything that was wrong right away rather than discovering it piecemeal. Then we could relax, knowing that every detail had been attended to and no gremlins lurked in the lockers.

Airing out and cleaning up

After we had cleared in and had gotten some sleep, we flushed the boat with fresh water and aired it out. If we had a hose available, we rinsed the boat thoroughly with fresh water, including all exterior stainless and teak, blocks, winches, genoa tracks, the wind vane, windlass, and the wheel-based autopilot. We opened up the bilge from one end to the other and removed everything from our forepeak settee locker. Then we poured buckets of water with a mild soap down through the chain hawser. We scrubbed the bilge with a long handled brush or a large sponge and flushed it with several buckets of fresh water. We left these areas open for 6 to 12 hours until they were thoroughly dry.

If we did not have access to a hose, we used a small amount of soap in two or three big buckets of water and didn't rinse the bilge afterwards. We could flush out the entire boat from chain locker to bilge pump with about 10 gallons of water—especially if we blocked the limber holes and scrubbed one area at a time.

The electric bilge pump got a thorough workout during this process. We checked the manual bilge pumps to be sure they were in working order. We ran the pressure water and used the handheld shower in the head to clean out areas that were difficult to reach.

We opened and aired out all lockers that held clothes or foul-weather gear. We sorted through all the clothes

in the forepeak lockers. Those stowed in dry bags or plastic bags needed only a cursory check to make sure they were still clean and dry. The rest we sorted into laundry and wool. Wool clothes were hung out in the cockpit for a day, where the sun and the wind eliminated any unpleasant odors (Figure 21-1, page 377). We also hung clothes from the hanging lockers out in the cockpit for several hours of sunshine. We gave foul-weather gear a thorough rinse with a hose or in a bucket before leaving it to air out for 24 hours. Inside the boat, we let all lockers air out for several hours.

We did a quick inspection of any locker or area that hadn't yet been aired out. If tightly packed books and papers had developed mildew, we pulled them out and propped the lockers open. We hung wool blankets out in the cockpit to air out if they needed it.

Through the course of airing out and cleaning up, we added a few more items to our to-do list. We identified any deck fittings that needed to be rebedded. We added to our laundry bag. Once in a while we found something more major—a turning block on deck to be replaced or a bilge or water pump to be rebuilt. By the end of the day, almost everything was back where it belonged, and the boat smelled as fresh and clean as when we left port.

The post-passage inspection

Once we had aired out and cleaned up the boat, we turned our attention to a thorough inspection of every piece of gear aboard. Even on the most successful passage, we added a few items to the repair list before we made landfall. But once the salt was cleaned off the boat and the lockers stood open while they aired out, we took the opportunity to make sure our repair list was complete.

If we were in a clean harbor, Evans dove and checked Silk's bottom. He made sure the rudder, prop, and zincs were all in good order, and he had a look at the bottom paint to see how it had held up. On most tropical passages, we would have acquired a crop of gooseneck barnacles, which Evans ignored. These require water flowing over them to live, so they would die and fall off within a few days of our dropping anchor.

We discovered any problems on deck when we hosed off all the hardware. If the passage had been more than

10 days or so or if we had any reason to suspect a problem, one of us went up the mast for a quick inspection of the masthead crane, lights, instruments, spreaders, and spreader lights.

We inspected every seam of our working sails and checked for chafe, broken threads, or small rips. If possible, we took our asymmetrical spinnaker ashore and spread it out on the grass where we could inspect it for pinholes or rips and allow it to air out. We fixed minor damage to any sails on the spot. We added to the to-do list any major damage that required patching.

By the second day in a new port, we had completed our post-passage inspection and the boat was back to normal. By our third day, we had organized the items on our to-do list, divided the tasks up, and began to work through the list of jobs.

Managing the repair list

We never completed a passage over five days without one or two small items needing attention when we got to port. After our early experiences, we never tried to get parts anywhere but in major ports where we intended to stay for a month or more. If we had made landfall on a tropical island without chandleries or boatyards, we would make do with whatever spares we carried and the few things that could be purchased from a local hardware store. Anything that we could not repair ourselves with the materials at hand would have to wait and go on the long-term repair list for the next major port. In the meantime, we would tackle one or two tasks every day until the immediate repair list was completed. Repairs hardly needed to be managed, they just needed to be done.

By the time we were approaching a mainland port such as Auckland or Durban, we always had an impressive list of necessary repairs. Most were minor, but a few would take several days or weeks to complete. We would find a few more items that needed attention after our post-passage inspection, and our repair list would often cover a page or more.

We learned not to leave the work until the end of our stay. Things always took longer than we anticipated. Trying to complete important tasks when rushed by an approaching departure date didn't yield results that could stand up to offshore demands. We made a complete list of supplies and spares required for repairs and for replenishing our spares locker. Then we spent time browsing in the local chandleries and talking to other voyagers to find out what was and was not available. We could then decide which tasks required long lead-times and focus on those first.

Long lead-time tasks generally fell into the following categories:

- **International deliveries.** Anything we had to order from outside the country and coax through customs always took far longer than we expected. We could not buy the strangest things locally, even in a country as boat-crazy as New Zealand. We carried a wealth of catalogs from which we could order parts. Having the part numbers ensured that we got the *right* parts into the country.

- **Specially made items and outside professionals.** We assumed anything that had to be custom made for the boat or that involved outside professionals would take more time, though sometimes we were pleasantly surprised. Custom stainless steel fittings fabricated by a machine shop, regalvanized chain, sails made by sailmakers, or canvas work by a local company all required several weeks of lead-time and almost inevitably arrived later than promised.

- **Haulout.** In areas where haulout facilities are scarce, such as Durban, we often had to schedule a haulout several weeks in advance. Even where facilities were plentiful, we had to decide where and when we wanted to be hauled out and make sure we had all necessary supplies for the work that had to be done on the hard.

During the first week, we tried to get as many long lead-time tasks under way as possible. We didn't worry about the jobs we could do ourselves with the materials we had on board or could get locally. Once we had everything else under way, we would return to these tasks and tackle one or two a day.

WHEN IN ROME . . .

For those who have not traveled very much, the idea of getting around in a foreign culture that speaks a different language can be intimidating. One of the greatest delights of traveling, however, is finding that the basics

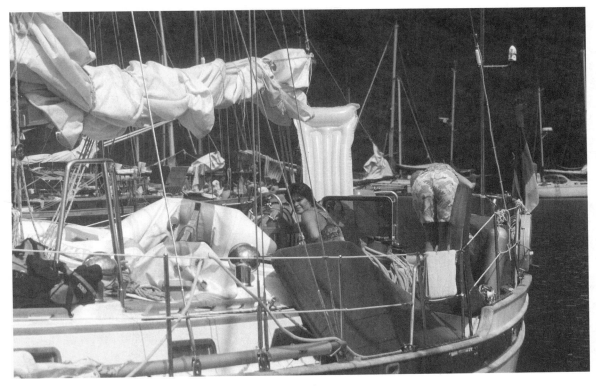

Figure 21-1. A boat in the process of airing out and cleaning up after an Atlantic crossing

get done much the same way the world over. People everywhere have to buy food, obtain fresh water, get from place to place, cook, sleep, build houses, and so on. If you start with the assumption that things are going to work in a similar way to what you are used to, you will find the first few experiences easier to deal with.

After you have grown comfortable with the similarities, the differences become more obvious. Every place has its own variations on the themes. On Bora Bora, French baguettes are delivered by a bakery van to each house and are put in a 2-foot-long "mailbox" with a little roof to protect the bread from the rain. In New Zealand, hot and cold faucets are reversed, and you turn on light switches by flicking them down instead of up. In Tonga, pigs wander the streets as dogs used to in the United States before leash laws. These textures define different cultures and add zest to traveling. If you are willing to make a few mistakes and lead the laughter each time you realize your faux pas, you will have no trouble acclimating to a new culture.

When you arrive somewhere new, your best information comes from other voyagers who have already mastered the culture and its idiosyncrasies. In most ports, voyagers congregate in one area and see each other frequently. That may be at the local yacht club or at a centrally located bar or restaurant. Chances are you'll know the details before you arrive, but if not, a hello to another boat and a couple questions will give you the information you need. Several weeks later, you'll be the one answering the same questions for another crew with the watery look of a recent passage still in their eyes.

Local money management

In any "civilized" culture, before you can buy the cold beer you've been craving on passage or pay for the berth where your boat is happily snuggled, you will need some local currency. Not so long ago, this could be a frustrating task. But today, several alternatives work in even the most remote places.

Almost every boat we knew of, regardless of nationality, carried an emergency stash of American dollars or American traveler's checks. U.S. dollars are still the only currency accepted worldwide. Like most of our friends, we stowed about $1,000 in cash in various secret places. Most of this was in $100 bills, but we always kept about $200 in $20 bills for those occasions when a small bit of American cash was the only solution to a problem—such as when a fee was required for clearing in before we were even allowed to go ashore. When we left, we assumed we would live off this money between major ports, converting it to local currency as we went. But we ended up keeping this as our emergency fund because dollars were often hard to replace, even in some mainland ports.

Traveler's checks or cash advances on a Visa or MasterCard offer the easiest ways to get local currency. American Express is still the gold standard with respect to traveler's checks. While you have to pay a fee up front to buy them, on many small islands they get a better exchange rate than cash. We were told that this was because the banks did not have to store the paper and ship it back to the mainland, as they did with dollars. You can purchase American Express traveler's checks at any American Express office. With a regular American Express green card, we could buy up to $1,500 at a time using a personal check. The gold or platinum cards had higher check-cashing limits. You can request a booklet from American Express that contains the addresses of every one of their offices throughout the world. Every major port we visited had an office, as did many of the smaller ports with resorts. We considered the fact that traveler's checks are replaceable if lost or stolen a major advantage.

With our Visa or MasterCard, we could get cash advances anywhere there was a bank—and we found banks on some pretty remote islands. The fees and interest charges on cash advances made this alternative less attractive than traveler's checks, though the exchange rate always seemed favorable. Our credit card statements rarely caught up with us before they were past due. We therefore had to keep track of how much we spent and send checks regularly.

On a small island, the bank will be the only show in town for changing money. You will find more alternatives in a larger city, including change kiosks and people trying to sell you currency in the street. Check around for the best rates before you change. In most places that will be the bank. When it is not, make certain that you are not dealing on the black market inadvertently.

Once you get your local currency, have a good look at it. Try to learn the differences between bills and coins as quickly as possible. You'll save yourself embarrassment and perhaps even money as you struggle to pull out the right bills at a store. Unlike American currency, which many foreigners find terribly boring, most countries differentiate between denominations using size, color, and even texture on their bills and coins. If you take the time to notice, you'll quickly learn the new currency.

If you plan to stay in one place for a number of months, consider opening a bank account. We did this in New Zealand, and it worked out very well. We enjoyed the convenience of a bank card, ATM machines, and checks for the six months we were there. Opening the account was difficult only because we used a wire transfer. We would have been better off using a cash advance, traveler's checks, or cash.

Wire transfers are probably the most awkward and inefficient way to move money around internationally. We did it twice in New Zealand. Each time it took 7 to 10 days and a myriad of angry phone calls—and that was between two countries with modern banking systems. If you think you might want the capability of making wire transfers, set it up before you leave at a large national or "super-regional" bank with a sympathetic banker who knows you reasonably well. The bank will have you fill out several forms. When you want money transferred, you will need to send a request by mail or fax with your signature. Ask for a list of your bank's correspondent banks. This will assist the foreign bank in determining how the money will actually be routed. Also, request that they wire the money in local currency to save you some exchange fees. Then follow up. Our money got derailed in some intermediary bank both times we tried it.

Local services

Yacht clubs are truly the home-away-from-home for the offshore voyager. Since the days of the earliest voyagers, many yacht clubs around the world have opened their doors and offered their services to long-distance sailors. The Panama Canal Yacht Club and the Balboa Yacht Club on either side of the Canal, the Royal Suva Yacht Club in Fiji, the Grande Baie Yacht Club in Mauritius (Figure 21-2), the Point Yacht Club in Durban (Figure 21-3), and the Hout Bay Yacht Club near Cape Town, to name a few, all welcomed us and dozens like us. When we entered a port where there was a yacht club, we knew everything was going to be just a little bit easier. Most yacht clubs hold mail for visitors, offer a laundry service, have dockage or a safe anchorage, offer fax and phone service, dispose of garbage, and invite visitors into the club bar or restaurant. All this is offered for free or for a small fee. We always found helpful people at the desk or behind the bar who knew exactly where to find a machine shop, a chandlery, or spares for a Yanmar engine.

Most yacht clubs have showers, and these were a

luxury after arriving from a long passage. Most tropical islands have only cold-water showers, but this is no hardship in the hot climate. Whenever you enjoy the unlimited water in these communal showers, wear flip-flops or thongs. Besides funguses like athlete's foot, many types of parasites grow in the moist ground around these facilities. Bare feet are an open invitation to infestation.

When there was no yacht club, we needed to figure everything out for ourselves. After finding a bank and getting some local currency, laundry and communications generally topped our list. Our favorite way to acclimate was just to wander. We found most of what we needed eventually and discovered lots of interesting things along the way. If we didn't have time to test the water, we would head straight for the local tourist office. Every place where there are tourists has an office. The staff will speak English, have free maps, and give you good advice for getting oriented.

Figure 21-2. The Grande Baie Yacht Club on Mauritius

Laundry

In Chapter 12, I discussed doing your own laundry with limited water. But the best solution to dirty laundry is a clean laundromat. These are not as unusual as we had expected. We found good laundromats in every major island port and throughout most developed countries. Paradoxically, we found laundromats more often than we found good fresh water. Laundromats can be hard to come by on remote islands, in Southeast Asia, and up the Red Sea. Where there are no laundromats, your choices will come down to a local "laundry service" or doing it yourself.

When doing laundry in laundromats, the following ideas make the entire process easier and ensure that your laundry arrives back at the boat in the same condition it left the laundromat:

■ **Stowing laundry.** When stowing dirty laundry on the boat for long periods, keep air circulating to minimize mold, mildew, and odors. Besides keeping the boat from smelling like a gym locker, this also limits the work required to remove stains. Mesh bags or milk crates both work well for stowing dirty clothes aboard.

■ **Laundry bags.** It can ruin your day if a stray wave rinses your freshly cleaned laundry as you are returning to your boat in the dinghy. The best bags for transporting laundry to the laundromat, therefore, are large, easily carried waterproof bags that can be closed. The largest size dry bags available from marine stores (13×13×20 inches) make excellent laundry transport bags. Ours came with a shoulder strap that made carrying them easy. Canvas bags, backpacks, mesh bags, and even pillowcases work. But bring along a few plastic garbage bags for the dinghy ride.

■ **Laundry detergent.** In many places, detergent is very expensive and of low quality, so you will want to bring your own to the laundromat. Purchase a couple of jumbo-sized packages before leaving a developed

Figure 21-3. The International Dock in Durban with the dinghy dock for the Point Yacht Club in the foreground

country and use this detergent everywhere else. Your laundry water will be "discharged" directly overboard without treatment, so buy phosphate free, environmentally friendly detergents. Transfer powdered detergents to plastic containers, or they will become a gooey mess in a few weeks. If you like fabric softener, whether in liquid or sheet form, take that along as well; you won't find it outside of developed countries. Take small quantities to the laundromat to minimize weight on the walk, which is often a half-mile or longer.

■ *Drying laundry.* In most laundromats, dryers are expensive and inefficient. If you are not in a yacht club or marina, put the clothes through one dryer cycle and take them back to the boat to finish drying on the lifelines in the sun. The UV radiation bleaches mildew stains out of white clothes and kills bacteria and viruses. If you are in a yacht club or marina, make sure the management does not object to clothes drying on the lifelines. Many do. If they prefer not to see the boats in the harbor "dressed" with laundry, that is their right and it should be respected.

If there is no laundromat ashore, there is often someone who does laundry. Most yacht clubs without their own laundry facility have an arrangement with a reliable local person. If you find someone on your own, make sure to get some references before turning over your clothes and bedding. We heard several stories of laundry taken hostage and returned only after an exorbitant ransom had been extracted. Keep a list of all of the clothes so there is no question if something is missing. Negotiate the price beforehand and agree on what service is expected. I was surprised to get back plastic bags full of soaking wet clothes in Tonga. Our clothes came back dried and ironed in Mauritius—even our underwear!

The service provided bears little relationship to the price, which varied widely. In some places, we had the equivalent of three or four pillowcases full of laundry washed, dried, and folded for less than $10. In other places, we would have spent $60 for the same service. The price was often more reasonable if we provided the laundry detergent.

Where local prices were high, we paid someone to do only the garments that were difficult to manage ourselves. We would pay a premium for towels, jeans, heavy cotton sweat pants, and sheets rather than do them in a bucket on the deck.

Communications

After a passage, we always wanted to let our families know we had arrived safely. On our first foray into the village, town, or city where we had made landfall, we searched out the most efficient way to make contact with the outside world. In most places we could make contact via phone or fax. If we were staying at a yacht club, both might be available right on the club grounds. If not, we had to find the best way to communicate ourselves.

In almost all European countries and on all the French islands, the post office has phones that can be used to make international calls. On many of the islands that were once controlled by the British, like St. Helena and Cocos Keeling, a telephone and telegraph office handles phone services separately from the post office. In either case, you first need to fill out a form with the number you want to call and how you want to pay for the call—collect, person-to-person, or cash—in which case they will want to know how long you want to speak for. Very few places allow you to charge the call to a calling card or a credit card. Where that is possible, an operator will input your card number and PIN since these phones do not have their own dials. That seemed a risky proposition, even more so after friends experienced problems in the Caribbean with fraudulent charges to their cards after giving their numbers to operators. We therefore called collect or paid for calls with cash.

After you've filled out your form, you wait until your name is called and you are told which booth to go to. You enter the booth, which is more like a closet than a traditional telephone booth. When the phone rings, you pick up and, with luck, your party is on the other end. At the end of your designated time, you get a beep or two as warning and then the call is cut off. In a town like Neiafu in the Vava'u group of Tonga, you might wait an hour or more for your call to go through on the only phone line out of the island group. If you are paying in cash, you go to the cashier and pay your money—usually somewhere between $2 and $4 per minute in the Pacific islands.

As an alternative, we found faxes absolute marvels of modern technology. Even in Neiafu, there was a dedicated fax line so faxes went out immediately. A fax page cost a fraction of a 10-minute phone conversation, and we could get more focused information across in a fax than during a surprise phone call. We found faxes even on the most remote islands, and we generally paid $2 a page; we were rarely charged more than $5 a page. Fax machines could be found in the same place as the phones, whether in the post office or at the telephone and telegraph office. Most tourist hotels and travel agencies also had fax services, and they were willing to send and receive for a fee.

In Australia, New Zealand, South Africa, and on a few of the larger islands frequented by tourists, we used our AT&T calling card at local pay phones. We could even use the AT&T USA direct service, which allowed us to dial a local number and talk to an American operator. In some places, we paid dearly for this service and didn't realize it until months later when the bill caught up with

us. For this reason, we tried to keep our usage to a minimum. Still, I would recommend taking a calling card along. In an emergency, it is often the fastest and easiest way to get through to someone who can answer a critical question or fix a serious problem. A British BT Chargecard will be accepted everywhere, as long as it's chargeable to a British phone line. Perhaps you could use a relative's or friend's?

A final word on phones and phone calls: One of the most frustrating things when calling from overseas are all those lovely toll-free numbers that make life at home so wonderful. An 800 number does not work when dialed from outside the country, and in all too many cases no alternative number is given on a catalog or repair manual. Before you go, check all your repair manuals and catalogs. Make sure you have a non-800 phone and fax number for each one. In addition, make sure you have non-800 numbers for your credit

Avoiding pests and plagues

Even paradise has a few not-so-pleasant realities. Among them are biting insects, cockroaches, and rats—and the very best you can hope for is to avoid them. If they find you, then you will have to be prepared to do battle.

The best way to avoid mosquitoes and biting flies is to anchor off and use screens, mosquito netting, and mosquito coils. Beyond that, there is little you can do except wait for night when the flies sleep or day when the mosquitoes sleep.

In the Pacific, particularly in the Marquesas, small sand fleas called no-nos (like the no-seeums of the Bahamas and the U.S. East Coast) have a painful bite that often gets infected. They stay near shore and tend to congregate near sources of fresh water. The local solution was to add Clorox to shower water. Our water had a good amount of Clorox in it, but the no-nos seemed unimpressed. Australian bug repellent—which was almost pure DEET and would never have been approved by the FDA—did keep these insects at bay. This also kept away the man-eating mosquitoes of northern Australia.

If you are tied up to a wharf or dock, you run a risk

of getting a rat or mouse aboard. Everyone cautions against using poison, since you can end up with a decaying rat in the most inaccessible part of the bilge. Several friends successfully used traps, so start there if you get a stowaway. As usual, prevention works best. Don't tie up if you can avoid it. If you are tied up briefly to a wharf area where there is garbage, keep an eye on your lines. If you are going to remain tied up for some period in such a place, fashion some sort of a rat guard on each line to prevent rodents from coming aboard.

Cockroaches are the most common plague, and we knew many people who suffered invasions. We struggled for a year and a half with our infestation. They came aboard in Antigua when we were on the hard. We tried every one of the cruising remedies, from boric acid, to flypaper, to roach motels, to curved jars with jelly or peanut butter inside. Then we tried more lethal attacks—including bug bombs and roach spray. What finally worked was another Australian product (the Australians really understand how to battle serious bugs). This roach bomb had to be left for a full 12 hours before we could take a peek inside.

card, bank, and calling card statements. You will save yourself a great deal of frustration.

Local supplies

After taking care of the necessities, our attention turned to resupplying the boat. We always needed to find diesel and water, and we often needed propane. If we were staying at a yacht club or in a marina, all three were straightforward. Otherwise, we asked other boats in the area where we could purchase fuel and water and asked about its quality. We often relied on rain-catching and tank water for several months between high quality water supplies. If there were fishing boats in the area, we could always get diesel—even if we had to transfer it from a drum. Propane was easier to come by than we had expected as it is used for cooking on so many of the islands. In many places, butane has been substituted for propane. We found that worked equally well, although the butane did not burn as cleanly.

Food came next. I felt I was truly exploring a town or a village when I strolled, canvas bag in hand, from shop to shop. I communicated in a combination of English, sign language, and the local language. From the canned goods on the grocery store shelves, to the fresh produce stacked in the stalls at the local market, to the materials and hardware in the local equivalent to the five-and-dime, I saw how people really lived, what things decorated their lives, what they ate, what they wore, and what they hoped for.

On small islands children would follow Evans and me—wide-eyed with wonder at our white skin and almost white hair—while the adults would observe our purchases and offer unsolicited advice. On larger islands, we would be lost in the bustle of traffic and tourists and enjoy some anonymity after weeks or

---

If you find yourself battling cockroaches, the following rules of engagement will help you win the war:

- **Single soldiers.** If you ever see one roach aboard, assume that you have a hundred. To find out for sure, leave something nice and sweet on the counter and turn on the galley light in the middle of the night. Seeing a few large roaches immediately after bombing don't necessarily mean disaster. Some of the bombs do not kill the largest adults; they only sterilize them.

- **Reproductive cycle.** Roaches are some of the most efficient reproductive organisms on earth. Eggs hatch a mere two weeks from the time they are laid. That means one bomb is never enough. Even if you wipe out every adult aboard, anywhere from two days to two weeks later you will once again hear the patter of little feet. While many of the products we used claimed to kill the eggs, after a half-dozen failures we stopped believing them. The only way to win the war is to bomb the boat at least twice, the second time about three to four weeks after the first—long enough that all the eggs have hatched but not so long that the new brood has already bred and laid more eggs.

- **Cozy corners.** Our early attempts failed in part because we left the beasties places to hide. Whenever we bombed the boat, we removed all food, utensils, plates, pots, pans, and so on. The first few times we left the quarter berth filled with blankets and sleeping bags, left lockers filled with line, and left other areas intact where the bugs could find enough of a pocket to survive. The last two times we bombed, we took the advice of an accomplished general in the cockroach wars and opened every locker, spread out blankets and sleeping bags, pulled out line and clothes, and then sprayed roach spray from a handheld can into every open locker. By the time we were getting ready to set off the bug bomb, groggy cockroaches were already fleeing the fogged areas, heading out in the open where the bomb could do its work.

Rather than go to all this trouble, prevent roaches from coming aboard in the first place. If you are careful about cardboard, you will out-fox most would-be stowaways. But you are not completely safe. As we found out, they can come aboard when you are hauled. Worse, in some parts of the world they have evolved a set of quite functional wings. In evolutionary terms, we humans have no hope of ultimately winning this particular war. But don't let that discourage you from making every effort to keep your own boat roach free.

months as the focus of attention in the outer islands. As voyagers, we shop our way into local cultures. We get to meet people and make connections while we go about the very real business of restocking our larder.

On a small island, you will find the local bakery, the market, and the island's few stores the first time you go ashore. In a larger port, you may need to wander through different parts of the town several times before you find the best supermarket or the most complete bakery. In most places, the focus of your reprovisioning will be the local market with its fresh produce and its nearby butchers, fish mongers, and bakeries.

When shopping in the local market, ask around to determine the best time to get the freshest produce. Most of the villagers bring their produce on a specific day. The widest selection and highest quality fruits and vegetables can be obtained early in the morning on that day. If you are told to be there by 6:00 in the morning, believe it. By 9:00 A.M. the good produce had already been purchased in most markets we visited.

No bags will be available at the market, so take along your favorite carrying bags. Bring a container for eggs or you will spend the day cradling a half-dozen wrapped in newspaper. If you do not recognize a particular fruit or vegetable, ask what it is and how it is prepared. The vendors will be delighted at your interest and will often cut one open and give you a bite.

Be prepared to negotiate. In America and Europe, we have become embarrassed about money. A price is a price, and we accept it or not. We have become removed from the barter system, the original basis of all economics that recognizes that the value of a specific item varies from person to person. Many Americans were insulted by the idea of bargaining in the local markets. Others were afraid of being cheated. In fact, negotiating is a game. As in many games, the social aspects matter more than the outcome.

Under the standard formula, you offer half what is being asked. Then you go back and forth until you end up about midway between your starting price and the asking price. You will get grumbles from some sellers and smiles from others, but all will end up pleased. Many vendors find tourists who will not negotiate painful to deal with; the rules of good conduct are being broken. They think you are being cheated, and they feel awful. In the Indian market in Durban, two Germans

were considering the price of a large soapstone carving. The wizened Indian proprietor said, "That's what I'm *asking.* Now you are supposed to tell me what you are *willing* to pay." The two Germans walked off and the proprietor looked at me sadly and said, "They just don't understand."

Early on, before I understood how the game was played, many of the vendors took pity on me. After charging me their asking price for six tomatoes, they would throw in two or three more just to make things right. So, view negotiating as a way to really understand value within the local culture. Use it to get to know the person behind the counter. Most of all, enjoy your hard-won trophies. There is something intensely satisfying about negotiating a better deal, even when the outcome is a foregone conclusion.

MANAGING THE HOME FRONT

At the same time as you are learning the ropes in a different culture, you will also need to be managing whatever you left behind when you set sail. A minor crisis often seemed to have arisen while we were on passage, so managing the home front almost always made the list of essential activities for our first week in port.

Ideally, you'll leave nothing behind that might worry you along the way. In the real world, you will need to stay in touch with your family, pay bills, attend to a house or a business, and pay taxes. To minimize the time spent managing the home front, entrust the details to someone reliable—even if you have to hire their services. One round-trip ticket from Fiji pays for a lot of professional assistance, so the tradeoff makes sense unless your affairs are simple indeed.

Mail

Mail constitutes a major event in the voyaging life. We made a beeline for the local mail drop as soon as we were legal. We'd then retire with our bulging envelopes to a café to linger for hours over letters and cappuccino. But we found the logistics associated with mail far more frustrating than we had expected. By comparison, managing our money was a breeze.

Someone must act as your forwarding agent at home. If you ask a friend or a relative, be sure they understand what is involved. My father acted as our dispatch agent, and he did a marvelous job. Our affairs were very simple. Even so, there were periods when it took several hours a week of his time. If you are leaving behind a business or any complex financial or legal affairs, hire someone and preserve your relationship with your relatives. Professional mail forwarding services are listed in the classified ads of national sailing magazines. Get some references and select the one that meets your needs. Some forwarding agents pay bills, take phone messages, and inform people where you are and when you can next be reached.

Once you have determined who is going to handle your mail, give that address to every person, organization, or business who might try to contact you. You will have only one person to inform of your next address, not several dozen. Mail can be bundled and sent off to you all at once. Mail does end up where it was meant to go, though it might take a roundabout route to get there. The following tricks ensured that our mail found us at the end of its journey.

■ *Address mail to last name and boat name.* Tell your forwarding agent to bundle the mail into large envelopes and address them to one last name followed by the boat name, in our case "Starzinger, s/v *Silk*." In almost every yacht club, post office, American Express office, and hotel around the world, mail is sorted into large bins by the first letter of the last name. If there is only one name on the envelope, there will be less chance that your mail will be misfiled. We used Evans's name because the first letter was the same as that of our boat name, eliminating another common area of confusion.

■ *Use a distinctive envelope.* Have the person who is forwarding your mail always use the same type of distinctive envelope. My father used oversized manila envelopes that were lighter in color than most, and I could often pick them out of a rack of mail without reading the names on the envelopes. White or colored 10×13-inch envelopes stand out. Other ideas are to address the envelope in colored ink—green catches the eye—or decorate the envelope with a distinctive logo. Avoid sailboats, though!

■ *Number the envelopes.* Every envelope should be

numbered consecutively, and your forwarding agent should keep a list of the numbers and the dates they were sent. When we arrived in port, we immediately knew if we were missing any from the middle of the group. In our first fax home we would ask how many had been sent to see if we had received everything.

■ *Send first class.* First class mail got through the most efficiently. We had several packages sent Global Priority, which actually took longer than first class and in some cases got stuck in customs. Don't believe the post office's estimate of the time it takes to deliver something by their different methods. They could only tell us when it would enter the country, not how long it would take to wend its way through customs and the local postal system. We ended up using first class exclusively. Two to three weeks would get a large envelope of mail from upstate New York to almost anywhere in the world.

■ *Put "Hold for pickup" in large letters on the envelope.* After the address, have your forwarding service put "Hold for pickup" on the envelope. This will usually keep the mail from being sent back if you don't show up for a month or so after the package is received.

Where do you have your mail sent? That depends on the place. Where there was a yacht club, we used their mail service. Where there was not a yacht club, we used American Express offices. Lacking either of those options, we used a local hotel. Cruising guides recommend addresses for mail forwarding for each place you plan to visit. We avoided "post restante" or "general delivery" at the local post office, because they will usually hold mail for only a few weeks before returning it. Where we could confirm through the cruising grapevine that a yacht club or hotel address was still operational, we were pretty comfortable having mail sent there before we arrived.

Of these options, the American Express offices are the most professional. They are generally local travel agents with clean facilities, fax machines, money exchanges, and other services for travelers. They keep the mail behind a counter, and you must show your card to get it, so no one can take yours accidentally—or on purpose. They are also very good about forwarding mail to another American Express office if you arrange it before you leave. To make use of these services, you do need an American Express card.

As mentioned under "Local money management," American Express has a free booklet listing all its offices worldwide. A little envelope symbol appears next to each office that holds mail for travelers. Be careful not to send mail to an office that doesn't show the little symbol, or it will be returned to the sender immediately. While we were out, American Express seemed to be reorganizing its network, and in several cases the address in the booklet belonged to an agent that had been dropped. These people were not very graceful about receiving our mail; in some cases, we had to work hard to get it from them. We learned to ask the office we were dealing with to call ahead and verify the name and address of the next American Express office before having mail forwarded there.

If we did not have an American Express office address or a verified yacht club or hotel address, we would not have mail sent before we arrived at a destination. We stayed in many places for a month or more, and first class mail took a couple of weeks. If we sent the new forwarding address in our first fax, we would receive mail before we left. We always gave a cutoff date for the last package to be sent, generally three weeks before our intended departure for the next destination.

Money matters

Beyond receiving mail, managing the home front came down to various aspects of managing our finances. We had to pay bills and file taxes. Others we knew had to manage real estate or businesses.

Bill payment

We had no regular bills that needed to be paid while we were gone. We had to pay our credit cards when we got cash advances or made purchases, and we had to pay our AT&T calling card if we used it to make phone calls. We therefore had occasional bills in amounts we couldn't predict. We never knew exactly how much the AT&T bill would be, and the credit cards were always complicated by exchange rates. Statements never caught up with us in time to make payments without incurring late fees, so we had to develop an alternative method of paying off these bills.

We tried to keep the balances on all of these cards at zero, so we made a guess on how much the bill was going to be and sent it off before we got a statement. By the time we made landfall, the bills would have caught up with the activity at our last destination. We faxed my father, and he sent us a summary of all the bills including the dates of the latest transactions, outstanding balance, and payments received. From that we could tell whether we needed to send more money. This did not work flawlessly. It sometimes took months for charges to find their way onto our statements and weeks for our payments to reach the company. But this system worked fairly well, and our balances were near zero most of the time.

If you have regular payments of fixed amounts, ask your bank to set up an electronic transfer from your account to the creditor's. Most banks can set up electronic transfers on a weekly, monthly, bimonthly, or semiannual basis. If the amount of the withdrawal changes, you or the payee will have to notify the bank in writing. You can handle health insurance payments, mortgages, boat insurance, and other regular bills this way.

Some mail forwarding services also do bill paying. If you have more than a half-dozen credit cards to manage, you may want to consider this option. Some people we knew relied on a full-service brokerage account to pay both regular and irregular bills. The personal service a broker provides can make bill paying and money management much easier. Several late payments in a row will send alarm bells off at the credit card companies and will appear on your credit history. To avoid this, you need to set up a reliable and straightforward way to manage bill payment before you leave.

Taxes

Depending on your income while you are voyaging, you may not need to file an income tax return. However, if you are earning income from investments, real estate, or an ongoing business, chances are you will have to file. If you want to income average when you return, you should also file. People residing outside of the country can get an automatic extension that will allow them to delay filing until August, as long as certain requirements are met. You can obtain tax forms, including extension forms, in American embassies and consulates.

If your tax situation is the least bit complex, hire an accountant to manage your taxes while you are away. Tell your forwarding agent to send any tax documents directly to your accountant. You will still have to sign the forms and return them, which can be difficult enough to manage if you are in a remote place.

Real estate or business

We knew several people who had to fly home to evict a tenant, see to a business that had run down in their absence, or repair water damage from a broken pipe in their house. The intricacies of mail and money cannot be avoided. However, for business and real estate, simpler is always better for long-term voyaging. If you cannot avoid the complexities, at least minimize the likelihood they will interfere with your trip by leaving your business affairs in competent hands.

There are many competent real estate management companies that will keep the house rented, oversee repairs, and evict a bad tenant. Their fee more than pays for itself and your peace of mind. For any type of major asset, consider leaving a general or specific Power of Attorney with someone you trust in the event it should be needed. All of this reduces the chance of your getting an unwanted dose of reality while you are enjoying paradise.

Assimilating ■ *Finding the way in* ■ *Respecting local laws and customs* ■ *Saying "thank you"* ■ **Sightseeing**
■ *Additional resources* ■ **Entertaining**

After a week in a new country, we were starting to feel at home. By this time, we had mastered some key words and phrases in the local language, figured out how the local currency translated into bread and beer, returned the boat to her normal shoreside state, reestablished contact with friends and relatives, and launched any major repairs that had to be completed before our next passage. We could finally devote our attention to the culture and the people we had come so far to see.

Exactly how we went about doing that depended on how developed the country was and on how much of the country was accessible by boat. In the many island nations we visited, *Silk* acted as our main mode of transport, offering unique glimpses into village life and intimate encounters with local people. For less-developed areas not accessible by boat, we needed to find another way to tour inland. In developed countries like Australia and New Zealand, the range of options for exploring were much the same as in the United States or Europe—rental cars, guided tours, backpacking trips, and so on.

Our social life sometimes included visits from friends and relatives. Having guests aboard allows you to see your world through their eyes, to experience anew the wonder of life afloat. You can lose sight of these things when your immediate circle of friends are all voyaging. The rewards of having guests share your home are accompanied by the challenges of managing the logistics of their departure and arrival.

ASSIMILATING

Most people who dream of sailing small boats across large oceans want to experience new cultures. They want to step back through time to see the South Pacific as Cook or Bligh did. They want to reach across the boundaries of language and tradition to touch real people living real lives. While this is easier to do on a sailboat than it is traveling any other way, an effort is still required beyond simply showing up. That wasn't true in the days when a handful of boats completed major voyages every year. But nowadays, hundreds of boats per year pass through the main harbor on most Pacific islands. Many of those ports are now cities. While cities have their unique local flavor, they have more in common with cities everywhere than they do with the culture of the island.

To really see a new culture, voyagers must make an effort to visit the small villages where local traditions are still practiced. Our most magical experiences always occurred in the least visited places off the beaten path. It requires effort to reach those places—obtaining a special permit in Fiji or sailing to windward for a day in Tonga. We were rewarded by local people who were eager to invite us into their homes and share their lives.

Once we find our way into a local culture, we are under an obligation to assimilate as far as possible for the period of time we are there. We must understand and adhere to local laws and respect local customs and traditions—even if we don't agree with them. When received with open hearts and giving hands, we need to respond in kind, to find ways to help those who have helped us. While this seems obvious, it can be difficult to say "thank you" without further obligating the receiver. Explorers and adventurers have always been cultural emissaries, and voyagers still act in that capacity the world over. We have a responsibility to make certain that our interactions reflect well on our own culture so those who follow us will be received with as much warmth and caring as we were.

Finding the way in

When we went ashore on the remote outer islands of Tonga or Fiji, we were always thronged by children. While I sat and put on my sneakers, they would circle around us and chatter excitedly in Polynesian. Then one or two, braver than the rest, would dart forward and try to touch our white skin. When we smiled and encouraged them, a group would come forward. Some tried to speak to us in a mixture of English and their native tongue, while others rubbed at our skin to try to get the white off. A few were brave enough to reach out and stroke my long, bleached-blond hair. As we wandered through the local village, the children would accompany us. We often felt like the Pied Piper followed by a band of prancing youngsters. After they had decided that we were basically harmless, one child would fall into step alongside me and a small hand would slip into mine. We had been accepted.

The magic of being accepted into another culture is a deeply touching experience. Time and time again, people opened their homes and their hearts to us, shared with us all the many aspects of their lives and relationships, and waved sorrowful good-byes when it was time for us to leave. If you visit only major ports, interact mainly with other voyagers, and don't enjoy being slightly off balance in a strange world, you will bypass most of the cultural experiences that make voyaging such a special way to travel. To make this kind of magic happen, you have to be willing to seek it out, take a few risks with your boat and your dignity, and open yourself up to the many experiences that unfold.

The more remote an island or an anchorage, the more likely you are to come face to face with people

Figure 22-1. Some of our many small friends in Muani, a village on the island of Kadavu in Fiji

who are interested in you and willing to let you into their lives. The fewer boats they have seen, the more of a stir you will cause, and the more you will be the center of attention for the duration of your stay. To experience cultural adventures, you must be willing to strike off on your own. That may mean traveling in waters that are less well charted, entering harbors with only a pilot and no real chart, visually navigating through coral to reach a village tucked well inside a lagoon, or trusting a local villager to guide you to a safe anchorage. All of this involves an element of risk, but the reward of meaningful personal interactions is all the sweeter for the effort your have invested.

How far do you have to go to get off the beaten path? In most cases, not nearly as far as you would think. Despite the sense of adventure intrinsic to offshore voyaging, the herd instinct often overtakes sailors when they arrive in a foreign port. We had to shake ourselves loose from our friends and the relatively sheltered life we were enjoying in the main harbor of an island group. A scant 20- or 30-mile sail would bring us to pristine anchorages and villages that had changed little since Cook first arrived.

In Tonga, for example, we made landfall in the northernmost island group called Vava'u. There we found an active community of close to a hundred cruising boats, many of whom we had first met in the Caribbean a year before. There was a morning net on the VHF run by one of the cruisers that featured weather, a swap shop, and local news spiced with generous amounts of gossip. In the main town of Neiafu, the Bounty Bar was the informal yacht club, offering cruisers camaraderie, entertainment, and libations. The dozen or so secure anchorages within 10 or 12 miles of Neiafu were referred to by the number on the local Moorings chart because the names were mostly unpronounceable. The villages in the area were fairly inured to visitors; only the children seemed interested in our presence.

After spending a month in this delightful area, we tore ourselves away and headed to the next Tongan island group. This area, called the Ha'apai group, is located only about 50 miles south of Vava'u. It is poorly charted and reef strewn, and there are very few anchorages that offer any sort of protection from a west wind. For the 10 days we spent sailing in this area, we saw only two other boats. When we went ashore here,

we found ourselves the center of attention everywhere we went.

We learned a valuable lesson in Tonga: The cultural experiences that we most treasure now were often a day or so to windward from where the voyaging boats congregated.

So how do you know where to go? Talk to others who have been there. In the Pacific, you will find boats from New Zealand and Australia who have spent more than one season in the islands. Those aboard can tell you whether you need a special permit to visit an area and offer advice on the best anchorages and the protocols for visiting a local village. The problem was never in knowing where to go. Everyone who visited the Marquesas knew that the Tuamotu atolls were still pristine. The other boats in Vava'u all knew that the Ha'apai group was waiting just to the south. Our friends in Fiji knew that several outlying islands had just been opened to yachts for the first time when we were there. But you can always find a reason not to visit, perhaps because the destination is to windward or poorly charted. So talk to those who have been there and weigh the risks against the possibility of an experience that most people in the twentieth century have only read about.

Even in more developed areas, you can still open the door to the local culture with a small effort. Children bridge the gap more easily than adults. If you are voyaging with children, you will never have to go to much effort to be invited into the local community. Your children and theirs will be interacting the minute you step ashore, and your own interactions will naturally follow.

Even if you do not have children, the children ashore offer ways to get involved with the local people. Throughout much of Polynesia, the children are taught in English. They can act as guides and interpreters. Even where language is an issue, children's natural curiosity tends to break down barriers. Some people carried candy and small toys such as yo-yo's or tops ashore with them and used these to make their first set of friends. We never did this but still found that children flocked to us on most islands we visited. If you follow the children to their school, you can suggest to the teacher that you talk a bit about where you are from and how you came to be here. That small bit of giving will often open an adult community to you, and you will leave the children with a significant memory.

You can easily cross the boundary of language and culture in local churches. In most places you will be welcomed at a local religious ceremony, as long as you dress appropriately and participate reverently. Many of the Pacific islanders worship in open-sided, palm thatched communal huts, and song plays an important part in the service. On Sunday, the whole world was clothed in harmony as the islanders sang for hours on end. We were touched by their voices and their worship—whether we were at anchor, ashore, or celebrating the sanctity of the day with them.

The camaraderie of the sea is shared by local fishermen who were often the first to reach out to us. They would stop by the boat and offer us some of their catch or ask if we had lures or fish hooks that we did not want. This was less a request for charity and more a way to begin a dialogue. If we met their gestures with equal interest in them and their lives, these seemingly casual encounters could lead to invitations to visit pearl farms in the Tuamotus or join the local fishermen in catching lobster on the reef in Fiji. In a few cases, we realized too late that what seemed like polite interest was an attempt to reach out to us and invite us into the village and its life. We regretted afterward missing those experiences. On the other hand, we never regretted reaching out, and we were never rebuffed.

Respecting local laws and customs

As visitors, we have a responsibility to respect the local laws and customs—whether we agree with them or not. In most cases, we thoroughly enjoyed abiding by the rules of a foreign culture. We found they even caused us to question our own cultural biases. But some of the traditions you are required to honor may be offensive to Western sensibilities, the most common example being how Moslem cultures treat women. With goodwill and a small amount of effort on your part, you will experience no real problems in most places. And you will not be held to exactly the same standard to which they hold themselves. But if something is going to offend you so terribly that you will not enjoy being there, avoid the area. You are not going to singlehandedly change traditions that have existed for hundreds of years.

Abide by all local laws. The penalty for possession of illegal drugs in some of the Far Eastern countries is death (Figure 22-2). Don't assume you will be protected because you are an American citizen. Recently an American teenager was flogged in Singapore for vandalizing cars. The embassy and American opinion could do nothing to prevent it. When you are in a foreign country, you are subject to their laws. Ignorance is no excuse. In most cases the laws do not differ significantly from those in the United States or Europe, but often the penalties are far more severe. For this reason, do not carry pornography or drugs (other than those in the medical kit), and be sure to declare weapons if you choose to have them aboard.

When you are in a new culture, approach everything with respect. Watch and learn how people do things. To avoid a faux pas, follow the leader and do as the others do. When you form your own conclusions about how the culture functions, as you inevitably will, share them only if asked—and then only if the person asking really wants to know.

While customs vary tremendously from place to place, some general protocols exist that will keep you out of trouble. Beyond that, there are three areas along the trade wind route where customs have the largest impact on voyagers and where a little knowledge helps to manage the situation: the kava ceremony in the South Pacific, Moslem cultures around the Red Sea, and boat boys in the Caribbean.

General protocols

In most cultures, the only unforgivable breaches concern religion or sacred places. Profane behavior in a holy place or inappropriate dress for women should

Figure 22-2. A sign like this must be taken seriously.

be avoided at all costs. On the other hand, issues of decorum—how you sit, how you greet people, how you eat your food—are viewed much less seriously. A failure in these areas is considered a breach of etiquette, which is easily forgiven. Before you get to your destination, determine which is which from guidebooks and other voyagers.

A few standard themes will help you get your bearings and avoid offending anyone:

■ *Paying respects.* In most remote island villages, a chief and several older men run things. By the time you have set your anchor, someone will probably come out and greet you. You should ask to be taken to the chief to pay your respects. In the western Pacific, the kava ceremony described in the next section formalizes this custom and offers you a framework of behavior. Elsewhere, you are not obligated to bring something as a gift. But you should seek out the village leaders and ask their permission to stay in their harbor and share in the village activities.

■ *Women's attire.* In most of the world, women are still expected to dress conservatively. Throughout the Pacific, women should be covered from shoulder to ankle. Outside of resort areas, bikinis, swimsuits, and tank tops are definitely not appropriate attire. In large towns or port cities, women wear long shorts and short-sleeved shirts. In small villages, women should dress as the local women do—in the one-piece pareu or lava-lava that is wrapped around the body and tied at the shoulder.

■ *Sunday behavior.* Throughout most of the Christian and Moslem world, Sunday is devoted to religion and prayer. Secular activities are frowned upon. In most places, you will not be able to shop or eat out. Even working on the boat is considered discourteous if done in full view of a small village where you are a guest. Drinking alcohol on Sunday is strictly forbidden in many cultures.

■ *Ownership.* On most islands in both the Caribbean and the South Pacific, everything is owned, either by the village itself or by individuals—every tree, every plant, every animal. Do not take anything without asking, whether it is a coconut, some fruit, or fish from a lagoon. We decry theft from our boats, then thoughtlessly

steal food from the local people. Take the time to ask, and you will generally be given more than you could possibly want.

■ *Hats and sunglasses.* Sunglasses inhibit communication, as anyone knows who has tried to carry on an emotional conversation with someone wearing them. Especially in cultures where they are uncommon, as on most remote islands, sunglasses can easily make you seem unapproachable and alien. The head is sacred in much of Polynesian culture, and anything that hides the head is viewed as an effort to conceal a person's character. Leave your hats and sunglasses aboard when going into a village until you know that the people there will not be offended.

Privacy is an area where, to a certain extent, a double standard applies. On many islands, to show up uninvited and start wandering around a small village without paying your respects to the local chief and being properly accepted is considered exceedingly rude—akin to wandering through suburban backyards and peering into windows. In most cases, villages consist of large extended families who view their village and the area around it as their private compound. They expect you to respect the privacy of that compound until you have been invited to share it, which you always will be if you approach the people respectfully and formally.

On the other hand, their curiosity about you and your boat will often blind them to the fact that you might like some privacy as well. Once you are accepted as part of the village, you truly become part of the family. You can expect "neighbors" to drop in on you at all hours of the day and night. They will be eager to step aboard and take a look at your home, just as you have looked at theirs. When we were anchored off a Fijian village where we had gone through the kava ceremony, we would be woken at dawn as the first fishing boat bumped into our hull and our first guests clambered aboard before we could even get dressed. For most of the rest of the day, we would be ashore with our hosts, walking to kassava plantations, smoking fish, weaving mats, and sharing meals. The minute we returned to the boat and collapsed with a sigh, another bump on the hull would alert us that our next set of guests had arrived. While you are anchored off a small village, you are the local entertainment and the center of attention. Be prepared and enjoy it. These memories will be some of the most wonderful souvenirs you take home.

Even in larger harbors, offshore boats arouse great interest. If you are not anchored off, there are times when you will feel like you are living in a fish bowl. On tiny Rodrigues Island in the southern Indian Ocean, groups of people stood on the quay to which we were tied and watched us while we went about our normal activities aboard. On their lunch hour, children would come from school and smile shyly at us. After work, men would gather and talk quietly about the boats in the harbor. In these cases, the people wear the reserve of the larger town and small city. Unless you approach them, they will leave you to your tasks. But if you encourage a dialogue or are open to questions, you can quickly break down that reserve and make lasting friends.

The kava ceremony

Throughout the western Pacific, the kava ceremony is an honored tradition that provides a beautiful initiation into the local culture. In parts of Tonga, most of Fiji, all of Vanuatu, and parts of the Solomon Islands, you will be required to present *yaqona* (pronounced yang-gona) to the village chief. These bundles of dried twigs are the root of a plant which is a member of the pepper family. When ground into a powder and combined with water, it forms a drink called *kava,* which is mildly euphoric. Some cruisers are insulted or intimidated by this requirement. Others are morally opposed to pro-

A day in the life—Ha'apai group, Tonga

After leaving Vava'u in Tonga, we arrived in the Ha'apai after an overnight sail. Our first impressions were recorded in my journal:

"The main town in this island group, Pangai, feels large and affluent. Laid out on a grid, it stretches four or five miles along the midsection of Lifuka Island and covers much of its width. Churches grace every other street—many new and beautifully built. In the tourist office, I signed the guest book as one of about a dozen visitors in August from all over the world.

"Next we headed to the police station and the post office for customs. They have just opened the customs office here, and they were quite delighted to have something to do. The customs men wanted to see the boat, so we drove with them back to the harbor. They were a bit put off when they saw our dinghy—it was quite a sight to see two ample Polynesians in the dinghy with Evans rowing. The man in the bow was even larger than the normal corpulent Tongan chief. Silky *was so bow down she would have been shipping water if there had even been a small chop.*

"Once on board, Evans said that they didn't really know what to do. They poked around the boat and talked for an hour or so. Then Evans rowed them back ashore. Cheerful good-byes, and we are set until we check out for Fiji.

"A walk through town revealed even more traditional clothing than in Neiafu. Groups of children followed us from store to store, gathering around the door to see what we were purchasing, then scattering when we returned to the street. 'Palangai, palangai' (white person) whispered down the street in front of us. Store owners dropped everything when we entered and hovered nervously while we wandered around. They were thrilled when we bought something, and we could hear the children calling out our purchases to the adults in the street. A chorus of 'oohs' and 'ahhs' greeted each pronouncement. The response to our presence here made the Vava'u Tongans seem nonchalant by comparison.

"Outside of town, Maria (age 10 or 12) introduced herself and walked with us for some time. Her English was excellent. Her uncle lives in New Zealand, and she dreams of visiting America someday. She wanted to know what church we went to, and she told us we would be welcome to worship with them on Sunday. After leaving Maria, we walked to an "ancient" fortress (1800s) that was built by the Ha'apai ruler who opposed the king who finally united Tonga. The sign at the site described moats and 6-foot-high walls with 18-foot bases, all surrounding an inner fortress and burial mounds. We read the sign and saw—nothing! Palm trees and brush, a clearing with a pedestal for a plaque (but no plaque), some plantings. That was all. I felt like the boy who cried 'The Emperor has no clothes!'"

viding a form of drug in "payment" for visiting a village. In fact, we found this practice to be a unique cultural experience that allowed us insight into Fijian village traditions that extend to the era before the coming of the Europeans.

In Polynesian culture, the village communally "owns" not just the land in and around it, but also the air above it, the sea and reef that protect it, and all the fish, animals, and plants within that space. In presenting the yaqona, the visitor is asking to become a temporary member of the village—to be allowed to fish, to anchor, to take water, to harvest coconuts. The visitor is also requesting the chief's protection—of vital importance when this culture practiced cannibalism. To ask permission to stay near the village, the visitor places the yaqona at the feet of the chief. If the chief picks up the gift, he has accepted total responsibility for the visitors' well-being and the visitor has become part of the village. If cruisers are lucky, they will be asked to participate in the ceremonial drinking of kava made from their yaqona. What follows describes a ceremony I attended in one of the more remote Fijian islands. With slight variations, this ceremony is practiced across the western Pacific.

For the ceremony, I wore a long skirt, sandals, and a long-sleeved shirt. Once ashore, we looked for the communal hut or *bure* where the kava ceremony is held almost every evening in most Fijian villages. Outside the communal bure, a young, shirtless man with muscles of iron was pounding the yaqona root in a metal bowl. Standing tall with arms straight in front of him, veins etched against his ebony skin oiled by sweat, he raised the heavy metal rod and let it fall down on the yaqona. Then he would lift it in such a way that it hit the side of the bowl with a metallic ring, like a gong, until it reached the top of the arc and was dropped again. Thump, ring, lift; thump, ring, lift: He tirelessly pounded the yaqona into a fine powder while the familiar sounds called the men of the village to kava.

The communal bure was a wooden rectangular shed some 20 feet wide and 40 feet long. As we entered, we took off our sandals and added them to the pile of footwear at the door. The room was divided into two parts by the presence of a ceremonial mat on the floor. We were directed to sit along the edge of the mat, a place of honor. The village elders, most of them wrinkled and toothless, sat cross-legged along the three sides of the mat that bordered the walls of the building. Halfway along the fourth side of the mat, exactly in the center of the floor, sat the carved kava bowl. About 3 feet in diameter, it stood on its four ornate legs like an old-fashioned bathtub.

In the other half of the bure, the men of the village sat in ragged rows facing the center of the room. Perhaps 30 men were already gathered when we entered. Then another dozen men sauntered in and sat down until the only open space in the room was the expanse of mat in front of the kava bowl. Last came two of the village women. The female guest of honor was not to be embarrassed by being the only woman in the room.

The crowd settled, and the chief started a long, sing-song chant in Fijian. This was punctuated by the crowd's response of "Naka" (roughly translated as "thanks") every minute or so and accompanied by a resonating, hollow-handed clapping. In the center of the room, the yaqona pounder wrapped the powdered root in a piece of cotton cloth, poured water into the kava bowl, and started swirling the cloth through the water in rhythm with the chanting. As the water was filtered through the root, it turned the color of a mud puddle during a hard rainstorm.

Suddenly, silence. Everyone waited. After what must have been the appropriate interval, the man at the bowl started a wailing moan over the liquid that ended in a final gesture of pushing the kava away and toward the chief—his body arched forward only a few inches off the mat, his arms outstretched in front of him, his fingers lightly brushing the bowl. It was a proud gesture of supplication, of entreaty, from which he was released by a resounding "Ho!" first from the Chief and then the rest of the villagers.

The man now took a coconut shell bowl and filled it to the brim with the brown liquid. He carried it to the chief and sat cross-legged in front of him. The chief clapped once, the same hollow-handed clap as before. Then he reached out and took the shell, and he raised it and drained it in one fluid motion while the cup-bearer clapped rhythmically. Once finished, everyone exclaimed "Ho!" as the chief handed the empty shell back. Finally the chief clapped three times more.

After the elders had each been served individually, the cup bearer presented a shell to me. I clapped once and raised it to my lips. The fluid felt gritty and tasted like clay. Almost immediately I noticed a tingling turning to numbness in my mouth and a buzzing somewhere in the back of my head.

Once the honored guests seated around the mat had been served, several men got up and began rapidly serving the rest of the people in the room. After everyone had drunk, another round of chanting punctuated by "Naka" and "Ho" began. Each of the elders in turn welcomed us to the village and offered us all that the village possessed. They spoke in Fijian, but one of the men patiently whispered into my ear the gist of what they were saying. We gave a small speech of thanks at the conclusion, and the kava was passed around again, the same way it was passed the first time.

By this point, our heads were buzzing and the sun was setting. We gave another speech of thanks and then we went around and shook every hand in the room. As we stepped back into our sandals by the door, the kava was making the rounds one more time. We slipped out of the bure, followed by the two village women who were no longer welcome.

As we returned to the boat, I was filled with a sense of well-being that was not entirely due to the kava. We had witnessed a ceremony kept alive by these people despite the protestations of missionaries and the guns of conquerors. We had been made welcome and honored, just as the Fijians had honored their most respected enemies and their most cherished friends for hundreds of years. We had been adopted by a community. I wished that our lives could be as simple in our own country.

Moslem cultures

While many of the islands we visited in the Indian Ocean had large Moslem populations, none of them were fundamentalist in their practices. We never saw women dressed in the chador, the full black gowns with eye slits, and did not travel in areas where alcohol was not sold because it violated Moslem law. But if you travel up the Red Sea, you will encounter such practices in the countries from Aden to Egypt. Our friends who have done the trip were rarely made to feel uncomfortable about their own behavior, so long as the women aboard dressed conservatively and everyone made an effort not to overtly break any of the local traditions. However, they often felt ambivalent about seeing how

women were treated—something they knew they could do nothing to change.

If traveling through this area, take the following tips from our friends who have been there:

- **Dress conservatively.** For women, this means loose, opaque clothes in conservative colors with a hat or a shawl to cover their hair. In some countries, mid-calf skirts are acceptable; in others, skirts should go all the way to the ground. In some places like Oman, the captain will be informed as to what women should wear, and women will not make it past the military check point dressed improperly. In other places, nothing will be said and there is no checkpoint—but you must still honor the Moslem customs. Men should wear long pants. Shorts are not acceptable in most countries.

- **Women should avoid traveling alone.** Wherever possible, travel with your partner. Even if you are not married, wearing an inexpensive wedding ring will save explanations. If you must travel alone, avoid eye contact with men. Where possible, sit with other women.

- **Men should never touch an Arab woman.** Men also need to be conservative, avoid looking at the Arab women, and never touch them. Even a gesture as innocent as putting a hand on a woman's arm to help her into a car is considered an insult.

- **Women should never touch men.** One woman we know of touched a man when she tried to stop a Suez Canal pilot from boarding their boat. She almost ended up in jail.

- **Respect Ramadan.** For one month a year, the Moslem world celebrates Ramadan, when they do not eat, drink, or smoke between sunrise and sunset. If traveling in these countries at this time, respect the local custom by refraining from eating, drinking, or smoking in public during the day.

- **Don't interfere with Moslems at prayer.** Moslems are required to pray five times a day while kneeling on a prayer mat facing Mecca. Do not photograph or walk in front of a Moslem at prayer.

- **Try to be sympathetic with those asking for alms.** Almsgiving is one of the duties of a good

Moslem. The beggars serve a respected function in the society. Give if you feel like it. Otherwise learn the words for "I have no money" and walk away.

Finally, remember that both pork and alcohol are forbidden to Moslems. Do not offend them by indulging in either, except in privacy.

The Caribbean boat boys

Some cruisers are troubled by the boat boys who ply their trade in the Windward Islands of the Caribbean from St. Lucia south through the Grenadines (Figure 22-3). There, boys in local boats offer to provide a variety of services to sailors for a fee—from tying a stern line to a palm tree to selling fish and coconuts. The offense comes from the implicit understanding that you cannot enter some harbors without enlisting a boat boy's aid: in essence, paying to be allowed to drop your anchor. We heard other cruisers refer to this as black-

mail and tell stories of stern lines cut in the night if the boat boys were not paid.

In our experience, the boat boys provided a window into the real culture of the Caribbean, and the services they offered were always useful and often ingenious. In Bequia and Tobago Cays, boat boys delivered hot bread and newspapers to us first thing in the morning. In St. Lucia near the mighty Pitons, the magnificent twin peaks that drop straight into the sea, boat boys guided us to a local waterfall where we showered with a group of village women who were entranced by our shampoo (Figure 22-4). One young man scaled a tree to get us the perfect coconut and then showed us how to open it with our windlass handle, a skill we used throughout the rest of our voyage (Figure 22-5). They helped us tie stern-to and took it upon themselves to guard our boat and our dinghy, with no additional money changing hands. To secure a line to a palm tree, they charged us a dollar (2 or 3 Eastern Caribbean dollars or EC, which is

Figure 22-3. Boat boys ply their trade in Marigot Bay, St. Lucia.

Figure 22-4. Communal showering in a waterfall near the Pitons on St. Lucia

the local currency). To take us to a waterfall, they charged up to 10 dollars. Their prices never seemed out of line with the service rendered, and we often ended up seeing aspects of the local area and culture that we never would have been privy to on our own.

The boat boys can be quite persistent. At times, the parade of people eager to do you some small service can become annoying if you are trying to enjoy an anchorage in peace. We learned to pick one person to be our assistant from among the dozen waiting as we approached an anchorage. Once tied up ashore, we would deal only with him for what we needed. If others came offering services, we said that so-and-so was already taking care of us, and that would be the end of the discussion. Within an hour or so, everyone in the area seemed to know that we were "taken care of" and our boat boy had assumed a proprietary interest in making sure that we were not disturbed. We would still be approached by people selling local handicrafts, but we al-

ways enjoyed seeing what they had to offer. We learned to bargain well, since the quality and prices varied tremendously.

Given the apparent disparity between the wealth of cruisers and the poverty of local villages, paying money for services fairly rendered seemed a small thing to us. By treating the boat boys fairly and with respect, we were treated fairly in return. Those who approach with hostility won't have their attitude improved by their interactions with these eager entrepreneurs.

Saying "thank you"

Throughout your travels, you will be the recipient of all types of hospitality. People will share their food, their homes, their families, and their lives. You will want to share with them in return, and you will often want to leave behind a small memento. In the communal cultures of many islands, tradition requires that they must feed and shelter a stranger who has been accepted into the village, even at the expense of their own needs. Many of these cultures are based on gift economies, where giving is the measure of one's wealth, and where gifts must be reciprocated or the pride and power of the village is diminished. In these cultures, we needed to find a balance, giving an appropriate gift that reflected the value of what we had received. We did not want to leave the village the poorer for our visit, nor did we want to obligate the village by giving something too extravagant.

For brief encounters with people who had shown us some small kindness, we carried several dozen photos of *Silk* with our name and address on the back. For trading or more substantial gifts, we carried an assortment of fishing lures, lines, hooks, and sinkers. We also carried extra corned beef and sugar, always welcome as gifts in remote villages. Friends we knew carried tee-shirts with their boat name on them, base-

ball caps, and cigarettes. We disagreed in principle with handing out cigarettes, but they are still a valued commodity throughout the world. If we asked to take someone's picture and they agreed, we would always try to send them a copy from the next major port; many villagers have never seen a photo of themselves. But don't make a promise to mail a photo lightly. The villagers will be greatly disappointed if you do not follow through and will be less likely to allow others to take photos.

When the hospitality was more extensive—such as times when we had been invited into somebody's house to share their lives for several days—we reciprocated in a number of ways. In some cases, we invited the family aboard our boat for dinner, for what seemed like basic food for us was always exotic and special to them. Just being able to eat on the boat and see how we really lived in our floating home was a thrill for most people we met. Taking a family or a group of children sail-

Photo by Leigh Leonard

Figure 22-5. Learning coconut etiquette from one of the boat boys

ing for a few hours or a day is both the easiest and the most treasured gift you can give someone who has shared much with you.

The medical kit can also be a way of saying "thank you." You can provide a unique service to the village by giving antibiotic ointment to someone with an infected cut or offering some cortisone cream to someone suffering from an itchy rash. While you have to be very careful playing doctor, most of the ailments you will see in island villages are minor and easily treated, and the relief to your new friends is tremendous.

Several times, we had spent a great deal of time with a family and felt we needed to give them something special. But we didn't know what was appropriate. We asked someone else in the village for advice. No one ever took offense at this, for they understand the need to give after having received. From those experiences, we learned that gaily colored pieces of material for making clothing were always welcome. News travels remarkably quickly through the coconut telegraph, and the recipient often knew what they were going to receive before we knew what we were going to give! Sending a postcard or letter from a few ports further along offers your friends a firsthand glimpse of another place, something they might never get any other way.

SIGHTSEEING

After the intensity of the one-on-one interactions in small islands, we enjoyed playing tourist for a few days or a week in more developed countries. The options are much the same for sightseeing the world over. Areas that cater to tourists offer van or bus tours, train rides, rental cars, backpacking trips, and so on. Talk to the local tour operators and travel agencies once you have arrived at your destination to learn about your range of options.

We preferred heading off on our own rather than taking a tour or going to the typical sights. We were always looking for ways to travel around the country that allowed us to interact with the people who lived there. The following solutions worked in many different places:

■ *Local buses.* On more developed islands, most local people rely on buses to get from place to place. On Faial in the Azores, a single bus circled the island several

Additional resources

There are many excellent guides to the areas that you are likely to visit on a trade wind circumnavigation. However, two unusual books are worth mentioning. *South Pacific Handbook* by David Stanley (Moon Publications, Inc., 1996) provides a comprehensive introduction to the Pacific islands meant for backpackers and budget tourists. It offers a wealth of information on local cultures and customs that will prepare you for getting the most from your sojourn on each island.

The second guide is more offbeat. *The World's Most Dangerous Places* by Robert Young Pelton, Coskun Aral, and Wink Dulles (Fielding Worldwide, 1997) is half adventure narrative and half traditional guidebook. While you can safely ignore the section on land mines, the book contains valuable information on areas that are politically unstable. Some of the countries covered that you might actually visit include Brazil, Colombia, Egypt, El Salvador, Eritrea, Ethiopia, Haiti, Israel, Mexico, the Philippines, Sri Lanka, Sudan, and Turkey. For each area, the author analyzes the political situation and its history, discusses local dangers and ways to avoid them, and provides a host of more mundane information ranging from medical risks to the location of the American embassy. Enjoy the hype, but cull the valuable information that may be more useful to voyagers than to just about anyone else—except, perhaps, Soldiers of Fortune.

times a day. On Réunion Island in the southern Indian Ocean, a dozen different buses traveled different routes and ended up in different places. These local buses became our favorite way to see the interior of an island: They traveled to all the villages and markets; were filled with local people who were often willing to act as informal tour guides; gave us a real flavor of how the island functioned; and were inexpensive.

■ *Bicycles.* On islands where there are roads and tourists of any sort, we could often rent bicycles and spend a lovely day pedaling sedately along quiet roads. Our favorite bike outing was on Bora Bora, where we rented bicycles from the Hotel Bora Bora and rode all the way around the island in about six hours.

■ *Car or motorcycle.* We purchased a car in New Zealand and used it to tour most of the North Island. In New Zealand, used cars cost very little, and buying and selling them is straightforward. Buying a car gave us complete freedom in sightseeing and errands and ended up costing far less than any alternative. Friends of ours purchased camper vans in Australia and toured that country during the cyclone season. Others purchased motorcycles in Europe and toured the continent for several months.

■ *Trains.* Train travel became one of our favorite modes of transport, second only to local buses. Some train trips take a day. Many use steam-driven engines to go to a nearby tourist area. A train goes into the mountains and to an old mining town from Cairns, Australia; from Knysna, South Africa, one goes to an old logging town. These were often touristy, but fun. Australia, Europe, and South Africa have extensive railroad systems for long-distance travel. This can be an economical way to travel that gives you the opportunity to meet local people and the time to really talk to them.

■ *Backpacking tours.* If we did decide that the best way to visit an area was to take a tour, we found that the tours aimed at backpackers were often the least expensive and the most fun. We wanted to see a great deal in South Africa, but we did not have the time to buy a car or a safe place to leave the boat for an extended period. So we selected a tour that used a van pulling a trailer that carried tents and sleeping bags. Eight people were on the tour. Each night we stayed at a campground, pitched a tent, made a fire, and cooked our meal. We ended up seeing a large part of the country over the course of 10 days for about $350 each. We came across backpacking tour operators in Australia and New Zealand as well.

When heading off for several days or longer, we had to decide how best to secure the boat. Everyone we knew struggled with this at one time or another. Most settled on one of the handful of standard solutions that follow.

A few of our friends hauled their boats and left them on the hard for all or part of cyclone season. They bought a car or a small camper van and set off to see the coun-try. One couple hauled their boat in Australia for three cyclone seasons in a row, touring New Zealand the first year, Australia the second, and Indonesia and Southeast Asia the third.

This solution requires generous amounts of money and time. We lacked both, so we generally found a secure marina where we could leave the boat and asked someone on another boat nearby to check her once in awhile. We didn't like leaving the boat where there was no real marina, particularly where boats were rafted three or four deep off a breakwall or a dock. In these situations, voyagers banded together to stagger their sightseeing, leaving several people behind to look after the boats. That didn't necessarily stop us from worrying, but nothing serious ever happened to *Silk* while we were gone.

In some areas, like Antigua or Tortola in the Caribbean, people leave their boats for several weeks or months while they return home to the States. If they do not have the boat hauled, they often hire someone to check the boat daily and run the engine. Make sure to get references for would-be caretakers. We heard several sad stories from distraught owners whose boats had been ignored or trashed in their absence. Generally those involved were not other cruisers; they were backpackers looking for crew positions or locals known in the community to be unreliable.

ENTERTAINING

You will want to share your new life with close friends and family. But when traveling by sailboat, the timetable for meeting in an exotic location can be easily upset. Then, both you and your visitors can be in a difficult situation. We heard too many stories about voyagers heading off to sea when they would not otherwise have done so to meet a schedule that had been arranged months in advance. Bad weather, broken gear, and an unhappy crew in no mood to entertain guests can be the unfortunate result.

One sensible rule for managing this problem is to allow guests to pick the place or the date, but not both. This allows you enough flexibility to determine where you are going to be when and decide what the best schedule will be for your rendezvous with your guests.

We approached the problem a bit differently. We invited people to join us when we reached an area where we were going to stay for an extended period. We had guests visit when we were in the Azores for six weeks, in New Zealand for six months, and in the Caribbean for four or five months. We would let them know as soon as we had arrived, and then they could make their own arrangements for any time over the next several weeks or months. We specified the time frame and the islands we could reach with a few days of sailing and let them decide the rest. We never left on a long passage knowing we had to reach a destination by a certain time to meet up with someone.

Given the limited space on offshore boats and the normal wardrobe that most Americans bring on vaca- tion, be explicit about what your guests will actually need and how much they can stow. For those who aren't sailors, tell them to bring only soft-sided luggage. Suggest they pack lots of sun block, cool clothes, good sunglasses, and hats. When they come aboard, give them a thorough introduction to the boat, including a demonstration on how to use the head, basic safety and emergency procedures, and any onboard rules with re- gard to smoking or other personal habits.

Once the introductions are over, sit back and enjoy your guests' wonder at your world and your skills. Through their eyes you will see an accomplished offshore voyager—an image that just might come as a surprise until you realize that it has been well and truly earned.

CHAPTER 23

KEEPING THE FAITH

Voyaging customs ■ *Voyaging etiquette* ■ *Anchoring* ■ *Rafting up* ■ *Coming aboard* ■ *Sea superstitions*
■ *Voyaging spirit*

A special camaraderie exists among those who ply the sea. This spirit is based on an understanding of our insignificance in the face of the great natural forces that still dominate life far from human habitation. When sailing the seemingly endless stretches of the world's oceans, we come to a new understanding of humankind's relationship to nature, and thus our relationship to each other. We share this camaraderie with those in whose wakes we follow—men and women who have tested themselves against the indifference of nature. We share it with other sailors, fishermen, and mariners who consider the sea their home. Those who share this bond will assist anyone at sea who is in trouble, and in turn they will never request assistance except in a life-threatening situation. Those of us who choose to venture offshore and test ourselves must be willing to keep that faith and be held to that standard. Otherwise, the time will come when we will be prohibited from heading off to sea freely. If that ever comes to pass, the magic of sailing around the world will be diluted: Spiritually, the world will be a poorer place.

Over time, keeping the faith has expanded to include other aspects of the way we interact with one another and with the cultures we visit. The Seven Seas Cruising Association promotes a tread-lightly attitude in their "clean wake" philosophy—the idea that we should leave nothing in our wakes that will not benefit those who follow. That includes everything from garbage to ill-will in a village. Every voyager should ascribe to this tenet. The hospitality with which we are greeted as we travel from place to place is both fragile and priceless. The thoughtless actions of the crew of one yacht can destroy the spirit of the sea. Just as we take responsibility for our

lives when we head offshore, we must take responsibility for our actions when we return.

Those of us who sail the world in small boats are a community. Like any community, we need shared values and rites of passage to reinforce our unity. Many of the mores of the community come directly or indirectly from the age-old concept of helping other mariners. In today's more crowded world, new standards have arisen to reinforce the need for courtesy in anchorages and marinas. When we return and once again live a shore-based life, the voyaging spirit returns with us. It is difficult, but we can bring some of the lessons from the sea back with us and use them to alter the way we interact with the world ashore.

VOYAGING CUSTOMS

One of the greatest joys of becoming a competent sailor lies in passing along customs, traditions, and assistance to those who follow.

Rendering assistance is the glue that holds the cruising community together. Whether the problem is an emergency at sea or a broken bilge pump, people who sail the ocean in small boats help one another. In any other community, this basic tenet would be abused. But it is counterbalanced by the fierce self-sufficiency of voyagers. The voyaging community's greatest asset is the stock of good will and generosity that, if it is to continue, must be contributed to by one and all. Everyone who has sailed around the world started out as a novice and received information, advice, encouragement, and physical assistance somewhere along the line. If that is not passed on in the same spirit of generosity and good will, then eventually the community will lose its traditions and values and will not renew itself.

The rites of passage start with christening the boat. This is supposed to take place at the vessel's launching, but it should also be done if the vessel is renamed (see sidebar, "Sea superstitions"). At launching, the christening is accompanied by the breaking of a bottle of champagne on the bow. Traditionally, a woman, most often the owner's wife, breaks the bottle. Given the relative strength of champagne bottles and the delicacy of fiberglass finish, scoring the bottle so it breaks easily is a wise precaution!

The bottle breaking is preceded by a speech describing why the boat's name was chosen, ending with, "I hereby christen this yacht _____." To rename a boat that is already in the water, the speech-making is accompanied not by breaking the bottle but rather by opening it and pouring some on the boat, some into the sea, and some into the owner's mouth. Then the bottle is shared with guests. Some people claim that's all you need to do to be official, but for purists a renaming can occur only after a denaming.

In a denaming ceremony, libations are offered to King Neptune, who is asked to forgive the sins the vessel has committed and the debts it has incurred. After four to eight days when King Neptune has everything in order, the renaming can proceed as above.

Other rites of passage celebrate the major landmarks on the sailor's journey. Crossing the equator has traditionally been celebrated by a baptism of the uninitiated carried out by Neptune (or Poseidon, if you prefer). Neptune is represented by a crewmember aboard who has previously crossed the line. In the standard celebration, Neptune appears on deck clothed in robes, wearing a long beard, and carrying a trident just as you are crossing the equator. Each uninitiated crewmember is forced to pay homage by offering the god of the sea various gifts and services. When Neptune is satisfied, the crewmember is "baptized," which might mean having a bucket dumped over his or her head, being immersed in a tub of water, or even (if you are becalmed) being shoved overboard.

When completing a circumnavigation, there are two major landmarks: crossing your outbound track and returning to your home port. In both cases, the standard celebration is similar to the christening, where a bottle of champagne is poured on the boat to celebrate her voyage, into the sea to thank the sea gods for a safe journey, and down the crew so that they can make merry. The same custom is often used for rounding one of the Great Capes, as the sea gods there are particularly jealous and require homage to forestall their fury.

Guest books have long been a tradition aboard, and many boats carry fancy, bound volumes. Visitors and friends are asked to complete a page, and the book serves as a record of the voyage and a keepsake for memories. Besides having a book aboard your own boat, be prepared to fill them out. The creativity and ingenuity you will find in most guest books will inspire you to come up with something unique for your own boat. Before you leave you may want to have business cards made up with your boat name and mailing address (and your call sign, if you are a Ham operator). These often form the centerpiece of a guest book entry, augmented by photos, drawings, maps, verse, and stories.

Guest books are also kept by those ashore who regularly interact with offshore boats and their crews. Village chiefs, hotel proprietors, and chandlery owners kept their own books and asked us to fill them out. Be prepared to do justice to your vessel and your trip in the records you leave behind.

VOYAGING ETIQUETTE

As the number of boats has increased in marinas and anchorages around the world, voyaging customs have been augmented by guidelines for common situations, such as anchoring, rafting up to other boats along a wall or wharf, and boarding someone else's boat. Most of these combine common sense and courtesy. We learned them as we went along, and sometimes we learned by violating them. Occasionally, someone got angry. More often, an experienced voyager took us aside and suggested a different approach. In that spirit, I share these thoughts with you—to use and to pass on to others who need to know.

Anchoring

When entering an anchorage or a marina, do so at a dead slow speed. Not only will this keep things under control, but you will minimize your wake and the effect you have on the boats already there. If you are not bored, then you are going too fast. As you select your spot, bear in mind that he or she who anchors first has rights. If you set your anchor and people on another boat are uncomfortable with your position, they have the right to ask you to move. If later you bump into them (or vice versa) and neither of you has dragged, you are the one who must reset your anchor. If you bump because one of you has dragged, whoever drags gets to reset their anchor since they have to do so anyway.

An empty mooring buoy should be given rights as if there were a boat on it, for a boat may return and you will have to move. With the proliferation of mooring buoys in some anchorages, it can be impossible to anchor without fouling one. The best you can do is to try to stay clear, and then deal with it if someone arrives to claim a buoy that your boat has just swung over. Don't pick up private mooring buoys without permission. Not only is this discourteous, but you have no way of knowing how the buoy is secured and for what size boat it is intended. Why take an unnecessary risk when you have perfectly good ground tackle aboard? If someone invites you to pick up their buoy, no true sailor will think you rude for asking about the buoy's construction and the date it was last maintained.

When anchoring, you want to make sure your boat is safe and you won't interfere with anyone else or cause them to interfere with you. If no one around you is using stern anchors or a second anchor off the bow, don't set one on your boat. If you do, your boat will not swing with the others. Eventually, something is going to go "clunk."

Unlike coastal sailing, offshore sailors do not generally raft up at anchor. This reflects most skippers' desire to set the anchor themselves if they are to get a good night's sleep. It also reflects a need for privacy. Most voyagers consider their deck and cockpit an extension of their private living space to be used for activities (like showering in the nude) for which they would prefer not to have a next-door neighbor.

If you have to run an engine or a generator at anchor, try to do so when you are least likely to disturb others. Doing so in the middle of the day is certainly better than early in the morning or late at night. As discussed in Chapter 6, when going ashore tie your dinghy on a long painter so others can reach the dock with their dinghies.

If you have to undo someone's painter to get to yours, make sure to redo it properly on the same cleat.

Rafting up

In European harbors, it is quite common to raft up to other boats along a breakwall or a fishing dock. Living cheek by jowl with your neighbors for an extended period of time requires a good deal of patience and courtesy.

That starts when you enter the harbor and decide where you want to raft up. The boat coming alongside is obligated to provide both fenders and lines. As you approach the boat you want to tie up to, ask permission if the owners are aboard. This should never be refused, and the owners should offer to assist you. If no one is aboard, go ahead and tie up.

If someone is assisting you, pass over a short length of line that the other person will make fast at the bitter end. You then pull the slack back aboard your own boat and cleat it off. This leaves the coil of line on your decks, not on your neighbor's. If things get a bit crazy because quarters are tight and you are shorthanded, ask the other person to take up the slack and cleat the line down and say you will clean it up once you get settled. As part of getting settled, make sure the topsides of both boats are well protected by fenders and the spreaders are staggered so as not to cause damage if the boats are rolled by a wake. Always take your own lines ashore from the bow and stern. These lines should be tight enough to take most of your boat's weight. As with lines tied to another boat, keep the extra aboard your boat rather than leaving it on the wharf.

The first time you go ashore, ask permission to cross each boat if the owners are present. Carry your shoes and cross quietly in front of the mast over the foredeck. Never cross through someone's cockpit. Again, if you have to run a generator or engine, pick your time. Never run your engine or generator at meal times, at the British tea time (late afternoon), or at cocktail hour.

Coming aboard

If you have been invited aboard another boat, say for cocktails at six o'clock, never go empty handed. Everyone brings something, whether it's dried bananas or a bottle of rum. Never board without permission, even if you have been invited. Knock on the hull or hail using the boat name as in "Hello aboard *Sea Spirit!*" When the owner emerges, ask permission to come aboard. Take your shoes off, unless the owner says there is no need to do so. When the party gets under way, remember not to get too loud—sound carries remarkably well over water. Loud music is considered discourteous after sundown.

Modern sailors have created and sustained their own set of superstitions, and you will encounter them when you go voyaging. Those who make a stop at the Azores island group will discover the importance of painting their boat's logo on the sea wall at Horta on Faial. We saw artwork left by boats that had passed that way in the 1950s and 1960s, including one of the Hiscocks' Wanderers. Not putting your logo on the wall was supposed to result in unnamed disasters. The only person we knew who did not follow the tradition was dismasted within two months. Good enough for me!

VOYAGING SPIRIT

Only when you return home do you find out how much you have really changed. Most voyagers find the transition back to shore much more difficult than the transition to voyaging. Life aboard is so full of color, intensity, and emotion that life ashore feels like a pale imitation.

Sea superstitions

Sailors are a superstitious lot—perhaps because after a certain point, luck plays such a large role in a boat's fate. There are a host of old superstitions, a surprising number of which are still believed by modern mariners. If you are the superstitious type, then take heed of the following age-old beliefs.

■ *Changing boat names.* Once a boat has been christened, it is supposed to be bad luck to change the name. We did change *Silk's* name, but the builder assured us that in Irish tradition this was not bad luck if the first letter of the name was retained and the boat was rechristened with generous libations for the sea gods.

■ *Leaving on Friday.* No self-respecting, superstitious sailor will ever set off on a passage on a Friday. A voyage begun just before the weekend is always supposed to end in disaster. I asked our British friends where this tradition came from, and the consensus seemed to be that the seamen resented leaving their sweethearts just before they might have some shore leave. So they deemed Friday—subconsciously or otherwise—an unlucky day to depart.

■ *Whistling for wind.* The seamen of the old British Admiralty believed that if you were becalmed, whistling would summon wind. They also believed that it was foolhardy to engage in this behavior, for the result was always supposed to be a gale or worse.

■ *No rabbits aboard.* The French have an absolute phobia about rabbits aboard boats, believing it the worst of bad luck. I asked several French sailors why this was so and got many different answers. The most likely answer seemed to be that the rabbits ate the wood of the ships, which could cause a boat to sink. But another answer offered by a charming Frenchman could be correct: The rabbits' passionate breeding behavior drove French sailors mad with desire for the women they had left behind.

■ *Naming your destination.* Respect for the sea and for the unforeseen combined with a good dose of humility make some sailors uncomfortable naming their destination before they reach it. Similarly, most people heading offshore for a number of years will not say that they are leaving to do a circumnavigation.

■ *Sacrificing to Neptune.* When becalmed or in a gale, many sailors claim that a sacrifice to Neptune will change the weather for the better. Luckily, the days of sacrificing crewmembers is past, and today the sea gods get mostly liquor. In our experience, Neptune was somewhat picky about accepting sacrifices—only the best would do. Inferior spirits seemed to infuriate him even more, so it's better to live with conditions than offer cheap brandy.

But in return for giving up the vivid extremes, we found luxuries we only dreamed of during our voyaging years. I still stand under the shower head mesmerized by the flow of hot water. Evans and I eat oranges by the case and apples by the bushel, reveling in their crisp taste and their year-round availability. I no longer cringe when a light is turned on or check the voltage drop on the batteries when I plug in my computer. Evans sleeps the night through without jumping up two or three times to check the anchor.

But the adjustments do not come easily. We came back to a culture shock more profound than any we ever experienced traveling abroad. We expected things to be different in different lands, but we somehow expected that things in our own country were not going to change while we were away. But we were wrong. The country had marched on without us: The Republicans and Democrats had changed political roles; 386 processors became 486 processors, then Pentium chips; people surfed the Internet and communicated on the worldwide web; O.J. Simpson was no longer just a guy who ran through airports chasing Hertz signs; the Generation-Xer's had replaced the baby-boomers as the disillusioned younger generation; rap had come and almost gone.

Even more disconcerting were the changes that existed because we had changed. After the one-room tin shacks that pass for grocery stores in the Pacific, I was overwhelmed by an average American supermarket. In all but the most developed countries, I asked for cereal and was lucky if I got a six-month-old plastic bag of imitation rice crispies. Here I honestly wonder if anyone ever went stark raving mad in the cereal aisle, completely unable to cope with a hundred different brands leering at them from the shelves. Most of the islands we visited had neither cats nor dogs, as these were generally considered a delicacy where meat is scarce. Here not only were there cats and dogs in plenty, but there were *fat* cats and dogs. What better proof could there be of America's general level of prosperity?

In the end, though, the most profound changes are the least tangible. We have long since left behind the materialistic yuppies who jet-setted around Europe and were bored by five-star restaurant meals. Since returning, we have lived a quieter, more introverted life than we did before we left. We have tried to keep the spirit of voyaging alive by keeping things simple and living

day to day. We take the time to go for walks and to watch sunsets. We do not own a television and have no interest in doing so. We try to insulate ourselves from the busyness that marks our culture in order to stay in touch with the calm stillness of our watery souls.

We also tread more lightly on our planet and are more conscious of the footprints we are leaving behind. We are sorely aware of how little impact we can have on our environment. Unlike living on *Silk,* we have so little control over how our electricity is generated, what happens to our sewage, or how much energy is used to transport our food. Like most Americans, we find that we must own a car to function effectively, particularly in the professional world.

Yet so many little things can be done, and these are the manifestations of our voyaging spirit. The canvas bags that carried pineapples and bananas back to the boat from village markets we now use every week at the local supermarket. We reuse plastic bags and recycle anything that is accepted at any recycling facility within 50 miles of us. We are very aware of water and electricity, and our bills for both are about half what they were before we left. We continue to entertain ourselves as we did on the boat, with books and conversations and journal writing and deep thoughts. We are painfully conscious of the pressure in our culture to be good consumers and to incur debt. We have to work to resist the almost overwhelming temptations of the American marketplace.

Sadly, trying to incorporate our voyaging spirit into our daily lives often means flying in the face of our current culture. Yet another gift of voyaging has been the tremendous appreciation we brought back with us of the wonder and wealth of this country. The word *civilization* takes on a whole new meaning after having seen places that were truly uncivilized. Civilized means that society functions: transportation moves to a schedule, public utilities provide adequate services, and a responsible group is entrusted with overseeing everyone's safety and adherence to society's laws. Civilized means that those laws must be obeyed. But it also means there is a value in those laws being fair and a struggle to realize fairness in the day-to-day world. Civilized means that we trust order instead of chaos, that we protect those who need protection. To see a place where these things are not the norm is to under-

A day in the life—the end of a voyage

This was the last journal entry I wrote aboard *Silk*, at Middleton, Rhode Island, on June 12, 1995.

"Sitting here and facing Silk's *bare shelves—surrounded by the last of the possessions that we have kept in this, our home of three years—I know that we have reached the end. This moment is the end of a journey and end of an era. With* Silk *and our own spirit of adventure, we had experiences that I never dreamed I would have. We met people and shared their lives, often for short periods of time. Yet the sharing had an intimacy that only comes with adventure—with living on the edge and dealing with life as honestly as with death. I wanted to find self-reliance. Instead, I found myself.*

"And this vessel, sitting quietly at her mooring while the rain drums on the coach roof, made it possible. She protected us in storms, raced with us toward new landfalls, sighed with us when the anchor bit deep into the sand at a passage's end. She has been my friend and confidant. And on many nights in a wild sea or a quiet anchorage, I have caressed her teak and felt her warm presence. She has given of herself to protect us, and we have tried our best to take care of her. Together, we have faced the most formidable forces on this planet: At times, we ran with wind and sea and rejoiced in the freedom of our flight; at other times, we battled to survive. Silk, Evans, *and I were a team. I will miss her gentle presence. I will miss feeling her watching over me while I sleep. I love this boat, and I will always be grateful to her.*

"The adventure became a reality. The demons have advanced and been vanquished—although a few linger to haunt the future. Silk *awaits her new owners, and Evans and I stand poised for our next challenge. Before it all slips away, I want to pause and mourn silently for the passing of one of the most intense, testing, growing periods in my life. I am proud of having completed this adventure, and I know that it will forever be with me. I will try now to find a life where I can continue to feel the sea in my soul and to know my own heart. But if I cannot do it, then I will find a way to return to voyaging. This adventure is ending, but the adventure will never end. I am far too alive now to let it."*

stand that the greatest good fortune at birth is not to be born rich or poor in a "civilized" country but to be born into such a country at all.

In the end, keeping the faith extends to your return ashore. Share what you have learned with others who are eager to go. Try to give those who will never go a glimpse of what it was like and how it changed you; perhaps they will be changed just a little by your experiences. Help others understand the most basic lesson that voyaging teaches: Ordinary people do the most extraordinary things. With a dream and a will, we can make things happen. We can control our destinies.

APPENDIX 1 | GALLEY SUBSTITUTES AND EQUIVALENTS

The best advice I can give you about provisioning is that there is almost nothing you cannot do without. I now know that I can make something nutritious and reason- ably palatable no matter what gets left behind. Table Appendix 1-1 should give you the confidence that no matter what, you can make *something*.

Table Appendix 1-1. Substitutes

If you need:	You can substitute:	Comments
1 cup granulated sugar	¾ cup honey, molasses, or maple syrup	Reduce liquid in recipe by ¼ cup
1 cup honey, maple syrup, or molasses	1¼ cup granulated sugar	Increase liquid in recipe by ¼ cup
1 cup granulated sugar	1¾ cup confectioners' sugar	
1¾ cup confectioners' sugar	1 cup granulated sugar plus small amount of flour	Use for frosting. Experiment with flour amount to get the right taste
1 square of unsweetened baking chocolate	3 tablespoons of cocoa plus 1 tablespoon of margarine	
1 cup whole milk	1 cup fruit juice or 1 cup potato water or 1 cup water plus 1½ teaspoons butter	For baking
1 cup buttermilk or sour cream (less than 10 percent butterfat)	1 tablespoon vinegar or lemon juice plus 1 cup whole milk	Heat milk slightly before adding; let stand for five minutes
1 cup sour cream	1 tablespoon of vinegar plus one can of Nestlé's reduced milk	Widely available throughout the Pacific; let stand for five minutes
1 cup light cream or half-and-half (10–12 percent butterfat)	1½ tablespoons of butter plus ⅞ cup of whole milk	For baking; if using nonfat dried milk add 1 more tablespoon of butter
1 cup coffee cream (20 percent butterfat)	3 tablespoons butter plus ⅞ cup of whole milk	For baking; if using nonfat dried milk add 1 more tablespoon of butter
1 cup coffee cream (20 percent butterfat)	1 cup of coconut cream	Can be purchased in islands or you can make it yourself
1 cup heavy cream (36–40 percent butterfat)	⅓ cup butter plus ¾ cup of whole milk	For baking
1 cup butter	¾ – ⅞ cup margarine or ¾ cup cooking oil	Margarine is more oily than butter so use a bit less
1 egg	2 tablespoons of cooking oil	Baked goods won't be quite as light

Table Appendix 1-1. Substitutes (continued)

If you need:	You can substitute:	Comments
1 teaspoon baking powder	$\frac{1}{4}$ teaspoon baking soda plus $\frac{1}{2}$ teaspoon cream of tartar	1 teaspoon baking soda will fizz in $\frac{1}{4}$ cup of hot water if active
1$\frac{1}{2}$ teaspoons arrowroot or corn starch	1 tablespoon flour	As thickening agent
$\frac{1}{8}$ teaspoon powdered ginger	1 tablespoon raw ginger	Makes a great gingersnap!
$\frac{1}{3}$ to $\frac{1}{2}$ teaspoon dried herbs	1 tablespoon of fresh herbs	
1 teaspoon vinegar	1 teaspoon lemon juice	
1 pound fresh mushrooms	3 ounces dried or 6 ounces drained canned mushrooms	
1 teaspoon dry powdered mustard	1 tablespoon prepared mustard	
2 cups tomato sauce	$\frac{3}{4}$ cup tomato paste plus 1 cup water	
1 can (10$\frac{3}{4}$ ounces) tomato soup	1 cup tomato sauce plus $\frac{1}{4}$ cup water	

Table Appendix 1-2. Equivalents

	Equals or yields	Comments
1 lemon	1–3 tablespoons juice plus 1–3 teaspoons grated rind	For lemonade: ½ cup lemon juice and ½ cup sugar per quart of water. Adjust sugar to taste.
1 lime	1½ to 2 tablespoons of juice	
8 ounces (3 cups) fresh mushrooms	1 cup sliced mushrooms	
1 pound uncooked macaroni	4–5 cups uncooked macaroni	
1 cup uncooked macaroni	2–2¼ cups cooked macaroni	
1 pound uncooked noodles	6–8 cups uncooked noodles	
1 cup uncooked noodles	1¼ cups cooked noodles	
1 pound dry spaghetti	5–6 cups uncooked or 6 cups cooked	
1 pound of rice	2 cups uncooked or 6 cups cooked	
1 pound instant non-fat dried milk	5 quarts reconstituted	
1 package active dry yeast	1 cake or ⅗ ounce or 1 tablespoon yeast	Proof yeast before using to protect your other ingredients.

Table Appendix 1-2 offers some equivalents of particular interest to the offshore voyager.

Besides understanding what can be substituted for what, you need to get used to metric equivalents. No table can really help you with that. You need to develop your own sense of how much a loaf of bread weighs in Imperial versus metric measurements. But two rules of thumb cover 80 percent of the situations: 500 grams or ½ kilogram is just over a pound; 25 grams is just under an ounce; and a litre is just over a quart (two pints). If you keep those two thoughts in mind when you go shopping, you won't be confused very often.

APPENDIX 2 | OFFSHORE MEDICAL KIT

The following tables summarize the contents of our offshore medical kit. This kit served us well during our three-year trip. The only areas that we had to supplement were the antihistamines and certain antibiotics. In retrospect, we could have taken smaller quantities of the dressings—such as the tape, sterile pads, and gauze—and less of the standard cold and digestive remedies. These were available throughout the world,

and we could have easily restocked if we had needed to do so. Beyond that, we felt comfortable with the scope of our medical kit. Of course, the various medications and supplies reflected our medical history. While you may want to use this list as a starting point, you should create your own medical kit in conjunction with your doctor that meets the needs of your own crew.

Table Appendix 2-1. General diagnostic equipment

Type	Materials	Quantity	Comments
Instruments	Stethoscope	1	
	Mercury rectal thermometer	1	
	Mercury oral thermometer	1	
Supplies	Tongue depressors	1 box	
	Q-tips	3 packages	Cleansing swabs to remove debris from deep wounds
	Cotton balls	1 package	
	Rubber gloves	1 box	To maintain sterility
	Dental floss	1 package	

Table Appendix 2-2. Materials for the treatment of wounds

Type	Materials	Quantity	Comments
Disinfecting materials	Betadine Scrub or Techni-care Surgical Prep	1 pint	For disinfecting hands or area around a wound
	Betadine Solution	1 pint	For applying directly to minor wounds
	Isopropyl alcohol	1 pint	
	Hydrogen peroxide	8 oz. bottle	
	Irrigation solution (saline)	1 quart	
	Burow's Solution	12 tablets	
	Large syringes (20 and 30 cc) for irrigation	6	

(continued)

Table Appendix 2-2. Materials for the treatment of wounds (continued)

Type	Materials	Quantity	Comments
Surgical supplies	Rubber tourniquet	2	
	3 cc sterile syringes with #23 or #25 1-inch needles[1]	2 dozen	For injecting local anesthesia or other drugs
	Lidocaine (xylocaine) injectable[1]	30 cc bottle	Local anesthesia
	Hemostat, curved, mosquito	1	
	Hemostat, straight	1	
	Surgical scissors	1	
	Needle holder/suture scissors combination	1	
	Scalpel holder	2	
	Scalpel blades #11	1 package of 6	
	Disposable single-edged razors	12	
	Airway resuscitation kit	1	
	Small pointed forceps	1	
	Medium blunt forceps	1	
	Steri-strip closures	2 boxes	For use on small wounds instead of stitches
	Suture 4-0 silk with needle[1]	1 box	
	Suture 4-0 gut with needle[1]	1 box	For internal sutures
	Gauze drains, ¼ inch	1 bottle	
Dressing supplies	Fabric bandages	4 boxes of standard 1-inch	Adhere much better in salt water than plastic backed bandages
	2-inch gauze rolls	6	
	3 x 3-inch gauze pads	2 packages	
	2-inch adhesive tape	6 rolls	
	Bandage scissors	1	

[1] By prescription only

Table Appendix 2-3. Medical supplies for specific anatomical problems

Type	Materials	Quantity	Comments
Orthopedic	Cold compresses (Kwik kind)	6	May want to carry more if children are aboard and/or if there is no freezer aboard
	Wrist splints, adult sized	2	
	Metal splints for fingers and toes	6	Can be cut to fit
	Wrist brace with reinforced Velcro closure	1	
	Cast liner, 3-inch rolls	6	To be used inside a fiberglass cast
	Fiberglass cast material	3 packages	
	3-inch ACE bandages	5	
	Triangular bandages	2	
Teeth	Temporary filling kit	1	
Eye	Sterile eye pads	6	
	10% sulfacetamide eye drops[1]	2 10-cc bottles	For pink eye
	Garamycin ophthalmic ointment[1]	4 3.5-gram tubes	For eye infection with granules
Ear	Pedi-Otic ear drops	2 15-cc bottles	To treat or prevent swimmer's ear
	Auralgan ear drops	1 10-cc bottles	Analgesic to reduce ear pain
Dermatological	1% hydrocortisone cream	2 1-oz. tubes	Wet, itching rash
	1% hydrocortisone ointment	2 1-oz. tubes	Dry, itching rash
	Zinc oxide	2 1-oz. tubes	Complete sun block
	Neosporin ointment	2 1-oz. tubes	Antibiotic ointment
	A&D ointment	2 1-oz. tubes	For burns and rashes
	Solarcaine spray	2 cans	For mild burns
	Aloe vera gel	2 large bottles	For sunburn
	Silvadene cream	1 jar	For second degree burns
	Lotromin antifungal 1% lotion	2 30-cc bottles	For fungus infection or athlete's foot
	Monistat cream and vaginal suppositories	3 kits	For vaginal yeast infection
	Diflucan tablets, 100 mg[1]	24 tablets	Single dose cure for vaginal yeast infections
	Kwell lotion and shampoo	1 pint of each	For treating head lice, scabies, pubic itching

[1] By prescription only

(continued)

Table Appendix 2-3. Medical supplies for specific anatomical problems (continued)

Type	Materials	Quantity	Comments
Digestive	Zantac, 150 mg	100 tablets	Antacid
	Pepto-Bismol	1 pint	
	Parapectolin[1]	8 oz.	Anti-diarrheal
	Lomotil[1]	3 cartons	Strong anti-diarrheal
	Senokot tablets	50	Laxative
[1]By prescription only			

Table Appendix 2-4. Medications

Type	Materials	Quantity	Comments
Antibiotics	Ampicillin, 250 mg[1]	500 tablets	
	Augmentin, 250 mg[1]	250 tablets	
	Bactrim DS[1]	100 tablets	
	Cephtriaxone injectable[1]	2 dozen single-dose vials	Injectable super-strength antibiotic
Analgesics	Ibuprofen, 200 mg	200 tablets	
	Tylenol with codeine #3[1]	200 tablets	
	Injectable Demerol[1]	30 cc in 15-mg doses	For extreme pain
Antihistamines and steroids	Hismanal, 10 mg[1]	80 tablets	
	Prednisone, 5 mg[1]	100 tablets	Steroid
	1:1000 adrenaline, 10 cc[1]	30-cc bottle	For life-threatening allergic reaction
	Medrol injectable, 40 mg[1]	3 40-mg vials	Steroid, to follow adrenaline or for use on serious recurrent hives
Seasickness remedies	Bonine	50 tablets	Mild medication
	Phenergan (Promethazine), 25 mg[1]	50 tablets	In combination with Ephedrine, effective strong medication
	Ephedrine, 50 mg[1]	50 tablets	
	Phenergan suppositories, 25 mg[1]	1 dozen	For use when oral administration is not possible
Cold remedies	Sudafed	100 tablets	
	Dimetane DC Cough Medicine[1]	1 pint	
	¼% Neosynephrine nose drops	2 30-cc bottles	
	Chloraseptic lozenges	3 packages	
	Chloraseptic mouthwash	1 bottle	
	Co-Tylenol	4 packages	
	Vicks Vaporub	1 jar	

[1]By prescription only